Strategies of
COMMUNITY
INTERVENTION

SIXTH EDITION

Strategies of
COMMUNITY
INTERVENTION
SIXTH EDITION

EDITORS

Jack Rothman
UNIVERSITY OF CALIFORNIA,
LOS ANGELES

John L. Erlich
CALIFORNIA STATE UNIVERSITY,
SACRAMENTO

John E. Tropman
UNIVERSITY OF MICHIGAN

THOMSON

BROOKS/COLE

Australia • Canada • Mexico • Singapore • Spain • United Kingdom • United States

Edited by John Beasley
Production supervision by Kim Vander Steen
Cover design by Cynthia Crampton Design
Composition by Point West, Inc.
Printed and bound by The P.A. Hutchison Company

ISBN: 0-87581-436-0

Library of Congress Catalog Card No. 00 134167

Wadsworth/Thomson Learning
10 Davis Drive
Belmont CA 94002-3098
USA

For information about our products, contact us:
Thomson Learning Academic Resource Center
1-800-423-0563
http://www.wadsworth.com

For permission to use material from this text, contact us by
Web: http://www.thomsonrights.com
Fax: 1-800-730-2215
Phone: 1-800-730-2214

Printed in the United States of America
10 9 8 7 6 5 4 3

Contents

THANKS TO THE FOLLOWING AUTHORS AND PUBLISHERS

"Approaches to Community Intervention" by Jack Rothman is an expanded version of Jack Rothman, "Three Models of Community Organization Practice," from National Conference on Social Welfare, "Social Work Practice 1968" (New York: Columbia University Press, 1968). Copyright © 1968, National Conference on Social Welfare. Revised 1974, 1979, 1987, and 1995.

"A History of Community Organizing Since the Civil War with Special Reference to Oppressed Communities" by Charles D. Garvin and Fred M. Cox was written for the fourth edition of this volume and is used by permission of the authors.

"Political Economy and Public Life" by Robert Fisher was written for the sixth edition of this volume and is used by permission of the author.

"Understanding American Communities" by Phillip Fellin was written for the fifth edition of this volume and is used by permission of the author.

"Organizations: Organizations as Polities: An Analysis of Community Organization Agencies" by Mayer N. Zald. Reprinted, with permission, from *Social Work* 11(4) (October 1966), pp. 56–65. Copyright 1966, National Association of Social Workers, Inc., Social Work.

"The Small Group in Community Organization Practice" by Rosalie Bakalinsky is from *Social Work with Groups* 7(2) (Summer 1984), pp. 87–96. © 1984 by The Haworth Press, Inc. All rights reserved.

"Community Problem Solving: A Guide to Practice with Comments" by Fred M. Cox is a revised version of the article that appeared in the fourth edition of this volume and is used with the permission of the author.

"Generic Social Work Skills in Social Administration: The Example of Persuasion" by Ronald L. Simons is from *Administration in Social Work* 11(3, 4) pp. 241–254. © 1988 by The Haworth Press, Inc. All rights reserved.

"Launching a Family-Centered, Neighborhood-Based Human Services System: Lessons from Working with Hallways and Street Corners" by Katherine L. Armstrong is reprinted with permission from *Administration in Social Work* 21(3/4) 1997, pp. 109–126. Copyright © 1997 by The Haworth Press, Inc., Binghamton, N.Y. All rights reserved.

"Social Action Community Organization: Proliferation, Persistence, Roots, and Prospects" by Robert Fisher was written for this volume and is based, in part, on Robert Fisher, "Community Organizing Worldwide," in R. Fisher and J. Kling, eds., *Mobilizing the Community* (Newbury Park, CA: Sage, 1993), pp. 3–22. Copyright © 1993 by Sage Publications. Used by permission of the author and publisher.

"The Tactics of Organization Building" by Warren C. Haggstrom is from "The Organizer," was previously published in the fourth and fifth editions of this volume, and is reprinted by permission of the author.

"Agency Under Attack: The Risks, Demands, and Rewards of Community Activism" by George Brager is reprinted with permission from *Reflections on Community Organization,* edited by Jack Rothman (Itasca, IL: F.E. Peacock Publishers, Inc., 1999). Copyright © by F.E. Peacock Publishers, Inc.

"Mobile Home Park Lot 'Rent Control': A Successful Rural Legislative Campaign" by Steven Soifer is reprinted with permission from *Journal of Community Practice* 5(4) 1998, pp. 25–37. Copyright © 1998 by The Haworth Press, Inc., Binghamton, N.Y. All rights reserved.

"Strategic Administration of Nonprofit Human Service Organizations: A Model for Executive Success in Turbulent Times" by David Menefee is reprinted with permission from *Administration in Social Work* 21(2) 1997, pp. 1–19. Copyright © 1997 by The Haworth Press, Inc., Binghamton, N.Y. All rights reserved.

"Leadership in the Managed Care Era: Challenges, Conflict, Ambivalence" by Stewart Gabel is reprinted with permission from the author and *Administration and Policy in Mental Health* 26(1) (September 1998), pp. 3–19. Copyright © 1998 by Human Sciences Press, Inc., Plenum Publishing Corporation.

"Walking the Line Between Capacity and Constraint: Feminist Social Work in a Conservative Era" by Susan E. Roche is reprinted with permission from *Journal of Progressive Human Services* 9(2) 1998, pp. 7–30. Copyright © 1998 by The Haworth Press, Inc., Binghamton, N.Y. All rights reserved.

"Program Development" by Yeheskel Hasenfeld was adapted from "Guide to Agency Development for Area Planners in Aging," Project T.A.P., funded by the Administration on Aging, Grant SRS-HEW 94-P-76007/5-01 to the Institute of Gerontology, University of Michigan/Wayne State University, and the University of Michigan School of Social Work Continuing Education Program. Reprinted by permission of the author.

Preface to the Sixth Edition

This marks the sixth edition of this book and thirty years of continuous publication. The written text has changed over the years in response to social and professional developments, so that different programs, issues, and illustrations have come to the fore. But the underlying perspective and the conceptual framework, generally, have been consistent.

As an example, the debate over whether to emphasize social services or social reform has resonated from the beginning of the century to the current time (Abramovitz, 1998; Berry, 1999). Is the practitioner's primary responsibility to the agency and its demarcated functions or does the professional have a broader concern regarding fundamental issues? We have subscribed steadily to the wider view encompassing support for social change and equity in society.

In the book *Controversial Issues in Communities and Organizations,* McMurtry and Kettner (1994) take the position that the key point of reference in macro practice is not communities but organizations. In their view, practitioners are employed in organizations, carry out their activities through organizational structures, and present themselves as representatives of an organization rather than as community-based change agents. It is not appropriate, therefore, they believe, to convey to students "the image of a social worker acting directly on communities to right wrongs, cure ills, and empower the oppressed" (p. 99). Their sponsoring organizations, they tell us, won't tolerate this.

In the same volume, Daley and Netting (1994) mount a counterargument. They agree that community intervention requires a sophisticated understanding of organizational behavior. But they envisage a broader scope, including engaging with informal networks, interest groups, and natural support systems that exist in and comprise the community.

Daley and Netting go on to project a more complex fabric of action: "Community organization is a richly diverse field of practice that includes policy analysts and developers; program planners; administrators and evaluators; resource developers and allocators; and community organizers and developers working with geographically or issue-defined interest groups and communities." This includes work with "oppressed and disenfranchised peoples and for the cause of justice" (p. 105).

Signing on as an employee of a human service organization does not require giving up a professional concern and personal commitment to promoting social change on behalf of disadvantaged members of society (Andrain, 1998; Deakin, 1999). Indeed, many organizations for which practitioners work, from the American Friends Service Committee to the Children's Defense Fund, are dedicated fundamentally to just such purposes (Mizrahi and Rosenthal, 1998). And professionals have the responsibility to look inward to change their organizations, as well as outward to change community conditions. Often, it is because of, and in collaboration with, citizens and groups in the community that internally directed organizational change ensues.

We stand with the broader perspective that was described, and the text attempts to articulate this orientation theoretically and in terms of practice strategies and skills. The sixth edition has as its base the intellectual framework that was established originally, but it also departs from it in various ways. The classic introductory "Three Models" article, which has provided the conceptual underpinning for all the previous editions, has been substantially revised and expanded by Jack Rothman. The "models" of action notion has been eased, in order to suggest broader "approaches" or "modes" of intervention. We still view strategies in terms of the community-building emphasis of locality development with its attention to community competency and integration, the data-based problem-solving orientation of social planning/social policy with its reliance on expertise, and the advocacy thrust of social action with its commitment to fundamental change and social justice.

But there is a great deal more consideration given to the overlapping and integration of these general approaches, with particular mixtures now articulated specifically and illustrated through examples taken from the world of contemporary practice. The middle section of the book focuses explicitly on these strategic considerations, as we will discuss shortly.

The first of the three parts comprising the book deals with **Parameters of Intervention**, setting out a fourfold contextual paradigm for analyzing community intervention. *Frameworks*, the first of these, includes alternative modes of action, historical trends, and the national political economy. *Arenas*, the second, encompasses community and organizational systems, which were touched on in beginning these comments. It also includes the task-oriented small group, which is an additional social entity through which much community intervention is carried out.

Core Elements of Practice is the third parameter, covering a cognitive schema for systematic problem solving, the use of persuasive forms of action depending on interpersonal influence, and the employment, contrastingly, of tactics of organized pressure and coercion. The fourth parameter deals with the interplay of *Micro and Macro Aspects of Practice*, including different concepts of integrated or generic practice, and the application of macro methods in micro settings.

The second or middle part of the book can be said to be the centerpiece, in that it concentrates explicitly on **Strategy**. For each of the three key intervention approaches there is an introductory conceptual overview, a piece on tactics and roles, one that presents a case illustration of carrying out the strategy in action, and another article that shows how that approach is combined with one or more of the others.

For example, locality development, while rooted in an immediate geographical base, includes linkages to organizations outside the local community setting; social planning and social policy are joined conceptually as a single intervention mode and, while relying on expertise, are shown to often include elements of citizen participation; and social action, while often employing militancy, may involve use of conventional modes of political advocacy and coalitions that include aggrieved or disadvantaged groups acting in concert with others.

The third and concluding part of the book covers the subject of **Administration and Management**, which it treats not as a separate mode of community intervention, but as an organizational means for implementing the various forms of community intervention that have been discussed. Administration relates as well to carrying out the varied service and program activities of social agencies.

The 90s were not a reassuring time for those who appreciate the role of the human services, and who are committed to responsibility exercised by the community and its elected government for disabled, and disadvantaged citizens. Both governmental and voluntary programs of support and aid have been contracted or eliminated (Weisbrod, 1997; Fabricant and Burghardt, 1998). For some of us, hope stirred with the election of a youthful president who seemed to exude intelligence and compassion. But the political, personal, and social forces at play have trapped progressive and humane propensities in a morass of gridlock.

Community professionals do not have a great deal of impressive ammunition available to advance their aims. The artifacts of prodigious political and economic power often elude them. But in the complicated game of community change, knowledge of how things work, skill in maneuvering the levers that set new directions, and the ability to make and use a wide range of contacts can have an enormous impact. Those who pursue community intervention need to know how to think, and to put their theoretical and practical savvy on the line in effective ways that advance human values.

It is trite to say that knowledge is power, but it is also profound. We hope that our effort in compiling this book will contribute to the process of progressive social change by intellectually empowering students and professionals—and through them ordinary citizens—to make a difference in a world that often seems foreboding and intractable.

—Jack Rothman
John L. Erlich
John E. Tropman

REFERENCES

Abramovitz, Mimi. "Social Work and Social Reform: An Arena of Struggle." *Social Work* 43(6) (1998): 512–526.

Andrain, Charles F. *Public Health Policies and Social Inequality.* New York: New York University Press, 1998.

Berry, Margaret E. "Service and Cause—Both Sides of the Coin." In Jack Rothman, ed., *Reflections on Community Organization: Enduring Themes and Critical Issues* (pp. 106–120). Itasca, IL: F.E. Peacock Publishers, 1999.

Daley, John M., & F. Ellen Netting. "Is Community Organizing Dead and Is the Future Organizational Practice? No." In Michael J. Austin & Jane I. Lowe, eds., *Controversial Issues in Communities and Organizations* (pp. 105–110). Boston: Allyn and Bacon, 1994.

Deakin, Elizabeth. "Social Equity in Planning." *Berkeley Planning Journal* 13 (1999):1–5.

Fabricant, Michael, & Steve Burghardt. "Rising from the Ashes of Cutback, Political Warfare and Degraded Services: Strategic Consideration for Community Building: An Editorial Essay." *Journal of Community Practice* 5(4) (1998): 53–65.

McMurtry, Steven L., & Peter M. Kettner. "Is Community Organizing Dead and Is the Future Organizational Practice? Yes." In Michael J. Austin & Jane I. Lowe, eds., *Controversial Issues in Communities and Organizations* (pp. 98–103). Boston: Allyn and Bacon, 1994.

Mizrahi, Terry, & Beth Rosenthal. "'A Whole Lot of Organizing Going On': The Status and Needs of Organizers in Community-Based Organizations." *Journal of Community Practice* 5(4) (1998): 1–24.

Weisbrod, B.A. "The Future of the Non-profit Sector: Its Entwining with Private Enterprise and Government." *Journal of Policy Analysis and Management* 16(4) (1997): 541–555.

PART ONE
PARAMETERS OF INTERVENTION

Introduction

In Part One we will set out the parameters of community intervention, delineating and illustrating the context within which practice is conducted. According to Fisher (1999), for change agents, "context is critical." A parameter is defined as a "constant" whose properties "determine the operation or characteristics of a system." Assuming that community intervention is a particular and unique system of practice, it is important to know the intellectual boundaries that constrain and shape it.

We begin with **frameworks.** Among these is the area of *strategy,* the fabric of action options that are available for the practitioner's choices in order to achieve change goals. We will spell out a comprehensive action spectrum in cross-sectional fashion. Next we will be informed by *history,* looking at the evolution of different strategies and their fluctuations as seen as longitudinal perspective. History offers a platform from which to make strategic choices as well as to forge new possibilities. There is also the framework of *societal ecology,* with its varied and complex structures, institutions, values, and norms that generate both problems to be confronted and opportunities to be exploited. In this analysis, the political economy of American society will be highlighted, recognizing that fundamental political and economic forces have a decisive impact on the local community situation.

From frameworks we move on to **arenas**, which are the specific social spheres in which the process of community intervention is played out. Three arenas are critical: the *community* itself; *organizations*, both formal and informal, within the community; and *small groups* of various kinds, particularly task-oriented units such as committees, commissions, boards, and the like. These social entities not only comprise the field of action, but also serve both as the vehicles through which community intervention takes place and as targets of change. It is inconceivable to think of engaging in community practice without having both knowledge of these arenas and skills in working with them.

This presentation draws in part on introductory notes by Fred M. Cox in a previous edition.

Community intervention acquires its particular character from certain common or **core elements of practice.** Among these we will examine *problem-solving methodology* to design change and modes of influence to affect change. Professionals typically emphasize a rational, systematic methodology of problem solving. The practitioner has to start with a sophisticated understanding of presenting problems before advancing to a solution stance. A problem has to be identified, bounded, and carefully analyzed so that logically derived initiatives with a high probability of producing effective outcomes are mounted. This kind of disciplined intellectual work distinguishes professional, competency-based practice from intuitive posturing that is well-meaning but often functionally flawed.

Also basic to community intervention are two broad modes of influence that are used to affect community affairs. One involves *interpersonal influence* that is educative, persuasive, and consensual in nature. It relies on the practitioner's use of self in personal encounters with others. The other mode involves *organizational pressure* and entails advocacy, political maneuvers, and even coercive measures. It relies on the practitioner's ability to mobilize and orchestrate change forces in the community. The use of a systematic problem-solving schema relates to what has been termed the analytic component of practice; the use of influence as an instrument of change has been termed the interactional component.

The pattern of **macro relationships to micro practice** follows. This final contextual factor relates macro-oriented community intervention, with its emphasis on structural change, prevention, and social reform, to micro-oriented intervention (casework, counseling, clinical treatment), with its emphasis on personal renewal and psychological repair. We know that problems and systems are interconnected: Society and community can cause or exacerbate the troubles of individuals, and distorted values and detrimental behaviors of individuals can undermine the common good. We will show various *generic practice approaches,* wherein the skills of individual and community intervention are combined. We will also note the *use of macro practice to support micro practice*, both by enhancing the agency structure and building a better social policy framework.

FRAMEWORKS

Strategy

Our interest here is community intervention, which has also variously been termed community planning, community relations, planned change, and community work. These are additional preferred terms such as neighborhood work, social action, intergroup work, and community practice. Under whatever label, we will be dealing with intervention at the community level oriented toward improving or changing community institutions and solving community problems. This activity is performed by professionals from many disciplines—social work, public health, adult education, public administration, city planning, and community mental health—as well as by citizen volunteers in civic associations and social action groups. Our own grounding is social work, but the issues and strategies we will cover are rather interdisciplinary in character.

These activities aim at a wide range of purposes. Among them are establishing new community services and programs; facilitating collaboration among them; and building the capacity of grassroots citizens' groups to solve community problems. Also of importance are seeking justice for oppressed minorities, bringing about social reform, and conducting programs of community relations or public education (Delgado, 1997; Rivera and Erlich, 1998).

The first piece, by Rothman, treats a variety of approaches to community intervention. A set of modes of action are suggested and analyzed in ideal-type form. These are termed locality development (building community competency and integration), social planning (which also includes elements of social policy and focus on rationalistic community problem solving), and social action (organized advocacy). The purposes and the tactical means within each approach differ in emphasis, as the text specifies and illustrates.

Rothman points out that the approaches rarely exist in pure form in practice, and that they tend to overlap, so that bimodal forms exist comprising action/planning, planning/development, and development/action mixes. Each of these has further variations based on the proportionality of the components in the mix. In addition, trimodal combinations of various kinds are common. Thus, a wide scope of strategy options are described, which can be used in a selective manner by the community practitioner. These options can be drawn upon differentially as a project goes through developmental phases or involves different problematic situations over time.

Rothman provides another useful perspective on practice, specifying a set of practice variables that are highly relevant for analyzing community intervention. The practice variables elaborated upon in the article include the following:

- Goal categories of community action
- Assumptions concerning community structure and problem conditions
- Basic change strategy
- Characteristic change tactics and techniques
- Salient practitioner roles
- Medium of change
- Orientation toward power structure(s)
- Boundary definition of the beneficiary system
- Assumptions regarding interests of community subparts
- Conception of beneficiaries
- Conception of the beneficiary role
- Use of empowerment

These practice variables operate differently in each mode of community practice, but in aggregate (the twelve practice variables across the three strategic approaches) generate an array of intervention initiatives that can be used selectively and in combination.

History

Grassroots civic action has been a constant element in community intervention, but to varying degrees and in varying forms over time. Community development and social action at the local neighborhood level reached an apex of sorts in the late 1960s, although certain precursors existed in the preceding decade and other developments have followed into the 1990s. Both social agency programming and independent social forces have contributed to this phenomenon of grassroots citizen involvement. For example, Point 7 of the Urban Renewal Act of 1954 required citizen participation in redevelopment as a condition of federal support. The Housing and Urban Development Act of 1968 reinforced this principle. Urban renewal authorities involved citizens at the grassroots in renewal planning in various degrees and with varying consequences (Wilson, 1963). Programs of the Office of Economic Opportunity around that time gave considerable momentum to the idea of including the poor in policy making and program implementation. Settlement houses have long emphasized organizational efforts in the neighborhoods to enable immigrants and the poor to improve their lot.

Other forces also contributed to the grassroots trend, particularly in the area of social action. The civil rights movement gave great impetus to social action in the black community. Some civil rights groups moved from tactics of protest to neighborhood organization and political action (Rustin, 1965). Growing black nationalism stimulated the beginnings of separatist institutions and programs, with a strong impetus for local control. African-American social action touched off similar activity among other oppressed racial minorities as well as among white ethnics. Student activism on hundreds of campuses underlined the participation concept. The women's movement became a powerful force for mobilizing local participation, as did organizing among gays. Grassroots approaches also developed in fertility control, community mental health, housing, public health, environmental protection, political practices reform, consumerism, and other institutional areas. Also of great significance was the peace movement, aimed at ending the war in Vietnam, with its political ramifications in the McCarthy and McGovern presidential campaigns and related events.

Grassroots civic action is often likened to a falling star—reaching its heights in the 1960s, then plummeting to earth, burned out and dissipated with the transition into the 1970s. A closer look reveals that the legacy of the earlier period has been carried forward, not in as dramatic or comprehensive a way, but nevertheless with vitality and prevalence. There's "A whole lot of organizing going on" (Miarahi and Rosenthal (1998).

One element of this is the provision for citizen involvement in governmental programs. A kind of participation revolution has been carried out, often somewhat imperceptibly, but usually at least at the level of formal specification or requirements. A broad assessment, which takes into account both governmental and voluntary community factors, has described grassroots activity as follows:

Despite a weakening of citizen input in many programs, new legislation in the mid-1970s strengthened the citizens' role in some instances; therefore, the situation remained mixed. Changes in Title XX of the Social Security Act mandated a period of public review before state plans for a variety of social service programs could be adopted. Some citizens continue to be active in decentralized city halls and neighborhood service centers. Others participate in consumer cooperatives or community development corporations in an attempt to make their neighborhoods more self-sufficient economically. Many citizens have turned to mass consumer education or political activities such as lobbying and legal action (Wireman, 1977).

Some concrete results have come about through these efforts. Wireman lists the following achievements of participation:

1. Bureaucrats are becoming sensitive to the need to take citizen and client opinions into account in planning and delivering services.
2. Improvements have been made in services in accordance with client needs and wishes.
3. Groups are learning how to influence and bypass traditional political and administrative channels.
4. A generation of leaders, especially from minority groups, holds positions of political or administrative authority in federal, state, and local government.

We must learn from history or be victims of its consequences (Berkhafer, 1995). Charles Garvin and Fred M. Cox provide a broad overview of the broad cultural and social factors that have shaped community intervention, particularly as it has developed in social work. They give particular attention to some of the institutions that emerged in the latter part of the nineteenth century in England and in North America that were the crucible out of which community practice grew. These institutions—charity organization societies, social settlements, councils of social agencies, community chests—gave birth to much of social work and most of what came to be called community organization in social work. The unique role of racial and ethnic groups in the development of community organization is portrayed. Finally, Garvin and Cox discuss the growth of professional community organization practice, as well as some of the main ideas that inform that practice.

Societal Ecology

The disparity between meritorious ideals and practical realities in our society has been termed "The American Dilemma." We espouse equality fervently, however economic and social differences remain sharp and pervasive (Weissberg, 1999). Gus Hall (1994) indicates that wealth in the United States is even more concentrated than income. He points out that the richest 1 percent of households held 36 percent of the nation's wealth in 1989, and that this percentage had increased phenomenally by some 70 percent over a six-year period. Concentration of wealth has continued into the new century.

Hall feels that this distribution of wealth is detrimental to societal progress and stability for several reasons. An increasing concentration of wealth brings with it an increasing concentration of political power. Further, when much of the population fails to participate in the gains of economic growth, this comes across to many people as politically and morally unjustifiable. Resulting friction can generate social disorder, including crime, conflict, and corruption. It may also result in a depression because of the disparity between the nation's capacity to produce and its ability to consume. In sum: "the growing concentration of wealth in America is politically anti-democratic, morally reprehensible, socially disruptive, and economically perilous" (p. 7).

The Nixon/Reagan/Bush administrations pushed to "get the government off the backs of citizens" and to increase the efficiency of public services through better management. As a means of reducing the scope and costliness of social programs, Nixon and his lieutenants made a deliberate effort to remove as heads of social programs professionals with human-service orientations, and to replace them with business-minded executives who had a predilection for the niceties of accountancy. The Nixon administration's ideological preference for the "hard-nosed" ways of the business world accounted in part for this stance, but there was also an overriding wish to cut back or dismantle many of the programs that had come into being during the Great Society period of the 1960s to aid the poor and reduce economic inequities. The Reagan/Bush administrations accentuated the gap between the wealthy and the impoverished.

Their gambit was given impetus by the overinflated claims of liberal programs, their inadequate funding, the hastily conceived and poorly managed character of many of them, and the political and organizational conflicts that surrounded them. The increasingly bad name of public assistance also served to discredit social programs and fuel welfare reform. When "New Democrat" Clinton replaced conservative Bush, it was on the basis of a platform promising to reinvent government and bring more order and managerial acumen to the federal programs than could the Republicans, and to diminish the scope of income transfer and social amelioration programs.

Disparities in status and wealth exist not only within nations, but also internationally across states. The North/South hemispheric division has both an objective and a psychological dimension, creating a climate of tension and antagonism. Chirot (1994) puts it this way:

The gap between the richest and poorest countries continues to grow. The perception of international unfairness is an important cause of anticapitalist and anti-Western ideological movements in the [less developed] parts of the world. It is clear that Western science and technology are superior and that they must be adopted to some extent. But the feeling that the established industrial powers are simply using their economic and political muscle to keep other societies poor exacerbates jealousy and resentful nationalism. It creates a climate of deep resentment among the proud intellectuals of [developing] countries, and this in turn makes them treat with contempt the ideologies of individualism and democracy practiced by the most successful Western countries (p. 92).

Fisher, in his analysis (article 3), stresses the importance of contextual factors such as these in defining the opportunities and potential outcomes in community intervention. He highlights the disparities in the way the benefits of economic growth have been distributed in the United States in the recent period. The rich have become wealthier and the poor have become more disadvantaged. The economic boom over recent decades, he shows, has been built on the sweat of those who earn poverty wages. At the same time, privatization and individualism have come to the fore, reducing the attention given to common concerns and the requirements of public life. Public spaces—such as city streets, libraries, and public parks—are downgraded as gated communities and shopping malls flourish. Globalization represents the expansion of these self-aggrandizing trends internationally. It involves the massing of private power on a world level, reflecting a drive for the private accumulation of wealth that is devoid of ties to localities. The need for corporations to support a healthy and educated workforce within their own borders and to encourage the development of desirable home communities has become less salient.

These facts of social ecology complicate the operations of locally based community organizations. Forces at the national and international level impinge more on the local situation and, at the same time, are not particularly accessible through local action. The diminishing economic status and political power of low-income people makes it more necessary to organize them to act on their behalf, but at the same time it makes it all the more difficult. There are racial overtones in all of this, inasmuch as those with lower economic means are disproportionately represented by racial and ethnic minorities. The deleterious circumstances and trends that have been described impact these minorities with particular force (Salomon, 1998; Pardo, 1998).

An analysis of the political economy along these lines reveals some unpleasant realities, but it defines the broad context of community intervention pointedly and highlights some important tasks.

ARENAS OF INTERVENTION

A major contribution of the social sciences to the practice of community intervention has been in understanding the context in which change agents work—often called the arenas of community practice. These are the social settings and systems in which practice takes place. These arenas include interpersonal relations, small groups, formal organizations, neighborhoods, communities, and societies. We have chosen three of these arenas—communities, organizations, and small groups—for special attention in this volume. We believe they are particularly salient for community practice.

In the past few years, the social sciences have added a great deal to our understanding of the contextual realities that confront community practitioners. We have been greatly assisted by some of the ways they have conceived of the "booming, buzzing confusion" that confronts us as we go into action in our work.

To view these environmental social units as arenas, instead of as means or ends as others have done, lends a special perspective. As arenas, they are viewed as the boundaries within which action occurs—the conditions of the practitioner's work to be understood and taken as given in doing community work. Time and resources—people, money, influence, and the like—are limited. What is selected for change must be chosen very carefully, calibrated not only to the hopes and aspirations of the clientele and those who assist them but also to available resources. To argue for regarding communities, organizations, and small groups as arenas, then, is to argue for understanding, analysis, and the careful assessment of objectives and possibilities. The impulse to act may prove frustrating and fruitless unless observation, diagnosis, and understanding have come first (Chambers and Taylor, 1998).

Communities

Community, as conceived here, emphasizes the territorial organization of people, goods, services, and commitments. It is an important subsystem of the society, and one in which many locality-relevant functions are carried on.

Communities are in serious trouble at this point in American history. Pollution; traffic congestion; flight from the cities to the suburbs, exurbs, and rural communities; disinvestment in the central cities; and serious unemployment, crime, racial tensions, drug abuse, and infrastructure deterioration are but some issues that confront citizens and community practitioners alike. If there is to be advancement of American society, the problems of the cities surely must be contained.

It is now painfully clear to community practitioners and community residents that the problems of the urban community will not yield quickly to solution. Part of the reason for this intractability lies in the fact that the community is one of the weakest competitors for the time and attention of the contemporary citizen. The family, the workplace, the church, and the school have all been able to attract long-time commitments from citizens. People have typically fled urban places, moved to the suburbs, and, if they commuted to jobs in the cities, left as soon as possible at the end of the workday. Large cities often lack stable populations with whom to plan.

This inability of the community to claim the commitment of its citizens is in itself a serious problem and symptomatic of deeper ills as well (Wuthnow, 1998). Fundamentally, the modern urban community contains many goods and services, but controls very few of them. Hence, it is increasingly unable to assemble resources to address its important concerns.

A variety of contemporary forces have contributed to the diminishing status of the local community (Warren, 1963). The federal and state levels of government have gained increasingly in authority, size, and importance since the beginning of the New Deal in the early thirties. Tax policies, court decisions, and legislative actions all contributed to the upward migration of governmental power and responsibility. As the upper levels of government in the 1980s began to find themselves pinched by a reduction in tax revenues and economic hardship caused by deindustrialization and an unfavorable balance of trade, they moved to withdraw the economic support they had provided to lower levels, leaving cities in a financial bind and constricting the services and amenities they are able to provide to residents.

The mass media have also played a significant role in this trend. Media enter the individual household directly and operate as a national homogenizing force. Television is privately viewed in one's own living room, enlarging the role of mass culture and reducing the influence of a locally based culture. Therefore, there is less need to go outside of the home into the community for socialization, entertainment, recreation, and other interpersonally shared pursuits. The "couch potato" phenomenon has been detrimental to the vitality of the community. The Internet, national and international in scope, additionally reduces the need for a local community to facilitate human connections. From a social systems standpoint, there is less horizontal interaction among community units and proportionately more interaction with extra-community entities.

Despite this shift, the local community remains a significant social entity in the lives of most people. In his contribution, "Understanding American Communities," Fellin shows why this is so and provides a broad overview of community functions. He covers this terrain using two broad theoretical categories that encompass ecological and the social system perspectives. In the ecological stance, people are the important unit of analysis and population characteristics are the prime analytical tool. Fellin treats population size, population density, and population heterogeneity. The latter involves social class considerations (an aspect of political economy) and race and ethnic factors.

The discussion of social systems, borrowing from Warren (1963), starts with a delineation of the basic and still-valuable functions of contemporary communities, including economic (production/distribution/consumption), socialization (family, education), political (social control), participation (voluntary associations), and mutual support (health and welfare). Fellin attends to the distinct subsystems within communities that specialize in carrying out each of the functions. The neighborhood is given coverage as a distinct form and level of social system, and one that has particular relevance for community intervention, especially when there are grassroots components.

Clearly, the community is more than a series of problem situations confronted by the practitioner, or a casual backdrop. A major perspective of this book sees the community as the arena in which people still carry out their daily lives and community practitioners do their work. The community and its various elements both limit possible actions and present opportunities for action. The practitioner's task is to acknowledge the former and seize upon the latter. From another perspective, the community and its various elements provide the means for action and are the vehicle through which goals are achieved.

Organizations

Most community practitioners, unlike many other professionals, are salaried employees of organizations, often large and complex ones—schools, community mental health and public health agencies, United Ways, public assistance agencies, hospitals, city planning departments, human relations commissions, and so forth. The major exceptions are university-based consultants and a few organizers who work on a freelance, fee-for-service basis. Even those who work outside of institutional settings—the movement organizers endeavoring to mobilize the latent discontent of oppressed minority groups, exploited workers such as farm laborers and environmental activists, and the like—typically work through some form of organization. Sponsoring organizations, or "change agencies," exert a profound influence on the practitioner's work.

Community organizers of all stripes frequently are engaged in influencing these organizations and others whose activities affect their clientele. Thus formal organizations are often the context within which organizers work, the targets of their efforts to bring about change, and the means used for changing undesirable conditions (Shin and McClomb, 1998).

In modern industrial society, complex organizations are essential tools and mediating instrumentalities for achieving collective purposes. They can contribute in significant ways to realizing the kinds of lives people want. However, too often, organizations are neither positive nor benign in their impact upon clients. Practitioners not only need to know how to get organizations to deliver services but often they must have the skills necessary to change the way organizations operate and the kinds of services they deliver to those needing aid or support.

Thus, an understanding of formal organizations is essential for community intervention. Practitioners sometimes become discouraged by the limitations that organizations impose. Although these limitations are often very real, the professional may be able to discover paths around organizational obstacles and find potentialities for action or change. Such discovery may begin with a detailed understanding of the factors affecting organizational behavior. Moreover, at the same time that organizations impose restrictions, they provide resources of various kinds—funds, facilities, contacts, goodwill, and political clout.

Zald, in his perceptive contribution, analyzes the community intervention agency as a sociopolitical entity. He examines its "basic zones of activity, goals, and norms of procedure and relationships." A series of propositions is offered that answer questions of great importance to practioners: Under various conditions, what kinds of goals and activities can one expect of the agencies with which one works? What kinds of roles and what styles of action are likely to be both possible and effective in response to external forces?

Zald treats four dimensions of organizational operation in depth. He is concerned with *constitutions*—the set of procedures or regular patterns that dictate the way the organization works. These patterns establish the boundaries within which community practitioners typically are obliged to function, and they determine whether practitioners can pursue change goals of a social action nature or service goals that have a planning/policy quality.

Next, the *constituency and resource base* are considered. They provide the wherewithal that determines not only what can be accomplished, but how much can be accomplished. These entities are composed of board members, financial contributors, grantors, interested legislators, and other community influentials. Zald goes on to discuss certain external objects of action. Third, in pursuing goals, community intervention agencies delineate a set of *target entities*—populations to be aided, enlisted, or coerced; organizations that can serve as allies or whose resistance needs to be overcome; and decision centers that need to be influenced in various ways.

The fourth dimension is *interorganizational relationships*. Community intervention organizations in the contemporary urban scene cannot function in isolation, but rather are connected to a welter of other organizations and institutions. These can facilitate, hinder, or provide context as an organization pursues its aims.

Small Groups

The group is the smallest and most intimate social unit that is an arena for engaging in community intervention. A variety of different types of task-oriented groups are employed for problem-solving and change purposes—grassroots block clubs, agency boards, municipal commissions, neighborhood committees and councils, staff groups, and others. All community practitioners work with groups of one or another type in the course of their career. It is a generic, ubiquitous element of practice, unlike some other roles that may arise only occasionally or not at all, such as designing a staff-training program, setting up a computerized management information system, or organizing a protest march (Tropman, 1997; Pendergrast and Farrow, 1997).

Small groups have certain attributes that distinguish them, particularly the element of face-to-face interaction. Homans (1950) has provided a definition that has stood up over time:

We mean by a group, a number of persons who communicate with one another often over a span of time, and who are few enough so that each person is able to communicate with all the others, not at secondhand, through other people, but face-to-face (p. 1).

A small group is not a population or a mass or an audience, but rather a tangible collection of people who can discuss matters personally and work together in close association. Larger entities sometimes subdivide into small groups in order to get necessary work accomplished.

Bales (1966) found that there are two broad functions involved in the functioning of groups: task functions that have to do with meeting the environmental purposes of the group (solving specific problems that the group was formed to tackle) and socioemotional or expressive functions that relate to keeping the group together and working in relative harmony on its external tasks. Parsons (1955) has referred to these more generally as system functions and uses somewhat different language to connote the same ideas: namely, a division between instrumental and maintenance functions.

Bales indicates that leadership roles in groups involve implementing the two types of functions. Task roles focus on things such as specifying the problem, breaking it into workable parts, deciding on what information is necessary to solve it, determining what kind of pressure needs to be brought to bear on decision makers, and so forth. Socioemotional or maintenance roles involve matters such as notifying people of meetings, keeping a friendly atmosphere, making sure there is enough room available to hold everyone comfortably, giving everyone a chance to speak, for example.

Researchers indicate that there are ordinarily an array of leadership roles that are distributed among members of the group, rather than one all-encompassing leader who alone carries out all of them. Such distribution of roles has also been found to be an effective way for groups to function, in that tasks can be divided efficiently among several members, the skills of the entire collectivity can be brought to play, and new leaders can develop on a continual basis.

The community practitioner needs to be aware of the need for both task and socioemotional functions and leadership roles in any group situation and to cultivate individuals who can perform these. This means encouraging members to take on responsibilities and supporting them as necessary through formal or informal training and psychological reinforcement.

Task-oriented groups typically go through regular stages as they engage in problem solving. It is important for the community practitioner to be aware of these in order to facilitate the process. Bales and Strodtbeck (1968) have charted the stages in the process and indicated some of the prominent member roles during each of them. The stages and related roles are as follows:

Orientation—An exploratory period focusing on determining what information is relevant and useful for dealing with the problem. Members come to understand the problem better and learn in common what is known or should become known by them about it. The key roles during this phase include giving information, asking for information, and clarifying the task.

Evaluation—A more feeling-level interplay during which differences in interests and values are discussed. Judgments now are made about the facts of the situation and about the viability of various courses of action. Key roles include giving opinions, asking for opinions, and expressing feelings about the problem and process.

Control—A coming to grips with the problem by deciding what should be done about it. Decisions made here are binding in that they can be said to be controlling of the actions of the members and potentially of the task environment. Key roles here include asking for suggestions, recommending actions, and giving direction.

The community practitioner can assist in this process by helping people to give the group enough time for orientation before moving into more advanced phases, encouraging appropriate roles at appropriate times, encouraging and protecting people in their expression of affect, and seeing that responsibilities and timing matters are pinned down in the control phase. Group members hopefully will be engaging in such leadership roles themselves; practitioners in general should supplement or fill in when there is a void in such actions by members.

In her contribution to this book, Bakalinsky discusses very broadly the place of small-group activities in community intervention. She considers the question of group size, pointing out that this involves the issues of both numbers of people as well as the scope of representativeness to be included in the group. Representativeness includes the issue of democratic participation by varied interests in the community and also the configuration of skills and competencies that are needed to attack the problem under consideration.

Group composition is also treated, including descriptive criteria such as age, gender, race, and experience, and behavioral characteristics related to group process roles such as conciliator, energizer, analyzer, and the like. The values and effects of emphasizing heterogeneity vs. homogeneity in the make-up of the group come into consideration here. Heterogeneity insures a greater range of views, interests, and resources, but may sometimes inhibit the evolution of collaborative relationships in the group.

This ties into another factor that is covered in the analysis—group cohesiveness. Members ordinarily have in common their concern over a given community issue or problem. That external preoccupation can be a binding element, but in many cases it is not itself enough to sustain continuing action. Members may need to have a sense of belonging to the group itself, to gain gratification in their association with other members, and to be attracted emotionally to the group situation. These elements of group climate and interaction are an additional consideration the community practitioner needs to address.

CORE ELEMENTS OF PRACTICE

Practice in large measure is an art and has many unique, particularistic attributes. Each problem encountered, and its context, has distinct qualities and requirements that cannot be ignored. At the same time, upon more abstract examination, there are basic or common aspects of practice, such as the presence of organizational constraints, the requirements of sufficient resources, and the necessity of leadership of one kind or another. These provide additional parameters within which community practitioners operate. We have chosen two basic practice elements to highlight—the use of a systematic problem-solving methodology to guide interventive behavior, and the exercise of professional influence to advance progress toward intended goals. Two influence modalities will be given attention in separate treatments, one interpersonal in nature (use of persuasion), and the other organizational in character (application of structured pressure tactics). Also, additional modes that are typically employed will be touched upon in this discussion.

Problem-Solving Methodology

Professional intervention as distinct from ordinary engagement in community affairs by volunteer citizens is characterized in part by use of a logical, orderly, and disciplined means of analyzing problems and developing a well-constructed solution strategy based on a solid factual understanding of the circumstances (Burch, 1999; Brueggemann, 1996). Pincus and Minahan (1973) refer to this as a "scientific method of investigation and problem-solving" (p. 91), which in this instance means proceeding in a systematic fashion and basing actions on existing theoretical knowledge and situational data.

For many individuals the community system is an amorphous, confusing, and intangible sphere that they do not comprehend or have direct contact with—as they do with a family or a small organization. Faced with the need to affect the community in some way, they do not have a clear sense of how to start or what to take account of. A problem-solving scheme provides a road map of sequential action steps and suggests variables to select out to examine and manipulate. This is analogous to working with individuals in psychotherapy, where a diagnostic framework for assessment and treatment planning is considered a necessary and useful component of practice.

Such an intervention planning framework provides structure and direction; it should optimize the probability of success in achieving intended objectives. In this sense, it injects a measure of control into the difficult and untamed process of steering community change. But we are speaking here of increasing chances of arriving at intended goals, not the certainty of reaching them. (Scott, 1998, has documented how "certain schemes to improve the human condition have failed.") Again, turning to clinical practice with individuals, a professionally disciplined somewhat stepwise process is assumed to aid in helping clients reach better mental health, but it does not insure that that end will be attained for each client.

After examining an array of different problem-solving frameworks, Glaser, Abelson and Garrison (1983) indicate that these can be grouped into a half-dozen basic steps.

1. Some problem or need is identified. It can be a concern expressed by an individual or group, an evident discrepancy between what is desired and how things are, or the realization that some new idea or program is not being applied in the local situation. It can be a concrete pressure resulting from defects, hardships, or tensions in the situation. In any case, without the surfacing of an awareness of a problem or need there is little likelihood that ameliorative action will be taken.

2. The problem needs to be defined, delineated, and clarified. Terms such as "assessment" or "diagnosis" are used to convey the notion of comprehending the problem in a realistic and sophisticated way. A faulty definition of the problem can lead to faulty solutions, or to conflicts and holdups resulting in no action at all. Certain involvements should be avoided, such as spending too much time on assessment, responding to demands for a crash program, or the practitioner imposing a favorite diagnosis on the situation. Also, ideological preferences, biases, and blind spots can lead to faulty appraisals that are not in tune with solid progress.

3. Systematic methods have to be employed to obtain accurate information about the problem. Tools of needs assessment, environmental impact study, or historical trend analysis can be employed at this stage. Community people can be drawn in and spoken with informally or through surveys and focus group techniques. Existing information can be gleaned (such as social indicators) or original data can be gathered. Such tools can assist participants in thinking through the issues. But they cannot be used in a mechanical way. In the end, judgment and a reasonable level of consensus among the people who are involved will carry the process forward.

4. From this information pool, alternative courses of action are delineated. These are weighed one against the other, with an examination of specific outcomes, possible side effects, resistances to be encountered, resources necessary and available, popular acceptance within the community, leadership skills that are required, and so forth. A preferred action strategy is chosen, and often contingency actions are identified, should the prime approach run into difficulty. In comparing alternatives, feasibility and promise need to be considered: Can the program be carried out simply and have rapid results? Do participants have high motivation and ample skills to mount it? Is there money to carry the program forward? Is the payoff real and substantial? and so forth.

5. Implementation actions are spelled out. This entails the specific behaviors and responsibilities of the practitioner and others, timelines, tactical techniques, programmatic details, etc. These may have to be framed in general terms, as the situation may not be sufficiently clear until the strategy is set in motion and the reactions of others are evident. The practical aspects of the action become more clear and

important at this stage, and can reveal whether the strategy design is realistic at all. Are there enough people who are willing to do the things that are necessary, are they willing to put up with threats or disapproval that might come about, are facilities and equipment at hand to enable movement to take place? If the plan is not feasible, this suggests moving back in the framework to reassess or choose another among the alternative strategies.

6. Terminal actions are set forth. This typically entails a careful evaluation of effects—what was achieved and what more needs to be done. Evaluation can be formal and use prescribed methods of evaluation research or it can be informal and use thoughtful judgments of those involved in or affected by the change effort. The evaluation may call for a continuation of the process in refined or reconstituted form. In this case the assignment of the practitioner may change or another professional might be assigned to the project. On the other hand, the evaluation may suggest that the practitioner detach from the project as it becomes institutionalized and routinized in the natural flow of the community. Just as there is a logical beginning, there needs to be a logical ending.

The selection by Fred Cox describes a specific problem-solving schema that incorporates these features and expands on them. It was developed initially by the editors of this book and has been used widely over the years. The Cox format includes a number of additional important elements, particularly the identification of the beneficiary system. This has implications for focusing on goals and developing an action system through which the change process is mounted. Cox also distinguishes between strategy and tactics and treats them in separate sections, the latter including such matters as the most effective entry into the change process, the training of participants, and means of dealing with opposition.

While a problem-solving format needs to be logical and orderly, it is not entirely linear. One step can feed back on the other and require a fresh start. As new information is gathered or unexpected results come about, it may be necessary to reassess and reformulate strategy and tactics. The scheme has to be considered suggestive, flexible, and cyclical in character, one that provides structure but is not a rigid blueprint or cognitive straightjacket.

Use of Influence: Interpersonal Interaction and Organized Pressure

The work of community intervention professionals, indeed of any practicing professional, is to produce intended effects. Their mission, sanctioned by society, is to redirect problematic conditions in a beneficial direction (improved health, better educated citizens, reduction of poverty, etc.). This means using the skills and the influence of the professional (in collaboration with others) to bring about these results. In the human services the practitioner ordinarily relies heavily on the use of the self as an instrument of influence and change.

We can conceptualize influence in terms of interpersonal interaction (on a one-on-one basis convincing people, giving them facts, inspiring them, showing them the way) or organized pressure (orchestrating political pressure, legal authority, or protest demonstrations). In the field of community intervention the employment of organizationally based means is recognized and accepted. It is an evident, expected modus operandi and does not have to be justified or explained. What is less clear to many people is that interpersonal influence is also a common and necessary component of community practice. The practitioner is constantly in person-to-person professional contact with individuals of infinite variety, and needs the capacity to comprehend their ways and motives and engage with them in a highly sophisticated way. We will dwell on the interpersonal component in this discussion because it is less well understood (Pearlmutter, 1998; Wittig and Bettencourt, 1996).

Specht (1988) highlighted this aspect of influence in his writings. He states that human-service professionals, in addition to dealing with individual clients, have to relate to collaterals of clients (family, friends, and neighbors), colleagues from within their own profession and in other professions, and "sociopolitical others"—who comprise the larger action system of community intervention. These may be local residents, legislative leaders, board members, clergymen, agency directors, PTA presidents, business executives, and many others, cross-cutting class, ethnic, political, and geographic lines. "Sociopolitical interaction can take place in boardrooms, bars . . . at all times of day and night; and in social contexts ranging from office interviews and formal meetings to dinners, parties and 'meeting for a drink'" (p. 61).

In many of these contacts the practitioner is engaged in exchange relationships, purposively seeking some kind of response or resource from others—willingness to participate in a meeting, to support a piece of legislation proposed by an action group, to contribute funds or time to a project, or to stay out of the way and let the action proceed. The interactions should be viewed professionally: They have the purpose of producing benefits for people needing services or who suffer some disadvantage in society.

In return, the practitioner also provides (or exchanges) resources or reacts responsively. This can "involve a range of concrete or symbolic items, including reassuring words, a wink, . . . a food basket . . . " (p. 64). Interpersonal transactions under exchange theory can entail the giving of information, money, goods, status, services, and affective qualities such as attention, approval, and empathy. The professional's organizational base, including the sponsoring agency or a citizen action group, provides many of the resources that can be drawn upon to carry out these exchanges. It is necessary to be able to size up the other person, to individualize sensitively, in order to determine the kind of resource that that person would likely find of value and react to favorably.

According to Specht, interpersonal interactions in the community intervention realm are in some ways more complex and demanding than with clients in clinical work. "The professional exercises less power and authority and maintains less control over the purpose and context of the interaction" (p. 60). The other person may have greater power or status (the mayor or a corporate leader) and there is less prior understanding, and less likelihood of a contract, concerning the rules of the game and expected outcomes than is typical in the clinical situation.

Also, the stakes can be high in a very tangible way—loss of funding for an agency, failure to enact significant legislation, or a decision not to build a low-income housing development or a shelter for the homeless. These results can also be personally embarrassing to the professional because knowledge of them is not confined to the clinical interviewing room; rather they can become public and contentious through reportage in newspapers, television, and community meetings.

These are personal encounters in a macro context, "in which actors share with others their feelings, beliefs, attitudes and fears, entrust others with . . . information about themselves, share secrets and privileged communications and rely upon one another to provide resources and carry out tasks that can affect their welfare [and that of those for whom they carry responsibilities] in significant ways" (p. 71). Interpersonal modes of influence clearly fall in the domain of community practitioner, as a resource to be used and a competency to be mastered.

Recognizing that influence can be either personal or organizational, a variety of different forms of influence can be exerted to obtain desired results. We will review an array of influence modes, five in number, that go from intrusive and forceful to nonintrusive and subtle, namely: coercive, incentive-based, rational, persuasive, and normative. An excellent review of theory and research on influence modes has been provided by Glaser, Abelson, and Garrison (1983), and we will draw on their analysis in this discussion. We have organized their ideas into the five categories mentioned above, which were constructed from their review. (See the Introduction to Part Two for an expanded treatment of influence and strategy.)

Coercive.   This approach involves the use of threat, force, fiat, or other means that may lead people to "go along," even against their wishes. Ordinarily, the target feels some degree of tension and stress in these circumstances. The approach may entail legal demands, administrative regulations, political clout, or economic pressure. Typical means applied include marches and other demonstrations, boycotts, legislative campaigns, strikes, and other forms of direct action. There may be the employment or potential employment of violence, civic disruption, or property damage. In other words, the individual experiencing coercive influence is faced with real, material loss or disadvantage in resisting the influence attempt. There is an effort by the change agent to gain compliance on the part of unwilling adversaries, and for this reason there may be a need for follow-up monitoring and recurring sanctions.

Incentive-Based.   A frequent mode of influence involves giving benefits or rewards in conjunction with engaging in intended or prescribed behavior. This might involve making a grant, allowing use of facilities, providing staff support, giving a testimonial, or writing off a loan. The entire behavior modification/learning theory school is rooted in this concept, as is exchange theory. The notion is to make it pleasurable and fulfilling for someone to engage in desired behavior. Incentives can be material, as in the examples given above, or they can be socioemotional (clearing the way for the target to belong to a high-status group) or symbolic (bestowing recognition through a medal or certificate).

The first two approaches are often organizational in form, in that they may involve changing structural features of the environment of the persons being influenced—for example their economic situation or political options. However, coercive means and use of incentives can also be applied on the interpersonal level. The approaches that follow are particularly applicable on the interpersonal level.

Rational.   This involves imparting information to individuals with the hope that this will enable the person to make a choice in the right direction. In this formulation, the information is not slanted and is given in an objective or neutral manner. The information may be empirical data, theory, or philosophical frameworks, for example. Some forms of counseling use this approach, as do sensitivity training (T-group) programs. Professionals engage in this form of influence when they indicate to an action group what programs are available to support given purposes, and what the specific consequences might be of choosing each of these. Providing information about health behavior, population trends, and governmental regulations all fit here.

Persuasive.   Here information and argumentation are provided in a proactive fashion. There is a clear message or point of view, using reasoning and rhetoric to convince the targeted individual to believe or act in prescribed ways. Data may be set forth, but they are likely to be selective and slanted in a particular direction. Belief about advisability of a given course is expressed, or proof is given that a particular action will be beneficial or effective. Efforts illustrating this approach include urging people to join an organization, vote for a particular candidate, boycott a product, make a financial contribution to a cause, or exercise daily.

Normative.   Normative influence is more subtle and varied in form. It involves making changes in the perceptions and beliefs of people, so that they internalize norms or values and come to make them their own. Among the different means used to accomplish this is encouraging participation in making decisions so that one is impacted by peer pressures and also becomes a stakeholder in the action plan that is decided upon. Or the change agent can present himself or herself as a friendly and admirable person whom the target individual likes and becomes identified with. The individual then is motivated to act in large measure because of attraction to the professional. When this is coordinated with modeling of the intended behavior by the change agent, the combination is particularly potent.

Two of these influence modes are examined in depth in selections in the text. Simons looks at means of persuasion, pointing out that direct-service professionals as well as macro-level administrators have to use this as a generic skill. He sets forth eight principles of effective persuasion, such as showing the advantages of the position that is advocated, being comprehensible, citing proven results, linking the message to influentials, and minimizing threats to the target. He illustrates with examples of the presentation of a funding proposal to a county board and developing a radio spot to recruit program volunteers.

Zander treats measures that make use of organized pressure. One of these is a coercive approach, including blocking the progress of targets, restricting their freedom of movement, and harming or threatening to harm them. Among the pressuring approaches he also includes are using third parties as a lever, demonstrating successful programs, and engaging in bargaining. Zander observes that pressuring methods cause targets to focus on their environmental circumstances rather than on the quality of the ideas being proposed. Therefore, he suggests, the methods are more effective in changing overt behavior than in modifying internal beliefs and values.

MACRO RELATIONSHIPS TO MICRO PRACTICE

Another contextual factor in community intervention involves the established approaches for achieving human development and social betterment. Typically change efforts along these lines have followed two paths: providing aid directly to individuals experiencing hardships and disabilities, or changing the social environment that may be causing or exacerbating these troubles. The first, a micro perspective, entails casework, counseling, and clinical treatment, with a psychological focus that aims to strengthen the individual. The second, a macro perspective, includes community intervention, policy practice, and administration, with a system focus emphasizing social change or preventive actions.

The approaches should be seen as complementary rather than in basic conflict. Optimal community well-being requires the coexistence of multiple approaches to deal with different problems and populations. The following statement by a long-time social work leader (Schottland, 1962) vividly articulates this orientation:

I view these two aspects of social work—practice and policy, psychological individualization and social reform, improvement of the individualized services and improvement of social conditions, direct rendering of services and broader programs of prevention, personal therapy and social leadership—as a coordinated approach to the solution of these problems, individual and community, with which social work is concerned.

While the casework aspect has tended to dominate, in the recent past opportunities have arisen for social work to strengthen its reform dimension. The social sciences, which had a great spurt following World War II, provide a knowledge base for the planning and social change areas comparable to the base provided earlier by psychoanalysis to the field of treatment.

Furthermore, society's disenfranchised groups have been exerting heavy pressures on the professions to address discrimination, social injustice, and social dysfunction. Contemporary problems such as poverty, blight, racism, delinquency, drug abuse, and educational decline simply do not lend themselves to overall solution through individualized services. While in the past the professions, including social work, have not fully embraced controversial areas involving social conflict, more recently they have begun to respond to such challenges. There is a more balanced micro/macro awareness than in some previous decades.

Generalist Practice—Combining Micro and Macro Methods

The interrelationship of individualized (micro) and community (macro) practice is best reflected in the generalist practice school, also identified by the terms integrated, unitary, generic, holistic, and multirole practice. All of these convey the notion of using both micro and macro practice together in ways that are mutually supplementing and reinforcing (Wharf and McKenzie, 1998; Kirst-Ashman and Hull, 1997). The practitioner starts with a broad assessment of the problem and develops an intervention approach that draws on the full range of practice options, often employing combinations of practice initiatives as appropriate. Teisiger (1983) describes the perspective as follows:

The appropriate starting point for interventions must be determined by examining the entire situation and must not be framed by what is initially presented. The problem . . . selected for intervention will determine the methodology of choice rather than the methodological bias or expertise of the worker... (p. 178).

An excellent overview of approaches to generalist practice is provided by Goldstein (1981), an analysis that indicates variations in emphasis and also suggests components of the approach. Some of the orientations he discusses are presented below.

Combined-Methods Generalist—This conveys the notion of using the discrete disciplines of casework, group work, and community organization in combined fashion, distilling them into a coordinated frame. The practice role that emerges is seen as a hybrid of sorts, comprising a lumped-together composite rather than a smoothly fashioned whole.

Case-Manager Generalist—This concept grows out of the case-manager role and the need to connect highly vulnerable and dependent clients to necessary community supports. This approach highlights integrating the services of fragmented agencies on behalf of clients while working with clients individually.

Generalist as a Role Composite—Here a very wide range of roles are merged to cut across problem and client types. Roles often thought of in clinical terms include supporter, advisor, therapist, and caretaker; then there is the administrator and consultant; further, there is the educator, coordinator, advocate, mediator, broker, and enabler. These roles are visualized as melding to form a coherent and well-articulated intervention package.

Problem-Focused Generalist—The idea here is to break away from specialist roles and agency functions as the determinants of intervention, and rather to build intervention from the requirements of the problem situation. An encompassing problem-solving schema is proposed, allowing the worker to move forward from a multifaceted person-in-environment assessment of client needs. The approach alternatively conceives of the building of practice from broad but common problem clusters, such as aging, physical disabilities, and child welfare.

Systems-Oriented Generalist—This approach starts from systems theory and assumes that human-service professionals relate to a range of different systems that may be dysfunctional, including individuals, families, groups, organizations, and communities. A client's problems may intersect various levels (family tensions, lack of informal social network support, and discriminatory hiring practices in the community) and may require an intervention plan that appropriately cuts across and impacts these levels, simultaneously or in sequence.

An incisive orientation to the generalist approach is provided in the selection on "Integrated Practice" by Parsons, Jorgensen, and Hernandez (1994). They offer a framework for analyzing intervention according to a continuum that ranges from small systems to large systems. Social problems are identified as the fundamental targets of intervention behavior. Further, the authors view education, habitation (growth promotion and inculcating problem-solving skills), and normalization as the guides to role-taking in practice. Empowerment across system levels is seen as central to practice, and a wide array of micro and macro practice roles is required to accomplish the empowering of people.

A different form of mixed practice is suggested in the contribution in this volume by Gutierrez. The starting point is the individual (women of color) and the need to focus on empowerment issues in direct practice with this type of client. Empowerment in this case is not a collective concept, as it is often in community-intervention literature (increasing the ability of a neighborhood to take action on its own behalf). Rather, the objective is to increase the individual's sense of control over her own life and to enhance her feeling of self-worth. This may involve the use of community-intervention perspectives and skills by the practitioner as a supplement to micro methods. Gutierrez suggests practice actions such as engaging in a power analysis of the client's objective situation and fostering within the client relevant skills such as competency in community and organizational change, assertiveness, and advocacy.

Viewing the issue of integrating macro skills into the clinical area more broadly, the whole information and referral aspect of micro practice draws heavily on the techniques and processes of macro practice. This includes helping clients to know how to make use of community resources—the approach to take with different agencies, whom to contact, how to state their case in a way as to gain the best service, how to counter negative responses, and the like. Linking clients with informal social supports such as neighbors, neighborhood organizations such as block clubs and other voluntary associations involves knowledge and skills from the macro area.

Micro-Macro Concerns for Social Justice

A concern with social justice has been recognized as intrinsic to macro practice. Clinical practice, however, shares in embracing this value. The outlook and experience of macro practice can support and reinforce the clinical orientation to social justice. Swenson, in article 12, discusses a variety of ways in which clinicians can advance social justice precepts in the agency setting. They can take action to fight oppressive beliefs and practices in agencies and act to develop new structures that promote democracy, equality, and client empowerment. In this, they would find it advantageous to draw on macro techniques that have been developed to promote organizational change and innovation.

Clinicians are advised by Swenson to aid oppressed clients to understand their objective circumstances and to consider means of liberating themselves from their exploiters. Relevant practice methods for accomplishing this are found in the writings of community advocacy theorists such as Freire and others. Swenson also suggests that clinicians employ typical community intervention techniques such as engaging clients in mutual aid groups and encouraging them to organize for collective social action.

Other suggested approaches involve assessing and understanding clients relative to their social status and position of power; helping clients who are in roles that embrace privilege and domination to consider taking steps to change; and acting to minimize status differentials in the relationship between clinicians and clients.

As clinicians move in some of these directions they may well encounter constraints imposed on them by agency policy, administrative prohibitions, and countervailing definitions of professionalism among their immediate peers. In these circumstances, it could be beneficial to pass the ball to macro colleagues, who often do not have their hands tied in the same way. This kind of cooperative interplay constitutes a special form of "interdisciplinary" collaboration among social work micro/macro subspecialties within the profession.

In her book, *Integrating Social Welfare Policy and Social Work Practice,* McInnis-Dittrich (1994) shows how legislative statutes and policy mandates impinge on the lives of clients and the operations of agencies. The author delineates a number of macro skills that can be employed to modify policies in order to benefit provision of service to clients, including written and verbal communication with legislators, lobbying, public hearings, using the media, supporting a political candidate, and going to court to change policy. The micro practitioner can participate in all of these activities, usually in collaboration with others, and as an adjunct or extension of the work done directly with individual clients.

We have shown ways in which micro and macro practice interconnect, and we have focused on how macro practice can enhance micro practice, but the converse also pertains. Micro methods can facilitate the interpersonal relationships aspect of community intervention and can help planners and organizations understand problems of clients at a very concrete and personal level. This information can contribute positively to the design of plans, the shaping of policy, and the organizing of residents. The complexity and interrelatedness of contemporary community problems invite collaboration and the kinds of cross-method approaches that have been discussed.

The contextual factors that we have presented provide a prism through which to examine community intervention and develop strategies and tactics. The parameters (frameworks, arenas, core areas of practice, and macro/micro relationships) can be seen as a kind of staging area from which informed strategic planning can take place. Part One elaborates on the parameters and Part Two articulates the strategic dimensions.

—Jack Rothman

REFERENCES

Bales, Robert F. "Task Roles and Social Roles in Problem-Solving Groups." In Bruce Biddle and E. J. Thomas, eds., *Role Theory: Concepts and Research* (pp. 254–63). New York: Wiley, 1966.

Bales, R. F., & F. L. Strodtbeck. "Phases in Group Problem-Solving." In Dorwin Cartwright & A. Zander, eds., *Group Dynamics Research and Theory* (3d. ed) (pp. 389–98). New York: Harper & Row, 1968.

Benne, K., and P. Sheats. "Functional Roles of Group Members." In L. P. Bradford, ed., *Group Development* (pp. 51–59). Washington, DC: National Education Association, 1961.

Berkhofer, R. *Beyond the Great Story: History as Text and Discourse.* Cambridge, MA: Harvard University Press, 1995.

Brueggemann, W. G. *The Practice of Macro Social Work.* Chicago: Nelson-Hall Publishers, 1996.

Burch, Hobart A. *Social Welfare Policy Analysis and Choices.* New York: Haworth Press, 1999.

Chambers, Lance & Michael A. P. Taylor. *Strategic Planning: Processes, Tools and Outcomes.* Brookfield, VT: Ashgate, 1998.

Chirot, Daniel. *How Societies Change.* Thousand Oaks, CA: Pine Forge Press, 1994.

Deakin, Elizabeth. "Social Equity in Planning." *Berkeley Planning Journal* 13 (1999): 1–5.

Delgardo, Gary. *Beyond the Politics of Place: New Directions in Community Organizing,* 2nd ed., 1997. Berkeley, CA: Chardon Press, 1997.

Fisher, Robert. "The Importance of History and Context in Community Organization." In Jack Rothman, ed. *Reflections on Community Organization: Enduring Themes and Critical Issues.* Itasca, IL: F.E. Peacock Publishers, 1999, 335–353.

Glaser, Edward M., Harold H. Abelson, & Kathalee N. Garrison. *Putting Knowledge to Use: Facilitating the Diffusion of Knowledge and the Implementation of Planned Change.* San Francisco: Jossey-Bass Publishers, 1983.

Goldstein, Howard. "Generalist Social Work Practice." In Neil Gilbert and Harry Specht, eds., *Handbook of the Social Services.* Englewood Cliffs, NJ: Prentice-Hall, 1981.

Hall, Gus. "Who Runs America?" *Forward* (April 1, 1994): 7.

Homans, George C. *The Human Group.* New York: Hartcourt, Brace, 1950.

Kirst-Ashman, K. K., & G. H. Hull Jr. *Generalist Practice with Organizations and Communities.* Chicago: Nelson-Hall Publisher, 1997.

Litwak, Eugene, & Henry J. Meyer. "The School and the Family: Linking Organizations and External Primary Groups." In Paul F. Lazarsfeld et al., eds., *The Uses of Sociology* (pp. 522–43). New York: Basic Books, 1967.

McInnis-Dittrich, Kathleen. *Integrating Social Welfare Policy and Social Work Practice.* Pacific Grove, CA: Brooks/Cole, 1994.

Mizrahi, Terry, & Beth Rosenthal. "'A Whole Lot of Organizing Going On': The Status and Needs of Organizers in Community-Based Organizations." *Journal of Community Practice* 5 (4) 1998: 1–24.

Pardo, Mary S. *Mexican American Women Activists: Identity and Resistance in Two Los Angeles Communities.* Philadelphia: Temple University Press, 1998.

Parsons, Ruth J., James D. Jorgensen, & Santos H. Hernandez. *The Integration of Social Work Practice.* Pacific Grove, CA: Brooks/Cole, 1994.

Parsons, Talcott. "Family Structure and the Socialization of the Child." In T. Parsons & R. F. Bales, eds., *Family, Socialization, and Interaction* (pp. 35–132). New York: Free Press, 1955.

Pearlmutter, S. "Self-Efficacy and Organizational Change Leadership." *Administration in Social Work* 22 (3) 1998: 23–39.

Pendergrast, Eudora S., & John Farrow. "Community Councils and Neighbourhood Committees: Lessons for Our Communities from Around the World." Toronto, ON: Canadian Urban Institute, 1997.

Pincus, Allen, & Ann Minahan. *Social Work Practice: Model and Method.* Itasca, IL: F. E. Peacock, 1973.

Rivera, Felix G., & John L. Erlich. *Community Organizing in a Diverse Society,* 3rd ed. Boston: Allyn & Bacon, 1998.

Rustin, Bayard. "From Protest to Politics: The Future of the Civil Rights Movement." *Commentary* 39 (February 1965): 25–31.

Salomon, Larry R. *Roots of Justice: Stories of Organizing in Communities of Color.* Berkeley: Chardon Press, 1998.

Schottland, Charles I. "Our Changing Society Challenges Social Work." Keynote Address, University of Pittsburgh School of Social Work Faculty-Alumni Conference, Pittsburgh, PA, March 30, 1962.

Scott, James C. *Seeing Like a State: How Certain Schemes to Improve the Human Condition Have Failed*. New Haven: Yale University Press, 1998.

Shin, Junseob, & George E. McClomb. "Top Executive Leadership and Organizational Innovation: An Empirical Investigation of Nonprofit Human Service Organizations." *Administration in Social Work* 22 (3) (1998): 1–22.

Specht, Harry. *New Directions for Social Work Practice*. Englewood Cliffs, NJ: Prentice Hall, 1988.

Teisiger, K. S. "Evaluation of Education for Generalist Practice." *Journal of Education for Social Work* 19 (1) (1983): 79–85.

Tropman, John E. *Successful Community Leadership: A Skills Guide for Volunteers and Professionals*. Washington, DC: National Association of Social Workers, 1997.

Warren, Roland L. *The Community in America*. Chicago: Rand McNally, 1963.

Weissberg, Robert. *The Politics of Empowerment*, Westport, CT: Praeger, 1999.

Wharf, Brian, & Brad McKenzie. *Connecting Policy to Practice in the Human Services*. New York: Oxford University Press, 1998.

Wilson, James Q. "Planning and Politics: Citizen Participation in Urban Renewal." *Journal of the American Institute of Planners* 3 (November 1963): 242–9.

Wireman, Peggy. "Citizen Participation." *Encyclopedia of Social Work* (1977): 178–9.

Wittig, Michele Andrisin, & B. Ann Bettencourt, eds., *Social Psychological Perspectives on Grassroots Organizing*. New York: Plenum Publishing Corp., 1996.

Wuthnow, Robert. *Loose Connections: Joining together in America's Fragmented Communities*. Cambridge, MA: Harvard University Press, 1998.

FRAMEWORKS

1.

Jack Rothman

APPROACHES TO COMMUNITY INTERVENTION

A PERSONAL PREFACE

This article presents a revision and refinement of the "Three Models" construct, which I introduced originally in 1968 and which has, with minor modifications and updating, provided the organizing framework for this book over its previous five editions. Through that time period, practices and conditions in communities have changed, and certain intellectual loose ends in the formulation have teased at me. My research studies pointed to gaps and uncertainties, and feedback from students and professionals in the field posed dilemmas that were difficult to resolve. It was as though I had packed a large and assorted pile of conceptual clothing into a cognitive suitcase and found there was a sock or the end of a tie sticking out after I had pressed it closed. The publication of this new edition has given me the impetus to try to tidy things up.

The basic ideas, it seems to me, hold up—but there is more complexity and variation than I had perceived. The best way to present the new perspective, I believe, is to do it in two sections. "Core Modes of Community Intervention" lays out the original schema, with some refinements and updating. "The Interweaving of Intervention Approaches" comprises an expansion and reformulation.

My first years of teaching were taken up with grappling to construct some type of unitary approach. But no matter how I labored, there were always contradictions and rough edges (the conceptual suitcase troubles started early). Someone who

recently sought to summarize the intellectual contribution of a complex American thinker was led to comment: "At the end of the exercise, worst of all, you may find you are left with a few extra pieces which seem to fit nowhere" (Gellman, 1984, p. xv). That's how I felt about the subject matter I was wrestling.

Meanwhile, as my students presented themselves in class, they also didn't compose a unitary entity. I came to realize that they broke roughly into three types, each of which was looking for different things from the school and from me. There were those who were concerned with the better delivery of services, including coordination among agencies and effectiveness in meeting the needs of various vulnerable populations. They were interested in doing social planning and policy development for organizations such as the United Way or comprehensive health planning councils. Another group had the Peace Corps or VISTA (Volunteers in Service to America) in mind and were focused on working at the grassroots level. They were motivated to bring people together to solve their local problems through discussion on a cooperative, self-help basis. A third group was influenced by the civil rights, antiwar and student movements (such as SNCC, Student Nonviolent Coordinating Council, and SDA, Students for a Democratic Society) and had a strong social action bent. Their aim was to aid the oppressed, promote social justice, and change society.

It gradually became clear to me that these different interests and motivations could not be encompassed comfortably by one practice orientation, and that it would be useful to think of different approaches that addressed each of the three empirically distinct groupings represented by the students. I began to stake out these three approaches conceptually, delineating a set of practice variables to be used to analyze variations among them. This was, perhaps, a risky departure from the prevailing casework mode, but, in time, clinical practice also broke from its solitary theoretical mold and began to include behavior modification, cognitive therapy, ecological practice, and other frameworks.

Social action presented a special challenge. Professional fields are typically conservative and eschew any taint of militancy—and that was especially true in the wake of the conformity-drenched decade of the 1950s, when any connection with radicalism was viewed with supreme suspicion. I needed to create an intellectual framework that would legitimate social action as an academic activity as well as an area of practice on par with other forms, something that did not exist in professional schools at that time.

I thought of the three approaches, or models, as ideal-types. They did not exist to a large extent in pristine, full-blown form in the real world, but were useful mental tools to help describe and analyze reality. Over time I have come to deemphasize or soften the notion of "models," which gives greater importance and internal validity to the approaches than seems warranted, and to accent the overlap and intermixture among approaches. The next section of this discussion will sketch out the original approaches as ideal-type constructs, and will also make a cross-comparison of them against a set of twelve practice variables. The last section, which is more practical and the place where the

analysis leads, will consider combined and variant patterns that serve to integrate the different modalities.

CORE MODES OF COMMUNITY INTERVENTION

THREE MODES OF INTERVENTION

Planning has been defined as the act of deciding what to do about some community affair while, meanwhile, life is bringing it around to a firm conclusion. And a typical committee assigned to deal with the task is, of course, merely a form of human organization that takes hours to produce minutes. These quips express a widespread popular view of social intervention as it is commonly carried out. Here, we will try to conceive of disciplined human reckoning that plays tricks on the natural course of life and actually begets intended effects, in furtherance of community well-being.

Differing and contrasting formulations of community intervention currently exist, which has been a source of perplexity and discomfort for the struggling practitioner and teacher. Taylor and Roberts (1985) describe the fluid nature of theory development, stating that in this field, "eclecticism, pragmatism and practice wisdom of professionals foster a turbulence and diversity that makes categorization and model-building especially difficult tasks" (pp. 24–25). In the founding issue of the *Journal of Community Practice*, editor Marie Weil states: that in order to "reclaim and strengthen community practice, theoretical approaches, guiding values and practice strategies need to be articulated so that they are both clear and carefully connected . . . a grounding . . . in reality and theory should be part of that movement forward" (Weil, 1994, pp. xxvii). A special issue of *The Journal on Conceptual*

Models of Practice was issued in 1996 (vol. 3, no. 3/4).

Three important approaches to purposive community change can be discerned in contemporary American communities, both urban and rural, and internationally. We will refer to them as approaches or Modes A, B, and C, and they can be given the appellations respectively of *locality development, social planning/policy, and social action*. Within each mode there are several variations and distinct emphases, but in this initial discussion we will select out and treat one prominent form within the mode for purposes of analysis. The three basic Modes of action do not necessarily exhaust all possibilities, but they offer a serviceable framework for a broad inquiry. These strategies are general in nature and are applicable across professional fields and academic disciplines. However, the author's grounding in social work and sociology will give a particular slant or tinge to the discussion.

In the presentation, community intervention is the general term used to cover the various forms of community level practice. "Community organizing" ordinarily implies social action and sometimes includes neighborhood work involving self-help strategies. But it excludes social planning/ policy development approaches. Community organization has traditionally been the inclusive nomenclature, but it often becomes confused with more narrowly focused radical community organizing. Community work is frequently used to convey a locality development outlook. On the other hand, social planning usually fails to embrace grassroots organizing efforts. Recognizing that there is no standard terminology, community intervention seems to be a convenient and useful overarching term to employ, although "community practice" has similar attributes and will be used occasionally as an alternative.

Administration (or management) is another form of social practice that takes place in the community within organizational settings. It involves developing organizations and keeping them running through obtaining funding and other resources, arranging staffing, establishing and carrying out procedures, maintaining records, and similar activities. Organizations constitute the vehicle through which social goals are pursued and relevant tasks are carried out. Thus, they provide the machinery for steering the endeavors of all three modes of community intervention— in addition to direct-service agencies and a wide spectrum of other programs in the community. Administration practice has a crucial bearing on the performance of all organizations, but it exists in a different dimension than community intervention and will be treated independently and apart from this analysis.

Mode A, Locality Development. This approach presupposes that community change should be pursued through broad participation by a wide spectrum of people at the local community level in determining goals and taking civic action. Its prototypic form will be found in the literature of a segment of the field commonly termed community development. As stated by an early U.N. publication: "Community Development can be tentatively defined as a process designed to create conditions of economic and social progress for the whole community with its active participation and the fullest possible reliance on the community's initiative" (United Nations, 1955).

Locality development is a community-building endeavor with a strong emphasis on what Selznick (1992) terms the "moral commonwealth." He describes this in words such as mutuality, identity, participation, plurality, and autonomy. Locality development fosters community building by promoting process goals: community competency (the ability to solve problems on a self-help basis) and social integration (harmonious interrelationships among different racial, ethnic, and social-class groups—indeed, among all people). Leadership is drawn from within, and direction and control are in the hands of local people (Dionne, 1998; Mattessich and Monsey, 1997; Minkler, 1997). It is a type of activity that has been initiated and sponsored by religious and service groups such as The Catholic Church and The American Friends Service Committee, and it reflects highly idealistic values. The style is humanistic and strongly people-oriented, with the aim of "helping people to help themselves." The process of educating participants and nurturing their personal development has high priority. "Enabling" techniques that are nondirective in character and foster self-direction are emphasized.

Many of the precepts of the feminist perspective on organizing overlap with the locality development approach, including stress on wide participation as well as concern for democratic procedure and educational goals—including consciousness-raising (Hyde, 1989; Naples, 1998; Halseth, 1993). The approach is also used, some would say misappropriated, by political and business leaders who espouse local initiative and privatization, relying on enterprise zones and like programs that essentially intend to scale back social programs for the poor that are carried out under governmental auspices.

Some examples of locality development as conceived here include neighborhood work programs conducted by settlement houses and other community-based agencies; federal government programs such as Agricultural Extension and The National Service Corps; and village-level work in some overseas community development programs, including the Peace Corps and the Agency for International Development (AID). To these can be added community work in the fields of adult education and public health education, as well as self-help and informal helping network activities conducted through neighborhood councils, block clubs, consumer cooperatives, and civic associations (Burns and Taylor, 1998).

Thinkers who contributed intellectual roots for locality development include John Dewey, Mary Follett, Kurt Lewin, and Eduard Lindeman. Among professional writings that express and elaborate this mode are Blakely (1979); Chavis et al. (1993); Cnaan (1991); Henderson and Thomas (1987); Lappin (1985); Mayer (1984); Ross (1955).

The terms "community development" and "locality development" have been used to identify the approach. The locality development nomenclature was employed in the original version of this analysis to convey this perspective on intervention in a precise way. Community development is a more polymorphic term, which sometimes connotes institutional and policy means to strengthen communities from above (Mier, 1993), or suggests industrial expansion through economic development (Bingham and Mier, 1993). Sometimes it has a national or international frame rather than an explicitly local one (Goetz and Clarke, 1993). Locality development will be the terminology of choice here, and when "community development" is used it will connote a Mode A strategy.

While locality development espouses highly respected ideals, it has been criticized for its performance record. Khinduka, in the prior edition of this book, characterizes it as a "soft strategy" for achieving change. He indicates that its preoccupation with process can lead to endless meetings that are frustrating for participants and conducive to a slow pace of progress. Khinduka further argues that concern with modifying attitudes and values may divert attention from important structural issues that need more direct engagement. Also, many projects draw their participation largely from racial and ethnic minorities and the poor, when it is the attitudes of the affluent and well-placed that need rearranging.

Embracing consensus as a basic modus operandi precludes arbitrary actions from occurring, but it puts those who stand to lose from needed reforms in a position to veto effective action. The heavy emphasis on the local community may be inappropriate at a time when the locality has lost much of its hold over people and patterns of life are influenced significantly by powerful national and regional forces. Khinduka admires locality development for playing a gentleman's game in the often sordid arena of community affairs, but he worries about whether it can win.

Mode B, Social Planning/Policy. This emphasizes a technical process of problem solving regarding substantive social problems, such as delinquency, housing, and mental health (Kettner, Monroney, and Marlin, 1999; Burch, 1996). This particular orientation to planning is data-driven and conceives of carefully calibrated change being rooted in social science thinking and empirical objectivity (unlike other existing forms of planning that are more political and emergent). The style is technocratic, and rationality is a dominant ideal. Community participation is not a core ingredient and may vary from much to little, depending on the problem and circumstances. The approach presupposes that change in a complex modern environment requires expert planners who, through the exercise of technical competencies—

including the ability to gather and analyze quantitative data and to maneuver large bureaucratic organizations—are needed to improve social conditions. There is heavy reliance on needs assessment, decision analysis, Markov chains, evaluation research, delphi techniques, computer graphics, and a plethora of sophisticated statistical tools.

The design of formal plans and policy frameworks is of central importance, as is their implementation in effective and cost-efficient ways. By and large, the concern here is with task goals: conceptualizing, selecting, establishing, arranging, and delivering goods and services to people who need them. In addition, fostering coordination among agencies, avoiding duplication, and filling gaps in services are important concerns in achieving service ends (Austin, 1997; Mandell, 1999).

Within the field of social work, educational programs in planning and policy typify the social planning/policy approach. It also finds expression in university departments of public administration, public health, urban affairs, city planning, and policy studies. It is practiced in numerous federal bureaus and departments, in United Ways and community welfare councils, and in city departments and voluntary agencies geared to planning for mental health, health, aging, housing, and child welfare. The National Association of Planning Councils has been formed to strengthen these local community planning efforts.

Intellectual roots for the approach can be found in the thinking of scholars such as Comte, Lasswell, Keynes, Herbert Simon, and Jesse Steiner. Some professional writings that reflect this mode include Gil (1976); Gilbert and Specht (1977); Kahn (1969); Lauffer (1981); Moroney (1991); Morris and Binstock (1966); and Tropman (1984).

While this approach emphasizes rationality in an explicit and formal way, and leans on it to lend legitimation for recommended actions (often by way of voluminous and impressive reports), the other approaches (Modes A and C) also need to be firmly embedded in rationality. Developing a means to successfully achieve broad civic participation or carrying out a protest demonstration to place pressure on public officials each require a high level of strategic calculation, linking chosen means logically to intended ends. The rationality may not be as overt and public, but it is equally related to effective and professionally sound intervention.

Planning and policy are grouped together in this discussion because both involve assembling and analyzing data to prescribe means for solving social problems. They overlap in some measure, but they also probably have distinct features. Frequently, in scholarly and practice writings, the two are treated as though they are mutually exclusive. Policy is often associated with higher social levels—with national and state, governmental structures, and the act of selecting goals and framing legislative or administrative standards rather than actually establishing programs and services.

No clear basis exists for this compartmentalization of policy functions. There is policy development at the local level as well as at higher echelons (Flynn, 1985). It is conducted under private auspices as well as under governmental sponsorship (Pierce, 1984). And it has implementation and monitoring functions in addition to the goal-setting aspect (Pressman and Wildavsky, 1984). Gilbert and Specht (1974) conceive of a "policy planner" and define policy as "a course or plan of action," thereby essentially blending the two.

In this discussion we are addressing policy as professional practice rather than as a method for conducting an analysis to understand social welfare programs (Tropman, 1984; Jansson, 1984). Ironically, many planning and policy scholars write as though the other area does not exist, although upon examination these authors cover a great deal of similar ground. A divergence or different emphasis (areas of less overlap) lies in policy practice's concern with megagoals or quasi-philosophical frameworks that guide legislative enactment and program development, while planning is interested to a greater degree in the details of program construction and service delivery.

In this discussion, "planning" will serve as a shorthand and convenient designation for the planning/policy approach.

The data-driven form of planning and policy practice has a certain currency and appeal, with its coherent intellectual structure and ostensible ease of implementation. Urban planning schools and policy studies programs place a great deal of emphasis on providing students with ever more complex and elegant statistical procedures and computer modeling methods. This may be because these are readily available, can be manipulated easily in a technical sense, and have an aura of mastery and completeness that is missing in more political forms of planning.

Webber and Rittel (1973) state that the data-driven approach is flawed because it is based on the assumption that problems are easily definable, well-bounded, and responsive to professional intervention. Instead, they say, contemporary problems are "wicked" in nature—unique, intractable, intermeshed with others, and situated in a constantly changing and turbulent social environment.

Two important factors place constraints on the prototypical rationalistic mode. The first is the intensification of constituency politics, a contemporary development that makes planning highly contentious and interactive. Interest groups of various kinds feel they should have a say and have acquired a voice, and they place themselves vigorously into the pluralistic process through which decisions are made. Many planners and policy professionals believe that interests of various kinds rightfully should go into the defining of goals and setting the community agenda, because these are socially constructed phenomena and involve value choices that extend far beyond the purview of the expert or bureaucrat.

Another factor confounding prototypical rationalistic intervention is the impact of fiscal constraint. There is public aversion to taxation and to governmental spending for social programs. Concrete economic conditions involving industrial decline and recessionary trends also place objective limits on social program options. These public attitudes and economic strictures have shifted planning from an optimizing stance to what Herbert Simon refers to as "satisficing." The dual effects of contentious community politics and a public leaning toward a "get by" level of social programming place into question the utility of elaborate, data-driven planning modalities.

Mode C, Social Action. This approach presupposes the existence of an aggrieved or disadvantaged segment of the population that needs to be organized in order to make demands on the larger community for increased resources or equal treatment (Bobo, Kendall, and Max, 1996). The particular approach we are describing has a militant orientation to advocacy with respect to goals and tactics (although not all advocacy is militant). It aims at making fundamental changes in the community, including the redistribution of power and resources and gaining access to decision

making for marginal groups. Social action intervention seeks to change legislative mandates of political entities such as a city council, or the policies and practices of institutions such as a welfare department or housing authority. Practitioners in the social action arena generally aim to empower and benefit the poor, the disenfranchised, the oppressed. The style is highly adversarial, and social justice is a dominant ideal (Karp, 1998).

Classically, stemming from the high point of social action in the 1960s, confrontational tactics have been emphasized, including use of demonstrations, picketing, strikes, marches, boycotts, teach-ins, civil disobedience, and other disruptive or attention-gaining moves. Disadvantaged and aggrieved groups frequently do not have at hand the funds, connections, and expertise available to others, and consequently they rely heavily on the resources of "people power," which has the potential to pressure and disrupt. Training institutes sponsored by the Mid-West Academy and Industrial Arcas Foundation have been established to equip low-power constituencies with the skills to impact higher circles of power.

The social action approach has been used widely by AIDS activists, feminist organizing groups, gay and lesbian organizations, consumer and environmental protection organizations, civil rights and black power groups, and La Raza and victim rights groups. It has been embraced by Industrial Areas Foundation and ACORN (Association of Community Organizations for Reform Now) projects, labor unions, including the United Farm workers, and radical political action movements.

Thinkers providing an intellectual foundation for this approach include Marx, Fourier, Bakunin, and Habermas and it was advanced in part by advocacy activities of Jane Addams and her Progressive Era allies.

Alinsky's *Reveille for Radicals* (1946) and *Rules for Radicals* (1972) have typified the orientation of the social action mode. Newer writings also reflect this orientation (Boyte and Riessman, 1986; Burghardt, 1987; Cloward and Piven, 1977; Delgado, 1986; Fisher, 1994; Freire, 1974; Kahn, 1992).

In recent years, social action movements have expanded their strategy bent beyond the confrontational style, and "new wave" organizing now employs a wider range of adversarial tactics. Political and electoral maneuvers that are more fine tuned and diversified are being used in considerable measure. This is because the groups have become more sophisticated over time, there is less public tolerance for disruptive methods, and power elites have become skillful in counteracting confrontations. Organizing has become less stridently ideological, and middle-class groups (and right-wing factions) have been drawn into campaigning on their own behalf or in joint actions.

However, there is a great deal of fragmentation among groups engaged in social action. Advocacy has taken on a particularistic caste, with each aggrieved constituency advancing its own special goals and interests in a "politics of identity" (Byrd, 1999; Gitlin, 1996). Even among people of color, African-Americans, Hispanics, Asian-Americans, and Native Americans go their own ways, independently and often competitively. Thus, coalition building has become a central concern in social action, since groups are typically not strong enough to achieve significant results on their own. But these coalitions are fluid, shifting, and irregular; new configurations have to be formed for different issues on a continuing basis—thus draining off energy that might be focused on external targets.

Fragmentation is especially handicapping because of the growing concentration of political and economic power locally, nationally, and even globally (see the discussion by Fisher on Political Economy). Relatively weak local entities that are disunited find themselves contending with powerful extracommunity entities that are functionally consolidated.

Human service professionals have not been prominent in the social action area, but there has been continuing participation on a small-scale basis over the years. Major national organizations such as ACORN and the United Farm Workers Union have been headed by social workers. There are relevant professional groups, such as the Union of Radical Human Service Workers in Boston and the Bertha Capen Reynolds Society nationally, and there is also a specialized periodical, the *Journal of Progressive Human Services*.

Modest salaries and the absence of professional perquisites are a deterrent to long-term involvement. But new graduates with an interest in basic social change are in a position to take this on as a communal responsibility for a limited time at the beginning of their career. The Nader organization's publication *Good Works* (Anzalone, 1985) and the "Community Jobs" newsletter list a multitude of positions and career opportunities. The richness of the experience, the chance to join hands with aspiring members of oppressed and dispossessed groups, and a sense of accomplishment in advancing a valued and meritorious cause can compensate for temporary material loss. Some professionals have and will continue to make this a lifetime commitment.

A PERSPECTIVE ON DISTINCT PRACTICE APPROACHES

Taking an overview, this three-pronged orientation, as a broad cognitive mapping device for community intervention, has a certain intuitive logic. Historically, several schools of social work have developed specialized programs for training according to the three modes. Thus, a community development program that was situated at the University of Missouri epitomized Mode A; the doctoral program in planning at Brandeis University, Mode B; and a social action program based at Syracuse University, Mode C.

Morris and Binstock (1966), based on an empirical examination of community organizations, suggested a similar threefold division. Friedmann (1987) attaches different language to these same approaches— social learning, policy analysis and social mobilization, as does Lyon (1987)—self-help, technical assistance and conflict. The formulation has also provided an effective conceptual framework for a historical volume on community intervention (Betten and Austin, 1990).

Empirical studies of the formulation lend general support. Cnaan and Rothman (1986) found that a sample of community workers in Israel distinguish between these approaches in their perception of their work and in their practice activities. Several studies in progress have replicated the inquiry with apparently similar results in Sweden, Egypt, Japan, Chile, India, and several other countries. (In the original study, social action appeared to be a more complex phenomenon than the other interventions.) In a series of case studies in Canada, Wharf (1979) observed that locality development and social planning were distinctly discernable, but that social action, while evident, again was more diverse. (We will discuss this disparity in the next section, "The Interweaving of Intervention Approaches.") Practitioners in Wharf's project found the framework particularly useful as an assessment tool, as did those in another Canadian study (Johnson, 1974).

The studies also suggest the existence of variations and mixed configurations, which is the subject of the next section. However, here, for analytical purposes, we view the three approaches as relatively "pure" expressions. The merit in this is suggested by Morris and Binstock (1966) when they refer to their own classification system:

> The categories are somewhat arbitrary, for it is sometimes difficult to say that a particular experience fits one category but not another. For these reasons it is particularly important to achieve as narrow a focus as possible in analyzing [intervention]: Otherwise a systematic treatment is virtually impossible (p. 15).

Examining ideal-types, while recognizing they are to some degree artificial, has the particular benefit of allowing us to perceive practice variables and intervention components within the modes in explicit and crystallized form. This generates a wide range of distinct practice options, across intervention orientations, that can be employed selectively and in combination. (This will be expanded upon subsequently.)

PRACTICE VARIABLES AND COMMUNITY INTERVENTION APPROACHES

In order to proceed with the analysis, we will specify a set of practice variables that help describe and compare each of the approaches when seen in ideal-type form. Each of the orientations makes assumptions about the nature of the community situation, goal categories of action, concepts of the general welfare, appropriate tactics, and so on. A set of twelve such variables will be treated in the passages that follow. The variables are based on the writer's long-term experience and review of the analyses of practice by others. They are assumed to be salient but by no means exhaustive. A number of themes from the previous discussion will necessarily be reiterated here, but they will be applied in a different and conceptually systematized way. Table 1.1 (p. 45) provides a summary and substantive overview, and the discussion offers further clarification and interpretation for those who wish to go into the details.

1. Goal Categories

Two main goals that have been discussed recurrently in the community organization and macro practice literature have been referred to as "task" and "process" (Rothman, 1964; Gilbert and Specht, 1977). Task goals entail the completion of a concrete task or the solution of a delimited problem in a community system: establishing new services, improving coordination of existing ones, passing specific social legislation, or changing the behavior or attitudes of residents, say, in regard to health practices. Process goals are oriented to system maintenance and enhancement and local empowerment, with aims such as creating self-maintaining, problem-solving structures, stimulating wide interest and participation in community affairs, fostering collaborative attitudes and practices among people, and enhancing indigenous leadership, all linked to enhancing community integration and local problem-solving capacity. Process goals are concerned with a generalized capacity of the community system to function over time; task goals are concerned with the solution of pinpointed functional problems of the system.

Locality Development. Process goals receive heavy emphasis. The community's growing capacity to become integrated and to engage in cooperative problem solving is of central importance. This view is expressed by Henderson and Thomas (1987) as follows:

> The challenge faced by professionals . . . is to realize that they must seek not just to deliver services to meet people's needs but to do so in a way that enhances people's autonomy, self-respect and their ability to work together to solve common problems (p. 7).

Social Planning. There is stress on task goals, focusing on the solution of substantive social problems. Social planning organizations often are mandated specifically to deal with concrete deficiencies, defects, or illnesses, and their official names signify this—mental health departments, municipal housing authorities, legislative committees, The American Cancer Society, commissions on physical rehabilitation or alcoholism, and so on.

> These aims of social planning have been described as: the solving of social problems; the satisfying of social needs; . . . coordination of services (including interdisciplinary cooperation), [and] the initiation and development of new services and facilities . . . (Weyers, 1992, p. 133).

It is difficult for many planners to attend to process goals because their organizational assignments often have official mandates, legislative directives, formal time lines, and prescribed procedures.

Social Action. The approach may lean in the direction of either task goals or process goals. Some social action organizations, such as civil rights groups and cause-oriented organizations, emphasize obtaining specific legislative outcomes (higher welfare allotments) or changing specific social practices (discriminatory hiring). Usually these objectives entail changes in policies of government or formal organizations. Other social action groups lean in the direction of process goals—aiding a constituency to acquire and exercise power—as exemplified by feminist organizing, ACORN, or the early black power movement. This objective of building local-based power and decision-making centers transcends the solution of any given problem situation.

A dual perspective encompassing both goal types has been put forth by Kahn (1982) as follows:

Organizing has both short- and long-range benefits. In the short run it's an effective tool for getting things done: for improving schools, for lowering taxes, for establishing rights on the job, for improving transportation and health care, for protecting and defending neighborhoods and communities . . . . But it is also an end in itself. As we organize, we clarify ourselves as individuals because we learn to speak for ourselves in ways that make us heard (pp. 7–8).

In recent years social action groups have given increasing attention to process goals and capacity building. The feminist movement's theme, "the personal is political," articulates that trend.

2. Assumptions Concerning Problem Conditions

Locality Development. The local community is seen to be overshadowed by the larger society, lacking in fruitful human relationships and problem-solving skills and peopled by isolated individuals suffering from anomie, alienation, disillusionment, and, often, mental illness. Technological change, it is believed, has pressed society toward greater industrialization and urbanization with little consideration of the effects on social relations. Henderson and Thomas (1987) state:

not only are people set apart from each other by conflicts and scapegoating, but we may wonder whether people know how to manage their relationships with each other. This state of affairs may have come about partly because social skills involved in neighboring and networking may have atrophied (p. 4).

Alternatively, especially in Third World international projects, the community is often seen as tradition-bound, ruled by a small group of autocratic elite, and composed of an educationally deprived population who lack skills in problem solving or an understanding of democratic methods.

Social Planning. The community is viewed as burdened by concrete social problem conditions. Warren (1972) reflects the outlook of social planners as follows:

It is apparent that certain types of "problems" are broadly characteristic of contemporary American communities. They appear in such forms as the increasing indebtedness of central cities, the spread of urban blight and slums, the lack of adequate housing which people can afford, the economic dependence of large numbers of people in the population, poorly financed and staffed schools, high delinquency and crime rates, inadequate provisions for the mentally ill, the problem of the aged, the need for industrial development, the conflict of local and national agencies for the free donor's dollar, the problem of affording rapid transit for commuters at a reasonable price and at a reasonable profit, and the problem of downtown traffic congestion. This list is almost endless, and each of the problems mentioned could be subdivided into numerous problematic aspects (p. 14).

Social Action. The community comprises a hierarchy of privilege and power in the eyes of those with a militant advocacy stance. There exist islands of oppressed, deprived, ignored, or powerless populations suffering social injustice or exploitation at the hands of oppressors such as the "power structure," big government, corporations, global capitalism, and racist or sexist institutions. This oppression can imply material deprivation or psychological dehumanization. Kahn (1982) states the social action position succinctly:

In the United States today power is concentrated in the hands of a small number of well-organized individuals and corporations. These corporations and the individuals involved in them have extraordinary power to make decisions that affect all our lives . . . regardless of the suffering that it has caused people . . . (p. 14).

Again, we caution that these are dominant motifs rather than discrete categories. Many social actionists are greatly concerned about apathy and substantive problems, even as some social planners are deeply concerned about the quality of social relations. We are defining tendencies in thinking rather than mutually exclusive cognitive compartments.

3. Basic Change Strategy

Locality Development.   The basic change strategy may be expressed as "Let's all get together and talk this over." This involves a concerted effort to bring a wide range of community people into determining their "felt" needs and solving their own problems. Local initiative and shared decision making are key.

Social Planning.   The basic change strategy in the data-driven modality we are describing is captured by "Let's get the facts and think through the logical next steps." Planners and policy practitioners in this framework focus on gathering pertinent data about the problem and then deciding on an empirically supported and feasible course of action. The practitioner plays a central part in assembling and analyzing facts, establishing goals or policy frameworks, and determining appropriate services, programs, and actions. This may or may not be done with the participation of others, depending upon the planner's sense of the utility of participation in the given situation and the organizational context within which he or she functions.

Social Action.   The change strategy is expressed through "Let's organize to overpower our oppressor and change the system," that is, crystallizing issues so that people know who their legitimate enemy is and mobilizing them to bring pressure on selected targets. Such targets may include an organization, such as the welfare department; a person, such as the mayor; or an aggregate of persons, such as slum landlords.

4. Characteristic Change Tactics and Techniques

Locality Development.   Tactics of consensus are stressed, including discussion and communication among a wide range of different individuals, groups, and factions. Blakely (1979) makes a case for cooperative, deliberative techniques in locality development: "Development specialists attempt within the conflict situation to place the stress on problem solving as opposed to win-lose strategies and attitudes" (p. 21).

Social Planning.   Fact finding and analytical skills are of central concern. Tactics of conflict or consensus may be employed, depending upon the practitioner's analysis of the situation. For example, writings on managerial planning often emphasize the value of cooperative participation (Peters and Waterman, 1982). At the same time, hostile takeovers are not unheard of in the business world, nor is there a dirth of aggressive moves by planning agencies and their client organizations to win over a larger share of United Way Funding. Policy specialists differentially seek allies from one or another faction to support a preferred legislative initiative as necessary.

Social Action. Conflict tactics are emphasized in the militant advocacy modality, including methods of confrontation and direct action. The ability to mobilize relatively large numbers of people is necessary to carry out rallies, marches, boycotts, and picketing. Success of social action groups is based on: "their ability to embarrass the target or their ability to cause the target political harm if the target is a public official, or financial harm if it is a business" (Bobo, Kendall, and Max, 1991, p. 29).

Alinsky (1962) felt it is important to "rub raw the sores of popular discontent." His strong philosophical/theoretical position was clear:

Issues which are noncontroversial usually mean that people are not particularly concerned about them; in fact, by not being controversial they cease to be issues. Issues involve differences and controversy. History fails to record a single issue of importance which was not controversial. Controversy has always been the seed of creation (p. 7).

5. and 6. Practitioner Roles and Medium of Change

Locality Development. The practitioner's characteristic role is that of an "enabler" or, as suggested by Biddle and Biddle (1965), "encourager." The role has been described in this way by Henderson and Thomas:

At a very basic level, locality development is about putting people in touch with one another, and of promoting their membership in groups and networks. It seeks to develop people's sense of power and significance in acts of association with others that may also achieve an improvement in their social and material well-being (p. 15).

The practitioner employs as a major medium of change the creation and guidance of small task-oriented groups, requiring skill in fostering collaborative problem finding and problem solving.

Social Planning. More technical or "expert" roles are emphasized. Referring to Ross (1955), the expert role contains these components: community diagnosis, research skill, information about other communities, advice on methods of organization and procedure, technical programmatic information, and evaluation. The practitioner employs as a salient medium of change the guiding and maneuvering of agencies, bureaucracies, and legislative bodies in addition to the collection and analysis of data. Weyers (1992) indicates that the role of the planner involves:

correlating identified needs and available resources. The nature and range of these needs are identified primarily with the aid of different forms of research, while the sources, on the other hand, are mainly the concern of formal systems and the structure of authority. To obtain these desired sources, the social worker has to employ available data (for instance in the form of need identification) in order to be able to claim support (p. 132).

Social Action. Roles entail the organization of disadvantaged groups to act on behalf of their interests in a pluralist political culture. The practitioner seeks to create and guide mass organizations and movements and to influence political processes. Mass mobilization is necessary because:

Power generally consists of having a lot of money or a lot of people. Citizen organizations tend to have people, not money. Thus, our ability to win depends on our being able to do with people, what the other side is able to do with money (Bobo, Kendall, and Max, 1991, p. 9).

Classic 1960s social action focuses on organizing disadvantaged populations to act on their own in their own behalf, which is seen as true empowerment. We will examine variations from this pattern within the social action mode later.

7. Orientation Toward Power Structure(s)

Locality Development. The power structure is included within an all-encompassing conception of community. All segments of the community are thought of, holistically, as part of the action system. Hence, power elites are considered allies in a common venture embracing the well-being of all. One consequence of this might well be that in this approach only goals that have mutual agreement become legitimate or relevant; goals that involve incompatible interests are ignored or discarded as inappropriate. Hence, aims involving fundamental shifts in the configuration of power and resource control, which can contribute materially to elevating the position of minorities and the poor, are likely to be excluded.

Social Planning. The power structure is usually present as the sponsor or employer of the practitioner. Sponsors may include a voluntary board of directors, an arm of city government, or a legislative unit. Morris and Binstock (1966) state the case this way: "Realistically, it is difficult to distinguish planners from their employing organizations. In some measure, their interests, motivations, and means are those of their employers." Planners are usually highly trained technical specialists whose services require considerable finances for salary as well as support in the form of supplies, equipment, facilities, and auxiliary technical and clerical personnel.

Frequently, planners can only be sustained in their work by those in the society possessing wealth, control of the machinery of government, and high prestige. As Rein (1965) suggests, much planning is by "consensus of elites" who are employers and policy makers in planning organizations. Usually this consensus is reinforced through technical language, selective use of factual data, and an expressed commitment to impartial rationality.

Social Action. The power structure is seen as an external target of action; that is, the power structure lies outside the beneficiary system or constituency itself and is an oppositional or oppressive force.

The person with the power becomes the "target" of an issue campaign. The target (sometimes called the decision maker) is always the person who has the power to give you what you want (If no one has such power, then you haven't cut the issue correctly.) (Bobo, Kendall, and Max, 1991, p. 11).

Power elites, then, usually represent a force antithetical to the group whose well-being the practitioner is committed to advance. Those holding power, accordingly, must be coerced or overturned in the interests of equity and social justice.

8. Boundary Definition of the Beneficiary System

Locality Development. The total community, usually a geographic entity such as a city, neighborhood, or village, is the beneficiary system. Accordingly, "Community Development is concerned with the participation of all groups in the community—with both sexes, all age groups, all racial, nationality, religious, economic, social and cultural groups" (Dunham, 1963).

Social Planning. The intended beneficiaries may be either a total geographic community or some area or functional subpart. Community welfare councils and city planning commissions usually conceive of their intended beneficiaries as comprising the widest cross section of community interests. On the other hand, sometimes the service populations of social planners are more segmented aggregates—a given neighborhood, the mentally ill, the aged, youth, juvenile delinquents, or the black community. Policy practitioners work with representatives who may view beneficiaries varyingly in universalistic commonweal terms or in terms of particularistic constituencies.

Social Action. Intended beneficiaries are usually conceived as some community subpart or segment that suffers at the hands of the broader community and thus merits the special support of the practitioner. According to Kahn (1982):

When people in government, such as community planners and developers, talk about community development, they often mean the development of an entire city. This idea is misleading. You can't develop an entire city. What's good for some people is not good for others. If something is good for one group, another group loses out. There are conflicts within groups. The poverty of one group may be caused by the profits of another (p. 80).

Practitioners are likely to think in terms of constituents, brothers and sisters, or allies rather than in terms of a "client" concept, which is seen as patronizing, detached, or overly clinical.

9. Assumptions Regarding Community Interests or Subsystems

Locality Development. The interests of various groups and factions in the community are viewed as reconcilable and responsive to the influence of reason, persuasion, communication, and mutual goodwill. Hence:

Community developers accept the notion that people, regardless of race, sex, ethnicity or place of birth, can find ways to solve their problems through group efforts. The community development movement is humanistic in orientation. This implies a genuineness or authenticity in

relationships that permits open, honest communication and feedback (Blakely, pp. 18, 21).

Social Planning. There is no pervasive assumption about the degree of intractability of conflicting interests; the approach appears to be pragmatic, oriented toward the particular problem and the actors enmeshed in it. Morris and Binstock set out the social planning orientation as follows:

A planner cannot be expected to be attuned to . . . the overriding interests of dominant factions. Considerable study and analysis of factions and interests dominant in various types of organizations will be needed before planners will have sufficient guidance for making reliable predictions as to resistance likely in a variety of situations (p. 112).

Social Action. The approach assumes that interests among community subparts are at variance and not easily reconcilable, that resources are limited or dominated, and that often coercive influence must be applied (boycotts, strikes, political and social upheavals) before meaningful adjustments can be made. Those who gain privileges and profits from the disadvantage of others do not easily give up their edge; the force of self-interest makes it foolish to expect them to do so. Saul Alinsky (1962) states:

All major controlling interests make a virtue of acceptance—acceptance of the ruling group's policies and decisions. Any movement or organization arising in disagreement, or seeking independent changes and defined by the predominating powers as a threat, is promptly subjected by castigation, public and private smears, and attacks on its very existence (p. 6).

10. Conception of Intended Beneficiaries

Beneficiaries are those who are in line to gain from the efforts of the practitioner and the intervention process.

Locality Development. Intended beneficiaries are likely to be viewed as average citizens who possess considerable strengths that are not fully developed and who need the services of a practitioner to help them release and focus these inherent capabilities. The Biddles (1965) express this viewpoint as follows:

1. Each person is valuable, and capable of growth toward greater social sensitivity and responsibility.
   a. Each person has underdeveloped abilities in initiative, originality, and leadership. These qualities can be cultivated and strengthened (p. 60).

Social Planning. The beneficiary group is more likely to be thought of as consumers of services, those who will receive and utilize those programs and services that are the fruits of the social planning process— mental health treatment, public housing, health education, recreation, welfare benefits, and so forth. Weyers (1992) makes this clear in highlighting the provision of social services as a key objective of social planning. "According to this point of view the efficiency of the community's social functioning will depend on the quantity and quality of professional services rendered to the community, as well as the way in which the community's concrete needs are provided for" (p. 132).

In policy settings beneficiaries may be conceived as both consumers and constituents.

Social Action. The intended beneficiaries are seen as aggrieved victims of "the system": of slum landlords, the medical establishment, government bureaucracies, racist institutions, patriarchal entities, and corporate polluters. Those on behalf of whom action is initiated are often characterized in "underdog" terms.

11. Conception of the Role of Intended Beneficiaries

Locality Development. Beneficiaries are viewed as active participants in an interactional process with one another and with the practitioner. Considerable stress is placed on group discussion in the community as the medium through which learning and growth take place. Beneficiaries engage in an intensive group process of exploring their felt needs, determining desired goals, and taking appropriate action.

Social Planning. Beneficiaries are clients, consumers, or recipients of services. They are active in using services, not in the determination of policy or goals.

Opportunities for members and consumers to determine policy are severely limited because they are not usually organized for this purpose . . . the opportunity to control policy is short-lived because the coalition will fall apart, lacking sufficient incentive to bind together the otherwise diverse constituent elements (Morris and Binstock, 1966, pp. 109–110).

Decisions, then, are made through the planner, often in collaboration with some community group—a board or commission, usually composed of business and professional elites, who are presumed to represent either the community-at-large or the best interests of those being served.

The data-driven policy specialist is likely to be looking over his or her back through this process, realizing that constituency interests and pressures could have an impact on policy enactment.

Social Action. The benefiting group is likely to be thought of as an employer of the practitioner or constituents. In unions the membership ideally runs the organization. The Industrial Areas Foundation will usually not enter a target area until the people there have gained a controlling and independent voice in the funding of the organization. The concept of the organizer as an employee and servant of the people is stressed. Kahn (1982) holds that the "staff director of the organization, if there is one, should be directly accountable to the board and should be held accountable by the board" (p. 70). Those not in key decision-making roles may participate more sporadically in mass action and pressure group activities, such as marches or boycotts.

12. Uses of Empowerment

Empowerment is a highly valued concept in contemporary thinking and parlance (Colby, 1997). However, in some ways it seems to be a buzzword that has to do more with creating a warm feeling than conveying a precise meaning. In the context of our discussion, each intervention approach values empowerment, but uses it in a different, sometimes contradictory, fashion.

Locality Development. Empowerment signifies the gaining of community competence—the skills to make decisions that people can agree on and enact together. It also implies the development of a sense of personal mastery within residents, as individual growth in people is considered a component of community building and a goal of practice.

Social Planning. With its reliance on facts and rationality, this approach tends to associate empowerment with information. Empowerment occurs when residents and consumers are asked to inform planners about their needs and preferences, so that they can be incorporated into plan design. Such information may be obtained through community surveys, including focus group techniques and public hearings, or through analysis of data from agency service records. Through this arrangement, consumers are afforded the right and means to have their views enter into the process by which decisions affecting them are made. Consumers are also empowered when information is provided to them about the various services that are available and particularities about these services, so they become equipped to make the best decisions about what programs and services to use. Information plays an important part in the other approaches also, but is given special emphasis in data-driven planning intervention.

Social Action. Empowerment means to acquire objective, material power—for residents to be an equal party in decision-making bodies such as agency boards or municipal commissions, or to have the political clout to directly affect decisions made by these bodies. Electoral campaigns are mounted to win seats on legislative units by representatives from the group, who will thereby have the authority to vote and engage in tangible trade-offs on the group's behalf. There is also attention to participants' personal sense of empowerment, because those individuals with a feeling of potency are more likely to lend themselves actively to the cause, and to contribute to the number count necessary for "people power" tactics of social action.

There is still another way that empowerment is viewed, emanating primarily from the conservative camp. Empowerment is equated with the elimination of governmental regulations and involvements, so that citizens presumably gain the freedom to conduct their lives without restraint. The popular slogan, "get the government off our backs," characterizes this way of looking at empowerment. It is reflected in the work of neoconservative planners and action groups on the radical right. Getting the government off the backs of some people at the same time removes protections and assistance given to other, disadvantaged, people and simultaneously disempowers them.

USES OF A MULTIMODAL APPROACH

This analysis puts us in a better position now to describe what an ideal-type intervention mode would look like. For an ideal-type mode to be in operation it has to include, in well-developed form, a large proportion of the variables attached to that mode in Table 1.1 (within its column), and to exclude all or nearly all of the components peculiar to any other mode. This is a tough and rare standard to reach in the emergent, disorderly arena of community affairs. Modal *tendencies* are a more realistic prospect.

Still, there are advantages to viewing intervention from the kind of multimodal perspective that has been presented. In the first place, it is important for practitioners who are grounded in a particular organizational situation to be aware of their moorings. This framework provides a means for assessing the strategic leanings in the practice context: What are the basic assumptions and preferred methods of action in the particular setting? In this way, the practitioner is more likely to perform appropriately, consistent with the expectations of supervisors, colleagues, participants, and other relevant actors.

Going beyond conformance to what exists, the practitioner may be in a position to create a form of action to deal with specific problems. Some rough rule-of-thumb guidelines can be posited. When populations are homogeneous or there is a willingness to exchange among various community subparts and interests, it would be useful to employ locality development. When problems are evident and agreed upon in the community and lend themselves to programmed solutions through the application of factual information, social planning/policy approaches would be a viable way to proceed. Finally, when subgroups are hostile and interests are not reconcilable through usual discussion and negotiation methods, it may be functional to engage in social action.

By assessing when one or another form of intervention is or is not appropriate, the practitioner takes an analytical, problem-solving stand and does not become the rigidified captive of a particular ideological or methodological approach to practice. Consequently, practitioners should be attuned to the differential utility of each approach, particularly to the tactics used in each, and should acquire the knowledge and skill that permit them to utilize these in disciplined and flexible fashion. We will be expanding on that theme in the next section.

This discussion has focused on a comparison of practice variables by following Table 1.1 horizontally across the community intervention approaches. For a feel of how each intervention mode would be implemented using its own set of variables interactively in combination, the table should be examined vertically, down the columns. This highlights the particularity and coalescence of each of the approaches, but it also encapsulates them synthetically. The next section demonstrates why that is so.

Before proceeding with the expanded treatment, it is useful to take a moment to clarify the domain of discourse and to indicate what is excluded. Any analysis carves its area of inquiry out of the infinite possibilities in the empirical world. The domain in this instance is the community

TABLE 1.1
Three Community Intervention Approaches According to Selected Practice Variables

	Mode A (Locality Development)	Mode B (Social Planning/Policy)	Mode C (Social Action)
1. Goal categories of community action	Community capacity and integration; self-help (process goals)	Problem solving with regard to substantive community problems (task goals)	Shifting of power relationships and resources; basic institutional change (task or process goals)
2. Assumptions concerning community structure and problem conditions	Community eclipsed, anomie; lack of relationships and democratic problem-solving capacities; static traditional community	Substantive social problems, mental and physical health, housing, recreation, etc.	Aggrieved populations, social injustice, deprivation, inequality
3. Basic change strategy	Involving a broad cross section of people in determining and solving their own problems	Gathering data about problems and making decisions on the most logical course of action	Crystallizing issues and mobilizing people to take action against enemy targets
4. Characteristic change tactics and techniques	Consensus: communication among community groups and interests; group discussion	Consensus or conflict	Conflict confrontation, direct action, negotiation
5. Salient practitioner roles	Enabler-catalyst, coordinator; teacher of problem-solving skills and ethical values	Fact gatherer and analyst, program implementer, expediter	Activist advocate: agitator, broker, negotiator, partisan
6. Medium of change	Guiding small, task-oriented groups	Guiding formal organizations and treating data	Guiding mass organizations and political processes
7. Orientation toward power structure(s)	Members of power structure as collaborators in a common venture	Power structure as employers and sponsors	Power structure as external target of action: oppressors to be coerced or overturned
8. Boundary definition of the beneficiary system	Total geographic community	Total community or community segment	Community segment
9. Assumptions regarding interests of community subparts	Common interests or reconcilable differences	Interests reconcilable or in conflict	Conflicting interests which are not easily reconcilable, scarce resources
10. Conception of beneficiaries	Citizens	Consumers	Victims
11. Conception of beneficiary role.	Participants in an interactional problem-solving process	Consumers or recipients	Employers, constituents, members

(continued)

TABLE 1.1 (continued)
Three Community Intervention Approaches According to Selected Practice Variables

	Mode A (Locality Development)	Mode B (Social Planning/Policy)	Mode C (Social Action)
12. Use of empowerment	Building the capacity of a community to make collaborative and informed decisions; promoting feeling of personal mastery by residents	Finding out from consumers about their needs for service; informing consumers of their service choices	Achieving objective power for beneficiary system—the right and means to impact community decisions; promoting a feeling of mastery by participants

and, in particular, purposeful community change. This analysis is concerned with how such change is brought about by people at the community level, rather than through societal currents or federal policies. In other words, the community is examined as both the vehicle and the target of change.

Further, the analysis is concerned with the domain of strategy, the broad interventive initiatives employed to create change. These entail general strategic options available to anyone, but the discussion emphasizes actions taken by professional change agents—who may be identified with any professional field or discipline. However, because of the author's background, the discussion is tinged by social work and sociological language and perspectives.

There are other interesting and important areas of community intervention that do not fall within this domain, at least in terms of substantive coverage. Some of these include work with special populations (cultural or ethnic groups, and women), coalition building, interorganizational coordination, metropolitanization, and so forth. Nor does the analysis attempt to provide a ubiquitous theoretical framework for all of macro practice. Any of these areas, and others, are worthy of sustained theoretical development in their own right, and cumu-

latively will provide a rich, expanding intellectual and conceptual base to inform community intervention.

The approach taken is at the level of middle-range theory. It does not try to develop a grand theory formulation that is highly abstract and comprehensively encompassing. In keeping with a middle-range perspective, there is use of grounded theory, which involves the observing of real-world empirical patterns, identifying them, naming them, and constructing indicative cognitive categories to reflect them. Other approaches to theoretical development could have started more deductively, with concepts such as power structure or exchange theory, and built complex constructs concerning community intervention from these.

Obviously, it would not be realistic to expect middle-range theory to carry the burden of embracing all the dimensions of community intervention, and if it tried to accomplish that it would certainly become unwieldy and incoherent. Conversely, hovering at the middle range, this construct does not provide the level of detail desired by some: how community developers should work with task groups, how planners should use data, how social actionists should organize demonstrations or form coalitions. These questions require exercis-

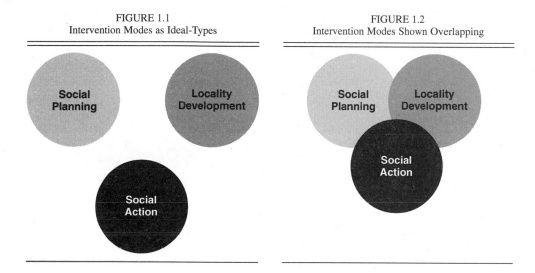

FIGURE 1.1
Intervention Modes as Ideal-Types

Social
Planning

Locality
Development

Social
Action

FIGURE 1.2
Intervention Modes Shown Overlapping

Social
Planning

Locality
Development

Social
Action

ing the art of application of the strategic initiatives, or developing specialized additional constructs.

THE INTERWEAVING OF
INTERVENTION APPROACHES

This analysis has attempted to delineate rather distinct and coherent categories of community intervention practice. Alfred North Whitehead offered a rationale for this: "The aim of science is to seek the simplest explanations of complex facts." But while supporting the effort to harness complicated processes, he also alerted us to the underside. We may come to actually believe the original facts are simple because our quest was to arrive at a simplified construction. The French social critic Raymond Aron once spoke of this as *delire logique*—logical delirium. Therefore, Whitehead went on to admonish: "Seek simplicity and distrust it." Following that dictum, we will now reexamine the previous discussion, bringing to it the eye of the skeptic.

Up until now we have treated each community intervention approach as though it were a rather self-contained ideal-type. That conceptualization is depicted visually in Figure 1.1. Actually, intervention approaches overlap and are used in mixed form in practice (Rothman, 1999). Figure 1.2 reflects broadly the movement toward overlapping.

Practice in any mode may require tactics that are salient in another approach. For example, neighborhood social actionists interested in aiding the homeless may find it necessary to draw up a social plan in order to obtain funding for desired service projects from DHHS (Modes C and B). Or social planners may decide that the most effective way of establishing a viable low-income housing project is to engage potential residents in deciding on the geographic layout and common facilities, and to organize a tenant action council to fight drug pushers (Modes B, A, and C).

A more true-to-life depiction of the character of overlapping is in Figure 1.3. Here we see that the ideal-type modes have a limited scope of frequency and that mixtures of various kinds, along the lines just described, predominate.

To clarify the place of the three practice modes in the overall schema of community intervention, it would be useful to turn to the physical world and the phenomenon of color and its properties. We know that there are three basic colors—red, green, and blue. Scrutinizing the properties of these primary colors is valuable because when the properties are mixed they generate an enormous array of hues and shadings. A set of composite secondary colors is yielded when the primary colors are blended in equal proportions. Further mixtures among all of these result in an almost infinite melange of tones.

Realizing that the analogy is not exact, the three intervention modes can be compared to the three primary colors (but they can only roughly approximate perfect composition in the real world). The basic modes are represented by the outer spheres in Figure 1.3. We can visualize them spawning multiple practice combinations. When two combine, the results are composite bimodal interventions, depicted in the figure by the designations Development/Action, Planning/Development, and Action/Planning. These are analogous to secondary colors.

The center of Figure 1.3 depicts mixed interventions that include a cross-section of variables from all three modes. These combinations involving complex balances of variables are difficult to categorize or even visualize in any succinct fasion.

Just as the primary colors make up only a very small proportion of the total universe of color, the basic intervention modes comprise only a fraction of the world of practice. Predominately, most practice situations probably entail three-fold mixtures. Bimodal composites, those situations consisting of relatively strong leanings

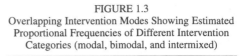

FIGURE 1.3
Overlapping Intervention Modes Showing Estimated Proportional Frequencies of Different Intervention Categories (modal, bimodal, and intermixed)

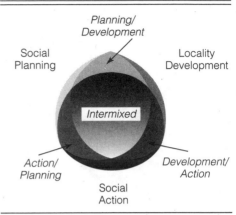

toward two intervention approaches, are probably intermediate in frequency.

These are guesses or loose hypotheses about intricate intervention patterns, rather than verified conclusions. The entire schema is basically a heuristic device that is meant to aid conceptualization. The heuristics, however, have grounded empirical referents and are subject to testing through controlled social research.

COMPOSITE BIMODAL MIXTURES

It would be helpful to further illustrate the overall paradigm in Figure 1.3 and the mixing phenomenon through some examples of the three composite bimodal forms. Note that the composite forms are not uniform in character or coloration, as Figure 1.4 depicts. The mid-area in each composite section of the diagram represents an equally balanced mixing of practice variables from the basic modes, but as we move away from the mid-area, toward one or another of the basic modalities, variables from that mode increasingly predominate in the blend. Myriad mixtures are possible. We will discuss each of the bimodal composites in turn below.

Development/Action in balanced form is portrayed in feminist organizing and in the Freire style of grassroots work. Hyde (1989) indicates that feminist organizing comprises a combination of traits that are traditionally considered feminine with those that are often considered masculine. The feminine aspect includes humanistic qualities such as caring and nurturance, coupled with the use of democratic processes and structures (an emphasis on consensus, the rotating of tasks, and respecting and engaging the skills of all participants). These aspects are all associated with the locality development mode.

At the same time, the feminist organizing perspective is concerned with fundamental cultural and political change—the elimination of patriarchal society. Hyde indicates, "feminist practice is revolutionary . . . it provides a vision of a radically different society in which the oppressive means of power and privilege are eradicated" (p. 169). These tougher, more militant elements of the practice in the past often have been associated with a masculine posture and the social action intervention mode. Following Hyde's line of analysis, we can say that the feminist organizing perspective, to a considerable degree, is a balanced composite of practice variables involving assumptions and goals of social action joined with the methods of locality development. (See Figure 1.4 for the location of feminist organizing in the Development/Action composite.)

Pablo Freire's work involves a similar blend, in that he has endeavored through an educational approach to empower impoverished peasants in Brazil and Chile to act against the forces of their oppression. He

FIGURE 1.4
Variations Within the Develoment/Action Mode

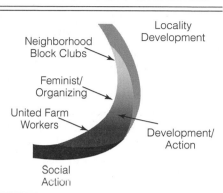

visualizes "education as the practice of freedom," and through "conscientization" seeks, in a sympathetic and enabling manner, to assist illiterate people to see clearly and realistically their objective state of being (Freire, 1974). Fortified with this information, they presumably will gain the motivation and wherewithal to take the steps necessary to transform the closed, unjust societies that repress them. Again, we see the means of locality development wedded to the goals of social action.

The composites we have illustrated represent a somewhat equal mixing of practice variables from Development and Action. They are akin to what is represented by "pure" secondary colors. But the mix might also involve a disproportionate weighting of variables from one or other of the two intervention modes. A composite leaning closer to locality development (see Figure 1.4) is found in Neighborhood Block Clubs. They promote socialization, sharing of information, neighborhood safety watches, mutual aid, and preservation of cherished neighborhood values and landmarks. The overall emphasis is on these Development features. However, when threatened by a porno movie house moving into the area, or the need for a traffic light to protect their children, the organization occasionally swings into a strong and even emotional ad hoc advocacy style.

On the other side of this dual composite stands an organization such as the United Farm Workers, as shown in Figure 1.4. Here the main thrust has been to raise the economic and social well-being of migrant farm workers, using a variety of advocacy measures, such as picketing, marches, and a sustained grape boycott. But there is also a less prominent or visible component that involves mutual aid and community-building among the membership, almost in the form of an extended intraethnic block club. Again, both modes coexist, but in different proportions from the typical block club on the other end of the spectrum.

The Action/Planning composite in balanced form is manifested in the various consumer protection programs of the Ralph Nader organization. This is shown in Figure 1.5, which depicts all the other illustrative organizations mentioned in this presentation. Figure 1.5 will serve as a useful reference guide through the remainder of the discussion. Advocacy in favor of consumer interests is a key thrust with Nader, including tactics that involve media exposure of corporate and governmental abuses, consumer boycotts, legislative campaigns, and the like. At the same time, there is heavy reliance on factual documentation through well-researched and sophisticated reports prepared by expert data analysts and policy specialists. There is also the dissemination of accurate empirical information to consumers so that they can make valid choices. The integration of Action and Planning methods is inseparable. Nader's Public Citizen organization carries out some grassroots programs— particularly on college campuses—which include a locality development component.

But locality development is in pale hue, overall. Another prominent example of a close mix of Action and Planning/Policy is The Children's Defense Fund, a high-profile child advocacy organization that uses research data most effectively.

A different type of balanced example is found in municipal-level citizen housing councils. While advocating for more and better housing, consistent with community welfare, these councils have to be prepared to engage in sophisticated interorganizational coordination and negotiation, and to bring to bear the tools and procedures of urban planning professionals, whose analyses and recommendations from within the planning bureaucracy they need to be able to convincingly counter or modify.

Action/Planning with an accent on social action is embodied in organizations on the left that draw up well-formulated policy blueprints for fundamental tax reform, massive low-income housing, and widespread single-payer health services provided under governmental auspices. The groups are essentially geared to social change, but they incorporate data-based reports and policy analyses into their work. The Institute for Democratic Socialism, a "think tank" of the Democratic Socialists of America, is an example. Similar in nature, but pointing to change in another direction (dismantling the welfare state, as an example), are a number of ideologically conservative institutes (the Hoover, for example), commissions, and foundations.

Another example is the area of "advocacy planning" (Davidoff, 1965), whereby grassroots organizations dedicated to change (or blocking intrusive projects) hire a planner or receive pro bono services from a professional, in order to design proposals that can be used with governmental bureaus of planning officials in support of given aims or positions. These planners may

FIGURE 1.5
The Paradigm of Community Intervention Showing Examples of Organizational
Types for Each Mode of Intervention and Mixed Forms

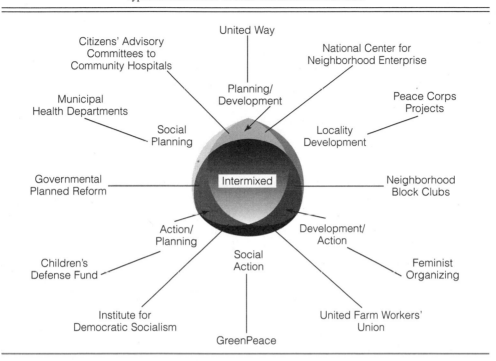

serve for only a limited time period or for only one of the many issues being advocated by the organization.

Shifting emphasis toward the planning dimension, Friedmann (1987) suggests a role involving a planner/policy analyst firmly ensconced within a governmental structure, where the professional essentially carries out technical planning functions, but with social reform in mind. Friedmann notes the role of Rexford Tugwell in Roosevelt's New Deal administration as an example. Robert Moses, in his role during the LaGuardia mayoralty in New York City, would be another. The Koerner Commission functioned similarly, transforming an investigation of urban civil unrest from a focus on social control to issues of equal opportunity. The practitioner's position, methods, and tone are fixed within a governmental bureaucracy, but there is a social advocacy dimension. Friedmann conceives of this government-sponsored planned reform as a distinct fourth intervention mode, in addition to the three we have discussed.

Planning/Development mixtures have a different patterning. The United Way, a convenient balanced example, is dedicated to systematic welfare decision making on the community level with regard to fundraising, budgeting, fund allocation, and coordination of services. However, it places a great deal of stress on citizen participation in these processes. Planning *and* volunteerism are the traditional hallmarks of the organization. Planning for the annual campaign and distributing financial resources to agencies are ongoing activities. But a considerable amount of energy is applied to recruiting community participants (who are most often business and professional elites), training leaders, giving workshops, and holding meetings and conferences of various kinds. Planning and Development are intimately intertwined.

Enterprise/empowerment zones also closely blend these modes of intervention, but in a different way. Their aim is to promote community building in inner cities through enhancing the capacity of minority residents to perform in economic and social realms, particularly by starting and running their own businesses. Local initiative and self-reliance are watchwords. But these programs also involve heavy inputs from the outside by corporate and government experts, and the design of elaborate processes to steer a process that is complex and quite technical in nature.

A composite that is weighted toward the planning side is found in citizen advisory committees that are established in the health field by departments of health, community hospitals, and hospital planning councils. These committees have an adjunct role in supporting the basic planning function, which often has a strong technical component. The committees do not ordinarily impact on policy, although they may play some part in policy implementation. They serve to provide legitimation in the community for decisions of planners and administrators; they also have a public relations element. For this reason, energy is applied by the organization to recruiting members, orienting them, and maintaining their bonds. This locality development component is, gener-

ally speaking, token rather than substantive in character.

On the other side of the spectrum, an organization such as the National Center for Neighborhood Enterprise is committed to furthering local initiative in urban neighborhoods, as well as seeking to empower poor and minority communities through self-help (while discouraging the means of political insurgency). The Center reflects the work and views of Robert L. Woodson, Sr., who is perhaps the chief organizer of locality development endeavors within African-American communities. In pursuing its goals, the Center actively compiles relevant data and employs the techniques of policy analysts and social planners. These, however, are subsidiary to and in support of the main development thrust.

Taking a different analytical stance now, the character of composite mixes result from the particular configuration of practice variables from each intervention mode. The exact coloration can be influenced by the sheer *number* or volume of variables from either mode of the *types* of variables from each (goals, assumptions, roles, tactics). The *potency* of different types of variables also may have an effect. For example, in feminist organizing, the goal of fundamentally changing gender roles in society is in ascendancy, sometimes dominating the question of tactics (as indicated by existing tactical variations between the position stated by Hyde and that of the radical lesbian movement).

Trimodal mixtures are even more varied than what we have already discussed. An example should suffice to illustrate the general notion. Community welfare planning councils bring social agencies together to share ideas and information, and to strengthen their bonds, in order to become a more successful and integrated service delivery system. The councils also hammer out specific plans and policy frames, in conjunction with the agencies, that are geared to providing more effective and efficient services to community residents. In addition, these organizations actively engage in advocacy, lobbying the city council and the state legislature for more funds and better mandates to meet client needs and expedite agency operations. Chambers of commerce use the same set of intermingled actions on behalf of the business community.

Illustrating intervention mixtures, with all their gradations, can go on endlessly. Examples given here should suffice to demonstrate the basic concept, to generate useful efforts by others, and to fuel critiques of the general formulation.

DILEMMAS IN EACH INTERVENTION MODE

There are other ways of analyzing the blending of forms of intervention. For each intervention mode we will frame a key issue that confounds the original modal formulation and has implications for expanding and mixing the intervention modes. The dilemmas we will pose spring in part from deliberately positing constructs in ideal or synthetic form, but they arise also from the complex, contentious, constraining, and obdurate social environment in which change agents currently find themselves. In response, practitioners have designed strategies that are more variagated, subtle, flexible, and inventive—and less one-dimensional—than in an earlier time.

Locality Development—External Linkages

We have seen that locality development places heavy emphasis on a self-contained local community context. This circumscribed, while holistic, community system is the arena in which features of grassroots initiative, self-help, intimate relationships, and enhanced competency are played out.

A dilemma is that often locality development programs are sponsored and funded by outside entities: municipal (city department of community development); national (The National Service Corps, Campaign for Human Development of the United States Catholic Conference); or international (The World Bank, The World Health Organization). This poses a threat to the conceptual integrity of the formulation. Jacobsen (1990) observes that "much of the initiative for community development actually originates from outside the community, which is a clear violation of the principles of community development" (p. 395).

Vertically linked organizations provide planning and administrative inputs that are hierarchical in nature. They chose the main goals to be pursued, recruit and select the staff, train them, set the program emphasis, and establish the rules of practice engagement.

Local groups are also often linked horizontally at the city or regional level with other similar local groups. Thus, a block club can affiliate with a council of neighborhood block clubs, or a neighborhood citizens association can become part of a citywide council of citizen groups or an interfaith umbrella organization of congregations. Here the coordination and information-sharing aspects of planning play a part, although elements of social action coalition-building may also be involved.

These relationships and entanglements contradict the self-enclosed quality of the original modal formulation. The broader formulation of locality development is shown in Figure 1.6, with the shaded area delineating the original construct.

FIGURE 1.6
Locality Development Intervention Showing Community-Bounded and Externally Linked Structural Forms
(original construct in shaded area)

Local and Community-Bounded	Horizontally Linked	Vertically Linked
Neighborhood Councils Block Clubs Self-Help Projects	Local Block Groups Affiliated with Regional Councils of Block Clubs Coalitions of Local Neighborhood Councils Information Clearing Houses	Peace Corps Projects Church-Sponsored Overseas Development Projects (American Friends Service Committee) United Nations Community Development Projects (World Health Organizations) National Service Corps

Social Planning/Policy—Participation

A dilemma in the original social planning concept is that even highly technical planning and policy development that is data-driven and expertise-based often includes elements of participation, in various forms and to varying degrees. This injects an important element of the locality development approach into the picture.

Political analyst Joel Kropkin observed, in the early Riordan mayoralty in Los Angeles, that there was a danger the new civic leader would lean too heavily on his previous corporate experience in his effort to reorganize city government operations and services. In industry, Riordan was able to use soundly conceived technical plans "for brokering deals between well-defined and somewhat logical, shareholders and other constituencies." Planning in a community context is different—more fluid and political—says Kropkin, with no evidence that "once a rational plan is developed, support for it will naturally follow." Instead, he maintains, it is essential that interests of various kinds be drawn into participation in this process, including municipal unions, churches, grassroots groups, city council members, and others (Kropkin, 1993, pp. 1, 6).

A reformulation of planning that includes the participation dimension is in Figure 1.7. We observe that decision making, as proposed in the original modal formulation, is sometimes concerted—in the hands of a small group of elite leaders and professional experts (see the shaded area of the Figure). Often city departments of child welfare, mental health, housing, and health operate in this way, as do the boards of private agencies like family service organizations, Jewish federations, and boys' clubs.

But planning can entail dispersed decision making, where other than elites alone take part in making judgments and choices. This broader form can involve both *substantive* participation in decision making, and *ancillary*, more peripheral involvement.

First, let us consider substantive activity. Residents and citizens can join in *policy decisions* of a basic nature, or they take

FIGURE 1.7
Social Planning Intervention Showing Concerted Decision Making and Dispersed
Decision Making Involving Various Forms and Degrees of Community Participation
(original construct in shaded area)

Concentrated Decision Making	Dispersed Decision Making			
	Substantive Participation in Decisions		Ancillary Participation in Decisions	
	Policy	Implementation	Facilitative	Symbolic
City and County Departments of Health, Housing, Social Services Boards of Voluntary Social Agencies— Family Service, Citizens' Planning, and Housing Councils	United Way Regional Planning Boards Free Clinics OEO projects— "Maximum Feasible Participation"	Local Branches of National Service or Planning Organizations— NAACP, Cancer Society Federal Program Implementation in the States— Title XX	Regional Meetings on Zoning Changes in City Planning Locally Conducted Congressional Hearings	Planners for Neighborhood Halfway Houses Real Estate Developers of Shopping Malls and Housing Complexes, Environmental Impact Reports

part in *implementation decisions* that relate to carrying out programs that grow out of policy decisions by others. The OEO "War on Poverty" spawned a multitude of grassroots organizations where "maximum feasible participation" at the highest policy-making levels was emphasized. Free clinics providing health services to low-income ill people have traditionally encouraged such participation. The United Way's Regional Planning Councils attempt to involve local residents in allocation and program decisions affecting the area.

Substantive implementation decisions, within established policy parameters, are frequently given over to members of local branches of national organizations, such as the American Cancer Society, The Urban League, League of Women Voters, and so

forth. Federal legislation, such as Title XX, has often left discretion for implementation in the hands of the states, counties, or municipalities.

Second, ancillary participation can be *facilitative* or *symbolic*. The facilitative form draws residents into the decision-making process by seeking their reactions to proposals, or asking for their advice. It may also entail providing information about impending changes in order to prepare people for them, thereby reducing stress or disruption in their lives. Regional meetings called by city planning departments to announce zoning changes or to ask people for their opinions about these changes are an example. Local hearings conducted by Congress or a city council are another, as are hearings related to environmental impact studies.

Symbolic participation serves to provide the appearance or aura of participation, but not its actuality. The aim is cooptation, whereby the opposition is won over or "cooled out." Real estate developers and housing officials often use this approach in trying to influence residents to accept a new project, as do social planners who attempt to establish group living "halfway houses" in urban neighborhoods for the mentally ill, delinquent adolescents, the homeless, and other vulnerable groups.

There is a tendency among human service professionals to instinctively reject the use of symbolic forms of participation, particularly when these are applied to them and their clients. There are, of course, vital ethical objections to the deceptive quality of this tactic but the question is intellectually complex.

Brager, Specht, and Torczyner (1987) address this issue in a penetrating discussion, taking the view that "manipulation is an unavoidable component of professional behavior" and that "political maneuvering" is inevitable in community intervention (p. 321). In seeking to advance the interests and well-being of those we seek to benefit, when facing inhospitable or potentially damaging actions by others, the practitioner is obligated to "employ artfulness in inducing desired attitudinal or behavioral outcome in others" (p. 317). The foes of our allies and constituents use powerful tools of accepted political in-fighting that challenge our capability to provide protection and nurturance. Brager and his associates recognize the importance and delicacy of this issue, and they delineate a set of factors to be weighed carefully in arriving at ethically sound conclusions about tactics. At the same time, they resist discarding the "planned ambiguity" tactic of symbolic participation, which, if it occurred, might mean abandoning to the winds of political fortune in pluralistic American communities the possibility of establishing group homes for the homeless and the mentally ill.

Social Action—Multiple Actors and Conventional Tactics

Social action is more complicated than the original model conveyed, as reflected in studies that found it to have complex qualities. For example, Cnaan and Rothman (1986) in a factor analysis inquiry discovered that planning and development can be explained through a single, consistent factor. However, social action comprised two or more factors, which were difficult to identify with clarity.

There are three dimensions that probably account for this complexity (see Figure 1.8). The original formulation did not take into account, and did not differentiate, the two essentially different types of goals of this intervention mode. These include radical change goals that aim at fundamental alterations in society or at specific policies or institutions within it, and more normative or reformist change goals that aim at incremental alterations. This is a basic context within which social action needs to be understood.

It is difficult to delineate precisely the division between radical and normative goal changes in social action. Radical change suggests breadth of alteration in the society and culture. Examples of this thrust include organizations that militate to eradicate racism or to transform the relationship between the races (as with the Nation of Islam), or to change the basic economic system of the country (as with the Democratic Socialists of America). However, a change that on the surface seems modest can have a broad impact. As an example, changing regulations about what can appear on TV, or the tone of presentation, can have

FIGURE 1.8
Social Action Intervention Divided by Type of Goal and Further
Differentiated by Tactical Means and the Composition of the Action Constituency
(original construct in shaded area)

| | | **GOALS** | |
		Radical Fundamental	**Normative** Incremental
Radical Disruptive Tactics	Disadvantaged Parties Mainly	American Indian Movement (AIM) ACT-UP	Industrial Areas Foundation Tenant Action Organizations
	Multiple Parties	Greenpeace The 60s Student and Anti-War Movements (SDS)	Ad Hoc Protests by Alliance for the Mentally Ill Animal Rights Groups
Normative Conventional Tactics	Disadvantaged Parties Mainly	Nation of Islam Center for Third World Organizing	La Raza American Association of Retired Persons
	Multiple Parties	Democratic Socialists of America Women's International League for Peace and Freedom	Childrens' Defense Fund Coalition for the Homeless

MEANS (row label at left spanning Radical and Normative means)

a rippling effect throughout the entire culture because of the widespread influence of the media.

In addition, fundamental change can be narrow and deep rather than wide in scope. The aim may be to alter a specific law or specific sphere of living in a radical way. As an example, the Pro-Life movement focuses on the single issue of abortion legislation, but is interested in drastically overturning existing legal arrangements rather than adjusting or tampering with them. Because of the saliency of the issue, the change being advocated would be seen by many as fundamental, and a deep threat.

Alternatively, radical change can be accomplished through a particular combination of breadth and depth that in aggregate goes beyond incrementalism. The precise calculus of this combination is elusive, but the possibility of it occurring seems plausible.

In any case, it is difficult to establish a firm dividing line between fundamental and incremental change, partly because incremental change is sometimes carried out as a strategic step leading to fundamental change. The extremes of each are easy enough to discern (the Communist Party as compared to the League of Women Voters); it is pinpointing the middle border that separates the two tendencies that is vexing.

Two other dimensions beside goal categories suggest revisions rather than additions to the original formulation. One of these concerns the constituency action system for the change effort. Going back to the sixties, social action movements focused on the disadvantaged or aggrieved group only as the vehicle of social change, as with the Black Panthers, AIM (American Indian Movement), La Raza, gay and lesbian groups and others, playing out the politics of identity. Going it alone was a way of ensuring that the fundamental interests of the group were safeguarded, that outsiders who might take over were contained, and group self-empowerment was promoted. This was the outlook incorporated within the original modal formulation.

Contemporary "new movement" organizing is seeking to become broader, more ecumenical. Fisher and Kling (1991) speak in support of "a more consciously ideological politics. New formations and groupings will only make community mobilization stronger . . . an explicitly challenging ideology is necessary if community movements are not to remain bound by the limits of personalized and localized consciousness" (p. 81). Advocacy groups across class and ethnic lines are forming, focused on environmental protection, crime prevention, neighborhood preservation, animal rights, and health issues. These new groupings and alliances involve community-building methods for achieving cohesion and continuity. Not only are the economically oppressed organizing to act on their own behalf, but, in addition, middle-class aggrieved persons, including right-wing

activists and the Ross Perot movement, are involved in victim rights, tax reduction, Pro-Life, government reorganization, and school reform efforts. The expanded constituencies include linkages and coalitions by grassroots groups that are national in scope.

The additional dimension is tactical in nature. Action groups have been characterized by their reliance on aggressive and abrasive advocacy measures, which was reflected in the original formulation. More recently, tactics have been refined and diversified. They are more normative in quality, utilizing conventional political maneuvers.

Many community organizers today cite a trend toward pragmatism that emphasizes electoral politics, consensus building, data collection and research, and the use of political and administrative channels. Confrontational tactics, while sometimes required, are considered ineffective in many cases. Although sit-in and demonstrations have succeeded in creating awareness of problems, administrators and officials also have learned how to defuse them (Hiratsuka, 1990, p. 3).

These new social action elements suggest the inclusion of practice variables from the other intervention modes. For example, conventional advocacy methods, such as factual documentation of environmental despoilment, include data-based techniques from planning and policy practice. Community-building within and among different advocacy constituencies brings to bear locality development practice.

These elements of social action are tied together and systematized in Figure 1.8. The top two shaded cells encompass the original intervention mode, and the additional six are expanded representations of the advocacy strategy. Each cell incorporates a different form of the admixture of: type of goal (radical/normative), type of advocacy (radical/normative), and type of constituency action system (disadvantaged parties mainly/multiple parties). Examples are provided for each of these social action amalgams. The information is essentially self-evident and does not require extended explication.

PHASING, VALUES, AND PRACTICE OPTIONS

The broad approaches, and sets of practice variables within them, offer a range of interrelated possibilities for designing intervention strategies. The point has been stated by Gurin (1966) as follows:

Our field studies have produced voluminous evidence that (various) roles are needed, but not always at the same time and place. The challenging problem, on which we have made a bare beginning, is to define more clearly the specific conditions under which one or another or still other types of practice are appropriate. The skill we shall need in the practitioner of the future is the skill of making a situational diagnosis and analysis that will lead him to a proper choice of the methods most appropriate to the task at hand (p. 30).

In addition to mixing approaches as discussed, there is a phasing relationship among them. A given change project may begin in one mode and then, at a later stage, move into another. For example, as a social action organization achieves success and attains resources, it may find that it can function most efficiently out of a social planning mode. The labor union movement, to a degree, demonstrates this type of phasing. As organizational growth and viability are achieved, headquarters operations (for example, the teamsters or UAW) become larger, more bureaucratized, and more technical, and social policy and administrative factors become more salient. The practitioner needs to be attuned to appropriate transition points in applying alternative modes.

As practitioners phase through their own careers, there will be demands to emphasize one or another modality. Historically, circumstances and preferences change, resulting in shifts in professional fashion and the employment requisites of agencies. For this reason, it is useful for practitioners to be broadly prepared, with the full range of competencies tucked into their professional portfolio.

Locality development was in vogue in the quiescent 1950s, when interactive, enabling practice was considered the quintessence of professionalism (Pray, 1947; Newstetter, 1947). Planning/policy was important during the Charity Organization Society and Community Chest and Council movements of the 1920s, as an aspect of emergent social work institution building. This mode came to the fore again during the New Deal spurt of policy development and program organization intended to cope with the Great Depression. It was called upon again in the Nixon and Reagan-Bush times of policy reversal and program curtailment, where efforts to promote efficiency, scrupulous evaluation, and cost containment were given prominence. Social action had its heyday during the roiling 1960s, and also in the early years of the century when progressives were advocating for legislation on child labor, workmans' compensation, and housing and municipal reform. Cycles in the relative rise and fall of different intervention modes will doubtless continue in the periods ahead.

In the past, professional actions and conceptualizations were often constrained by particular value orientations to practice— for example, acceptance of only collaborative, nondirective practice (Pray, 1947). Alinsky followers derided all others as "sell-outs," while planners were often disdainful of militants for fomenting disorder and antagonism. The current outlook, however, is more accepting of varying value orientations. An examination of empirical findings on professional values leads to the conclusion that "human service professions do not appear to be highly integrated with regard to the existence of a delimited, uniformly accepted value system" (Rothman, 1974, p. 100). The approaches suggested in this presentation are in the spirit of such a position.

The locality development practitioner will likely cherish values that emphasize harmony and communication in human affairs; the planner/policy specialist will give priority to rationality; the social actionist will build on commitments embracing social justice. Each of these value orientations finds justification in the traditions of the human service professions. It would be difficult to claim monopoly status for any one or other. Indeed, contemporary thinking suggests that values are plural and conflicting, and may well come in pairs of divergent commitments (Tropman, 1984). Mixing occurs on those frequent occasions when more than one value is being pursued at a given time.

The various intervention approaches can all be applied in a way to pursue values conducive to positive social change and human betterment. Our position accepts the validity of each of the stated value postures and encourages their interrelated employment.

Values aside, the intervention modes have to draw from one another because of the inherent functional limitations within each. Planning and policy initiatives have created worthy programs, particularly when pushed by the other two modes, but have accomplished little in redistributing wealth and power or in preventing the victimization of the have-nots. They have typically concealed the vested interests of the professionals and failed to address the widespread alienation of society. Locality development has had its successes in countering isolation and depersonalization in specific places, but not in removing the social conditions that continue to generate anomie and inequality. Social action has confronted power and economic inequities in some measure at the local level, but has not had sufficient potency to cope with larger national power issues or to shape a strategy to rehumanize those it cannot defeat. Each modality alone faces obstacles that the others can contribute to addressing.

Another reason for seeking new configurations of action is that, at the highest societal levels, established institutions and modes of operating are showing grave defects. Eastern European communism, with its outrageous tyrannies and rigidities, has collapsed from within and left a widespread landscape of upheaval and turmoil. But the Western market–dominated countries, who are now the only game in town, are saddled with the cruel by-products of an acquisitive ethic, and they display persistent pathologies of economic and social disparity, industrial decay, recurring joblessness, cultural decline, racism, and anomie—to use the short list.

New social forms are called for that combine the liberal ideal of political democracy and the socialist ideal of economic democracy, ensuring a balance of liberty and equality in both spheres. Barbara Ehrenreich (1993) has stated the challenge aptly:

We must outline how we believe that the community of human beings can live together more equitably and peacefully than it does now. *The vision has to be a vision beyond capitalism, with its inevitable economic injustice. This is a time when people looking for change don't have some kind of precise model to inform that struggle for change.* Everyone has some responsibility to start imagining, dreaming, inventing and visualizing the kind of future we would like.

This discussion prompts us to look back at Table 1.1, the listing of practice variables across intervention modes, and read it in a different light now. The table, in aggregate, provides a repertoire of practice options, for flexible application. Each of the thirty-six cells describes an analytical or behavioral intervention initiative. (This is not a complete enumeration of the possibilities by any means, but it is a suggestive one.) The practice options, when used critically and selectively, can provide vital components to interweave creatively into the design of strategy.

This moves us toward a contingency formulation where practitioners of any stripe have greater range in selecting, then mixing and phasing, components of intervention. An important next step is to identify a set of situational criteria to inform such tactical packaging. A number of social parameters of the situation readily come to mind, among them the type of change goal and its scope, the quality of constituency leadership, availability of knowledge regarding relevant problems and solutions, the extent and character of resistance, the degree of financial and other resource support at hand, and stage of development of the action system.

There is a need for research concerning which situational criteria, or clusters among them, are most critical for strategy development. Beyond that, it would be useful to study how these criteria specifically inform the selection and meshing of practice options from the repertoire of intervention components, in the interests of designing change strategies with greater impact.

In summary, the goal of this piece has been to lay open and chart a multifaceted change process that plays a large role in inducing the progressive development of society. Historically, what humans have been able to capture cognitively, they often have been able to master behaviorally—which is a reason for persisting in the endeavor. However, there are no panaceas inherent in this text. The world is an unpredictable place, and humans have struggled through time to gain greater control over and better their social environs. One can only believe and hope that a sound, informed analysis coupled with disciplined action will provide some increment of probability beyond intuitive strivings. Through systematic evaluation and other research we can hone our techniques and monitor our results, thereby learning cumulatively from experience and improving our record.

Such efforts are analogous to the realm of interpersonal helping in psychotherapy. It is assumed that use of theory and tested practice will improve on the natural advice and support that neighbors and family provide to one another. Still, despite the best efforts of dedicated therapists some clients remain mired in despair and confusion. Those of us in the human services hold the limited aspiration that, to some unknown degree, what we do will enhance the probability that beneficial results will come to pass.

The sharpening of change methods is an endless and evolving process. The mental skirmishing involved in this revision of an earlier construct is captured in T. S. Eliot's wise and edifying words:

> We shall not cease from exploration. And the end of all our exploring will be to arrive where we started and know the place for the first time.

From that ground, naturally, the exploration begins anew.

BIBLIOGRAPHY

Alinsky, Saul D. "Citizen Participation and Community Organization in Planning and Urban Renewal," p. 7. Chicago: Industrial Areas Foundation, 1962.

Alinsky, Saul D. *Reveille for Radicals.* Chicago: University of Chicago Press, 1946.

Alinsky, Saul D. *Rules for Radicals.* Chicago: University of Chicago Press, 1972.

Anzalone, Joan, ed. *Good Works: A Guide to Careers in Social Change,* 3d ed. New York: Dembner Books, 1985.

Austin, Michael. J., ed. *Human Services Integration.* New York: Haworth Press, 1997.

Betten, Neil, & Michael J. Austin. *The Roots of Community Organizing, 1917–1939.* Philadelphia: Temple University Press, 1990.

Biddle, William W., & J. Loureide. *The Community Development Process: The Rediscovery of Local Initiative.* New York: Holt, Rinehart & Winston, 1965.

Bingham, R. D., & R. Mier. *Theories of Local Economic Development.* Thousand Oaks, CA: Sage Publications, 1993.

Blakely, Edward J. "Toward a Science of Community Development." In Edward J. Blakely, ed. *Community Development Research: Concepts, Issues and Strategies,* pp. 15–23. New York: Human Sciences Press, 1979.

Bobo, Kim, Jackie Kendall, & Steve Max. *Organizing for Social Change: A Manual for Activists in the 1990s.* Washington, DC: Seven Locks Press, 1991.

Bobo, Kim, Jackie Kendall, & Steve Max, eds. *Organizing for Social Change.* Washington, DC: Seven Locks Press, 1996

Boyte, H., & F. Riessman. *The New Populism.* Philadelphia: Temple University Press, 1986.

Brager, George, Harry Specht, & James L. Torczyner. *Community Organizing,* 2d ed. New York: Columbia University Press, 1987.

Burch, Hobart A. *Basic Social Policy and Planning: Strategies and Practice Methods.* New York: Haworth Press, 1996.

Burghardt, S. "Community-Based Social Action." In *Encyclopedia of Social Work,* 18th ed. NASW, 1987.

Burghardt, S. *Organizing for Community Action.* Beverly Hills, CA: Sage Publications, 1982.

Burns, Danny, & Marilyn Taylor. *Mutual Aid and Self-Help: Coping Strategies for Excluded Communities.* Bristol, England: Policy Press, 1998.

Byrd, Michael. "Urbanism, Alletropolitan Development, and Identity Politics: Social Psychological Considerations of Left- Wing Mainline organizing in Metropolitan Nashville. " *Journal for the Scientific Study of Religion* 38 (1) 1999: 146.

Chavis, D. M., P. Florin, & M. R. J. Felix. "Nurturing Grassroots Initiatives for Community Development: The Role of Enabling Systems." In T. Mizrahi and J. Morrison, eds. *Community Organization and Social Administration: Advances, Trends and Emerging Principles,* (pp. 41–67). New York: Haworth, 1993.

Cloward, Richard, & Frances Piven. *Poor People's Movements.* New York: Pantheon, 1977.

Cnaan, R. A. "Neighborhood Representing Organizations: How Democratic Are They?" *Social Service Review, 65* (1991): 614–34.

Cnaan, R. A., & J. Rothman. Conceptualizing Community Intervention: An Empirical Test of "Three Models" of Community Organization. *Administration in Social Work, 10*(3) (1986): 41–55.

Colby, I. C. "Transforming Human Services Arough Empowerment of Neighborhoods," *Journal of Community Practice* 4 (2) 1997: 1–12.

Davidoff, P. "Advocacy and Pluralism in Planning." *Journal of the American Institute of Planners, 31*(4) (1965): 331–37.

Delgado, D. *Organizing the Movement: The Roots and Growth of ACORN.* Philadelphia: Temple University Press, 1986.

Dionne, E.J. *The Revival of Civil Society in America.* Washington, DC: Brookings Institution Press, 1998.

Dunham, Arthur. "Some Principles of Community Development." *International Review of Community Development,* No. 11 (1963): 141–51.

Ehrenreich, B. From a letter to the membership of Democratic Socialists of America, dated December 1, 1993, New York.

Fisher, R. *Let the People Decide: Neighborhood Organizing in America,* rev. ed. Boston: Twayne, 1994.

Fisher, R., & J. Kling. "Popular Mobilization in the 1990s: Prospects for the New Social Movements." *New Politics* 3 (1991): 71–84.

Flynn, J. *Social Agency Policy: Analysis and Presentation for Community Practice.* Chicago: Nelson Hall, 1985.

Freire, Paolo. *Education: The Practice of Freedom.* London: Writers and Readers Publishing Cooperative, 1974.

Friedmann, John. *Planning in the Public Domain: From Knowledge to Action.* Princeton, NJ: Princeton University Press, 1987.

Gellman, Barton. *Contending with Kennan: Toward a Philosophy of American Power.* New York: Praeger, 1984.

Gil, David. *Unraveling Social Policy.* Cambridge, MA: Schenkman, 1976.

Gilbert, Neil, & Harry Specht. *Dimensions of Social Welfare Policy.* Englewood Cliffs, NJ: Prentice-Hall, 1974.

Gilbert, Neil, & Harry Specht. *Dynamics of Community Planning.* Cambridge, MA: Ballinger, 1977.

Gilbert, Neil, & Harry Specht. "Process Versus Task in Social Planning." *Social Work,* XXII (3) (1977): 178–83.

Gitlin, Todd. *The Twilight of Common Dreams: Why America is Wracked by Culture Wars.* New York: Henry Holt and Company, 1996.

Goetz, E. G., & S. E. Clarke. *Comparative Urban Politics in a Global Era.* Thousand Oaks, CA: Sage Publications, 1993.

Gurin, Arnold. (1966) "Current Issues in Community Organization Practice and Education," Brandeis University Reprint Series, No. 21, p. 30. Florence Heller Graduate School for Advanced Studies in Social Welfare.

Halseth, Judith H. "Infusing a Feminist Analysis into Education for Policy, Planning, and Administration." In T. Mizrahi, & John Morrison, eds. *Community Organization and Social Administration: Advances, Trends and Emerging Principles.* New York: The Haworth Press, 1993.

Henderson, Paul, & David N. Thomas. *Skills in Neighborhood Work.* London: Allen & Unwin, 1987.

Hiratsuka, Jon. "Community Organization: Assembling Power." *NASW News* (September, 1990): 3.

Hyde, Cheryl. "A Feminist Model for Macro-Practice: Promises and Problems." In Yeheskel Hasenfeld, ed., *Administrative Leadership in the Social Services: The Next Challenge,* (pp. 145–81). New York: The Haworth Press, 1989.

Jacobsen, Michael. "Working with Communities." In H. Wayne Johnson, *The Social Services: An Introduction,* (3d ed.), (pp. 385–403). Itasca, IL: F. E. Peacock, 1990.

Jansson, B. *Theory and Practice of Social Welfare Policy: Analysis, Processes and Current Issues.* Belmont, CA: Wadsworth, 1984.

Johnson, Marilyn S. *Development of an Action Research Proposal: An Analysis of Practice.* Master of Social Work Thesis. Calgary, Alberta: School of Social Welfare, 1974.

Jones, Wyatt C., & Armand Lauffer. "Implications of the Community Organization Curriculum Project for Practice and Education." Professional Symposium of NASW, National Conference on Social Welfare, 1968.

Kahn, Alfred J. *Theory and Practice of Social Planning.* New York: Russell Sage, 1969.

Kahn, S. *Organizing.* New York: McGraw-Hill, 1982.

Kahn, S. *Organizing: A Guide for Grassroots Leaders.* Silver Spring, MD: National Association of Social Workers, 1992.

Karp, David R., ed. *Community Justice: An Emerging Field.* Lanham, MD: Rowman & Littlefield, 1998.

Kettner, Peter M., Robert M. Monroney, & Lawrence L. Martin. *Designing and Managing Programs: An Effectiveness-Based Approach,* 2d ed. Thousand Oaks, CA: Sage Publications, 1999.

Kropkin, Joel. "Riordan's Next Challenge: Become the Political Man." *Los Angeles Times,* December 19, 1993, pp. M1 and M6.

Lappin, Ben. "Community Development: Beginnings in Social Work Enabling." In Samuel H. Taylor & Robert W. Roberts, eds., *Theory and Practice of Community Social Work,* (pp. 59–94). New York: Columbia University Press, 1985.

Lauffer, A. "The Practice of Social Planning." In Neil Gilbert & Harry Specht, eds., *Handbook of the Social Services,* (pp. 588–97). Englewood Cliffs, NJ: Prentice Hall, 1981.

Lyon, Larry. *The Community in Urban Society.* Philadelphia; Temple University Press, 1987.

Mandell, Myrana, P. "Community Collaborations: Working Through Network Structures." *Policy Studies Review* 16 (1) 1999: 42.

Mayer, N. *Neighborhood Organization and Community Development.* Washington, DC: Urban Institute, 1984.

Mettessich, Paul W., & Barbara Monsey. *Community Building: What Makes it Work: A Review of Factors Influencing Successful Commnity Building.* St. Paul, MN: Amherst H. Wilder Foundation, 1997.

Mier, R. *Social Justice and Local Development Policy.* Thousand Oaks, CA: Sage Publications, 1993.

Minkler, Meredith, ed. *Community Organizing and Community Building for Health.* New Brunswick, NJ: Rutgers University Press, 1997.

Moroney, Robert M. *Social Policy and Social Work: Critical Essays on the Welfare State.* New York: Aldine de Gruyter, 1991.

Morris, Robert, & Robert H. Binstock. *Feasible Planning for Social Change.* New York: Columbia University Press, 1966.

Naples, Nancy A. *Grassroots Warriors: Activist Mothering, Community Work and the War on Poverty.* New York: Routledge, 1998.

Newstetter, Wilber I. "The Social Intergroup Work Process," *Proceedings, National Conference of Social Work,* pp. 205–17. New York: Columbia University Press, 1947.

Peters, T. J., & R. H. Waterman. *In Search of Excellence.* New York: Harper & Row, 1982.

Pierce, D. *Policy for the Social Work Practitioner.* New York: Longman, 1984.

Pray, K. L. M. "When Is Community Organization Social Work Practice?" *Proceedings, National Conference of Social Work.* New York: Columbia University Press, 1947.

Pressman, J., & A. Wildavsky. *Implementation.* Berkeley, CA: University of California Press, 1984.

Rein, Martin. "Strategies of Planned Change." American Orthopsychiatric Association, 1965.

Ross, Murray G. *Community Organization: Theory and Principles,* pp. 80–83. New York: Harper and Brothers, 1955.

Rothman, Jack. "An Analysis of Goals and Roles in Community Organization Practice." *Social Work* IX (2) (1964): 24–31.

Rothman, Jack. *Planning and Organizing for Social Change: Action Principles from Social Science Research,* p. 100. New York: Columbia University Press, 1974.

Rothman, Jack, ed. *Reflections on Community Organization: Enduring Themes and Critical Issues.* Itasca, IL: F.E. Peacock Publishers, 1999.

Selznick, Philip. *The Moral Commonwealth: Social Theory and the Promise of Community.* Berkeley, CA: University of California Press, 1992.

Taylor, Samuel H., & Robert W. Roberts, eds. *Theory and Practice of Community Social Work.* New York: Columbia University Press, 1985.

Tropman, John E. *Policy Management in the Human Services.* New York: Columbia University Press, 1984.

Tropman, John E. "Value Conflict in Decision-Making." In F. M. Cox et al. *Tactics and Techniques of Community Practice,* (2d ed.) Itasca, IL: F. E. Peacock, 1984.

Tropman, John E. "Policy Analysis: Methods and Techniques." In Anne Minahan, ed. *Encyclopedia of Social Work,* 18th ed., (pp. 268–83). Silver Spring, MD: National Association of Social Workers, 1987.

United Nations. *Social Progress Through Community Development,* p. 6. New York: United Nations, 1955.

Warren, Roland L. *The Community in America,* rev. ed. Chicago: Rand McNally, 1972.

Webber, M. M., & H. W. J. Rittel. "Dilemmas in a General Theory of Planning." *Policy Sciences* 4 (2) (1973): 155–69.

Weil, Marie. "Editor's Introduction to the Journal." In Marie Weil, ed., "Diversity and Development in Community Practice." *Journal of Community Practice* 1 (1): xxi–xxxiii. New York: The Haworth Press, 1994.

Weyers, M. L. "Field Practice Models and Strategies in Community Work." In A. Lombard, *Community Work and Community Development: Perspectives on Social Development,* (pp. 124–44). Pretoria, South Africa: HAUM-Tertiary, 1992.

Wharf, Brian, ed. *Community Work in Canada.* Toronto: McClelland and Stewart, 1979.

2.

Charles D. Garvin and Fred M. Cox*

A HISTORY OF COMMUNITY ORGANIZING SINCE THE CIVIL WAR WITH SPECIAL REFERENCE TO OPPRESSED COMMUNITIES

This paper traces the development of community organization within American communities since 1865. It is concerned both with community activities in which professionals were engaged and also with indigenous community efforts. Sometimes these two activities are seen as separate. Fisher, for example, identifies three dominant approaches to organizing: social work, political activism, and neighborhood maintenance.[1] He characterizes the social work approach as one that is reformist with a professional at the core; activism as one oriented to a government; and maintenance as a middle-class oriented approach to neighborhood improvement.

In this article, in contrast, we see these three approaches as affecting one another in ways that are determined by historical and contemporary forces. We shall, therefore, present our analysis of interactions among various kinds of organizing activities in the United States, yet pay special attention to indigenous efforts within oppressed groups. This is because of our conviction, somewhat yet not entirely contrary to Fisher's characterization of social workers as organizers, that the most effective kind of organizing is that which complements and supports such indigenous efforts. We seek to describe, therefore, from a historical view (1) how relevant professional social work efforts were to indigenous ones and (2) how responsive both were to the issues embedded in the larger society.

In order to organize this analysis, we shall emphasize the many important community efforts in which ethnic communities have been engaged. Such organizing has occurred in virtually all ethnic communities. For example, there are many organizations devoted to improved conditions within Jewish, Italian, and Polish enclaves. In this article, however, we focus upon the history of organizing in ethnic communities which are now economically and socially oppressed. These include black, Chicano, Native American, and Asian American ones.

Other ethnic groups also have organized to secure their rights. The same has been true of the elderly, gay persons, and the handicapped. Space limitations, however, make it impossible for us to explore each. We have, however, included the women's movement because of our conviction regarding its broad scope and impact.

For purposes of this analysis, we divide American history since the Civil War into five stages. For each stage we outline the social forces and ideologies which affected community organizing; the specific community organization activities; and the institutions that sponsored the organizing

---

*The authors are grateful to John Tropman, Barry Checkoway, and Howard Brabson for contributing their views on the most recent developments in community organizations.

[1]Robert Fisher, "Neighborhood Organizing: Lessons from the Past," Social Policy (Summer, 1984), pp. 9–10.

efforts. We also describe the types of organizing occurring in oppressed communities. Finally the effects of these social forces, activities, and institutions upon the education of community organization practitioners are described.

1865 TO 1914

During the period between the end of the Civil War and the beginning of World War I, a number of social issues emerged in the United States that had strong impact upon welfare practices. Ideologies developed in response to these social conditions, and solutions were proposed for those defined as problematic. These social issues were the rapid industrialization of the country, the urbanization of its population, problems growing out of immigration, and changes in oppressed populations after the Civil War. These are described and their relevance for the emergence of community organization practice highlighted.

Social Conditions

Industrialization. The growth of technology and the centralization of industry brought with them a wide range of social problems. These included problems of working hours and conditions, safety, and child labor.[2]

Urbanization. A direct consequence of industrialization was the movement of large parts of the population from the country to the city.[3] The many unskilled workers who moved into the city from rural areas, particularly from the South and from Europe, were often forced to take up residence within the oldest and most crowded sections. These districts were inadequate in sanitation, building conditions, and city services. As Jane Addams wrote:

The streets are inexpressibly dirty, the number of schools inadequate, sanitary legislation unenforced, the street lighting bad, the paving miserable, and altogether lacking in the alleys and smaller streets, and the stables foul beyond description. Hundreds of houses are unconnected with the street sewer.[4]

Immigration. In the early part of the nineteenth century, many immigrants came from northwestern Europe and spread out across the country. By 1890 the frontiers were gone. A large number then came from southern and eastern Europe until the tide of immigration was stemmed by legislation passed shortly after World War I. Asian and Mexican people went to the West and Southwest; small numbers of Puerto Ricans settled in the East.

These people brought with them not only their own social and religious institutions, but a variety of problems. Many came from peasant origins and sought a rural environment. However, most of those who came in the later waves were unable to escape the cities where they landed. Impoverished and often sick from the crossing, they were forced to take whatever work they could find. They clung to their former ways. This later brought them into conflict with their children who took on American habits and manners.[5]

---

[2]For a social worker's perception of these conditions, see Jane Addams, *Twenty Years at Hull House* (New York: The Macmillan Co., 1910), pp. 99, 109ff

[3]For details, see Allan Nevins and Henry Steele Commager, The Pocket History of the United States (New York: Pocket Books, 1942), pp. 326–357..

[4]Addams, op. cit., pp. 97–100.

[5]See Oscar Handlin, *The Uprooted* (New York: Grosset and Dunlap, 1951).

Minorities After the Civil War

Blacks. During reconstruction there were many organizations that sought to support and sustain newly won civil rights. After the period of reconstruction there were many efforts on the part of black people to organize themselves "to the point where they could demand those rights which had slipped away since reconstruction."[6] The Supreme Court decision which declared the Civil Rights Act of 1875 unconstitutional was a major source of frustration for it placed the responsibility for protecting the rights of black people largely on the states.

During this period, the Populist Movement in the South was a major political force which attempted to secure black support. Fishel and Quarles quoted the white president of a Populist convention in Texas as saying that the black "is a citizen as much as we are." However, these authors noted that "the elections of 1892 saw their [Populists'] defeat in the South and the end of any political effort to work with the Negro on an equitable basis."[7]

A major concern of the black community was to solve the problem of educational deficits, particularly in vocational and higher education. In this context, an important event was the founding of Tuskegee Institute in 1881. Also, in the fifteen years before 1900 over fifteen hundred black people were lynched, and between 1900 and 1910 another nine hundred black people perished in the same way. "The sickening brutality of the act of lynching was matched only by its lawlessness and, in too many cases, the innocence

of its victims."[8] Black support of other oppressed minorities during this period is illustrated by black poet Alberry Whitman's *The Rape of Florida*, an exposition of white degradation of the Seminoles (published in 1884).

Toward the end of this period many industries in the North encouraged black people to migrate from the South. Workers were needed because of the termination of the large European immigrations and the expansion of war industry. As a consequence their urban living conditions were deplorable.

Chicanos.[9] Although we describe community organizing primarily since the Civil War, we must recognize that the history of protest among Chicanos began with the Treaty of Guadalupe Hidalgo, signed on February 2, 1848, which brought a formal end to the Mexican-American War. Under this treaty, Mexico lost 45 percent of its territory including the wealth of the oil fields of Texas and the gold of California. More than a hundred thousand persons who had previously been citizens of Mexico were added to the United States. From this beginning, the rights of these "conquered" people were heavily infringed upon with little legal redress available. Protest took the form of guerrilla activity by so-called bandits and armed rebellions that were vigorously repressed by the government. According to one authority, "Organized hunts, murders,

---

[6]Leslie H. Fishel, Jr., and Benjamin Quarles, *The Negro American: A Documentary History* (Glenview, IL: Scott, Foresman & Co., 1967), p. 308.

[7]Ibid., p. 309.

[8]Ibid., p. 358.

[9]Although the term *Chicano* has not been used throughout all of the historical periods described in this chapter, we use it whenever we refer to those United States residents and citizens who are descended from Mexicans. For details of the evolution of the Chicano movement, see Gilberto Lopez y Rivas, *The Chicanos: Life and Struggles of the Mexican Minority in the United States* (New York and London: Monthly Review Press, 1973), pp. 57–74.

robberies, and lynchings of Mexicans were everyday happenings, and cattle rustling and assaults on Mexican merchants were carried out with brutality and savagery."[10]

Native Americans. In the period just before the Civil War, the status of Native Americans was largely determined by the Removal Act of 1830. This act gave the president the right to remove any Indians who lived east of the Mississippi.[11] The Seminoles of Florida and the Sac and Fox of Illinois fought, but most were moved peacefully. A particularly shameful action was that taken against the Cherokees, who were forcibly removed in 1838 from Georgia to what was to become Oklahoma, with a great loss of lives on the way despite their enormous effort to adapt to the new culture forced upon them.

After the Civil War, the removal to reservations continued until the passage of the Dawes Act of 1887 which authorized the president to distribute 160 acres to each Indian adult and 80 acres to each child. This followed a series of major fights with tribes such as the Sioux in 1876, Nez Percé in 1877, Cheyenne in 1878, and Apache a few years later.

The Dawes Act was a failure in that it did not convert the Indians to agriculture as intended. Much of the land given was poor, and funds for its development were unavailable. As a result, between 1887 and 1932, "approximately 90 million acres out of 138 million initially held by Indians passed to white ownership."[12] In view of the exploitation they suffered the survival of many Indian tribes seems miraculous.

Asian Americans. The Chinese, the first immigrants from Asia to come in large numbers, arrived on the west coast in the 1840s. Their labor was sought as the California economy soared with the gold rush. It was in the mining regions that serious hostility to the Chinese first developed. When the Civil War began there were more than fifty thousand Chinese in California, mostly men. By the 1870s violence directed at Chinese was intensified by an economic depression. For example, "some twenty Chinese were killed by gunfire and hanging on October 24, 1871."[13]

Agitation from workers who sought anti-Chinese legislation continued for the rest of the decade. Consequently in 1882, Congress enacted the Chinese Exclusion Act, which was renewed in 1892 and made permanent in 1902.

About two hundred thousand Japanese arrived in America between 1890 and 1924 in an atmosphere hostile to Orientals. The early immigrants were mostly young males from rural backgrounds. Like the Chinese, they were recruited as a source of cheap labor. However, the migration of Japanese women was soon encouraged.

California's Alien Land Bill of 1913 exemplifies general attitudes toward the Japanese. It provided that Japanese aliens could lease agricultural lands for a maximum of three years, and that lands already owned or leased could not be willed to other persons. As the California attorney general indicated in a public speech, the intention was to limit the number of Japanese who would come to or stay in California.[14]

---

[10]Ibid., p. 33.

[11]John R. Howard, ed., *Awakening Minorities: American Indians, Mexican Americans, Puerto Ricans* (New Brunswick, NJ: Transaction Books, 1970), p. 17.

[12]Ibid., p. 19.

[13]Harry H. L. Kitano, *Race Relations* (Englewood Cliffs, NJ: Prentice-Hall, 1974), p. 196.

[14]Harry H. L. Kitano, *Japanese Americans* (Englewood Cliffs, NJ: Prentice-Hall, 1969), pp. 7, 17.

Ideological Conditions

These problems were relevant to the emergence of community organization practice as they were affected by ideological currents prevalent during this period. These currents included Social Darwinism, radicalism, pragmatism, and liberalism. These ideologies were, at least in part, a response to problems of industrialization, poverty, urbanization, race relations, and cultural conflicts brought on by immigration.

Social Darwinism. As Max Lerner pointed out:

When the gap between laissez faire and social welfare became too obvious after the Civil War, conservative thought called into play the new popular interest in Darwinian theories. The jungle character of the economic struggle was frankly admitted, but it was justified and even glorified by Social Darwinism on the ground that nature had decreed it. The new natural law came to be "natural selection" and the triumph of the "fit" who survived.[15]

This philosophy led to the view that social failure was due to some inherent inferiority in the individual and that assistance to such people was an interference with natural law. This was compatible with the American ideal of "rugged individualism" as well as minimum government. The latter meant that the role of government was to protect property and ensure the enforcement of contracts, but not to interfere in any way with the content of such contracts.

Radical Ideology. While Social Darwinism may have served the interests of the economically secure, other ideologies provided a rationale for the activities of those who sought to change the lot of those who were not. One indigenous American radical, Henry George, "spoke for a 'reforming Darwinism' which saw the social order as the outgrowth of evolution but wanted to use it deliberately in a humanizing effort for the weakest as well as the strong."[16] The radical ideas of this period also stemmed from labor organizers. A Socialist Labor Party (SLP) was organized in the United States in 1876.[17] Within this group were Marxist as well as other ideological influences. Among the demands of the party were that "all industrial enterprises be placed under the control of the government as fast as practicable operated by free cooperative trade unions for the good of the whole people."[18] The Socialist party was founded in 1900 and united several groups, including the SLP.

This discussion cannot deal thoroughly with the history of American labor. However, community organizing aimed at mobilizing the oppressed drew upon this movement.

Pragmatism. This indigenous philosophy, first articulated by Charles S. Peirce and William James and developed by such men as John Dewey and George Herbert Mead, anticipated many efforts at social engineering. As Lerner stated:

Through these variations there ran the common thread of the "revolt against formalism" and against fixed principles or rules—that truth did not lie in absolutes or in mechanical formulas but in the whole operative context of individual growth and social action in which the idea was embedded. This movement of thought was, in a

---

[15]Max Lerner, *America As a Civilization: Life and Thought in the United States Today* (New York: Simon & Schuster, 1957), p. 722.

[16]Ibid., p. 726.

[17]Called for one year the Workingman's Party of America.

[18]*The Socialist*, July 29, 1876. See also John R. Commons, *History of Labor in the United States*, Vol. II (New York: The Macmillan Co., 1935), p. 270.

sense, the American counterpart to the Marxist and historical schools of thought in Europe which tried to apply the evolutionary process to social thinking. This intellectual base made possible, as it also expressed, the political reform movement from Theodore Roosevelt to Franklin Roosevelt.[19]

Liberalism. According to Lerner the credo of liberalism "has been progress, its mood optimist, its view of human nature rationalist and plastic; it has used human rights rather than property rights as its ends but has concentrated on social action as its means."[20] Despite its problems, he states, "liberalism has nevertheless emerged as a central expression of the American democratic faith."[21] Liberal ideas have been important in building support among the privileged for the voice of the underclasses to be heard in the councils of government and for them to reap the benefits bestowed by government.

Community Organization Institutions

As we have stated, community organization activities during the period between the Civil War and World War I can be divided into two categories: the first are those which were carried on by individuals or institutions related to present-day social welfare activities. The charity organization societies, settlement houses, and urban leagues are important examples.

A second category of activities are those that were conducted by those with no direct connection to contemporary community organization programs but which have become areas of interest for community practitioners. Examples include the organi-

zation of political, racial, and other action groups.

The Charity Organization Society. A number of factors noted above contributed to the emergence of charity organization societies in England in 1869 and, by 1873, in the United States.[22] These societies initially came into existence to coordinate the work of the private agencies which provided for the needs of the poor. Soon, however, these societies began to offer direct relief and other services, as well as to coordinate the work of other agencies.[23] Murphy summarized their program as follows:

They established social service indexes or exchanges listing individuals or "cases" known to cooperating agencies. They evolved the "case conference," in which workers from different agencies interested in the same "case" or the same family—workers from the settlement house, the relief-giving agencies, the child-placing agencies, the agencies established to protect children from cruelty, the visiting nurse association, and others—would meet to plan a constructive course of action in behalf of the "case." In some instances, too, the charity organization societies made broad studies of social and economic problems and recommended specific remedial measures.[24]

These social forces contributed to this development in several ways. The movement of large populations into the cities, as well as the waves of immigration which met the manpower needs of growing industries, led to many social problems associated with poverty, inadequate housing,

---

[19]Lerner, op. cit., pp. 722–723.

[20]Ibid., p. 729.

[21]Ibid., p. 730.

[22]Charles Loch Mowat, *The Charity Organization Society, 1869–1913* (London: Methuen and Co., 1961), pp. 16–21 and 94.

[23]The direct services which had significance for the emergence of social casework will not be pursued in this paper. Only the community organization antecedents will be noted.

[24]Campbell G. Murphy, *Community Organization Practice* (Boston: Houghton Mifflin Co., 1954), p. 35.

illness, and exploitation. Both humanitarian impulses and fear of what these people might do in desperation produced agencies directed to ameliorating conditions. In a sense, this was an effort to counter the more radical ideologies.

Separate efforts also were made by groups associated with different neighborhoods and ethnic and religious groups, and those with different problems. Difficulties which arose repeatedly were: (1) The same people were approached over and over again to provide resources for such agencies, and they began to look for ways to make charitable solicitations more efficient and less demanding on the few. (2) Duplication of aid was apparent, and those who offered it sought ways to avoid this and prevent the pauperization of the recipients which they believed was the inevitable result of indiscriminate relief. (3) Paid functionaries arose who sought to rationalize these activities, drawing their inspiration from the same wellsprings that fed a developing pragmatic philosophy. (4) The resources of some charitable societies were insufficient for the maintenance of required services, prompting an incessant search for new sources of funds.

During this period, leaders of charity organization societies harbored serious reservations about the wisdom of public activity on behalf of the poor. In general, they doubted government's ability to administer aid so that it would be rehabilitative. Darwinian ideology and a hedonistic theory of motivation strongly influenced their views on the matter. The Social Darwinians regarded relief as interference with the operation of natural law, and the hedonists held that the only assurance of hard work among the poorer classes was the fear of hunger and exposure. This was tempered somewhat by humanitarian impulses. The charity organization societies distinguished between the "worthy" and the "unworthy" poor and chose to aid the former who, for reasons beyond their control, were unable to support themselves and who, through the moral example of the societies' "friendly visitors," could be rescued from pauperization. The rest were relegated to the not-too-tender mercies of the public poor law authorities, never to be supported at a level equal to the lowest wages in the community so that they would constantly be goaded toward self-support.

The functions of the charity organization societies were cooperative planning among charitable institutions for the amelioration or elimination of various social problems and the creation of new social agencies and the reform of old ones. Charity organization leaders were actively engaged in securing reforms in tenement housing codes, developing antituberculosis associations, obtaining legislation in support of juvenile court and probation work, establishing agencies and programs for the care of dependent children, cooperating with the police in programs for dealing with beggars and vagrants, and supporting legislation requiring absent fathers to support their children.[25]

Some of the most significant contributions of the charity organization societies to community organization were the development of community welfare planning organizations and of social survey techniques. One of the earliest and most important examples was that of the Pittsburgh organization. Writing in 1922, Frank Watson discussed the significance of the Pittsburgh survey:

---

[25]For details on these activities see Frank D. Watson, *The Charity Organization Movement in the United States* (New York: The Macmillan Co., 1922), pp. 288–323.

Few of the offspring of the charity organization movement have had more far-reaching consequences or given greater promise of the future than the Pittsburgh Survey, the pioneer social survey in this country. Interpretation of hours, wages, housing, court procedure and all the rest, in terms of standards of living and the recognition that the basis for judging of social conditions is the measure of life they allow to those affected by them, constitute the very essence of the developments that have since taken place in social work.[26]

Out of the Pittsburgh survey came a council of social agencies which took upon itself the responsibility for acting upon the recommendations of the survey and conducting additional studies and reforms.

The Social Settlements.[27] Settlements emerged fifteen years after charity organization societies. Samuel Barnett opened Toynbee Hall, one of the first settlements, in the slums of East London in 1884. Stanton

---

[26]Ibid., pp. 305–306.

[27]This section rests heavily on the analysis of Allen F. Davis in his Spearheads for Reform: The Social Settlements and the Progressive Movement 1890–1914 (New York: Oxford University Press, 1967). Although Toynbee Hall is commonly referred to as the first social settlement, it was opened, although only half-completed, on Christmas Eve of 1884 by two Oxford University students (see Davis, p. 3). A. F. Young and E. T. Ashton, in their British Social Work in the Nineteenth Century (London: Routledge & Kegan Paul, 1956) claimed that Oxford House was opened in October 1884, while Toynbee Hall was not opened until January 1885 (p. 230). Thus Toynbee Hall was one of the first settlements to open its doors. Although Oxford House was technically the first, Samuel Barnett, who fathered the settlement house movement in Great Britain, was associated with Toynbee Hall. This may account for the fact that a number of scholars erroneously regard Toynbee Hall as the first settlement house. See: Frank J. Bruno, Trends in Social Work (New York: Columbia University Press, 1948), p. 114; Arthur Hillman, "Settlements and Community Centers," in Harry L. Lurie (ed.), Encyclopedia of Social Work (New York: National Association of Social Workers, 1965), p. 690. The authors thank David Gilbert for bringing this to our attention.

Coit, who visited Toynbee Hall in 1886, established the University Settlement on the Lower East Side of New York later that year. Although charity organization societies and social settlements were prompted by the same social conditions, their analyses of the problems created by industrialization and immigration were quite dissimilar, leading them to different objectives and programs. Barnett, an Anglican clergyman influenced by the Christian Socialists, and John Ruskin sought to bridge the gap between the social classes and restore human values to a society dominated by materialism. Coit, strongly affected by Felix Adler and the Society of Ethical Culture, believed that nothing short of a moral and intellectual renaissance in city life was required. This could best be approached, he believed, by bringing together people of all descriptions into joint efforts, breaking down the barriers of interest, age, social class, political and religious affiliations.[28] Rather than looking to individual character as the root cause of social problems, settlement house leaders typically saw environmental factors as responsible for the conditions they deplored.

Thus, while the charity organization societies seemed more ideologically related to the Darwinian ideology, the settlement appeared to draw more heavily upon the liberal, or even the radical, ideologies of the day. The types of individuals who became involved in these two movements also were different. Charity organization leaders were persons closer to the upper classes in society and epitomized noblesse oblige. They favored either reforming the poor or modifying the most adverse of their social circumstances. Although exceptions on both sides can be cited, the settlement house

---

[28]Stanton A. Coit, *Neighborhood Guilds: An Instrument of Social Reform*, 2d ed. (London: Swan, Sommerschien and Co., 1892), pp. 7–16, 46–51.

workers were a different breed. Typically well educated and drawn from the middle classes, they were frequently critics of the social order who identified with and shared the lives of the poor in some measure. Their writings usually lack the condescension so often found in those of the charity organization workers.

Perhaps the most striking quality of the settlement program was its pragmatism. Unlike the charity organization societies, settlements had no predetermined scheme for solving the problems of society. In fact, they had no coherent analysis of the problems they confronted. Instead, with a general concern about the impact of such phenomena as industrialization, urbanization, and immigration upon society, they searched for answers that would be both feasible and effective.

Services were a major theme in their activities. They organized kindergartens and clubs for children, recreational programs, evening schools for adults, public baths, and art exhibitions.[29]

Social reform was, perhaps, the most basic and self-conscious thrust of the settlements. Services were often initiated as experiments which, if successful, could serve as models for other institutions. Indeed, many of the programs demonstrated by the settlements were taken over by other agencies.

The settlements' reform efforts went much beyond the organization of new or improved services. They included legislative campaigns at the local, state, and national levels. In the field of education,

they worked for the development of vocational education and guidance in the public schools, as well as for the addition of school nurses, hot lunch programs, and education for the retarded and handicapped. They urged the creation of small neighborhood playgrounds, housing code improvements, reduction of congestion through city planning, and the transformation of public schools into neighborhood social centers. Although settlement workers could not agree on the value of immigration restrictions, they organized such groups as the Immigrant Protective League to ease the immigrant's adjustment to the new world. Settlement workers fought for laws to protect employed women and abolish child labor, and they helped organize the National Child Labor Committee and the National Women's Trade Union League. They were often involved in municipal reform activities, both at the ward and the city-wide levels, and many contributed to the platform and organizational work of the Progressive party in 1912.[30]

One theme ran through both the service and reform efforts of the settlements—participation and democracy. Many of their service activities were designed to permit dialogue between working people and settlement residents. The residents involved themselves in the life of the community so that they might know what services were needed. They worked to reduce the barriers that separated them from their neighbors, and the neighbors from one another. They invited labor leaders and radicals of their day to use their facilities.

[29]Contemporary group work also traces its origins to these settlement activities. On the other hand, the major thrust of group work is toward personal and interpersonal problems, and community organization, toward social conditions in a wider context. There is some indication, however, that group work may again be emphasizing its earlier social commitments.

[30]A study indicates that, after his defeat in 1912, Roosevelt terminated his relationship with social workers and returned to a more traditional Republicanism. See W. I. Trattner, "Theodore Roosevelt, Social Workers, and the Election of 1912: A Note," *Mid-America* 50, No. 1 (1968), pp. 64–69.

Finally, in everything they undertook, settlements tried to help their neighbors develop their potentialities to the fullest. There was great emphasis on education of all kinds. One of the major reasons for opposing child labor was its negative effects upon the development of children. Municipal reform was viewed, in part, as a process of helping communities gain the capacity to deal with their problems more effectively.

The settlement idea spread rapidly. In 1891 there were six settlements in the United States; by 1910 the number had jumped to over four hundred. Most of them were located in the large industrial cities of the East and Midwest; there were very few in the South or West.

The Organization of Ethnic Minorities and Women. A variety of forms of organization among black Americans was tested during this period as black people coped with their shifting status in American life. One of the earliest of these forms was developed by a group of prominent black people in 1865 and led by Frederick Douglass and George T. Downing who were "charged" with the duty to look after the best interests of the recently emancipated.[31] Almost twenty-five years later, in 1883, a very different kind of step was taken by the Louisville Convention of Colored Men which "concentrated on large issues of political, as distinct from partisan, rights, education, civil rights and economic problems."[32] Five years later, the Colored Farmers Alliance and Cooperative Union came into existence. In 1890, the Afro-American League organized in another direction, emphasizing legal redress rather

than politics.[33] In 1890, blacks from twenty-one states and the District of Columbia organized the Afro-American League of the United States. Issues which concerned this group included school funds, and legal and voting rights. In 1896, the National Association of Colored Women was formed.

Crosscurrents, similar to those which affect the organizations of black people today, were operative between the Civil War and World War I. On the one hand, many efforts were under the influence of Booker T. Washington, who sought an accommodation with white interests in order to maintain their support. In contrast, W. E. B. DuBois epitomized an opposition to this approach in 1905 when he called for "a conference 'to oppose firmly the present methods of strangling honest criticism.'"[34] The Niagara movement grew out of this meeting and by 1909 resulted in the formation of the National Association for the Advancement of Colored People. Such social workers as Jane Addams, Florence Kelly, and Lillian Wald assisted in these organizing efforts.

The Committee on Urban Conditions among Negroes in New York City, later to become the National Urban League, was another organization in which social workers were involved during this period. Its first executive, George Edmund Haynes, "was on the faculty of Fisk University and particularly interested in training black social workers."[35]

As noted earlier, Mexican-Americans, as well as Native Americans, were confronted with efforts that took away their lands. One response to this trend was the development

---

[31]Fishel and Quarles, op. cit., pp. 259–260.
[32]Ibid., p. 308.

[33]Ibid., p. 312.
[34]Ibid., p. 357.
[35]Ibid., p. 361.

of small groups for protection and support. Some, for survival, became bandits. Organized protest, however, for Mexican-Americans began in agriculture or, as Howard states, "The roots of the Chicano movement lie in the fields."[36]

In 1903, for example, Mexican- and Japanese-American sugar beet workers struck in Ventura, California.[37] In addition, throughout this period, but particularly from the 1880s on, many organizations came into existence whose function was, according to Alvarez, to preserve a Mexican-American way of life through "celebrations, social events, provision of facilities, information and communication networks."[38] The function of such organizations was to preserve a bicultural and bilingual existence. Some examples include the Penitente Order in New Mexico in the 1880s and Mano Negra, also in New Mexico, in the 1890s.[39]

The Native Americans during this period continued to have well-developed forms of tribal organization, partly as a heritage of their early struggles for survival against white encroachment. However, the tribes were separated from one another geographically and structurally, thus often rendering them easy prey for governmental manipulation. Nevertheless, the militancy of the period in actual warfare, as well as persistent legal action, represents an impressive, though unsuccessful, effort to secure a greater measure of justice from American society.

The early Chinese immigrants were organized into family or benevolent associations, tongs, or business interests.[40] For the Japanese, the Japanese Association for Issei (first-generation Japanese in the United States) had some similar functions.

Thus, for these Asian groups, a major function of community organizations during this period was mutual benefit and cultural participation. For example,

people from the same *ken*, or Japanese state, often cooperated in various ways, and this was noticeable in particular trades. For example, Miyamoto writes that the first Japanese barber in Seattle was from Yamaguchi-ken. After he became established, he helped his friends from the same ken with training and money, so that, eventually, most of the Japanese barbers in Seattle were from Yamaguchi-ken.[41]

During this era, when associations existed or were created in many ethnic groups, organizations for the benefit of women also emerged. In 1868, Susan B. Anthony was a leading organizer of a working women's association to fight economic discrimination against women. In addition, during the next decade unions of women working in a number of industries such as laundries and shoe factories were organized. By 1886, there were 113 women's assemblies in the Knights of Labor.[42] Other organizations also were concerned about the poor working conditions

---

[36]Howard, op. cit., p. 95.

[37]Ibid.

[38]Salvador Alvarez, "Mexican-American Community Organizations," in *Voices: Readings from El Grito, A Journal of Contemporary Mexican American Thought, 1967–1973*, ed. Octavio Ignacio Romano-V (Berkeley: Quinto Sol Publications, 1971), pp. 205–214.

[39]Ibid., p. 209.

[40]For a discussion of evolving forms of Chinese-American community organizations, see Melford S. Weiss, "Division and Unity: Social Process in a Chinese-American Community," in *Asian Americans: Psychological Perspectives*, ed. Stanley Sue and Nathaniel N. Wagner (Palo Alto: Science & Behavior Books, 1973), pp. 264–273.

[41]Kitano, *Japanese Americans*, op. cit., p. 19.

[42]For details of these and other endeavors, see "A Century of Struggle: American Women, 1820–1920," in Barbara Deckard, *The Women's Movement: Political, Socioeconomic, and Psychological Issues* (New York: Harper & Row, Publishers, 1975), pp. 243–284. This section draws heavily on that chapter.

of women. For example, in 1894, the New York Consumer's League presented information on these conditions. By 1896, this organization had branches in twenty states. In 1900, the International Ladies' Garment Workers' Union was organized and throughout the pre-World I period it continued to organize despite many obstacles.[43]

While working women were organizing themselves in their workplaces, more affluent women organized to secure the vote. The women's suffrage movement and the movement for the abolition of slavery had originally been one. The split came partially because northern business interests stood to gain from the black vote but could see no value in women having the same right.[44] This was symbolized when the American Equal Rights Association, working for black and women's rights, split in May 1869. Later that year moderate women organized the American Woman Suffrage Association while radical women formed the National Women Suffrage Association. These organizations remained separate until 1890 when they merged to form the National American Woman Suffrage Association. Unfortunately, the class bias of these organizations was evident in attacks on blacks as less fit to vote than women and in other statements made to ensure the acceptability of the women suffrage movement in the South.

The women's suffrage movement was able to see to it that the Nineteenth Amendment was proposed every year from 1886 to 1896, although it was defeated each time. The lack of strength to pass the amendment, according to one authority, was due to "their own conservative tactics and racist, elitist positions, which alienated

their potential allies."[45] With the emergence of militant supporters, however, such as radical farmers, the Progressive Party, and the socialists and a shift to more militant leadership, many states did come to adopt woman suffrage. By 1916, both major parties supported suffrage. In 1917, the Women's party turned to more militant tactics and picketed the White House. Partly, also, because of women's activities in the war and the public support of President Wilson, the House of Representatives finally passed the Nineteenth Amendment in January 1918. It took, however, another eighteen months for Senate approval.

Development of the Profession and Professional Education

For this period it is impossible to discuss community organization as a specialization in social work, which had itself not yet emerged as a separate entity. There were individuals concerned with coordinating charity, organizing neighborhood settlements, or mobilizing protest in racial matters, but these people had little common professional identity. Some training activities began to emerge in 1898 when the New York Charity Organization Society started a summer training course. This was expanded to a one-year program a few years later, and by the end of World War I seventeen schools of social work had come into existence in the United States and Canada. The Association of Training Schools for Professional Social Work was formed at that time also. The emphasis, however, was more on what became casework than on methods of community organization.

While the ethnic organizing of the period as well as that among women may

---

43Ibid., p. 270.
44Ibid., p. 262.

45Ibid., p. 269.

have secured the support of social workers as *individuals*, this did not represent activities of the profession or of a social work method called community organization. Nevertheless, many precedents were being created for and lessons learned by those who sought to create a more humane society and this included social workers.

1915 TO 1929

Social Conditions

After World War I, several new conditions emerged that had a significant impact on community organization practice: urbanization increased markedly, industrial potential escalated, and racial conflicts intensified. By 1920 more than half of the population of the United States lived in cities, and industrial innovations were accelerated by the heavy demands on production created by World War I.

The twenties, nevertheless, was a decade of confidence in the economic system. As Lerner stated, "Big business of the 1920s, certain that it had found the secret of perpetual prosperity, claimed the right to the policymaking decisions not only in the economy but in the government."[46]

Ironically, this period also brought some major crises in civil liberties. "After World War I there was a wave of raids and deportations; it arose from the uneasy feeling that the Russian Revolution had caused a shift in the world balance of power and spawned a fanatic faith threatening American survival."[47] The period also witnessed the intensification of activities of groups such as the Ku Klux Klan with antagonism directed against blacks, Jews, and the foreign born.

The Condition of Minorities

Blacks. This was a period during which black Americans made strong attempts to improve their lives and were simultaneously subjected to major efforts at repression. Seventy-six black people were lynched in 1919,[48] and "the white national secretary of the NAACP was badly beaten on the streets of Texas."[49] Chicago experienced a severe "race riot" in 1919 which resulted in the death of 15 white and 23 black persons as well as injury to an additional 537.[50]

However, progress occurred in many spheres of American life. The term *the New Negro* became prevalent in the 1920s, and this was supported by the increased self-respect of many black war veterans. During this period, distinguished people such as Langston Hughes, Countee Cullen, and Paul Robeson began their careers. Black school attendance jumped from 45 to 60 percent of the eligible school population between 1910 and 1930.[51] In fact, in many ways the current emphasis on black power and black identity has ideological antecedents in this period.

Chicanos. These years saw a large immigration of persons from Mexico into what had become the United States. Between 1910 and 1919, almost two hundred and twenty-five thousand persons came, and in the next decade the number was almost double.[52] According to one writer, "that striking increase is directly related to the miserable economic conditions in Mexico after ten

---

[46]Lerner, op. cit., p. 279.

[47]Ibid., p. 455.

---

[48]Fishel and Quarles, op. cit., 403.

[49]Ibid.

[50]Ibid., p. 405.

[51]Ibid.

[52]Lopez y Rivas, op. cit., p. 85.

years of armed struggle."[53] Specifically, the Mexican economy was in a poor state after the Mexican Revolution while the southwestern United States was experiencing considerable economic growth.

There was an expansion and development of nonagricultural worker organizations during this period. As Moore notes:

In 1920 Mexican workers struck the Los Angeles urban railway. In later years the strikes in the fields and mines of the Border States were both more numerous and more sophisticated. The earlier ones were significant, however, because Mexicans were generally denied normal channels of political expression in any of the Border States except New Mexico.[54]

Native Americans. During this period, the conditions of Native Americans continued to deteriorate as the government persisted in its policy of implementing the Dawes Act of 1887 which distributed land to individuals. The attempt to undermine the widely practiced custom of holding land in common for the good of all was continued. The act not only created severe economic problems but eroded traditional tribal government.[55] In fact, "The Indian Agent and his staff were 'the government' for most tribes from the cessation of treaty making to the 1930s."[56]

In addition to the effects of the Dawes Act, two other actions also diminished tribal ties. From 1917 to 1921, the trust on land allotments of Indians of less than one-half Indian blood was terminated. Many Indian agents were also eliminated and their wards

placed under school superintendents and farmers reporting directly to the Commissioner of Indian Affairs.[57] This focused activities on individuals, not tribes, and presumably moved Indians as individuals into non-Indian education and agriculture.

Asian Americans. The Immigration Act of 1924 epitomized the attitudes of the American government, if not of the society, to the foreign born. No immigration was to be permitted for Asians; low quotas were set for southern Europeans, and high ones for northern Europeans. This made it impossible, particularly for the Chinese who had not come as families, to form or reunite families. In Japanese communities, these years marked the birth and early development of many *Nisei*, or second-generation Japanese-Americans. With great determination, many Nisei moved into middle-class occupations.

Ideological Currents

The ideologies that were prevalent in the earlier period continued to exert a strong influence. The sense of complacency and optimism stemming from economic growth and affluence did find perceptive social critics, however. In addition, the following are ideas which developed during this period and which also molded social work practice.

Psychoanalysis. Some may find it strange to regard psychoanalysis as an ideology; nevertheless, the conditions of the period were conducive to the introduction of psychoanalysis as a major intellectual force in social work. This was a period of affluence, and many believed that the social environment offered so many opportunities and was other-

---

[53]Ibid., p. 39.

[54]Joan Moore, *Mexican-Americans* (Englewood Cliffs, NJ: Prentice-Hall, 1970), p. 24.

[55]Theodore W. Taylor, *The States and Their Indian Citizens* (Washington, DC: United States Department of the Interior, Bureau of Indian Affairs, 1972), p. 17.

[56]Ibid.

[57]Ibid., pp. 17–18.

wise so benign that any problems must be the result of individual failure. Psychoanalytic practice was clearly oriented toward changing the individual and not the system. Social workers, as Jesse Taft observed, became preoccupied with the person and all but forgot the situation: "The most daring experimental caseworkers have all but lost connection with social obligation and are quite buried in their scientific interest in the individual as he has evolved through his own unique growth process."[58] The social worker disassociated herself from charity to be reborn a psychotherapist.[59]

Anti-Intellectualism.   Despite the increasing popularity of Freud's ideas, this was not a period of intellectual activity in the United States. Vice-President Coolidge attacked the colleges and universities as "hot beds of sedition."[60] Many intellectuals, along with T. S. Eliot, fled to Europe, finding America a "wasteland."[61] American writers such as Sinclair Lewis castigated the American middle class, as F. Scott Fitzgerald did the upper class. It should also be remembered that the Scopes trial, testing the legal right to teach evolution in the schools, took place in 1925. According to one authority "only one event in the 1920s succeeded in arousing intellectuals of every kind of political loyalty: the arrest, trial, and execution of two Italian anarchists, Nicola Sacco and Bartolomeo Vanzetti."[62]

---

[58]Roy Lubove, *The Professional Altruist: The Emergence of Social Work As a Cause, 1880–1930* (Cambridge, MA: Harvard University Press, 1965), p. 89.

[59]Ibid.

[60]Samuel Eliot Morison, *The Oxford History of the American People* (New York: Oxford University Press, 1965), p. 909.

[61]Ibid., p. 910.

[62]For a brief summary of the case and its effects on opinion, see Frederick J. Hoffman, *The Twenties: American Writing in the Post War Decade* (New York: The Viking Press, 1955), pp. 357–364.

Development of Community Organization Institutions

The Community Chest and United Fund. This period saw a continued increase in the number of welfare institutions. This proliferation of agencies generated insistent demands for coordination. The increase in such institutions was prompted primarily by accelerating urbanization. The war increased the pace as "some three hundred American communities organized war chests to cope with the mounting flood of appeals from national and local agencies."[63] The agencies' increasing needs for financing, despite the affluence of the period, prompted demands from both the philanthropists and the professionals for better fund-raising methods. The interests of these two groups were not identical, and this led to the development of two separate yet interrelated institutions—the community chest or united fund, on the one hand, and the community welfare council on the other. The separation of interests between the suppliers of philanthropic dollars and the dispensers of them had effects which can be seen to this day in community welfare institutions.

Lubove reflected this situation accurately when he declared:

Financial federation captured the imagination of businessmen by promising efficient coordination and organization of the community welfare machinery, immunity from multiple solicitation, economical collection and distribution of funds, and the development of a broad base of support which would relieve the pressure on the small circle of large givers. The corporation, increasingly regarded as a source of gifts, appreciated the conveniences of federated finance.[64]

There was also opposition to this development. National organizations resented

---

[63]Lubove, op. cit., p. 189.
[64]Ibid., p. 183.

the competition for local funds. Of particular importance to the contemporary scene in community organization is resistance to the erosion of "democracy" implicit in the development of a fund-raising bureaucracy. Lubove cited one chest executive who stated, "We are facing here the age-long and inevitable conflict which exists in any society between the urge for individual independence and initiative on the one hand, and the need for social control on the other."[65]

Philanthropists wanted their funds spent efficiently and desired relief from the constant appeals of charitable solicitors. United appeals for financial support were created to serve these objectives, originating with the United Jewish Appeal in Boston in 1895.[66]

Community chests evolved in several ways. First, welfare agencies joined to solicit funds, hoping to raise more money than each could obtain separately. In 1887, the Charity Organization Society in Denver initiated joint fund-raising among fifteen of its twenty-three cooperating agencies, an effort which proved financially successful in its first year of operation.[67] Community chests were also organized by councils of social agencies. In 1915, two years after its organization, Cincinnati's Council of Agencies brought twelve agencies together in a united appeal for funds. Before 1927, councils in St. Louis, Minneapolis, Columbus, New Haven, and Detroit had followed suit.[68]

For the most part, however, community chests were initiated by large contributors. Often their first step was a charity endorsement bureau which later reorganized as a community chest. Businessmen and industrialists believed that welfare services, like public utilities, should be held accountable to the public. Because contributors rarely had time to investigate agencies that asked for support, local chambers of commerce organized bureaus to (1) establish standards for welfare agencies; (2) investigate individual agencies and measure their operations against their standards; (3) recommend those agencies that met the test; and (4) encourage members and the public to support organizations that received endorsement.[69]

The endorsement bureau had its critics. Because it mainly represented the large business and industrial contributors, agencies viewed the bureaus as potentially autocratic and a threat to their autonomy. Furthermore, agencies believed that the organization might dampen contributors' interest and enthusiasm.[70] The demands upon a small number of contributors also became very great. The first major effort to remedy these conditions was taken by the Cleveland Chamber of Commerce. After initiating a study of the problem in 1907, the chamber launched the Federation for Charity and Philanthropy in 1913. Cleveland's federation is generally considered to be a major landmark in the history of community chests,[71] a name which was first used in Rochester, New York, in 1919.[72]

[65]Ibid. p. 196. Lubove, here, was quoting Raymond Clapp, "Who Shall Decide Personnel Policies?" *Survey* 65 (1930), p. 103.

[66]Lyman S. Ford, "Federated Financing," in Harry L. Lurie (ed.), *Encyclopedia of Social Work* (New York: National Association of Social Workers, 1965), p. 331.

[67]William J. Norton, *The Cooperative Movement in Social Work* (New York: The Macmillan Co., 1927), pp. 50–54.

[68]Ibid., pp. 93–99.

[69]Ibid., pp. 24–29.

[70]Ibid., pp. 29–30.

[71]Ibid., pp. 68–71.

[72]Guy Thompson, "Community Chests and United Funds," *Social Work Year Book, 1957*, ed. Russell H. Kurtz (New York: National Association of Social Workers, 1957), p. 176.

Community chests were dominated by three kinds of people: contributors, particularly those who gave large sums; solicitors, the small businessmen, service club members and middle management types who helped to raise the chests' funds; and volunteers representative of the health, welfare, and recreation agencies that were supported by the chests. The membership delegated much of the decision making to a board of directors, which hired an executive. In the beginning, most of the work was done by volunteers. Volunteers still continue to play an important part in community chests.

World War I gave a great impetus to the development of chests. Overseas relief and other war-created welfare needs stimulated the development of nearly four hundred "War Chests." During the 1920s the number of communities with community chests increased from 39 to 353.[73]

The Council of Social Agencies and Community Welfare Council. The first decades of the twentieth century saw the development of an increasing professionalism among those who helped the poor. The friendly visitor was replaced by the paid agent. The charity organization societies founded schools of philanthropy which, beginning around the turn of the century, became graduate schools of social work. The development of the social survey—a disciplined effort to obtain factors necessary for planning—was another manifestation of the growing professionalism. In short, the growing cadre of welfare professionals, with the support of many volunteers who served as board members of charitable societies, was interested in organizing a rational, systematic approach to

the welfare needs of communities. Their interest included providing for the gaps in service, detecting problems, and looking to future needs. This combination of professionals and volunteers formed councils. The first councils were organized in Milwaukee and Pittsburgh in 1909. By 1926 there were councils in Chicago, Boston, St. Louis, Los Angeles, Detroit, Cincinnati, Columbus, and New York.[74]

Because of the potential conflicts noted earlier, one of the problems experienced by councils was their relation to community chests or united funds. Often councils have been regarded as the planning arm of the chest or fund, and this limited their relationship to publicly supported health and welfare agencies. Yet when councils maintained some degree of independence from chests and funds, they seldom could provide the necessary incentives to gain compliance with their plans. Those councils that were heavily influenced by chests or funds were often assigned responsibility for distributing the money raised in the united appeal, a function seldom performed by independent councils.

Another problem of welfare councils was their relation with constituents. In the beginning, most councils were confederations of welfare agencies, largely those supported by chests. Within such a federated structure, councils often found it difficult to take forceful action, not wanting to seriously offend their agency constituents, which had a major stake in welfare plans. With the growing professionalization of councils, they often were reorganized as councils of individual citizens with an interest in welfare problems and services. This shift was indicated in the change in name from "council of agencies" to "com-

---

[73]Ford, op. cit., pp. 327–328.

[74]Ibid., p. 37.

munity welfare council." Efforts were made to recruit those with a reputation for influence, and decisions have increasingly reflected the views of professional planners and their volunteer constituents rather than welfare agencies. In spite of this, welfare councils have not enjoyed a reputation for effective planning.[75]

The Social Unit Plan. Roy Lubove[76] described a local development which anticipated one trend that later became important in community organization. This plan was launched in 1915 when the National Social Unit Organization was founded. A pilot area was selected in Cincinnati. The sponsors desired to test:

the theory that a democratic and effective form of community organization which stimulated people to define and meet their own needs has to divide the citizens into small, primary units, organize the occupational specialists, and insure an "organic" and coordinate working relationship between the representatives of groups having special knowledge or skill for service to the community and the representatives of the residents.[77]

The social unit plan led to the development of block councils, block workers, and federations of such groups, referred to as the Citizens Council of the Social Unit. Occupational groups also elected a council. This program lasted three years and "concentrated on health services."[78] The movement did not expand in this form, perhaps indicative of the fact that the time for this idea had not yet come.

The Organization of Ethnic Minorities and Women. Particularly in the South, many institutions developed among blacks because of the patterns of discrimination and segregation which existed during this period. Out of school segregation, educational organizations arose. Black newspapers also came into existence because news of the black community was ignored by the white press. The exclusion of blacks from white churches led to a variety of black religious organizations.[79]

Many black soldiers hoped that their return from World War I would see a change in the patterns of racism they had suffered for so long. This was not to occur, as the Klan and other groups intensified their campaigns and "returning Negro soldiers were lynched by hanging and burning, even while still in their military uniforms."[80] One reaction to this was the Universal Negro Improvement Association of Marcus Garvey. This organization rapidly became the largest nonreligious black organization. The purpose of the movement was to send blacks back to Africa, and the attraction of this to many blacks was a clear indication of their disaffection with America.

There was also militancy, and as Franklin stated:

This was the spirit of what Alain Locke called "The New Negro." He fought the Democratic white primary, made war on the whites who consigned him to the ghetto, attacked racial discrimination in employment, and pressed for legislation to protect his rights. If he was seldom successful during the postwar decade and the depression, he made it quite clear that he was unalterably opposed to the un-American character of the two worlds of race.[81]

---

[75]These changes did not occur until the late 1940s and 1950s, but are reported here to complete the discussion of community welfare councils.

[76]Lubove, op. cit., pp. 175–178.

[77]Ibid., p. 176.

[78]Ibid.

[79]Much of the material in this section has been drawn from John Hope Franklin, "The Two Worlds of Race: A Historical View," *Daedalus* 94, No. 4 (Fall 1965), pp. 899–920.

[80]Ibid., p. 912.

[81]Ibid., p. 913.

During this same period, a major thrust of Mexican-American organization was toward integration.[82] This represented the desires of the growing middle class to secure their share of the American wealth. An example was the Order of the Sons of America, founded in San Antonio in 1921. An intent of this organization was to show Anglos that its members were different from Mexicans who cause problems.[83] The League of Latin American Citizens had similar objectives.

Meanwhile, Chicano laborers were waging their own struggle. Lopez y Rivas points out that "all over California, Arizona, Texas, New Mexico, and other states they went on strike for better wages and living conditions as well as an end to racist employment practices." These efforts, however, met with "violent repression."[84] Nevertheless, an important development was the founding in 1927 of *La Confederacion de Uniones Obreras Mexicanos*. This organization held its first general convention in May 1928. Delegates attended from twenty-one unions as well as mutual aid societies. Farm labor groups also struck the fields throughout California. The *Confederacion* itself engaged in major organizing activities throughout the 1920s and 1930s.[85]

The actions of the federal government which had the effect of undermining Native American institutions continued during this period. One piece of legislation, the Snyder Act of 1921, continued to affirm the objective of the Bureau of Indian Affairs to provide "for the general support and civilization of Indians."[86] However, the Meriam Report of 1928 recommended "an acculturation program on an understanding of the Indian point of view."[87] Even though these actions may have been inspired by good intentions, their patronizing nature was unsupportive of indigenous institutions.

One author, in an attempt to characterize efforts to organize women after the adoption of the Nineteenth Amendment, titles her chapter "Forty Years in the Desert: American Women, 1920–1960."[88] In the first place, there was no indication of a women's bloc vote, which some had feared. This was not to deny the fact, however, that in specific elections in those states that had adopted women's suffrage, the proportions of women voting differently than men made a difference in the outcome. An example was the defeat of antisuffrage senator John Weeks in 1918.[89]

The National Women's Party, however, continued to operate. It maintained a platform committed to full equality and supported the first introduction of the Equal Rights Amendment into Congress in 1923. However, it was quite small and in 1923 had only eight thousand members as compared to fifty thousand three years before.[90]

The League of Women Voters was founded in 1920. This group was much less militant than the National Women's Party and it declared in 1931 that "nearly all discriminations have been removed."[91] The League was less concerned about women's issues than child labor laws, pacifism, and other general reforms.

The general conservatism of the 1920s took its toll on the women's movement. The

---

[82]Lopez y Rivas, op. cit., p. 62.

[83]Ibid.

[84]Ibid.

[85]Alvarez, op. cit., pp. 211–212.

[86]Taylor, op. cit., p. 19.

[87]Ibid.

[88]Deckard, op. cit., p. 285.

[89]Ibid., p. 286.

[90]Ibid., p. 287.

[91]Ibid.

prohibition against child labor, which women's groups favored, was attacked as a subversive plot.[92] It was even charged that all liberal women's groups were part of a Communist plot.[93] Despite this, women continued to found organizations including the National Federation of Business and Professional Women's Clubs (1919) and the American Association of University Women (1921).

Development of the Profession

Most of those who trained for social work in the first two decades of the twentieth century were studying to become caseworkers. However, by 1920 Joseph K. Hart had written a text entitled *Community Organization*, and between then and 1930 at least five books were written on the subject.[94] It is easy to see why the casework emphasis existed in view of the prevalent ideologies and issues of the period, emphasizing individual conformity to the "system." In fact, community organization practice during this period was aimed largely at enhancing agencies oriented toward personal adjustment. Except, perhaps, for the workers in settlement houses, the "social unit plan," and the organizations developing in the black community, little thought was given to the changing social institutions to meet the needs of individuals. Even in the case of settlements, the workers there often thought of themselves as educators, recreation leaders, or group workers. In the black community, organizers rarely identified with social work.

Nevertheless, some different ideas were beginning to emerge. Mary Follett foresaw the advantages to democracy of the organization of primary groups in the local communities.[95] Eduard Lindeman, who taught for many years at the New York School of Social Work, also spoke of the value of "an attempt on the part of the people who live in a small, compact local group to assume their own responsibilities and to guide their own destinies."[96]

The emphasis of this period, however, was aptly summed up by Lubove when he wrote the following:

Federation employed the rhetoric of the early community organization movement, but its intensive concern with the machinery and financing of social welfare diverted attention from cooperative democracy and the creative group life of the ordinary citizen to problems of agency administration and service. It substituted the bureaucratic goal of efficiency through expert leadership for what had been a quest for democratic self-determination through joint efforts of citizen and specialist. Community organization had barely emerged as a cause before it had become a function absorbed into the administrative structure of social work.[97]

1929 TO 1954

Social work, as well as other institutions in the United States, was deeply affected by the two major cataclysms of this period: the depression and World War II. To regard these years as a single period in American history may seem odd to some readers, but they cover a coherent period in the devel-

---

[92]Ibid., pp. 288–289.

[93]Ibid.

[94]Meyer Schwartz, "Community Organization," *Encyclopedia of Social Work*, op. cit., 1965, p. 177.

[95]See for example, her book, *The New State: Group Organization, the Solution of Popular Government* (New York: Longmans, Green and Co., 1918), p. 217.

[96]Eduard C. Lindeman, *The Community: An Introduction to the Study of Community Leadership and Organization* (New York: Association Press, 1921), p. 58.

[97]Lubove, op. cit., p. 180.

opment of ideas and issues in community organization practice. A departure from this pattern took place in the fifties, marked by the desegregation decision of the Supreme Court and the end of McCarthyism, that period of ideological repression which received its name, as well as much encouragement, from the late Senator Joseph McCarthy of Wisconsin.

Social Conditions

To set the stage for the discussion of the history of community organization during the period, one should call attention to several social forces.

Depression Issues. The most apparent of the social forces at play was the vast increase in unemployment. The bank and stock market failures also removed whatever reserves people might otherwise have utilized in such a crisis. Mortgage foreclosures deprived many of their homes, farms, and small businesses.

The Growth of Government. The expansion of government programs was a direct result of the depression. Government expenditures, programs, and controls grew in unprecedented ways. The government became an employer, a producer of goods and services, and a vast resource to restore the industrial processes. The federal government also became the most significant planner and promoter of welfare programs through the enactment, in the mid-thirties, of such legislation as social security and the minimum wage.

The Growth of Unionism. The depression also stimulated a major upsurge of trade unionism. The founding of the CIO showed that the labor movement was at last free from the limits of a craft basis for organiza-

tion. The passage of the National Labor Relations Act in 1935 marked the beginning of an era in which government facilitated the development of unions and thereby became less the biased protector of business interests. The development of strong unions in the auto, steel, electrical, meat-packing, and other industries had a major impact upon the industrial scene. The organization of the Brotherhood of Sleeping Car Porters gave the black community an important labor spokesman, A. Phillip Randolph.

The International Scene. During this period, it became evident that the Communist party was firmly entrenched in the USSR. In Spain, Italy, and Germany, facist governments seized power. American counterparts of these movements were apparent in the developments within the United States.

On the international level, these developments had consequences of the most serious nature for the United States. Just at the time in the thirties that many programs to solve the social problems of the country were being tested, the need to prepare for and then wage World War II increasingly absorbed the attention and resources of the American people. In fact, only with the war did the country clearly come out of the depression.

The Condition of Minorities

Blacks. The creation of many New Deal agencies "added credence to the emergent fact that for the first time the federal government had engaged and was grappling with some of the fundamental barriers to race progress."[98] On the other hand, there

---

[98]Fishel and Quarles, op. cit., p. 447.

were many times when Roosevelt, who was highly regarded by many black leaders, failed to deliver on expectations because of political considerations. Where local control was strong, the effect of some of those programs was to continue the exclusion of black people from necessary benefits.

It is undeniable, however, that important strides were made during this period. There was a considerable expansion of opportunities for black people in important governmental positions. Civil service brought many black people into white-collar positions in government. World War II increased this momentum. The Committee on Fair Employment Practice, established by Roosevelt in 1941 to improve employment opportunities in defense industries, was a significant development. In 1948, Truman created the civil rights section of the Justice Department and established the President's Committee on Equality of Treatment and Opportunity in the Armed Services. The courts struck down restrictive housing covenants and outlawed segregation on buses in interstate travel.

Chicanos. During this period, Chicanos began to move beyond the Southwest into many parts of the United States. This was due in part to the processes of acculturation but also to the fact that new Mexican immigrants were willing to work for lower wages than second-generation persons, who then tended to move to new areas. Particularly in the North, jobs were more available and wages better. A pattern of migrant farm labor was also established emanating from the Southwest and spreading to other parts of the country, as Chicanos followed the crops.

Much of the immigration during this period was illegal but responsive to employers seeking cheap labor. Employers

aided the smuggling in of such persons.[99] The need for labor was heightened as Asian immigration ended.

In summarizing the period prior to 1940, however, one authority states:

The lot of the Mexican-Americans, except as they were affected by the immigration, changed little during this period prior to 1940. In a real sense, they were forgotten Americans; there was little assimilation to the majority society. They remained a Spanish speaking, largely rural, and generally poor minority. The decline of the small farmer and sheepherder forced many off the land altogether. But even as wage earners, they received no proper return in comparison to their contribution to the building of the economy of the Southwest.[100]

Native Americans. Early in the period being described here, a new approach was adopted to Native Americans: the Indian Reorganization Act of 1934. The intent of this act was to reverse the land policy of the Allotment Act of 1887 and the intent of trying to "stamp out everything that was Indian."[101] The 1934 act specifically provided authorization for the purchase of new land, the initiation of tribal organization, the creation of loan funds for individuals *and tribes*, and extended the trust of Indian lands "until otherwise directed by Congress."[102]

This new policy of a more humane concern for Indians was a part of FDR's New Deal. The Commissioner of Indian Affairs from 1933 to 1944, John Collier, was an anthropologist with a long career of interest in Indian affairs, and this may also have made a difference. Collier was critical of

---

[99]Wayne Moquin with Charles Van Doren, *A Documentary History of the Mexican Americans* (New York: Praeger Publishers, 1971), p. 252.

[100]Ibid., p. 253.

[101]Taylor, op. cit., pp. 20–26.

[102]Ibid.

many American values and was identified with the aspirations of many Indian groups, as well as having his own ideas about the potential of Indian society.[103]

Tribal governments, established under this act, were helped to develop constitutions and carry on many operations required of modern governments, economic as well as political. In contradiction to this, however, was the policy of promoting assimilation by urging states to provide the same services for individual Indians as for other citizens.

Asian Americans. This period saw the gradual improvement of the economic status of Chinese-Americans although not necessarily of their social status. As Kitano states:

In the late 1930s and during World War II the Chinese became our friends and allies, although the general tone of the friendship was condescending. . . . Their peace loving nature was emphasized; they had fought valiantly against the "sly, tricky Jap;" they were different from their more aggressive neighbor. . . . In many ways, this praise deflected from the everyday humiliation, harassment, and deprivation faced by many Chinese, even with the relatively favorable attitude toward all Orientals (except the Japanese) at this time.[104]

The most devastating event affecting the Japanese-American community was the wartime evacuation of all persons with as little as one-eighth Japanese blood from the West Coast. By March 1942, one hundred and ten thousand such persons, most citizens of the United States, were in virtual concentration camps in such states as Colorado, Utah, and Arkansas. There was widespread compliance by most Japanese-Americans, even though they had to abandon their homes and possessions. This terrible injustice continued until 1944 when the Supreme Court revoked the policy. Most families who survived the experience had to begin all over again. Little remained of their property or belongings.

Ideological Currents

The most important ideological issues of the period were those stimulated by the conditions of the depression. The emphasis of the twenties upon the individual's responsibility for his or her own destiny could not hold up under the circumstances of the thirties. The literature of this period emphasized the effects of the social order on people and the need to modify that order to solve the spiritual as well as the economic problems which plagued Americans.[105] Many came to regard government, rather than business, as the preferred means for developing a better society. However, except for small minorities, people wanted their government to operate through much the same political processes as it always had, and the economy to remain capitalist, though under strong government controls.

These ideas were not basically shaken by the war. Fascism as an international enemy was further proof that there are forces which transcend the individual and must be controlled by collective action. Although congressional investigations of "un-American activities" received support, the external enemy and wartime prosperity took many people's attention away from problems within the United States. Moreover, Americans' faith in their

---

[103]Ibid., p. 22.

[104]Kitano, *Race Relations*, op. cit., p. 200.

[105]It was noted earlier that the ideological antecedents of some black militancy were in the twenties. Current white militancy had similar antecedents in the thirties.

own political and economic system may have been reinforced by wartime victory. However, the specter of an external enemy acting in concert with internal agents returned with a vengeance with the cold war and the Korean War, dampening criticism of the "American way of life" and making it difficult to gain support for proposals to confront the country's social problems.

Development of Community Organization Institutions

Community organization agencies, like others in social welfare, found themselves unable to cope with the massive needs of the country during the depression. This period marked a shift of emphasis in operations from local and private to regional or national and public. The federal government through its agencies became the main impetus for social planning. At first through the Federal Emergency Relief Administration and later through the Federal Security Agency, standards for welfare activity were set, coordination was promoted, fact finding was conducted, and plans for public education were launched.

World War II advanced the trend toward community planning under national auspices, both public and private. The need for welfare services grew as new and expanding communities of defense workers and soldiers sprang up. The Office of Community War Services in the Federal Security Agency was created to handle some of the planning for recreation and public health needs in affected areas.

Organization of Ethnic Minorities and Women. Organization in the black community remained primarily on a national level, and some authorities have noted a degree of apathy regarding anything beyond that.[106] The NAACP continued to wage campaigns in the courts, the Congress, and the press for the rights of blacks. The Urban League expanded its programs of employment, family welfare, health, and education. The thirties and forties did not foster any prominent new organizational efforts. In addition to the external threats noted earlier, this may have been due to the development of governmental programs, trade union activity, and local activity, which black people believed would provide long-hoped-for access to the "American Dream."

During the 1930s, the organizing activities of the *Confederacion de Uniones Obreras Mexicanas* continued. Efforts to build union organizations also included those of the National Farm Workers' Union. Other organizations emerged, and some examples of these are the League of United Latin American Citizens (Texas, 1929), the *Associacion de Jornaleros* (Texas, 1933), the *Sociedad Mutualista Mexicana* (Ohio, 1936), the Pan American Student Forum of Texas (1943), and the Community Service Organization (California, 1947).[107] The vitality of Chicano life is apparent in the organizations that were created during these years. These developments may well have provided support for the new programs which emerged in the 1960s.

These years also saw movements within Native American tribes. Through new government policies, many tribal governments were established or strengthened. Tribes assumed authority to:

employ legal counsel; prevent sale or encumbrance of tribal land or other assets without the consent of the tribe; negotiate with federal, state,

---

[106]Fishel and Quarles, op. cit., p. 450.

[107]Alvarez, op. cit., pp. 209–210.

and local governments; determine tribal membership; assign tribal land to individuals; manage economic affairs; appropriate money for salaries or other public purposes; levy taxes, license fees, or community labor in lieu thereof; control conduct of members of the reservation by enactment of ordinances . . . [108]

As was true of Mexican-Americans, it seems likely that the organizational development of the depression, war, and postwar years was a precursor to militant organizing in the next decade.

A somewhat different type of organizational experience characterizes Chinese-American life. Chinese-Americans had been living within their own communities, but a trend toward some dispersion began at this time. The control exerted by the traditional associations weakened in many Chinese-American communities. Some who had gained status in the broader community did not have it in the ethnic community because of age and cultural difference, including language. Thus, new institutions began to emerge to meet their needs.[109] In many ways, the situation was similar for Japanese-Americans, although recovery from the "relocation" of the war years was a long and hard process.

The period between the depression and the 1950s was not a good one for the women's movement. During the war years many women were employed, and this may have diminished demands for equal employment opportunities for women. However, such issues as adequate child care were central. The conservative swing after the war discouraged militancy among women. Even the League of Women Voters, hardly a radical organization, showed a decline in membership during this time.

Development of the Profession and Professional Education

This, while not a period of innovation in community organization beyond the shift from a local to a national emphasis, was a time of intensive efforts to conceptualize the nature of community organization practice. Writers had three overriding concerns.

The *first* bore upon the relation between community organization and social work. Some contended that community organization was not really a legitimate form of social work practice, and others took pains to establish community organization's affinity to the basic values and concerns of social work.

The *second* was an interest in the objectives of community organization. On the one hand, practitioners regarded the Industrial Revolution as destructive of personal, face-to-face relations between people and believed that community organization practice should strengthen community cohesion. At the same time, they were disturbed about a number of social problems and thought that community organization practice should prevent or at least ameliorate them.

Third, they struggled with the appropriate role for the practitioner. Neighborhoods and communities needed the help of practitioners if localities were to achieve their objectives. And yet practitioners must not impose their views on those served. One must somehow strike a balance between giving help and fostering self-determination.[110]

1955 TO 1968

The beginning of this period coincides with the end of the McCarthy era and the Supreme Court decision on school desegregation.

---

[108]Taylor, op. cit., pp. 23–24.

[109]For a discussion of this development, see Weiss, op. cit., pp. 264–273.

[110]For further details, see Schwartz, op. cit., pp. 177–190.

Whether or not causally related, these events appear to have anticipated a number of other phenomena.

Social Conditions

The Growth of the Civil Rights Movement. Marked by the 1954 Supreme Court decision ending legal school segregation, the rising dissatisfaction of black Americans gave birth or renewed vitality to a number of organizations which have sought to end the inequality of opportunity afforded black people. The Montgomery, Alabama, bus boycott, which began in December of 1955, brought Martin Luther King, Jr., and the Southern Christian Leadership Conference forward as leaders in the civil rights struggle.[111] The Congress of Racial Equality (founded in 1943) sponsored nonviolent resistance in the form of sit-ins, freedom rides, and demonstrations.[112] The Student Non-Violent Coordinating Committee, the Mississippi Freedom Democratic party, the Black Panther party, the Black Muslims, the Republic of New Africa and other black nationalist groups, and the NAACP were among the organizations affected by the rising tide of civil rights activities. The quest for black power grew out of the experiences of the Student Non-Violent Coordinating Committee and other active groups who came to despair of achieving genuine integration. As they began to fight for black pride and capability, they demanded autonomy in black affairs, including neighborhood control of schools and economic institutions.[113]

---

[111]Martin Luther King, Jr., *Stride Toward Freedom* (New York: Ballantine Books, 1958).

[112]James Peck, *Freedom Ride* (New York: Simon & Schuster, 1962).

[113]Stokely Carmichael and Charles V. Hamilton, *Black Power: The Politics of Liberation in America* (New York: Vintage Books, 1967).

Subsequently other minority groups asserted themselves, claiming their rights and developing pride in their special identity. The Chicanos of the Southwest made substantial progress in organizing. Stimulated by Cesar Chavez and his success in organizing California farm workers, Chicanos organized groups such as *La Raza Unida* in such places as south Texas, New Mexico, and even where migrant farm workers traveled in search of employment, such as Michigan, where many Chicano farm workers settled down and sought education and regular jobs. American Indians, whose living conditions are generally worse than those of any other minority in this country, likewise demonstrated solidarity in such ways as occupying Alcatraz Island in San Francisco Bay and obtaining legislative support for expanded fishing rights in Michigan.

As the period continued, one trend was clear: a growing effort to create ethnic minority institutions. Examples include neighborhood control of schools, black-owned business, black professional societies, black-led Model Cities programs, powerful interest groups such as the National Welfare Rights Organization, and black labor unions. Nevertheless, conflicts were evident among the leaders of these groups, often traceable to ideological differences. For example, some black leaders sought parallel black economic organizations, i.e., black capitalism, while others worked for changes in the power bases of all American institutions to include major input from black people and other minorities.

Late in this period, other groups asserted themselves, feeling deprived in comparison with their fellow citizens and encouraged by the achievements of blacks and other minorities. Gay men and lesbians demanded social and economic rights and fought discrimination in jobs and housing. The elderly, sometimes with the support of Grey Panther groups, demanded greater attention to their needs, especially for health care. The handicapped also drew attention to the discrimination they suffer in education, employment, and public facilities. Women, oppressed by the requirements of their traditional roles, demanded liberation and equality. A not fully successful achievement was congressional approval of the Equal Rights Amendment to the federal Constitution and its ratification by many state legislatures. "Middle America" became a potent political force. Disgruntled citizens such as Irene McCabe mobilized large numbers of people who opposed the busing of school children to achieve racial integration. Political candidates (George Wallace, for example) captured the support of large numbers of disenchanted voters who felt strongly about school busing and high taxes and were distrustful of government. An anti-gay movement secured defeat of legislation favoring gay rights in Florida.

The Vietnam War. It is difficult to judge the impact of this war on social work and community organization. Nevertheless, seldom in American history have so many felt so antagonistic to a major involvement of their country. Aside from concerns about the justice of the war, its implications for the allocation of resources to deal with problems on the home front were of grave concern. Some regarded this war and, more generally, what President Eisenhower had referred to as the expanding influence of the "military-industrial complex" and the consequent retreat from dealing effectively with problems of our cities, as the most serious crisis the nation had faced. Certainly, the war led many to doubt the citizen's ability to influence governmental decisions.

The Growth of Student Movements. Stimulated by student involvement in the civil rights movement, student activism among whites as well as blacks and across the whole political spectrum increased phenomenally. Many student activists turned to social work and particularly to community organization in search of a career compatible with their personal commitments. Some students entering school in the mid-1960s were affected by the community organization projects carried out by the Students for a Democratic Society. Many had experiences relevant to community organization through the Peace Corps or VISTA. Still others were influenced by the dynamic organizing style of Saul Alinsky and many organizations he helped found.

Increasing numbers of black students sought admission to professional schools, including programs offering training in community organization. Puerto Rican and Chicano students did likewise, and there is an indication of similar developments among Japanese- and Chinese-American students, particularly on the West Coast.

Development of Community Organization Institutions

The federal government took increasing responsibility for dealing with a wide range of domestic social problems, primarily through grants-in-aid to state and local governments. This had an important bearing on the growth of community organization practice. For example, early in this period the federal government sharply increased appropriations for mental health, primarily for research, professional training, and mental health clinics. More recently, federal programs encouraged preventive measures and efforts to treat the mentally ill in their local communities, a process requiring community organization skills. Similar developments occurred in programs for the mentally retarded, the physically disabled, and the alcoholic. The construction of hospitals and other health facilities, together with encouragement of health services planning at the state level, also received federal support. Programs of slum clearance, urban renewal, neighborhood development, housing subsidies, and regional planning were created and expanded with federal assistance. Although by no means exhaustive, this list of activities exemplifies the role of the federal government in the fields of health and urban development. Similar changes in related fields such as education and child welfare also occurred, which stimulated additional demand for community organization skills.

The trend toward federal responsibility for welfare problems was escalated by the War on Poverty, a product of the Kennedy and Johnson administrations. This program captured the interest of many community organizers. Among the specific programs were Head Start; VISTA; Neighborhood Youth Corps, Job Corps and other work-training programs; adult basic education; assistance to the rural poor, including migrant farm workers; and a wide variety of locally conceived "community action programs" offering opportunities for local initiative in legal aid, health, housing, consumer education, and so forth. Perhaps the single most important influence these programs had on community practice was the very large number of jobs they offered for people trained as organizers. One much-debated ingredient of these programs was the provision for "maximum feasible participation" of service recipients in program decisions. The how, where, and why of this was often confusing to both professionals and citizens.

Other programs created during this period tried to solve urban problems, which continued to intensify. A major effort was the Model Cities program established in 1966, which provided funds to groups representative of particular neighborhoods

within cities. These groups used such funds either to develop new programs within existing civic institutions or to create new institutions where necessary.

In some Model Cities neighborhoods, a vision grew of a "parallel" government manned by the poor within the neighborhoods. This vision was muted, however, by developments which made the existing city governments powerful partners in any operation, under the rationale that coordination and accountability were necessary. This challenged community organizers to help constituents exert influence under these newly instituted rules.

All of these moves to solve urban problems raised the same issues: Which strata of society will have power? How are the poor to be represented? How are priorities to be determined? Community organizers were involved in answering all these questions, offering a variety of answers to each of them.

Ideological Currents

This was a time in which virtually all the previous ideas about community organization practice reappeared. On the one hand this was when American people supported the development of vast new responsibilities for government in solving the problems of welfare. On the other hand, there was a renewed emphasis upon participatory democracy. Local organization, black power, community control, and such concepts as "maximum feasible participation" (which Daniel P. Moynihan has paraphrased "maximum possible misunderstanding") had a wide appeal.

As might be anticipated, those ideological developments were reflected in the political groupings of the period. The Eugene McCarthy campaign for president in 1968 brought together many who saw themselves, at least for the moment, as working within existing institutions.

Various groups identified with "the New Politics" continued this effort. On the other hand, as frustration over the lack of federal commitment to civil rights and ending the Vietnam war grew, violent ideologies and solutions also were perpetuated. An alternative "dropout" culture grew as a spin-off of this process. Some community organizers, for example, developed and lived within a growing network of communes.

Alongside interests in added government responsibility and participation of the people has been a strong tide of disengagement from society on the one hand and of violent opposition to those who control society on the other. These currents were reflected in social work, with some students planning government jobs, others looking forward to participation in anti-establishment grassroots organizations, and still others asking if social work and "revolution" are compatible orientations. Moderation and social planning formed the dominant orientation of community organization students, while social work as a whole experienced a marked increase of interest in professionalization, psychotherapy, self-realization and "making a good living."

Development of the Profession and Professional Education

Training for community organization practitioners in social work grew markedly at first. Both the number of programs and the number of students rose sharply. By 1969 the number of schools of social work providing training programs for community organizers increased to forty-eight, from thirty-six in 1965.[114] Community organiza-

tion was taught in some form in virtually all schools.

Parallel with the increase in numbers were efforts to clarify the nature of community organization, identify what community organizers need to know to be effective, and give recognition to the development of community organization as a specialized form of practice within social work. In the late 1950s, the Council on Social Work Education embarked upon a wide-ranging study of the curriculum in schools of social work which included separate attention to community organization.[115] The National Association of Social Workers created a Committee on Community Organization which prepared working papers and bibliographies designed to codify practice knowledge and establish the position of the community organization specialty within social work.[116] In 1962 the Council on Social Work Education gave formal recognition to community organization as a method of social work comparable with casework and group work.[117]

An ambitious effort to develop curriculum for training community organizers was initiated in 1963. It, too, was sponsored by the Council on Social Work Education and received financial support from HEW's Office of Juvenile Delinquency and Youth Development.[118] This study culminated in the publication of five book-length reports and numerous journal articles and confer-

---

[114]Arnold Gurin, *Community Organization Curriculum in Graduate Social Work Education: Report and Recommendations* (New York: Council on Social Work Education, 1970), p. 10.

[115]Harry L. Lurie, ed., *The Community Organization Method in Social Work Education*, Vol. IV, Project Report of the Social Work Curriculum Study (New York: Council on Social Work Education, 1959).

[116]See especially National Association of Social Workers, Defining Community Practice (New York: NASW, 1962).

[117]Council on Social Work Education, *Curriculum Policy Statement* (New York: CSWE, 1962).

[118]Gurin, op. cit., pp. vii–viii.

ence reports.[119] Earlier efforts pointed up the similarities of community organization practice and other forms of social work practice. Perhaps the most significant theme of this latest curriculum study was the recognition that community organization practitioners required professional training that is, in many ways, differentiated from training for other social work specializations.

1969 AND AFTER

We have chosen 1969 as the beginning of the current phase of community organization history because of the political events that began that year and the many social changes related to these events. That year was the first one in which Richard Nixon held office as president of the United States. In his, as well as succeeding administrations, many of the programs initiated by Kennedy and Johnson were terminated, particularly those that were associated with the Office of Economic Opportunity and the Department of Health and Human Services (formerly the Department of Health, Education, and Welfare). Nixon's administration did, however, present some alternatives that were intended to link community and social planning more fully to the traditional political structures through such devices as revenue sharing and a community development block grant program.

This trend abated somewhat in the one-term administration of Carter but continued in an even more extensive manner as President Reagan sought to implement his philosophy of reducing the role of government, particularly the national government, in offering programs to solve social prob-

lems. This view was closely related to other ideas regarding how to cope with the economic crises brought on by severe unemployment and inflation, namely to reduce government spending while increasing purchasing power through reduction in taxation.

Social Conditions

John Naisbitt in his treatment of trends in society does an excellent job of highlighting the social conditions as well as ideological currents of this period and we draw heavily upon his work in the discussion that follows.[120] We have chosen to emphasize these kinds of trends at this point rather than specific events or programs because of the impact we believe they are having on social work practice at community and societal levels.

The Emergence of an Information Society. This development is associated with a shift in the occupational structure of the United States along with technologies that make this possible. By the 1980s, more than 60 percent of those employed work with information ". . . as programmers, teachers, clerks, secretaries, accountants, stock brokers, managers, insurance people, bureaucrats, lawyers, bankers, and technicians . . . Most Americans spend their time creating, processing, or distributing information."[121]

This trend has had major effects upon people who were already employed but lacked some of the skills now required, upon those seeking employment, and upon the skills people must obtain in order to be employable. This last point has obvious implications for an assess-

---

[119]For a summary and reference to the various publications of this project, see Gurin, op. cit.

[120]John Naisbitt, *Megatrends: Ten New Directions Transforming Our Lives* (New York: Warner Books, 1982).

[121]Ibid., p. 14.

ment of the adequacy of educational institutions as well as the educational preparation of the population.

Important technological developments associated with this shift to an information society are those of "high technology." In almost every sphere of life, technological developments have changed the ways we live. Some examples of this are the utilization of computers for virtually every information processing task; the creation of many devices for monitoring and improving our health; the use of video associated mechanisms for entertainment, education, and marketing; and the employment in the factory of countless new ways of mechanizing production. These changes, in addition to the ways they have altered our lives, have also produced counterforces, according to Naisbitt, in that people have also sought new ways to be together doing simple things with each other.[122]

Growth of a World Economy. The changes that have taken place in the economic status of the United States are that it no longer plays the dominant role in the world economy, its economic growth has stalled, and its domestic market is dominated by foreign products in many sectors. The role of Japan, for example, is well known as a producer of many of the technological products used in the United States. What may not be as well known is the growth of South Korea in steel, of Brazil and Spain in ship building, and of China in textiles. This is leading to vast shifts in investment patterns, interorganizational relationships on a global scale, and the effects that economic developments within the United States have on those in others.

Decentralization. Despite the seeming concentration of power implied by a world economy, the actual trend is toward decentralization. According to Naisbitt, "the decline of American industry and the rise of the new information economy neutralized the pressure to centralize and we began to decentralize."[123] Some of the examples he cites of this are the proliferation of cable TV stations and lower-powered broadcast TV stations; the increased role that state as opposed to national government is playing in our lives; a vast increase (that we shall discuss later) in neighborhood organizations; the interest in local magazines; and the shift of population to rural areas and small towns.

Ideological Currents

Perhaps the ideological development with the most impact on the current phase of community organizing is the belief in the value of self-help activities—although this might, in a classic social work sense, be thought of as *mutual aid.* In a limited way, this development has been seen by some as an outgrowth of President Reagan's emphasis on reducing people's reliance on government, but we join Naisbitt in seeing this as a culmination of a long historical process in which people reacted to their alienation from their government, their welfare institutions, and their occupations.

Some of the spheres in which we can see the development of self-help are in the ways people are seeking to improve their health through running, eating natural foods, monitoring their weight, and acting to prevent illness. They are also providing each other with mutual support in a manner that often imitates the highly successful program of Alcoholics Anonymous, such as Gamblers Anonymous,

---

[122]Ibid., pp. 39–53.

[123]Ibid., pp. 98–99.

Parents Anonymous, Tough Love, Compassionate Friends (for those whose children have died), and groups for those who have had cancer, a mastectomy, a colostomy, Acquired Immune Deficiency Syndrome (AIDS), or who lost a close friend or relative because of suicide. These are only a few of the hundreds of organizations that have arisen for mutual aid in the last few years and that continue to be created on almost a daily basis somewhere in this country.

As we mentioned earlier in this article the federal programs of the sixties required "maximum feasible participation" of their consumers. While this requirement has abated, in most societal spheres the move toward participation has grown. Naisbitt illustrates this in the creation and development of new political parties, the increase in splits among legislators of the same political party, the rise in the use of initiatives and referenda, and the tax "revolts." He also points to what he refers to as the "participatory corporation" which offers "workers, shareholders, consumers, and community leaders a larger say in determining how corporations will be run."[124] He sees this as occurring through consumerism, the appointment of more outside board members, shareholder activism, and worker participation.

Another trend noted by Naisbitt is toward "networking" in which people seek ways of locating others who can help them achieve desired ends. This has been facilitated by computer utilization in which computer files are maintained that can locate others of similar interests and needs. Examples cited by Naisbitt are the Denver Open Network, the National Women's Health Network in Washington, D.C., and the Newton, Massachusetts WARM LINES.[125]

---

[124]Ibid., p. 175.
[125]Ibid., p. 193.

Finally, we are becoming a society of even more diversity in all of life's spheres. A major example is that of the family in which the traditional notion of a household composed of two adults of different sexes who are married to each other (each for the first time) and who have children is the exception rather than the rule. Blended families, one-parent families, gay male and lesbian couples, and "living together" families are increasingly likely to be found in every community. The options available to women to work in every occupation and to play any and all family roles are accepted and, if not, are fought for. And people living each of these life styles, and many others that exist or are emerging, are developing networks, literature about their aspirations, and unique ways of coping.

Development of Community Organization Institutions

The major shift in community organization practice after 1969 was the withdrawal of federal funding from many community organizations and the termination of many community-oriented federal programs. This trend became most pronounced during the Reagan administration. The casual observer might conclude *incorrectly*, therefore, that there was a decrease in the quantity of community organizations. Nothing could be farther from the truth!

As Perlman states:

The contemporary grassroots movement is new, growing, diverse, and effective. Although its lineage can be traced back to the social movements of the 1960s, the early Alinsky organizations of the 1950s, and the union struggles of the 1930s and 1940s, in its present form it is not yet a decade old. Most of the groups we shall be describing started in the early 1970s, and many are five years old or less. They are growing in numbers and expanding in size so rapidly that any estimates of their size and numbers are outdated as quickly as they are calculated.[126]

Although, as Perlman states, the number of grassroots organizations is expanding, efforts have frequently been made to assess their quantity. She quotes a figure cited by the National Commission on Neighbor-hoods of 8,000 groups, and the Department of Housing and Urban Development (HUD) has begun a clearinghouse with 4,000 groups. In addition, the Alliance for Volunteerism estimated there were six million voluntary associations in the United States in 1975. Perlman adds that there are some 10,000 block clubs in New York City alone.[127]

Many local groups are affiliated with regional or national organizations. Among these are Association of Community Organizations for Reform Now (ACORN); National People's Action, and Massachusetts Fair Share. Some organizations also were created to provide support and technical assistance to grassroots groups such as the Center for Community Change, the National Center for Urban Ethnic Affairs, National People's Action, and the National Association of Neighborhoods.[128]

The important difference, however, between this and earlier periods is that these organizations cannot rely on federal financing but, instead, have generated many alternative forms of support. This often comes from state and local governments but also from voluntary donations, fund-raising efforts, and support from various constituencies such as labor organizations, churches, and businesses.

The focus of many of these organizations is on specific issues such as housing, the creation of cooperatives, obtaining adequate health care in the community, and a host of consumer related topics. They exist in all ethnic communities and among all socioeconomic groups.

Organization of Ethnic Minorities and Women

The growth of neighborhood organization that we have just described also characterizes some of the major developments within oppressed ethnic communities. A few examples demonstrate the geographical spread as well as breadth of purpose of this. Native American organizations include the Seminole Employment and Economic Development Corporation (Florida); the Menominee Restoration Committee (Wisconsin); and the Zuni Craftsman Cooperative Association and the All Indian Development Association (New Mexico). Hispanic ones include the Mexican American Unity Council (Texas); Chicanos Por La Causa (Arizona); and the Council for the Spanish Speaking (California). Asian-American examples are the East Bay Asian Local Development Corporation and the Asian Neighborhood Association (California).

Within the black community, as well as the others we have named, these organizations have been highly issue oriented. The issues in that community have included reducing poverty through neighborhood job creation and training, reversing the trend toward the dismantling of services for children, and reducing illiteracy. Many black organizations have also sought to identify ideologically with peoples of the third world.

An example of these developments is PUSH in Chicago and the activities of its

---

[126]Janice E. Perlman, "Grassroots Participation from Neighborhood to Nation," in Stuart Langton, *Citizen Participation in America*, (Lexington, MA: D.C. Heath, 1978), p. 65.

[127]Ibid., p. 67.

[128]More information on these organizations may be found in Robert A. Rosenbloom, "The Politics of the Neighborhood Movement," *South Atlantic Urban Studies*, Vol. 4 (1979), pp. 103–119.

leader Jesse Jackson. That organization has heavily focussed on creating economic opportunities through such campaigns as encouraging black people to spend their money within the black community. Many black churches in keeping with this approach have created credit unions within their communities.

Many developments are continuing to occur within the women's movement and women's organizations. As progress was made in securing women's rights in the workplace, in academic institutions, and in government, this has provided impetus to even stronger commitments of women and women's organizations to refuse to settle for anything less than full opportunity. A recognition that, despite this progress, the "feminization of poverty" continues to be an issue for the entire society has contributed to the specific agendas of women's organizations. The candidacy of Geraldine Ferraro for vice-president has reinforced the conviction that women can and should seek every role available within the political and economic structure of society, and is likely to have effects that have not yet been predicted.

Development of the Profession and Professional Education

We shall not explore this topic at any length here as it is expressed throughout all of the chapters in this book. We believe that an important shift took place during this period, however, that we should draw attention to in this historically oriented analysis. This was the shift to thinking of community organization activities as part of "macro" practice that also includes interventions at organizational and societal levels.

This shift is important because it recognizes that social change takes place through a set of activities that sometimes focuses on a single organization, sometimes on a community, and sometimes on a society as a whole. The skills the practitioner uses when engaged in these activities are sometimes unique to the level (i.e., organization, community, society) but more often are appropriate to several levels. Such skills include needs assessment, group leadership, budgeting, and class advocacy—to name a few. The current edition of this book attests to this evolution.

Students and others learning to practice at these macro levels are likely to be taught this range of skills while being afforded opportunities to practice roles that are defined as management within an organization, organizing within a community, or policy creation and/or implementation within regional and societal institutions.

The tools available to these practitioners have grown over this period and include utilization of computer and other technological resources for communication and data manipulation purposes as well as knowledge regarding organizational, community, and societal phenomena drawn from major advances in the social sciences, particularly sociology, social psychology, anthropology, political science, and economics. Whether this "new world" leads to more successful efforts at social change than those engaged in by previous generations of organizers remains to be seen.

A unity of thinking among all social workers regarding micro and macro practices of change is, at least, encouraged by the spread of systems-oriented and ecologically based thinking throughout the profession. Presumably all social workers are coming to see the necessity for systems changes and the participation of the consumer of social services in these changes. The negative side of the picture is some tendency for social work students and practitioners to be highly concerned about career advancement and to emphasize *therapy* rather than social change in their career goals.

SUMMARY AND CONCLUSIONS

Community organization practice has been examined in its social and ideological context during four periods of its history, separated by events with particular significance for that practice: the First World War and the end of the Progressive Era (1914); the stock market crash (1929) and the Supreme Court decision ending legal racial segregation in the public schools (1954).

It is impossible to understand community organization as an isolated phenomenon or merely as a technique of social engineering, for it is so closely related to what is most important in the lives of those it touches. Industrialization, urbanization, immigration, and minority emancipation created great opportunities and problems. The perspectives of Social Darwinism, socialism, pragmatism, and liberalism through which social conditions were perceived set the stage for many institutional developments important for community organization practice. Among these were charity organization societies designed to coordinate unplanned efforts to rescue the poor, and social settlements intended to help the urban poor get themselves together, unite rich and poor in a common enterprise, and reform the oppressive conditions of life that victimized the poor. Minorities organized, in some cases, to accommodate themselves to the system and, in others, to fight it.

Following World War I, the American people expressed a strong desire to return to "normalcy" and the principles of free enterprise, and they developed a sense of profound optimism toward capitalism. The newly emerging profession of social work withdrew from its prior efforts to change pernicious social conditions. In its place, the profession cultivated a preoccupation with the individual psyche. In this context, efficiency-oriented community chests were organized by busi-nessmen to spread the cost and reduce the annoyance of charitable solicitations. A growing cadre of welfare professionals promoted councils of agencies to rationalize their efforts, fill the gaps in services, and promote disinterested and effective services supported by dependable and expanding resources. The social unit plan, oriented toward grassroots participation, found little sympathy in the climate of the times.

The depression brought the federal government into welfare planning and strengthened grass-roots activities, particularly through the labor movement. World War II and the government's response to the demands of blacks and others for equality were the beginning of important developments in community organization. Small programs for training community organization practitioners to work with community chests and welfare councils were organized, and their teachers produced the beginnings of a professional literature.

Recent periods are characterized first by the civil rights movements and those of oppressed minorities and by student activism and discontent with the war in Vietnam, generating strong professional interest in grass-roots organizing and planning with local citizens, plus a pervasive sense of anger and alienation.

This was followed by major reverses in the government's commitment to community organizing. Shifts in social attitudes, particularly among young people, were not conducive to organizing. Nevertheless, particularly within ethnic groups and among women, these commitments were kept alive and are now intensifying through the growth of neighborhood organizations.

Where does all this lead? Several major questions dangle precariously overhead like the sword of Damocles: How will impatient underclasses, and particularly large ethnic minorities, respond to current social conditions? Will the necessary wisdom and determination be forthcoming to put our resources to work on the social problems that threaten to divide the nation? What are the most effective ways to accomplish our objectives consistent with our values? The first is a question that only those who are oppressed can answer, and the most persua-sive answers are likely to be deeds rather than words. The second is a question for the whole nation, especially the president and Congress, the governors, the state legisla-tures, the city councils, and the neighbor-hood groups themselves. The last is a particular responsibility of macro practi-tioners, including community organizers.

3.

Robert Fisher

POLITICAL ECONOMY AND PUBLIC LIFE:
THE CONTEXT FOR COMMUNITY ORGANIZING

As organizers and community workers we always need to consider the importance of context in shaping not only the success or failure of any effort but the very opportuni-ties that exist for organizing. At any given moment the larger context helps determine what seems salient or acceptable in terms of organizing goals, strategies, tactics, and so forth. Every organizer should have as good a grasp as possible of the challenges and opportunities in the larger political-economic context. This article seeks to aid that knowledge development.

THE POLITICAL-ECONOMIC CONTEXT: UNEASE AND INEQUALITY IN THE 1980s AND 1990s

We are living in a time of dramatic and unpredictable change, and nowhere is this more evident than the American economy. Despite pundits and economic advisers who tout the recent strength of the economy, the most positive indicators during the past two decades are characterized by dramatic fluc-tuation. The negative indicators reflect an economic crisis for many that has lasted a few decades. Take the 1980s first. True, the economy expanded from 1983 through 1990 and price inflation fell from the dou-ble-digit highs of the late 1970s. The approximately 30 million people who earned between $50,000 and $200,000 per year did well enough during the decade. And those at the top flourished, so much so that being a millionaire, the epitome of wealth 20 years before, was dubbed "mean-ingless" by one conservative commentator. By the end of the decade there were some 100,000 "decamillionaires," those with wealth above $10 million (Phillips, 1990, 4). These were the symbols of the decade's economic success. The goal of neoconserv-ative economic policy was to unleash the creativity and daring of American entrepre-neurs, whose success, wealth, and reinvest-ment would "trickle down" to all segments.

In fact, "the much vaunted economic recovery of the 1980s did little or nothing to pull the country out of the economic crisis that began in the late 1960s and deepened during the 1970s and early 1980s" (Bowles, Gordon, Weisskopf, 1990, 4–5). Throughout the decade the average weekly wage fell, so that by 1990 it was back to $258, which wiped out about half the gains U.S. workers had made since World War II. The percentage of employees working full-time and earning a low wage—defined as less than $12,195—increased from 12 percent in 1979 to 18 percent in 1990. Low-wage work even increased among college graduates, from 6.2 percent to 10.5 percent (Kuttner, 1992, 1). More banks failed between 1989 and 1991 than in all the years from the end of the Depression until 1980 (Mead, 1991) This was notwithstanding the savings and loan scandals and bailout, which cost the American people some $500 billion. Key economic indicators such as output, productivity growth, investment, and profit rates, in addition to real wage growth, all were well below levels of the 1950s and 1960s. Home ownership declined precipitously. Overwhelming trade deficits turned us from the largest creditor to the greatest debtor nation.

Under Reagan's presidency, which may now seem to some as ancient history but whose "supply-side economics" is essential to understanding the contemporary context, the top personal tax bracket dropped to 28 percent from 70 percent in only seven years. The 1986 tax reform law, sponsored by both Republicans and Democrats, reduced the tax on the top income bracket from 38.5 percent to 28 percent, while those in the next lower income bracket paid a higher rate of 33 percent. Corporate and capital gains taxes followed suit. At the very moment when funds were increasingly needed to finance a nation in increasingly dire economic straits, the policy was to *spend more* and *collect less* from those who could afford it most. Numerous studies, by authors on both the right and left, document the extraordinary redistribution of income upward in the United States during the 1980s (see Phillips, 1990; Center on Budget and Policy Priorities, 1990). The top 1 percent of income after taxes in 1990 almost equalled that of the bottom 40 percent; in 1980 the top 1 percent had only one-half the total income of the bottom 40 percent. Of the total income gain from 1977 to 1989, 70 percent went to the richest one percent of Americans (Kuttner, 1992). The incidence of poverty, declining in the late 1960s and early 1970s, jumped upward again to 1964 levels, hitting women, children, and people of color the hardest (*Houston Chronicle*, 1992; Sidel, 1986; Reed, 1999).

The figures are staggering. In terms of children alone, 20 percent of all children in the United States are poor and 40 percent of the poor are children. Moreover, about 40 percent of poor families have incomes equivalent to half the poverty line or less. It is impossible, for example, to raise two teenage kids in a major U.S. city on less than $5,000 a year. The United States has the terrible distinction of being the only major industrial nation where children are the largest impoverished group. And disproportionately these are black and Latino children. In most of our major cities 50 percent of the children of color are growing up in poverty, often in households way below the poverty line. In Texas, where one in four children live in poverty, 42 percent of black children, 43 percent of Hispanic children, and 9.7 percent Anglo children are poor (Rosenberg, 1989; Mickelson, 1992; Sidel, 1986).

Worst hit in the 1980s were cities, from which most elites and the middle class fled. As the federal government removed support and as city tax bases eroded, affordable housing became increasingly scarcer and jobs, especially manufacturing jobs, left town. Inner-city poverty rose from 30 percent of all poor people in 1968 to 43 percent in 1988. Federal spending on cities fell more than 60 percent from 1981 to 1992; the federal share of city budgets plummeted from 18 percent in 1980 to 6.4 percent in 1990 (*New York Times*,1992; Tilly, 1990). Crime rates, drug use, racial and ethnic conflict, gang violence, infant mortality, teen pregnancy, homelessness, inadequate health care, and AIDS, to name but the most publicized problems, all increased in staggering and alarming proportions. Urban infrastructures collapsed after years of neglect.

The much-vaunted economic recovery of the mid-to-late 1990s has helped address some of the economic crises of the prior two decades. The American economy has been characterized by sustained growth, low inflation, increases in certain forms of investment, and real spending on producer durables. These economic advances are grounded in the rapid and dramatic technological innovation that characterizes the age, as well as draconian neoconservative business strategies that boost parts of the economy while ignoring others. For example, the corporate pursuit of cutting costs—"efficiency" through downsizing, hiring more contract workers, employing more part-time employees who receive fewer benefits, and so forth—has led, when coupled with technological innovations, to recent increases in worker productivity and declines in unemployment levels. But these increases in productivity coexist with declines in individual purchasing power and job security for most people. Wages and salaries for most Americans are either unaffected or hurt by economic developments in the 1990s. "Resources are allo-

cated in a more marketlike manner, but overall performance is nonetheless mediocre and living standards are mostly stagnant (Kuttner, 1996, 24). Actually, in terms of economic inequality and conditions of the poor and most people of color in the United States, conditions in the 1990s look largely like those of the 1980s. The widening of income inequality that began in the early 1970s, accelerated dramatically in the 1980s, and continued apace in the early 1990s seems to have slowed in the past few years. Nevertheless, the rich continue to get richer as the poor stagnate. Between 1983 and 1995 the net worth of the top 1 percent swelled by 17 percent, the bottom 40 percent lost an astounding 80 percent, and the middle fifth lost more than 11 percent. An economic boom "has been built on the sweat of the 30 percent of American workers who earn poverty or near poverty wages" (Schor, 1999, 4) . While there is some good news recently— statistics related to infant mortality, elder poverty, high school dropouts, and births to teenage mothers are improving (Miringoff and Miringoff, 1999)—the number of people, especially children, living in poverty, average weekly earnings, and median family income are no better now than they were in 1990, and the 1990 figures reflect a decade and a half of worsening conditions. As if such conditions did not pose sufficient challenges for organizing, the vulgar free market response to vast global changes further perpetuates social problems and undermines meeting social need.

COMMUNITY ORGANIZATION IN A PRIVATE WORLD

The growing inequalities and unease that characterize American life reflect broader developments globally: The world is experiencing an epochal transformation equal to that of the industrial revolution of the nineteenth century. No one knows exactly what the transformation is or where it will lead; most analyses are more aptly descriptions of what is happening, whether labeled globalization, the information/communications revolution, postindustrialism, postmodernism, and so forth (Bauman, 1998). The dramatic contextual changes demand, however, that we understand as best possible the shape and opportunities of the contemporary world. To this end, I offer the following analysis of how the world is becoming more private, how the economic hardships and unease described in the first part of this chapter result from it, and what challenges and opportunities the contemporary world holds for community workers (Fisher and Karger, 1997).

In a nutshell, we increasingly live in a private as opposed to a public world. A public world, Ryan (I 992) offers, encourages "open, inclusive, and effective deliberation about matters of common and critical concern" (p. 259). Habermas (1989) further suggests that the public represents what is open to all, as opposed to exclusive or closed affairs. Or the public is tied to the state, as with a public building, which is not necessarily completely open to all but does house the government and is fundamentally about "promoting the public or common welfare of its rightful members" (p. 2). The public is about the creation and maintenance of society, existence in a social world larger than one's self or one's family. Public life is life at work, at school, in communities, and as citizens of the nation and the world. The public realm is the world of contact with acquaintances and strangers, including a broad diversity of people. It is the *social* in social work.

In a multitude of ways, the world in which community workers live and work is increasingly moving away from the public, away from the social, toward a preoccupation with the private. This is the new and challenging context for contemporary community organization: How to practice *social* work in a world increasingly antagonistic to the public. How to create empowered public citizens in a context that increasingly values independent and autonomous private consumers, workers, and family members.

The privatization of life has one central feature: It reflects a society highly focused on and dominated by *a culture of private individuals, a physical world of private spaces*, and *a society characterized increasingly by private instead of public institutions*. These developments are certainly not new. The recent privatization of life, however, is occurring with a massive speed and grander reach than ever before. In the past generation an extraordinary social, political, and economic transformation dramatically accelerated and expanded the privatization process, profoundly reshaping the context in which community workers live and practice.

THE CULTURE OF PRIVATE INDIVIDUALS

Sociologist David Riesman wrote in *The Lonely Crowd* (1950) of the penchant of Americans to act not on goals or ideas of their own but on the commitments and passions of others. He wrote of a society becoming increasingly "other directed" rather than "inner directed." More recently, social commentators (Sennett, 1974; Sennett, 1990; Lasch, 1978; Bellah et al., 1985; Bookchin, 1987; Specht & Courtney, 1994) argue the opposite. Americans, and much of the rest of the world as well, are becoming increasingly self-absorbed with the private and the personal. They are moving increasingly away from concern with the larger society, away from commitment to a public life. Bellah and his associates (1985) see this vividly in the contemporary penchant for psychotherapy—the sharing of a "first language of individualism" and the goals of self-actualization—by large numbers of the citizenry across the political spectrum. Reality is explained through a lens of individual will, personal life, and personal morality. "Be all you can be" promises a recruiting poster of the United States Army, an organization that seeks to subvert the individual will of soldiers to the Army's collective goals.

Sennett (1974) and Lasch (1978) see this penchant for the personal as a retreat into narcissism. Ironically, they argue, the obsession with personal needs and wants blocks their fulfillment as people become more and more distanced from, and less and less grounded in, society. Elshtain (1994) proposes that contemporary versions of individualized rights erode civil society, freeing citizens from all and any ties of mutual interdependence and reciprocal obligation. Political philosopher Hannah Arendt (quoted in Sennett, 1990) argued that the retreat into the personal, what she called "the fear of making contact," reflects "a lack of the will to live in the world" (p. 135). As society seems to become more difficult, divided, and dangerous, the increasing fear of the social world causes people to turn inward to a preoccupation with themselves and their families. But the prominence and dominance of individualist strategies and visions throughout society continually narrow, attention to the personal and private. Martin and O'Connor (1989) propose that the focus on individual rights, freedom, and opportunity discourages Americans from "seeing the impact of the social con-

text on their lives." The fear of difference coupled with the concern for the personal—both exaggerated in the 1980s and 1990s—turn the private domains of self and family, of private intimate matters, into the *proper* arenas and concerns of life.

If the private domain becomes *the* natural and good arena, what does that say for public life? How does one practice community work in a world focused on private matters? If public life is the "open, inclusive, and effective deliberation about matters of common and critical concern" (Ryan, 1992, p. 259), what come to pass for matters of concern in a private world are personal intimate ones. Public life becomes all about private life—the more immoral the better. One only has to watch*Oprah*or *Geraldo*, or any of the other comparable television programs that engage millions daily in the most intimate matters of personal life that pass for, or at least take the place of, public deliberation about common and critical concerns. Or look at what takes the place of public deliberation about public matters of elected officials in the nation's capital! A general sense of the public gets lost in the discourse on private life.

For those interested in community organizing, the culture of individualism clearly makes social change and all collective efforts more difficult. Bellah et al. (1985) propose that the middle class can talk only in terms of individualistic achievement and self-fulfillment. Because Americans increasingly lack a language for the collective and community, people find it difficult to maintain commitment to others, either in a public sphere or in intimate relationships (Bellah et al., 1991). Even when people tend to form a community, they often do so around discussion of personal needs (12-step groups) and personal salvation (churches). To the extent that discourse and language remain focused on individuals, so do discussions of problems and solutions. Witness contemporary debates about the nature of problems such as poverty, homelessness, AIDS, and so forth. When government is not being blamed, the victims are held responsible for their alleged individual shortcomings. They are lazy, unintelligent, mentally unstable, promiscuous, or simply tied to a deviant culture (underclass, homosexual, homeless, etc.). The discourse of individualizing problems dominates most contemporary debates about social problems. This discourse is functional for the agenda of global privatization, since if problems are individual in nature, then so must be the cures. Government programs, collective social policy, and social expenditures are dubbed the source of problems, certainly not the solution. In short, no social problems would exist if everyone who had a problem solved it individually.

Social work practice and education mirror this development, posing a barrier within as well as outside the profession. As Specht and Courtney (1994) argue, building on the work of Bellah, Lasch, and others, the emphasis on the psychoanalytic and therapeutic in social work practice and education distances it from the immediate social world. Individualistic processes of counseling and therapy, individualized diagnoses of pathologies, and individual-based strategies for solving problems all perpetuate the individualistic trend and distance clients from community work and the collective social world. As a result, students often come to schools of social work with primary training in psychology. Many want to be private practitioners, distanced from the poor and the public bureaucratic work of a welfare office or child-protective services. They want to work with clients like themselves: middle-class clients who have insurance and can pay for private services.

Public work looks more risky and less attractive. Students steer clear of courses or programs in community organization or macro practice, because at the least they seem to offer less professional opportunity. But to the extent that social work professionals also shun the public and retreat into the private, then the very *social* in social work—the macro part of social work—is further devalued, delegitimized, and ridiculed. Community organization declines in importance and salience in its own professional home.

Americans live and work in a world of individuals who, in their quest for self-fulfillment and their fear of society, turn inward and away from the social, and *ipso facto*, participate in the dissipation of a sense of public life and a public good. This is partly because in the privatizing context the public spaces requisite for public life are disappearing.

A PHYSICAL WORLD OF PRIVATE SPACES

The turning away from public life is equally visible in the places people inhabit and their relationships to each other. Spatial arrangements matter, although people tend not to think about such things—even in a field such as community organization, which should be more attentive to issues of geography and urban planning. For example, cities are spatially structured. The nature and patterns of physical facilities such as housing, highways, and shopping and work areas or the very form of a city, its neighborhoods and suburbs, impinge directly on social life and community work. "It is of course a truism that spatial relations are necessarily social," geographer Kevin Cox (1988, p. 71) argues. Spatial arrangements both reflect and produce social problems and determine the feasibility of social strategies to address them.

In the new privatized context, public space declines as private space takes over. This is especially serious for the poor and working-class citizens excluded from the new private spaces and for community workers interested in rebuilding a sense of the public and a progressive vision of the public good. Boyte (1992) describes public spaces as "environments that are open, accessible and involve a mix of different people and groups" (p. 6). They also are spaces, such as city streets or public parks and beaches, that are "owned" by the people. They have a primarily public function, for people to gather, walk, jog, play, and talk *in public*. Private spaces, conversely, are intentionally designed as limited access, closed places that are restricted to homogenous groups. This can include the house or apartment where one lives, or such increasingly proliferating private spaces as gated communities or shopping malls. In all private spaces, there is a desire to provide a controlled space of order and clarity, one removed from an unpredictable and complex public space. "On the most physical level," Sennett (1974) writes, the private "environment prompts people to think of the public domain as meaningless" (p. 12). Private spaces are also designed to make money, as with malls or suburban developments, or to provide a closed, exclusive space for the reproduction of class relations, such as a restricted country club.

The decline of public space, or at least the ongoing tension in a capitalist society between public and private space, is not new. The United States, like most capitalist nations in the modem era, appropriates space primarily as a private commodity. Parks, space for public buildings such as libraries and schools, and open "commons" for citizens are expensive *and* produce no income. They sell nothing; they must be supported by public taxation, by the people for the public good. City streets and sidewalks, historically, were the most basic unit of public space. Walking is a most public of acts. With the invention of the automobile, one of the most private means of transportation, the city street has been transformed from a public milieu to an "artery" for motion. Walking in public becomes an anachronism. As the automobile has come to dominate American life, so has the detachment people feel to the milieus they travel through. "One ceases to believe one's surroundings have any meaning save as a means toward the end of one's own motion" (Bennett, 1974, p. 15).

To the extent that the environment has meaning, beyond being a thoroughfare, it usually beckons fear, danger, or distaste. Office workers in the downtown areas of Houston, Dallas, and Montreal, for example, walk from one corporate structure to another in the privacy and protection of an underground tunnel system connecting the "fortified cells of affluence" in which they work (Davis, 1992, p. 155). The tunnels are the new public spaces, where people interact, shop, and eat on their lunch hours. Owned by private firms, they are closed to city problems and citizens of the street. They are not public spaces. New private spaces keep "street people" and diversity out; controlled private spaces sacrifice diversity and real public interaction. Sidewalks, parks, even libraries are left to minorities, the poor, and students.

Judd (1994) argues that "the enclosure of commercial and residential space is becoming a defining and ubiquitous feature of American cities" (p. 2). Blakely and Snyder (I 997) call it "Fortress America." Increasingly, enclosed private spaces replace older open public space throughout our cities. Shopping malls, walled and gated communities, skyscrapers that turn away from the city streets, these are the spaces in which people increasingly work, live, and even play. They offer safe havens and guarded spaces in an unfriendly world. Security is important to the new private spaces. Witness the proliferation of private police patrols in neighborhoods that can afford them, electronic security systems for houses and cars, and gated communities with police attendants. But fear proves itself omnipresent. Surveys show that suburbanites in Milwaukee are as frightened of violent crime as those living in the inner-city of Washington, where the level of crime is 20 times greater (Davis, 1992).

People who once lived in relatively densely settled cities have left them for more private suburbs. They live and work in areas characterized by freeways, shopping malls, detached single-family housing, and postindustrial business areas devoted primarily to finance, banking, and information processing. They enter the city only occasionally, pay few or no taxes to it, and are free of its political control. What used to be a nation of city dwellers is now a nation of suburbanites. The cities, the areas most heavily affected by social problems and in need of social change, are avoided and ignored. "Are cities dead?" became the Nietzchean-like question of the early 1990s. This "disaggregation" of space spreads life outward with a centrifugal force that removes concern with the urban center and with those who remain there.

Mike Davis (I 992) captures the condition brilliantly in his book on Los Angeles:

In Los Angeles, once-upon-a-time a demi-paradise of free beaches, luxurious parks, and "cruising strips,"genuinely democratic space is all but extinct. The Oz-like archipelago of Westside pleasure domes—a continuum of tony malls, arts centers and gourmet strips—is reciprocally dependent upon the social imprisonment of the third-world service proletariat who live in increasingly repressive ghettoes and barrios. In a city of several million yearning immigrants, public amenities are radically shrinking, parks are becoming derelict and beaches more segregated, libraries and playgrounds are closing, youth congregations of ordinary kinds are banned, and the streets are becoming more desolate and dangerous. (p. 227)

Increasingly, Sorkin (1992) writes, people live in a geographical spaces—cities and towns and neighborhoods that all look and seem the same. They live with increasingly loosened ties to any specific space. These "analogous" spaces are similar to television in their structure. Television homogenizes difference, provides a conceptual grid of boundless reach in which all combinations make sense. It makes a coherent view of the social order difficult to picture, just as it blends all of this difference together. Skyscrapers, houses, factories, strip centers, and malls seem almost to float in a nonplace urban realm. A universal sameness of place occurs. Plasticized strip centers, the ubiquitous fast-food eating places, and franchise capitalism provide an interchangeable, departicularized reality all over America (Sorkin, 1992, p. xiii).

The more time people spend watching television in the "privacy" of their living rooms, driving in private cars, talking into cellular phones, communicating through electronic mail, and living in "detached" housing and independent living spaces, the more they fall prey to the domination of private space. Contrary to the belief that new communication inventions such as electronic mail and the Internet foster a public communication hitherto unknown, they are essentially a highly private act that occurs in the privacy of a home or office. Users of these systems choose with whom they "interact." Ultimately, it is a highly private form of potentially public communication. There are good reasons why many prefer the new private spaces and lifestyles.

But there are costs as well, not only for those left out and kept out of the skyscrapers, atrium hotels, malls, affluent suburbs, and computer networks, but also for the millions who feel cut adrift from a sense of community and bereft of connection to a social world whose very nature transcends, and thereby adds to, individual life.

Current "recentralization" efforts, designed to bring citizens back into downtowns areas, plan for "safe city centers" devoid of urban diversity and problems. We get public spaces for only that part of the public with dollars to spend. As people remove themselves from public life, as they are distanced from the real public, they lose what is vital—the social mix and the surprises of democratic space—the very things that give city life its human connection. Public urban life requires physical proximity and democratic public realms. Public space affords the unique opportunity to grapple with difference. With less of it, people find a highly limited discourse in the new privatized spaces, limited in both its range of vision and the variety of its participants.

For those interested in community organizing, the divided city—separated by class, race, ethnicity, and neighborhoods—has always posed extraordinary challenges to its inhabitants and to those social activists who wanted to change it. As space becomes more privatized, the gulf deepens and *social* life declines. Privatized and scattered spaces make building social and public solidarities more difficult. Community life has always been important as an assumed base of is support for social work clients. Economic restructuring, more aptly labeled "destructuring," shatters community life as it does the decline of social supports. Working with people who have little connection to the larger society makes community work more difficult. For social

workers interested in community organizing, trying to organize in the private spaces of suburbia or shopping malls is not the same as organizing in working-class neighborhoods or on the city streets of the past (Suarez, 1999).

Moreover, as space disaggregates and people are separated by larger distances, the simple act of trying to physically bring people together to build a sense of public life is made much harder. To the extent that citizens and space are reduced to their market function (citizens as economic men and women, city space as shopping centers), the struggle to redefine citizenship in terms of social responsibility becomes more difficult. The decline of attachment to specific space (e.g., a neighborhood) and the geographic hypermobility of the population further contribute to a decrease in the sense of social ownership and public responsibility. Even the most basic ecological theories popular in social work observe that clients need a connection to their environment. Helping clients, not to mention building solidarity with them and promoting social change, has always been difficult work. As the environment becomes more dominated by others for private purposes and less known by both community workers and neighborhood people, organizing becomes even more challenging than before.

A POLITICAL ECONOMY OF PRIVATE INSTITUTIONS

One of the most significant international developments in the past two decades has been the rise of the "privatization" strategy. As a result of pressures from profound economic and social changes that began in the early 1970s, the very idea of public social programs, not to mention the socialist or welfare state, was delegitimized. In the

Reagan-Bush era especially, but continuing in the United States during the Clinton years, "big government" became *the* problem. Neoconservatives and neoliberals sought to dismantle the welfare state as much as possible (Piven & Cloward, 1982). The free market, as both economic theory and policy, became the unchallenged ruler and guide of the world.

The argument is that in the new global economy, nations cannot afford costly social programs. The intent of "privatization" is to dismantle the state as much as possible to reduce "social costs" on the corporate sector and the affluent, those who are, in theory, responsible for stimulating the economy. If nations do not adopt such policies, if capitalism is not "unbridled," then investments will supposedly go elsewhere. These are clear strictures from the World Bank, the IMF (International Monetary Fund), and global corporate investors. Not only in the United States and Europe, but in Asia, Africa, and South America, the context of privatization forces almost all social and political agendas away from social welfare conceptualizations toward laissez-faire capitalist ones.

This strategy for "survival in the global economy" has swept across the globe, dominating not only national policy but local, urban options as well. Adopted early on by "sunbelt" cities such as Houston, Texas, this trend has emerged in most American cities, formerly social democratic cities in Western Europe, formerly communist cities in Eastern Europe, and third-world cities. Accordingly, neoconservative and neoliberal agendas seek to return cities to a "golden age of free enterprise." Social problems are ignored as much as possible as new business agendas of unfettered capitalism come to dominate global, national, and local decision making. Cities as disparate as New York, Cleveland, London,

and Vienna reprivatize by cutting public programs, turning public programs over to for-profit private interests, and by ignoring festering social needs (Fisher & Kling, 1993). The problem of worsening poverty in the United States, for example, is deemed unsolvable; it is labeled the product of an "underclass" subculture and blamed on the victims of poverty and government programs.

Privatization refers not only to transferring governmental operations and roles over to business, but also to the reorientation of political, social, economic, and cultural institutions to corporate needs, values, goals, and leaders. Barnekov et al. (1989) propose that privatization "reflects a general policy orientation rather than a finite set of policy alternatives" (p. 4). This policy direction contains four key elements. First, priority is placed on economic considerations in almost all aspects of domestic activity. Second, private markets are preferred over public policies wherever possible in terms of allocative social choices. Third, if public intervention is deemed necessary it must supplement private market processes and include maximum private-sector participation. Fourth, public programs are expected to be modeled on the methods of private sector businesses.

Under such a framework, government becomes the problem and champions of social programs become the enemies. Why are the poor impoverished? Because government programs create dependency (Murray, 1984). Why is the American economy in its third decade of economic crisis? Because government taxation increases the national debt by destroying entrepreneurial incentive and risk-taking (Gilder, 198 1). Why are key American corporations not more competitive in the global economy? Because government regulations foist unrealistic and costly programs on the backs of business (Friedman, 1962; Gilder, 1981). Public schools, the U.S. Post Office, and most public social services, especially those directed at providing income support for the poor, all are said to be not only ineffective but wrongheaded. The public sector and advocates of allocative programs are seen as doing more harm than good. In fact for many—not simply libertarians but most free marketers—the public sector has no legitimate functions other than policing.

Of course, public institutions need to be challenged. Government defense expenditures in the 1980s did dramatically increase the federal debt. Bureaucracies can be autocratic and inefficient, whether public or private. Governments are coercive. But the argument for privatization conveniently forgets the different missions and roles of the public and private sectors. The mission of the public sector is to serve the public good, the general welfare. This is why elected officials were sometimes called "public servants." The public sector is the primary sector of a polity that has some resources to effect significant social change, and at least in theory, has the mission to do so. The private sector has a very different mission. It is designed to make profits, not address social problems. Unlike the public sector, it is not accountable to the citizenry and is responsible only to investors and stockholders. How can corporations be expected to address social problems in a highly competitive economy in which they are under severe economic pressure to restructure and downsize their operations? Social policy and programs are not the business of the private sector.

The argument for dismantling the public sector and turning problems over to the private and voluntary sector is a ruse. This strategy is fundamentally a political rationale for load-shedding government social responsibility, decreasing taxes on the wealthy and powerful, selling off valuable state-owned industries or land, and deregulating trade and investment. Ultimately, such policies have a corrosive effect on public life and the very fabric of society. Problems in the privatized context mount and simply go unattended and unaddressed. For those with fewer resources, opportunities to address the problems decline. Instead, they see a diminution of jobs that pay living wages to the unskilled; a shortage of adequate and sufficient housing for the working class, working-class poor, and homeless; less available and adequate public services in the areas of health, education, and welfare; and a declining sense of safety and security in the streets (Fisher & Kling, 1993).

In the new fee-for-service political economy, those who have the money to pay for quality services from private sources—whether it is private schools, private security systems, or private health care—are among the fortunate. People who must rely on the public are told that the public sector is being "restructured," and no longer has the resources to address such problems. Moreover, it no longer has the legitimacy. Such activity by public institutions is now deemed inappropriate. Recipients of public services, including the middle class, get less and less for more and more tax money. Look at public schools. Look at continuing cuts in social welfare programs. But this is not the primary or even secondary concern of the corporate designers of the privatization strategy. Profits and elite jobs come first. In the short-run this is good business policy—That is cutting costs and regulations in order to maximize profits. In the long run, and more importantly, as social or public policy, it is absurd. What is startling is how effective the arguments for the privatization of institutions have been; they have become global common sense despite their obviously destructive aspects.

For those interested in community organizing, the decline and delegitimization of the public sector—the undermining of people's sense of the proper and important role of government and other public institutions in American life—pushes discourse on problems and solutions into an asocial focus on the individual and the family. Moreover, the decline and delegitimization of government forces community workers to rely on private funders for resources and promotes private solutions to serious public problems. In part, this reliance is based on the direct relationship in the United States between public sector social programs and private sector financial support for social welfare efforts (Wolch, 1990; Salamon, 1989). In those areas with more social democratic cultures, such as New York City, charity giving is also higher. In the United States, the liberal culture of public social responsibility tends to encourage more, not less, civic activism and support. Former President George Bush's concept of "a Thousand Points of Light" rests on the belief that the private sector will pick up the social responsibilities of a declining public sector. Bush's assumption was that private charities, such as United Way and voluntary food banks, will simply replace public programs. They will not. In periods of economic contraction (when assistance is needed the most), charity giving is among the first things to decline. This occurred in the Great Depression and in the recession of the 1980s (Karger & Stoesz, 1994).

Equally challenging for community workers is the belief that private programs will solve social problems. It is clear that the private sector does not have the funds at its disposal, given its responsibility to its stockholders rather than the homeless or the unemployed, to effectively address social problems in more than a token way. The penchant for private charity produced, Schram (I 993) argues, a mentality of "welfare by the bag." Massive collective problems such as homelessness and hunger are expected to be addressed by private individuals giving a can of tuna fish or beans, producing a bag of goods to tide over the alms recipient. Moreover, the very idea that government is the problem and the marketplace is the solution to social problems poses perhaps the greatest barrier to the mission of community organizing and social change. This policy is not only harmful in its failure to address social problems, it undermines democracy. Proponents of privatization argue that getting government off people's backs enhances democracy. The dismantling of the public sector in the United States, however, simply makes it more difficult for people to hold politicians and leaders accountable. Where can citizens go in a privatized context to make claims and demands or to engage in democratic debate? Suffice it to say that the barriers posed to democracy by the privatization of social life and institutions have harmful consequences ultimately to democratic citizenship throughout the world.

Globalization also creates worldwide pressures for the adoption of strategies of consensus and moderation and the rejection of conflict options. The argument is that for localities to be competitive in the global economy, social costs, such as protests or strikes, must be minimized. To polish its image and affect public life, business seeks to create partnerships, especially in the area of charitable giving. For social workers and agencies experiencing a decline in public funding, forming partnerships with those who have at least some resources becomes critical. Strategies of moderation and consensus ensue. No "rubbing raw people's resentments," as Saul Alinsky once proposed. The goal is to work together for the good of the whole. Working together now means focusing on community economic development instead of social action, for example, and working with banks and absentee landlords instead of targeting them. Moreover, the consensus line must be toed even by those who understand that the good of the whole is not what brings most businesses into partnership with social service agencies. Conflict and protest are relegated to being inappropriate icons of 1960s radicalism. By limiting of community organizers and their constituents, funders profoundly influence their ability to effect social change. New "partners" may be willing to support "worthy" mainstream organizations, such as the Red Cross or the American Cancer Society, but be disinterested in the strategy options "unworthy" welfare mothers or a Latino gay advocacy community center.

To the extent that the public debate on issues remains on the right that is, discussions on whether to revive orphanages, cut taxes for the rich, teach creationism instead of evolution, and dismantle welfare programs—then it is difficult to raise more progressive issues of interest to community organizers and the people with whom they work. Having the political discourse stuck on the political right undermines the mission of community work and the goals of social change. Meanwhile, problems worsen and programs falter, which only contributes further to public suspicion of governmental efforts.

GLOBALIZATION: ECONOMIC DISTANCING FROM THE SOCIAL

What is the stem root of the new privatized context? In a nutshell, it is economic globalization, the hegemonic response to it of neoconservative policy, and the weak state

of resistance to both. While it is still unclear how the global transformation that is underway will evolve, the first phase has pointed to a shift from an industrial to a postindustrial or information economy, a dramatic centralization of power worldwide among global corporations, an accelerating impoverishment of those people and regions of the world that do not fit into the upper echelons of the global economic restructuring, and a marked opposition to both the public sector and social matters.

The more obvious effects of the global political economy began in 1973 on the heels of the OPEC oil embargo and the impending defeat of the United States in Vietnam. Prior to that, the global order was relatively stable, dominated politically and economically by the United States. The period after World War II was to be, Henry Luce said, the beginning of the "American century." The booming and dominating American economy of the postwar era was able to triple the median family between 1950 and 1970 (Barnet, 1994). However, the economic growth of the unchallenged American empire lasted less than a generation.

Around 1973 a number of factors coalesced to trigger the new global political economy. For one, the OPEC embargo stalled the American economy. Secondly, the end of the Vietnam War vividly underscored the long-term drain of military expenditures on productive investment. As a consequence, the United States went off the fixed exchange rate of the goal standard. All of these factors occurred in a context of rising global economic competition and precipitated a crisis in capitalism of global proportions. Economic growth rates, corporate profits, and manufacturing fell off dramatically in almost every Western industrialized nation. To address the decline in profits that lay ahead for U.S. corporations, business leaders argued that a new political economy of unbridled capitalism needed to be introduced, one that minimized government regulation and high social expenditures, and negated the compromises made with labor unions since the 1930s. The era ahead was clearly going to be difficult for American business. If sacrifices were to be made, the members of the elite Business Roundtable proposed, they should not be made by those at the top of society. Profits or corporate salaries, the highest in the world, should not be cut. They proposed instead that the social welfare obligations of society needed to be curtailed to allow American businesses to compete more effectively worldwide (Fisher, 1994). This strategy, also known as economic restructuring or globalization, would soon become the ground rules for all nations and localities (Kuttner, 1996; Brecher, Childs, Cutler, 1993; Brecher & Costello, 1994).

Globalization is not only a political response to economic changes; it also represents a dramatic shift in technology and information processing. As such, it embodies a new postindustrial context and a shift from an economy of industrial goods production to one of service production. Moreover, globalization entails the transformation of social life through computer and telecommunication innovations. Technological breakthroughs in transportation and communication alter the nature of work and the skills needed for employment in the high-technology service economy. Because of these changes, the velocity of capital has increased exponentially in the new global economy, moving from investment sites through electronic mail, seemingly in the blink of an eye. In response, cities had to restructure, as downtowns withered and factory towns collapsed due to deindustrialization (Logan & Swanstrom, 1990).

Businesses also restructured, through "downsizing" or some other soft-sounding term. The results of this corporate strategy were the undermining of labor unions, the large-scale layoff of workers, and various other means of cost-cutting necessary to maximize profits in the new world economic order. The central issue for society became economic survival. A nation or city would be measured not by the quality of life it provided for its citizens or its commitment to promoting the social good, but by how it could cut costs to make it more attractive as an economic investment site for business.

"Privatization around family, status, and consumption produces its own distinctive politics: one which is antithetical to the solidarities of class and long-term commitments, and more amenable to the opportunism and search for the immediate "fix" which capitalist interests have always found so congenial and easy to exploit" (Cox, 1988, p. 62). This philosophy fits with the 15-year lifespan of what used to be called buildings but now are "stores" on strips and at strip mall centers. This also fits with attitudes toward social problems and those in need. Whatever is quick, simple, easy, and least costly is what will be done. With this "enterprise" strategy foisted on the world, the inequality and centralization of capital throughout the globe continues to increase dramatically.

The velocity of capital traveling through computerized systems transcends physical space, loosening capital investment from obligations and ties to communities and locales. Sandel (1988) argues that privatization ignores the "corrosive" affects of capitalism. Unrestrained capital mobility not only ignores the social, it disrupts community. Power rests in corporations unaccountable to society (Lasch, 1991). Not only has capital become distanced from the social, it has become almost unchained by government, even at the national level. The increased mobility of capital and the new types of international investment transcend the nation-state, eroding its power to control economic, let alone social, matters (Brecher, Childs, & Cutler, 1993). Stateless corporations, some of them with economies that rival the GNP of significant nation-states, force nations to compete with each other for their business. Like the private a geographical spaces discussed earlier, these are corporations without ties to place. Of course, corporations are not as mobile as capital since physical moves remain expensive. Place matters somewhat to corporate investors. Nevertheless, as Martin Davis, former chairperson of Paramount Communications, put it: "You can't be emotionally bound to any particular asset" (Barnet, 1994, p. 754).

What this ultimately means is a nearly complete distancing from the *social* at the very moment that these global entities are responsible for so much social change and damage worldwide. Globalization demands the adoption of economic objectives over social ones and focuses on corporate over public needs. It ignores festering social and urban problems, which now, like almost everything else, are left to the so-called marketplace. It represents the turning back of oppositional movements and claims of the 1960s, deemed as too costly and as impediments to the shift in priorities of global capitalism. The new political economy that developed after 1973 was partially a catching-up to the economic and technological trends that had been in play since the 1950s, but which had not been felt because the Cold War had proved so profitable. Politically it represents not only an effort to promote a corporate and right-wing agenda, but relatedly, to delegitimate and defund progressive social change and

proponents of social welfare programs (Starr, 1987).

At this stage, globalization is primarily the massing of private power on a global level. The concentration of wealth so evident in the United States in the 1980s and 1990s reflects worldwide economic trends. As stateless megacompanies "search the world for bargain labor, sell their stock on exchanges from London to Hong Kong, and pin more and more of their hopes on customers in the emerging markets, most of them in Asia, they are walking away from the enormous public problems their private decisions create for American society" (Barnet, 1994, p. 754). What this ultimately yields is a push away from the *social*—an overemphasis on the individual as the source of problems and the source of solutions, the similar restructuring of urban space throughout the world, and the end of public costs, as much as possible. What makes the problem also possible is the relative quietude and ineffectiveness of alternatives and challenges to the neoconservative vision of a new world order. On a very significant level, the new private world of today, so singular in its view and so increasingly concentrated in its power and control, has greatly diminished our democratic experiment, which is what the discussion of public life is all about.

Curiously, as capital and power centralize in the new global economy, the functions of both implementing its tasks and cleaning up its mess are increasingly decentralized. This leads, paradoxically, to significant new forms of public life. Voluntary-sector social efforts proliferate worldwide to address problems as diverse as ecological disasters, inadequate public education, crime prevention, and AIDS. Total quality management (TQM) strategies spread in the workplace, part of the effort to decentralize decision making around work strategies and performance. Public schools increasingly have site autonomy to develop participatory decisional structures that include administrators, teachers, parents, and business representatives. The voluntary sector expands exponentially, helping to address the needs of society through multitudinous nonprofit grassroots efforts. This proliferation is a mixed blessing, for while the tasks in the new global economy are handled on a more decentralized basis, power to make the essential decisions regarding the allocation of resources and organizational objectives is increasingly centralized. "Decentralization of production" accompanies "concentration of control" (Montgomery, 1995, p. 461).

CONCLUSION

For those interested in community organizing, global capital devastates communities while it forces people back into them as a first line of coping with and resisting external economic forces. At first glance, community-based efforts seem to neatly replicate the second part of the globalization strategy: decentralize task structures. But grassroots efforts may yet prove the best means for meeting the challenges of contemporary privatization. They may be the seeds of resistance to the antisocial perspective and provide necessary opportunities for a public life in which people come to understand the value of an inclusive, democratic, and egalitarian public good and public life. The community is an essential component of how people collectively deal with globalization. Michael Sandel (1988) suggests that increasing globalization requires the building and rebuilding of communities to provide a basis of stability and identity in a global context that challenges both. Without such

community building, "we will find ourselves without any form of political community that expresses our shared identity, and knits us together in the families, schools, and neighborhoods that democracy requires" (quoted in Friedman, 1993, p. 1; Sandel, 1988). The more the nation moves into a global economic model, the more people need community to give structure to everyday life. Community provides a base to stabilize and organize public life, to give people training in citizenship and social responsibility. Because global capitalism generally ignores its impact on community life, and because it is fundamentally unaccountable, unrestrained, and corrosive to the traditional stability of the community, grassroots organizing becomes a means for dealing with the antisocial aspects of global privatization (Lasch, 1991; Sandel, 1988).

Nevertheless, given the larger contextualization of this chapter, it must be emphasized that the physical community—for example, a neighborhood—is ultimately too narrow and too lacking in resources to perform such functions on its own. And communities of culture for example, a community built around identities of gender, race, ethnicity, or sexual orientation—serve as important collective gels in an era where people no longer stick together well, but are by themselves not sufficient. Community and cultural identity are too narrow to meet the challenge of global privatization. Clearly, any public philosophy and social change movement for the contemporary era must recognize the value and importance of communities and cultural identity in helping to rebuild public life. But there are critical issues of power on a larger scale which need to be addressed if an equitable society is to be fashioned. These include challenging the absolute prerogative of private decisions, emphasizing social responsibilities as well as rights, refashioning the welfare state to support basic human needs, and limiting the power and scope of corporations and global capital. Community organizations can help meet the challenges of the contemporary world by tying their work to a critique of the undemocratic and antipublic nature of our contemporary political economy. As Lasch remarks, "in a world in which there are no values except those of the market . . . [there is] an almost irresistible pressure on every activity to justify itself in the only terms it recognizes: to become a business proposition, to pay its own way, to show black ink on the bottom line" (cited in Judge, 1995, p. 35). We must not only act locally and think globally, but, this chapter argues, we must do what we can to help create an alternative vision and movement to that of the politics of global privatization. In such an effort, not only are the importance of political economy and public life reasserted, but they are tied to people's daily experience through connection with community life.

REFERENCES

Barnekov, T., Boyle, R., and Rich, D. (1989), *Privatism and Urban Policy in Britain and the United States*. New York: Oxford University Press.

Barnet, R. J. (1994). "Lords of the Global Economy." *The Nation* December 19, p. 754–757.

Bauman, Z. (1998). *Globalization: The Human Consequences*. New York: Columbia.

Bellah, R., Madsen, R., Sullivan, W., Swedler, A., and Tiplon, S. (1985). *Habits of the Heart: Individualism and Commitment in American Life*. New York: Harper & Row.

Bellah, R., et al. (1991). *The Good Society*. New York: Knopf.

Blakely, E. J., and Snyder, M. G. (1997). *Fortress America: Gated Communities in the United States*. Washington D.C.: Brookings Institution Press.

Bookchin, M. (1987). *The Rise of Urbanization and the Decline of Citizenship*. San Francisco: Sierra Club Books.

Bowles, S., Gordon, D., and Weiskopff, T. (1990). *After the Wasteland: A Democratic Economics for the Year 2000*. Armonk, NY: M. E. Sharpe.

Boyte, H. (1992). "The Pragmatic Ends of Popular Politics." In C. Calhoun, ed., *Habermas and the Public Sphere*. Cambridge, MA: MIT Press, pp. 340–354.

Brecher, J. (1993). "Global Village or Global Pillage." *The Nation*, December 6, pp. 685–88.

Brecher, J., Childs, J., and Cutler, J., eds., (1993). *Global Visions: Beyond the New World Order*. Boston: South End Press.

Brecher, J., and Costello, T. (1994). *Global Village or Global Pillage: Economic Reconstruction From the Bottom Up*. Boston: South End Press.

Center on Budget and Policy Priorities. (1990). As quoted in *Chicago Tribune*, July 24, p. 5.

Cox, K. (1988). "The Politics of Turf and the Question of Class." In J. Wolch and M. Dear eds., *Power of Geography: How Territory Shapes Social Life* (pp. 61–90). New York: Routledge.

Davis, M. (1992), City of Quartz. New York: Vintage.

Elshtain, J. (1994) *Democracy on Trial*. New York: Basic Books.

Fisher, R. (1994). *Let the People Decide: Neighborhood Organizing in America*. New York: Twayne.

Fisher, R., and Karger, H. (1997). *Social Work and Community in a Private World: Getting Out in Public*. New York: Longman.

Fisher, R., and Kling, J., eds. (1993). *Mobilizing the Community: Local Politics in a Global Era*. Newbury Park, CA: Sage.

Friedman, M. (1962). *Capitalism and Freedom*. Chicago: University of Chicago Press

Friedman, T. (1993). "The Designs Behind the Surprises." *New York Times*, November 28, Section 4, pp. 1–3.

Gilder, G. (1981). *Wealth and poverty*.New York: Basic Books.

Habermas, J. (1989) "The Structural Transformation of the Public Sphere." Boston: Harvard University Press.

Houston Chronicle. (1992). September 4, p. 1.

Judd, D. (1994). "Enclosing the Commons of the Public City." In H. Liggett and D. Perry, eds., *Representing the City.* Newbury Park, CA: Sage.

Judge, C. (1995). "Soul Men." *In These Times* (January 23), 35.

Karger, H. J., and Stoesz, D. (1994). *American Social Welfare Policy: A Pluralist Approach,*, 2nd ed., New York: Longman.

Kuttner, R. (1992). "The Splitting of America," *Boston Globe,* May 18th, in *The Organizer Mailing* VI July, 1992, p. 1.

Kuttner, R. (1996). *Everything for Sale: The Virtues and Limits of Markets.* Chicago: University of Chicago Press.

Lasch, C. (1978). *The Culture of Narcissism.* New York: W. W. Norton.

Lasch, C. (1991). *True and Only Heaven.* New York: W. W. Norton.

Lasch, C. (1994) *Revolt of the Elites.* New York: W. W. Norton.

Logan, J. R., and Swanstrom, T., eds., (1990). *Beyond the City Limits: Urban Policy and economic Restructuring in Comparative Perspective.* Philadelphia: Temple University Press.

Martin, P. and O'Connor, G. (1989). *The Social Environment.* White Plains, NY: Longman.

Mead, W. R. (1991). "Recession obsession blurs economic decay," *Houston Chronicle* April 21, p. 1E.

Mickelson, J. S., (1992). ed., *Houston's Children 1992.* Houston: Children at Risk.

Mills, C. W. (1971). *The Sociological Imagination.* New York: Penguin Books.

Miringoff, M., and Miringoff, M. (1999). *The Social Health of the Nation: How America Is Really Doing.* New York: Oxford University Press.

Montgomery, D. (1995). "What The World Needs Now." *The Nation,* April 3, pp. 461–463.

Murray, C. (1984). *Losing ground.* New York: Basic Books.

New York Times. (1992). May 6, Editorial, p. A18.

Phillips, K. (1990). *The Politics of Rich and Poor: Wealth and the American Electorate in the Reagan Aftermath.* New York: Harper.

Piven. F. F., and Cloward, R. (1982). *The New Class War: Reagan's Attack on the Welfare State and Its Consequences.* New York: Pantheon.

Reed, A., ed., (1999). *Without Justice for All: The New Liberalism and Our Retreat from Racial Equality.* Boulder, CO: Westview Press.

Riesman, D. (1950). *The Lonely Crowd: A Study of the Changing American Character.* New Haven: Yale.

Rosenberg, T. (1989). *Poverty in New York City, 1985–1988: The Crisis Continues.* New York: Community Service Society of New York.

Ryan, M. (1992). "Gender and Public Access: Women's Politics in Nineteenth Century America." In C. Calhoun, ed., *Habermas and the Public Sphere.* Cambridge, MA: MIT Press, pp. 259–288.

Salamon, L., ed. (1989). *Beyond Privatization: The Tools of Government Action.* Washington DC: Urban Institute Press.

Sandel. M. (1988). "Democrats and Community." *The New Republic,* February 22, pp. 20–23.

Schor, J. (1999). Foreword to Shifting Fortunes: The Perils of the Growing American Wealth Gap (http://www.stw.org/html/shifting_fortunes_report.html).

Schram, S. (1993). "Inverting Political Economy: Looking at Welfare from the Bottom Up." Paper presented at American Political Science Association meeting.

Sennett, R. (1974). *The Fall of Public Man.* New York: W. W. Norton.

Sennett, R. (1990). *The Conscience of the Eye.* New York: W. W. Norton.

Sidel, R. (1986). *Women and Children Last: The Plight of Poor Women in Affluent America.* New York: Penguin.

Soja, E. (1985). *The Spatiality of Social Life.* In D. Gregory and J. Urry, eds., *Social Relations and Spatial Structures.* New York: St. Martin's.

Sorkin, M., ed. (1992). *Variation on a Theme Park: The New American City and the End of Public Space.* New York: Noonday Press.

Specht, H., and Courtney, M. (1994). *Unfaithful Angels: How Social Work Has Abandoned Its Mission.* New York: Free Press.

Starr. P. (1987). *The Limits of Privatization.* Washington, DC: Economic Policy Institute.

Suarez, R. (1999). *The Old Neighborhood: What We Lost in the Great Suburban Migration, 1966–1999.* New York: Free Press

Tilly, C. (1990). "Down and Out in the City: Examining the Roots of Urban Poverty," *Dollars and Sense,* No. 155, April, p. 6.

Wolch, J. (1990). *The Shadow State: Government and Voluntary Sector in Transition.* New York: Foundation Center.

4.

Phillip Fellin

UNDERSTANDING AMERICAN COMMUNITIES

At the macro practice level, social work requires an understanding of communities in American society. Communities constitute an important arena or context for social work at all levels of intervention, but especially with regard to social policy, community organization, and administration and management. In conceptions of social work, communities are viewed not only as arenas for macro practice, but also as targets and vehicles of change (Cox et al. 1987; Kramer and Specht, 1975; Netting, Kettner, and McMurtry, 1993; Rothman and Tropman, 1987). Consequently, conceptual frameworks and empirical findings about communities from the social sciences are useful for human service professionals. This article presents two major theoretical perspectives on communities: human ecology and social systems theory. These perspectives are well developed in the social sciences and are widely used as conceptualizations of the social environment in social work education and practice (Germain, 1979; 1991; Longres, 1990; Chess and Norlin, 1988).

DEFINING COMMUNITIES

There is an emerging consensus in the literature that communities are constituted when a group of people form a social unit based on common location, interest, identification, culture, and/or common activities (Garvin and Tropman, 1992). Following this definition, communities may be classified into two major categories,

distinguished by common locality or place, and by interest and identification. These community types often overlap with each other, while displaying significant similarities and differences.

Communities may also be characterized in terms of three dimensions: (1) a functional spacial unit meeting sustenance needs; (2) a unit of patterned social interaction; and (3) a symbolic unit of collective identity (Hunter, 1975, p. 538). Communities of "place" vary along these dimensions, as well as by size, density, and heterogeneity. Locality-based communities are often referred to as neighborhood communities, community areas, local municipal communities, and metropolitan communities. Generally the population size and geographical areas of these communities increase from the neighborhood unit to the metropolitan area. Locality-based communities are usually overlapping, such as neighborhoods within municipalities. Consequently, people generally reside in multiple communities of place—that is, communities within communities.

In addition to membership in locality-based communities, many people have membership in one or more communities of interest and identification (Longres, 1990). These communities are based on some feature of common identity or belief, such as ethnicity, race, religion, lifestyle, ideology, gender, sexual orientation, social class, profession, or workplace. Members of these communities not only have a common identity with their group, but often engage in some level of organizational activity, such as social participation in professional groups, sports clubs, religious groups, and ethnic organizations. Communities of interest and identification often coincide with neighborhood communities. For example, people who identify themselves in terms of common racial, ethnic, religious, or social class membership may live in residential areas that have a high proportion of people with one or more of these characteristics.

The two sets of theory, human ecology and social systems, provide useful perspectives about spacial and geographic communities, as well as communities of identification and interest. This knowledge is directly related to macro social work practice tasks and strategies. For example, knowledge about communities of place forms a basis for social planning, that is, districts for urban planning, service delivery areas for health and social welfare planning, and catchment areas in mental health planning. Understanding of communities of identification, such as racial and ethnic groups, religious groups, social class groups, enhances the practice of organizing for social action. These community groups also become the focus of self-help and mutual aid activities carried out in the practice of locality development (Rothman, 1993).

ECOLOGICAL SYSTEMS

From an ecological standpoint, community may be defined as "a structure of relationships through which a localized population provides its daily requirements" (Hawley, 1950, p. 180). This ecological definition of community focuses on the relationship of populations to their environment, especially in regard to spacial organization—that is, how people and services are distributed. Emphasis is placed on the "division of labor" within a community—types of occupational groups, and how a structure of occupational stratification emerges through an interdependence within and between communities (Hawley, 1950; 1986).

Theories of human ecology focus on the development of locality-based community structures through several processes, such as competition, centralization, concentration, segregation, integration, and succession (Park, Burgess, and McKenzie, 1925; McKenzie, 1926; Poplin, 1979). A major area of *competition* in communities is over the use of land, as individuals, groups, and social institutions seek an "advantage of place" for commercial, industrial, institutional, and residential purposes. Competition results in dominance when social groups have the power to control the use of the most valued land in a community. Communities are considered dominant when they develop controlling influence over other communities.

Centralization describes a clustering of institutions and services in a central location, such as a business district, a transportation center, or communications center. Decentralization is a process by which organizations move out from a central location. The concept of *concentration* refers to the influx of individuals, especially through migration and immigration, into an urban area. The process of *segregation* describes how individuals, groups, and institutions, distinguished by social characteristics such as race, ethnicity, social class, or religion, become congregated in separate physical locations. *Integration* refers to a situation whereby individuals with a mix of one or more of these characteristics, such as white and minority residents, reside in the same community. *Succession* refers to a process of change, when one social group or set of institutions is replaced by another within a geographic area. These concepts not only denote a processes of change in communities, but are also used to describe end states, such as integrated or segregated neighborhoods.

Application of an Ecological Perspective

An ecological perspective allows us to describe locality-based communities in terms of social geography, that is, the distribution of people, organizations, and resources in space. This perspective calls attention to the physical layout of the community, that is, the location of residences, industry, commercial and business areas, social and health services, churches, recreational areas, and schools. Choldin (1985) refers to these features of the community as the "built environment." Within this environment, one can observe changes over time in the use of space and in the distribution and movements of people. The technique of mapping is used to describe land-use patterns, boundaries of racial, ethnic, religious, and social class groups, rates of crime, rates of poverty, and child maltreatment (Coulton et al., 1990; Green, 1982; Wilson, 1987; Zuravin and Taylor, 1987).

An ecological perspective provides an understanding of the demographic development of communities. Data from the U.S. Bureau of the Census are used to describe a range of characteristics of communities, such as size, density, and heterogeneity. Thus the examination of data about metropolitan areas, urbanized areas, suburban areas, small communities, and rural areas highlights the interrelationships and differences between communities, including exchanges, communications, and interdependencies with one another (Martinez-Brawley, 1990). Analysis of census data leads to an understanding of past as well as ongoing phases of urbanization, including demographic changes in specific communities, such as large, urban, inner city areas.

Population Size

Population size is an important descriptor of locality-based communities. The U.S. Bureau of the Census provides census tract data on the size of population in local neighborhoods, community areas, municipalities, townships, and metropolitan areas. Changes in population size of these communities have accompanied the process of urbanization. Historically, this process has been defined in terms of an increased proportion of the population in urbanized areas in contrast to rural areas. Increasingly, the size of communities has changed due to several patterns, such as technological advancements, changes in transportation and communication, and development of large-scale economic organizations and residential areas away from the central cities. In addition, population changes have occurred due to patterns of fertility of ethnic minority groups, migration within the United States, movement of white and ethnic-minority middle-class populations from central cities to suburbs, and recent immigration of non-European and refugee groups. A major change has been the decline in population size of central cities in major metropolitan areas, especially through "white flight" from cities to suburbs and beyond. These population-size changes have been accompanied by changes in other census demographic characteristics of communities, such as the residential separation of people by race, ethnicity, and social class.

Population Density

Population density is an environmental variable that refers to the number of people within a physical space. Based on the writings of Wirth (1938), density has been thought to lead to a more complex community structure, to a more economically specialized population, to residential overcrowding, and, hence, to "friction and irritation." Density of population is frequently associated with negative factors of city life, such as "too much noise, too much dirt, too much pollution," that is, "an environment that is stress-producing" (Krupat, 1985, p. 95). Krupat has noted that density may lead to crowding, a "psychological or subjective experience that results from a recognition that one has less space than one desires" (p. 100). Crowding occurs in housing arrangements, in transportation, in use of facilities, and in neighborhood communities. Urban inner-city living areas tend to be high in density, in contrast to low density of suburban neighborhoods.

The question of what effects density and crowding have on people and their social relationships has been of particular interest to social workers, social reformers, and urban sociologists, especially from the turn of the century to the present time (Choldin, 1985; Fischer, 1978; Krupat, 1985). Krupat's (1985) review of the research literature on density and social pathology suggests there may be no causal effect of one on the other, but that "high-density living definitely has the capacity to be stressful," especially for people living in poverty (p. 112). Two dimensions of urban life that have attracted special attention for social workers are the adverse living conditions of the poor, and the limits on positive social relationships sometimes imposed upon people in communities of large size and density.

Population Heterogeneity

The composition of the population in a community is often described in terms of its homogeneity or heterogeneity. Such variables as social class, race and ethnicity, religion, age, and gender are used to classify people and describe such groups in relation to their presence in neighborhoods, municipalities, and metropolitan areas. From an ecological point of view, these characteristics are aggregated to indicate the social structure of geographic communities. Groups classified in these terms also represent communities of identification, and in the instance of social class and race/ethnicity there is often an overlap with locational communities. The study of community stratification systems of social class and race/ethnicity has special relevance to the macro practice of social work, inasmuch as membership in these groups affects the quality of life of people in positive and negative ways. People benefit or suffer as a result of their social positions within communities, through differential life chances, employment opportunities, access to social and material resources, and social relationships.

Social Class. Stratification by social class refers to inequalities among people measured in such terms as socioeconomic status and lifestyle. Commonly used indicators of social class include occupation, income, education, and lifestyle. The U.S. Bureau of the Census provides data on these factors, allowing for the development of social profiles of communities. A classic illustration of how census statistics can be used to describe social class differences in communities is provided in the Social Area Analysis framework of Shevky and Bell (1955). This approach involves the use of three major constructs: social rank (education and occupation), urbanization or family status (type of housing, marital status, children, members of household working), and segregation or ethnicity (proportion of minorities in the area compared to the total community population). Of particular concern to human-service professionals is the residential segregation of population groups, by social class and by ethnic minority status, and the impact of residence on community life.

Community profiles of social class illustrate ways of using aggregate data to determine the proportions of people in various social class levels or social ranks. Of course, social class ranking of individuals and households may be influenced by other factors, most notably race, ethnicity, family background, religion, and lifestyle. In fact, individuals in racial and ethnic groups may construct their own rankings within a social stratification system. Factors of occupation, income, and education have in common the fact that they are quantitative indicators that point to inequalities among individuals and among population groups. There is little agreement, however, about where to draw the lines in order to distinguish one class from another, or what to call the various class levels. One commonly used set of names includes the poor, working class, middle class, upper-middle class, and upper class (Jackman and Jackman, 1983).

Social class is often associated with the life chances and lifestyles of community residents. Indicators of lifestyles include such factors as the value and location of homes, clothing styles, consumer spending patterns, travel and vacation styles, and choices of reading. The most prominent of these factors is the value and location of one's residential dwelling. In large urban communities, high value of housing and prestigious location are the signs of upper class membership, just as the Single Room Occupancy housing in a skid row or the low-cost housing in slum areas are signs of underclass membership.

Social class can be a community of identification, based on subjective measures such as class consciousness, class awareness, class identity, and cognitive maps— all images individuals have about their location in the class structure. The concept of social class appears to have considerable meaning in the way community residents view themselves. For example, using residents' reports on their subjective interpretations of social class, Jackman and Jackman (1983) found that social classes, as interest groups, form the basis for the development of social communities.

In recent years, social scientists and human service professionals have given considerable attention to a special group of people within the lower classes (Devine and Wright, 1993; Jencks and Peterson, 1991; Wilson, 1989). Some individuals and families living in poverty appear to fall outside the traditional class hierarchy and are viewed as members of an underclass. These people appear to be restricted by social, economic, and personal barriers from entry into the traditional class structure. As Wilson (1989) has noted, an early and "dominant image of the underclass became one of people with serious character flaws entrenched by a welfare subculture and who have only themselves to blame for their social position in society" (p. 182). More recently, an alternative view based on empirical research has emerged, a view that emphasizes the "severe constraints and limited opportunities that shape their lives," based on "class and racial subjugation in the ghetto" (p. 183).

Wilson's (1987) explanation of the relationship of demographic changes to the social dislocation of African Americans in the inner cities illustrates the use of an ecological perspective to explain the emergence of a ghetto poor minority underclass. Wilson seeks to explain differences in inner-city neighborhood communities prior to 1960 with communities of the 1980s. He notes that "inner-city communities prior to 1960 exhibited the features of social organization . . . including a sense of community, positive neighborhood identification, and explicit norms and sanctions against aberrant behavior" (p. 3). In contrast, these inner cities became the locale for a ghetto underclass associated with problems of social dislocation, such as high rates of "crime, joblessness, out-of-wedlock births, female-headed families, and welfare dependency" (p. 16). These problems are seen as the result of societal, demographic, and neighborhood factors, especially historic and contemporary discrimination, the flow of migrants, changes in the age structure, economic system changes, and concentration effects of living in areas with high rates of poverty (Wilson, 1987, 1989, 1993; Wacquant and Wilson, 1989). Most importantly, Wilson suggests that these concentration effects have led to a lack of social organization in neighborhoods, that is, social isolation and a lack of community resources from social networks, social institutions, and workforce participation.

Given the considerable diversity in the underclass population, social workers participate in a variety of programs directed toward alleviating the problems of these individuals, and in changing the social conditions that retain them in this devastating state of poverty. Social workers may be involved in the development of housing programs and in job training and jobs programs, along with other social welfare programs, in order to help people escape from their underclass conditions. While these programs have helped some individuals move into mainstream society, the presence of a substantial underclass population within urban communities continues to be a major social and community problem, the solution to which requires public policy changes in all community subsystems. Social workers in policy-making roles can participate in supporting these changes, which, in Wilson's (1993) terms, will enhance social rights for all ethnic and racial groups, that is "the right to employment, economic security, education, and health" (p. 30).

Race and Ethnicity. Race and ethnicity comprise two major concepts used in describing heterogeneity of populations in the United States and within communities (Snipp, 1989). Because of the significance of cultural features that distinguish racial groups from each other, concepts of ethnic group and minority group are often used instead of the concept of race. The term "minority" has come to refer to people of color who are a minority in number within society and have experienced high degrees of discrimination, prejudice, and oppression (Bernal, 1990). The term "ethnic" is combined with "minority group" to refer to people of color—groups identified by the Equal Employment Commission established by the Equal Rights Act of 1964 as African American, Asian American, Native American, and Hispanic (Glazer, 1983). There is considerable diversity within each of these ethnic minority categories, attributable to national origin, social class differences, and state of acculturation and assimilation, as well as to other sociocultural factors.

The Bureau of the Census collects information about the affiliation of individuals with racial and ethnic groups. The population of the United States is classified in terms of racial categories of American Indian or Alaska Native, Asian or Pacific Islander, Black, White, and Other. Hispanic origin is considered as ethnicity, and persons identifying themselves as Mexican, Puerto Rican, Cuban, or Other Spanish/ Hispanic origin are classified as of Hispanic origin. "The concept of race the Bureau of the Census uses reflects self-identification by respondents, that is, the individual's perception of his/her racial identity. The concept is not intended to reflect any biological or anthropological definition" (Statistical Abstracts, 1992, pp. 4–5). One of the consequences of classification is that "nonwhite" status carries with it certain compensations as a result of affirmative action policies, minority contracting set-asides, and anti-discrimination policies (Barringer, 1993). Currently, in the United States, ethnic groups are classified as ethnic minority groups but also in terms of white ethnic groups. These later groups historically have been differentiated in terms of European nationality, for example, white immigrant groups such as Polish, Italian, German, Irish.

A significant dimension of the demographic development of communities in the United States is the diversity of ethnic and racial populations brought about by immigration (Maldonado and Moore, 1985; Tobin, 1987). Census data of 1990 display large changes in the racial and ethnic composition of the United States from 1980 to 1990, with nearly one in four Americans of African, Asian, Hispanic, or American Indian ancestry in 1990 compared to one in five in 1980 (Barringer, 1991). A significant part of this growth came from nearly ten million ethnic minority immigrants, especially in the Hispanic population. Equally dramatic in change is the new diversity of the Asian population due to immigration, with fast growing groups of Vietnamese, Indians, and Koreans.

An important aspect of this growth in ethnic populations from immigration is the distribution of immigrants. An analysis of 1990 census data by Frey (1993) shows that "Most immigrants are flooding into just a handful of states, while the rest of America is largely untouched by the new immigration" (Tilove and Hallinan, 1993, p. F/1). This change has led some demographers to believe there is a new "white flight" occurring, not just from city and suburban communities, but from states and regions of the United States. In the light of these population changes, Frey (1993) predicts that

"What is really developing here is two very separate societies, two separate Americas" (Tilove and Hallinan, 1993, p. F/1).

In summary, ecological perspectives focus on macro-level variables with regard to population, environment, social organization, and technology. Attention is given to "fundamentally important community phenomena such as whether the community is growing or shrinking, whether the population is young or old, whether different segments are integrated or segregated, how densely the population lives, and what sort of transportation and communications systems are used" (Choldin, 1985, p. 59).

SOCIAL SYSTEMS PERSPECTIVES

Social systems theory provides another useful framework for understanding American communities. While this theory is unusually complex, its major concepts provide a guide for examining the structural and functional attributes of locality-based communities. We begin with the idea that a social system involves the interaction of two or more social units, that is, the interactions within and among social groups and social organizations. In order to apply systems concepts to locality-based communities, we are interested in how well the subsystems of a community are functioning, as well as the community as a whole, in meeting the needs of its residents. This involves examination of community subsystems, such as the economic, political, educational, health, and social welfare systems. The major social units within each of these subsystems are formal organizations, such as businesses, governmental offices, churches, schools, health care organizations, and social welfare agencies. Informal groups, including families and social groups, also contribute to the functioning of community subsystems and the total community.

An important feature of social systems theory is the specification of boundaries of the system in relation to its environment. To illustrate, a municipality in a metropolitan area may be defined as a community system, with boundaries that are likely to be both geographical and psychological. The external environment includes other municipalities, as well as state, regional, and national entities with which the municipal community interacts. One of the central functions of such a community system is boundary maintenance. A community engages in activities that will assure its continuance as a separate entity or social organization. Boundary maintenance is exemplified by physical boundaries as well as legal, political boundaries.

Study of the community social system includes attention to the interaction of the system beyond its own boundaries with outside systems, such as other communities and society. This outside system, designated by Chess and Norlin (1988) as the suprasystem, provides inputs into a community system and receives outputs. Thus this interaction provides for inputs into the system, such as culture, money, material resources, and information. Outputs may be thought of as the results of the interactions within a system, such as the goals of a community and/or its subsystems. These goals are related to employment, health, safety and security, social welfare, education, housing, and other indicators of quality of life (Chess and Norlin, 1988).

The concepts of input and output are related to the ways in which interactions of the units within a social system are patterned. Classical social systems theory, particularly as developed by Talcott Parsons (1951), describes these patterns in terms of systems functions. Patterns having to do with the system's external activities serve adaptive and goal-attainment functions, with internal activities serving integrative and pattern-maintenance/tension-management functions. These patterns represent the problems a community must solve in order to maintain itself.

Systems patterns of interaction can be thought of as "task functions" and "maintenance functions." Task functions of adaptation and goal attainment involve relationships with the outside environment through the economy and the polity. Integration functions occur in the juridical system, and pattern-maintenance/tension-management is handled by groups such as the family, education, and cultural units of the community. Communities as systems must relate to changes within and without the system, and maintain themselves through systems functions. From this perspective, a community constantly seeks a level of stability or equilibrium. Thus when the various subsystems of the community change, there is an impact on the total community. When the task or maintenance functions of the subsystems are not carried out successfully, this leads to a lack of goal attainment and may lead to community disorganization.

Application of a Social Systems Perspective

The functions of social systems formulated by Parsons (1951) are applied to locality-based communities by Warren (1963). Community functions include: production/distribution/consumption (economic system), socialization (family, educational system), social control (political system), social participation (voluntary associations), and mutual support (health and welfare agencies, primary groups). These functions are carried out through the subsystems of the community and their various formal organizations, as well as through the actions of primary groups, such as family and other household groups, friendship groups, kinship groups, neighborhood groups, peer groups, self-help groups, and informal social club groups.

Communities interact with other communities, and these external relationships have important implications for the way in which a particular community system maintains its boundaries and its equilibrium. Equally important are the interactions of formal organizations of community systems with similar social units outside the community. These extra-community relationships are identified by Warren (1963) as vertical, in contrast to the horizontal interactions within a community. For example, in regard to mutual support, a typical community unit is a voluntary health association; a unit of horizontal pattern; a community welfare council; a unit of a vertical pattern: a national health association.

Understanding a locality-based community as a social system is enhanced through knowledge about the various community subsystems. The social work professional needs to have a thorough grasp of the health and welfare services subsystem of a community, including knowledge about the organizations that make up various fields of service, and about the horizontal and vertical patterns of organizations of the subsystem. At the same time, such knowledge is also needed about community political, economic, educational, and religious subsystems, since the major community functions identified by Parsons (1951) and Warren (1963) are carried out through these systems. This knowledge base provides the answers to a number of questions about communities. These include:

1. To what extent and under what conditions do voluntary associations contribute to the healthy functioning of a community, of the various community subsystems, and of individual citizens?
2. To what extent do the formal organizations within a subsystem of the community succeed in carrying out their community functions, through their own performance, and through cooperation with each other and with other subsystems through horizontal interorganizational relationships?
3. In what ways are community actions, as played out in the various subsystems, influenced by vertical relationships with organizations and systems (economic, political, health and welfare, education) outside the community?
4. How do communities and their subsystems handle social conflict among population groups and create and maintain social order?
5. How is the functioning of a community and its subsystems coordinated or influenced by the power and/or decision-making structures of a community? Under what conditions does one or another subsystem become dominant in the community?
6. What mechanisms exist in the community to handle controversies and tensions within and between community subsystems and with other communities?
7. How is social integration created and maintained in communities? How do community systems and their subsystems operate to minimize or eliminate barriers to the full participation of vulnerable populations subjected to discrimination and oppression?

NEIGHBORHOODS

Locality-based communities are made up of neighborhoods, an important context for macro social work practice. Ecological and social systems perspectives can be applied to the understanding of the structure and functioning of neighborhood communities as significant parts of the social environment. Increasingly, neighborhoods provide the location for community-based services for people with special needs, such as people with developmental disabilities, mental illness, and physical illness. Practice activities are often directed toward strengthening of neighborhood social networks, and social controls, including block clubs, church groups, school organizations, and other voluntary associations.

Boundaries need to be established for neighborhoods in order to apply ecological and social systems concepts to these communities. Neighborhoods can be distinguished in terms of geographical area, with immediate neighborhoods referring to areas where a small number of household dwellings are in close proximity to each other. When a household area includes several blocks, it may be referred to as an extended neighborhood. Somewhat larger areas of 30 blocks or more may be designated as community neighborhoods (Litwak, 1985). Boundaries of neighborhoods are established by various groups, including residents, social planners, school boards, political parties, churches, health and welfare service agencies, and the mass media. Once such boundaries are established, census tract data can be used to describe a neighborhood in terms of population size and density, racial, ethnic, and religious composition, education, income, occupational status, level of employment, age structure, and household composition.

Another way of defining neighborhoods is as primary groups. Often, residents define their neighborhood as a small, personal arena that allows for ongoing, personal relationships, neighboring, informal helping, and exchanges of goods and services. The boundaries of a personal neighborhood are likely to cover a small geographical area. These primary-group neighborhoods, as well as extended neighborhoods, provide a number of community functions, such as a sociability arena, an interpersonal influence center, a source of mutual aid, an organizational base, a reference group, and an area signifying status (Warren and Warren, 1977). Consequently, residents of neighborhoods have a potential set of resource and social supports (individuals and organizations) within their local environment.

Social systems perspectives cannot be applied to neighborhood communities in the same ways as are used to understand municipal or metropolitan communities. Neighborhoods do not have similar subsystems that carry out locality-relevant functions in the ways they are performed by larger communities of place. Ecological perspectives more appropriately allow us to examine neighborhoods, especially their demographic characteristics, such as size, density, and heterogeneity. We are also able to examine various types of structures of neighborhoods through attention to community variables such as social class, ethnicity and race, social interaction, identity, and links to the broader community.

MODELS OF NEIGHBORHOOD TYPES

Neighborhood communities have social structures, although social scientists are not consistent in their choices of social dimensions to describe these structures. Several models for analyzing neighborhood structures are available to the macro social practitioner. In a model developed by Warren and Warren (1977), neighborhoods are differentiated in terms of the nature and level of social identity, social interaction, and linkages to the wider community. The six types of neighborhoods—integral, parochial, diffuse, stepping-stone, transitory, and anomic—offer differential benefits as well as social barriers to helping resources for residents (Warren and Warren, 1977). Practice applications of this model are illustrated by Warren and Warren (1977) and Warren (1981) in relation to such questions as when to organize, how to identify leadership resources, how to reach out to a neighborhood, how to assess neighborhood functions, and how to select practice roles and tactics for working in a neighborhood.

A second model for typing neighborhoods, developed by Litwak (1985), emphasizes two dimensions of neighborhood primary groups—the level of membership change or turnover, and the capacity to retain primary group cohesion/social integration. Using these characteristics, three neighborhood types are created: mobile neighborhood (high mobility, capacity to handle change), traditional neighborhood (stability, low capacity for change), and mass neighborhood (high mobility, low capacity for change). The usefulness of this typology for social work practice is illustrated by Litwak (1985) in relation to planning and service needs for older adults. The model can be applied to the various stages of the life cycle. For example, neighborhoods can be assessed in terms of working with young families in need of rapid integration into surburban or inner-city neighborhoods. This typology is useful in selecting interventions that speed up neighborhood social integration, such as creation of voluntary associations.

A third typology focuses on organizational, value, and change dimensions of primary group neighborhoods (Fellin and Litwak, 1963). The organizational base of neighborhoods involves informal contacts and local formal organizations, such as voluntary associations. Neighborhoods can be classified in terms of both their level of organization and their capacity to implement their values, such as orientations toward education, good citizenship, and crime and violence. Recognition of the values of residents in a neighborhood is helpful for both interpersonal and community practice. For example, in areas with high rates of crime and delinquency, the social worker can assess the values of residents toward law and order and toward the tolerance of deviant behavior, and their willingness to organize to implement values to combat violence and crime.

A fourth model, developed by Figueira-McDonough (1991), uses an ecological perspective for classifying communities. Her typology can be applied to neighborhood communities, as it focuses on population and organizational factors. Population factors include poverty and mobility, and organizational factors include informal networks (kin, friends, informal groups), secondary networks (schools, church groups), and external links (external support, resources). These variables are used to create neighborhood types, identified as (1) stepping-stone (nonpoor and mobile, low primary, high secondary networks, high external links); (2) established community (nonpoor, stable; high primary, high-secondary networks, low-external links); (3) disorganized community (poor, mobile; low primary, low secondary networks, low external links); and (4) parochial community (poor, stable; high primary, low secondary networks, low external links). This typology emphasizes sources of resources, by taking into account features of individual households (poverty) and of other members of the community (networks and external links). Hence this typology has particular relevance to social work practice at both the micro and macro levels, since it points to the need for assessment of the level and source of social supports available to community residents.

SOCIAL CLASS AND ETHNIC MINORITY NEIGHBORHOODS

As we have noted, often communities of identification and interest overlap with communities of place. A useful classification of neighborhoods comes from examining the social class characteristics of neighborhoods, as well as the ethnic minority composition. Often these two dimensions of neighborhoods, social class and ethnic minority composition, are combined, since ethnic minority groups are disproportionately represented in the middle-, lower-, and underclass neighborhoods. Attention to the social class level of neighborhoods is important for social workers, since neighborhood location and social class have a powerful effect on the resources and liabilities that affect the quality of life of neighborhood residents.

Ethnic minority neighborhoods are found mainly in the central cities of large urban areas. They are often referred to as "communities," based on a high proportion of residents identified by a single race or nationality group (Rivera and Erlich, 1992). Increasingly, ethnic minority working- and middle-class people, especially African Americans and Hispanics, have moved away from ghetto areas into racially and ethnically integrated communities, as well as to suburban neighborhoods where there is a high concentration of middle-class minority populations (Nathan, 1991). In the newly emerging middle-class minority neighborhoods, residents have membership in both a spacial community and a

sociopsychological community (Taylor, 1979), not unlike many minority residents in inner-city working-class and poverty neighborhoods.

SEGREGATION IN NEIGHBORHOODS

Contrary to the popular image of American society as a "melting pot" of races and ethnic groups, data from the 1990 census indicate that most communities in the United States continue to be highly segregated (Harrison and Weinberg, 1992). The concepts of segregation and integration serve to describe these neighborhood communities, with segregated neighborhoods having a high proportion of ethnic minority and/or cultural group membership (Rusk, 1993). Empirical studies of housing patterns in North American communities continue to leave no doubt that housing segregation is due in large part to discrimination and prejudice based on race and/or ethnicity (Tobin, 1987; *New York Times,* 1991; *Wall Street Journal,* 1992).

Federal legislation, such as the 1968 Fair Housing Act, as well as ongoing court decisions, have brought about some changes in the extent of discrimination in housing. However, the activities of several major groups involved in housing continue to maintain residential segregation, such as real estate brokers, home builders, banks and savings and loan associations, and local, state, and federal governments (Darden, 1987; Karr, 1993). "White flight" of city residents to suburban areas is only one (albeit a major) explanation for the segregation of American communities. Nonracial causes for household moves also contribute to segregated neighborhoods. The ecological concept of succession provides a framework for observing and explaining changes in population composition, especially in changes in population from white to ethnic minority groups.

Programs that seek to intervene in the process of succession and to create and/or maintain residential integration provide opportunities for involvement of professional social workers. Goals for these programs include "achieving a racial balance," "achieving integration," "integration maintenance," and "reduction of segregation." Examples of interventions to reach these goals are related to attempts to attract African Americans into white neighborhoods and whites into areas with high proportions of African Americans (Klibanoff, 1984; Hayes, 1990; Jones, 1990; Pepper, 1990; Dozier, 1993; Hirsch, 1992). In one of the most sophisticated studies of neighborhood integration maintenance efforts, Saltman (1991) identified a number of factors that facilitate the attainment of integration goals and concluded that racially diverse neighborhoods are maintained only with enormous difficulty.

REVIEW

Ecological and social systems perspectives have been presented as approaches to understanding the structure and functioning of the "multiple communities" that make up the social environment. Specific attention has been given to municipal communities (often referred to as "the community"), to neighborhood communities, and to ethnic minority communities of interest and identification. Ecological and social systems perspectives assist in the assessment of the overall functioning of these communities. A useful concept for making this assessment is community competence, that is, the capacity of a community to engage in problem solving in order to achieve its goals (Cottrell, 1983). In their use of this concept, Barbarin et al. (1981) emphasize that the capacities of social systems, and of the individuals and groups within a community, constitute a dual dimension of competence. In this sense, "Community competence refers both to the ability of social systems to respond to differential needs of the varied populations they serve, and [to] the ability of citizens or groups to use existing resources or develop alternatives for the purpose of solving problems of living" (Barbarin et al., 1981, p. 3). Social systems perspectives provide an understanding of municipal communities that is useful in the assessment of community competence. At the same time, ecological perspectives describe social conditions that may enhance or detract from the competent functioning of locality-based communities, especially municipal and neighborhood communities.

Competent communities are not easy to create or maintain. One of the most significant barriers to community competence involves the values, attitudes, and practices of people toward special population groups. Communities vary in regard to their level of discrimination, prejudice, oppression, acceptance, and tolerance. Many American communities lack an appropriate response to the differential needs of such groups as ethnic minorities, cultural and religious groups, women, physically and mentally disabled persons, gay and lesbian individuals, children, young adults, and older adults. Competent communities make special efforts to create equal opportunity and reduce barriers to the quality of life and full participation in community affairs of people discriminated against and oppressed. Macro-level social workers can contribute to community competence by participating in activities, tactics, and strategies that contribute to improved functioning of communities, especially in their capacity to help vulnerable population groups gain access to and utilize community resources.

REFERENCES

Barbarin, O., P. R. Good, O. M. Pharr, and J. A. Siskind, eds. *Institutional Racism and Community Competence.* U.S. Department of Health and Human Services, Pub. # (ADM) 81-907, 1981.

Barringer, F. "Immigration Brings New Diversity to Asian Population in the U.S." *New York Times*, June 12, 1991.

Barringer, F. "Ethnic Pride Confounds the Census." *New York Times*, May 9, 1993.

Bernal, M. E. "Ethnic minority mental health training trends and issues." In F. C. Serafica, et al., *Mental Health and Ethnic Minorities.* New York: Praeger, 1990.

Chess, W. A., and J. M. Norlin. *Human Behavior and the Social Environment.* Boston: Allyn and Bacon, 1988.

Choldin, H. M. *Cities and Suburbs.* New York: McGraw-Hill, 1985.

Cottrell, L. S., Jr. "The Competent Community. In R. Warren, and L. Lyon, eds. *New Perspectives on the American Community.* Homewood, IL: The Dorsey Press, 1983.

Coulton, C., S. Pandey, and J. Chow. "Concentration of Poverty and the Changing Ecology of Low-Income, Urban Neigh-borhoods: An Analysis of the Cleveland Area." *Social Work Research and Abstracts*, 26(4) (1990).

Cox, F. M., J. L. Erlich, J. Rothman, and J. E. Tropman. *Strategies of Community Organization.* Itasca, IL: Peacock Publishers, 1987.

Darden, J. T. "Choosing Neighbors and Neighborhoods: The Role of Race in Housing Preference. In G. A. Tobin, ed., "Divided Neighborhoods: Changing Patterns of Racial Segregation." *Urban Affairs Annual Reviews* (32) (1987).

Devine, J. A., and J. D. Wright. *The Greatest of Evils: Urban Poverty and the American Underclass.* New York: Aldine De Gruyter, 1993.

Dozier, M. "Fund to Boost Oakland Integration." *Detroit Free Press*, April 23, 1993.

Fellin, P., and E. Litwak. "Neighborhood Cohesion Under Conditions of Mobility." *American Sociological Review*, 28(3) (1963).

Figueira-McDonough, J. "Community Structure and Delinquency: A Typology." *Social Service Review* (March 1991).

Fischer, C. "Urban to Rural Diffusion of Opinions in Contemporary America." *American Journal of Sociology* 84(1) (1978).

Frey, W. H. *Newhouse Study.* Newhouse News Service, August 23, 1993.

Garvin, C. D., and J. E. Tropman. *Social Work in Contemporary Society.* Englewood Cliffs, NJ: Prentice-Hall, 1992.

Germain, C. *Social Work Practice: People and Environments.* New York: Columbia University Press, 1979.

Germain, C. *Human Behavior in the Social Environment.* New York: Columbia University Press, 1991.

Glazer, N. *Ethnic Dilemmas.* Cambridge: Harvard University Press, 1983.

Green, J. W. *Cultural Awareness in the Human Services.* Englewood Cliffs, NJ: Prentice-Hall, 1982.

Harrison, R. J., and D. H. Weinberg. *Racial and Ethnic Segregation in 1990.* Washington, DC: U.S. Bureau of the Census, April 1992.

Hawley, A. *Human Ecology: A Theory of Community Structure.* New York: Roland Press, 1950.

Hawley, A. *Urban Ecology.* Chicago: University of Chicago Press, 1986.

Hayes, A. S. "Is Town's Housing Plan the Key to Integration or a Form of Racism?" *Wall Street Journal*, October 4, 1990.

Hirsch, J. S. "Columbia, Md., at 25, Sees Integration Goal Sliding from Its Grasp. *Wall Street Journal*, February 27, 1992.

Hunter, A. "The Loss of Community: An Empirical Test Through Replication. *American Sociological Review* 40 (1975).

Jackman, M., and R. Jackman. *Class Awareness in the United States.* Berkeley: University of California Press, 1983.

Jencks, C., and P. E. Peterson. *The Urban Underclass.* Washington, DC: The Brookings Institution, 1991.

Jones, L. "Balancing Act." *Detroit Free Press*, September 29, 1990.

Karr, A. R. "Consumer Group Finds Marketing Bias in Mortgage Lending in 16 Large Cities." *Wall Street Journal*, August 13, 1993.

Klibanoff, H. "Chicago Suburb Actively Seeks Racial Diversity." *Detroit Free Press*, October 8, 1984.

Kramer, R. M., and H. Specht, eds. *Readings in Community Organization Practice*, 2nd ed. Englewood Cliffs, NJ: Prentice-Hall, 1975.

Krupat, E. *People in Cities.* New York: Cambridge University Press, 1985.

Litwak, E. *Helping the Elderly.* New York: Guilford Press, 1985.

Longres, J. F. *Human Behavior and the Social Environment*. Itasca, IL: Peacock Publishers, 1990.

Maldonado, L., and J. Moore. *Urban Ethnicity in the United States*. Beverly Hills, CA: Sage Publications, 1985.

Martinez-Brawley, E. E. *Perspectives on the Small Community*. Silver Spring, MD: NASW Press, 1990.

McKenzie, R. D. "The Scope of Human Ecology." *Publication of the American Sociological Society* 20 (1926).

Nathan, R. P. "Where the Minority Middle Class Lives." *Wall Street Journal*, May 22, 1991.

Netting, F. E., P. M. Kettner, and S. L. McMurtry. *Social Work Macro Practice*. New York: Free Press, 1993.

New York Times. "Study Finds Bias in House Hunting," September 1, 1991.

Park, R., E. W. Burgess, and R. D. McKenzie, eds. *The City*. Chicago: University of Chicago Press, 1925.

Parsons, T. *The Social System*. Glencoe, IL: Free Press, 1951.

Parsons, T. *Structure and Process in Modern Societies*. New York: The Free Press, 1960.

Pepper, J. "Common Ground: Cleveland Suburbs Work to Achieve a Racial Balance. *Detroit News*, August 19, 1990.

Poplin, D. Communities: *A Survey of Theories and Methods of Research*, 2nd ed. New York: Macmillan, 1979.

Rivera, F. G., and J. L. Erlich. *Community Organizing in a Diverse Society*. Boston: Allyn and Bacon, 1992.

Rothman, J. Personal Correspondence, 1993.

Rothman, J., and J. E. Tropman. "Models of Community Organization and Macro Practice Perspectives: Their Mixing and Phasing." In F. M. Cox, J. L. Erlich, J. Rothman, and J. E. Tropman, eds., *Strategies of Community Organization*, 4th ed. Itasca, IL: Peacock Publishers, 1987.

Rusk, D. *Cities Without Suburbs*. Baltimore: Johns Hopkins University Press, 1993.

Saltman, J. "Maintaining Racially Diverse Neighborhoods." *Urban Affairs Quarterly* 26(3) (1991).

Shevky, E., and W. Bell. *Social Area Analysis: Theory, Illustrative Application and Computational Procedures*. Stanford, CA: Stanford University Press, 1955.

Snipp, C. M. *American Indians: The First of This Land*. New York: Russell Sage, 1989.

Statistical Abstracts. U.S. Bureau of the Census, 1992.

Taylor, R. "Black Ethnicity and the Persistence of Ethnogenesis. *American Journal of Sociology* 84(6) (1979).

Tilove, J., and J. Hallinan. "A Nation Divided." *Ann Arbor News*, August 22, 1993.

Tobin, G. A., "Divided Neighborhoods: Changing Patterns of Racial Segregation." *Urban Affairs Annual Reviews* (32) (1987).

Wacquant, L. J. D., and W. J. Wilson. "The Cost of Racial and Class Exclusion in the Inner City." *Annals* 501 (1989).

Wall Street Journal. "Mortgage Gap on Racial Basis Persisted in 1991," October 1, 1992.

Warren, R. *The Community in America*. Chicago: Rand McNally, 1963.

Warren D. *Helping Networks*. South Bend, IN: University of Notre Dame Press, 1981.

Warren, R. and D. I. Warren. *The Neighborhood Organizers' Handbook*. South Bend, IN: University of Notre Dame Press, 1977.

Wilson, W. J. *The Truly Disadvantaged*. Chicago: University of Chicago Press, 1987.

Wilson, W. J. "The Underclass: Issues, Perspectives, and Public Policy." *Annals* 501 (1989).

Wilson, W. J. "The New Poverty and the Problem of Race," *O.C. Tanner Lecture*. Ann Arbor: University of Michigan, 1993.

Wirth, L. "Urbanism as a Way of Life." *American Journal of Sociology*, 44(1) (1938).

Zuravin, S. J., and R. Taylor. "The Ecology of Child Maltreatment: Identifying and Characterizing High-Risk Neighborhoods." *Child Welfare*, November/December 1987.

5.

Mayer N. Zald

ORGANIZATIONS:

ORGANIZATIONS AS POLITIES: AN ANALYSIS OF

COMMUNITY ORGANIZATION AGENCIES

The interdependence of subject matter in the fields of community organization and sociology has long been recognized by teachers and practitioners. Possibly to a greater extent than with any other segment of social work, the problems of this field of practice are grist for the mill of the student of society and the community. And yet there is no systematic sociology of community organization (hereinafter referred to as "CO"). Such a sociology would include a social history of the emergence and growth of the field of practice, an analysis of its ongoing social system, and diagnostic categories and criteria for investigating community problems and structure.

This paper focuses on one aspect of the social system of the field, presenting, in particular, a set of concepts and propositions about the structure and operation of CO agencies. These concepts and propositions are designed to explain some of the determinants of agency processes and, consequently, the styles and problems of professional practice.

Indeed, much more of the variability of practice in CO is determined by its organizational context, as compared with many professional fields. The needs and problems of the community are not funneled and defined directly between the practitioner and the community segment to which he is related; instead, needs are defined and shaped by the constitution and goals of the employing agency. Furthermore, the means selected to deal with community problems depend on organizational requirements, stances, and definitions. Whatever the practitioner's activity, he is guided by the structure, aims, and operating procedures of the organization that pays the bills.

Therefore, any useful theory of CO practice must include concepts and propositions about how CO agencies shape practice and how such organizations are themselves constrained. The question then becomes: *How are we to analyze community organization agencies?*

ORGANIZATIONAL ANALYSIS

The general approach used here is that of organizational analysis.[1] It is a form of analysis that takes the total organization, not some subpart, as its object. Typically,

[1]Organizational analysis has been developed most explicitly by Philip Selznick and his students. For example, see Philip Selznick, *T.V.A. and the Grass Roots* (Berkeley: University of California Press, 1949); Selznick, *Leadership in Administration: A Sociological Interpretation* (Evanston, IL: Row, Peterson & Co., 1957); and Selznick, *The Organizational Weapon* (New York: Rand Corporation, 1952). See also Burton Clark, *The Open Door College* (New York: McGraw-Hill Book Co., 1960); and Charles B. Perrow, "The Analysis of Goals in Complex Organizations," *American Sociological Review*, Vol. 66, No. 6 (March, 1961), pp. 854–866. The following works also are informed by this perspective: David L. Sills, *The Volunteers* (Glencoe, IL: Free Press, 1957); Martin Rein and

studies using this approach focus on the relation of goals to structure and the pressures to change goals arising from both the environment and the internal arrangements of the organization. A common focus is the allocation of power to different groups and the manner in which subgroup loyalties and power affect the operation of organizations. Furthermore, organizations are seen as developing distinctive characters—styles and strategies of coping with recurring problematic dilemmas of the organization.

Central to organizational analysis, but often only implicitly treated, is an analysis of the polity of organizations—the patterned distribution and utilization of authority and influence. The frame of reference taken in this paper is explicitly quasi-political. CO agencies are among a class of organizations in which goals are often in flux; in which the patterns of power of influence ebb and flow, but are central to understanding the problems of the organization; in which conflict is sometimes subterranean, sometimes overt, but almost always there; and in which organizations are in unstable relations to their environments. Thus, it seems warranted to give explicit attention to problems of power and the modes of binding people together for collective action. CO agencies can be analyzed as miniature polities.

Four interrelated concepts form the core of this analysis:

1. Organizations have *constitutions,* that is, they have basic zones of activity, goals, and norms of procedure and relationships that are more or less institutionalized in the organization and that are changed only with great effort and cost.

2. Constitutions are linked to the *constituency and resource base* of the organization. The constituency is not the clientele; rather, the term refers to the groups and individuals who control the organization and to whom the agency executive or executive core is most immediately responsible—the board of directors, key legislators, officeholders, major fund-raisers or grantors.

3. CO agencies wish to affect *target populations,* organizations, or decision centers.

4. Finally, CO agencies exist among a welter of other agencies; they have foreign or *external relations* that can facilitate, impede, or be neutral to the accomplishment of their goals.

These concepts are not mutually exclusive, yet each focuses on somewhat different observations. For purposes of exposition they can be treated separately.

ANALYSIS OF CONSTITUTIONS

In a sense, the constitution of an organization represents its social contract—the basic purposes and modes of procedure to which the major supporters and staff of the organization adhere.[2] When attempts are made to change the constitution of an

---

Robert Morris, "Goals, Structures and Strategies for Community Change," *Social Work Practice, 1962* (New York: Columbia University Press, 1962), pp. 127–145; and Robert D. Vinter and Morris Janowitz, "Effective Institutions for Juvenile Delinquents: A Research Statement," *Social Service Review,* Vol. 33, No. 2 (June, 1959), pp. 118–130.

[2]Not much attention has been paid to organizational constitutions by sociologists because they often work in organizations whose constitutions are not problematic. E. Wright Bakke uses a conception of constitution or "charter" that is even broader than the author's, but has the same intent. See *Bonds of Organization: An Appraisal of Corporate Human Relations* (New York: Harper & Bros. 1950), especially chap. 6, "Organizational Charter," pp. 152–179.

organization, the agency can expect conflict and disaffection, unless clear benefits adhere to the major supporters. The constitution of an organization is made up of the agency's commitments to major programs and modes of proceeding (goals and means). This is, of course, more than just the formal or written statement of goals and procedures, for these may have little to do with the organization's actual constitution. On the other hand, many patterned aspects of agency operation may not be part of the constitution, for these patterns may not deal with basic agreements about goals and means.

Analysis of constitution and goals is important for a sociology of CO practice because it clarifies several important aspects of it—the problems agencies confront when they attempt to change goals and structure, the possibilities of effectiveness vis-à-vis specific goals, and the styles of the professional's work. To be fruitful, analysis of constitutions must be broken down into more specific analytic problems. This paper will treat two: analysis of agency goals and constituency and agency autonomy.

Dimensions of Goals

Organizations come into being to pursue collective ends. A central part of the constitution of any organization is the sets of agreements about goals that are understood by major constituents. Not only do goals represent a set of constituting agreements, they focus organizational resources on a problem field. That is, organizational goals along with beliefs about how to attain them set tasks and problems for agency personnel.

Although there are several conceptual and methodological approaches to the study of goals, two aspects are especially

crucial here.[3] First, the goals of the organization determine some of the basic types of CO work. Second, attempts to shift the objectives of the organization can threaten its body politic. The goals of CO agencies can be classified along three analytically distinct dimensions: (1) change or service orientation (that is, according to whether the goal is to give the recipient of service essentially what he or his representative wants—information, program, and the like—or whether the community or individual is changed regardless of whether it or he initially wanted to be changed); (2) institution or individual and group orientation; (3) member (internal) or nonmember (external) orientation. The dichotomous cross-classification of these three dimensions yields the typology shown in Figure 5.1.

Of course, it is clear that some of these organizations are more likely to be sites for group work than for CO practice. But community organizers can be found in all of them.

The typology classifies organizations by their target and the ends they wish to achieve with each group. For instance, a community center (Cell D) usually offers services to individuals, rather than attempting to change them; it is oriented to groups and individuals who are members rather than to institutions (other large-scale organizations). On the other hand, in Cell B are agencies that attempt to mobilize people to change the society and its institutions.

The typology brings to the fore regularities of practice problems shared by agencies "located" in the same cell and

---

[3]See Mayer N. Zald, "Comparative Analysis and Measurement of Organizational Goals: The Case of Correctional Institutions for Delinquents," *Sociological Quarterly*, Vol. 4, No. 3 (Summer 1963), pp. 206–230.

FIGURE 5.1
Goal Dimensions of Community Organization Agencies

	CHANGE ORIENTED		SERVICE ORIENTED	
	INSTITUTION	INDIVIDUAL AND GROUP	INSTITUTION	INDIVIDUAL AND GROUP
	A	B	C	D
INTERNAL (MEMBER)	Regional planning groups for specific areas New-style welfare councils (planning is change oriented)	Neighborhood block clubs Settlement houses	Old-style welfare council (coordinate, no enforcement power)	Community centers Adult education
	E	F	G	H
EXTERNAL (NONMEMBER)	Lower-class social movements Governmental community projects	Agencies working with street gangs Family service agencies	Regional or community research agency	National health agencies (excluding research)

differences among agencies in different cells. For instance, typically CO organizations aimed externally, at change, and at institutions (e.g., to change the school system) have to be able to mobilize sanctions against the target. On the other hand, those aimed at providing services to individual members (e.g., community centers) have the problem of finding attractive programs to bring people in the door—no question of conflict or of mobilizing sanctions arises in such cases.

In general, *the more change oriented the goals are, the greater the incentives needed by the practitioner and his agency to accomplish these goals.* (Of course, incentives can come from within the target or client group, e.g., an alcoholic may strongly desire to be cured of his alcoholism.) Furthermore, *the more member oriented an organization is, the greater the likelihood of a consensus on action,* because the act of joining implies some agreement about goals. Member-oriented agencies are more likely to use persuasive techniques than nonmember-oriented organizations (who

must use appeals to self-interest or sanctions). Finally, *the more institution oriented the target is, the more likely the bonds of organization are not solidaristic—based on the emotional attachments between agent and client—and the more likely they are based on exchange relations, on criteria of institutional rationality.*

These dimensions also relate to the problems of organizational maintenance in the face of attempts to attain specific goals or to change goals. The constitution of the organization consists of a set of expectations that, if violated, threaten the maintenance and stability of the organization. For example, Peter Clark has discussed the case of a local voluntary organization composed of businessmen interested in taxation and governmental efficiency.[4] The standard activity of the organization was information-gathering and education on different tax and governmental programs. Clark

[4] See "The Chicago Big Businessman as Civic Leader." Unpublished doctoral dissertation, University of Chicago, 1959.

found that when any specific tax legislation or assessment was proposed it was difficult to get the organization to take a definite stand on the proposal. Instead, often a group of businessmen who favored or opposed the tax would form a specific ad hoc committee to lobby for or against the issue. Clark concluded that although the organization was concerned with taxation, any specific piece of legislation tended to have differential effects on members and internal conflict would result if any attempt were made to take a definite stand. Instead of fighting an issue through and creating dissension, members took action outside the organization. Clark's case represents a situation in which the constitution did not allow for change attempts. Similar problems occur in other organizations. The general point is that as an organization begins to change its basic goals, constitutional problems emerge.[5]

The foregoing discussion of dimensions of goal analysis will also be of relevance in the discussion of constituency and target groups that follows.

Constituency and Agency Autonomy

Some CO agencies have the goals of integrating and coordinating major constituents. However, even when agencies have other goals, the question of constituency-agency relations is a focus of organizational constitutions. A pattern of normative expectations develops about consultation, discretion, and

the locus of initiation of agency goals and programs. This pattern is largely a function of the resource dependency of the agency.[6] *To the extent that an agency is heavily dependent on its constituency it is likely to develop a constitution giving little room for discretion.*[7]

Constituency-agency relations are crucial to understanding executive roles. Professional CO role-taking varies in terms of how much and how often the executive must report to the constituency. Professional roles may vary from a situation in which the executive does little more than facilitate constituency decision making to one in which the constituency is consulted seldom, if at all.[8] What determines these roles?

Three factors (excluding personality style) appear to be important in affecting the level of executive decision making— the fund-raising base, the role of the constituency in accomplishing organizational goals, and the knowledge base differential between constituency and staff.

1. *The more routinized and relatively independent of the constituency the agency's fund-raising base is, the less likely the staff is to consult with and involve the constituency*

---

[5]On the succession of goals in organizations, see David L. Sills, "The Succession of Goals," in Amitai Etzioni, ed., *Complex Organizations* (New York: Holt, Rinehart & Winston, 1954), pp. 146–158. See also Mayer N. Zald and Patricia Denton, "From Evangelism to General Service: On the Transformation of the Y.M.C.A." *Administrative Science Quarterly*, Vol. 8, No. 2 (September 1963), pp. 214–234.

[6]For one treatment of the problem of organizational autonomy see Charles Perrow, "Organizational Prestige: Some Functions and Dysfunctions," *American Journal of Sociology*, Vol. 66, No. 4 (January 1961), pp. 854–866. See also, Selznick, *Leadership in Administration*, pp. 120–133.

[7]Note that the proposition does not apply to the formal or stated charter of the organization alone, but rather to the expectations that develop out of the actual dependency bases of the organization. The point is important, for many organizations, notably business corporations, formally "decentralize" and on paper sometimes resemble what are called "federated" systems. Yet through the judicious, and sometimes injudicious, use of central power these corporations never really build up a constitution of federalism.

[8]See Rein and Morris, op. cit.; and Sills, op. cit.

systematically in decision making. Thus, agencies that have an immediate and vital appeal to the public (such as the national voluntary health organizations) or have legal and routinized access to funds are less likely than others to have broad participation by their constituencies in decision making.

2. *When the agency is directly dependent on its constituency for achieving organizational goals, greater attention will be paid to constituency wishes and participation.* An agency is dependent on the constituency for achieving goals when its prestige and influence must be utilized to mobilize other segments of the community. After all, the only moderate prestige and influence of CO professionals is usually insufficient to generate widespread community support. An agency is also dependent on the constituency when it is their change that is sought (when the constituency and the target group are the same).[9] Attention to the constituency may be only formal or surface; nevertheless it affects the conduct of office.

3. *The greater the knowledge differential between staff and constituency, the more likely the staff will be given autonomy in the exercise of their work and the more likely the constituency will be consulted only on "boundary" conditions—changes that affect the relation of the agency to the community.* In general, the more decisions are defined as "professional" problems, the less likely are constituencies to be involved.

It would be wrong, however, to assume that an executive cannot influence agency-constituency relations. Constitutions are not immutable! Furthermore, the executive might not want autonomy; the constituency might represent a resource that can be cultivated usefully.

Constituency Characteristics and Agency Operation

The constitution of an organization emerges and is maintained partly to satisfy the constituency. At the same time that they give the organization its continuing mandate, the characteristics of the constituency may lead to a limit on goals and means.

Class Basis of Constituency. A large body of literature testifies to the greater difficulty of involving working-class individuals in voluntary organizations as compared to middle- or upper-class persons.[10] Extending these findings to CO agencies, the following proposition emerges: *the lower the socioeconomic status of the constituency, the more difficult it is likely to be to maintain their interest and participation.* In other words, the CO practitioner with a lower socioeconomic class constituency will devote more of his energies to motivating the constituency than he would in other organizations.

Not only is level of participation affected by the socioeconomic basis of the constituency, but there is some reason to think that the style of participation is also likely to differ. In general one would expect that *when a CO agency aimed at changing some aspect of the community has a middle- and upper-class constituency it will be more likely to attempt to gain its*

---

[9]It should be clear, however, that there is an analytic difference between a target group and a constituency. A target group or institution is the change object of the organization. The target group is not directly involved in the choosing of means, the personnel, or the goals of the agency. Target groups become part of the constituency when they become part of the decision-making apparatus of the agency.

[10]For a careful summary of much of this literature and an attempt to understand the dynamics of the phenomenon, see William Erbe, "Social Involvement and Political Activity," *American Sociological Review,* Vol. 29, No. 2 (April 1964), pp. 198–215.

*ends through persuasion, informal negoti-
ation, and long-range harmonizing of
interests.* On the other hand, *the more an
organization has an essentially lower-class
basis, the more it will resort to direct
action, open propaganda, and agitation*
(when it takes action at all).[11] First, the
higher up one goes in the stratification system, the more likely it is that the constituency has easy access to office-holders,
can command respect from them, and can
threaten use of sanctions that the target
person will recognize. Thus, the more élite
the constituency the more likely it is that
informal negotiations will take place and
can be fruitful.

Second, people from higher socioeconomic groups begin having organizational
experiences from an earlier age. The higher
up in the status system, the more likely the
constituency will have had experience in
organizational negotiation, the more time
they can comfortably spend in organizational participation, and the more rewarding to them is such participation.[12]

Obviously, the CO practitioner must take
these factors into account. The attempt to
get concrete results, the amount of time
spent in agitational versus more neutral

activities, and the mechanisms of involving
the constituency will each differ depending
on the class base of the constituency.

*Organizational versus Individual Con-
stituencies.* For many CO agencies the
crucial characteristic of the constituency is
not so much that of its class base but
whether its basis is individual or organizational. All else being equal, *the more an
agency has a constituency made up of
agencies, the harder it is to get commitment
to an action program that does not have
widespread societal consensus and the
more likely the agency is to serve as a
clearing-house for information and coordination.*[13]

One of the advantages to a CO agency of
having a constituency comprised of organizations is that it then has a built-in multi-
plier effect. That is, those programs that are
agreed to can be disseminated through a
wide range of other organizations—the
population that can be reached is greater.
On the other hand, a constituency made up
of organizations requires the agency to
work through the problem of new and
extreme programs with all constituent
agencies. If the new program threatens the
autonomy of the organizations or challenges *their* constituencies, there will be little incentive for commitment. Because of
the desire to protect organizational autonomy, agencies comprised of organizations
are more likely to have a structure similar
to a representative assembly, which permits

---

[11]See the discussion in Herbert J. Gans, *The Urban
Villagers: Group and Class in the Life of Italian-
Americans* (New York: Free Press of Glencoe, 1962),
especially chap. 5, pp. 104–120. The necessity of
active and direct modes of expression in the appeal to
lower socioeconomic groups is one of the essential
elements in Saul Alinsky's approach to CO.

[12]Catherine V. Richards and Norman A. Polansky
have shown that among adult women, those who participated in organizations as adolescents and whose
parents also participated were more likely to participate in voluntary associations than those who did
not have either of these characteristics in their
background. The over-all rate of parent and adolescent
participation is, of course, directly related to socioeconomic status. See "Reaching Working-class Youth
Leaders," *Social Work*, Vol. 4, No. 4 (October 1959),
pp. 31–39.

---

[13]The author has less confidence in this proposition
than in the previous one. For one thing, it may cause
comparison of disparate organizations, for instance,
neighborhood block clubs with welfare councils.
Ideally, to test such a proposition one would take CO
agencies in similar types of communities with similar
types of goals and see if variation in their constituencies
did in fact lead to different types of action programs. Such a design might be difficult to realize.

veto powers, while agencies comprised of individuals are more likely to have either straight majority rule or an oligarchic structure.[14]

The "all else being equal" clause in this proposition is especially important. If the organizations have joined the CO agency with the expectation that extreme programs would be proposed, then such an agency might be as likely as one comprised of individuals to initiate new and extreme programs rapidly. Thus, some community councils organized for purposes of neighborhood protection and development have been constituted out of organizations and still have initiated "radical" action programs.

TARGET GROUPS AND CO PRACTICE

The purpose of the professional and his agency is to improve the functioning of groups, individuals and communities. To do this he attempts to change individuals and the relationships among individuals and groups. His goal may be reached not only by changing relationships and attitudes, but by changing the facilities—hospitals, schools, trading associations—used by people in carrying out their daily lives. Thus, he may be attempting to mobilize the community for a relatively specific substantive proposal and the target group may only be changed insofar as it has reached a fairly specific decision. Values, norms, and social relations may not be changed; only questions of efficiency may be involved. Differential diagnosis of target problems has important organizational implications. Let us examine two aspects of agency-

target relations—the role definitions of line workers and the tactics of institutional penetration.

Role Definitions of Line Workers

The problem can be posed as a question: Should line workers be substantive specialists or should they be "multipurpose" workers coached by substantive specialists? Should the worker be a technical specialist, knowledgeable in the specific problems of the community, or should he be a generalist, knowledgeable about how to relate to communities?

At least partly the answer depends on the extent to which the target group accepts and is committed to the purposes of the agency. *To the extent that an organization's goals are accepted and its functions in a community understood, a specialist organization can most efficiently communicate information and methods that can then be utilized by a target group.* However, *to the extent that members of a target group are suspicious of an agency, communication channels will be blocked.* In such a situation a generalist will be required whose main job is to establish an organization-target group linkage. As that linkage is established, it then becomes possible to reintroduce specialists, now trading on the generalist's relations.[15]

But what of the qualifications of such multipurpose workers? Who should they

---

[14]See Rein and Morris, op. cit., for a discussion of the problems of agencies whose constituencies are made up of organizations.

[15]See Albert Mayer and associates in collaboration with McKin Marriott and Richard Park, *Pilot Project India: The Story of Rural Development in Etawah, Uttar Pradesh* (Berkeley: University of California Press, 1958). See also Elihu Katz and S. N. Eisenstadt, "Some Sociological Observations on the Response of Israeli Organizations to New Immigrants," *Administrative Science Quarterly*, Vol. 5, No. 1 (June 1960), pp. 113–133; and Gans, op. cit., chap. 7, pp. 142–162.

be? To the extent that the target group is difficult to penetrate because of problems of distrust, and to the extent that major sanctions are not controlled by the organization, the most effective generalist is likely to be one who minimizes social distance at the same time that he represents the "ego ideal" of target group members. "Personalistic" as opposed to "professional" criteria become crucial.

As many field workers have noted in working with lower-income ethnic groups and delinquent gangs, and as Katz and Eisenstadt have suggested for Israeli administrative agencies, the overcoming of distrust may require the worker to appear to identify more with the problems and perspective of the target group than with the agency. As the level of distrust decreases, however, the target group becomes amenable to the norms and procedures of the agency and more normal agency-client relations can be established. Thus, in order to be effective, CO agencies must evaluate the extent to which target groups are receptive to their policies. Staff role definitions must be fitted to this diagnosis. Sometimes, however, CO diagnosis involves the question of how one makes specific decisions, not how one reaches a group. When the target question switches to penetrating institutional decision centers, a new set of diagnostic criteria becomes relevant.

Tactics of Institutional Penetration

The legacy of Floyd Hunter and C. Wright Mills to the practice field can be summed up as "to the power structure!" Many CO workers, civil rights workers, and others who are trying to change communities seem to be saying: "If you want something done you must get the power structure behind you." If community organizers followed this dictate, they would find themselves pursuing a chimera. If they tried to mobilize the same élite on every decision, they would fail both to mobilize them and to attain their objectives.

Furthermore, the power structure is often relatively irrelevant to many decisions, for it is often isolated and in an official decision center or is most sharply affected by the sentiments of that most diffuse of all decision centers, the voting populace. Thus, the job of analyzing decision centers requires the most precise diagnosis of the chain of influence and mechanism of decision making for each specific decision.

If the decision involves a referendum, different kinds of issues appeal to different groups. Machiavellian advice to a community organizer interested in promoting school bonds is to see that the middle class is overrepresented (as it is when the turnout is low), since they tend to vote for school funds. On the other hand, when, as in some states, referenda are held on welfare matters, the lower class should be motivated to vote, for they tend to vote "yes" on these measures.[16]

In mobilizing a target group, the CO practitioner and agency must face squarely the dilemma of their relative commitment to "the democratic process" versus their commitment to specific social values. The advice given above obviously conflicts with faith in the democratic process. This is a dilemma not only for CO practitioners, but for all advocates of social welfare. However, in part the problem of whether to pursue specific goals regardless of an idealized conception of the democratic process

---

[16]For a study that looks at the relation of income and ethnicity to "public" and "self-interest" voting on referenda see James Q. Wilson and Edward C. Banfield, "Public Regardingness as a Value Premise in Voting Behavior," *American Political Science Review*, Vol. 58, No. 4 (December 1964), pp. 876–887.

resolves itself according to agency goals and mandates. For instance, the more specific and concrete an organization's objectives and the greater the demands on the organization by the constituency, the more likely it is that workers' concerns about "process" will be relegated to the background.

EXTERNAL RELATIONS

In attempting to mobilize a target group, reach a specific objective, or integrate services, CO agencies must deal with other agencies. The CO agency may be but one among many and it may be without a mandate to guide, direct, or lead the other agencies. Often a CO agency has as part of its mandate the integration of the disparate institutions, but the mandate may be honored more in the breach.

One of the basic premises of organizational analysis is that only under very special conditions do organizations purposely attempt to decrease their scope, actually admit that they are ineffective, or willingly give up "turf." These special conditions involve low ideological or career commitment to the organization on the part of staff, an increasingly difficult fund-raising problem, and a constituency that increasingly finds better alternative uses of time and money. As a working assumption it is reasonable to assert that most organizations will attempt to maintain autonomy and increase their scope.[17] Even when it is obvious that one agency is more capable of achieving a shared goal than another, it would be rare indeed for the latter to donate

its income for the expansion of the former. And it is rarely obvious that one agency has some superiority over another.

Given the assumption that agencies generally wish to increase autonomy and scope, the integration and coordination of agency policy and programs depend on the enlightened self-interest of the treaty signers—the independent agencies. As a general postulate, coordination, sharing of facilities, and proper integration are likely to take place only when both of the autonomous agencies stand to gain. Specific conditions follow.[18]

1. *If two agencies are essentially in a competitive relation to each other for funds, constituency, and staff, full-scale coordination and merger of programs would indeed be unlikely.* (Nor, given the nature of funding processes in which multiple appeals increase the total amount of funds available for the welfare sector, would a merger of identities necessarily lead to a more effective welfare economy.)

2. *The greater the marginal cost of coordination and integration or the lower the marginal profit, the less chance of integration and coordination of programs.* (Cost and profit do not necessarily refer to money; there can be costs of time and energy, for instance.) It follows that coordination will

---

[17]In addition to Perrow, op. cit., see Norton E. Long, "The Local Community as an Ecology of Games," *American Journal of Sociology*, Vol. 64, No. 3 (November 1958), pp. 251–261.

[18]This discussion draws on the following articles, which have recently discussed problems of co-ordination and interorganizational relations: William J. Reid, "Interagency Co-ordination in Delinquency Prevention and Control," *Social Service Review*, Vol. 38, No. 4 (December 1964), pp. 418–428; Eugene Litwak and Lydia Hylton, "Inter-Organizational Analysis: A Hypothesis on Coordinating Agencies," *Administrative Science Quarterly*, Vol. 6, No. 4 (March 1962); Sol Levine and Paul E. White, "Exchange as a Conceptual Framework for the Study of Inter-Organizational Relationships," *Administrative Science Quarterly*, Vol. 5, No. 4 (March 1961), pp. 583–601.

most easily be achieved on problems that are least expensive to both parties. Coordination is more easily achieved on a specific case than on over-all programs.

3. *The greater the organizational commitment to a fixed program or style of operation, the less likely the coordination and integration.* Agencies develop commitment to programs on ideological grounds and, because the programs help the agency to solve problems of identity, they thereby become part of the organizational character.[19] To the extent that a program must be changed by a merger, the costs mount.

These three propositions state the conditions that impede coordination and integration. Stated somewhat differently, they indicate conditions contributing to coordination, cooperation, and integration:

1. *The greater the symbiotic relation between agencies, the more likely the coordination.* For instance, interestingly enough, the police and an agency working with delinquent gangs have more to gain from cooperating than a family service agency and a street work agency. The latter agency can actually contribute only occasionally to aiding the family service agency in its work with its case load and, at best, the family service agency can help "cool out" an offender. On the other hand, the police and the street worker have a strong symbiotic relation. The street worker gains status with the boys with whom he is working by being able to negotiate with the police, while the police have fewer problems with the gang. The same principle applies to the relation of membership groups to the "Ys," of mental hospitals to general hospitals, and so on.

2. *The greater the marginal profits, the more likely the coordination.* Sometimes funds are granted only to cooperating agencies. If the funds are great enough they overcome the costs of integrating or joint planning. Marginal profits of coordination may be seen in the face of a crisis in facilities. When programs become overburdened, when facilities are inadequate and multiple expansion funds are not available, a negotiated settlement may allow specialization between agencies, reducing overall financial needs and making coordination profitable.[20]

There is also some evidence to suggest that overlapping constituencies contribute to such coordination.[21] *The less constituencies overlap, the more likely it is that the constituencies are either neutral to or distrust each other and thus the longer it will take and the more difficult it will be to gain cooperation.*

This last point suggests that external relations may also be related to the concepts discussed earlier; that is, costs and profits are defined in the context of and affected by organizational constitutions and goals, constituency, and target groups.

CONCLUSIONS

In this paper one part of a sociology of CO practice has been developed—the organizational analysis of CO agencies. In each section several testable propositions were presented about the conditions under which

---

[19]On the concept of organizational character see Selznick, *Leadership in Administration.*

[20]See Robert Morris, "New Concepts in Community Organization Practice," *Social Welfare Forum, 1961* (New York: Columbia University Press, 1961), pp. 128–146.

[21]Ibid.

different kinds of CO agency problems and processes arise. However, this paper has not presented a complete analysis of CO agencies. First, there are not enough empirical studies of these agencies to permit this. Second, the internal role structure of agencies has not been dealt with. Nevertheless, the writer is convinced that analysis along these lines will be valuable for both sociol-ogy and CO practice. For sociology the reward will be rich in that studies of sets of organizations will permit an examination of problems of mobilizing support and community consensus; for community organization the reward will be rich in that an analytic and differential basis will be developed by which to assess CO agencies and evaluate practice roles.

6.

Rosalie Bakalinsky

THE SMALL GROUP IN COMMUNITY ORGANIZATION PRACTICE

Community organization, within social work, has not as yet developed a comprehensive theory of its practice. Part of the problem has been difficulty in defining the essential nature of such practice for it incorporates a wide range of activities with diverse population groups. Rothman (this volume) has conceptualized three different app-roaches or models of community organization, each implying a different set of goals, practitioner roles and strategies of intervention. While a community organizer may tend towards one model over another, an indispensable aspect of his or her practice will be the creation, maintenance and influence of small groups in order to achieve certain objectives. The practitioner may at one or different times be engaged in forming a neighborhood group of low income residents, in staffing an agency board, or in establishing a planning group whose purpose is either the creation of a new service or coordination of existing services. It would seem then, that knowledge and skill in work with small groups would be an important requirement of any type of community organization practice.

While groups in community organization may differ on goals, structure and composition, there are certain characteristics and processes which can be considered generic to all types of groups. This paper will attempt to discuss some of the significant features of groups and their implications for community organization practice. Where implications cannot be readily drawn, questions will be raised which might suggest directions for further exploration and study.

GROUP STRUCTURE AND DYNAMICS: SELECTED FEATURES

The use of groups in any change effort assumes the belief that the group is a more effective or more desirable means of achieving that change than is individual effort. In many organizations, sheer necessity or practicality impels the use of group effort to achieve its goals. Furthermore, democratic values dictate that "rule by the many" is more desirable (even though it may not be more effective or efficient) than "rule by the one."

To create or develop a highly effective group out of an aggregate of individuals is no simple task. Groups, like individuals, have their own unique characteristics and personalities. They can be mature or immature, functional or dysfunctional. As individuals need to be nourished and nurtured to maturity, so do groups. While many factors impact a group's development and functioning, four dimensions will be highlighted for discussion: group size, composition, cohesiveness and leadership. These dimensions can be considered variables which affect or determine the degree to which the group will be functional and effective in attaining its goals.

As a frame of reference for the discussion it might be useful to clarify what is meant by a highly functional, mature group. Bradford (1976) has identified the following characteristics:

1. Members are highly involved in the group and share responsibility for its operation.
2. Members assume responsibility for their own behavior and for its effect on both the group task and on the other members.
3. There is an atmosphere of trust and concern which allows members to express ideas, feelings and fears.
4. Conflict is neither suppressed nor repressed. Diversity of opinion is expected and encouraged.
5. Communication is free, open and non-defensive.
6. There is a willingness and capability to

examine and evaluate the group's functioning (Bradford, 1976, pp. 29–32).

These criteria are considered essential for maximum group productivity and high member satisfaction.

Group Size

The dimension of size presents a dilemma for the community organizer working with any task or problem-solving group. Research has indicated that the optimum size of a group is from five to seven (Hartford, 1971, pp. 168–169). This range allows for fuller participation and involvement and therefore is more satisfying to all members. As the size increases there is less participation; "the most active participants become more active, while the least active become less active and may even become silent" (Hartford, 1971, p. 165). Larger groups tend to encourage aggression, competition and inconsideration among some members. Furthermore, increase in size requires more formal group structure, greater need for coordination of group tasks and activities, and more time to reach agreement or consensus.

On the other hand, studies have shown that larger groups (that is, of about twelve to fifteen) are more effective in solving complex problems.

Groups may have a greater possibility of accuracy in problem solving because of the greater number of checks and balances. There is the possibility of greater variety of opinion and more ideas if the focus of the group is on some cognitive task (Hartford, 1971, p. 167).

The difficulty is one of assuring a small enough group that will provide the members with a sense of satisfaction and a feeling that their participation is important to the group while at the same time assuring there are sufficient resources within the group to enable task and goal attainment.

In community organization practice, the agency board is one area in which the dilemma of size is most apparent. The number of persons included on a board is determined by many factors: interest in the agency, financial contribution or access to needed funds, representation of significant elements in the agency's constituency, and so on. Frequently members are added because they enhance the prestige and status of the board and agency. These factors, while necessary considerations, can increase the size of the board beyond the optimum. Of perhaps greater significance is the tendency not to remove board members who have proven themselves to be dysfunctional. Rather, the inclination is to add new members. Houle (1960) has written

Sometimes it is necessary to enlarge a board, but the ineffectiveness of the present membership is not very good grounds for doing so. The net result is often a big ineffective board rather than a small ineffective board—and ineffectiveness grows worse as it grows larger (p. 28).

The agency board was used as an illustration; the variable of size has similar implications for other community organization groups. The point at which it is best not to add another member to a group, even though he may contribute a valuable resource, is a question that merits further study.

Group Composition

In selecting members for a group, descriptive and behavioral attributes of potential members are important considerations. Descriptive attributes refer to a position an individual occupies within a classificatory group. Age, sex, ethnicity, education, occupation, etc., are examples of descriptive attributes. Behavioral attributes refer to the way in which an individual behaves in a position. The compromiser, competitor,

evaluator, harmonizer, etc., are examples of behavioral attributes (Pincus and Minahan, 1973, pp. 204–205). Homogeneous descriptive attributes facilitate communication, interaction and compatibility among members. Heterogeneous behavioral attributes increase the possibility that members will perform both group task and maintenance roles. The degree of homogeneity and heterogeneity on both descriptive and behavioral characteristics is a key question in group composition. Research has shown that problem-solving groups ". . . with heterogeneous behavioral attributes produce a higher proportion of high quality, acceptable solutions than do homogeneous groups" (Pincus and Minahan, 1973, p. 206).

In community organization, high value is placed on citizen, consumer or client participation in the development and delivery of services that are important to them. A planning, task or advisory group that is comprised of the ethnic minority client or consumer, the professional expert and other important community figures (descriptive heterogeneity) will encounter problems in the group's internal functioning. To the extent that the community organizer will be successful in creating a group climate in which all members respect and trust each other and feel free to express their ideas and opinions, then the diversity in descriptive attributes will not be dysfunctional. If such endeavor fails, then the diversity will handicap the group's functioning even though there may be high agreement on, and interest in, group goals and tasks.

The maxim of homogeneous descriptive attributes has relevance for organizing low-income, ethnically mixed neighborhoods. Brager and Specht (1973), writing about the primary group phase in community organizing have stated

Social bonds are more easily developed among persons who have similar characteristics and beliefs. Groups composed of people of the same ethnicity, color, class, sex, age, and so forth, will be more cohesive than those in which membership characteristics are disparate. . . . Thus, there may be no alternative in ethically mixed communities but to organize ethnically homogeneous groups which later come together to pursue superordinate goals (p. 128).

Organizing separate ethnic groups within a community runs the risk of increasing the competition that may already exist between them. This may handicap later efforts to bring them together on shared concerns and interests.

The trend towards ethnic affirmation, in contrast to "integration" or "assimilation," further complicates the matter. Ethnic affirmation places high value on difference— difference in attitudes, values and lifestyle. Focus on differences tends to lead to less intimacy, less trust and less cohesion among group members, factors having negative effect on group functioning. Creating ethnically diverse groups, at any stage, may then be most difficult.

At what point in time ethnically mixed groups can be formed for effective problem solving is an important issue warranting further research.

Cohesiveness

Group cohesiveness is reflected by the pride members feel in belonging, by the gratification derived from the group and by coordinated, synergistic group activity or effort. The extent to which members are attracted to the group will determine the extent of its cohesion. A group that fails to coalesce runs the risk of ultimate disintegration and demise.

Hartford (1971), referring to the research reported by Cartwright and Zander has stated that

the individual member's attraction to the group will depend upon four major factors: (1) the incentive nature of the group, its goals, program, size, type of organization, and position in the community; (2) the motivation of the person, his needs for affiliation, recognition, security, and other things he can get from the group; (3) the attractiveness of other persons in the group; and (4) if the group serves as a means for satisfying needs outside of the group (p. 246).

Research has indicated that attraction to a group will increase when a member has prestige, or can potentially obtain it, within the group, and when he or she enjoys acceptance, recognition and a sense of worth by the group. Also, groups in which there are cooperative relationships are more attractive than groups where competitiveness predominates.

The research would indicate that many people volunteer or agree to participate in community organization groups in order to satisfy personal, psychological needs. Even in instances where the primary motivation may be interest in the goals of the group, unless basic psychological needs of acceptance and recognition are satisfied, attraction to the group will decrease. Awareness and assessment of such needs and ability to intervene in the group process to assure their gratification are important prerequisites for the practitioner. Quite often community organizers work with groups as a consultant or on an advisory basis. Freedom to directly intervene in the group process is limited. The equality in relationship power between the members and the practitioner may further limit his or her influence. Thus, the practitioner will have to resort to indirect means through which members' needs can be gratified.

A unique aspect of community organization groups is that in many of them, individuals are members by virtue of the fact that they are representatives of other groups or organizations. In an interagency coordination group, for example, members represent different organizations that frequently are in competition with each other. Competitive relationships could be expected, at least initially, in the coordination group. As was mentioned earlier, competitive relations weakens group cohesion. Creating or developing cooperative relationships would become a critical, albeit difficult, task. An interesting area for further research might be determination of factors or variables that promote cooperative relationships amongst a group of representatives whose surrogate organizations are in competition with each other.

Leadership

One of the most definitive studies on group leadership was conducted by Robert Bales. In summarizing the findings of his research, Hartford (1971) writes

In any group there emerges task or instrumental leadership and socioemotional or affective leadership. The task leadership facilitates the work. It helps to organize and divide the labor, specify the goals, and move the group toward achieving its goals. The affective leadership. . . . focuses on feelings, mediating differences, soothing ruffled tempers, supporting members, and helping them feel good (p. 212).

An important discovery was that it was rare for one person to fulfill both types of leadership roles, but both are essential for group stability and optimum functioning (Bales, 1966, p. 131).

This conception of leadership implies that at any stage in a group's development both roles need to be performed even though one role may be more needed at a particular point in time than another. It is this point that, I believe, has created some confusion among some community organization writers.

Burghardt (1979) has attempted to relate stages of group development, leadership styles and models or strategies of community organization. He appears to believe that task leaders are not as important or valuable as affective leaders in the locality development model because it is ". . . a method that from the start emphasizes process over task, social interaction over concrete goal directions" (Burghardt, 1979, p. 220). The fact that solution of problems is secondary to development of community capacity and integration does not negate the value of task leadership roles. A group that has been created in order to enhance a sense of community pride in its members, and to increase competence in dealing with community problems, has goals, the goals representing some change in the participants or members of the group. An activity that moves the group closer towards attainment of that goal can be considered a task leadership activity. An activity that contributes to group solidarity is an affective leadership activity. Conceivably, one can have a group in which members feel very good being and working together but still lacking in competence; indicating a need for task leadership activity. Similarly, I would argue that in social planning groups, where problem solving takes precedence over process, there is just as much need for affective as well as task leadership. For, unless the group achieves integration and a sense of well-being, it will not be effective as a problem-solving medium.

The confusion might be semantic. Rothman distinguishes locality development and social planning by defining the former as involving process goals and the latter task goals. Process goals refer to the development of community self-help and integration; actual solution of problems is a lesser priority. Task goals refer to actual solution of community problems (Rothman, 1974, p. 26). "Task" and "process" as related to group leadership have a different connotation though there is a conceptual similarity. As has already been noted, task leadership refers to activities that move the group towards goal attainment; affective leadership, towards group integration and maintenance. All groups, whether formed for purposes of changing attitudes or feelings in the participants, or for achieving some change external to the group members, require both types of leadership. Thus, in locality development and social planning groups, both task and process are dimensions of *equal* importance.

Given the validity of this argument, then it is essential that a community organizer maintain an appropriate balance between the two forms of leadership in the groups with which he or she is engaged; and if one or both are lacking, he or she may need to perform the necessary role. Brager and Specht (1973) support this position. In analyzing the instrumental and expressive roles of the community worker they state

Paradoxically, the community worker must attempt to fill either role—or however inconsistent it may seem, both at once—depending on the state of equilibrium (or lack of it) which exists within his group at a particular time (p. 85).

The research on leadership vitiates the concept of the leader as a person with unique or superior qualities or attributes. There is wide acceptance of the idea that leadership is not vested in one person but is shared by all members in the group (Bradford, 1976, pp. 10–14). Many groups in community organization have formal, designated leaders. The committee chairperson, elected or appointed, is frequently referred to as the leader of the group. If the chairperson is perceived by self and others as carrying major responsibility for task and/or affective functions, the risk of a passive, apathetic, ineffective group with disgruntled members is

greatly increased. A crucial responsibility of the chairperson then, is to help group members perform the necessary leadership functions. In other words, the chairperson's role is that of facilitator, not leader.

This raises a dilemma for the chairperson because it implies relinquishment of certain prerogatives as a group member. As a facilitator, the chairperson cannot forcibly advocate one position over another. His or her responsibility is one of encouraging expression of all positions and assuring that all receive equal hearing. Jay (1979), writing on committee meetings, addresses this dilemma and offers a questionable solution. He states

Regardless of whether leadership is in fact a single or a dual function, for our purposes it is enough to say that the chairman's best role is that of social leader. If he wants a particular point to be strongly advocated, he ensures that it is someone else who leads off the task discussion, and he holds back until much later in the argument (p. 264).

Jay suggests that the chairperson can always find opportunity to express his or her preference when summarizing the meeting. Though his point seems to be that it is more important for the chairperson to maintain affective rather than task leadership, the rationale for his position is not clear. Jay's solution to the dilemma is open to question for it assumes that the chairperson ought to adopt one of the two types of leadership roles; an assumption negated by the studies on effective group leadership.

Suffice it to say, however one may conceive of the chairperson's role, it demands much skill in and knowledge of group dynamics. The fact that many chairpersons of community organization groups are not professionally trained or skilled in this area raises the question of their capability to develop a highly productive, effective group.

CONCLUSION

Small groups constitute an ubiquitous element in community organization. Yet, very little of group theory is reflected in both its theory and its practice. One wonders if many committees and other groups flounder because insufficient consideration is given to important aspects of group structure and process. In this paper, only a few components have been discussed. There are others, such as group conflict and its resolution, norm development, decision making, and so on, that are of equal relevance. Given the different nature of client groups, goals and strategies of intervention in community organization, there is need for more rigorous study and research on the application of small group theory within this area of social work practice.

REFERENCES

Bales, R. F. "The Committee Meeting." In William A. Glasser and David L. Sills, eds. *The Government of Associations.* Totowa, New Jersey: The Bedminster Press, Inc., 1966.

Bradford, L. P. *Making Meetings Work.* La Jolla, California: University Associates, 1976.

Brager, G. and H. Specht. *Community Organizing.* New York: Columbia University Press, 1973.

Burghardt, S. "The Tactical Use of Group Structure and Process in Community Organization." In Fred M. Cox, John L. Erlich, Jack Rothman and John E. Tropman, eds. *Strategies of Community Organization,* 3rd ed. Itasca, Illinois: F.E. Peacock Publishers, Inc., 1979.

Hartford, M. E. *Groups in Social Work.* New York and London: Columbia University Press, 1971.

Houle, C. O. *The Effective Board.* New York: Association Press, 1960.

Jay, A. "How to Run a Meeting." In Fred M. Cox, John L. Erlich, Jack Rothman and John E. Tropman, eds. *Tactics and Techniques of Community Practice.* Itasca, Illinois: F. E. Peacock Publishers, Inc., 1977.

Pincus, A. and A. Minahan. *Social Work Practice: Model and Method.* Itasca, Illinois: F. E. Peacock Publishers, Inc., 1973.

Rothman, J. "Three Models of Community Organization Practice." In Fred M. Cox, John L. Erlich, Jack Rothman and John E. Tropman, eds. *Strategies of Community Organization,* 2nd ed. Itasca, Illinois: F. E. Peacock Publishers, Inc., 1974.

7.

Fred M. Cox

**COMMUNITY PROBLEM SOLVING: A GUIDE
TO PRACTICE WITH COMMENTS**

This problem-solving guide was developed by the original editors and their students. Community practitioners will find that the guide directs their attention to a number of factors central to assessing community problems and developing a course of action for attacking them.

There have been a number of efforts to provide a model to guide community organization practice. Murray G. Ross developed a set of principles to guide community organization and a discussion of the roles of the organizer (16, pp. 155–228; 17, pp. 157–231). Ronald Lippitt and his collaborators studied a wide range of planned change efforts, which include efforts at the community level. From this study, they formulated a discussion of the phases of planned change, the role of the change agent, an approach to diagnosis in planned change, and an analysis of the forces operating for and against changes (9). Roland Warren provides a five-stage model of the "development and change of community action systems" (25, p. 315 and pp. 303–39). Robert Perlman and Arnold Gurin offer a "problem solving model" in their study of community organization, prepared under the auspices of the Council of Social Work Education (12, pp. 61–75). This list is by no means comprehensive (19, pp. 504ff.), but it includes those that have been most influential in shaping the present effort.

The guide is ordered sequentially as the factors considered are likely to be encoun-tered in practice. The guide should be used flexibly. The experienced practitioner may not need to explore each point as carefully as one new to a situation. Few will have the opportunity to employ it systematically in every practice context. Nevertheless, we believe the practitioner will find it useful as a reminder of issues that may otherwise be overlooked or questions that provoke thought that may have an important bearing on practice decisions and outcomes. Some practitioners will be confronted with more "givens" and fewer choices than others. A clear understanding of the "givens" as well as the options is crucial for effective practice.

Like most general models, this one may fail to call attention to certain questions of importance in specific situations. Many practitioners will want to refine and elaborate the guide to suit the particulars of the practice situation in which they are involved. In general, however, we believe that the guide can contribute to a more logical and coherent approach to confronting problems in the multiple pressures and confusions of community practice.

THE GUIDE

This section briefly outlines the main categories comprising the guide to community problem solving. It will be followed by a more elaborate commentary that provides further detail about each of the steps in the process. In preparing a problem-solving statement at the outset of a project, the practitioner uses this commentary as a basis for deciding about what to include in the initial analysis.

I. Preliminary Considerations

A practitioner starts out by spelling out certain givens in the intervention situation that serve to structure and shape further actions. Intervention is typically carried out within an agency or organization that establishes the ground rules and gives the worker an assignment (whether specific or broadly conceived) to implement. The sponsoring agency has a preexisting mission and formulates the broad goals that are to be aimed for. It also typically has evolved preferences about strategies and tactics, which the practitioner has to take into account. Within the agency, factors of various kinds color the work: specific decision makers who create policy, lines of authority, norms of operation, and programmatic structures. The practitioner, as an employee of the agency, brings to bear on the assignment personal motivations and capacities, which intersect with the opportunities that are provided in the organizational environment and form a unique meld. Such factors should be made explicit at the outset as part of designing a plan of action.

II. Problems

An early step in all practice entails a problem analysis and needs assessment in order to provide a firm basis for action steps. It is important to identify the type of problem, its location geographically and socially in the system, and its scope, and to determine those who are affected by it. Past change efforts should be clarified so that they can be built upon in an effective way. The practitioner brings to the situation only one per-

spective among others; therefore it is useful to discern the perceptions of those who are participants in the action or who will be affected by it in one way or another.

III. Social Context of the Problem

To gain a meaningful understanding, the problem has to be examined in a sophisticated way. What was the origin of the problem? Can it be explained through some theoretical perspective such as communication blocks, institutional racism, or interorganizational conflict? What structures and factions either maintain or can potentially alleviate it? What are the consequences of taking action or failing to do so for different elements in the community: Who gains and who loses?

IV. Intended Beneficiaries

Who are the people or groups that stand to gain from the intervention? These can be identified with respect to demographics, spacial location, ethnic identity, economic and political standing, and so forth. Cleavages within the beneficiary group should be described, as well as their relationships with various parts of the community system.

V. Goals

The goals of various parties in the situation should be clarified, including the beneficiary system, the agency, and significant others. Based on the overall analysis, the practitioner needs to delineate a set of professional preferred goals, with an order of priority. These should include task goals related to concrete problems and process goals related to community competency and system maintenance.

VI. Strategy

The practitioner needs to go on to design potential strategies to address problem situations. A set of relevant tasks have to be laid out and an action system conceived that is made up of participants and allies. In addition, it is important to identify people and forces who will interfere with or resist the action plan. Needed resources and their availability have to be assayed. In light of this examination a preferred strategy should be outlined.

VII. Tactics

Tactics comprise the mechanics of carrying out a strategy. First there is the question of entry—where to start and with whom? The beginning phase also entails the notion of leverage—what initial actions give the best chance of sustaining the strategy? There exists the important matter of determining how to work interactively with the action system. Specific expectations have to be formulated, including an informal "contract" between the practitioner and those making up the action system. Some implementation steps include training and supporting participants, scheduling actions over time, using resources effectively, and dealing with the opposition in appropriate ways.

VIII. Evaluation

Action in itself is not the essence of intervention. Actions are calculated to bring about beneficial outcomes. It is important in thinking ahead to consider means whereby to examine results in order to determine objectively and empirically whether goals were achieved and to what extent. The practitioner should indicate how the effectiveness of the strategy will be measured, as well as the effectiveness of the tactics. Only in this way will learning be derived concerning the viability of various practice options, thereby improving practice.

IX. Modification, Termination, or Transfer of Action

As an intervention experience nears resolution (as indicated through evaluation), it may be necessary to formulate new goals and strategies in order to move into a next phase. On the other hand, it may be time for the practitioner and agency to withdraw. In that case certain termination actions are necessary, including preparing the action system for the change. Concluding steps may involve transferring responsibility to a new agency, or institutionalizing the results within the community to insure the stability of the change. It might be useful in doing a problem-solving analysis to look ahead and devise a scenario that predicts potential results and suggests terminal actions.

ELABORATIONS[1]

As part of the effort to increase the professional character of community organization practice, we need to develop guidelines for decision making that are grounded upon tested generalities. As our knowledge base expands, it should be possible to rely more heavily on insights drawn from the social and behavioral sciences. The problem in basing decisions on tested knowledge is to find a way to join the hodgepodge which is the reality of community practice and the generaliza-

---

[1] The author acknowledges the contributions made by his colleagues John L. Erlich and Jack Rothman, whose critical comments and suggestions were used extensively in preparing this supplement to the preceding guide.

tions derived from research, which necessarily oversimplify, and select a few factors believed to be of overriding importance.

This problem is a difficult one for at least two reasons. First, our knowledge of what factors are most influential and their effects upon matters of importance to the practitioner, together with the various conditions that affect such cause and effect relationships, is very limited. Typically, we must be content with a combination of practice wisdom and partially tested theory validated under conditions quite different than those faced by each practitioner. For example, conclusions about group behavior are often based on laboratory data rather than field studies.

Second, even when knowledge is very full and based on rigorous study, there are serious problems in applying it. Scientific knowledge is the knowledge of probabilities, of the chances that certain actions or events are likely to be followed by particular consequences. But even a high probability of B being followed by A leaves room for the possibility, in some minority of instances, that A will not produce B. And there are always newly emerging contingencies, the effects of which are unknown, and relatively unique configurations of events and conditions that were not anticipated in the research studies. Thus, even under the best conditions, we must guard against expecting too much from scientific knowledge in guiding practice decisions.

What does the problem-solving guide contribute to this process? First, it suggests the major types of information that must be obtained by the practitioner if he or she is to reach informed decisions. Second, it offers the outline of an interconnected set of frameworks within which to collect this information. It does not, however, provide propositions or generalizations to which decisions must be referred; these comments

will suggest some additional sources we have found useful for this purpose. The comments are organized in the same order and under the same headings as the guide above. Wherever possible we relate these comments to the three modes of community organization around which this book is organized.

I. PRELIMINARY CONSIDERATIONS

A. Summary of Assignment

The practitioner provides a brief orientation to the nature of the assignment. If the guide is used for training purposes, the instructor may find this summary particularly useful.

B. Agency

The organization that sponsors the practitioner's work is the agency referred to. Its primary significance is in the possibilities it opens and the constraints it places upon practice.

Social action is typically sponsored by groups of like-minded people who feel generally oppressed by the wider society, are offended by particular governmental decisions or social norms, or share common interests they believe can be achieved more effectively through collective action. The group is held together by some common identity (ethnic or racial characteristics, ideological or cultural similarities, goals, a piece of turf, a shared sense of being oppressed by the larger society). While the sponsor is likely to be homogeneous in some respects, necessary funds may be generated by the group itself or may come from outside sources which may not fully identify with the sponsor, its goals, or, particularly, its methods. This constitutes a problem for some social action groups because, as they engage in controversial activities, they may jeopardize their financial support. On the other hand, to the extent they are homogeneous they are able to pursue their objectives single-mindedly, without undue debate over ends and means.

Locality development may be sponsored by a national government, as in the case of many community development programs in developing countries or in industrialized countries with groups of people isolated from modernization. In such cases there may be conflict between the aims and values of the national government and the people toward whom locality development is directed. Governmental sponsorship, however, may bring otherwise unavailable resources to bear upon problems of underdevelopment. In other cases, locality development is sponsored by groups who seek self-development, often at the initiative and with the continued assistance of some outside group (American Friends Service Committee, a community development program in a land-grant college). Under these conditions, considerable emphasis is placed upon representing various segments of local people and upon their voluntary choice of aims and activities. Given the diversity of people within a locality, problems often arise in finding consensus and in sustaining motivation to work on common problems, but, because these are necessary, the programs chosen represent what local people really want and may be more permanent than those imposed from outside.

Social planning may be sponsored by government at various levels or by private organizations. Backed by constituted authorities or the socially or politically elite, these agencies tend to view their mandate as deriving from the established political process or from democratic procedures in which all citizens are at least nominally free to participate. They typically focus on bringing technical skills to bear upon social

problems and are dependent upon the sources of legitimacy, so that they often overlook the views of those who are the presumed beneficiaries or targets of their planning efforts. Insistent demands for wider participation may create operating problems for social planning agencies. If the agencies can secure substantial support, both financial and political, and highly qualified specialists, however, they may be able to resolve social problems to a greater degree than if support from those affected by the plans were required or fewer resources were available.

The extent to which organizations are bureaucratized has a major impact upon the kinds of tasks they can undertake and the strategies and tactics available to the practitioner. Organizations vary not only in internal structure but in relations with the social environment. They emerge out of the needs of particular constituents, with whom they have a variety of understandings about goals and methods. As noted in the text above, social action agencies are oriented toward their members, while social planning agencies are created by elites to control social problems experienced by nonelites. Zald discusses this with special reference to factors affecting the autonomy of the strategies available to the community organization agency (Article #5). Rein and Morris discuss the effects of the planning organization's goals and structure upon the strategies it employs (13, pp. 127–45).

Parenthetically, it should be noted that formal organizations may be important to the practitioner not only as sponsors of action but as allies in a joint effort or as targets of strategy.

C. Practitioner

The practitioner's activities can be analyzed from two perspectives. The first, which examines the practitioner's motivation, capacity, and opportunity, was developed by faculty members at the University of Chicago's School of Social Service Administration (14). This perspective raises three general questions: (1) To what extent do the personal and professional goals of practitioners coincide, reinforce, compete, or conflict with the goals of those they are trying to help and with those of the sponsoring agency? (2) Does the practitioner have the basic qualities of intelligence, ability to empathize with others, a sense of personal identity, and the special skills and knowledge necessary to operate effectively in a particular community organization assignment? (3) Does the practitioner have the support of the agency, the human and financial resources that are necessary to do the job with a reasonable expectation of effective performance? If there are impediments in the situation, what, if anything, can be done to correct them? Ronald Lippitt and his collaborators give attention to some of these questions (9, pp. 92–99).

The motivation, capacity, and opportunity required will vary with the type of practice and the nature of the sponsoring agency. For example, the practitioner's ideological predilections and world view will affect the motivation to work for various types of agencies and the willingness to use different strategies and tactics. Skills in working with different kinds of people (poor people, local elite) and in using various techniques (making population projections, teaching people how to handle unfamiliar situations) affect the capacity to work in different settings. The types and amounts of resources needed for effective practice vary for agencies with various scopes, goals, and strategies.

Role theory provides perhaps an even more useful perspective for analyzing the practitioner's work. The ambiguity and conflict in role definitions by various persons with whom the practitioner interacts, the discontinuity between the various roles one plays currently and between past and present roles, and the personal strain involved in learning a new role and coping with the problems inherent in role ambiguity, conflict, and discontinuity must be taken into account in understanding the practitioner's behavior and decisions (22, pp. 17–50; 9, pp. 91–126).

II. PROBLEMS

This section of the guide directs the community organization practitioner's attention to an analysis of the difficulties he or she is trying to remedy. The problems of concern are usually social rather than personal, affecting a substantial portion of the people served and out of harmony with their preferences. They may be substantive in character, i.e., problems such as mental illness, insufficient housing, or delinquency, or they may involve process, affecting the way the society, the community, and its institutions are organized, formally or informally, for dealing with social problems. Often the two are closely connected as, for example, when it is assumed that the negative reaction to the mentally ill stems from the lack of community-based institutions for dealing with them—well-organized family care homes, recreation programs, emergency services for coping with personal life crises, etc. Community practitioners are typically concerned with problems of both substance and process.

At this point the guide calls for careful observation and description. Explaining the problem is reserved for the next section. The practitioner describes the kind of problem dealt with as clearly as possible, where it is located, how widely it is distributed among different kinds of people, and the degree to which one group is affected in comparison to another. The practitioner looks at past efforts to improve conditions, who made them, the extent of their successes or failures, and the probable reasons for these outcomes. He or she gives particular attention to differences in perceptions of the problem among the affected groups.

The varying ways in which the problem is perceived will be of particular importance. The agency, various subgroups of the client, and the practitioner may all see the problem a little differently and thus favor different solutions.

In the context of social action, the problem typically will be viewed as one of social injustice—an oppressed minority not receiving its fair share of political, economic, and educational resources, a group that has been deprived of some benefit or has had some social cost inflicted upon it, or a group seeking some benefit for itself at the expense of others for reasons it considers justified. Of increasing importance recently, many negatively regarded groups seek improved status and respect.

In a locality development context, the problem often will be defined as a failure to modernize, to develop the necessary capital and skills to facilitate industrialization at an appropriate rate or to build the necessary services ("infrastructure") needed to support an urbanizing population. The problem may be regarded as opposition to change (strong traditional or new but counterproductive forms of social organization), anomie (languishing social organization), or loss of local autonomy (an organized community losing control to national business, philanthropic, and governmental institutions). A normative view held by some community developers is that the problem stems from the failure of local

democracy, the lack of concern about and a sense of responsibility for local problems.

Social planning agencies tend to define the problem as one or more fairly discrete social problems (mental illness, crime and delinquency, poverty, poorly organized services) for which they seek various technical solutions. The problems with which social planners deal are seen as forms of deviant behavior or social disorganization. Deviant behavior, such as mental illness, delinquency, or child abuse, is at variance with prescriptions for particular social roles. Merton makes a useful distinction between two types of deviant behavior, nonconformist and aberrant, which is particularly appropriate in the light of unrest among women minority groups, gays and students (10, pp. 808–11). The nonconformist announces his or her deviant behavior, challenges the legitimacy of rejected social norms, tries to change norms regarded as illegitimate, and calls upon higher social values as justification for actions. Conventional members of society recognize that the nonconformist is dissenting for disinterested reasons. In contrast, the aberrant individual hides his or her acts from public view, does not challenge the legitimacy of broken norms, tries to escape detection and punishment, and serves personal interests through aberrant behavior.

Social action groups of oppressed people may define their behavior as nonconformist and seek responses from the rest of society that first confirm this definition and ultimately redefine the behavior, prompting the nonconformity as acceptable rather than deviant. For example, those seeking abortion law reform, acceptance of homosexual preferences, or equality in job opportunities may use nonconformist means to secure redefinitions of abortion, homosexual behavior, and equal employment opportunities as nondeviant. Social planners may assist them through legitimate ("conformist") means that are possible within the context of their work—drafting legislation, taking matters to court, enlisting the support of community leaders, and so forth. Social planners may also participate in efforts to redefine the behavior of some deviants who, by this definition, are aberrant but whose crimes are trivial and are not regarded as morally reprehensible, or as victimless. The smoking of marijuana in moderation may increasingly be regarded as a trivial offense at best or a victimless crime at worse. Those who engage in drug abuse, prostitution, gambling, and homosexuality are often hurting no one but themselves. Even where behavior cannot be redefined as acceptable, social planners may assist in relieving exacerbating responses, through plans for bail reform and community care for the mentally ill, for example. Finally, planning services to modify the behavior of deviants, using new techniques such as behavioral modification, will continue to be useful for a number of forms of deviant behavior.

Other social problems are regarded as symptoms of social disorganization, not necessarily involving deviations from prescribed norms but rather reflecting incompatibilities between various parts of a social system, such as different rates of change (for example, technology changes more rapidly than social values). Poverty, housing shortages, water pollution, unemployment, and racial discrimination are often regarded as examples of social disorganization that constitute social problems social planners seek to solve.

Locality development practitioners typically view social problems from this standpoint, focussing on those that retard the maintenance or enhancement of a society or community (sharply increasing birth rates, general apathy, lack of entrepreneurial skills, or a failure of leadership). They are also concerned with the inability of a locality to obtain resources or achieve results from self-help efforts.

Another way of looking at social problems is offered by Arnold Rose (15, pp. 189–99), who defines two perspectives. One, which we will call "disjunctive theory," regards social problems as arising from different meanings being attached to objects that form the context of social interaction or from different values being assigned to the behaviors displayed in relation to those objects. Marijuana (an object) is regarded by some as a potentially dangerous mind-altering drug and by others as a means to a pleasant "high." The smoking of marijuana (behavior in relation to the object) is disvalued by some and enjoyed by others. Poverty in the United States today (a set of objects or conditions) is regarded by some as an unfortunate but inevitable by-product of the free enterprise system and by others as a needless hardship inflicted upon substantial (though decreasing) numbers of people by the economic system. Living in poverty (behavior in relation to that condition) is regarded as avoidable and remediable by individual effort or as essentially irremediable "tough luck" by some and as unnecessary deprivation remediable by collective effort by others. In each case, the problem is regarded as arising from lack of agreement on meanings, values, or both.

The disjunctive theory is often held, at least implicitly, by those practicing locality development and leads to emphasis upon the socialization process, education, and communication. If meanings attached to the same objects differ, efforts can be made to give people "the facts" so that increasingly meanings can be shared. If values associated with particular behaviors conflict, communication between those who disagree may ultimately lead to a greater degree of consensus.

The other perspective Rose calls "conflict theory." From this point of view, social problems are the product of competition for scarce resources (wealth, prestige, power) which results in painful struggles over their distribution, with some being dissatisfied at the outcome.

Conflict theory assumes that values are held in common, that is, most people want the same things and will fight over their distribution, while disjunctive theory assumes that social problems arise from wanting different things or defining the same things in different ways. Those engaged in social action tend to regard social problems from the perspective of conflict theory. Although these practitioners may agree that some secondary grounds for conflict may arise from different meanings being attached to the same events (for example, the lack of a common understanding about the "facts" of poverty), they argue that the basic problem is one of maldistribution (of jobs or income). Social action practitioners try to solve social problems by mobilizing power to induce a redistribution of the valued objects in favor of their constituents or intended beneficiaries.

III. SOCIAL CONTEXT OF THE PROBLEM

A. Origins

The practitioner must take care to interpret the origins of a problem. He or she may understand how a problem came to be by examining its origins, but cannot thereby explain its persistence. Conditions that brought about a problem originally often fade, so that present conditions can only be explained by reference to factors currently operating. The practitioner must search for contemporary conditions that are causally connected with the problem and try to change them.

An effort should be made to understand the historical roots of the problem, particularly if there is a long or significant history affecting the present state of affairs. Coleman discusses what he calls residues of organization and sentiment that build up as people interact in community life and may take the form of collaborative patterns, expressed in latent or manifest forms of social organization or in organized cleavages such as those between rival political parties or ethnic groups. They may also be expressed in sentiments of liking and respect or of hostility (4, pp. 670–95).

B. Theory of the Problem

It is at this point in the analysis that attention is directed toward a search for controlling factors. Assuming that most problems are sustained by a wide variety of factors and that some are more influential than others, the practitioner's task is two-fold: First, one must locate factors that have a major effect on the problem to be corrected. Second, one must choose problems one can reasonably expect to influence, given the time, money, personnel and other resources at one's disposal.

In many social action contexts, the problem will be understood as some form of conflict between "haves" and "have-nots." But greater specificity is required. Which particular interests are pitted against one another? What are the dynamics of the conflict? Are there any aspects of the problem or any facts that do not seem to fit into a conflict perspective? What are the implications for intervention? In many cases of locality development, the problem will be regarded as arising from barriers to communication or different rates of change, i.e., some form of disjunction or social disorganization. But it is important which specific theory or set of theories is selected, for this will exercise an important influence on strategies and tactics chosen. Most practitioners engaged in social planning will consider alternative theories explaining various social problems they are charged with ameliorating. But, again, the specific theory chosen is of great importance in shaping the action taken. If, for example, lower-class male delinquency is conceived of as arising from a lack of legitimate opportunities for success in American society, efforts will be made to expand those opportunities. If, on the other hand, delinquency is thought to arise from psychological problems or parental rejection, efforts will be directed toward various forms of counseling or the strengthening or substitution of parental relations. Or, if the labeling of youngsters as delinquent and the consequent processing through the criminal justice system are thought to be responsible for the perpetuation of delinquent behavior, efforts will be made to decriminalize certain behavior and handle young people who transgress social norms outside the criminal justice system.

Unfortunately, the explanation of the problem chosen by (or more typically implicit in the behavior of) the practitioner is usually limited by the ideology and values of the employing organization or the practitioner. The practitioner should explore his or her own preconceptions and those of the employer to determine what limits such preconceptions place on the choice of an explanation for the problem. However the theory of the problem arises, whether it is implicit in various predisposing values or is more rationally developed, it will have a major influence on the goals and strategies chosen for dealing with the problem.

C. Structural-Functional Analysis of the Problem

The practitioner begins with an assessment of available "theories of the problem." One selects the most reliable theories, and within them the factors that are both potent and potentially controllable. The next step is careful observation of the particular social problem in its context, collecting information within the framework of the theories and hypotheses selected earlier. The outline suggests that both the impact of various factors on the social problem in question and the effect of the problem on these factors be assessed. For example, we might identify particular social structures (schools, employers) that systematically deny opportunities to persons of lower socioeconomic or ethnic minority status, thus creating discontent, delinquent behavior, and so forth. We might then show the impact of such behavior on schools, ethnic minorities, and so forth, emphasizing the differential effects on various groups. This, of course, has implications for which groups, individuals, or organizations may be recruited into organized efforts to alleviate the problems.

Two useful terms in this section of the commentary are functional and dysfunctional: The functional consequences of action strengthen and unify social systems; dysfunctional consequences produce conflict or threaten disruption of existing social patterns. However, these terms should not be confused with "good" and "bad." Functional consequences can perpetuate what is, from the practitioner's perspective, an undesirable system, such as patterns of racial discrimination in housing and employment. Likewise, dysfunctional consequences may be exactly what the practitioner desires. For example, the early sit-ins, in addition to disrupting preexisting patterns of race relations, tended to enhance the self-esteem of black people and provide experience in contentious organized action.

IV. INTENDED BENEFICIARIES

The "client" is defined as the intended beneficiary of the practitioner's activities. It may be a group of people, a formal organization, or a population category. Clients can be analyzed in terms similar to other forms of social organization. Some of the factors that may be most important are outlined in the guide. The major implication of this section is that the beneficiaries must be identified and understood both in their context, i.e., their relations to other social phenomena, and in their internal structure. We must also be sensitive to changes that have taken place in the group and the reasons for them.

The definition of intended beneficiaries forces the practitioner to be clear about whom he or she is trying to help and to differentiate them from others who are regarded in more instrumental terms. There was a time when it was conventional for the community organizer to say that the client is the community. This rhetoric tends to hide the fact that particular actions may benefit some, harm others, and have little effect on still others. The suggested definition makes the practitioner consider whose interests will be sacrificed last if decisions must be made requiring that someone pay a price. It also demands that the practitioner consider how much to expect others to "pay" for the sake of the intended beneficiaries and decide whether the price is justifiable.

If they are a group of individuals with strongly held common interests that can be rather precisely defined, the practitioner will have little difficulty in knowing what benefits to work for on their behalf. On the other hand, one is likely to have difficulty in gaining allies and support for the group. If they are a heterogeneous group with common interests that can be defined only at the most general level, the practitioner probably will have trouble in defining precisely what to aim for. The chances of alienating some faction of the clientele are increased, but the group is likely to be much more inclusive, and thus the practitioner will have less difficulty in gaining needed outside support.

As Rothman notes (Article #1), the beneficiary group is viewed differently in the several contexts of practice. In locality development, they are citizens and participants in local problem solving. In social planning, they are consumers and recipients of services. In social action they are victims of oppression and employers or constituents of the practitioner.

The kind of beneficiaries one is able to serve is limited, in important ways, by the type of organization that employs one. That is, it is most difficult for a practitioner to give primacy to the interests of a group that is not the primary beneficiary of his or her employer. Blau and Scott have developed a typology of organizations based on the identity of the groups that are the primary beneficiaries of organizations (2, pp. 42–57). The main implication for practice is that the practitioner experiences grave difficulties in making clients out of groups other than those that are naturally the primary beneficiaries of the type of organization employing him. For example, the primary beneficiary of a mutual benefit association is its members. If practitioners employed by, say, a labor union define some nonmembers as the client—perhaps the people living in an impoverished neighborhood—they are likely to run into difficulties with members who resent the diversion of their dues for purposes not directly related to their welfare. Community practitioners employed by such agencies as public assistance bureaus sometimes experience difficulties when they select goals with which the public is out of sympathy. Part of the reason for these difficulties is a failure to recognize the true character of such social service agencies as commonweal organizations whose prime beneficiary is the general citizen instead of, as commonly believed, service organizations whose primary beneficiary is the clientele.

V. GOALS

At some point in his or her work, the practitioner must define as clearly as possible the particular goals to be achieved with the beneficiary. Lack of clarity may lead to goal displacement, i.e., the unintended replacement of goals by new, often unrecognized objectives. Under some conditions—when the situation is very unstable, when there is little experience to guide action, or when knowledge of aims would help those opposed to them—it may be necessary to be vague in public statements or to move toward goal definition through a process of successive approximation. Many other factors also lead to goal displacement—insufficient resources to pursue multiple goals, factional differences in interests, procedures which come to be valued by those who benefit from them, and so forth. Precise goal definition is one defense against goal displacement, however, and provides some criteria against which results can be measured. Resistance to goal displacement should not be used as an excuse to avoid adopting new goals when old ones have been achieved or are no longer appropriate, or new resources make it possible to add goals.

The practitioner must take into account not only his or her personal objective but also the views of the sponsoring organization, the participants, and other groups whose support is needed or whose resistance or objections must be anticipated. It is not necessary to accommodate the interests of the opposition or of those who are largely indifferent to or unaffected by the action, but one must do so for those whose cooperation, whether as active collaboration or passive awareness and the absence of hindering responses, one must have. Those whose interests must be taken into account if the practitioner is to achieve his or her objectives are called the "action system." (This term is used in the guide under the heading "Strategy.")

As suggested above, various groups have different *goals*, attach varying *importance* to particular goals, and have contrasting sets of *priorities*. Factions within groups may also differ in these ways. In taking these differences into account, the practitioner may decide on a strategy of "something for everyone," or may begin with one easily achieved goal of fairly high importance to all elements in order to build confidence in the organization's capability. One may develop some other rationale for selecting goals, but information about the relative priorities and salience of the goals of different factions is essential to a reasoned decision (11, pp. 25–31).

Social problems may reside in a group's relations with its environment (inadequate police protection or unresponsive public officials) or among its members (uncoordinated activities, low morale, lack of commitment). Goals are of two parallel kinds. For example, a welfare council may appeal for additional public funds for a child care center or try to develop support for a human relations commission. These are commonly referred to in the literature as "task goals."

Other goals affect the maintenance and enhancement of the organization (resolving destructive factional rivalry or transforming member apathy into involvement and commitment). These are called "process goals." In general, both types of goals must be served, but at particular times one type may be more important than another. At one time it was generally believed that the community practitioner should pursue only process goals, that is, be concerned exclusively with facilitating or "enabling" clients to achieve self-defined goals. Rothman argues persuasively that the practitioner need not be limited in this manner (18, pp. 24–31).

VI. STRATEGY

Perfect rationality (or anything approaching it) is unattainable in most practice situations. Computer technology may enable some to come a bit closer. But most of us must, as Herbert Simon puts it, "satisfice" rather than "maximize" the efficiency and effectiveness of our decisions (20, p. xxv).

However, some practitioners approach questions of strategy with predetermined formulas, agency traditions, and little imagination. While it is not feasible to consider every possibility and identify the single best way to achieve objectives, it does not follow that one strategy is as good as the next. We ask the practitioner to consider at least two good possibilities and exercise judgment in choosing the best one.

Perhaps more than any other activity, strategy development offers the practitioner an opportunity for creativity. In applying the guide, he or she sketches each strategy, outlining the minimum tasks required to achieve success; the necessary elements of the action system; the resistance (opposition), interdependence (entanglements),

and interference (competition and indifference) forces that may be encountered; and the plans to handle them (9, pp. 71–89). Finally, the practitioner evaluates his or her ability to carry them out and develops a rationale for choosing between the various strategies being considered. As a general approach to decision making this applies to all types of practice. However, the relative emphasis given to various tactics (research, client participation, confrontation with organizations and their leaders) will vary with the model of practice used.

To the extent that success depends upon a correct theory of the problem and an effective strategy, success may be limited by the choices permitted by the elites or the political process. Because social planning strategies normally depend upon the effective manipulation of large-scale bureaucracies, success may also depend heavily on whether the strategy chosen can be effectively administered. And finally, because those whose actions are required for success—the functionaries and the targets— are not ciphers but people with interests and values that guide what they will respond to and what they will do, strategies that assume values about which there is little consensus or which assume a nonexistent community of interests are likely to enjoy limited success.

Some recent analyses suggest that strategies that operate as much as possible in a way analogous to a competitive market situation are most likely to succeed. They maximize individual choices and allow for individual differences. They require a minimum of bureaucratic complexity, especially detailed rules and numerous functionaries to enforce or monitor compliance. It has been suggested that this is the reason for the failure of such programs as the War on Poverty, the success of Social Security, and the potential of income maintenance programs based on negative income tax principles (7).

VII. TACTICS

Strategy shades imperceptibly into tactics. The inspiration for much of this part of the guide comes from Lippitt and his colleagues (9). Among the questions the practitioner is asked to consider are: Where is it possible to gain a foothold in the targets? At what point are efforts likely to be most effective? For example, the practitioner may have access to other practitioners working in low- or middle-echelon positions in a target organization. His or her analysis, however, may lead to the conclusion that, to achieve the objective, the practitioner must gain access to the top executive. One may, therefore, bypass colleagues in the target organization and approach a member of one's board with the necessary social and political contacts to gain the ear of the target agency executive.

In order to avoid misunderstandings, it is important for the practitioner to communicate with key people in the action system (those whose cooperation is needed to carry out the strategy) so that they may develop common ideas about such things as definition of the problem, objectives, approaches, roles each participant will perform, and amount of time each participant will commit to the endeavor. The resulting set of agreements is referred to as the contract. Although the concept is borrowed from the law, it does not imply legal or even written form. The expectations must be as clear and unambiguous as possible, and all necessary participants must understand and commit themselves to the terms of the contract.

In carrying the plan into action, it may be necessary to train and support participants who feel more or less uncertain about what they are doing. This is particularly relevant for those who are inexperienced in the sort of activities required by the contract. The timing of various actions must be carefully planned. Resources of several kinds may require difficult coordination—it may be necessary to induce competing professionals to work together or to provide the press with newsworthy events involving large numbers of people so that politicians will take the action system's demands seriously.

It is desirable to consider an "action-reaction-action pattern" borrowed from Alinsky (1). We refer to these patterns when one group makes a move, intended to elicit a response from an adversary, that makes possible further action to achieve objectives that could not have been otherwise undertaken. For example, a group might leak information to an adversary that it plans a massive disruption of the adversary's business. The expected response is an offer to negotiate which, in turn, makes it possible to obtain concessions favorable to the group that would not have been secured by an initial request for negotiations. Such tactics depend on credibility; if the adversary does not believe that there is a genuine threat, it is not likely to negotiate.

The practitioner should anticipate that some form of opposition to the program undertaken by the action system may emerge and make plans to handle it. Under some circumstances, no such opposition will develop—organizing a council on aging or applying for funds from the federal government to mount programs for the aging should arouse no controversy or opposition. If insurmountable opposition can be expected, however, plans should be changed unless the practitioner is deliberately trying to heighten awareness of impotence and stimulate anger as a prelude to other, perhaps stronger forms of action. If opposition is inevitable, a variety of approaches is available to cope with it in ways that may further the action system's objectives.

VIII. EVALUATION (3, 5, 6, 21, 24)

Evaluation should be an ongoing process. Plans must be worked out for the collection of information from participants in the action system regarding effectiveness with respect to both task and process goals. This may be quite informal (setting aside a portion of a meeting to discuss "how we're doing") or much more rigorous (standardized data collection, written reports) depending upon the size, complexity, and other requirements of the effort in which the practitioner is engaged. The important thing is that assessment not be overlooked, for the process allows the practitioner and the organization to revise their program if activities are found to be less than satisfactory.

Practitioners often find annual or semiannual meetings good opportunities for taking stock. The results may be set forth in a periodic report. There is a tendency at such meetings to "put the best foot forward" and overlook difficulties in order to maintain or enhance morale, build financial resources, and avoid offending those who have been active in the organization. Ordinarily it is best to find ways to say what may be the unpleasant truth in a manner that minimizes problems. For example, it is possible to express gratitude for individual contributions while calling attention to persistent difficulties that exist "in spite of the best efforts of everyone involved."

IX. MODIFICATION, TERMINATION, OR TRANSFER OF ACTION

Evaluation of program and organizational effectiveness may lead to any one of several conclusions. First, the practitioner may conclude that the program is operating much as expected, is achieving its intended purposes, and should be continued. Second, he or she may find that some aspects are faulty, because of an erroneous analysis of the situation, a poor strategy, or particular actions that were inappropriate or poorly carried out. This conclusion should lead to necessary revisions. Third, the practitioner and those he or she is working with may conclude that the program has served its purpose or, alternatively, is hopelessly inept. In either case, the conclusion should be to discontinue operations and the practitioner must plan carefully for this. Finally, for a variety of reasons the practitioner may be leaving the job. Under these conditions, it is necessary to arrange either the transfer of professional responsibilities to another practitioner or the termination of the program.

CONCLUSION

These comments suggest how the guide may be used and offer some additional references which are intended to give it a broader scope and greater utility. We hope that practitioners will use the guide to remind themselves of some of the more important factors they need to take into account in planning their work.

Obviously the busy community practitioner will be unable to utilize fully the analysis suggested here in daily work. However, many of the steps in the problem-solving process will become part of the professional "equipment" he or she may apply, perhaps less formally and less rigorously but nonetheless effectively, in making day-to-day practice decisions. This is the hope we have had in preparing the guide and using it in teaching community practice.

BIBLIOGRAPHY

1. Alinsky, Saul D. *Reveille for Radicals.* Chicago: University of Chicago Press, 1946; and *Rules for Radicals.* New York: Random House, 1971.

2. Blau, Peter, M., and Richard W. Scott. *Formal Organizations.* San Francisco: Chandler Publishing Co., 1962.

3. Campbell, Donald T. "Reforms as Experiments." *American Psychologist* 24 (April 1969): 409–29.

4. Coleman, James S. "Community Disorganization," in Merton and Nisbet, op, cit., pp. 670–95.

5. Herzog, Elizabeth. *Some Guidelines for Evaluative Research.* Children's Bureau Publication No. 375. Washington, DC: U.S. Dept. of Health, Education, and Welfare, 1959.

6. Hyman, Herbert H., and Charles R. Wright. "Evaluating Social Action Programs," in *The Uses of Sociology,* edited by Paul F. Lazarfeld, William H. Sewell, and Harold Wilensky. New York: Basic Books, 1967, pp. 741–82.

7. Levine, Robert A. *Public Planning: Failure and Redirection.* New York: Basic Books, 1972.

8. Levine, Sol, Paul E. White, and Benjamin D. Paul. "Community Interorganizational Problems in Providing Medical Care and Social Services," *American Journal of Public Health* 53 (August 1963): 1183–95.

9. Lippitt, Ronald, Jeanne Watson, and Bruce Westley. *The Dynamics of Planned Change: A Comparative Study of Principles and Techniques.* New York: Harcourt, Brace and World, 1958.

10. Merton, Robert K. "Epilogue: Social Problems and Sociological Theory," in *Contemporary Social Problems,* 2d ed., edited by Robert K. Merton and Robert A. Nisbet. New York: Harcourt, Brace and World, 1966.

11. Morris, Robert, and Robert H. Binstock. *Feasible Planning for Social Change.* New York: Columbia University Press, 1966.

12. Perlman, Robert, and Arnold Gurin. *Community Organization and Social Planning.* New York: John Wiley and Council on Social Work Education, 1972.

13. Rein, Martin, and Robert Morris. "Goals, Structures and Strategies for Community Change." In *Social Work Practice 1962.* New York: Columbia University Press, 1962.

14. Ripple, Lillian. "Motivation, Capacity and Opportunity as Related to the Use of Casework Services: Theoretical Base and Plan of Study," *Social Service Review* 29 (June 1955): 172–93.

15. Rose, Arnold. "Theory for the Study of Social Problems," *Social Problems* 4 (January 1957): 189–99.

16. Ross, Murray G. *Community Organization: Theory, Principles and Practice.* New York: Harper & Bros., 1955.

17. Ross, Murray G., with B. W. Lappin. *Community Organization: Theory, Principles and Practice.* 2d ed. New York: Harper & Row, 1967.

18. Rothman, Jack. "An Analysis of Goals and Roles in Community Organization Practice," *Social Work* 9 (April 1964): 24–31.

19. Sanders, Irwin T. *The Community: An Introduction to a Social System.* 2d ed. New York: The Roland Press, 1966.

20. Simon, Herbert A. *Administrative Behavior,* 2d ed. New York: The Macmillan Co., 1957.

21. Suchman, Edward A. *Evaluative Research: Principles and Practice in Public Service and Social Action Programs.* New York: Russell Sage Foundation, 1967.

22. Thomas, Edwin J., and Ronald A. Feldman, with Jane Kamm. "Concepts of Role Theory," in *Behavioral Science for Social Workers,* edited by Edwin J. Thomas. New York: The Free Press, 1967.

23. Thompson, James D., and Arthur Tuden. "Strategies, Structures and Processes of Organizational Decision," *Comparative Studies in Administration,* edited by J. D. Thompson et al., pp. 195–216. Pittsburgh: Pittsburgh University Press, 1959.

24. Tripodi, Tony, Phillip Fellin, and Irwin Epstein. *Social Program Evaluation: Guidelines for Health, Education and Welfare Administrators.* Itasca, Ill.: F. E. Peacock Publishers, 1971.

25. Warren, Roland L. *The Community in America.* Chicago: Rand McNally, 1963.

8.

Ronald L. Simons

GENERIC SOCIAL WORK SKILLS IN SOCIAL
ADMINISTRATION: THE EXAMPLE OF PERSUASION

Increasingly there is consensus in the literature on social welfare management that social service administration differs in significant ways from general administration and hence requires a particular type of educational preparation (Hasenfeld & English, 1974; Patti, 1983; Steiner, 1977). Having agreed that social service administrators need to be educated in a fashion that differs from that of the general administrator, there is much disagreement concerning the form that education for social welfare management should take (Perlmutter, 1984). Even if a consensus could be reached concerning the ideal curriculum for students interested in social administration, it is not clear that this would have a significant impact upon the way programs are managed as the administrators of most human service organizations are direct service workers who have been promoted into supervisory positions (Patti, 1983).

This paper takes the position that both social welfare administration and direct service social workers require a common set of skills. Of course, both the administrator and direct-service worker must also know the proven theories and techniques associated with his or her level of practice. However, these specialized procedures only serve to compliment or build upon generic skills that characterize all social work practice. Hence, the social worker who receives a rigorous education in the generic skills of social work practice would be prepared, with little additional training, to practice as a direct service worker or social administrator.

In an effort to develop this contention, the next section of this paper defines and discusses the concept of generic skills as it relates to the service effectiveness of human service administration. A set of persuasive strategies is then developed as an example of empirically based generic procedures appropriate to the demands of both administration and direct service work.

GENERIC SKILLS AND SOCIAL ADMINISTRATION

As noted above, most experts in the area recognize social welfare administration to be different from administration in general. One of the major differences is that human service organizations assume a commitment to client welfare or service effectiveness rather than profit or some other outcome (Patti, 1985). In the course of pursuing this performance objective, the social administrator must also be concerned with efficiency, productivity, resource acquisition, and staff morale (Rapp & Poertner, 1985). All of this requires the execution of tasks such as obtaining funds and clients, supervising and motivating personnel, juggling the conflicting demands of multiple constituents, managing information on program performance, and the like. At first glance, this diverse set of activities seems to demand a set of competencies quite different from those assumed in direct service work. However, a closer examination shows that to a large degree these administrative tasks rest upon the ability to carry out the general skills of the problem-solving process. Importantly, these problem-solving skills are the same ones employed by direct service workers.

As Perlman (1957) noted some years ago, social work is a problem-solving activity. This is true whether one is employed as an administrator or a direct-service worker. The steps and skills associated with problem solving remain the same regardless of level of practice (Simons & Aigner, 1985). To see how this is so, consider the problem-solving process:

First, data must be collected in order to assess the problem. The principles of interviewing, observation, questionnaire construction, and sampling are the same whether one is collecting data on clients, employee morale, or the impact of a management information system. Next, based upon the assessment of the problem, specific goals must be established and a sequence of tasks identified for reaching the goals. The skills associated with goal setting and task planning are the same for direct service and administrative problems. Action systems must often be formulated to carry out the tasks that have been identified, and a common set of skills are required in order to pull together and run a group whether it be a committee or treatment group. Usually some individual or group must be influenced to change if the problem of concern is to be resolved. The target may be a client, a board member, or a funding agency, but the principles for effective persuasion, inducement, or constraint remain the same.

An important component of the problem-solving process is the evaluation of the attempted solution. This involves collecting data concerning the impact of the problem-solving effort. Thus one schooled in the general skills of problem solving must know quasi-experimental research procedures required for evaluation. The canons of quasi-experimental design remain the same whether one is evaluating a direct-service intervention or some component of organizational performance.

All this suggests that the human service administrator and the direct-service worker employ a similar set of skills. These problem-solving skills, which are relevant to any setting or level of practice, should be considered the generic skills of social work. Unfortunately, the term "generic skills" does not have a common meaning among social work educators. Often times it is used to refer to processes such as facilitating, mediating, relationship enhancement, and the like. When defined in this fashion, the skills suggest little in terms of specific practice guidelines and have limited utility for social workers employed in the areas of policy and administration. Stated differently, such formulations are not really informative or generic.

To be generic, a set of skills must be organized around the activities that characterize social work in various settings and level. Thus the skills should relate to the problem-solving process endemic to all social work practice (Simons & Aigner, 1985). To be useful, to facilitate effective practice, the skills must indicate specific, empirically based tasks and activities. The skills should involve clearly identified practice principles based upon empirically proven theories and techniques (Simons & Aigner, 1985).

As an example of a set of principles which meet these criteria, the following section develops a list of practice guidelines with regard to the skill of persuasion. The ability to exercise influence through persuasion is important in human service administration as funding bodies must be persuaded to invest in the program, legislative and policy-making groups need to be persuaded to establish priorities and guidelines which facilitate quality programming, community agencies must be persuaded to refer clients, community residents may need to be persuaded to serve as board members or as volunteers, and so on. The social administrator is constantly attempting to persuade some person or group to contribute the time, energy, or other resources required for effective service delivery. Hence, the ability to exert influence through persuasion, like the other generic skills, is an essential component of successful human service administration.

Given how often program viability and success hinges upon the manager's ability to influence certain individuals and groups, it is essential that social administrators be schooled in techniques for maximizing the efficacy of the persuasive communications. Recently, the author employed theory and research from the literature on attitude formation and change to deduce various strategies for exercising influence (Simons, 1982; Simons & Aigner, 1985). These strategies were presented as generic approaches, i.e., as procedures that might be employed to enhance the effectiveness of social workers practicing in any role or setting. Since the publication of these articles, the author has decided that the principles regarding persuasion should be reformulated so as to increase their utility to macro practitioners. It is not that the principles as originally stated are now viewed as incorrect; rather it is a matter of recasting them in a fashion that allows for greater flexibility and ease of use.

The previous statements emphasized the way that role reversal, giving both sides of an issue, stressing consistency, and identifying self-defeating behavior might be utilized to persuade a target system to change. The principles were presented as alternative approaches to constructing a persuasive appeal, or as strategies which might be employed in a serial fashion in the course

of dialogue with the target. Although well suited to the needs of the direct-service worker, a good bit of ingenuity was required in order to combine the principles into a single persuasive appeal as macro practitioners must do in funding proposals, presentations before boards, media campaigns, etc. In the section to follow, the principles of persuasion are reformulated and integrated with research and theory regarding the adoption and diffusion of new ideas.

PRINCIPLES FOR EFFECTIVE PERSUASION

As noted above, persuasion involves producing change through the provision of new information—that is, the target receives information that influences him or her to think, feel, or act in a new way (Gamson, 1968; Pincus & Minahan, 1973). Or, as Larson (1983) states, "the process of persuasion involves your presenting good reasons to people for a specific choice among probable alternatives" (p. 281). Theory and research on persuasion are concerned with identifying the characteristics of messages which persons find appealing, with discovering the nature of communications which are perceived to contain "good reasons" for adopting the position being advocated. Based upon the findings of several decades of research, the following factors appear to be important components in effective persuasion appeals.

Emphasize Advantages or Rewards

People are constantly processing the information available to them and making decisions as to how they might best satisfy their needs and achieve their goals. Hence, the probability that individuals will change their behavior in response to a communication is increased when the message provides information indicating that the change will enable them to more effectively satisfy their needs and desires.

Several studies show that a target audience is more apt to adopt a favorable attitude toward a behavior or procedure when they perceive it to have a relative advantage over existing or alternative practices (Coleman, Katz & Menzel, 1966; Rothman, 1974). Rogers (1968) notes that the advantages or rewards associated with an action may not be economic or material. The benefits of adopting the line of action being advocated may be largely psychological, leading to an increase in prestige, status, or satisfaction. People must have sufficient reason for modifying their behavior or for adopting a new procedure. One good reason for doing so is because the new approach yields rewards at a level unavailable through existing practices or alternative actions.

Be Comprehensible

The action being advocated must be presented in a language that is readily understood by the target audience. Technical jargon should be avoided if possible. People will not adopt a line of action which they do not fully comprehend. Simple, easily understood ideas are more likely to be accepted than arguments which are complex and hard to follow (Glaser, Abelson & Garrison, 1983; Rogers, 1983; Zaltman, 1973).

Show Compatibility of Values

There is substantial evidence that people are more apt to accept an idea if it is perceived as consistent with their present beliefs, values, and ways of doing things

(Rogers, 1983; Rothman, 1974; Zaltman, 1973). For instance, Woolfolk, Woolfolk and Wilson (1977) found that students who were shown identical videotapes of a teacher using reinforcement procedures evaluated the teacher and the technique more favorably when the videotape was described as an illustration of "humanistic education" than when it was labeled behavior modification. And Saunders and Reppucci (1977) reported that the reaction of school principals and superintendents to a program proposal varied according to whether or not the program was identified as employing a behavior modification approach. Such studies are a clear demonstration of the way that one can destroy an audience's receptivity to an idea by using words or phrases which the group perceives as representing beliefs or practices contrary to their value commitments. Indeed, the label or name selected for a program or activity should be chosen with great care (Rogers, 1983).

Various groups, whether human service agencies, funding bodies, or civic organizations, are often committed to a particular sociopolitical, treatment, or practice ideology (Rappoport, 1960; Hasenfeld, 1983). An idea is more apt to be accepted or assimilated by a group if it is perceived to be compatible with the assumptions, principles, and procedures that make up the group's ideological orientation (Glaser, Abelson & Garrison, 1983). Compatibility promises greater security and less risk to the receiver while making the new idea appear more meaningful (Rogers, 1983).

Cite Proven Results

An audience is more apt to accept an idea if its consequences have already been observed. When people can see the positive results of an action or procedure they are more likely to adopt it (Glaser, Abelson & Garrison, 1983; Rogers, 1983). Given this finding, a stepping-stone approach is often the most effective way of selling an idea. First, a small group is persuaded to test the procedure. The positive results obtained in this demonstration project or pilot program are then cited in persuasive communications designed to promote the idea across a broader population (Rothman, 1974; Rothman, Erlich & Teresa, 1981).

Allow for Trialability

The target group will perceive less risk if the new idea can be tried on a piecemeal basis prior to wholesale adoption of the procedure (Rogers, 1983; Rogers & Svenning, 1969). As Glaser, Abelson, and Garrison (1983) observe:

The extent to which a proposed change is known to be reversible if it does not prove desirable may affect its adoption. Not all innovations can be discarded later with impunity; the bridges back to the status quo ante may have been burned. Situations in which the user need not "play for keeps" provide more opportunity for innovation (p. 61).

People are reluctant to commit themselves to a line of action which does not allow for a later change of mind. An idea is more apt to be adopted if it can be broken into parts which can be tried one step at a time, with the group having the option of discontinuing the new procedure at any time in the process should they decide that it is not producing the anticipated results (Rogers, 1983; Rothman, Erlich & Teresa, 1981).

Link Message to Influential Others

Consistent with the predictions of Balance Theory (Heider, 1958), several studies indicated that people tend to adopt the same attitude toward an object or idea as that held by someone they like, and that they tend to adopt the opposite attitude toward an object or idea as that held by someone they dislike (Tedeschi & Lindskold, 1976). In this way, individuals maintain cognitive balance.

These findings suggest that an idea is more likely to be accepted if it is linked to persons that the target likes. The most direct method for doing this is to have someone the target likes or respects deliver the persuasive appeal. When this is not feasible, reference might be made to influential others as part of the communicated message. For instance, if a city council member is known to be a firm supporter of the state governor, and the governor is known to have the same views on an issue as the social worker who is trying to influence the council member, this information could be presented to the council member. This general tactic can be used whether the favored person is the president, a movie star, a well-known expert on some topic, or the target's colleague, friend, or spouse.

The social worker might cite individuals similar to the target when information about whom the target likes or respects is lacking. This strategy is based on the extensive body of research indicating that people tend to be attracted to people they perceive as similar to themselves. Thus, when attempting to persuade a landlord to make repairs, the worker might name other landlords who have made such repairs; when attempting to persuade a principal to institute a drug education program, the worker might cite principals from other schools in the city who have begun such programs, and so forth.

Avoid High-Pressure Tactics

Research based upon Reactance Theory shows that when individuals feel pressured to select a particular course of action, whether through the promise of rewards, the threat of punishment, or intense appeals, they tend to increase their valuation of alternatives to the position being advocated (Brehm, 1966; Wicklund, 1974). High-pressure tactics create a boomerang effect. The use of pressure to persuade people to adopt an idea frquently creates resistance and a determination to act in a manner which is contrary to the proposed action. Human beings value their freedom and will resist attempts to circumscribe their choice of self-determination. Therefore, messages should be presented in a manner that minimizes any threat to the target's feeling of freedom. Phrases such as "It's your decision," "But, of course, it's up to you," and "Think about it and see what you want to do," serve this function; whereas words such as "must," "should," and "have to" are likely to arouse resistance (Brehm, 1976).

In addition to using phrases such as those just cited, reactance can be lowered through the use of two-sided messages (Secord & Backman, 1974). Two-sided communications acknowledge the limitations of one's own position and grant some merit to alternative points of view. A two-sided argument is more effective when the opposing view is presented first and the view preferred by the communicator is presented last (Johnson & Matross, 1975). Thus, when attempting to persuade an audience who is committed to another point of view, the social worker should begin by acknowledging the perspective to the group. The worker should assure them that he or she understands and appreciates their point of view. Such a beginning lowers audience defensiveness and makes the worker appear less one-sided and more objective.

Minimize Threats to Security, Status, or Esteem

Change agents often commit the "rationalistic bias" of assuming that people are reasonable beings who, when presented with the logic of a new and better approach, will recognize its merits and embrace it without hesitation (Zaltman & Duncan, 1977). However, events frequently fail to unfold in this fashion. People's logic and reason are often distorted by less rational processes. Sound judgment may be clouded by a defensive emotional response. Emotional defensiveness may be produced because a group fears the new procedure will signal a diminution in their prestige or power (Bright, 1964; Berlin, 1969). Those persons who have benefited the most from existing practices are likely to be threatened by a change in procedures. Other individuals may fear that the new approach will devalue their knowledge and skills and that they will have a difficult time learning the new procedures (Bright, 1964; Glaser, Abelson & Garrison, 1983). In still other instances, persons may be reluctant to adopt a course of action because they feel they will lose face with their friends or some constituency.

The wise change agent will construct his or her communications in a manner that alleviates such threats. Whenever an idea might be interpreted as threatening to the target group's security, esteem, or sense of competence, these fears should be discussed and objectively examined as part of the communication process. By acknowledging and evaluating these concerns through the two-sided approach discussed above, defensiveness may be reduced and reason allowed to prevail.

We began this section by noting that people are persuaded by a message when it provides them with "good reasons" for selecting the advocated course of action over alternatives. Based upon attitude change research and studies of the adoption and diffusion of innovations, eight principles for enhancing the persuasiveness of a communication have been identified. These principles of communication are listed in Table 8.1. The principles might be summarized as suggesting that people are most apt to perceive that they have good reason to adopt the position being advocated when it has advantages over alternatives, is easily understood, is compatible with existing values and practices, has been shown to have positive results, can be adopted on a trial basis, is endorsed by admired others, may be accepted or rejected, and contains no threats to security or esteem.

EXAMPLES OF THE PRINCIPLES IN USE

As observed earlier, social administrators frequently employ persuasion in an effort to obtain the resources necessary for a viable program, such as funding, clients, personnel, and community goodwill. In this section, two illustrations are provided of the way in which the principles identified above might be combined to maximize an administrator's persuasiveness. The first considers the situation of presenting a fund-ing proposal to a county board while the second concerns the formation of a radio spot designed to solicit local citizens to serve as program volunteers.

Assume that a social worker is interested in persuading the board of supervisors in his or her county to provide funding for a new community corrections halfway house. After reviewing the eight principles of persuasion, the individual might construct a presentation which contains the following: First, the advantages of the program must be noted. Community correctional programs are cheaper and often produce lower recidivism rates than alternative facilities (Advantages Principle). Since the residents of the halfway house would be working during the day and living in the house at night, attention might be drawn to the way in which the program is consistent with community values of work and supporting oneself (Compatibility Principle). Concerns about the dangers posed by convicted criminals living in the community would need to be acknowledged and addressed through a description of the screening procedures to be employed in selecting residents for the house (Threats Principle). The positive results obtained by similar programs in other communities should be cited (Proven Results Principle). Mention might be made of any influential politicians or

TABLE 8.1
Principles for Constructing Persuasive Communications

1. Emphasize Advantages.
2. Be Comprehensive.
3. Show Compatability of Values.
4. Cite Proven Results.
5. Allow for Trialability.
6. Refer to Influential Others.
7. Avoid High-Pressure Tactics.
8. Minimize Threats to Security, Status, or Esteem.

organizations who support the correctional halfway house concept (Influential Others Principle). The idea could be presented as reversible. At the end of a certain period an evaluation might be planned and a decision made as to whether the results obtained warrant continued support (Trialability Principle). Finally, an effort would be made throughout the presentation to be clear and understandable (Comprehensibility Principle) and to emphasize that it is the board's decision, that they should only adopt the proposal if they perceive that it is a good idea (Minimal Pressure Principle).

Of course, the presentation would need to contain information in addition to the material just mentioned. The board would probably want details regarding where the facility would be located, how it would be staffed, the costs to be incurred, and the like. However, many proposals are largely limited to a consideration of such items. If a proposal is to be persuasive it should also address the issues identified in the eight principles discussed above.

As a second example, assume that a radio spot is to be constructed in an effort to solicit volunteers to work in a psychiatric halfway house. The announcement might begin by describing the problems in living faced by the residents of the facility and the way that volunteers can help solve such difficulties (Advantages Principle). Attention might be drawn to the way in which volunteering is consistent with the American tradition of helping one's neighbor to get back on his feet during hard times (Compatibility Principle). The valuable consequences that have been obtained through the use of volunteers, either in this program or in similar others, could be noted (proven Results Principle). In citing these consequences, the rewards for both the resident and the volunteer should be described (Advantages

Principle). The announcement might acknowledge listener concerns regarding the time that may be involved and doubts about being able to function as an effective volunteer (Threat Principle). These issues could be addressed by briefly noting how many hours a week are required and by assuring the listener that volunteer training and supervision are provided. The listener might be informed that the commitment is time limited, say six months or a year, with the option of volunteering again at the end of the period (Trialability Principle). An influential community person might be recruited to read the announcement (Influential Others Principle). Everyday language, rather than psychiatric argot, would need to be used to describe the program and the services provided by the volunteers (Comprehensibility Principle). The appeal should be made in a warm, factual fashion which avoids the appearance of a hard-sell campaign (Minimum Pressure Principle).

As these two examples demonstrate, the eight principles of persuasion, so long as they are employed in an honest and forthright manner, do not violate the values of the social work profession. None of the principles involve the use of trickery or hidden agendas. Rather, they merely suggest the types of information that the target will desire prior to committing to the idea being presented. Of course, the principles might be used in an unethical fashion. For instance, a person might claim that a program has been shown to produce certain results when it has not, or that a procedure can be tried on a trial basis when in reality it can only be discontinued through great expense and inconvenience. The principles imply no value dilemmas, however, so long as an individual utilizes them with sincerity and honesty.

CONCLUSIONS AND
RECOMMENDATIONS

This paper has exemplified the generic skills approach to social work practice as it relates to the need for administrators to manage their influence with an array of internal and external constituents in order to enhance service effectiveness. The eight principles of Persuasion articulated here may be used by social workers in a variety of administrative and direct-service settings. Given the fact that often conflicting demands are placed upon administrators from the political environment in which human service organizations operate, the ability for administrators to use persuasion in their efforts toward improving service effectiveness for clients is a critical skill.

To be truly generic, skill training for administrators and students must be organized around the components of the problem-solving process. It is problem solving that characterizes all levels of social work practice. And, if it is to be really useful, this training must focus upon specific techniques and activities which have some empirical basis. In the present paper, several principles concerning the skill of persuasion were presented as an example of a set of practice principles meeting these criteria. Elsewhere an effort has been made to identify such practice guidelines with regard to other steps in the problem-solving process (Simons & Aigner, 1985).

Given the fundamental nature of generic, problem-solving skills for the profession, there is a critical need for more social workers to become involved in research concerned with the design and development of such procedures. However, we already know a lot that can be passed along to administrators and students. This material should be taught in a rigorous fashion with a profusion of role plays and exercises directed toward various direct-service, planning, and administrative problems.

To ensure that students appreciate the general applicability of the skills, instructors in clinical, community, and planning and administration classes should underscore the way in which the material in their courses builds upon and serves to compliment the basic social work skills. Educating students in this fashion would begin to address the problem of most social administrators being promoted to direct-service workers with little administrative training.

REFERENCES

Berlin, I. N. "Resistance to Change in Mental Health Professionals." *American Journal of Orthopsychiatry*, 1969, 39, 109–115.

Brehm, J. W. *A Theory of Psychological Reactance*. New York: Academic, 1966.

Brehm, S. S. *The Application of Social Psychology to Clinical Practice*. New York: Halsted, 1976.

Bright, J. R. *Research, Development, and Technological Innovation: An Introduction*. Homewood, IL: Irwin, 1964.

Coleman, J. S., E. Katz, & H. Menzel. *Medical Innovation: A Diffusion Study*. New York: Bobbs-Merrill, 1966.

Gamson, W. A. *Power and Discontent*. Homewood, IL: Dorsey, 1968.

Glaser, E. M., H. H. Abelson, & K. N. Garrison. *Putting Knowledge to Use*. San Francisco: Jossey-Bass, 1983.

Hasenfeld, Y. *Human Service Organizations*. Englewood Cliffs, NJ: Prentice-Hall, Inc., 1983.

Hasenfeld, Y., & R. A. English, eds. *Human Service Organizations*. Ann Arbor, MI: University of Michigan Press, 1974.

Johnson, D. W., & R. P. Matross. "Attitude Modification Methods." In F. H. Kanfer & A. P. Goldstein, eds. *Helping People Change*. New York: Pergammon, 1975.

Larson, C. U. *Persuasion: Reception and Responsibility*, 3rd ed. Belmont, CA: Wadsworth, 1983.

Patti, R. J. *Social Welfare Administration: Managing Social Programs in a Developmental Context.* Englewood Cliffs, NJ: Prentice-Hall, Inc., 1983.

Patti, R. J. "In Search of Purpose for Social Welfare Administration. *Administration in Social Work*, 1985, *9*, 1–14.

Perlman, H. H. *Social Casework: A Problem-Solving Process.* Chicago: University of Chicago Press, 1957.

Perlmutter, F. D. "Social Administration and Social Work Education: A Contradiction in Terms?" *Administration in Social Work*, 1984, *8*, 61–69.

Pincus, A., & A. Minahan. *Social Work Practice: Model and Method.* Itasca, IL: F. E. Peacock, 1973.

Rappoport, R. *Community as Doctor.* London: Tavistock Publications, 1960.

Rapp, C. A., & J. Poertner. *A Performance Model for Human Service Management.* Manuscript, University of Kansas, 1985.

Rogers, E. M. The Communication of Innovations in a Complex Institution. *Educational Record*, 1968, *48*, 67–77.

Rogers, E. M. *Diffusion of Innovations.* 3rd ed. New York: Free Press, 1983.

Rogers, E. M., & L. Svenning. *Managing Change.* Washington, DC: U.S. Office of Education, 1969.

Rothman, J. *Planning and Organizing for Social Change.* New York: Columbia University Press, 1974.

Rothman, J., J. L. Erlich, & J. G. Teresa. *Changing Organizations and Community Programs.* Beverly Hills: Sage, 1981.

Saunders, J. T., & N. D. Reppucci. "Learning Networks Among Administrators of Human Service Institutions." *American Journal of Community Psychology*, 1977, *5*, 269–276.

Secord, P. F., & C. W. Backman. *Social Psychology.* New York: McGraw-Hill, 1974.

Simons, R. L. "Strategies for Exercising Influence." *Social Work*, 1982, 27, 268–274.

Simons, R. L., & S. M. Aigner. *Practice Principles: A Problem-Solving Approach to Social Work.* New York: Macmillan, 1985.

Steiner, R. *Managing the Human Service Organization.* Beverly Hills: Sage, 1977.

Tedeschi, J. T., & S. Linskold. *Social Psychology: Interdependence, Interaction and Influence.* New York: Wiley, 1976.

Wicklund, R. A. *Freedom and Reactance.* Hillsdale, NJ: Lawrence Erlbaum and Associates, 1974.

Woolfolk, A. E., R. L. Woolfolk, & G. T. Wilson. "A Rose by Any Other Name. . . . Labeling Bias and Attitudes Toward Behavior Modification. *Journal of Consulting and Clinical Psychology,* 1977, *45*, 184–191.

Zaltman, G. *Processes and Phenomena of Social Change.* New York: Wiley, 1973.

Zaltman, G., & R. Duncan. *Strategies for Planned Change.* New York: Wiley, 1977.

9.

Alvin Zander

PRESSURING METHODS USED BY GROUPS

We turn now to methods which agents of change are likely to use when they are sure of the ends they seek and wish to induce target persons to accept and work toward those goals. In the sequence of procedures we examine here, the activists increasingly employ incentives that are desirable (or repulsive) to the target persons in order to get them to change things.

CHANGE AGENTS SEEK THE HELP OF LEGITIMATE THIRD PARTIES

Persons who wish to develop acceptance for an idea may realize that they are being ignored by those they hope to influence. The advocates, because they feel that their goal is just, turn to a method that will earn their cause due attention. They employ one of the procedures available in every community to help persons with grievances confront those whom they want to reach. These are *legitimate* methods in the sense that residents of the area have established and approved of them, often by passing laws. The common denominator among these approaches is that a third party (or its stand-in) is asked for judicious help through the use of formal rules, the presence of mediators, or both.

Consider examples in which the third party is represented by, let us say, a set of rules. Take the guidelines prepared by a city planning commission, which citizens in the community are to follow if they wish to bring business before the board. These regulations require that would-be speakers request permission in writing to take the floor, describe the topic of their comments, and promise to talk no longer than five minutes. They are not allowed to speak at a meeting of the board unless they adhere to these rules. Persons who wish to prove that there is a need in the town for a new bus line may circulate a petition among neighbors, asking them to sign it if they approve of the idea. To make these petitions valid, the individuals circulating them have to follow requirements concerning signers' age, place of residence, and length of residence. Likewise, if reformers want to apply pressure on state legislators to pass a law on conservation of water, they must obtain the required number of signatures and present these to the legislators. Comparable procedures are to be used if they wish to place the name of a candidate on the ballot.

At other times, reformers may try to bolster their case by getting target persons to agree that they will accept the help of a mediator. This official is to keep the discussion between presenters and listeners flowing smoothly. He or she may function in accord with rules that discussants develop ahead of time or in line with rules that have the weight of state or local law. Management and labor, for instance, can create their own procedural plans before a bargaining session begins and pledge to abide by the outcome of this process. In so doing, they also must conform to general laws governing mediation of labor-management disputes. An arbitrator provides the same help as a mediator but also has the

177

right to reach a decision, hand it down, and require that it be obeyed by all concerned. This process is called *binding arbitration.* Members of elected boards in public agencies are usually prohibited from submitting to binding arbitration, since they are legally beholden to the people who elected them, not to an arbitrator.

Another kind of third party is a judge in a court of law. Agents of change may request an injunction from the court to stop a practice that they think should be restricted, such as dumping toxic waste in a river, running machinery before it has been inspected for safety, or harassing homeless people who try to get a hearing before the social services commission. An increasingly common technique used by groups that have been created to complain about the negligence of companies is to sue a firm, provided that the plaintiffs can show they have been hurt by the actions of those they bring to court. For example, Meier (1987) reports that over six hundred suits were filed against businesses by citizens before 1987 in matters of environmental control. Although companies that have been sued have protested these suits, saying they were frivolous, were in support of the plaintiffs' pet projects, or were forms of extortion, the number of suits is expected to continue rising, along with the stakes involved. The Clean Water Act, passed . . . by Congress, provides for daily fines of $10,000 to $25,000 for each violation. Before this legislation existed, similar complaints were directed to local, state, or federal government in an effort to make officials enforce laws already on the books. More recently, the emphasis has shifted to the polluters themselves, usually manufacturers, because the new law now allows that shift. Sometimes a company forestalls a lawsuit by promising to clean up its act and making a contribution to the organization

that brings the complaint. This practice keeps the firm out of court, saves the expense of hiring lawyers, costs less than what a jury might award the plaintiffs, and allows the firm to claim that it has made a tax-deductible contribution to a nonprofit agency. Other companies have reached agreements whereby they put sums of money aside that must be handed over if they break the law again. Such suits and agreements provide a way for citizens to have a useful part in ensuring that laws are well enforced.

The use of a legitimate method by agents of change requires that certain general conditions be present. Clearly, rules must exist before the process begins, whether these are created by officials of the larger community and have a regular place in a legal code or are developed by activists themselves. These regulations, by solemn pledge on both sides, are to be obeyed in implementing both the discussion and the content of the final agreement. The legitimacy of the rules may also derive from contracts, tradition, or custom. The important point is that all participants promise to abide by the regulations. Legitimate methods, to be used well, ordinarily require knowledge and skill. People must understand them and be able to follow where they lead. In many instances, complainants hire a person trained in the law who puts their case forward, for a fee, in court. Such moves require money, patience, and plenty of time, since the wheels of justice grind slowly. Above all, complainants must have a good case: Otherwise, it is a waste of resources to appeal to a third party for help.

Why are legitimate procedures used? They are usually employed because other methods have failed, and the innovators are not able to get a reasonable hearing from target persons about changes they wish to propose. The innovators may also have been heard by target persons, who then keep the complainants waiting too long. A request by change agents is considerably more potent if they ask that an accepted rule be obeyed than if they press for a change on the grounds of logic or preference (Frank, 1944). A legitimate method is also useful if agents of change do not trust the target persons and want a disinterested entity involved in the discussion, to keep the talks fair and aboveboard. The reason labor-management bargaining sessions use a mediator or an arbitrator, for example, is that neither side is confident that its counterpart is telling the truth. Many formal organizations are governed by laws that state whether and how changes can be made in the way they operate. Funk (1982) describes a number of these regulations and their effects.

The main reason for using a legitimate approach is that (in principle, at least) the issue is settled once and for all. After an agreement is reached, there should be no more pressuring, on the one hand, and no more opposing or resisting, on the other (unless the verdict is appealed). Participants must obey the decision. There is also a reasonable chance that justice will prevail. The method offers an opportunity for change agents to have an impact that they might otherwise never achieve, provided that they have a good case.

The effects of using such processes are noteworthy. As mentioned, participants come away feeling that the matter is settled. Everyone must abide by the outcome, whether it is palatable or not. Furthermore, the decision provides criteria for determining what is proper behavior, and these criteria can be used later to assess how closely participants are sticking to the rules. The use of a mediator or a referee may have other good consequences (Deutsch, 1973). A mediator can help participants face up to

the issue and understand it, including some aspects of it that are hidden or embarrassing to reveal. He or she can help bargaining move along by providing favorable circumstances, devices, tools, or tricks that allow participants to reach a full understanding of the issue. In so doing, he or she can assist all parties by correcting misperceptions that they develop about one another's statements. A mediator can establish rules for courteous interaction, so that discussants show respect for one another. He or she can help determine which ideas are worthy of consideration as possible solutions and which ones are unlikely to lead anywhere. A mediator can press leaders to promise that they will abide by the decision, whatever it is. He or she makes the final agreement palatable to all, so that no one will regret the outcome, and helps make the decision acceptable to bystanders who have a vested interest in this discussion. Although the issue is settled, there may be a residue of hard feelings among those who lose. Persons recall things said during the process that were derogatory or unfair. The winners, for their part, may feel that they have not gained everything they wanted.

How is a third party used most effectively? The agents of change should have a good case and be able to demonstrate that the matter under discussion is a source of a serious deprivation for them and others or that it offers an opportunity for improving a current state of affairs. When taking a suit to court, moreover, they hire a lawyer to guide them through the legal system, and they furnish that person with effective witnesses, data, money, and encouragement. Finally, agents of change who use a third party need to be persistent and patient. A third party (or strict rules) can slow progress. Target persons may also stall or employ tactics that embarrass agents of change, so that the latter give up the fight.

To sum up, a number of issue-settling procedures are legitimate because they have been approved by citizens in the community as ways to judge the validity of complaints and to get relief from these. Such methods ordinarily require participants to abide by the outcome. They are unlike some other methods often used by agents of change who are trying to influence target persons. They are based on strict regulations, and participants must abide by these rules. They require knowledge of the process before they can be used wisely. They demand that participants have a good case, and they require time, patience, money, and expert help. The value of these procedures is that they usually solve the problem once and for all, unless the decision fosters anger and a desire for retribution among those who did not get their way.

REFORMERS NURTURE PERSONS IN NEED

Some groups are created to improve conditions for persons outside the unit. They may describe to officials the situation facing disadvantaged individuals and tell these listeners what ought to be done for the needy ones, or they may develop a demonstration of a helpful service, with a view toward inspiring decision makers to support a similar program in the future. We are interested here in the altruistic acts of change agents and how these can influence target persons. This display of nurturance is, in a way, another example of modeling. We are taking it up here as a separate method, however, because reformers who demonstrate how to care for needy persons may plan to improve things for others with no help from neighbors, or they may wish to show decision makers how to be caring persons. The

deprived individuals may become target persons themselves if they are urged to help in plans and actions for the nurturance of their disadvantaged colleagues, or citizens at large may become target persons if they are pressed for money and labor to support the helping program. Finally, a model activity to care for the deprived takes much energy, time, and compassion. Persons who create a model must feel deeply that what they are doing is important: It is not simply a temporary, interest-arousing process.

The kinds of demonstrations that helping persons develop are well known. They provide resources to persons who need them, such as food, clothing, shelter, or money. They care for personal needs of individuals through educating, healing, reforming, or saving their souls. They provide emergency assistance in case of a fire, flood, storm, or accident. To provide such nurturance quickly or frequently, they may form enduring organizations whose members are trained to do what is needed.

The motivation of members in these groups is to benefit disadvantaged persons, without receiving any payment themselves other than the satisfaction of helping deprived ones. This help is provided either by the innovators or by the target persons who agree to furnish care for those in need of it (Bar-Tal, 1976; Macaulay and Berkowitz, 1970). The reformers also help decision makers by showing them how they can better provide a particular kind of nurturance. It is not always easy for reformers to interest officials in offering a new service. If the officials agree to a change, they are admitting, in effect, that they have not been operating as wisely or compassionately as they should, and the implementation of a new plan reveals this. The target persons also may believe that individuals who require help are lazy, greedy, or unwilling to take care of themselves and therefore do not deserve to be nurtured. Caring programs, moreover, cost money and have a way of becoming more expensive once they are under way.

Activities to help others are complicated and require their initiators to have sufficient good will, patience, know-how, and resources to accomplish what they set out to do. Why do agents of change choose to provide nurturing? The most obvious reason is that deprived persons appear unable to improve their situation on their own. They do not have the knowledge, tools, or money to get the kinds of services they need. What is more, the deprived often do not ask for help because they do not want to be obligated to benefactors, are embarrassed to admit that they cannot help themselves, or do not think that they can get the kind of aid they need. The helpers, for their part, prefer to be kindly volunteers in these efforts because they prize the satisfaction they derive from helping. Their cause is also more convincing to target persons if they do not accept payment for the services they provide.

What are the consequences of such an approach? If the disadvantaged persons value the help given to them, they will be grateful but at the same time will feel obligated to those who provide it. Because of this, they may refuse further assistance or accept as little as possible, for fear that they will be expected to reciprocate but will be unable to. Sometimes the help of reformers is not welcomed by those to whom it is offered because it creates a burden for the receivers, who must agree to be saved, give up past beliefs, or take care of a "gift horse." Not uncommonly, the effort of do-gooders is more bother than it seems to be worth, yet those who provide assistance feel good about themselves. They are proud of their efforts, even when the outcome is not all they had hoped for.

Several conditions cause such a demonstration to be more effective in the sense that the disadvantaged are actually assisted or the target persons agree to sponsor further assistance. Helping behavior is more likely to succeed if the innovators derive satisfaction from aiding disadvantaged persons. Thus, they examine what deprived persons need and plan what they should do to meet those needs. In a successful nurturing group, members provide help in ways that do not make the assisted persons feel incompetent or dependent on their helpers. If the initiators intend to rescue people who are in an emergency, they practice how to perform this mission speedily and work to improve their operation. The reformers make sure that official persons know about the demonstration, learn what favorable outcomes it provides, and recognize that such services need wider and continuing support from the community.

To summarize, agents of change may influence decision makers by providing or demonstrating services that help individuals who cannot help themselves. Initiators of nurturing expect no reward other than the satisfaction they derive from knowing that deprived persons have been assisted. They intend their appeal or demonstration to persuade target persons to provide continuing support for such a program.

...

AGENTS OF CHANGE BARGAIN WITH TARGET PERSONS

Suppose that individuals advocating a change tell listeners that they are willing to eliminate some parts of their request if the listeners will drop their objections to other parts. The approached persons, in turn, offer to adopt some of the suggestions made by the agents of change, if the latter will alter some of the ideas they have brought to the conference. This process, in which persons on each side give some things and gain others, is called *bargaining*. Members of a new neighborhood association, for instance, say they will stop making a plea for new sidewalks if the city will promise to pave their streets. Participants ostensibly work toward a solution that is equally valuable to persons in both parties. Often, however, one side gains more and yields less than the other; it obtains a better bargain. As another instance, members of both parties refuse to change their initial stand, so that the bargaining stalls and becomes an empty exercise.

Why do agents of change try to bargain with target persons? In most cases, they do so because they believe that the others are willing to think about modifying their practices in some way, may give up something during a bargaining discussion, or may make a deal with the innovators. Bargaining often develops after other methods fail. Those on each side feel that they can have some control over their rivals by making attractive offers and counteroffers. Reformers are also likely to try bargaining if they believe that they have enough power to influence the acts of target persons and are not merely weak pleaders. They may have this power because there are many members in their group of change agents, they represent an official body that is known to be powerful, they have sponsored frequent and influential media campaigns urging the decision makers to introduce changes, or they have been coercive toward target persons to make them willing to bargain.

Change seekers may also want to bargain because they recognize that they have something the target persons covet, such as votes, funds, expertise, community support, or labor; therefore, bargaining is sensible

for all concerned. The proposers may perceive that their ideas can be improved through the discussion involved in bargaining because the process gets target persons thinking about changes they may be willing to make, or agents of change may bargain because they believe that they can get their own way, without giving up much.

The consequences of bargaining depend in good part on the content of the bargain. Participants may hit on a mutually agreeable plan that satisfies those on both sides, or those in one party may be pleased because they have won what they wanted, while members of the other party are dissatisfied because they have lost on a point they value. If this loss is great enough, the losers may become angry and force the winners to defend themselves against their wrath. It is not uncommon for bargaining to deteriorate into conflict, in which persons on each side try to coerce the other side, rather than make concessions. After a bargaining session, the winners feel satisfied with themselves and rest contented, but the losers examine, evaluate, and improve on their argument, so that they can bargain better in the future. In the long run, losers are indirectly helped because they must overhaul their case and their strategy. Winners, however, may not see the need to engage in such self-appraisal and passively rest on their laurels (Zander, 1982).

When is bargaining most effective? Consider the circumstances needed if the outcome is to be equally satisfying to change agents and target persons alike. Both sides must be fairly equal in their ability to influence the other; otherwise, those with the greater influence will listen little, talk a lot, and push the matter in ways that suit themselves. Effective two-way bargaining also requires members on one side to make an offer to compromise—to give in on some matter, in the hope that those on the other side will do likewise. The initial offer is something that the providers know or hope the others want. A responding offer will likewise be on a matter that is probably desirable to the others. Ideally, then, the sacrifice and the satisfaction should be equal on both sides. There is a danger in making the first offer, however, because persons on the other side may see this as a sign of weakness and believe that those making the first offer are giving in. The ones who receive the original compromise may accept it but make no counterproposal, since they are now ahead of the game.

It helps for people on both sides to have a clear understanding of what people on the other side want and to be able to satisfy this desire amply during the bargaining session. Neither side should offer anything that is considerably more valuable than what the other side can give, since doing so makes it appear that the offer is a bribe.

Pruitt (1972) describes several ways for bargainers to be sure that concessions are equal. One is to make a small unilateral concession, with the statement that no further offer will be made until the target individuals advance something in return. Another is to propose an exchange of concessions; persons on one side say that they are ready to concede on a given point, if those on the other side will also make a concession. It helps to make this proposition through an intermediary, whose offer can be disowned if the other side is not interested, or to call in a mediator who talks with those on both sides and thus opens communication on issues that have been avoided.

If bargainers approach a session as though it were a contest that they intend to win, their tactics are different. To come out ahead, they must gain more and give up less than the others do. Accordingly, the would-be winners make sure that they know the preferences of the persons with whom they are bargaining, know what the others are offering, top that offer, and emphasize that this will be the last chance for a settlement. Initial stakes of a truly competitive bargainer are set high, so that the respondents will feel compelled to bargain, for fear of losing if they do not. Demands stated in strong terms at the outset lead those on the other side to recognize that they cannot hope to get all they want from such hard bargainers, and so they keep their own aspirations low.

Strong bargainers tend to become assertive, in order to bolster their stand. Assertive tactics are described by Bailey (1983):

1. Make a frontal attack on the premises and values of those on the other side. Urge them to abandon their views, on the grounds that they are not convincing. Display raw emotion, to create fear or shame in the others, or to play upon their pity and compassion. Ask the listeners if they can bear the consequences that will follow from an unfair bargain.

2. Argue on grounds that are prized by all concerned, such as democratic values, the need for equality, or the golden rule.

3. Appeal to the importance of using reason and logic, and to the value of an open mind that considers both sides of an issue.

4. Remind listeners that they have a duty toward others who will be affected by the agreement being formed.

5. Appeal to the other side's cunning self-interest. Be smart; look after yourself first. This is especially useful when past obligations can be invoked, and when others can be pressed to undertake new obligations or can be invited to enter into a special deal.

6. Appeal to the mutual interdependence among the persons involved, and stress that each side needs the other.

If people on one side hope to benefit more as a result of bargaining, they cannot let themselves give in to threats, pressure, or other forms of coercion, and they cannot let differences escalate in such a way that those on both sides will not listen to the give-and-take while a conflict grows. The winner in a bargaining session wants to prevail without generating resistance that may interfere with easy access to the gains.

In summary, while bargaining over a proposed change, members of two units holding incompatible views try through discussion to reach a mutually agreeable decision by giving up some things in order to gain others. Agents of change usually are not able to get target persons into a bargaining relationship unless they have power fairly equal to that of the persons they hope to influence. To reach an agreement that pleases both sides, participants must be ready to compromise. To win, those on one side make the other side see that it cannot get what it wants while ignoring their desires. In the long run, it is better if each side wins equally.

AGENTS OF CHANGE REWARD TARGET PERSONS

People working for reform may try to make their proposals acceptable to target persons by offering to reward them if they do as they are asked. Such rewards include having their pictures in the newspaper; receiving public praise, medals, plaques, statues, or banquets in their honor; having streets named after them; or receiving a day of celebration for the new development. Target persons will reject such benefits, however, if they see them as bribes, payoffs, inadequate prizes, or illegitimate offers. Sometimes rewards are given to target persons after they have behaved in an

admirable fashion, with an eye toward teaching them to continue their good efforts.

Apparently, a reward promised in order to induce a particular action is not always taken to be a bribe, if the offer is made for a good cause. For example, when staff members of a government agency and a private foundation told townsfolk that they would be given a grant if they planned ways to improve social services in their community and followed procedures prescribed by the granters, the offer was accepted without guilt (Marris and Rein, 1967). It is not unusual for an official body in a community to offer rewards to groups of citizens. For instance, police patrols are often increased if neighbors requesting such protection help by monitoring their own streets.

The reasons behind the use of rewards are well known. Persons who want to influence specific others sense that those others are uninterested, and so they offer a reward to arouse their enthusiasm (Gamson, 1975). The offer may be made as part of a proposal for change, in which case it will be provided only if the decision makers actually do introduce the innovation; or the reward may be used as a reinforcement for approved past behavior, and the recipients are led to understand that they will be rewarded again if they repeat their good actions. One advantage of publicly rewarding target persons is that bystanders see certain actions rewarded and assume that anyone else (themselves, for instance) who behaves in the same fashion will also be rewarded.

What are the consequences of receiving a reward? We know from research that a person who gets a reward is grateful toward those who provide it, but not if the reward is seen to be payment for services agreed on and rendered or deserved for some other reason. In such a case, the gain is not a reward; it is a payment ("I had it coming"). A reward will not be effective if it is not valued by the receiver. Moreover, if the same reward is offered repeatedly, its value falls, and it is no longer satisfying. Those who are rewarded many times eventually raise their price and want more for the same amount of service.

Persons who move into action solely because of an offered reward are ordinarily motivated only to earn the reward, not to carry out an action that is valuable or sensible in its own right. The reward, not the change, is the incentive. When this is the case, people do only what is necessary to get the reward. They behave in the ways requested by the reward giver. They make these actions visible, so that the agent of change knows that their behavior deserves to be rewarded. The agent of change keeps an eye on the target persons, to be sure that they do the things that warrant the prize. Because target persons' overt acts can be observed, rewards are useful ways to encourage behavioral innovations. If a reformer seeks transformation of the beliefs or attitudes of the target persons, however, it is difficult to determine whether they have in fact made such changes. People can say that they have revised their thinking in order to win a reward when actually they have not. The point is that rewards are more effective in changing target persons' overt actions than in changing their covert beliefs.

Agents of change can be expected to use rewards in several ways to enhance their influence over target persons. They make sure that the object or event they offer as a reward is valued by target persons, since a reward is not a reward unless the receivers believe it is. They make sure that the persons being rewarded know why they have won approval, so that the awarded behavior

will be repeated. They make sure that bestowal of the reward is made public, so that it will provide a lesson to bystanders. They make sure that the reward is not offered in such a way that it is taken as a bribe, since such offers are demeaning, unethical, and often ineffective. They take care to have plenty of rewards available, so that their supply does not run out. They do not offer the same reward repeatedly. They recognize that by using rewards they can influence overt behavior better than hidden feelings, ideas, or beliefs.

In summary, change agents try to influence the behavior of target persons by providing events or objects that the latter value, on the assumption that rewards will stimulate target persons' interest in creating a change. The persons who benefit feel grateful toward the providers of the reward, unless the receivers do not place much value on the reward or feel that they have earned it as payment for their efforts.

AGENTS OF CHANGE COERCE TARGET PERSONS

Activists become coercive when they intend to constrain freedom of choice among persons they wish to influence. In using coercion, change agents threaten to punish target persons if they do not do what they are asked to do or do not stop behaving in undesirable ways. The coercers inflict a penalty or punishment on the ones being coerced, until the latter change their behavior. There is no limit to the ways in which reformers can be coercive. For example, citizens interfere with a session of the city council by interrupting unwanted speakers. Workers employed downtown block access to the city's parking structure after the city raises rates on streetside parking meters. Homeless squatters build shacks on university property, to make their deprivation visible. Parents threaten the school board with recall if the board does not fire the football coach. Students raid a building where animals are housed for use in medical research. A neighborhood organization stops making contributions to the town's United Fund because the local athletic club was not given a grant that it requested. A nuclear power plant is set on fire by activists opposed to such sources of electricity. Bus drivers run late because of alleged discrimination by the traffic commission in the hiring of homosexual women.

We shall consider three types of coercive action here. First, activists interfere with efforts of target persons, so that the latter cannot do their regular work. Second, they physically limit the freedom of target persons or hostages. Third, they threaten harm or inflict it on target persons, other individuals, or things of value. But first, a few comments on the nature of coercion.

Any coercive act places constraints on the behavior of those toward whom it is directed. The threatened penalty is repulsive, and in order to avoid this punishment, the persons being coerced do what is asked of them. The driver obeys a traffic cop. A university's board of regents stops talking when students crowd its meeting room to shout insults. Constraints are stronger as the proffered punishments are more undesirable. If the target persons see the penalty as not repellent (or not likely to occur), they will pay little attention to coercive demands. Like rewarding, coercion changes overt behavior more effectively than it changes covert beliefs, since visible actions can be monitored by the coercer, but ideas and attitudes cannot. Therefore, those who use coercion typically spy on persons they put under pressure, to make sure that punishment is promptly delivered

when it is deserved. . . . [T]he threat of coercion, its actual use, and the subsequent surveillance put on persons who have been pressed to change generate poor interpersonal relations between the agents of change and the target persons. These in themselves become a separate cause for concern.

We get an insight into how often activists use coercion from the study done by Gamson (1975). Gamson examined the strategies employed by a number of protest movements. Most of these bodies had hundreds or thousands of members, and so they are not replicas of the units we have been considering. Nevertheless, much of what they did took place in community settings, and so Gamson's findings are not wholly irrelevant to our purpose. Gamson looked for two kinds of success in the work of these groups. One kind is the community's *acceptance of the change agents' group* (that is, the unit was seen as a set of spokespersons who represented legitimate interests). The activists were therefore respected and given attention. The other kind of success is that Gamson calls *attainment of new advantages* (that is, the group achieved its objectives to some degree or won other valued outcomes). Thus, the unit won respect as a group, accomplished something worthwhile, or both. The organizations in Gamson's sample had similar rates of success in winning acceptance (47 percent) and in achieving new advantages (49 percent). Gamson was interested in two ways of protesting. One way limited the freedom of target persons and included instances of strikes, boycotts, vituperation, discrediting of antagonists, or restricting the moves of those being pressed. The other way was more violent and included harmful attacks or threats to persons or property. The freedom-limiting behavior was used by 42 percent of the groups, and violence was used by 25 percent. The larger the organization, the more its members were likely to engage in violence; the smaller the group, the more likely it was to be the recipient of violence. We shall review more of Gamson's results later.

Blocking the Progress of Target Persons Toward Their Goals. In some methods of coercion, activists set out to make it difficult for target persons to conduct their regular business or achieve their normal objectives. The blockers say (or shout) that they will continue their obstruction until they get their way. I can think of five different blocking maneuvers.

In one form, called a *sit-in*, participants seek services in a place where they have been forbidden to enter. They remain until they are forced to leave. For example, black students walk into restaurants, libraries, or bus stations that they are not supposed to use. Workers slow their actions to a snail's pace, so that production is reduced to a trickle. Dissidents stand or sit on a highway, so that trucks and cars cannot move into a nuclear power plant or remove weapons from a munitions depot.

In a second way of creating a barrier, agents of change interfere with the business of target persons. They strike, walk out, sabotage machinery, or take over a meeting and allow only their own members to talk.

In a third type of blocking maneuver, reformers interfere with the work of persons in an organization whose practices they wish to change. They attend the meetings of a decision-making body, such as a city council or a board of education, and prevent business as usual by making loud comments (from the audience), seizing the microphone, occupying all the seats in the hall, refusing to be quiet, making it impossible for speakers (on the wrong side of the issue) to be heard, or bringing along a brass band.

Alinsky (1971) urges members of inner-city neighborhood community councils to make their grievances known to governmental officials in no uncertain terms. He says, "Our concern is with the tactic of taking; how the have-nots can take power from the haves" (Alinsky, 1971, p. 126). He provides a set of rules (actually, they are maxims) for what he calls *power tactics*. He means, in our terms, successful coercion of decision makers through interference with their meetings. Alinsky's list of rules includes the following: "Power is not only what you have but what the enemy thinks you have" (p. 127); "Make the enemy live up to their own book of rules" (p. 128); "Ridicule is man's most potent weapon" (p. 128); "Keep the pressure on" (p. 128); "The threat is usually more terrifying than the thing itself" (p. 128); and "The price of a successful attack is a constructive alternative" (p. 130).

The leaders of an organization of tenants in a housing project created a rent strike, refusing to pay what they owed until their apartments were rehabilitated. Brill (1971), in a book-length description of this strike, says that central members prevented the eviction of tenants for nonpayment of their rent by threatening to create a riot if nonpayers were forced to move out of the housing project. This threat worked so well that they used it repeatedly thereafter.

A fourth form of blockage is a *boycott,* in which dissatisfied persons agree to buy nothing from or provide no services to individuals who are responsible for an unpleasant state of affairs. Familiar examples are refusals to shop in certain stores, ride local buses, or work for particular bosses.

A fifth form of blocking maneuver is a hostile demonstration, in which disadvantaged persons reveal the depth of their displeasure by breaking windows, vandalizing furniture, or destroying equipment used by target persons.

The common feature of these five blocking moves is that reformers willfully create barriers that interfere with the productivity of those they want to influence. Why do activists use such approaches? They use them mostly because these are ways of getting attention from individuals who are ignoring the demands made by the change agents. Blocking actions force the affected people to pay attention to ideas that they prefer to ignore (Carter, 1973). These methods also allow activists to indicate clearly that they are angry and dissatisfied and want a change. Change agents use barrier-producing procedures if they know how target persons work and can therefore see how to block their work. They also hope to create confusion, which arises out of the obstructed persons' uncertainty about how to respond to the interventions. The target persons want to prevent interference with their work, but they also feel guilty if they do not provide a fair hearing to the reformers, and they become anxious if they provoke criticisms among bystanders who feel that the complainers have had too little (or too much) sympathetic attention.

The members of a group devoted to social action will be more ready to interrupt the work of target persons, according to Levitt (1973), if they feel and are willing to express moral outrage at the behavior of these decision makers. The change seekers are sure that their view is superior in its virtue to all others, and yet it is being ignored. They also are more inclined to intervene in the work of target persons if they want a solution to their troubles very soon but the officials are dragging their feet or are only pretending to give the matter consideration. The change seekers therefore feel that they can open the issue only by confronting the officials. They do not mind having their tactics or themselves disparaged, disapproved, criticized, or resented, and their courage to act is based on their faith in the cause they represent. Although their actions are a form of blackmail, they are prepared to use this method to get their way.

Robertson (1988) believes that protests are frequent in and around San Francisco because there are many universities in the area that create a ferment of ideas. There is a tradition of strong unions, with an emphasis on group discipline and a "them against us" attitude. There is a variety of races, politics, ethnic bodies, and sexual preferences, which make conflict a regular part of life. Moreover, the climate allows year-round outdoor gatherings and demonstrations. Robertson remarks that many San Franciscans ally themselves to causes because they get a sense of identity from doing so and they enjoy rebelling against authority in outrageous ways. It is fun and provides excitement.

What effects do methods like these have on persons at the receiving end? Of course, they are seldom welcomed. To limit the length of the following discussion, I shall concentrate on procedures used in interrupting a meeting, since the psychology of such an action is typical of what happens in other ways and places. Furthermore, any blockage of work eventually must be settled at a conference table, where changers and target persons meet face to face. As we have remarked, blocking behavior is hard for recipients to handle. The aggressive recklessness that characterizes such behavior generates anger or defensiveness among target persons, as well as a temptation to respond in kind. The inclination to imitate the style of the interrupters is exacerbated if the ideas that the reformers propose are not useful. Indeed, it often happens that activists have no innovations at all to offer; they simply want to stop what is going on, to counter an operation that is responsible for their dissatisfaction. They block a meeting and demand that the program they dislike be cancelled, but they have no suggestions for a better way of doing things when they are asked what improvements they recommend. For example, college students want "irrelevant" teaching stopped, but they cannot say what ought to be taught or how, or interrupters make proposals, based on misinformation, about the organization they are attacking, and the target persons are embarrassed by trying to respond soberly to these far-out ideas.

A group of target persons whose members are prevented from working is faced with several alternatives: giving in to the interrupters and acceding to their demands, trying to reason with them, sitting and being reviled, or clearing the room. Any effort to suppress noisy confronters can backfire if bystanders are drawn into helping the suppressed persons and if these newcomers sharpen the aggressiveness of the activists. Then each side becomes increasingly hostile in response to the actions of the other. Under laws requiring that public organizations hold open meetings, it is not permissible to meet secretly and thereby dodge such interference. A likely resolution of this intervention is for the target persons to propose a meeting with the protesters, in order to engage in constructive problem solving. The target persons may be uneasy about proposing to do this, since past actions of the disrupters do not suggest that they will behave in ways necessary for a sensible session. Nevertheless, I believe that assertive interventionists can become calmly objective once they have an opportunity to present their case to target persons and can evaluate it against other proposals (see Lancourt, 1979).

How can barriers be used effectively? Consider two broadly different types of action: those in which change agents are disobedient (but their behavior is civil), and those in which the success of their intervention depends on a discourteous style. In civil disobedience, activists visibly violate customs or laws governing behavior, continue to do so when asked to desist, and respond to aggression against them with no hostility, since angry behavior could make them guilty of assault and battery or generate public reaction against them. For example, a number of citizens occupied a mayor's office, refused to leave when asked, and went limp when dragged from the building. At the first opportunity, they reentered the office and began their vigil once more, singing, chanting, and smiling to those whose work was interrupted. Such group action requires members who have strong faith in their convictions, so that they can withstand criticism and attempts to repress them. They are civilly passive in order to demonstrate their moral strength and the faith they have in the rightness of their cause, not because they are weak and hesitant. Civil disobedience is more effective, as we noted earlier, if it generates feelings of guilt in target groups who ignore requests for relief. Reformers induce guilt by emphasizing the unfairness of the situation they wish to change. Their perseverance in the face of demands that they stop protesting increases guilt among target persons, and the reformers generate even more shame among target persons if they are forced to cease and desist. A demonstration of civil disobedience requires participants to engage in shared planning and to agree to stick to their plan. Passive resistance, as we saw earlier, may cause low morale among the resisters because their progress is bound to be slow. Therefore, managers of such a procedure repeatedly reassure members that their plan is a wise one, that their unit's success will be all they have hoped for, and that they are gradually winning their way, even though this may not yet appear to be the case. How to maintain morale among the courteously disobedient should be given more study.

Levitt (1973, p. 77) believes that the success of face-to-face confrontation depends on the use of "pushiness, jarring rhetoric, and sometimes outright violence." The actions are carefully staged, to get wide publicity at the expense of adversaries. This style of influence goes beyond mere persuasion because those who use it anticipate open disapproval of their methods and intend to ride roughshod over such criticism. The appearance of resistance among target persons is taken by the activists as evidence of the effect they desire to have. Levitt (1973) states that interrupters depend on exaggeration in word or deed. They overstate their case, sharpen the issue and force listeners to respond. The confronters hammer away at only one or two issues and refuse to be drawn into discussing other topics. They express righteous anger and say repeatedly that the target persons are at fault. If and when members of the audience change their minds, they do so in order to stop this harassment.

Restricting Target Persons' Freedom of Movement. In this approach, change agents seize one or more persons and keep them isolated or under guard. They often take persons other than decision makers and declare that they will not set these victims free, or will harm them, if stated demands are not met by officials within a given period of time. The incentive presented to decision makers in order to make them act on these threats is to stop the suffering of the captured persons. In a related approach, activists may conduct a coup d'état, in which a band of militant persons captures key leaders in the governmental bureaucracy and forces them to do as they

are told or replaces them with individuals who will act as ordered. Because this instructed subset occupies a central place in the organization, the remaining members follow the instructions issued by their usual superiors, and the administrative machinery continues to run as it always has (Luttwak, 1968).

Other examples of the use of physical restraint to force a change are noteworthy. The regents of a university are locked in their meeting room by students who are demanding that the school recruit a larger proportion of black, Asian, and Chicano students. Individuals whose behavior in the community does not suit self-appointed reformers are seized as a way of making them obey rules laid down by the vigilantes. Managers of a company are barred from their offices until they develop new methods for protecting workers from accidents. A well-known individual is taken as a hostage, so that the complaints of the kidnapers will be given wide notice. Trains, planes, or ships are hijacked, and passengers are kept under armed surveillance until the grievances of their kidnapers are resolved (or the aggressors themselves are apprehended).

Why do change agents adopt such methods? A major reason is that a small band can accomplish much in this way. It gains immediate attention from the news media, which make a wide audience available at no cost and describe the unsatisfactory state of affairs about which the hijackers are complaining. The hijackers thereby get a hearing from persons they otherwise could not reach, and sometimes they win sympathy from observers who have never heard of them or their cause. The act itself is a form of propaganda by deed, since it implies that the perpetrators have a good reason for taking such measures; they are asking for help in eliminating an entrenched deprivation.

Because hostage taking is illegal in most places, officials concerned with protecting public safety soon become involved. They must choose among stalling and saying nothing to the kidnapers, in the hope that the latter will decide that their attempt has failed; talking with the captors in ways that keep them calm; bargaining, in order to see what freedom for the hostages would cost; and attacking the place where the hostages are kept, in order to rescue them and arrest the criminals.

What conditions cause such hostile behavior to be successful? Gamson (1975) reports that the social movements he studied were more likely to attain at least some of their objectives through blocking, vituperation, or violence if they had strongly centralized (formal) supervision of their organizations, aimed to displace the leaders among target persons, and were not disposed to altruism. The writings of Hyams (1975), Laqueur (1979), and Luttwak (1968) suggest what takers of hostages usually have going for them. The actions are mounted by a small, well-drilled, closely directed group whose members have rehearsed their operations well. The small size of the unit makes it inconspicuous, hard to find, and not easy to identify. The squad works quickly and carries out actions that the actors know will stimulate outrage and repugnance among hostages and observers. Each member of the unit knows exactly what he or she is to do. Leadership is strong because the uncertain situation may make it necessary to revise the initially planned procedure after the operation begins. The squad's members are obedient and willing to do what they are told, no matter how repulsive these actions may be. They feel deeply about the importance of the group's objectives and are therefore willing to be fanatics.

Because publicity is necessary for the success of such an activity, participants are schooled in how to talk to reporters and how to state their demands clearly. The kidnapers are also trained in bargaining because a hostage-taking event involves oral give-and-take (at a distance) with police or other officials. Success often depends on the ability to drive a hard bargain, and so the kidnapers must be articulate, unflappable, aware of what they can and cannot concede, and apparently fearless. They learn the tricks of haggling, such as offering concessions at one time and cancelling them later, showing an iron fist at one moment and a velvet glove at another, changing their minds whenever an agreement is near, setting a deadline for action by target persons, and stalling for time when stalling is useful. Above all, they attempt to encourage sympathy among bystanders by making it appear they have been and are being treated unfairly. One problem for persons who use these methods is that there is no clear point at which to stop or give up. They are breaking the law, and so part or all of their energies are engaged in avoiding penalties.

A coup d'état (a type of activity not often used in democratic society) demands a precise set of circumstances if it is to be used effectively, according to Luttwak (1968). First, "The social and economic conditions of the target [organization] must be such as to confine political participation to a small fraction of the population" (p. 32). Second, "The influence of foreign powers in its life must be relatively limited" (p. 32). Third, "The target state must have a political center. If there are several centers these must be identifiable and must be politically, rather than ethnically, structured. If the state is controlled by a nonpolitically organized unit, the coup can only be made with its consent or neutrality"

(p. 45). The strategy of a coup is controlled by two considerations: the need for speed, and the need to neutralize any opposing forces. Care is taken to avoid bloodshed (which can arouse resistance) during the coup. If there is a delay, the intentions of the rebels will become visible, and there may be enough time for opposition to be organized. If things move swiftly, however, enemies and friends alike will hold their fire, to see what leaders of the coup intend to do. (They learn this too late, after the new regime is already in command.)

Harming or Threatening to Harm. In the most extreme form of constraint, initiators inflict pain or damage on persons and objects, or they warn that they will do such things if their wishes are not met. Bombs are exploded in public places, citizens who have no relevance to the activists' grievance are injured, community leaders are harmed, informants are grilled or tortured, undesirable people are lynched, and prominent figures are assassinated or replaced by members of the opposition as part of a coup d'état. Threats are delivered through anonymous telephone calls, unsigned letters, burning crosses, or hostile graffiti. For example, a leader of organized crime and politics in China warns dissidents by depositing a black coffin in the living room of a misbehaver, or members of the Mafia deliver a dead fish to convey the same kind of message.

Brill (1971) tells how leaders of a rent strike at a city-owned housing project tried to frighten city officials into meeting the strike group's demands. They used planned behavior to show that they were powerful and angry. They all stared stonily at the mayor while refusing to answer questions (silent stubbornness was perceived to be a way of displaying strength), exaggerated the number of persons taking part in the strike, used military terms when addressing one another in a public meeting, boasted publicly about the effectiveness of their hostile acts, and showed up at bargaining sessions wearing African tribal costumes.

Actions like these are often said to be forms of terrorism because they terrify those who are harmed, are threatened with harm, or observe such events. The term *terrorism*, however, has different meanings among students of such behavior. Here are a few typical definitions; all describe terrorism as a *political* act. Terrorism is the "use of terror by political militants as a means of overthrowing a government in power, or of forcing that government to change its policies" (Hyams, 1975, p. 46). It is "the use of covert violence by a group for political ends and [it] is usually directed against a government, less often against another group, class, or party" (Laqueur, 1979, p. 79). It is "the use or threatened use of violence in behalf of a political or ideological cause" (Newhouse, 1985, p. 46). "Terrorism is the deliberate and systematic murder, maiming and menacing of the innocent to inspire fear for political ends" (Netanyahu, 1978, p. 48). Hitchens (1986) remarks that it is difficult to find a definition of terrorism that is not tautological or vacuous (the use of violence for political ends), a cliché (an attack on innocent men, women, and children), or a synonym for the actions of swarthy opponents of United States foreign policy. He reviews five recent books on terrorism and concludes that the term is essentially a cliché in search of a meaning. It is a handy label that obliterates the need for making distinctions among various kinds of violent acts employed to encourage social change. (A synonym in the urban drug culture of today is simply "criminal gang behavior.") This vague and emotionally loaded notion of terrorism has generated numerous misconceptions. Laqueur (1979, p. 219) lists several such beliefs: "Terrorism is a new and unprecedented phenomenon." (In fact, it has a long history in many parts of the world.) "Terrorism is used only by persons at the left end of the political spectrum." (In fact, dictatorships of the right always depend on it to ensure their power, and so do criminal leaders.) "Terrorism is employed by persons who have a legitimate grievance; removing the cause for the complaint will therefore eliminate the terrorism." (In fact, the complaints of terrorists are often hard to understand, impossible to remedy, or exceedingly self-centered.) "Terrorism is always effective." (In fact, it is useful only in limited circumstances, when a mass movement makes it part of a grand strategy or when it follows a political assassination.) "Terrorists are really human idealists and more intelligent than ordinary criminals who perform terrorist acts." (In fact, some of the worst horrors in history have been carried out by persons with strong ideals, and most of the successful terrorists of our time have the overt and full support of a specific religious group.) "Terrorism is used as a weapon only by the poor and weak." (In fact, many ardent terrorists are wealthy and powerful leaders.)

All in all, the term *terrorism* is too obscure and sweeping for our purposes. Its frequent use in daily discourse indicates that some agents of change choose to inflict deliberate harm on those they intend to influence. Fortunately, we seldom see such violent acts in American community groups engaged in social action except among (or between) criminal gangs, which use many of the methods that political terrorists use.

Why do activists plan to do harm to persons or objects? This question has many answers because reasons differ in different settings. One explanation points to the personal characteristics of those who use violent behavior or threats. Attempts to learn whether violence-prone people are similar in their personalities and different from the nonviolent have yielded few reliable or useful findings. It is evident, however, that harmdoers are most often young middle-class males (Laqueur, 1979). They frequently begin their careers by pressing for social change in legitimate ways, but because they are not successful with that approach, they turn to more extreme methods, assuming that doing damage to people or property will work. They know that hostile behavior will win the attention of the persons they hope to influence. Hyams (1975) asserts that agents of change use violence in order to weaken the status of local officials. Citizens observe that their leaders have not protected them from danger, and so they doubt the ability of the office holders and no longer want them in office.

Users of violence give other reasons for choosing an aggressive style. They think it will overcome the inertia of target persons and force them to attend to issues they have been avoiding. The aggressors also believe that this style will earn them the support of observers if their hostile actions are met with force. They assume that the products of modern technology make it easier to do harm without being caught. Examples of such products are plastic explosives, bombs that can be triggered at a distance, devices to interrupt or tap into enemy computers, poison darts, mind-altering drugs, and instruments that allow eavesdropping on private conversations over radio waves or telephone lines. In several parts of the world, and in some ethnic neighborhoods of the United States, a man who is wronged is disapproved of by his peers until he has had his revenge on the ones who offended him.

Doers of harm are skilled in rationalizing their behavior to themselves and to critics. Their usual argument is that the ends they seek are so valuable (fair, beneficial, overdue, correct) that they may properly use any method that will work (Pfaff, 1986). Any harm this procedure causes to target persons is a fair price, they think, for getting rid of a deplorable situation. The ends justify the means. As a variation on this theme, hostile change agents believe that the persons they are treating violently are so evil, wrong, and despicable that they have no rights. Such views have been expressed over the years by writers who support the infliction of pain as a method of introducing change.

Hyams (1975) reviews arguments expressed by philosophers of violence around the turn of the century, including Max Stirner. Writing in 1906, Stirner based his ideas on the necessity for ultraindividualistic behavior. Each person, he said, is alone against all others. A state or a government is not needed to provide for or protect a citizen. If an individual cannot get others to provide what he demands of them, he should take it by force. Faults in society are not due to the strength of the masters but to the weakness of the underlings. Each person must make his own way, depending on nobody else. (Where have we heard such ideas more recently?)

Nechayev (also cited by Hyams) advised individuals to transform themselves into ruthless egos dedicated to creating a revolution by creating fear in any who resist. First, revolutionaries are to assassinate all intelligent and important persons. They also must get rid of the would-be reformers because such persons may be successful in introducing desirable modifications and may thereby weaken people's interest in rebelling. Stupid and unimportant citizens should be left alone because their behavior warrants revolution and should visibly illustrate the need for reform. A more recent writer who offers comparable rationalizations is Fanon (1966), who declares that violence is "a cleansing force" that "frees the black from an inferiority complex, restores his self-respect, and invests his character with positive and creative qualities" (p. 73).

What effects do harmful actions have? They often intimidate target persons or cause them confusion about how to deal with such acts. Weak and hesitant responses occur if the persons under attack are not prepared to handle hostility or if they are not able to resist the change agents. They may unwillingly do what is asked, in order to keep the peace or avoid harm. They will not let themselves be so influenced, however, if they can deviate from the wishes of change agents without this deviance being detected. If the target persons are strong enough to ignore the activists' threats, they will meet aggression with their own aggression, which often encourages further and hotter hostility from the agents of change, and a cycle of escalation begins. The issue at hand is ignored because of anger and the desire on both sides to meet fire with fire.

Gamson (1975) found that participants in 25 percent of the protesting social movements he examined used violence against people. Movements that used violent behavior won about as much acceptance and respect as those that did not employ it, but violent actions allowed activists to accomplish more. Among groups that threatened to harm people, 75 percent gained their objectives and 25 percent did not. Among those that used civil methods, 53 percent reached their objectives and 47 percent did not. In Gamson's groups, violence paid off; it helped groups get the changes they sought.

We see, then, that violence can be successful as a stimulator of change. What may account for this success? Perhaps harmdoers prevent escalation of anger by indicating after an aggressive act that they are willing to negotiate or bargain with the target persons. Coercive activists often get their way simply because they have the power to use hostility in a telling fashion. They employ force to win and have enough control over future events to maintain the victory thereafter. The social changes introduced by criminal gangs or dictators are examples.

The most effective groups that use violent behavior are able to suppress quarrels among their own members. They avoid tiffs caused by anxiety over the commitment of their members to group values and objectives. Such conflict is kept under control because the members need one another for protection from the external threats that their groups face and that enhance group cohesion. Even so, several writers believe that most members of a violent team drop out sooner or later, unless they can keep up their enthusiasm for their cause. Leaders of violent gangs try to avoid having their units fall apart by assuring colleagues that they all have the same objectives and by preventing quarrels among participants over who is most faithful to group goals. One wonders how the dynamics of a ruthless, coercive group differ from those of an altruistic body. Do the two have similar problems in keeping the unit effective?

In summary, agents of change may threaten harm or do actual harm to individuals they want to influence, to observers, or to objects of value. They do these things in order to get the attention of target persons and the support, perhaps, of bystanders, and to create an incentive—a negative one—for change. These efforts may generate timid acceptance of their demands or aggressive counteractions. Even though most officials do not like to bargain with users of violence, they usually do. Activists who employ violent methods probably get their way as often as they fail.

SUMMARY

When activists use constraining methods to try to influence target persons, target persons pay less attention to the quality of the ideas proposed by the initiators than to the incentives (to win a reward, or to avoid a penalty or punishment) that accompany the proposals. The receivers agree to introduce changes, in order to attain effects that they value or to avoid ones they dislike.

When they employ pressuring methods, activists realize that target persons may acquiesce in order to win a favorable response or avoid an unfavorable reaction. Thus, they try to determine whether target persons have really changed or are only pretending to have done so. The use of constraining methods requires close monitoring of target persons' behavior. If they do not want to change in the ways proposed by activists but do wish to win favorable reactions or avoid unfavorable responses, then they will pretend to have changed. Activists can monitor overt actions by target persons more reliably than covert shifts in target persons' beliefs, attitudes, or values. Therefore, activists who use constraining methods are often more effective in influencing the overt behavior of target persons than in changing their covert beliefs or feelings.

REFERENCES

Alinsky, S. *Rules for Radicals.* New York: Random House, 1971.

Bailey, F. *The Tactical Uses of Passion.* Ithaca, NY: Cornell University Press, 1983.

Barbrook, A., and C. Bolt. *Power and Protest in American Life.* Oxford, England: Martin Robertson, 1980.

Bar-Tal, D. *Prosocial Behavior: Theory and Research.* New York: Wiley, 1976.

Bellah, R., and others. *Habits of the Heart.* New York: Harper & Row, 1985.

Berry, J. "Beyond Citizen Participation: Effective Advocacy Before Administrative Agencies." *Journal of Applied Behavioral Science,* 1981, *17,* 463–477.

Berscheid, E., and E. Walster. *Interpersonal Attraction.* Reading, MA: Addison-Wesley, 1978.

Bollinger, L. *The Tolerant Society: Freedom of Speech and Extremist Speech in America.* New York: Oxford University Press, 1987.

Boulding, E. "Image and Action in Peace Building." *Journal of Social Issues,* 1988, *44,* 17–38.

Brehm, S., and J. Brehm. *Psychological Reactance: A Theory of Freedom and Controls.* Orlando, FL: Academic Press, 1981.

Brill, H. *Why Organizations Fail.* Berkeley: University of California Press, 1971.

Caldwell, L., L. Hayes, and I. MacWhirter. *Citizens and the Environment.* Bloomington: Indiana University Press, 1976.

Capraro, J. "The Revitalization of Chicago Lawn: A Private Sector Response to Local Decline." *Commentary,* 1979, *3,* 11–14.

Carter, A. *Direct Action and Liberal Democracy.* New York: Harper & Row, 1973.

Cartwright, D., ed. *Studies in Social Power.* Ann Arbor: Institute for Social Research, University of Michigan, 1959.

Cartwright, D. "Influence, Leadership, and Control." In J. March ed., *Handbook of Organization.* Skokie, IL: Rand McNally, 1965.

Cartwright, D., and A. Zander. *Group Dynamics: Research and Theory.* New York: Harper & Row, 1968.

Chamberlain, D. "Town Without Pity." *Image,* Aug. 2, 1987, pp. 23–28.

Commager, H. *The Era of Reform, 1830–1860.* New York: Van Nostrand Reinhold, 1960.

Cordes, C. "Responding to Terrorism." *The Monitor,* 1986. *17,* 12–13.

Crowfoot, J., M. Chesler, and J. Boulet. "Organizing for Social Justice." In E. Seidman, ed., *Handbook of Social Intervention.* Newbury Park, CA: Sage, 1983.

Deci, E. *Intrinsic Motivation.* New York: Plenum, 1975.

Delbecq, A., and A. Van de Ven. *Group Techniques for Program Planning.* Glenview, IL: Scott, Foresman, 1975.

Delgado, G. *Organizing the Movement: The Roots and Growth of ACORN.* Philadelphia: Temple University Press, 1986.

Deutsch, M. *The Resolution of Conflict.* New Haven: Yale University Press, 1973.

Diringer, E. "Earth Lovers Tell Why They Turned Tough." *San Francisco Chronicle,* Dec. 7, 1987, p. A-8.

Douglas, M., and A. Wildavsky. *Risk and Culture.* Berkeley: University of California Press, 1982.

Fanon, F. *The Wretched of the Earth.* New York: Grove Press, 1966.

Flinn, J. "Playing Mental Games." *San Francisco Examiner,* Jan. 21, 1988, p. B-8.

Frank, D. "Experimental Studies of Personal Pressure and Resistance." *Journal of General Psychology,* 1944, *30,* 23–41.

Fraser, J. *The Chinese: Portrait of a People.* New York: Summit Books, 1980.

French, J., and B. Raven. "The Bases of Social Power." In D. Cartwright, ed., *Studies in Social Power.* Ann Arbor: Institute for Social Research, University of Michigan, 1959.

Fuchs, L. "The Role and Communication Task of the Change-Agent Experience of the Peace Corps Volunteers in the Philippines." In D. Lerner and W. Schramm, eds., *Communication and Change in the Developing Countries.* Honolulu: East-West Center, 1967.

Funk, D. *Group Dynamics Law: Integrating Constitutive Contract Institutions.* New York: Philosophical Library, 1982.

Gamson, W. *Power and Discontent.* Homewood, IL: Dorsey Press, 1968.

Gamson, W. *The Strategy of Social Protest.* Homewood, IL: Dorsey Press, 1975.

Gerlach, L., and V. Hine. *People, Power, and Change: Movements of Social Transformation.* Indianapolis: Bobbs-Merrill, 1970.

Goodenough, W. *Cooperation in Change.* New York: Russell Sage Foundation, 1963.

Gotshalk, D. *Human Aims in Modern Perspective.* Yellow Springs, OH: Antioch Press, 1966.

Gusfield, J. "The Study of Social Movements." In D. Silk, ed., *International Encyclopedia of Social Sciences,* Vol. 14. New York: Macmillan, 1968.

Hammond, K., and L. Adelman. "Science, Values, and Human Judgment." *Science,* 1976, *194,* 389–396.

Hanley, R. "The Hot Dirt Rebellion." *San Francisco Chronicle and Examiner,* Sept. 14, 1986, p. A-5.

Hine, R. *California's Utopian Colonies.* New Haven: Yale University Press, 1953.

Hirschman, A. "Reactionary Rhetoric." *Atlantic Monthly,* May 1989, pp. 63–70.

Hitchens, C. "Wanton Acts of Usage." *Harper's,* Sept. 1986, pp. 66–76.

Holsti, E. "Crisis, Stress, and Decision Making." *International Social Science Journal,* 1971, *23,* 53–67.

Hornblower, M. "Not in My Backyard, You Don't." *Time,* June 27, 1988, pp. 44–46.

Hyams, E. *Terrorism and Terrorists.* New York: St. Martin's Press, 1975.

Janis, I. *Victims of Groupthink.* Boston: Houghton Mifflin, 1972.

Janis, I., and L. Mann. *Decision Making.* New York: Free Press, 1977.

Kahneman, D., and A. Tversky. "Prospect Theory: An Analysis of Decision Under Risk." *Econometrica,* 1979, *47,* 239–291.

Kanter, R. *Commitment and Community.* Cambridge, MA: Harvard University Press, 1972.

Kiesler, C. *The Psychology of Commitment.* Orlando, FL: Academic Press, 1971.

Knoke, D., and J. Wood. *Organized for Action: Commitment in Voluntary Associations.* New Brunswick, NJ: Rutgers University Press, 1981.

Kweit, M., and R. Kweit. *Implementing Citizen Participation in a Bureaucratic Society.* New York: Praeger, 1971.

Lancourt, J. *Confront or Concede.* Lexington, MA: Heath, 1979.

Langton, S. "Current Reflections on the State of the Art." In S. Langton, ed., *Citizen Participation in America.* Lexington, MA: Heath, 1978.

Lanternari, V. *The Religions of the Oppressed.* New York: Knopf, 1963.

Laqueur, W. *Terrorism.* Boston: Little, Brown, 1979.

Lebow, R., and J. Stein. "Beyond Deterrence." *Journal of Social Issues,* 1987, *43,* 5–71.

Levitt, T. *The Third Sector: New Tactics for a Responsive Society.* New York: American Management Association, 1973.

Lindgren, H. "The Informal-Intermittent Organization: A Vehicle for Successful Citizen Protest." *Journal of Applied Behavioral Science,* 1987, *23,* 397–412.

Lippitt, R., J. Watson, and B. Westley. *The Dynamics of Planned Change.* San Diego, CA: Harcourt Brace Jovanovich, 1958.

Lipset, S., and E. Raab. *The Politics of Unreason.* New York: Harper & Row, 1970.

Liversidge, D. *The Luddites: Machine Breakers of the Early Nineteenth Century.* New York: Watts, 1972.

Luttwak, E. *Coup d'état: A Practical Handbook.* New York: Knopf, 1968.

Macaulay, J., and L. Berkowitz. *Altruism and Helping Behavior.* Orlando, FL: Academic Press, 1970.

Madison, A. *Vigilantism in America.* New York: Seaburg Press, 1973.

Marris, P., and M. Rein. *Dilemmas of Social Reform.* New York: Lieber-Atherton, 1967.

Mayer, A. "The Significance of Quasi-Groups in the Study of Complex Societies." In M. Banton, ed., *The Social Anthropology of Complex Societies.* London: Tavistock, 1966.

Meier, B. "Citizen Suits Become a Popular Weapon in the Fight Against Industrial Polluters." *Wall Street Journal,* Apr. 17, 1987, p. 17.

Moreland, R., and J. Levine. "Socialization in Small Groups: Temporal Changes in Individual-Group Relations." In L. Berkowitz, ed., *Advances in Experimental Social Psychology,* Vol. 15. Orlando, FL: Academic Press, 1980.

Morgan, G. *Images of Organization.* Newbury Park, CA: Sage, 1986.

Moscovici, S. *Social Influence and Social Change.* Orlando, FL: Academic Press, 1976.

Moynihan, D. *Maximum Feasible Misunderstanding.* New York: Free Press, 1970.

Netanyahu, B. *Terrorism: How the West Can Win.* New York: Farrar, Straus & Giroux, 1987.

Newcomb, T. *The Acquaintance Process.* New York: Holt, Rinehart & Winston, 1961.

Newhouse, J. "The Diplomatic Round: A Freemasonry of Terrorism." *The New Yorker,* July 8, 1985, pp. 46–63.

Nisbet, R. *The Quest for Community.* New York: Oxford University Press, 1953.

Nisbett, R., and L. Ross. *Human Inference: Strategies and Shortcomings of Social Judgment.* Englewood-Cliffs, NJ: Prentice-Hall, 1980.

Olsen, M. *Participatory Pluralism.* Chicago: Nelson-Hall, 1982.

Osborn, A. *Applied Imagination.* New York: Scribner's, 1957.

Perlman, J. "Grassroots Participation from Neighborhoods to Nations." In S. Langton, ed., *Citizen Participation in America.* Lexington, MA: Heath, 1978.

Pfaff, E. "Reflections: The Dimensions of Terror." *The New Yorker,* Nov. 10, 1986, pp. 122–131.

Piven, F., and R. Cloward. *Poor People's Movements: Why They Succeed and How They Fail.* New York: Pantheon, 1977.

Prestby, J., and A. Wandersman. "An Empirical Exploration of a Framework of Organizational Viability: Maintaining Block Organizations." *Journal of Applied Behavioral Science,* 1985, *21,* 287–305.

Priscoli, J. "Implementing Public Involvement Programs in Federal Agencies." In S. Langton, ed., *Citizen Participation in America.* Lexington, MA: Heath, 1978.

Pruitt, D. "Methods for Resolving Differences of Interest: A Theoretical Analysis." *Journal of Social Issues,* 1972, *28,* 133–154.

Pruitt, D., and J. Rubin. *Social Conflict: Escalation, Stalemate, and Settlement.* New York: Random House, 1986.

Robertson, M. "A Penchant for Protest: Why the Bay Area Likes to Demonstrate." *San Francisco Chronicle,* Mar. 25, 1988, pp. B-3–B-4.

Rogers, E. "Social Structure and Social Change." In G. Zaltman, ed., *Process and Phenomena of Social Change.* New York: Wiley, 1973.

Rogers, E. *Diffusion of Innovations.* New York: Free Press, 1983.

Rosenblatt, R. "The Demogogue in the Crowd." *Time,* Oct. 21, 1985, p. 102.

Rosener, J. "Matching Method to Purpose: The Challenge of Planning Citizen Activities." In S. Langton, ed., *Citizen Participation in America.* Lexington, MA: Heath, 1978.

Rothman, J., J. Erlich, and J. Teresa. *Promoting Innovation and Change in Organizations and Communities.* New York: Wiley, 1976.

Rude, G. *The Crowd in History: A Study of Popular Disturbances in France and England, 1730–1848.* New York: Wiley, 1964.

Ruffner, F., ed. *Encyclopedia of Associations,* 5th ed. Detroit: Gale Research Co., 1968.

Schachter, S. *The Psychology of Affiliation.* Palo Alto, CA: Stanford University Press, 1959.

Seligman, M. *Helplessness: On Depression, Development, and Death.* New York: W. H. Freeman, 1975.

Sieber, S. *Fatal Remedies: The Ironies of Social Intervention.* New York: Plenum, 1981.

Stone, C. *Should Trees Have Standing? Toward Legal Rights for Natural Objects.* Los Altos, CA: Kaufmann, 1974.

Thum, G., and M. Thum. *The Persuaders: Propaganda in War and Peace.* New York: Atheneum, 1972.

Toch, H. *The Social Psychology of Social Movements.* Indianapolis: Bobbs-Merrill, 1965.

Trotter, R. "Stop Blaming Yourself." *Psychology Today,* 1987, *21,* 31–39.

Tversky, A., and D. Kahneman. "Causal Schemata in Judgments Under Uncertainty." In M. Fishbein, ed., *Progress in Social Psychology.* Hillsdale, NJ: Erlbaum, 1978.

Unger, D., and A. Wandersman. "The Importance of Neighbors." *American Journal of Community Psychology,* 1985, *13,* 139–169.

Vander Werf, M. "Sign Man Calls 'Em, Wears 'Em." *Arizona Republican,* Oct. 4, 1987, p. B-1.

Vogel, E. *Modern Japanese Organization and Decision Making.* Berkeley: University of California Press, 1975.

Walton, E. "Establishing and Maintaining High Commitment in Work Systems." In J. R. Kimberly, R. H. Miles, and Associates, eds., *The Organizational Life Cycle: Issues in the Creation, Transformation, and Decline of Organizations.* San Francisco: Jossey-Bass, 1980.

Wandersman, A. "A Framework of Participation in Community Organizations." *Journal of Applied Behavioral Science,* 1981, *17,* 27–58.

Wandersman, A. "Citizen Participation." In K. Heller, R. Price, S. Rienharz, and A. Wandersman, eds., *Psychology and Community Change: Challenges of the Future.* Homewood, IL: Dorsey Press, 1984.

Wandersman, A., and others. "Getting Together and Getting Things Done." *Psychology Today,* Nov. 1985, 64–71.

Wandersman, A., and others. "Who Participates, Who Does Not, and Why? An Analysis of Voluntary Neighborhood Organizations in the United States and Israel." *Sociological Forum,* 1987, *2,* 534–555.

Warren, R. *Social Change and Human Purpose: Toward Understanding and Action.* Skokie, IL: Rand-McNally, 1971.

Warren, R., S. Rose, and A. Bergunder. *The Structure of Urban Reform.* Lexington, MA: Heath, 1974.

Weick, K. *The Social Psychology of Organizing.* Reading, MA: Addison-Wesley, 1979.

Wicker, A. "Behavior Settings Reconsidered: Temporal Stages, Resources, Internal Dynamics, Context." In D. Stokols and E. Altman, eds., *Handbook of Environmental Psychology.* New York: Wiley, 1987.

Wilson, J. *Introduction to Social Movements.* New York: Basic Books, 1973.

Woito, M. *To End War: A New Approach to International Conflict.* New York: Pilgrim Press, 1982.

Wood, J., and M. Jackson. *Social Movements: Development, Participation, and Dynamics.* Belmont, CA: Wadsworth, 1982.

Zander, A. *Motives and Goals in Groups.* Orlando, FL: Academic Press, 1971.

Zander, A. *Groups at Work: Unresolved Issues in the Study of Organizations.* San Francisco: Jossey-Bass, 1977.

Zander, A. *Making Groups Effective.* San Francisco: Jossey-Bass, 1982.

Zander, A. "The Value of Belonging to a Group in Japan." *Small-Group Behavior,* 1983, *14,* 3–14.

Zander, A. *The Purposes of Groups and Organizations.* San Francisco: Jossey-Bass, 1985.

Zander, A., J. Forward, and R. Albert. "Adaptation of Board Members to Repeated Success or Failure by Their Organizations." *Organizational Behavior and Human Performance,* 1969, *4,* 56–76.

Zander, A., and T. Newcomb, Jr. "Group Levels of Aspiration in United Fund Campaigns." *Journal of Personality and Social Psychology,* 1967, *6,* 157–162.

10.

Ruth J. Parsons, Santos H. Hernandez, and James D. Jorgensen

INTEGRATED PRACTICE: A FRAMEWORK
FOR PROBLEM SOLVING

Social workers in the year 2000 will practice in a postindustrial era. As Bell (1973) and Naisbitt (1982) pointed out, the late 1900s are a new societal era characterized by different problems and needs than those to which social work has responded in the past. Naisbitt characterized this era as the information society in which adaptive generalists instead of potentially obsolete specialists will be needed. The complexity of technological advancement has the potential to increase alienation by decreasing connectedness between people and their communities. These views of the emerging society challenge the basis of social work practice and call for a new look at social work intervention. The authors submit that social workers in the new era must be generalists prepared to design interventions for solving social problems, not indepth specialists within a limited dimension of a particular social problem. As Walz and Hoffman (1982) suggested, a society in transition must rebuild and redesign the social institutional base. Thus social workers must grasp a broader domain in which human problems and solutions require the investments of many institutions and professions, only a small portion of which will be social workers. Generalists will need to guide and engineer the problem definition and means of solution, as well as the development and management of community resources for mutual problem solving. Such a view describes social work generalists as creative problem solvers in a specific practice arena (Heus & Pincus, 1986).

Integrated practice, a practice model organized around this view of social work, focuses on a social problem as a target, and uses differential role taking in intervention (Hernandez, Jorgensen, Judd, Gould, & Parsons, 1985). The model suggests that both prevention and habilitation are optional intervention points. Professional social workers are educators and mobilizers of resources, not specialized therapists. Practice principles are guided by a habilitation model that includes promotion of competency, normalization, and empowerment. Integrated practice builds and expands on contemporary social work practice models including Anderson's (1981) micro and macro frameworks, Germain and Gitterman's (1980) life model, and Maluccio's (1981) competency-oriented practice. Practice strategies include differential role taking, teaching problem-solving models, networking, team building, and mutual aid and self-help.

SOCIAL PROBLEMS AS TARGETS

In integrated practice, the target of social work intervention is the whole of social problems, rather than the rehabilitation of victims of social problems alone. Traditionally, social work has defined itself as promoting the interaction between individuals and their environment for the betterment of both (Bartlett, 1970) and has distinguished itself from other related professions by that attribute. This definition implies that the question of location of the problem is open. Rather than assuming that the problem is within an individual, the problem also may be defined as located in the interaction between the individual and the environment or within the environment. Moreover, the question of where to intervene is open. The location of the problem and the focus of intervention need not always be the same.

Using systems concepts as a theory base, social work practice is framed as boundary work (Gordon, 1970). Intervention in either macrosystems (the broader society and communities), mesosystems (neighborhoods, organizations, and groups), or microsystems (individuals and families) can effect results at other levels. A social problem calls for multilevel systems intervention that links systems for a synthesis of energy aimed at problem resolution or reduction. However, in actuality, current social work intervention tends to follow the methodological expertise of the practitioner. This is the "law of the instrument" principle, which uses the expertise of the practitioner to define the area in need of intervention (Kaplan, 1964, p. 23). Described as "specialization by solution," this tendency has guided social workers to work only with the victims of social problems (Heus & Pincus, 1986, p. 15). Victims of social problems are those targeted as the "deviants" in U.S. society. They are the drinkers in the social problem of alcoholism. They are the abusers in the social problem of child abuse. They are depressed or angry women and minorities in the social problems of sexism and racism. They are the most accessible and easily labeled participants in social problems, and society is more willing for social workers to work with these victims than with other components of social problems. Using the medical model as a theoretical screen, "curing" of the sick is more politically acceptable than targeting either the cause or the major contributing factors to social problems. This social pathology view of social problems blames the victims of social problems for their own role in the dynamics of the problem (Rubington & Weinberg, 1981).

Integrated practice, by contrast, views social problems from the labeling perspective suggested by Becker (1963, p. 19). This perspective defines social problems as reactions to an alleged violation of rules or expectations and focuses on the conditions under which behaviors or situations come to be defined as problematic or deviant. A problem is a situation evaluated as undesirable by someone, and may be an unsuccessful solution to another problem. Problems and solutions become different dynamics of the same set of variables. The discrepancy between the expected norm and the labeled behavior can be viewed as the interaction between an individual and the environment, which is the traditional arena of social work practice.

Viewing social work practice in this context opens up the option of prevention as a viable practice arena. Prevention has been dismissed too often as an intervention point in social work because of lack of knowledge regarding causality. Pinpointing the cause of social problems is viewed as a political and theoretical enigma. In fact, it is not necessary to know the cause of social problems to create prevention intervention. It is, however, necessary to target certain contributing factors related to the problem that may be ameliorated, even though these factors may not be readily identified as causal.

Support for this approach can be found in the mental health prevention literature.

Albee (1982) proposed that determining intervention points in prevention can be facilitated by viewing mental dysfunction as a product of several factors (Table 10.1).

Individual differences and environmental stress are relatively difficult to affect. Situational factors, coping skills, self-esteem, and support systems are more likely to be amenable to change. Change in any of these factors affects the incidence though not necessarily the cause. Using this formula, the incidence of concern can be reduced by compensating for organic factors. Compensation can be achieved by reducing environmental stress and/or increasing coping skills, self-esteem, or support systems.

Bloom (1979) suggested that a new paradigm for prevention in mental health should abandon the search for cause and pay closer attention to precipitating factors. The paradigm assumes that people are variously vulnerable to stressful life events and that people may all respond differently to the same event. Therefore prevention programs can aim to facilitate mastery or reduce the incidence of particular stressful life events without focusing on understanding their origins. Linking preventive services with stressful life events such as

TABLE 10.1
Mental Dysfunction

$$\text{Incidence of mental dysfunction} = \frac{\text{organic factors} + \text{stress}}{\text{coping skills} + \text{self esteem} + \text{support system}}$$

school entrance, parenting, divorce, and widowhood, Bloom argued that competence building may be the single most effective preventive strategy for dealing with individual and social issues in most communities. He proposed that availability of community resources, and knowledge and skills for accessing those, are keys to building power, self-esteem, and competence of individuals.

Integrated practice, then, is constructed on the assumption that problems are interactional between an individual and the environment. Intervention takes on dimensions of choice and decision making, and raises a question about where intervention should occur. Intervention is not viewed as directed toward either small or large systems. Instead, intervention is viewed on a continuum (Table 10.2). At one end, intervention engages victims of social problems for habilitative purposes. On the other end,

TABLE 10.2
Integrated Practice Intervention Continuum

Small Systems ◄───► Large Systems

Work with:			
Individuals or groups of victims	Groups of victims	Victims and nonvictims	Victims and non-victims or nonvictims only

For what purpose:			
Habilitation, educations, and sensitization	Enabling victims to create support systems	Creation of and access to needed services structures	Social problem reduction, alleviation, and prevention

intervention engages both victims and non-victims in action-directed environmental changes that mitigate against the contributing factors in the problem.

An illustration of this practice model can be found in viewing the problem of single room occupant (SRO) elderly in inner-city neighborhoods. A traditional view of the problem views the SRO elder as the problem, and therapeutic interventions are created to bring them in line with society's expected norms for behavior. The labeling perspective opens up the definition of the problem and arenas for solution. From an integrated practice perspective, the problem is defined as the elderly's isolation and lack of access to services. SRO elders are seen to be potentially competent persons who are caught in an interactive dynamic of lack of economic resources, preferred autonomous life-styles, chronic illnesses, powerlessness, and learned helplessness. Intervention then would be targeted toward all points along the intervention continuum. The elderly themselves should be offered programs designed to build trust, assess need, educate, and raise awareness about their situation. Support groups can be created in the hotels and apartments to raise awareness and decrease isolation. The service sector should be educated about the population and its isolation. Creative ways to deliver services can be created and taught to the service sector. Finally, advocacy for creation of housing facilities should be conducted.

EDUCATION AS A GUIDE IN ROLE TAKING

An important theoretical assumption in this model is the function of the social worker as educator-generalist. Generalist skills are required; the specialized area of knowledge of practitioners lies in the dynamics of the social problem as a whole and in problem solving. Moreover, as social workers assume different roles along the intervention continuum, an educational emphasis shapes each role or point of intervention.

Rationale for this assumption can be found in the critical consciousness concept of Friere (1972), which suggested that oppressed persons often live in a "culture of silence" and do not possess the capacity for critical awareness and response. They do not see that their situation can be different from what it is, nor do they perceive themselves as having potential power to intervene in the social world and change it. To raise a critical consciousness, education of oppressed people, Friere suggested, should begin with development of self-concept in which they become subjects able to determine their situation, not mere objects at the mercy of whatever happens to them. Education can be an antidote for learned helplessness.

McKnight (1977) strongly critiqued traditional professionalized service. He questioned the service culture that translates need into deficiency, places that deficiency in the client, and then separates that deficiency into components requiring specialties for intervention. Specialization of problems in the minds of professionals provides rationale for their specializing in minute arenas. They develop expert tools, instruments, and a complex language that is not understood outside of their arena. McKnight criticized such professional help for its disabling effects. His views caution social work as a profession not to emulate related specializations and reinforce the role of social workers as generalists who seek to understand social problems from a complex perspective of individual dynamics interacting with sociopolitical forces. In addition, McKnight suggested that if victims and nonvictims are to participate in problem resolution, social workers will have to educate both groups all along the breadth of the intervention continuum, rather than withhold information in the role of expert diagnostician and solution specialist. Social workers' expertise is in the defined problem and the ability to mobilize victims and non-victims for problem reduction.

HABILITATION VERSUS REHABILITATION

Practice principles for the integrated practice model are based on habilitation. Habilitation implies growth promotion or provision of means for problem solving. Rehabilitation, by contrast, implies rebuilding or restoration. Habilitation does not deny the existence of impairment resulting from victimization, but it changes the focus of intervention from the impairment to the competency of the impaired individual (Table 10.3).

Habilitation builds on three conceptual components: (1) a view of human behavior in a normalized political and socio-economic context (as opposed to a view of behavior through a labeled deviancy screen); (2) an assumption of competency on the part of victims of social problems; and (3) empowerment as a goal of intervention.

TABLE 10.3
Habilitation and Rehabilitation Principles

	Habilitation	Rehabilitation
View of client	Problems between person and environment	Problem in the person
	Victim of social problem	Devalued deviant with dysfunctional condition
	Expectation of fundamental competence and learning of coping skills	Expectation of helplessness
View of client behavior	Behavior on a normative continuum	Behavior as dichotomous; abnormal or normal
	Behavior viewed in environmental context, code of cultural conventions	Behavior attributed to need, deficiency, or pathology
	Current events cause current behavior	Past events cause current behavior
	Behavior as troubling to society	Behavior as the client's problem
Relationship between social worker and client	Coequal problem solvers, each with unique expertise	Dysfunctional client and the social worker as healer
	Treatment expertise not needed, but instead education and mobilization	Expert therapist; client a recipient of service
	Risk and responsibility expected from client	Fostering of dependency of client
	Client expected to learn new coping skills and resources	Client expected to be dysfunctional due to pathology
Intervention	Intervention independent of etiology	Cause necessary for determination of cure
	Education and acquisition of new skill	Treatment and cure implied

Normalization

The view of behavior from a normative environmental context, instead of a normal/abnormal dichotomy, attempts to decrease labeled deviancy. Positivistic thinking views dysfunctional behavior as caused by either individual factors or environmental factors. A normalized approach suggests that behavior cannot be viewed objectively, but must be viewed in terms of a person's intentions, motives, and reasons. Three factors must be considered in this view of behavior (Ingleby, 1980). First, behavior viewed in its environmental context becomes understandable in its specific circumstances and, given that set of circumstances, most people would respond similarly. Second, behavior is purposive. It is intended to convey a message about the specific situation. Behavior can be viewed as a form of protest against environmental pressure or as a way of coping with the environment. Third, behavior is understandable when viewed in its cultural code of conventions. These factors invite the examination of behavior in its political and socioeconomic context, which is important for social work because a large number of social work clients are women and racial minorities, and thus are economically and socially discriminated against.

Competence

According to the integrated practice perspective, victims of social problems are fundamentally competent persons who are participants in an interaction in a problem, a condition broader than their behavioral reactions. The principle of competency in assessment suggests that client systems have the capacity for learning, understanding, and solving problems. It assumes that clients' coping skills can be increased and that they have a right to risk and fail. They

are viewed as the best experts on and resources for their problems. In what Maluccio (1981) referred to as a new/old approach to social work practice, competence-oriented social work is based on an ecological transaction that contains three components: (1) clients' capacities and skills, (2) clients' motivation, and (3) the environmental qualities that impinge on clients' functioning. He suggested that client and social worker roles must be redefined as persons who share a task. Power invested in the social worker must be decreased; social distance reduced; and clients' identity, autonomy, and reciprocity in the relationship promoted.

Empowerment

Empowerment is the major principle guiding work with client systems. According to Solomon (1976), empowerment is a

process whereby the social worker engages in a set of activities with the client or client system that aims to reduce the powerlessness that has been created by negative valuations based on membership in a stigmatized group (p. 19).

Solomon (1976, p. 19) further described powerlessness as the inability to manage emotions, skills, knowledge, or material resources in a way that effective performance in valued social roles will lead to personal gratification. Therefore, powerlessness can be viewed as one's inability to obtain and use resources to achieve personal goals, and powerlessness in groups and communities can be viewed as the inability to use resources to achieve collective goals. Empowerment then is "the process of development of an effective support system for those who have been blocked from achieving individual or collective goals" (p. 19).

Power is central to a helping process that enables clients to solve their own problems.

If clients lack power, then social workers must enable them to achieve it in relationship to themselves and to oppressive systems. Ryan (1971) proposed that power is a central component in the helping process when he suggested that self-esteem is to some extent an essential to the human survival; [self-esteem] depends partially on the inclusion of a sense of power within self-concept; and mentally healthy persons must be able to perceive themselves as at least minimally powerful and capable of influencing their environment to their benefit. Furthermore, a sense of power must be based on the actual experience and exercise of power. Competence, power, and self-esteem are linked inextricably and their loss may be a powerful stress.

Empowerment as the primary principle of intervention carries two key assumptions. As was suggested earlier, it makes the job of the social worker one of power broker. It suggests that it is the job of social workers to provide supports so that clients may have access to the benefits and prerequisites accorded to the mainstream of society.

If client problems are viewed as a disparity between coping skills and environmental pressures, social work intervention may be at either end of that relationship (Maluccio, 1981). Empowerment intervention, however, must go beyond simply a choice of intervention points: Social workers must leave capacity to solve problems in place when they leave. An evaluation of empowerment asks the question "Did the client system retain increased capacity for solving problems when the social worker no longer was present?" "Was expertise given to the client?" The belief that client systems have capacity for problem solving is based on the use of self-fulfilling prophecy as a positive expectation. Learned helplessness must not be reinforced, but must be decreased. To empower SRO clients, it is necessary to educate them about their situation and teach them new skills to access resources and act on their own behalf.

INTEGRATED PRACTICE AND CONTEMPORARY STRATEGIES

Several social work practice theories have emerged during the late 1970s and early 1980s that provide appropriate bases for this practice model. Germain and Gitterman's life model (1980) is based on the interaction between individuals and their environments, and suggests that coping skills of individuals and environmental resources can be enhanced to empower clients' process through life transitions. Pincus and Minahan's (1973) framing of the target system as different from the client and change systems supports the idea of choice of intervention across a continuum. Middleman and Goldberg's role quadrant (1974, pp. 15–31), further elaborated upon by Anderson (1981), provides a practice framework for intervention across a continuum of decision points. The view of a social worker as a generalist problem solver is supported by Heus and Pincus (1986).

These theories contribute to the view that problem-solving approaches not only must involve all five client systems (communities, organizations, groups, individuals, and families), but that social workers also must assume a variety of roles with client systems. Reduction of powerlessness must be approached from a variety of roles. Effective problem solvers cannot afford to rely on one role as the means to solution.

Roles are those behaviors through which social workers empower clients. They include conferee, enabler, mediator, broker, advocate, and guardian. Roles are assumed to be appropriate interventive behaviors across the five client systems depending on the chosen points of intervention. Roles can be clustered into four groups. The conferee/enabler role includes consultation with the client system regarding a problem and decisions about strategies for solutions. This role includes education of the client system about resources and information regarding others with similar problems, and enabling support and encouragement of clients to seek out solutions. The mediator role includes facilitating conflict resolution and enabling clients to negotiate solutions to problems. The broker/advocate role includes the brokering and creation of services and advocacy for individual clients or groups of clients toward problem-solving resources. Guardianship is a necessary role social workers assume in the absence of other guardians when a client's level of functioning is so low that competency is destroyed. All of these roles are assumed to be applicable to all five client systems on the intervention continuum.

The breadth of knowledge and skill suggested here may appear too broad for one social worker's expertise. The authors are not proposing a practice model that requires social workers to know everything, but, instead, a narrowing focus to select strategies used within the roles along the continuum of intervention. In this way, this practice model goes beyond the social worker's position as an advanced generalist. The model calls for strategy selection within role taking with the five client systems to be problem solving in nature, and employs a principle of education. Strategies are selected that educate clients and can be shared with clients.

Solomon's (1976) critique of traditional social work roles as not empowering clients adds an important dimension to this model. She argued that work with oppressed populations must be educa-

tional. Linking clients to resources is not empowering, but education about resource access is. The failure of an individual to learn cognitive, interpersonal, and technical skills in the ordinary course of events increases dramatically the probability that that individual will need professional help. The capacity of individuals, groups, and larger institutions to cope with problems can be increased substantially by providing needed information, knowledge, and skill to both victims and nonvictims of social problems.

A problem-solving framework similar to Compton and Galaway's (1984) problem-solving process is a guiding framework for social workers and provides a basis for deciding how to intervene. Such a framework includes exploration, assessment, goal formulation, planning, implementation, and evaluation. Specific strategies that follow this problem-solving model are selected for intervention. For example, in the conferee/ enabler role, the task-centered system of Reid and Epstein (1978) is used to confer with client systems regarding problems. This model is selected because it is problem solving in nature and can be taught to clients. Self-help, mutual aid, education, and skill development groups are significant strategies because they also are educational. In the mediator role, the focus is on educating client systems about alternative means for negotiating and resolving conflicts. In organizational and community intervention, strategies that educate are team-building, conflict resolution, networking, self-help groups, and process organizational development. Role-taking strategies share education as a goal. By teaching problem-solving strategies, social workers empower clients and themselves to cope with social problems and reduce their impact on clients and society.

REFERENCES

Albee, G. (1982). "Preventing Psycho-Pathology and Promoting Human Potential." *American Psychologist, 37,* 1043–1050.

Anderson, J. (1981). *Social Work Methods and Processes.* Belmont, CA: Wadsworth.

Bartlett, H. (1970). *The Common Base of Social Work Practice.* New York: National Association of Social Workers.

Becker, H. S. (1963). *Outsiders: Studies in the Sociology of Deviance.* New York: Free Press.

Bell, D. (1973). *The Coming of a Post-Industrial Society: A Venture in Social Forecasting.* New York: Basic.

Bloom, B. (1979). "Prevention of Mental Disorders: Recent Advances in Theory and Practice." *Community Mental Health Journal, 15,* 179–191.

Compton, B., & Galaway, B. (1984). *Social Work Processes.* Homewood, IL: Dorsey.

Friere, P. (1972). *Pedagogy of the Oppressed.* New York: Herder & Herder.

Germain, C. B., & Gitterman, A. (1980). *The Life Model of Social Work Practice.* New York: Columbia University.

Gordon, W. (1970, April). *Social Work as Boundary Work.* Paper presented at the Third Annual Institute on Services to Families and Children, School of Social Work, University of Iowa, Iowa City.

Heus, M., & Pincus, A. (1986). *The Creative Generalist.* Barneveld, WI: Micamar.

Hernandez, S. H., Jorgensen, J. D., Judd, P., Gould, M., & Parsons, R. J. (1985). "Integrated Practice: Preparing the Social Problem Specialist Through an Advanced Generalist Curriculum." *Journal for Social Work Education, 21,* 28–35.

Ingleby, D. (Ed.). (1980). *Critical Psychiatry.* New York: Pantheon.

Kaplan, A. (1964). *The Conduct of Inquiry: Methodology for Behavioral Science.* San Francisco: Chandler.

Maluccio, A. N. (Ed.). (1981). *Promoting Competence in Clients.* New York: Free Press.

McKnight, J. (1977). Professionalized Service and Disabling Help. In I. Illich, ed., *Disabling Professions* (pp. 69–91). London: M. Boyars.

Middleman, R., & Goldberg, G. (1974). *Social Service Delivery: A Structural Approach to Social Work Practice.* New York: Columbia University.

Naisbitt, J. (1982). *Megatrends.* New York: Warner.

Pincus, A., & Minahan, A. (1973). *Social Work Practice: Model and Method.* Itasca, IL: F. E. Peacock.

Reid, W. (1978), *The Task-Centered System.* New York: Columbia University.

Rubington, E., & Weinburg, M. (1981). *The Study of Social Problems,* 3rd ed. New York: Oxford University Press.

Ryan, W. (1971). *Blaming the Victim.* New York: Random House.

Solomon, B. (1976). *Black Empowerment: Social Work in Oppressed Communities.* New York: Columbia University.

Walz, T., & Hoffman, F. (1982). "The Professional Social Worker and the Year 2000." In D. Saunders, O. Kurren, & J. Fischer, eds., *Fundamentals of Social Work Practice* (pp. 236–245). Belmont, CA: Wadsworth.

11.

Lorraine M. Gutiérrez

WORKING WITH WOMEN OF COLOR:
AN EMPOWERMENT PERSPECTIVE

Women of Color—black, Latina, Asian American, and Native American—make up 20 percent of the total female population of the United States (Lin-Fu, 1987). Although the populations encompassed by this umbrella term differ in many respects, they have similarities in status and power. Women of color experience the "double jeopardy" of racism and sexism in U.S. society. They are hampered by average earnings that are lower than those of white women, by overrepresentation in low-status occupations, and by an average low level of education (Gordon-Bradshaw, 1987: Kopasci & Faulkner, 1988; Lin-Fu, 1987). Correspondingly, women of color are underrepresented in positions of power in government, corporations, and nonprofit institutions (Gordon-Bradshaw, 1987; Zambrana, 1987). These facts suggest that if social workers are to work effectively with women of color, they need to address how the powerless position of these women in society contributes to individual client problems.

Powerlessness has direct and concrete effects on the experiences of women of color. Lack of access to many social resources is both a cause and an effect of the powerlessness of this population. The poverty rate of women of color is more than double that of white women: 32.3 percent of all black women and 26.4 percent of all Latinas live below the poverty line (Wilson, 1987). Therefore, women of color are more likely than white women to suffer from poor or no housing, insufficient food and clothing, and inadequate access to health services (Gordon-Bradshaw, 1987).

Even for women who are not poor, powerlessness contributes to poor mental health outcomes. Women, the poor, and members of ethnic and racial minority groups have much higher rates of mental illness than do men, whites, and the more affluent (Pearlin & Schooler, 1978; Thoits, 1983). Most studies of the connection between membership in these groups and mental health have focused on the stressful life circumstances of these groups and the strain that these circumstances put on their capacity to cope (Pearlin & Schooler, 1978; Silver & Wortman, 1980). However, this link may be analyzed from the perspective of power and the effect that powerlessness has on reducing the ability to exercise personal control, on the development of negative stereotypes of women and minorities, and on gaining necessary social and material resources.

Within existing models of social work practice, especially those focused on the individual, the problems of women of color are couched in individual terms and analyzed in relation to a specific client situation; the role of objective powerlessness often is overlooked. Intervention often focuses on assisting women to cope with or accept a difficult situation rather than on working to change the situation (Gould, 1987a, 1987b; Morell, 1987). A social worker may be aware that a client's problem is rooted in the lack of actual power, but increasing the client's actual power is rarely the goal of an intervention. Social work education is partially responsible for this oversight: methods for increasing the power of individual clients are not taught in most programs.

An empowerment perspective, which assumes that issues of power and powerlessness are integral to the experience of women of color, can address this oversight. It proposes concrete and specific ways in which practice can help resolve the personal problems of women of color by increasing their power on a number of different levels. The author outlines the assumptions of the empowerment perspective, the internal processes that it involves, and specific techniques for empowering women of color. Because women of color make up one of the fastest-growing segments of the American population (Lin-Fu, 1987), skills to work with this group will be of increasing importance for social workers.

DEFINING EMPOWERMENT

Empowerment is a process of increasing personal, interpersonal, or political power so that individuals can take action to improve their life situations. Empowerment theory and practice have roots in community organization methods, adult education techniques, feminist theory, and political psychology. Therefore, use of the term empowerment is often vague and can mean different things. Authors on the macro level often define *empowerment* literally and depict it as the process of increasing collective political power (Fagan, 1979; O'Connell, 1978). Conversely, on the micro level, *empowerment* often is described as the development of a personal

feeling of increased power or control without an actual change in structural arrangements (Pernell, 1985; Pinderhughes, 1983; Sherman & Wenocur, 1983; Simmons & Parsons, 1983a, 1983b). A third group of authors has begun to grapple with the interface of these two approaches: how individual empowerment can contribute to group empowerment and how the increase in a group's power can enhance the functioning of its individual members (Bock, 1980; Gould, 1987a, 1987b; Kieffer, 1984; Longres & McLeod, 1980; Morell, 1987; Schechter, Szymanski, & Cahill, 1985).

This article is written from the third perspective on empowerment, which, according to Rappaport (1985),

suggests a sense of control over one's life in personality, cognition, and motivation. It expresses itself at the level of feelings, at the level of ideas about self worth, at the level of being able to make a difference in the world around us. . . . We all have it as a potential. It does not need to be purchased, nor is it a scarce commodity (p. 17).

This definition of empowerment includes combining a sense of personal control with the ability to affect the behavior of others, a focus on enhancing existing strengths in individuals or communities, a goal of establishing equity in the distribution of resources, an ecological (rather than individual) form of analysis for understanding individual and community phenomena, and a belief that power is not a scarce commodity but rather one that can be generated in the process of empowerment (Biegel & Naperste, 1982; Kieffer, 1984; Rappaport, 1981).

Empowerment theory is based on a conflict model that assumes that a society consists of separate groups possessing different levels of power and control over resources (Fay, 1987; Gould, 1987a, 1987b). Social problems stem not from individual deficits, but rather from the failure of the society to meet the needs of all its members. The potential for positive change exists in every person, and many of the negative symptoms of the powerless emerge from their strategies to cope with a hostile world (Pinderhughes, 1983). Although individual clients can be helped to develop less destructive strategies, changes in the social order must occur if these problems ultimately are to be prevented (Rappaport, 1981; Solomon, 1982).

The process of empowerment occurs on the individual, interpersonal, and institutional levels, where the person develops a sense of personal power, an ability to affect others, and an ability to work with others to change social institutions. The literature describes four associated psychological changes that seem crucial for moving individuals from apathy and despair to action:

1. Increasing self-efficacy. Bandura (1982, p. 122) defined *self-efficacy* as a belief in one's ability "to produce and to regulate events in one's life." Although this term was not used in some of the empowerment literature, all authors described a similar phenomenon, using such concepts as strengthening ego functioning, developing a sense of personal power or strength, developing a sense of mastery, developing client initiative, or increasing the client's ability to act (Fagan, 1979; Garvin, 1985; Hirayama & Hirayama, 1985; Mathis & Richan, 1986; Pernell, 1985; Pinderhughes, 1983; Shapiro, 1984; Solomon, 1976).

2. Developing group consciousness. Developing group consciousness involves the development of an awareness of how political structures affect individual and group experiences. The development of group consciousness in a powerless person results in a critical perspective on society that redefines individual, group, or community problems as emerging from a lack of power.

The development of group consciousness creates within the individual, or among members of a group or community, a sense of shared fate. This consciousness allows them to focus their energies on the causes of their problems, rather than on changing their internal subjective states (Burghardt, 1982; Friere, 1973; Gould, 1987a, 1987b; Keefe, 1980; Longres & McLeod, 1980; Mathis & Richan, 1986; Solomon, 1976; Van DenBergh & Cooper, 1986).

3. Reducing self-blame. Reduction of self-blame is tied closely to the process of consciousness raising. By attributing their problems to the existing power arrangements in society, clients are freed from feeling responsible for their negative situation. Because self-blame has been associated with feelings of depression and immobilization, this shift in focus allows clients to feel less defective or deficient and more capable of changing their situation (Garvin, 1985; Hirayama & Hirayama, 1985; Janoff-Bulman, 1979; Keefe, 1980; Longres & McLeod, 1980; Pernell, 1985; Solomon, 1976).

4. Assuming personal responsibility for change. The assumption of personal responsibility for change counteracts some of the potentially negative results of reducing self-blame. Clients who do not feel responsible for their problems may not invest their efforts in developing solutions unless they assume some personal responsibility for future change. This process is similar to Friere's notion of becoming a subject, or an active participant, in society rather than remaining a powerless object (Bock, 1980; Friere, 1973). By taking personal responsibility for the resolution of problems, clients are more apt to make an active effort to improve their lives.

Although these changes have been described in a specific order, the empowerment process does not occur in a series of stages. Instead, the changes often occur simultaneously and enhance one another. For example, as individuals develop self-efficacy, they may be more likely to assume personal responsibility for change. Researchers who have studied the process also suggest that one does not necessarily "achieve empowerment" but rather that it is a continual process of growth and change that can occur throughout the life cycle (Friere, 1973; Kieffer, 1984). Rather than a specific state, it is a way of interacting with the world.

EMPOWERING TECHNIQUES

As stated above, social work practitioners may be aware of how a lack of power affects clients, but they may lack knowledge of how individuals can gain power, especially in the context of individual practice. When social workers attempt to help women of color who may be overwhelmed by their particular situation, this lack of knowledge can lead to frustration and can disempower the social worker. Fortunately, the literature suggests specific techniques and forms of intervention that can lead to empowerment.

The Helping Relationship

The basis of empowering practice is a helping relationship based on collaboration, trust, and the sharing of power. To avoid replicating the powerlessness that the client experiences with other helpers or professionals, it is critical that the worker perceive himself or herself as an enabler, an organizer, a consultant, or a compatriot with the client. The interaction between worker and client should be characterized by genuineness, mutual respect, open com-

munication, and informality. It presumes that the worker does not hold the answers to the client's problems, but rather that in the context of collaboration, the client will develop the insights, skills, and capacity to resolve the situation (Bock, 1980; Fagan, 1979; Keefe, 1980; Pinderhughes, 1983; Schecter et al., 1985; Solomon, 1976).

Along the same lines, the worker also can facilitate empowerment by helping the client to experience a sense of personal power within the helping relationship. This technique is based on the assumption that from the experience of power within the intervention the client can generalize to feelings of power in the larger social environment. Workers can facilitate this experience by having clients role play and practice powerful behaviors, by engaging clients in roles in which they help others, and by having clients take control of the helping relationship by setting the agenda, sharing the leadership of groups or meetings, and researching resources (Pernell, 1985; Pinderhughes, 1983; Schechter et al., 1985; Shapiro, 1984; Simmons & Parsons, 1983a, 1983b).

Actively involving the clients in the process of change is another aspect of the helping relationship that encourages empowerment. According to Solomon (1976), empowerment is a

process whereby the social worker engages in a set of activities with the client or client system that aim to reduce the powerlessness that has been created by the negative valuations based on membership in a stigmatized group (p. 19).

Like other authors, Solomon describes empowering interventions as those that are focused on activities ranging from the exploration of a problem to the development of alternative structures in a community (Beck, 1983; Checkoway & Norsman, 1986; Fagan, 1979; Garvin, 1985; Hirayama & Hirayama, 1985; Mathis

& Richan, 1986; Pinderhughes, 1983; Solomon, 1976). What is common to this range of activities is praxis, the blending of reflection and action. Because clients are actively involved in change, they also are reflecting on and analyzing their experience, and the results of their analyses are then integrated into the development of future efforts (Bock, 1980; Burghardt, 1982; Friere, 1973; Keefe, 1980; Longres & McLeod, 1980; Resnick, 1976; Rose & Black, 1985).

Suggested Modalities

The literature on empowerment suggests interventions on the individual, group, family, and community levels. Practitioners are advised to develop intervention skills on all these levels and to feel comfortable moving from one modality to another. However, small-group work is presented as the ideal modality for empowering interventions, because it is an effective means for integrating the other techniques. It can be the perfect environment for raising consciousness, engaging in mutual aid, developing skills, and solving problems and an ideal way for clients to experience individual effectiveness in influencing others (Coppola & Rivas, 1985; Garvin, 1985; Hirayama & Hirayama, 1985; Pernell, 1985; Sarri & du Rivage, 1985). The emphasis on small-group work holds true in the literature across all levels of intervention, whether the goal is empowering individuals or changing institutions.

In the same spirit, the literature recommends involvement of clients in mutual aid, self-help, or support groups. In the context of empowerment, mutual aid, self-help, and support groups are formed by people experiencing similar problems, who then focus on providing emotional and concrete support (Garvin, 1985; Sherman

& Wenocur, 1983). The groups facilitate empowerment by creating a basis of social support through the change process, a format for providing concrete assistance, an opportunity to learn new skills through role playing and observing others, and a potential power base for future action (Hirayama & Hirayama, 1985; Keefe, 1980; Pinderhughes, 1983; Solomon, 1982). They also can provide the context for developing group consciousness, by involving clients in dialogue with others who share their problems.

Techniques

Within the context of a collaborative helping relationship and a small-group work modality, the specific techniques described below have been suggested for empowering clients.

Accepting the Client's Definition of the Problem. Accepting the client's definition of the problem is an important element of an empowering intervention. By accepting the client's definition, the worker is communicating that the client is capable of identifying and understanding the situation. This technique also places the client in a position of power and control over the helping relationship, and it does not preclude bringing up new issues for exploration, such as the connection between personal and community problems (Beck, 1983; Fagan, 1979; Garvin, 1985; Shapiro, 1984).

Identifying and Building upon Existing Strengths. By identifying and building upon existing strengths, the empowering practitioner gets in touch with the client's current level of functioning and current sources of functioning and current sources of individual or interpersonal power (Mathis & Richan, 1986; Pinderhughes,

1983; Shapiro, 1984; Sherman & Wenocur, 1983; Solomon, 1976). This technique is most effective if the worker can recognize that the client has been involved in a process of struggle against oppressive structures and that this struggle has required considerable strength. By analyzing elements of the struggle, client strengths can be more easily identified, communicated to the client, and then used as a basis for future work.

Engaging in a Power Analysis of the Client's Situation. Engaging in a power analysis of the client's situation is a critical technique for empowering practice. It first involves analyzing how conditions of powerlessness are affecting the client's situation. A second crucial step is to identify sources of potential power in the client's situation. An indirect technique is dialogue between the worker and the client that is aimed at exploring and identifying the social structural origins of the client's current situation (Keefe, 1980; Longres & McLeod, 1980; Resnick, 1976; Solomon, 1976). Another, more direct, technique involves focusing the client's analysis on a specific situation—either the client's own situation or a vignette developed for the intervention (Bock, 1980; Pinderhughes, 1983; Schechter et al., 1985; Solomon, 1976). Clients and workers should be encouraged to think creatively about sources of potential power, such as forgotten skills, personal qualities that could increase social influence, members of past social support networks, and organizations in their communities.

An effective power analysis requires that social workers fully comprehend the connection between the immediate situation and the distribution of power in society as a whole (Garvin, 1985; Keefe, 1980; Mathis & Richan, 1986; Pernell 1985). The

process may require consciousness-raising exercises to look beyond the specific situation to problems shared by other clients in similar situations. Also, it is crucial that workers not adopt feelings of powerlessness from clients, but rather that they learn to see the potential for power and influence in every situation.

Teaching Specific Skills. Teaching specific skills is one means of helping the client to develop the resources to be more powerful (Mathis & Richan, 1986; Pernell, 1985; Shapiro, 1984). The skill areas most often identified in working with women of color include problem solving; skills for community or organizational change; "life skills," such as parenting, job seeking, and self-defense; and interpersonal skills, such as assertiveness, social competency, and self-advocacy (Checkoway & Norsman, 1986; Fagan, 1979; Garvin, 1985; Hirayama & Hirayama, 1985; Keefe, 1980; Schechter et al., 1985; Sherman & Wenocur, 1983; Simmons & Parsons 1983a, 1983b; Solomon, 1976). When teaching these skills the worker should adopt the role of a consultant or facilitator rather than an instructor, so as not to replicate the power relationships that the worker and client are attempting to overcome (Schechter et al., 1985; Sherman & Wenocur, 1983; Solomon, 1976).

Mobilizing Resources and Advocating for Clients. Mobilizing resources and advocating for clients also are useful strategies if the worker and the client together lack adequate resources for empowerment. Mobilizing involves the worker in gathering concrete resources or information for clients, as well as in advocating on their behalf when necessary. Although some have argued that advocacy can be in conflict with the goal of empowerment because it can reinforce feelings of powerlessness

(Rappaport, 1981; Solomon, 1976), it may be carried out in a collaborative way that includes the client and that involves learning new skills. Through advocacy and resource mobilization, the worker and client together ensure that the larger social structure provides what is necessary to empower the larger client group (Checkoway & Norsman, 1986; Mathis & Richan, 1986; Pinderhughes, 1983; Sherman & Wenocur, 1983; Solomon, 1982).

CONCLUSION

The techniques described above form the basis for empowering practice with women of color on the personal, interpersonal, or political level. For social workers to have an impact on conditions of powerlessness, they need to rethink both the mode and the focus of practice. These techniques would require practitioners to move beyond work with individual clients and problems, to thinking of ways to engage women of color in group efforts toward both individual and community change.

If empowering practice is to be effective, it calls for some changes in the current structure and content of social work practice and education (Gould, 1987a; Hasenfeld, 1987; Morell, 1987). Social workers must pay attention to the effects of powerlessness and oppression on clients' lives and to techniques for overcoming them. Social workers also need to develop skills in the area of small-group work and community practice if they are to work in empowering ways, and the organizations that employ them must support their efforts to engage themselves in the social contexts of their clients and to move among levels of intervention. These changes, and others, are critical for the implementation of empowering practice.

Working with women of color can be challenging and gratifying. The literature on empowerment suggests specific ways in which social workers can move individual women from feelings of hopelessness and apathy to active change. When these techniques are applied effectively, they can contribute to the empowerment of individual women and to their involvement in solving the problems of all women of color.

REFERENCES

Bandura, A. (1982). "Self-Efficacy Mechanism in Human Agency." *American Psychologist, 37*, 122–147.

Beck, B. (1983). *Empowerment: A Future Goal of Social Work.* New York: CSS Working Papers in Social Policy.

Biegel, D., & Naperste, A. (1982). "The Neighborhood and Family Services Project: An Empowerment Model Linking Clergy, Agency, Professionals and Community Residents." In A. Jeger & R. Slotnick, eds., *Community Mental Health and Behavioral Ecology* (pp. 303–318). New York: Plenum.

Bock, S. (1980). "Conscientization: Paolo Friere and Class-Based Practice." *Catalyst, 2,* 5–25.

Burghardt, S. (1982). *The Other Side of Organizing.* Cambridge, MA: Schenkman.

Checkoway, B., & Norsman, A. (1986). "Empowering Citizens with Disabilities." *Community Development Journal, 21,* 270–277.

Coppola, M., & Rivas, R. (1985). "The Task-Action Group Technique: A Case Study of Empowering the Elderly." In M. Parenes, ed., *Innovations in Social Group Work: Feed-back from Practice to Theory* (pp. 133–147). New York: Haworth.

Fagan, H. (1979). *Empowerment: Skills for Parish Social Action.* New York: Paulist Press.

Fay, B. (1987). *Critical Social Science.* Ithaca, NY: Cornell University Press.

Friere, P. (1973), *Education for Critical Consciousness.* New York: Seabury.

Garvin, C. (1985). "Work with Disadvantaged and Oppressed Groups." In M. Sundel, P. Glasser, R. Sarri, & R. Vinter, eds.,

Individual Change Through Small Groups, 2nd ed. (pp. 461–472). New York: The Free Press.

Gordon-Bradshaw, R. (1987). "A Social Essay on Special Issues Facing Poor Women of Color." *Women and Health, 12,* 243–259.

Gould, K. (1987a). "Feminist Principles and Minority Concerns: Contributions, Problems, and Solutions." *Affilia: Journal of Women and Social Work, 3,* 6–19.

Gould, K. (1987b). "Life Model vs. Conflict Model: A Feminist Perspective." *Social Work, 32,* 246–351.

Hasenfeld, Y. (1987). "Power in Social Work Practice." *Social Service Review, 61,* 469–483.

Hirayama, H., & Hirayama, K. (1985). "Empowerment Through Group Participation: Process and Goal." In M. Parenes, ed., *Innovations in Social Group Work: Feedback from Practice to Theory* (pp. 119–131). New York: Haworth.

Janoff-Bulman, R. (1979). "Characterological Versus Behavioral Self-Blame: Inquiries into Depression and Rape." *Journal of Personality and Social Psychology, 37,* 1798–1810.

Keefe, T. (1980). "Empathy Skill and Critical Consciousness." *Social Casework, 61,* 387–393.

Kieffer, C. (1984). "Citizen Empowerment: A Developmental Perspective." In J. Rappaport, C. Swift, & R. Hess, eds., *Studies in Empowerment: Toward Understanding and Action* (pp. 9–36). New York: Haworth.

Kopasci, R., & Faulkner, A. (1988). "The Powers that Might Be: The Unity of White and Black Feminists." *Affilia: Journal of Women and Social Work, 3,* 33–50.

Lin-Fu, J. (1987). "Special Health Concerns of Ethnic Minority Women." *Public Health Reports, 102,* 12–14.

Longres, J., & McLeod, E. (1980). "Consciousness Raising and Social Work Practice." *Social Casework, 61,* 227–267.

Mathis, T., & Richan, D. (1986, March). *Empowerment: Practice in Search of a Theory.* Paper presented at the Annual Program Meeting of the Council on Social Work Education, Miami, FL.

Morell, C. (1987). "Cause Is Function: Toward a Feminist Model of Integration for Social Work." *Social Service Review, 61,* 144–155.

O'Connell, B. (1978). "From Service Delivery to Advocacy to Empowerment." *Social Casework, 59,* 195–202.

Pearlin, L., & Schooler, C. (1978). "The Structure of Coping." *Journal of Health and Social Behavior, 19,* 2–21.

Pernell, R. (1985). "Empowerment and Social Group Work." In M. Parenes, ed., *Innovations in Social Group Work: Feedback from Practice to Theory* (pp. 107–117). New York: Haworth.

Pinderhughes, E. (1983) "Empowerment for Our Clients and for Ourselves." *Social Casework,* 64, 331–338.

Rappaport, J. (1982). "In Praise of Paradox: A Social Policy of Empowerment Over Prevention." *American Journal of Community Psychology,* 9, 1–25.

Rappaport, J. (1985). "The Power of Empowerment Language." *Social Policy, 17*(2), 15–21.

Resnick, R. (1976). "Conscientization: An Indigenous Approach to International Social Work." *International Social Work,* 19, 21–29.

Rose, S., & Black, B. (1985) *Advocacy and Empowerment: Mental Health Care in the Community.* Boston: Routledge & Kegan Paul.

Sarri, R., & du Rivage, V. (1985). *Strategies for Self Help and Empowerment of Working Low-Income Women Who Are Heads of Families.* Unpublished manuscript, University of Michigan, School of Social Work, Ann Arbor.

Schechter, S., Szymanski, S., & Cahill, M. (1985). *Violence Against Women: A Curriculum for Empowerment* (facilitator's manual). New York: Women's Education Institute.

Shapiro, J. (1984). "Commitment to Disenfranchised Clients." In A. Rosenblatt & D. Waldfogel, eds., *Handbook of Clinical Social Work* (pp. 888–903). San Francisco: Jossey-Bass.

Sherman, W., & Wenocur, S. (1983). "Empowering Public Welfare Workers Through Mutual Support." *Social Work,* 28, 375–379.

Silver, R., & Wortman, C. (1980). "Coping with Undesirable Life Events." In J. Garber & M. Seligman, eds., *Human Helplessness: Theory and Application* (pp. 279–375). New York: Academic Press.

Simmons, C., & Parsons, R. (1983a). "Developing Internality and Perceived Competence: The Empowerment of Adolescent Girls." *Adolescence*, 18, 917–922.

Simmons, C., & Parsons, R. (1983b). "Empowerment for Role Alternatives in Adolescence." *Adolescence*, 18, 193–200.

Solomon, B. (1976) *Black Empowerment*. New York: Columbia University Press.

Solomon, B. (1982). "Empowering Women: A Matter of Values." In A. Weick, & S. Vandiver, eds., *Women, Power, and Change* (pp. 206–214). Silver Spring, MD: National Association of Social Workers.

Thoits, P. (1983). "Dimensions of Life Events that Influence Psychological Distress: An Evaluation and Synthesis of the Literature." In H. Kaplan, ed. *Psychosocial Stress: Trends in Theory and Research*. New York: Academic Press.

Van DenBergh, N., & Cooper, L., Eds. (1986). *Feminist Visions for Social Work*. Silver Spring, MD: National Association of Social Workers.

Wilson, J. (1987). "Women and Poverty: A Demographic Overview." *Women and Health*, 12, 21-40.

Zambrana, R. (1987). "A Research Agenda on Issues Affecting Poor and Minority Women: A Model for Understanding Their Health Needs." *Women and Health*, 12, 137–160.

12.

Carol R. Swenson

CLINICAL SOCIAL WORK'S CONTRIBUTION
TO A SOCIAL JUSTICE PERSPECTIVE

Social justice is increasingly being seen as the organizing value of social work. For clinical social workers, this conceptualization clarifies and focuses a unique contribution that clinical social work can make to the mental health professions. In this article "clinical social work" is used in this sense to include case management, advocacy, teamwork, mediation, and prevention roles, as well as therapeutic and counseling roles. Clinical social workers engage in supervision, organizational change, directing programs, and community education. They also join with other social workers and their clients in social action (Swenson, 1995). Clinical social work should not be equated with practice based on a medical model, a focus on pathology, "blaming the victim," or social conservatism. Clinical social workers can consider what a social justice perspective means and how it can be enacted in clinical contexts. They can think about work with individuals, families, and groups from a social justice perspective. They can provide leadership in assessing theories, practices, and service delivery arrangements from the point of view of increasing social justice.

DEFINING SOCIAL JUSTICE

First, the profession must consider what "social justice" is and why it is being considered the organizing value for social work. Furthermore, what is an organizing value? The term comes from Wakefield (1988a, 1988b), who has written one of the most definitive statements about social justice in social work, particularly in regard to clinical social work. He described the "defining function" or primary purpose of a profession as its "organizing value," in the sense in which the organizing value of medicine is curing disease; of education, learning; and of law, legal justice.

Traditionally, when social work has tried to define its function, it has emphasized the "person-in-situation" construct. That construct became more conceptually rigorous as systems and ecological theories and theories of attachment, coping, adaptation, and resilience, as well as "two-person psychologies" in psychodynamic thinking developed. So, for instance, we had Gordon's (1969) definition of social work purpose as matching people's coping capacities and the qualities of impinging environments.

The person-in-situation conceptualization has always had some difficulties. Social work is not the only profession adopting systems thinking or any of the other theories mentioned, and many professions could be said to improve the goodness of fit between people and environments. In fact, in one way or another, all professions do. Education gives people skills and knowledge to navigate their world more competently and effectively, and law helps people make claims against some unjust environments. Medicine cures people of diseases they have caught from noxious environments, makes environments more healthy, and helps people overcome health challenges that compromise their functioning in various environments. Social justice would seem to be a more convincing organizing value for social work than the person-in-situation construct. But then what does "social justice" mean? Social justice defines a goal to which the person-in-situation construct can be directed, a goal both broader and more specific than "producing growth-inducing and environment-meliorating transactions" (Gordon, 1969, p. 10).

Dorothy van Soest (1995), in the *Encyclopedia of Social Work*, said that there are three components of social justice: legal justice, which is concerned with what a person owes to society; commutative justice, which is concerned with what people owe each other; and distributive justice, which is "what society owes a person" (p. 1811). She said that distributive justice involves decisions about allocating resources and that it is the most important, in the sense that it underlies the other two. Others divide social justice into different components, but distributive justice— social workers' concern—is always one component. (See, for example, Tyler, Boeckmann, Smith, & Huo, 1997.)

Social justice figures prominently in the revised NASW *Code of Ethics* (NASW, 1996) and in the current "Curriculum Policy Statement" of the Council on Social Work Education (1992). In the curriculum policy statement, promotion of economic and social justice are mandated content areas, as are diversity, populations at risk, and ethics and values. All of these can be seen as different perspectives on the concept of social justice. Populations at risk are people from whom social resources have been unjustly withheld; diversity entails respecting the cultures of everyone, not just the privileged few; and social work ethics and values emphasize the dignity and worth of each person, respect for difference, promoting social change, and multicultural competence. All these are elements of a just society. The newly revised *Code of Ethics* includes substantially more attention than the previous one to social justice as a responsibility of all social workers, including attention to diversity, oppression, and populations at risk. All social workers are expected to influence social policy, engage in social action, and advocate for disadvantaged groups.

The philosopher John Rawls (1971) made a major contribution to theories of social justice when he rebutted libertarian and utilitarian views on the grounds of equality. He said that hardships of some people cannot be justified by a greater common good. Rawls is a social contract theorist "in the tradition of Locke, Rousseau, and Hobbes," which Rawls integrates with "the Kantian moral tradition, where . . . every person is taken to be morally equal and deserving of respect" (Wakefield, 1988a, pp. 196–197). Rawls's views provide a rigorous philosophical argument for long-standing social work values.

Rawls (1971) developed two principles: (1) Basic liberties must be equal, because citizens in a just society must have equal rights; (2) there should be equality of opportunity and of social resources for each person. Inequalities in resources should not be allowed, unless they benefit those who are worst off (Dworkin, cited in van Soest, 1995, p. 1811).

Social resources are most often thought to be economic in nature, but Rawls's analysis can be applied to noneconomic goods as well. Wakefield (1988a) said,

In particular, Rawls's analysis implies that some psychological traits, such as self-respect, that are closely linked to the structure of social institutions and to how people react to each other are a kind of social benefit for which justice requires an attempt at fair distribution. If this is so, then psychotherapy-style interventions aimed at imparting such psychological goods would play an integral role in a justice-oriented profession.

I believe that a Rawlsian approach to distributive justice has the power to make sense of the social work profession and its disparate activities in ways not yet generally appreciated. Social work can be conceived as a profession engaged in alleviating deprivation in all its varieties, from economic to psychological; social workers identify people who fall below the social minimum in any justice-related good and intervene in order to help them rise above that minimally acceptable level. (p. 194)

SOCIAL JUSTICE CRITERIA

So, if we are persuaded by Rawls (1971) and Wakefield (1988a) that alleviating various "deprivations," not just economic deprivations, can be a form of social justice work, social workers need to identify other types. Rawls's terms are somewhat unfortunate. It is very important to be clear that Rawls's language, and mine following Rawls, does not imply any shortcoming whatsoever on the parts of the people or groups who are "deprived." (I want to thank Claudia Cassel, MSW, whose careful attention to language identified this and other instances when words "make a difference.") These deprivations can be of many different kinds but may be clustered in the broad categories of political, social, psychological, physical, and spiritual. Then the question becomes, What types of clinical theories, interventions, and service-delivery arrangements are most congruent with the value of social justice? And how do we allocate scarce resources? Would all people with all kinds of deprivations be equally deserving of intervention? I address the second issue first.

Who Deserves Intervention for Social Justice?

Rawls (1971) offered a direction for thinking in his concepts of "relative deprivation" and "minimally acceptable level" of resources. Thus, the more deprived a person is in the various dimensions of economic, political, social, spiritual, and psycholog-ical resources, the more compelling is his or her claim. A person who is poor and a victim of childhood sexual abuse has a greater claim than a sexual abuse survivor who is not poor; a depressed, divorced woman caring for children and elderly parents has a greater claim than a depressed male president of a major company. More subtly, if relieving someone's deprivation, even if it is relatively less compelling, might enable her or him to reduce the deprivation of others, a justice-based argument could be made for providing clinical intervention. For example, if relieving the previously mentioned company president's depression enabled him to develop a more compassionate stance toward his employees, perhaps reducing their relative deprivation in important ways, clinical intervention would be consistent with a social justice perspective.

What Theories, Interventions, and Arrangements Are Congruent with Social Justice?

The other issue is the adequacy of various theories, interventions, and service delivery arrangements when considered from a social justice perspective. But first, is it legitimate to evaluate theory and practice from the point of view of a value, which social justice clearly is? The modern scientific tradition has held that theories and practices should be evaluated on the basis of empirically measured outcomes. The view is widespread that theories are "value free" and that choosing among them is not a question of match with values but of their "explanatory power" or "rigor" (Prilleltensky & Gonick, 1994). One unfortunate result has been that social workers, perhaps especially clinical social workers, have been burdened with theories that are not particularly congruent with social work values.

Fortunately, some important contemporary views recognize that all theories embody values. These include postmodernism, critical theory, social constructionism, and hermeneutics, or interpretive social science (Berger & Luckman, 1967; Derrida, 1974; Foucault, 1980, 1981a, 1981b; Gergen, 1985; Habermas, 1971, 1983/1990; Lyotard, 1984). Social constructionism has alerted the profession to the ways that knowledge is socially created, as people filter "data" through the lenses of their experiences, values, and prior knowledge. Hermeneutics directs attention to the complexity of meanings inherent in supposed "facts." And postmodernism and critical theory have emphasized that ideas that become privileged as "knowledge" are those that support powerful interests (and which powerful interests support). All of these perspectives challenge the belief in the objectivity and neutrality of data. They offer support for using values as a standard for evaluating the adequacy of theories and practices.

If we use advancing social justice as a core value for clinical practice, we can determine which clinical theories and practices are most congruent with that value. There are many clinical theories and practices that we can claim or reclaim.

RELEVANT THEORY AND PRACTICES

Strengths Perspective

The strengths perspective (Saleebey, 1992, 1994; Weick, Rapp, Sullivan, & Kisthardt, 1989) is a key element of social justice-oriented clinical practice. Without a strengths perspective, social workers are left with theories that pathologize, emphasize deficits, and "blame the victim." These theories suggest a relative deprivation of respect and often are internalized as not being worthy of respect. They also cut people off from potential internal and external resources, thus increasing their relative deprivation.

Weick and Saleebey (1995) used the following language (a strength and resource in itself!): "the imagery, power, and richness of human experience" (p. 3), "array of capacities, ingenuities, and resources," "mobilization and articulation of inherent talents, abilities, aspirations, resources, wiles & grit," "capacities, competencies, possibilities, visions, values, hopes," "what people know and can do" (p. 4). Contrast this with the language of the DSM-IV (American Psychiatric Association, 1994), for example. Weick and Saleebey also found possibilities in people's life-worlds: "stories and narratives; values and beliefs; informal, natural resources; visions and hopes; abilities and gifts; cultural lore and lessons" (p. 5). They identified ways communities can amplify resilience: Acknowledge and use assets of members, have an ethos of involvement and participation, and offer individuals many ways to contribute to the moral and civic life of the community. Weick and Saleebey also offered this poetic but straightforward and intensely practical description of a helping role: "uncovering, naming, embellishing, and celebrating abilities, talents, and aspirations in the service of desired change" (p. 8). And finally, they emphasized the "transforming interaction between community development, group empowerment, and individual resilience" (p. 6).

Ethnic-Sensitive Practice

Ethnic-sensitive practice (Devore & Schlesinger, 1996; McGoldrick, Giordano, & Pearce, 1996) emphasized the significance of race and ethnicity as a mediator of people's day-to-day objective experience and of their subjective sense of self. Such

practice restores to people an appreciation for their particular cultural experience and identity. Lee (1994) added class as an equally significant mediator. Lee said that class-sensitive practice must understand and address the realities of being "locked in" and marginalized by oppression.

More universalistic approaches deprive people of the meaning of these social dimensions of their existence by acknowledging neither their negative effects (racism, classism, and so forth) nor their strengths as a positive resource. Universalistic approaches also unwittingly impose cultural norms and values of the dominant culture while claiming to be culturefree. A non-English-speaking recent immigrant from a culture where time is measured by the rising and setting of the sun, a single parent with three children under school age, who must take two buses to go to the clinic is held to the same expectations of timeliness as a college student unencumbered with job or caretaking responsibilities and able to afford a car.

Feminist Practice

Feminist practice attends to difference, as ethnic- and ethnic/class-sensitive practices do. However, it also includes an analysis of power and offers a critique of power relations characterized by domination and subordination. Feminist practice suggests an alternative way of understanding and using power based on collaboration and cooperation rather than on competition (Bricker-Jenkins, Hooeyman, & Gottlieb, 1991; Van Den Bergh & Cooper, 1986). Feminist thought has been particularly helpful in its insistence that "the personal is political"— that is, the linking of personal relationships with social structures.

Although feminist practice particularly emphasizes gendered patterns of power, most feminists are committed to identifying and addressing practices that disempower or oppress anyone, whether on the basis of race, religion, sexual orientation, or any other category. Feminist practice is also effective as a tool for consciousness raising about other oppressions. Feminist ideas are particularly important because so many clinicians resonate to them, and this awareness can be used to raise consciousness about other oppressions.

Until now, we have particularly focused on ideas that can inform direct work with clients. The clinician-activist model seeks to move beyond direct work and to address larger societal issues. Walz and Groze (1991) wanted to counter a "conservative retreat" in social work. They noted that professional social workers have left or been forced out of public welfare positions, that social work services are increasingly directed to middle-class clients, and that social work students are less altruistic and less activist than in the past. They said, "Social work belongs . . . serving the needs of the most oppressed and needy [sic] people in society. . . . The clinician is data gatherer and analyst, in addition to therapist. The client becomes the centerpiece of change, revealing to the therapist the types of system-wide changes or reforms that are necessary" (p. 501). Walz and Groze concluded, "The current clinical social worker must be convinced that 'client interest' advocacy research is a legitimate clinical activity, [as is] institution building, broad public education, and political action" (pp. 501–502).

Justice-Oriented Practice

Justice-oriented practice can be seen as one implementation of the clinician-activist model. Hopps, Pinderhughes, and Shankar (1995) offered data on effective interven-

tions with overwhelmed clients, who are often poor women of color with multiple problems. These are the people who suffer the most deprivation, receiving less than Rawls's (1971) "minimally acceptable level" of many resources. Hopps et al. (1995) called for comprehensive services incorporating clinical work with health, employment, anticrime, and housing initiatives; providing group and community change activities, as well as individual and family work; and offering extensive availability, affirmation, and high expectations to clients.

Although both approaches move beyond direct work to consider whole programs, they also share a continued emphasis on the professional as an expert. The next several approaches attempt to alter the power arrangements between client and clinician, between client and others, or between client and society.

Self-Awareness

Self-awareness, or reflexivity, is one of the most central concerns in clinical social work, as it is in critical theory. A social justice perspective requires that practitioners pay careful attention to their own experiences of oppression and of privilege or domination. Most clinicians have learned to engage in scrutiny about interpersonal patterns and internal processes. Many have considered the implications of experiences of being oppressed. Less common is the expectation that clinicians will learn about their own privilege and the power inherent in the clinician role.

Millstein (1994, 1997) developed methods that clinicians can use for systematic reflection on their practice—in particular their experiences of racism and oppression. These are structured processes, which, if repeated at regular intervals, can serve as a document of changing experiences and attitudes about racism over a professional life span. Garcia and Swenson (1992) offered another means, this time for partners to create a dialogue in writing. The writing gives both a record of the dialogue and a special "space" that verbal dialogue does not afford—the opportunity to reflect in private and for a period of time before responding or initiating ideas. This makes it particularly suitable for conversations on difficult and sensitive topics. Although both techniques address racism, they could easily be adapted to other experiences of privilege or oppression. Other means of deepening self-awareness include peer therapy, or cotherapy, as it is sometimes known, and, of course, personal therapy. It is particularly helpful if that therapy is undertaken with therapists who are able to do the social justice work of identifying social experiences of oppression and privilege.

It is often difficult for clinicians to see themselves as powerful, privileged, or oppressive. And yet clinicians do their clients and the goal of social justice a disservice when they cannot bear to see this. Clients are more burdened than clinicians are, and they see our privilege and power. It is a sad commentary that the very services that may enhance social justice may instead serve to increase the psychological experience of injustice. It is particularly important to have done this personal and professional work about one's own privilege and power when undertaking work with oppressors as a form of clinical social justice work.

Narrative Approaches

Interventions from the "narrative" approach (Freedman & Combs, 1996; White, 1995; White & Epston, 1990) are particularly effective in embodying ideas of social justice. Michael White, who practices social work in Australia, draws his theoretical analysis from Foucault, especially Foucault's ideas about the inextricability of power and knowledge. White (1995) described several ways to make power and knowledge more available to clients, ways that will move in the direction of a more just society. One of these ideas is "externalization," or separating problems from the person so that the person can exercise increasing influence over the problem. As the person becomes more influential, she or he becomes liberated from the oppression and power of the problem. The "problem" may be the kinds of social processes we have been discussing, such as racism or sexism. They may also be more idiosyncratic problems such as encopresis in children or the experience of infertility for adults. White and others have developed a process of questioning that enables the client to gain more power over the problem. The questions try to find in the client's language, or to create, an emotionally resonant name for the problem (like "Sneaky Poo," for encopresis).

The narrative therapists have also devised particularly creative ways to reduce the clinicians' power in relation to clients. Their stance is one of respectful curiosity. They convey a belief that the client wants to change, can change, and has valuable but subjugated knowledge and skills to draw on. They have developed methods of recordkeeping that record the session and serve as letters to the clients. With practice, these take no longer than ordinary recordkeeping, but they do away with the pathologizing language and implicit expert power of most records. Thus, they serve as excellent tools to enact a strengths perspective.

Oppressors as Clients

Work with "oppressors" as clients is particularly challenging work for the social justice-oriented clinician. Again the narrative therapists have come up with helpful perspectives. White (1995) and Jenkins (1990/1993) offered the idea of "inviting responsibility" as a general stance that the therapist can take toward people whose behavior is oppressing others. After careful questioning designed to elicit the client's wish to be responsible, the therapist works to identify "restraints" to acting on that wish (a parallel to externalizing the problem). It is especially important that the clinician has done her or his own work on ways she or he is privileged and even an oppressor, so as to be able to work with these clients.

"Just" Therapy

"Just" therapy has been developing in New Zealand and has been introduced to American audiences by narrative and collaborative therapists (Tamasese & Waldegrave, 1994; Waldegrave & Tapping, 1990). Tamasese and Waldegrave (1994) said, "Therapy can be a vehicle for addressing some of the injustices that occur in a society. It could be argued that in choosing not to address these issues in therapy, therapists may be inadvertently replicating, maintaining, and even furthering, existing injustices" (p. 5).

The "just therapists" have identified three underlying assumptions: spirituality, justice, and simplicity. Waldegrave and Tapping explained, "Since spirituality informs every aspect of life in Maori and Pacific Island cultures, we have learned to respect the sacredness of all life. . . . We view the process of therapy as sacred. People come, often in a very vulnerable state, and share some of their deepest and most painful experiences. For us, these stories are gifts that are worthy of honour. The therapists honour them by listening respect-fully for their meaning, and offering new meanings which enable resolution, hope, and self-determination." Justice involves "naming the structures and actions that oppress and destroy equality," whether it be at the micro level of the family or the macro level of the society. And therapy reflects simplicity, because people and societies have been resolving their difficulties without the necessity for therapists from time immemorial. "The therapy we offer finds its expression in the movement in meaning from problem-centered patterns, to new possibilities of resolution and hope" (Waldegrave & Tapping, 1990, p. 7).

Mutual Aid Groups

Mutual aid groups build and build on the strengths of individuals to give help to each other (Gitterman & Shulman, 1994; Schwartz, 1971, 1985/1986; Shulman, 1992). They offer instrumental, informational, and expressive support. Mutual aid groups are particularly useful for naming the problem, or consciousness raising, and collective problem solving. Almost any shared situation can be a focus of mutual aid groups: AIDS education for teenagers, parents of chronically ill children, severely mentally ill adults, people in recovery from substance abuse, men who abuse their wives, partners of people with Alzheimer's disease. On occasion, groups may be helped to organize themselves to take collective action. When they do so, they are on their way to being empowerment groups.

Empowerment Practice

Empowerment practice (Gutiérrez, 1990; Lee, 1994; Simon, 1994; Solomon, 1976) emphasized reducing direct and indirect power blocks, or those caused by external and internalized oppression. In the tradition of the critical theorists, reflecting on and understanding one's own situation in relation to social processes is considered essential for effective change at either the personal or the collective level.

There is some controversy over the use of the term "empowerment." Some authors include personal empowerment, that is, an enhanced self-respect and increased efficacy in negotiating one's immediate environments, social and physical. Others wish the term to be limited to practice that enables people to take collective action on behalf of others, as well as themselves. Still others maintain that these distinctions are arbitrary and open to question. Lee (1994) described a continuum of empowerment from the personal to the interpersonal to the social and a continuum of actors from the single person to the group to broad coalitions.

Empowering practices, which also may be called liberatory or emancipatory practices, are emerging in many different fields. A common link is critical theory. Critical theory, which can be related to postmodernism (Doherty, Graham, & Malek, 1992; Rosenau, 1992), tries to connect the emancipation of individuals with social and political change through developing critical consciousness. Critical theorists emphasize reflexivity, the human capacity to reflect on our own history, as essential for truly liberating social change (Dean & Fenby, 1989).

These ideas have led to interest in emancipatory or liberatory practices in areas as diverse as religion (liberation theology [Boff, 1996]), rhetoric (emancipatory dialogic rhetoric [Simons, 1991]), psychology (liberation psychology [Martin-Baro, 1994]), literature (narratives of liberation [Taylor, 1989]), education (conscientization, pedagogy of the oppressed, transformative education [Freire, 1970/1973; Hooks, 1994]), and psychiatry (revolution-

ary psychiatry [Fanon, 1968]). In social work there are such contemporary and historical writers as Breton (1989), Moore and Wallace (1993), and Reynolds (1934/1982, 1951/1973). There is a social justice–oriented journal, the *Journal of Progressive Human Services*, which publishes some clinically relevant material.

This account of theories and practices is necessarily incomplete. The work that lies ahead includes continuing to explicate the values underlying theories and practices. Then the profession must evaluate them for their contribution to "the affirmation of self-determination for diverse and oppressed groups, to the just allocation of resources, and to the expression of marginalized voices" (Prilleltensky & Gonick, 1994, p. 168). Social workers also must ensure that their methods of developing knowledge are compatible with their value and theoretical commitments (Witkin, 1993).

SYNTHESIS AND CONCLUSION: CLINICAL SOCIAL JUSTICE PRACTICE

What does social justice mean when we sit with a client? It means profound appreciation for a client's strengths, contexts, and resources. Experiences of race, ethnicity, gender, class, religion, sexual orientation, and ability, because these shape clients' worlds and meaning-making, are seen as central. It means we engage in thorough analyses of professional and organizational power and actively work to increase client power relative to professionals and agencies. It means we acknowledge and articulate the client's social realities. We engage in the work of exploring our own experiences of oppression, and of privilege and power as well. We assess clients' "relative deprivation" and "minimally acceptable levels of resources" in the economic, political, physical, social, spiritual, and psychological domains. We acknowledge political, moral, and ethical issues as political, moral, and ethical and let clients know where we stand, when appropriate (Dougherty, 1995). It means we encourage clients to experience the reciprocal help of mutual aid groups and to organize for collective social action.

Clinical social justice work also includes planning services and advocating for services that decrease clients' relative deprivation in political, economic, social, spiritual, and psychological spheres. It means examining all the ways that professionals interact with clients from a position of expert power and attempting to do things differently. It means examining agency structures and attempting to create structures that are socially just. Following the lead of the just therapists (Tamasese & Waldegrave, 1994), we seek to raise issues of socioeconomic status, race, and gender in the agency and devise strategies of accountability from the more to the less powerful groups. Social action for social justice is a central component.

Sadly, in the contemporary world, social justice–oriented clinical practice is under assault. Managed care and other cost-cutting measures appear to be increasing social injustice, rather than increasing social justice. It is important to preserve, articulate, and attempt to implement a vision of clinical social justice–oriented practice. I suggest some ways to do so.

We can capitalize on the ways that social justice–oriented practice is congruent with the ideology of managed care. Some elements are an emphasis on strengths; planning comprehensive, continuous, and integrated community services; and supporting people to remain in the community. At present, the implementation of managed care often seems to run counter to its own ideology. Services are brief, "remedical-ized," and focused on reducing pathology and achieving concretely measurable outcomes. The best services are going to people who can afford to buy them privately or can be persuasive advocates for themselves, rather than to people with the greatest needs. Unjust social conditions, such as poverty and violence, which are known to increase mental distress and physical illness (Albee, 1986), are not only not being addressed, but are being permitted to intensify.

However, the creative and committed social justice–oriented clinician can find ways to maintain her or his vision and practices. One approach is to become "bilingual": to be able to think and speak the managed care language as well as social justice language. One can then use the languages selectively: the social justice language with clients and "kindred spirits" and the managed care language with administrators. Another strategy is to argue for social justice thinking or interventions using the managed care ideology, when these are congruent. For example, the "medical offset effect" research is encouraging some HMOs to offer more psycho-educational, prevention, and mental health services to reduce medical costs (personal communication with Rita van Tassel, then chair, Massachusetts NASW Managed Care Committee, October 21, 1997). Social justice-oriented clinicians can support enhanced services as intrinsically worthwhile and cost-effective as well.

We can also educate other professionals about a social justice perspective. They may have entered their work out of a wish to "make the world a better place" but found little support from their profession for understanding their work in this way. And we must continue social action focused on changing social values and institutions so that social justice—in the economic, political, social, physical, psychological, and spiritual domains—becomes available to all.

I share with Wakefield the hope that social justice—that is, alleviating deprivation in its many forms—will gain credence as the organizing value of social work. I believe it offers a means for clinical and non-clinical social workers to understand themselves more fully as partners in the same profession. And as clinical social workers clarify the meaning of clinical social justice work, they have a contribution for non-social work clinicians who seek to understand their practice as social justice work.

REFERENCES

Albee, G. (1986). Toward a just society: Lessons from observations on the primary prevention of psychopathology. *American Psychologist, 41*, 891–898.

American Psychiatric Association. (1994). *Diagnostic and statistical manual of mental disorders* (4th ed.). Washington, DC: Author.

Berger, P., & Luckman, T. (1967). *The social construction of reality*. Garden City, NY: Doubleday.

Boff, L. (1996). *The future of liberation theology*. Unpublished lecture, Harvard Divinity School, Cambridge, MA.

Breton, M. (1989). Liberation theology, group work, and the right of the poor and oppressed to participate in the life of the community. *Social Work with Groups, 12*(3), 5–18.

Bricker-Jenkins, M., Hooeyman, N., & Gottlieb, N. (1991). *Feminist social work practice in clinical settings*. Newbury Park, CA: Sage Publications.

Council on Social Work Education. (1992). *Curriculum policy statement for master's degree programs in social work education*. Alexandria, VA: Author.

Dean, R., & Fenby, B. (1989). Exploring epistemologies: Social work action as a reflection of philosophical assumptions. *Journal of Social Work Education, 25*, 46–54.

Derrida, J. (1974). White mythology: Metaphor in the text of philosophy. *New Literary History, 6*(1), 5–74.

Devore, W., & Schlesinger, E. (1996). *Ethnic sensitive social work practice* (4th ed.). Boston: Allyn & Bacon.

Doherty, J., Graham, E., & Malek, M. (Eds.). (1992). *Post-modernism and the social sciences*. New York: St. Martin's Press.

Dougherty, W. (1995). *Soul searching*. New York: Basic Books.

Fanon, F. (1968). *The wretched of the earth*. New York: Grove Press.

Foucault, M. (1980). *Power/knowledge: Selected interviews and other writings*. New York: Pantheon Books.

Foucault, M. (1981a). Technologies of the self. In L. Martin, H. Gutman, & P. Hutton (Eds.), *Technologies of the self* (pp. 16–49). Amherst: University of Massachusetts Press.

Foucault, M. (1981b). The political technology of individuals. In L. Martin, H. Gutman, & P. Hutton (Eds.), *Technologies of the self* (pp. 145–162). Amherst: University of Massachusetts Press.

Freedman, J., & Combs, G. (1996). *Narrative therapy: The social construction of preferred realities*. New York: W. W. Norton.

Freire, P. (1970/1973). *Pedagogy of the oppressed*. New York: Seabury Selections.

Garcia, B., & Swenson, C. (1992). Writing the stories of white racism. *Journal of Teaching in Social Work, 6*(2), 3–17.

Gergen, K. (1985). The social constructionist movement in modern psychology. *American Psychologist, 40*, 266–275.

Gitterman, A., & Shulman, L. (Eds.). (1994). *Mutual aid groups, vulnerable populations, and the life cycle* (2nd ed.). Itasca, IL: F. E. Peacock.

Gordon, W. (1969). Basic constructs for an integrative and generative conception of social work. In G. Hearn (Ed.), *The general systems approach: Contributions toward a holistic conception of social work* (pp. 5–11). New York: Council on Social Work Education.

Gutiérrez, L. M. (1990). Working with women of color: An empowerment perspective. *Social Work, 35*, 149–153.

Habermas, J. (1971). *Knowledge and human interests* (J. Shapiro, Trans.). Boston: Beacon Press.

Habermas, J. (1990). *Moral consciousness and communicative action* (C. Lenhardt & S. Nicholson, Trans.). Cambridge, MA: MIT Press. (Original work published 1983)

Hooks, B. (1994). *Teaching to transgress: Education as the practice of freedom*. New York: Routledge.

Hopps, J., Pinderhughes, E., & Shankar, R. (1995). *The power to care: Clinical practice effectiveness with overwhelmed clients.* New York: Free Press.

Jenkins, A. (1990/1993). *Invitations to responsibility.* Adelaide, Australia: Dulwich Centre Publications.

Lee, J. (1994). *The empowerment approach to social work practice.* New York: Columbia University Press.

Lyotard, J. (1984). *The post-modern condition: A report on knowledge.* Minneapolis: University of Minnesota.

Martin-Baro, I. (1994). W*ritings for a liberation psychology.* Cambridge, MA: Harvard University Press.

McGoldrick, M., Giordano, J., & Pearce, J. (Eds.). (1996). *Ethnicity and family therapy* (2nd ed.). New York: Guilford Press.

Moore, L., & Wallace, G. (1993). *Emancipatory social work: The application of post-modern theory to social work education and practice.* Paper presented at Council on Social Work Education Annual Program Meeting, New York.

Millstein, K. (1994). Building knowledge from the study of cases: A reflective model for practitioner self-evaluation. *Journal of Teaching in Social Work, 8*(1/2), 255–280.

Millstein, K. (1997). The taping project: A method for self-evaluation and "informed consciousness" in racism courses. *Journal of Social Work Education, 33*, 491–506.

National Association of Social Workers. (1996). *Code of Ethics.* Washington, DC: Author.

Prilleltensky, I., & Gonick, L. (1994). The discourse of oppression in the social sciences: Past, present, and future. In E. Trickett, R. Watts, & D. Birman (Eds.). *Human diversity: Perspectives on people in context* (pp. 145–177). San Francisco: Jossey-Bass.

Rawls, J. (1971). *A theory of justice.* Cambridge, MA: Harvard University Press.

Reynolds, B. C. (1934/1982). *Between client and community: A study in responsibility in social casework.* Silver Spring, MD: National Association of Social Workers.

Reynolds, B. C. (1951/1973). *Social work and social living.* Silver Spring, MD: National Association ot Social Workers.

Rosenau, P. M. (1992). *Post-modernism and the social sciences.* Princeton, NJ: Princeton University Press.

Saleebey, D. (1992). *The strengths perspective.* New York: Longman.

Saleebey, D. (1994). Culture, theory, and narrative: The intersection of meanings in practice. *Social Work, 39*, 351–359.

Schwartz, W. (1971). On the use of groups in social work. In W. Schwartz & S. Zalba, (Eds.), *The practice of group work* (pp. 3–24). New York: Columbia University Press.

Schwartz, W. (1985/1986). The group work tradition and social work practice. *Social Work with Groups, 8*(4), 7–27.

Shulman, L. (1992). *Skills of helping individuals and groups* (3rd ed.). Itasca, IL: F. E. Peacock.

Simon, B. (1994). *The empowerment tradition in American social work.* New York: Columbia Universify Press.

Simons, H. (1991, March). *Arguing about the ethics of past actions: An analysis of a taped conversation about a taped conversation.* Paper presented at Temple University Conference on Dialogic Rhetoric, Philadelphia.

Solomon, B. (1976). *Black empowerment. Social work in oppressed communities.* New York: Columbia University Press.

Swenson, C. (1995). Clinical social work. In R. L. Edwards (Ed.-in-Chief), *Encyclopedia of social work* (19th ed., Vol. 1, pp. 502–513). Washington, DC: NASW Press.

Tamasese, K., & Waldegrave, C. (1994). Cultural and gender accountability in the "just therapy" approach. *Dulwich Centre Newsletter, 2 & 3*, 55–67. (Adelaide, South Australia)

Taylor, P. (1989). *The narrative of liberation: Perspectives on Afro-Caribbean literature, popular culture, and politics.* Ithaca, NY: Cornell University Press.

Tyler, T., Boeckmann, R., Smith, H., & Huo, Y. (1997). *Social justice in a diverse society.* Boulder, CO: Westview Press.

Van Den Bergh, N., & Cooper, L. B. (Eds.). (1986). *Feminist visions for social work.* Silver Spring, MD: National Association of Social Workers.

van Soest, D. (1995). Peace and social justice. In R. L. Edwards (Ed.-in-Chief), *Encyclopedia of social work* (19th ed., Vol. 3, pp. 1810–1817). Washington, DC: NASW Press.

Wakefield, J. C. (1988a). Psychotherapy, distributive justice, and social work: Part 1. Distributive justice as a conceptual framework for social work. *Social Service Review, 62*, 187–210.

Wakefield, J. C. (1988b). Psychotherapy, distributive justice, and social work: Part 2. Psychotherapy and the pursuit of justice. *Social Service Review, 62*, 353–382.

Waldegrave, C., & Tapping, C. (1990). Social justice and family therapy. *Dulwich Centre Newsletter* (Special issue), *1*. (Adelaide, South Australia)

Walz, T., & Groze, V. (1991). The mission of social work revisited: An agenda for the 1990s. *Social Work, 36*, 500–504.

Weick, A., Rapp, C., Sullivan, W. P., & Kisthardt, W. (1989). A strengths perspective for social work practice. *Social Work, 34*, 350–354.

Weick, A., & Saleebey, D. (1995, October). *A postmodern approach to social work practice.* Paper presented at Adelphi University, School of Social Work, Garden City, NY.

White, M. (1995). *Re-authoring lives: Interviews and essays.* Adelaide, Australia: Dulwich Centre Publications.

White, M., & Epston, D. (1990). Story, knowledge and power. In *Narrative means to therapeutic ends* (pp. 1–37). New York: W. W. Norton.

Witkin, S. (1993). A human rights approach to social work research and evaluation. *Journal of Teaching in Social Work, 8*, 239–253.

PART TWO
STRATEGIES

Introduction

In the black winter of 1909
When we froze and bled on the picket line
We showed the world that women could fight
And we rose and won with women's might.
　　　　　　 — From the poem, "The Uprising of the 20,000,"
　　　　　　　　 honoring the waistmakers' strike of 1909

Whether we are moving face first or the other end first in engaging the twenty-first century is a matter of some contention. Indeed, in trying to confront the critical problems of our era we might be well advised to keep in mind the admonition of Pogo (and his cartoonist Walt Kelly): "We have met the enemy and he is us." The unfortunate (and sometimes very counterproductive) tendency to either promise much more than we can deliver or attempt to avoid all major controversial issues is still very much a part of macro-level social work. One important reason for this is that our idealism (and often our ideology) goes far beyond our change technology. If we are to join the struggles by which we are confronted in any significant way, the question of strategy must not be neglected.

A fundamental problem for nations, for organizations, and for individuals is that of getting from where they are now to where they would like to go. The action-idea or process-idea by which nations and individuals (and everything in between) guide the actions they take in order to drive toward chosen objectives may be referred to as strategy. Because strategy involves an action-idea, it is dynamic, and depends upon assessments of the actions of others involved in the situation. These assessments are both anticipations (judgments about what others will do, and what you will then do, made in advance) and on-the-spot action/reaction sequences. This sense of the word "strategy" is derived from game theory, which distinguishes games of individual skill, games of chance, and games of strategy—the last being those in which the most effective course of action for each player depends upon the actions of other players and the initial players' anticipation and assessment of those moves. As such, the term emphasizes the interdependence of allies' and adversaries' decisions and their various expectations about each others' behavior.

The centrality of strategy for the community practitioner is undeniable. Without it, ideology and commitment are reduced to empty rhetoric. On the other hand, actions without strategies are not helpful either. Used by themselves, interventive actions tend to become merely forays against *ad hoc* "targets of opportunity" without any sense of how they may fit into some larger plan. The vigor with which problems of strategy are endlessly debated is but one example of their critical importance to community practice. Only through a consideration of alternatives that is both thoughtful and pragmatic can a reasonable evaluation of various plans of action and their respective strengths and weaknesses be made.

Just what is strategy? How may it be distinguished from tactics? When and how should one change strategies? What tools, what action "rules of thumb" are available to guide practitioner actions? Each community intervention mode can be thought of as a strategic approach to the problems of social injustice, uncoordinated services, and lack of community. But when should one be used and others set aside? When should one be an initial strategy, to be followed by others at a later time?

These are the questions faced by community practitioners every day. However, efforts to pose these issues sharply, or explicate them fully, are few and far between in the literature. Part Two is an attempt to accomplish just this task.

In keeping with the construct presented in Part One, we will view strategy in terms of three basic intervention approaches and combined forms among them. Separate chapters are devoted to each of these modes—development, planning and policy, and action—with examples of mixing given for each. Our discussion highlights means of influence as a core element of strategy, and we will show that different means of influence are associated with different strategic modes of intervention.

However, before undertaking this core analysis, we will examine some underlying elements of strategy that contribute to our understanding of the concept. Among these elements are strategy as a goal, as orchestration, as an amalgam of conflict and consensus tactics, as a task and process phenomenon, and as a means-ends spiral. We will also consider contextual variables that influence the exercise of strategy. With these ideas in place, we will be in a position to elaborate on social influence—modes of intervention, which provide the organizing framework for the readings in Part Two.

UNDERLYING ELEMENTS OF STRATEGY

Strategy as a Goal

Basically, we regard strategy as an orchestrated attempt to influence a person or a system in relation to some goal which an actor desires. It is "orchestrated" in the sense that an effort is made to take into account the actions and the reactions of key allies and adversaries as they bear upon the achievement of the proposed goal. That goal tends to be general, such as a particular "state of the system" desired by the change agent. It is sometimes called "strategic intent" (Hamel and Prahalad, 1989). For example, exorcising white racism from a big city educational bureaucracy may be a state-of-the-system goal.

Articulating a strategic intent, however, is not an easy task. While it is beset by numbers of difficulties, four deserve special mention—the articulation of goals, the substitution of ideology for goals, the trivialization of goals, and the measurement of goals.

The Articulation of Goals.   Practitioners should select and articulate goals at a level of public understanding such that they have a possibility of being achieved, and so that the public will know (and the worker will know) when they *have been achieved.* For example, a worker who sets as a goal the global aim of eliminating racism in a particular community is bound to be disappointed. This is not to say that the elimination of racism should not be a goal, but rather that it should not be *the* goal. On the other hand, if the goal is one of bringing integration to a suburban housing area, or providing new job or educational opportunities for African-Americans, then the results can be monitored more effectively. Without intermediate and feasible proximate goals, the worker's interventions cannot be evaluated to any significant degree and progress cannot be assessed. Specifying general strategic purposes, and more concrete strategic goals, is an important part of the community intervention process.

Ideological Substitution.   Because goals are hard to articulate and specify ideological commitment to some general value is substituted for the actual goal. Practitioners become "true believers" in the sense in which Eric Hoffer (1958) has suggested. Progress toward the desired goal becomes transformed into an assessment of the "purity" or motivation of the practitioner. While not more typical of community organizers than any other group of change agents, this solution tends to move the goal out of the realm of the "practical" or empirically concrete and to develop a series of personalistic assessments. From this perspective, "commitment" becomes a culmination for the believer; without it, progress becomes impossible. However, all too often, this commitment concern becomes ideological enmeshment, and is associated with a lack of real progress toward visible accomplishments (for example, full employment).

Goal Trivialization.   With goals hard to specify, the substitution of means for goals is not that uncommon. It is sometimes called "means ritualism." Here we find, for example, the agency that relies heavily on a continuing series of community meetings from which nothing ever seems to emerge.

Measurement.   Part of the problem, of course, is that achievement and accomplishment are hard to measure. Goals must have measures, milestones, and benchmarks that can be used to assess progress. Without such measurement, goals become hollow.

Strategy as Orchestration

While most practitioners are well acquainted with thinking about strategy as goal setting, the notion of orchestration probably bears further attention. In a sense, it is intended to convey a dramatic "arrangement"—with different performers, each with various skills and roles, each of whom may enter and leave the scene according to some action plan. Solos articulate with the movement of the whole piece. The change agent's roles include prompter and producer-conductor. He or she lays out a "score" for the performance and attempts to integrate its diverse elements as the performance goes forward. In all likelihood the score itself will have to be changed—in response to shifting conditions—one or more times during any given performance.

But more is implied here than the interplay of many persons, or persons and institutions, at any given movement. There is a progression over time—as each phase of the action scheme is completed. Indeed, it suggests the notion of a "means-end chain," where all of the simultaneous performances are at once ends in themselves, and means to a more general end. A familiar example to practitioners is the community clean-up or safe neighborhood campaign. The project is an end in itself, as well as a means to the more general goal of community cohesion and pride. Thus community strategy often involves a complex and dynamic pattern of performances within performances. However, in this general framework there are several critical issues that need to be explored in more detail.

Strategic Focus: Conflict Versus Consensus Approaches

The problem of strategy is often dichotomized into a choice between conflict and consensus approaches. This trend toward polarization invites many of us to think in terms of "choice" between "brave" and "cowardly" strategies, or "radical" versus "establishment" modes. The tension between conflictual approaches and consensus-seeking ones is real. As Weber points out, "Conflict cannot be excluded from social life . . . 'peace' is nothing more than a change in the form of conflict or in the antagonists or in the objects of the conflict, or finally in the chances of selection" (Coser, 1956, p. 21).

Yet consensus is, paradoxically, a part of conflict, as much as the converse is true. Without subsequent negotiation, agreement, and some form of reconciliation, the fruits of conflict are likely to be meager indeed. Even when total revolution or the transfer of substantial power is effected (or attempted), the "outs" who are now "in" must move to consolidate their gains through at least a modicum of consensus and reconciliation. (The situation in the former Soviet Union provides an excellent example.) At the same time, the current powerful thrust toward "conflict management" is also to be closely scrutinized. Any attempt to move everything by consensus and agreement, to keep everything "nice," may be used to mask significant problems and avoid the possibility of arriving at decisions on critical issues. It has been previously pointed out that the use of conflict or consensus may be predominant in a given mode of practice—such as conflict in social action or consensus in community development. Seen more broadly, conflict and consensus are viewed as the Siamese twins of social progress. If both these task and maintenance functions are not attended to, progress toward social goals may be sharply truncated, if not halted, as William Gamson points out in his article on "Rancorous Conflict in Community Politics" (Gamson, 1966). Clearly both are needed. To assume a battle-ready posture, where there is (or may be) no conflict, is often to create a hostile environment in which movement by consensus cannot take place.

Strategic Focus: Task Versus Process Approaches

In working with collectivities and groups, as planners and organizers almost always are doing, tension rises between focus on the "task" (paint, fix up, for example), and the "process" (building communities and networks through common activities). In a task emphasis, community building and bonding take a second seat; in process orientations, task accomplishment is in second place. Task goals refer to "hard" production-oriented functions in which decisions are made, individual interests neglected, and feelings disregarded. Process goals involve the repair of ruptures caused by task activities and an attempt to create a higher level of group solidarity through which task business can proceed more effectively. Clearly it is here, also, that a mix of strategic approaches is needed. An outline of some possibilities is suggested in Figure 1. This grid outlines some of the choices of emphasis that the practioner can make. "Locality development" typically occupies the bottom half of the grid, with a focus on the right-hand corner. Sometimes, though, group bonding is developed through opposition to other groups. "Policy and planning" occupy the upper part of the grid, with policy tending to center in the upper-left quadrant (because policy requires decisions, and decisions often involve conflict), and planning occupying the right half (because planning requires cooperation to get the program together and running.) "Social action" tends to occupy the left two quadrants, focusing on both task accomplishment and the challenge of getting specific improvements, and on process activities that include conflict, involving challenging power holders and beneficiaries on socially unjust practices and processes.

FIGURE 1
A Strategic Grid of Conflict/Consensus and Task/Process Foci

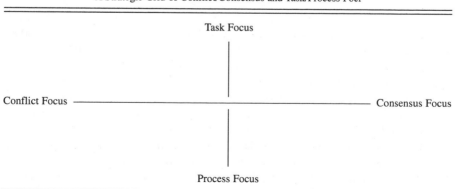

Task Focus

Conflict Focus ——————————————————— Consensus Focus

Process Focus

However, it is also important to note that the whole system tends to turn (or rotate) and turn again in a spiral fashion. For example, dramatic social action efforts to draw attention to hate crimes may give way to more consensus-oriented policy and planning decisions to combat it. Moreover, ongoing programs to support and welcome diversity may need to move back and forth between modes embracing both conflict and consensus, and modes emphasizing either task or process—or both from one issue to the next.

The Means-Ends Spiral

Most practitioners recognize the operation of means-ends chains as common practice experiences. Putting the two notions together, strategy can be redefined as an outward means-ends spiral, alternatively emphasizing task and process, conflict and consensus modes.

The concept of strategy as an orchestrated means-ends spiral has a number of important consequences for community intervention. For one thing, it suggests that total reliance on a strategy of either consensus or conflict will in most circumstances be unsuccessful. It anticipates the skill of the organizer in moving with the community or group between task and process phases. And it offers the idea of progression toward concrete intermediate objectives as a measure of strategic success. Now let us turn to an examination of the contexts in which strategic successes must be achieved.

Contextual Variables in Strategic Assessment

Strategy is not devised in a vacuum. The strategic thinker works in some specific community, with specific groups and probably for some organization. As a plan is developed, there are a number of factors that should be taken into account.

Strategic thinking and development must begin with a consideration of the agency resources in people, money, and equipment which the agents have at their disposal. Often there are inter-agency fights over the allocation of these resources. And, whatever the level, we know that in community practice there are rarely sufficient amounts of any one of the resources to meet the demand. Since they are scarce, competition for them becomes intense. The more scarce the resources (and thus, the more intense the competition), the more a strategy of power-building self-help is indicated.

The resources of the broader system in which the organizer must act are another consideration. Such resources may be the availability of money, on the one hand, and that amorphous but all-important resource, public support and understanding on the other. Sometimes the agency and the system have resources differentially available to them. In some developing countries, community agents have access to expensive and sophisticated equipment which the indigenous population does not know how to use. Thus, even the presence of resources does the worker no good if they cannot be used. More frequent, and characteristic of many urban change programs in America, is the target system that has more resources than the change agency. Hence, from a strategic point of view, the system (or particular elements within that system) can "hold out" much longer than any agency-backed client organization and win most struggles. In general, when the target has more resources than those available to the change agent or agency, a social action strategy is indicated.

The amount of resistance to change objectives is a third factor of critical importance. Generally, we assume some resistance to change proposals as a matter of course. Sometimes, however, the complexity of the problem itself gives the appearance of resistance. We must be careful to distinguish between a situation where a social problem is complex, but there is no substantial resistance (for example, many public health problems fall into this category) and one where many solutions are known but there is strong resistance (for example, income maintenance). Then, too, areas where important gains can be made, and where the system is neutral to mildly opposed (for example, tutorial enrichment programs), a social planning strategy should be considered.

In modern urban America, class variables are a very strong predictor of behavior and institutional preferences, from sex habits to styles of child rearing, from religion to responses to pain (Bendix and Lipset, 1966). It is thus with some concern that we note the absence of literature which substantially attempts to exploit these differences in the conceptualization of strategic alternatives.

Generally speaking, the change agent can represent a constituency which is of higher, equal, or lower social class than the change target. For the community practitioner this situation offers certain strategic "hints." They devolve upon the fact that change strategies are "handicapped" by their class of origin—particularly as viewed by the recipient of the change proposal. For example, a change proposal coming from a high-status change agency (or agent) to a low-status community has a good likelihood of "success," particularly if the agency is willing to utilize its prestige in achieving the desired goal over the objections of community residents. On the other hand, a change proposal coming from a lower-class constituency directed toward a middle-class formal organization is likely to be stalled, sidetracked, and indefinitely tabled or ultimately defeated. It is all too easy for the class "handicap" (either positive or negative) to obfuscate the merits of any given change proposal. Many of the demands for "power" of various sorts—as enunciated by the poor, gays and lesbians, racial and ethnic minorities, and women—can be understood as a demand for a new set of handicapping arrangements in the system. Problems of lower-class constituencies may be handled by developing social action strategies to build a new handicapping system (that is, causing shifts in power and/or resource allocations), followed by appropriate strategies of development and planning.

Variability in problem complexity is a relevant issue and poses questions of problem "tractability." Community problems are comprised of many unique and interrelated elements. Sometimes even the simplest technical problems—garbage collection, for example—are confounded by political complexities of great magnitude. On the other hand, problems which have substantial support across a wide range of publics—job-training projects—may falter on technical insufficiencies. Other complexities—from agency staff changes to national upheavals—also may enter the picture. Fundamentally, the change agent, taking the problem in all its ramifications, must be able to assess the degree of complexity involved, and how amenable to solution it may be. Different degrees of complexity require different kinds, timing, and sequencing of strategies.

Legitimacy—of either a target of change or a change agent—is a key variable for the community practitioner. Indeed, a change target of dubious legitimacy has a built-in vulnerability that may be exploited. On the other hand, a target with broad legitimacy in the community may be especially difficult to attack. Change agents need to make a realistic assessment of their own legitimacy and act accordingly. That is, an inadequate legitimacy must often be strengthened for effective action to take place; a charismatic legitimacy can carry the change agent a long way before an action begins.

In our modern bureaucratized society, organizational strength of either change target or change agent is often a vital contextual problem. As a change target, weaker organizations are more vulnerable to a variety of change efforts. Strong organizations, however, typically present special difficulties even for the most enterprising of change agents. Since organizations are many times vehicles through which change is carried out, their strength must be carefully appraised as part of the planning for change efforts. Six substantive problems—resources, resistance, class, complexity, legitimacy, and organizational strength—in the development of a successful community intervention strategy have been discussed (for others, see Weil and Gamble, 1995). There is no implication that these six are the only important factors; nevertheless they seem significant in that they cut across any functional area of community action and are common to most social-change situations. Clearly, it also seems important to note that race and/or gender issues must often be taken into account as well. At times, they are neglected at great peril to both the change effort and the practitioner. Still, a key question remains. How can all these "problem" factors be dealt with in a conceptually interrelated way? One source of help is in emerging social science theories and approaches.

MEANS OF INFLUENCE AND MODES OF INTERVENTION

Strategy and Means of Influence

Often we become confounded by the variety of styles of influence (as well as current vogues) and fail to recognize that there are fundamentally three, and only three, core modes of influence. To get another person, group, or organization to do what is desired, force, inducement, and agreement (or "hit, buy, and woo") may be used (Etzioni, 1961; Fisher, 1994). These three modes occur not only on the individual level as strategies of influence, but they are main change initiators at the societal level as well. Let us consider each in some detail.

Force, or coercive power, has been a vital concept in the analysis of human events. The possession of force, or control over the means of force, gives the change agent an important weapon. Often it is not necessary to actually use available force, but simply to make a *credible threat*. At other times, the actual application of force is necessary (for example, to establish credibility through a "show of strength"). Modes of force may range from physical violence and war, on one end of a continuum, to sit-ins, confrontations, and personal harassment at the other end. Drawing on our previous distinction, force constitutes a conflict strategy, and its use typically creates resentment. The use of force also suggests the existence of resistance. Indeed, there are strong moral sanctions against using force when resistance is absent, as in the case of "shooting an unarmed man" or attacking a "defenseless" nation. In all well-integrated social systems, the subsystem which has primary responsibility for control over the use of force is the polity, or governmental structure. Agents of force, such as the police and the army, for example, are under this kind of political control. Access to certain positions in the polity are sought because of the relationship they have to the potential mobilization of force, even though the notion of force may be obscured or veiled.

The second means by which social goals may be achieved is inducement. Often, goals can be purchased or traded. Force need not be used, although value consensus may not be present. For example, people who argue that integrated housing is a "good investment" are using an inducement strategy. On a more fundamental level, the entire economic system is an inducement system. People contribute to the system and receive differential payments in return. This pay can be traded for many other goods in the system. The purchase of goods is, in turn, an inducement to the manufacturer to create new and more profitable goods. Inducement frequently involves the use of facts and information to persuade people to lend themselves to certain programmatic approaches. The factual information sets forth convincingly the benefits to be gained through accepting a particular plan or course of action.

In using coercive power, one has to control the means of force. To use an inducement strategy, one needs to manipulate the goods by which people may be induced. Money is one such "good." Interestingly, power is another. (This suggests an interaction between the three main modes, which we shall discuss momentarily). Status positions, prestigeful associations, jobs, symbols of recognition and access to personnel and equipment are also among the most desired goods. In earlier times, salvation and indulgences were coin of the realm. Increasingly, control over information (and the emerging information highway) is coming to be an important and negotiable commodity. As society comes to be more and more complex, more and more specialized, more and more technological, detailed information is required to solve even apparently simple problems. Hence, it becomes a desired good, and a most significant one.

Perhaps the most subtle and sophisticated method for achieving social goals is through value consensus or agreement. A consensus mode proceeds through the development of an agreement between the actors that a course of action should be followed. Typically, the consensus is based upon fundamental agreements on underlying values in the social system. Then the parties attempt to demonstrate that the position they wish to take is closely attuned with the value or operates according to it. One simple example deals with the vote. In the United States, it is common and widely accepted practice to settle matters in dispute with a vote of those present. This procedure requires a plurality achieved through the rule of one-person-one-vote. However, the strong biases inherent in this procedure are often ignored. The intensity of preference on an issue—the fact that some people may feel very strongly while others take the matter rather lightly—is simply neglected in this procedure.

Similarly, with each member having a single vote, differences in knowledge, experience, and analytical ability are not accorded any special weight. The presumption is made that somehow the most desirable alternatives possible will receive a full hearing.

Value consensus usually emerges through some kind of socialization process. In the most obvious case, of course, it is the socialization of infants and children to the norms and mores of the dominant culture or their own ethnic group. Less explicit, but socialization nonetheless, is a host of processes that go on in adult life—the peer group of friends, the informal "clique" at the workplace or factory. Then too, many of us have a broader and more undefined group which we use as a reference point to assess our own attitudes and progress (political parties, a profession, the church, etc.).

Relating Influence and Modes of Intervention

These three types of influence have some very interesting additional properties. For one thing, each may be a goal as well as a means to the others. Thus, inducements can be used to secure power and the control over force. Force can be used to secure agreement, although in perhaps a more limited fashion. Inducements, when applied over time, tend to produce value agreement. This is the time-honored process of "cooptation."

Second, each is the basis for an important part of the stratification system in society. Certainly people possess different amounts of power and can be located somewhere on a power continuum ranging from most to least. People also have differential control over various inducements, such as money and information. A rank ordering can be done of those "commanding" salient inducements. Finally, people are closer to, or farther from, valued positions in society. This is often referred to as "status." For this reason, each of these means of influence is an important "good" in the system. One might conceptualize the task of the community worker in terms of equalizing the distribution of these "goods," or improving the position of his or her constituency on one or more ranking scales. Often the worker will attempt to capitalize on the properties of one system to produce increments in another.

Third, none of these influence means can exist without the others. Not only do they interpenetrate on a goals-means basis, but they also are mutually supportive. Hence, the use of force generally exists within some context of agreement about the conditions under which force may be used and the amount of force necessary to produce certain results, etc. On the other hand, the amount of force often produces a new situation with which the existing web of value agreements must cope. Both are supported by a framework of inducements. Without inducements, the potential user of force cannot often muster the necessary elements of force.

Finally, force, inducements, and value agreement are the means by which society at large insures order and stability in the social system, and the means by which the society is changed. Force, for example, can be a means by which order is maintained, or disrupted. Inducements are used to develop commitments to the system, or to lure people to other competing systems. Values are at once sources of common bonds and of great divisiveness in the society.

It might be useful at this time to relate these three means of influence to the earlier discussion of the three models of community intervention (Article 1). On the intervention level, social action is most closely related to the force variable. Police, courts, and the military are typical examples of force used to maintain the system. As a change variable, civil disobedience and other forms of disruptive militancy are typical. Social action usually attempts to build up the pressure of cumulative force through massing large numbers of people in united and often dramatic activity. Although in a quite different fashion, policy is also related to the force variable. That is, legal and legislative machinery are often the impelling force behind the use of policy as an intervention system maintenance mode. As a change mode, the courts can be used, in this case, to support such efforts as class action suits.

Planning as an intervention technique articulates best with the inducement means of influence. Planning involves a complex of processes (which may include, as elements, development, action, policy, and administration). Fundamentally, the planner attempts to induce the system to adopt a proposed plan through a variety of techniques. Typically the situation is one of high complexity, and the planner brings to bear significant expertise on the location and extent of the problem, past attempts to deal with it, and the most desirable alternatives in view of current circumstances (especially resource availability).

The value means of influence best articulates with the locality development mode of intervention. In both cases, the achievement of value agreement and common orientations is a central focus of either change or system-maintenance objectives.

The development of these two sets of terms—one pertaining to means of influence and the other to modes of intervention—permits us to develop a framework for considering the types of styles and strategies available to the change agent. This framework is displayed in Figure 2.

Figure 2 suggests that there are at least nine basic strategic themes that may be employed. While as we pointed out, each mode of intervention is characterized by a particular means of influence (as indicated by its location on the diagonal in Figure 2), in actuality other means of influence are also typically utilized. Thus, while militancy often is expressed in social action, inducements through negotiation take place, as well as value consensus through moral exhortation.

In addition, each mode of intervention offers special leverage on a key contextual variable or general problem situation. Thus social action is concerned especially with unequal distribution of goods and resources in the society as reflected in class stratification; planning deals with matters of high complexity; policy may be especially important in either augmenting or undermining the legitimacy of the political system and its institutions; and locality development is particularly useful with a situation of limited communal resources.[1]

---

[1]Furthermore, each intervention mode is often associated with particular patterns of linkage. Thus, social action typically involves local primary groups banding together to make demands upon (or link up with) formal organizations. Planning often includes a number of cross-linkages to improve, for example, service delivery. Policy usually involves the linkage between some larger aggregate (like a legislative body) that takes action for change and formal organizations through which the new mandate is carried out. Locality development usually requires the establishment of good working relationships among primary groups and, at a later stage, cooperative arrangements with appropriate formal organizations.

FIGURE 2
A Matrix of Intervention Strategies, Means of Influence, and Contextual Variables

MODES OF INTERVENTION

Basic Means of Influence	Action	Planning/Policy	Development
Force (power)	*Militancy* Disruption, sit-in, "liberation" of institutions, para-military activities	*Power Elite* Involve influential elites	*Reconciliation* (Client system with power groups)
Inducement	*Negotiation* Bargain, confrontation with "facts"	*Expertise*	*Pilot Projects* (Illustrative of potential gains, build to larger tasks)
Value Consensus	*Moral Exhortation* Expose, "Radical thought"	*Representation* "Federation" of interests	*Group Development*

CRITICAL CONTEXTUAL PROBLEMS

	Low social class High resistance	High complexity	Low resources

THE MIXING AND PHASING OF STRATEGIES

Strategy Confrontation: The Mixing and Phasing of Strategies

It is often the case, as we have suggested in the means-ends spiral notion, as well as in the Introduction to the entire volume, that the practitioner must move from one strategy to another as shifts occur in the conditions affecting his overall objectives. Figure 2 suggests a possible scheme for mixing and phasing the strategies under two fundamental problem conditions.

The first set of problematic situations requires moving horizontally across the chart. It assumes that society or some target system is using one of the means of influence to maintain a problem condition. If the change agency, for example, is dealing with a problem defined by the system as one of force and power, one begins with a militant action strategy to build power and influence, and then moves to a planning strategy to consolidate the acquired influence and build a power block, to a development strategy for building value consensus and establishing channels for negotiating the allocation of scarce resources.

In contrast, where inducement is the main mode of maintaining the status quo, one begins with a planning strategy, bringing expertise to bear on a detailed analysis of the problem. One might then seek to build consensus through a development strategy, backed up with the potential of action, if needed.

In the case where values form the main vehicle of conservative influence, value "liberation" needs to take place (often in small groups) followed by a more action-oriented strategy of moral confrontations and radicalization, to a planning framework in which a number of interests are represented as negotiations take place.

The second problem orientation begins not with the mode through which society maintains the status quo, but rather with the mode of intervention to which some change agent or agency is committed. This orientation helps to illustrate the type of strategic configuration which remains within one intervention mode. If an agency is committed to a social action mode, its scenario begins with militancy. After a militant demonstration, one moves to a position of bringing values in line with action, and then to a negotiating position. On the other hand, a development-oriented agency, because of its limited resources, usually begins in a group organization phase and moves through an inducement phase before coming to an action phase. Planning starts with the calling together of experts, moves to building a power block, and concludes with some representation of all significant interests.

The main point is that one can use either the characteristics of the problem or the type of change agency (action, planning and policy, or development) as a point of departure. In either case, to achieve closure on particular problems, a differential set of strategies needs to be used, perhaps relying on different agencies and different persons at different phases of action. Two elements remain constant in either perspective: One is the notion of the means-ends spiral, and the other is that the *beginning* strategy should be articulated with the primary maintenance means (and this initial target of change) in the system.

All of these change processes (or change attempts) may be seen in struggles surrounding such current issues as managed care, case management, violence containment, health care reform, and welfare reform. In the final analysis, what is being contested is, "Who will pay for what services to be offered to whom?"

ANALYSIS OF MODES OF INTERVENTION IN PART TWO

Three means of influence and modes of intervention are described and illustrated in the articles in Part Two. In addition, variations in the modes of influence are discussed, which suggests mixtures among them, either cross-sectionally at a given juncture or longitudinally over a period of time.

Locality Development

Locality development is characterized by Cnaan and Rothman as an intervention approach that emphasizes community building and social integration. Arriving at widely agreed upon goals and forms of action through broad citizen participation is central to this approach, including a process wherein value consensus plays a prominent part. These authors draw on Durkheim's concept of organic community to encapsulate the goals of locality development. The organic notion signifies solidarity among residents, including interdependence, mutual responsibility, and interpersonal exchange, with noncoercive norms guiding social interaction.

The discussion goes on to point to two core features of locality development: Local residents rather than professional change agents decide on the ends to be pursued, and collaborative tactics predominate in moving toward change. The practitioner seeks to establish local representative groups to deliberate and act, thus group development and interactional skills are highly important.

An example of locality development tactics is given in the article by Martí-Costa and Serrano-García. They place needs assessment in an ideological context, showing that in locality development this technique is used both to engage citizens actively in determining what problems are of importance to them, and to help make them conscious of the impact of these problems on their lives.

Rather than being only an objective research tool, needs assessment is simultaneously an action instrumentality. Needs assessment provides a basis for going through four intervention phases: (1) increased familiarity by residents with the community, (2) creation of a core group of community people and professional interveners to manage the assessment, (3) formation of grassroots task groups to analyze findings and devise relevant goals and action plans, and (4) involvement of new and expanding groups in a cyclical manner as action proceeds and new circumstances evolve.

A vivid illustration of locality development is presented in the article by Kaul. He describes efforts to organize an oppressed minority community in the East Akron area through a neighborhood settlement house. Kaul provides step-by-step information about the process he went through to encourage self-help efforts by residents, employing the means of forming block clubs throughout the area. These were later incorporated into a block club council having greater scope and containing greater human resources than the single units. Through their own efforts, residents carried out a wide range of beneficial actions that involved recreational and cultural programs, health and sanitation, neighborhood beautification, safety, and housing. Local leadership was nourished and developed in the process.

An example of both mixing and phasing in a locality development context is shown in the article by Minkler. This is a case study of organizing elderly residents living in single-room occupancy hotels in the Tenderloin district of San Francisco. The project began with some typical locality development programs decided upon by the residents. One early thrust involved food and nutrition, with participants operating their own "minimarkets" in hotel lobbies and running a cooperative weekly breakfast program at reduced prices. Residents also started a Safehouse Project, whereby 48 neighborhood businesses and agencies were recruited to become places of refuge, marked by colorful posters, where residents could receive assistance in times of emergency.

Over time, the project staff felt that participants also ought to be developing a power base and engaging broader issues. The project phased into undertaking social action initiatives such as carrying out a protest against a raise in rent. They also pressured to change a landlord's harsh eviction policy and to have bathrooms made wheelchair accessible.

But locality development involvements continued concurrently, with support groups of residents conducting such interrelational activities as planning holiday parties and organizing memorial services for group members who passed away. This mixture of community intervention modes appears to have achieved a useful balance in the Tenderloin situation.

Planning/Policy

The planning/policy intervention mode is depicted in the article by Rothman and Zald, in which they discuss a data-driven, rationalistic approach to promoting change. Planning/policy in this context relies on facts and logic to persuade individuals to take certain actions—the inducement being alleviation of difficult and vexing problems that affect them directly or indirectly, such as crime, urban blight, homelessness, and child abuse. These authors indicate that comprehensive societal planning has not been characteristic of the American experience, but that it has been attempted in sectoral areas, such as state prison systems, social security, and corporate planning. At the community level, The United Way, welfare councils, and hospital planning councils have injected a rationalistic dynamic into the process of community problem solving.

These authors indicate that the rationalistic approach has received criticism in recent years because it wrongly assumes that sufficient information can be assembled to resolve highly complex problems. Also, communities are in a state of flux and turbulence, thus the orderly and painstaking accumulation of data that planners bring to bear on problems contains a time lag. Finally, this approach fails to take into account sufficiently the input of citizens who are in constant touch with and affected by problems—hence, it is in conflict with basic democratic values. While planning and policy development serve to bring evidence and objectivity into the realm of decision making, a rigid and stereotypic adherence to rationalistic means is described by these authors as self-limiting.

The practitioner in planning and policymaking clearly does not operate as a mechanistic being, even in a highly rational change process. Personality characteristics and values of the practitioner are an element in the exercising of change roles, and personal qualities of the policymaker also enter into the amalgam by which decisions are made. In the analysis in his article, Snare identifies three different types of policy professionals: the expert (a neutral technician who most closely represents the rationalistic mode); the advocate (one who brings a commitment to given objectives to the situation); and the troubleshooter (a problem-solver focused on making things run smoothly). Two types of policymakers are brought into the picture by Snare: the pragmatist (who is a facilitator and negotiator, typically one who seeks viable compromises in political interplay); and the crusader (a partisan with loyalties to given aims and compatriots).

Snare lays out a series of stages in the planning and policymaking process, including agenda-setting, collecting information and formulating alternatives, making decisions, accomplishing the task, and evaluating results. He believes that practitioner roles are played out differently in each of these phases. We can assume from the analysis that certain practitioner types will work more comfortably with given policymaker types. For example, troubleshooters may take to pragmatists, while experts may not mix well with crusaders. Using this perspective, we can see that even a highly deliberative effort will be influenced by the complex interaction between the policy analyst, the policymaker, and the planning process.

An example of prestructured social intervention is provided by Bielefeld, Scotch, and Thielemann in their description of HIV/AIDS planning in Dallas. During the first stages of the epidemic, health and human service agencies were overwhelmed.

Treatments were expensive; clients needed a range of integrated services, including multiple medications together with counseling and other social and psychological assistance. Resources were inadequate, and a great deal of social stigma and anxiety impeded attending to those requiring aid.

Ryan White legislation was passed at the federal level to increase resources and provide a more comprehensive approach to confronting the illness. The Dallas case study illustrates how well-defined legislative mandates led nonprofit organizations to expand their programs, particularly in providing economic assistance and social services in the health care field. Local agencies, particularly, were encouraged and given the means to increase benefits to minority clients. The administrative standards imposed on participating nonprofit agencies evoked more stringent efforts on their part in terms of fiscal control and monitoring outcomes. The program also channeled the human service organizations toward more and improved interagency coordination. This infusion of federal funds on a carefully planned basis helped institute a vital and needed HIV/AIDS service delivery system in this community.

Armstrong describes a planning effort that was more flexible and participatory than the AIDS case, one that mixed elements of planning and locality development. The focus was on developing a family-centered, neighborhood-based service delivery system involving a high degree of interagency collaboration. Youth issues and health concerns were of high moment. In the project, community members were systematically brought into creating the service plan and program infrastructure. A countywide needs assessment was conducted at an early point, using methods whereby the view of residents were brought into the picture through focus groups, interviews, and town meetings.

Within each of the neighborhoods designated to participate in the program, a community development element was an integral part of the program. This entailed creating a local self-governance structure and clarifying community priorities. The design also called for employing neighborhood residents, developing neighborhood leadership, and bolstering self-help and mutual assistance. Collaborative links were formed with local businesses, civic groups, and other community-based organizations. The blending of intervention modes appeared to have good results in the particular local context.

Social Action

Fisher, in his overview article, describes the classic conception of social action, and shows how it has evolved and changed in recent decades. Early notions of social action viewed it as "grassroots-based, conflict-oriented, with a focus on direct action, and geared to organizing the disadvantaged or aggrieved to take action on their own behalf." It relies on the means of force or pressure to obtain concessions from individuals having a great deal of power and prestige in society. Examples are given from the Alinsky school of organizing, liberation struggles of people of color, urban decentralization actions, and the New Left.

Fisher goes on to describe "new social movements," which embrace efforts in feminist, ecological, gay and lesbian, and oppressed minority organizations.

Developments in recent organizing efforts include national and global elements, a longer time frame for organizational activity, and a changing context within which to function. Democracy and diversity are central themes in this trend, however culturally oriented, identity-based actions result in fragmentation and stalemate. Fisher believes there has been a concomitant reduction in emphasis on meeting the material needs of the poor. He advocates practice initiatives directed at building coalitions, entering into electoral politics, and reinvigorating an ideological commitment to social justice and community solidarity.

Some tactics and techniques of organization building in this mode are detailed by Haggstrom. He indicates that the process begins with the organizer bringing people together at a meeting. Individuals are encouraged to express their acute concerns, admitting them openly to themselves and others, and to engage in responsible planning to seek relief. The organizer highlights the conflicts in the situation, because the problems of low-income, low-power people cannot be resolved without threat to the self-interests of those in advantaged positions.

Haggstrom warns about symbolic concessions that are made tacitly by elites when faced with organized pressure. The organizer has to help the group at that time to move to a new line of action focused on forcing the opponent to follow through on these agreements. Haggstrom views social action as a morality drama wherein the organizer strives to see that the action episode is projected publicly as a struggle between the forces of good and the forces of evil. The script is written in such a way that the action group controls the conflict, and the other parties are put in the position of responding to and containing it. Haggstrom addresses the ethical and moral dimensions of everyday organizing head-on and in a philosophical key. He also deals with hard political and personal tactical choices that confront the social action practitioner.

Social action as a morality drama is depicted vividly in the Mobilization for Youth case study described by Brager. The narrative provides a close view of the harsh and damaging tactics that power elites will bring to bear when they feel threatened by advocates for the poor. A range of radical actions were carried out by the Mobilization program, including rent strikes, demands on schools and service agencies to change their programs, and competition with city officials around who should control certain resources. The aim was to open opportunities for upward mobility for minority youth.

There was a strong reaction from establishment groups. They labeled the staff as subversive, enlisting the support of the right-wing press in a vitriolic media campaign. Further, they called for a political means test for all staff, which would be a way to weed out the most committed and militant. The agency fought back through lobbying, holding rallies, and conducting a petition drive, but these efforts were not enough to fully vanquish the onslaught. Change advocates in devising social action initiatives clearly need to anticipate the strength of potential counterattacks from their opponents, and to assess the tactical means they have available to overcome these.

A social action project having favorable results is described in the article by Soifer. Here a statewide effort achieved rent stabilization legislation for low- and middle-income mobile home park residents throughout Vermont. The strategy employed a combination of grassroots organizing involving disruptive tactics, together with normative lobbying techniques typically used in planning and policy processes. Soifer refers to this as an "insider-outsider" strategy. The staff organized 23 tenant organizations across the state, following the action model of ACORN (Association of Community Organizations for Reform Now). Militant pressures were reflected in an unannounced visit to the governor's office by 25 activists and a newspaper reporter. But the organization also hired a lobbyist, drew on expert testimony, and worked for incremental political change through collaborative and persuasive means.

The author indicates that the project in this way was able to shift power relations between renter and landlords, at least in the short term. Soifer takes the view that flexibility is necessary in employing change strategies. He maintains that the community practitioner must be capable of using a variety of methodologies and knowing how to "integrate, synthesize, and shift between them as necessary."

SOME TASKS AHEAD

As always, times of great unrest and turmoil, such as those in which we live, may be regarded primarily as periods of either great danger or enormous opportunity for change. To personally and professionally maximize the possibilities for positive change, there are certain steps we can take as part of our strategic efforts. One is to help in the translation of private (individual, small-group, community) troubles into public issues where they can be seriously addressed (community care for AIDS patients, for example). A second is to resist the pressure to cannibalize each other in response to the demands for privatization, downsizing, and cost containment. A third is to seek ways of bringing to reality—when and where we are able—the promise of a multicultural society. The last step is to remember that, if we use well the tools at our command, we can play a vital roll in determining the shape of human services for the first quarter of the twenty-first century.

—John E. Tropman
John L. Erlich

REFERENCES

Bendix, Reinhard, & Seymour M. Lipset, eds. *Class, Status and Power*. New York: The Free Press, 1966.

Coser, Lewis. *Functions of Social Conflict*. New York: The Free Press, 1956.

Etzioni, Amitai. *A Comparative Analysis of Complex Organizations*. New York: The Free Press, 1961.

Fisher, Robert. *Let the People Decide: Neighborhood Organizing in America*, 2nd ed. Boston: Twayne Publishers, 1994.

Garrison, William. "Rancorous Conflict in Community Politics." *American Sociological Review* 31 (1) (February 1966): 71–81.

Hamel, Gary, & C. K. Prahalad. "Strategic Intent." *Harvard Business Review*, 67 (3) (May–June 1989): 63–76.

Hofer, Eric. *The True Believer*. New York: The New American Library, 1958.

Weil, Marie, & Dorothy Gamble. "Community Practice Models." In R. L. Edwards et al., eds. *Encyclopedia of Social Work*, 19th ed. Washington, DC: NASW 1995: 577–593.

13.

Ram A. Cnaan and Jack Rothman

LOCALITY DEVELOPMENT AND THE BUILDING OF COMMUNITY

THE FUTURE OF COMMUNITY

Social critics and moral philosophers have lamented detrimental contemporary trends, including ever-encroaching technology, disintegration of the family, ecological destruction, and widening economic and social disparities. They cite among these the erosion of community life, indeed, the "eclipse" of community as a viable social institution. Locality development is a community intervention modality that specifically aims to address that concern.

Before dealing with locality development as an intervention mode, it would be useful to define the term "community" and establish the need for efforts aimed at the enhancement of communities. One source is Warren's (1978) classical work, *The Community in America*, which defines community broadly as "that combination of systems and units that perform the major functions having locality relevance," namely, "production-distribution-consumption, socialization, social control, social participation, and mutual support" (p. 170).

Cox (1987) states that "the community may be perceived of as a place where a group of people live and conduct various activities of daily living: earn a living, buy goods and services they are unable to produce for themselves, school their children, transact their civic and governmental affairs, etc." (p. 133). Clearly such a holistic, self-contained community is a rarity in our time.

One hears it widely lamented that modern communities do not offer what, in some past golden days, "gemeinschaft" had presumably provided, namely, an environment characterized by intimate, spontaneous, inclusive, and enduring personal relationships. In this type of community people knew each other well, their fates were intertwined, and there was a great deal of solidarity, mutual concern, and social responsibility. Tonnies (1957) distinguished between this harmonious "gemeinschaft" and the alienated and transitory "gesellschaft."

The decline in the importance of local communities manifests itself not only in waning interpersonal relationships, but also in the weakening of the local community as a force that bears on the destiny of its members. In modern societies, local institutions are significantly impacted by wider social, economic, and political systems—urban, regional, national, and international. Culture no longer evolves locally, but is a product of powerful vertical, extracommunity influences such as the mass media.

Two key questions arise from this. First, if the community is declining as an institution, why be concerned with community practice? Second, if the local community is still a relevant institution, how can it be enhanced? The remainder of this section will answer the first question, while the rest of the chapter will answer the latter.

An old Jewish parable, attributed to Rabbi Menachem Mendel of Kotzeck

(Sade, 1993), uses an allegory that conceives of a person as a spiritual tree. When asked about moving to another location, Rabbi Menachem Mendel responded that moving from one city to another is a major event involving not only one's body and personal belongings that are on the ground but also one's more celestial spirit. People are planted in their community, and being forced to move entails cutting both their earthly and their psychic roots.

One may be able to grow new roots in another community, but frequent relocation results in weaker roots, and each move may be painful, especially at a later stage of life. It takes years to develop a network of meaningful social ties, and although modern means of transportation and communication allow us to keep in touch with people who are afar, most of our meaningful social contacts are with those we can meet on a frequent basis within a circumscribed geographic space. Informal mutual aid, such as baby-sitting in case of emergency, is provided locally by people who know and care for each other. Newcomers find it difficult to blend into such informal systems.

In some instances, people can easily define their community; in others they find it difficult. When asked to identify their community, most people mention its boundaries. Milton Kotler notes, "The most sensible way to locate the neighborhood is to ask people where it is, for people spend much time fixing its boundaries. Gangs mark its turf. Old people watch for new faces. Children figure out safe routes between home and school. People walk their dogs through their neighborhood, but rarely beyond it. Above all, the neighborhood has a name" (cited in Morris and Hess, 1975, p. 40).

The issue of a geographically defined area with discernable boundaries raises distinct possibilities for community practice.

We know that boundaries and borders are commonly used in distinguishing among nations, but they are important at the community level as well. A border between countries serves three key functions: (1) to assure physical safety (this denotes what is defensible and where to position security forces in advantageous posts); (2) to secure natural resources (such as fishing territories or national ownership over mines); and (3) to protect national heritage and solidarity (including language, norms of behavior, and citizenship-membership).

We suggest that borders of local communities serve the same functions in a less pronounced way. Historically, the borders of local communities (which often included walled defenses) were designed to assist in assuring security, and they still do. Local watch groups and police departments in American cities and universities reflect this.

Communities attempt to give preference to locals in enjoyment of facilities and amenities. In rural communities, the use of open spaces is a guarded privilege of local people, and in many urban congested neighborhoods parking spaces are reserved for area residents. Further, many studies have found that people who own living units or work in a certain community are more invested and willing to volunteer to uphold the local community for the benefit of its residents (Freidmann, Florin, Wandersman, & Meier, 1988). Accordingly, Morris and Hess (1975) observed that the first stage of community identity often begins with residents organizing to maintain the integrity of their area against intrusive outside interests and to preserve its resources for themselves and their neighbors.

Some local communities seek to maintain their heritage through historical societies, museums, monuments, and celebrations. Local parks, coffee houses, bars, and barber shops become part of the community's collective identity and sense of distinctiveness. People identify themselves (proudly or otherwise) by the community to which they belong, usually the one in which they live. One's identity, especially during childhood, is established by the community of residence. However, people today often were not born into the community in which they live as adults, but rather they settle there by choice. This choice is not always purely a matter of personal preference, but rather a compromise between aspirations and financial ability. Thus, people end up in localities (an affluent suburb, the country-side, downtown) that serve to define their social and economic status and to reflect their self-image.

Before concluding this section, it is important to note that some contemporary definitions view the community somewhat more abstractly in terms of common activities and purposes. Using this orientation allows one to conceptualize a community not only as a geographical entity with phys-ical boundaries but also as a community of interest or affinity, such as people with a similar political ideology (liberals), social-class position (workers) or a physical or mental disability (cancer patients). Murray Ross (1967) has referred to these as func-tional communities, which though intang-ible have psychological boundaries and group identities that separate insiders and outsiders. The focus of this chapter is on geographical communities, but the discus-sion can be readily applied to functional and affinity communities.

Communities of today are not what they used to be; one may ask if they ever were what some people idealistically think they "were in the past." While people are more mobile and share their energies and invest-ments among various separate social entities (residential, work, recreational), communi-ties still hold importance for many people.

Even if people are unaware of it, they share many needs and problems by the mere fact of geographical proximity or common fate. If the water system breaks down in a certain area and becomes pol-luted, all residents of the area have the same need for fresh water, and their lives are intermingled regardless of whether they acknowledge it or wish it to be so. Frequently the needs and problems shared by people do not necessarily unite them to take corrective steps. Often, a concerted effort by a professional is required to mobilize people into problem-solving action, which is the rationale for locality development practice.

CONCEPTUALIZING LOCALITY DEVELOPMENT

Locality development is a method used as part of community organization interven-tion. It gives high priority to building com-munity solidarity and competence. It seeks

to educate and motivate people for self-help; to develop responsible local leadership, to incul-cate among the members of rural communities a sense of citizenship and among the residents of urban areas a spirit of civic consciousness; to introduce and strengthen democracy at the grassroots level through the creation and/or revi-talization of institutions designed to serve as instruments of local participation; to initiate a self-generating, self-sustaining, and enduring process of growth; to enable people to establish and maintain cooperative and harmonious rela-tionships; and to bring about gradual and self-chosen changes in the community's life with a minimum of stress and disruption (Khinduka, 1987, p. 353).

Rothman in Article 1 of this book notes that locality development involves "broad participation by a wide spectrum of people at the local community level in determin-ing goals and taking civic action." The most common interventions are increasing communication among residents, educating, forming groups, seeking consensus, encouraging group discussion, and focusing on common concerns and problems. The individual who engages in locality development practice has to be a good group facilitator, coordinator, teacher, and conciliator and has to have patience with a slow pace of change, as the process of community building is more important than any single given problem. Locality development brings to mind the metaphor of teaching a hungry person the skill of fishing as opposed to occasionally plying the poor soul with a fish for dinner.

Practice aimed at these objectives has been identified by the terms "community development" and "locality development." The locality development nomenclature was employed originally by Rothman in the first edition of this book to clearly designate this process-oriented approach to practice. Community development is a more eclectic or amorphous term, which sometimes connotes institutional and policy means to strengthen communities from above (Mier, 1993), or implies the promotion of industrial expansion through economic development (Bingham & Mier, 1993). Sometimes it incorporates a national or international perspective rather than a strong local emphasis (Goetz & Clarke, 1993). For this reason, we will favor the locality development terminology, and when we alternatively use "community development" it will be in this more delimited sense.

Locality development has been practiced in both rural, less developed areas of the world and urban settings. In developing countries, locality development often was related to economic development, while in urban areas it contained an element of political empowerment. Yet, in cities, economic issues such as rent control or unemployment are important matters, just as in rural areas the political process and control by traditional elites can be a critical factor. Rubin and Rubin (1992) observe that in urban centers, recently, "local groups . . . have started Community Development Corporations (CDCs) to run or finance local businesses and housing. Among many other projects, CDCs have built or rehabilitated housing for poor and moderate-income families, established and managed neighborhood shopping centers, and worked to establish local businesses" (p. 27). Thus, currently we consider both settings (urban-rural) and both areas of concentration (politicial-economic) as integral to locality development.

An important set of assumptions or values drives locality development. First, people who suffer from a common problem often may be unaware of it, attempt to ignore its existence, or even believe there is nothing they can do about it. Locality development is thus a purposive process by which awareness emerges along with a desire to act in order to resolve problems.

Second, community workers engage a very broad cross-section of community members and do not lean in the direction of elite, influential members. In this respect, they apply the principle of the "more the merrier" and believe that the more extensive the representation the better.

Third, practitioners start "where the people are" and gradually move to where they come to want to go—not necessarily to where the practitioner would like them to be. Local self-determination is strongly valued.

Fourth, locality development eschews exclusionary or discriminatory approaches; minorities of all sorts are welcomed and their unique perspectives and needs are acknowledged and incorporated into the general agenda. Multiethnic and cross-cultural perspectives are highlighted.

Fifth, locality development seeks to empower local residents to gain the capacity to solve problems and successfully cope with powerful authorities and institutions that affect their lives. Self-help is a core concept.

Sixth, the prime constituents of the locality development practitioner are the local residents and not established organizations and authorities in the community who may pay the salary of the community developer. Keeping this type of arrangement operative requires a high degree of sophistication, involving both interpersonal and political skills on the part of the practitioner, as well as a clear sense of direction.

Seventh, locality development assumes that planned intervention in the community is better than allowing a flawed status quo to prevail. This assumption is sometimes questioned, especially in developing countries, by those who claim that often the results of locality development practice are iatrogenic and involve breaking down an existing indigenous system and replacing it with an inferior one (Goulet, 1989). The critique needs to be recognized and attended to, within a framework that is explicitly change-oriented and optimistic about human potential. Also, promoting genuine active involvement of local participants helps to insure that changes are in keeping with indigenous culture and aspirations.

THEORETICAL GROUNDING FOR LOCALITY DEVELOPMENT

Community organization in general and locality development in particular are often criticized for lacking a theoretical or conceptual base. In this section we draw upon Durkheim's (1933) categorization of organic and mechanistic communities as an element in constructing a theoretical

underpinning for locality development. Durkheim's most famous works involve the study of the etiology of suicide and the phenomenon of anomie (the breakdown in guiding norms and mores resulting from the combination of urbanization, secularization, and industrialization, combined with the decline of the extended family and the rise of new forms of social problems). These works led Durkheim to study ways by which people in the emerging industrial society could function advantageously and live a good life.

Durkheim suggested that people in a centrifugal type of situation need some form of social glue to hold them together: This he called solidarity. Solidarity is the means by which people feel shared commitments and willingly join together to improve their common quality of life. Solidarity can be achieved in two ways, organic and mechanistic. It is the role of community development to sustain organic solidarity and minimize mechanistic solidarity.

Locality development is consistent with Durkheim's (1933) concept of an organic community, a community manifesting high degrees of interdependence among individuals—with exchanges, legal contracts, and norms guiding these interrelations. Legal codes in an organic community are comparatively less punitive and more "restitutive," specifying noncoercive ways to redress violations of normative expectations and reintegrate violators back into the network of interdependencies that typify organic communities. Individual freedom in such a community is highly valued and, in fact, norms stressing respect for the personal dignity of the individual dominate the highly abstract collective conscience. In such a community, contracts (such as the norms of disposing of garbage) are not only a means of communication and bargaining; they also serve to foster a cohesive outlook reinforcing the mutual responsibility and commitments of members of the same community.

In an organic community residents know each other and, if a common problem emerges, they discuss it and attempt jointly to cope with it. The ongoing interaction assists in facilitating communitywide involvement and concern so that the power of the community to cope with threats is the power of the collective, and is often stronger than the simple sum of individual members. This type of community was beginning to disappear in Durkheim's time, and he feared that anomie would result in a new kind of social order, the mechanistic community.

A mechanistic community bases the essence of solidarity upon a repressive collective conscience that regulates the thoughts and actions of individuals located in the structure. A mechanistic community utilizes repressive legal codes and punitive sanctions, thereby limiting individual freedom, choice, and autonomy. The collective conscience dominates people and their actions, and needs are constrained by its dictates and those of cohesive subunits. Durkheim seems to have been anticipating elements of German National Socialism and the Russian Leninist scenario.

Tonnies (1957) had a related formulation in his distinction between Gemeinschaft and Gesellschaft. The Gemeinschaft (the organic community) allows the individual to experiment and decide internally whether to conform. The Gesellschaft (the mechanistic community) keeps the individual in line by exerting external pressure that is internalized involuntarily or obeyed in an uncritical way.

According to Durkheim, a community with a low degree of organic solidarity is bound in the long run to generate many social problems and be detrimental to its residents. He predicted that mechanistic communities will show higher rates of anomie and, consequently, experience more social problems. He looked for means to increase organic solidarity, and one of his ideas was a single-industry town, in which all residents are bound by the common interest of their source of employment.

Using this scheme, we can see that locality development practitioners attempt to shift the balance from a mechanistic-type community toward an organic-type community. This is accomplished by helping to make people jointly aware and responsible for their quality of life, thereby increasing residents' solidarity. By fostering widespread participation among residents and building a consensus among them, norms are self-generated and the need to use coercive measures is mitigated.

This theoretical formulation, of necessity, has been presented in brief, contracted form. It should, however, suggest in a general way how the framework can be applied to locality development issues. It also illustrates the manner in which other sociological constructs can be drawn upon to contribute to theory building in this area of practice.

RESIDENT INITIATIVE AND COLLABORATIVE TACTICS: THEMES AND VARIATIONS

In this section we will treat two important aspects of locality development: the source for determining the program and the preferred tactical approach. Locality development favors working with clients to decide what they need and not deciding for clients what is good for them. The emphasis is on direct initiation of goals by local people rather than the more indirect or circumlocutious shaping of goals by the practitioner or other external parties. The preferred mode of problem solving and program implementation is consensual, not conflictual.

Garkovich (1989) states, "if community development as a discipline and a practice is to be relevant to the needs of the communities of tomorrow, the challenge is to shift the focus of training and activities to the more difficult and time-consuming, yet eminently more effective, strategy of local capacity building" (p. 215). This requires that local people take the initiative and be allowed the time required to plan their own destiny.

Khinduka (1987), on the other hand, is critical of what he perceives to be an overemphasis on process in community development and the lack of focus on task goal attainment. In his words, "the community development approach to social change, by and large, is still dominated by a process orientation which evaluates the actual outcome of a community project primarily in terms of what happens in the minds of men rather than in terms of its impact on the social structure" (p. 354).

However, it is clear that modifications in people's behaviors and attitudes can be correlated with successful changes in their environment. These two outcomes are not necessarily antithetical. Also, encouraging self-help does not blindly preclude other options regardless of the circumstance.

Sometimes local residents in complex situations or at an early stage of development are not in a position to move forward, and a practitioner will take the lead. For example, active negotiating by a community developer with a landlord on behalf of residents to supply heat during the winter months may be preferable to waiting until tenants become miserable and ill enough in the bitter cold to decide to petition the landlord. Thus, occasionally and as a variant,

the community development practitioner acts assertively on the behalf of residents (Batten, 1967; York, 1984).

Collaboration has long been a watchword in this area of practice. Kettner, Daley, and Nichols (1985) suggest that collaborative and educational tactics have the advantage of minimizing potentially negative side effects. These approaches build and strengthen communities by cementing relationships among people and increasing their knowledge about the problems they face. Collaborative tactics engender attitudes of good will and mutual support, and foster creative and democratic decision making. But, as in the previous discussion, the approach cannot be applied in a single-minded and uncritical manner. Occasionally pressure tactics may be called for.

The reader of this volume is already aware that social action, the primary arena for conflictual methods, is discussed in the next section of this book. Yet, conflict as a practice method may overlap with locality development and cannot be ignored in that context. Sometimes intractable problems do not yield to tactics having a high degree of civility, and participants tire and become impatient with drawn-out processes of accommodation and compromise (Bryant, 1979; Epstein, 1970).

Coleman (1957) notes that conflict is one of the most powerful tools available to powerless segments of society when dealing with societal problems. It is understood, however, that conflict should be reserved for infrequent application in locality development practice, and used as an option of last resort. Conflict is very difficult to retreat from and, once begun, difficult to set aside in order to resume a collaborative mode (Kettner, Daley, & Nichols, 1985). Furthermore, there is a risk that changes brought about by conflict may be reversed by those on whom they were applied (Marris & Rein, 1973).

There is another way of looking at this issue. Conflict is associated with an *advocacy* role for the practitioner, while collaboration is associated with an *enabling* role. Enabling and facilitating constitute the prime thrust in locality development, but, as we have seen, advocacy with its conflictual *modus operandi* cannot be dismissed. While for many years locality development literature viewed enabling and advocacy as distinct and competing approaches, today it is commonly accepted that the two can be used jointly in keeping with the principle of mixing and phasing various models and strategies.

The term "enabler," advanced in 1947 by K. L. M. Pray from the functional school of social work at the University of Pennsylvania, distinguishes the community social worker from the community organization agitator such as a union organizer (Dunham, 1959; Lappin, 1985; Pray, 1948). The enabler, using a direct mode with residents, applies an objective approach and helps awaken and focus discontent about existing conditions that are harmful to the community, attempts to assist local residents in getting organized by providing them with information and technical skills, and supports their struggle to improve existing conditions or combat oppressive policies.

The term "advocate" is associated with the social movements of the 1960s. In that period, simply enabling local residents to cope with the paternalism of formal and private agencies was viewed as no longer enough to evoke the cooperation or sympathy of neighborhood people. Residents, radicals, and local professionals looked for committed people who would not question the need to act on behalf of clients—to remedy injustices stemming from previous

actions taken by government authorities, businesses, voluntary organizations, and powerful individuals (Perlman & Gurin, 1972). This approach also assumes it legitimate for locality developers to act as "political tacticians." That is, they are expected to seize opportunities and apply pressure, when possible, to guarantee maximum benefits to the residents of the neighborhood (Brager, 1968).

A traditional enabler might face a credibility problem, as residents come to doubt the practitioner's motives because of not taking a militant or partisan posture when problems are serious and unyielding. A committed advocate might face problems in making necessary linkages with significant agencies, systems, and individuals that had been attacked and offended through previous actions. Henderson and Thomas (1980) aptly note that, "the worker often has to handle such [. . . unpredicted and contrasting . . .] situations within a short span of time, and he or she is therefore always working with different audiences and constituencies from varied role positions" (p. 3). The dominant themes of locality development have to leave room for necessary variations.

PROBLEM-SOLVING ROLES IN LOCALITY DEVELOPMENT

It is said that community intervention entails analytical and interactional roles. The analytical ones concern the issues, needs, and objectives being addressed and encompass problem-solving activities. The emphasis is on task goals. Interactional roles concern human and process-oriented aspects of the work, including promoting good working relationships, and encouraging group development. The emphasis is on process goals.

In locality development, even analytical, problem-solving elements have strong interactional aspects, in that problem solving typically is done with the participation of residents rather than independently on their behalf. Community building, the major aim, is by definition permeated with process goals. In this section we will discuss problem-solving elements, and in the next one we will examine interactional and group development factors.

Authors have approached the analytical aspect in different but overlapping ways. Lindeman (1921) introduced an early model that had a balanced treatment of analytical and interactional features. He employed 10 stages to describe the steps in community development: developing a firm consciousness of need, spreading this consciousness of need, projecting this consciousness, stimulating an emotional impulse to meet the need expeditiously, presenting alternative solutions, allowing for dispute on solutions, engaging in fact gathering, holding an open discussion of issues and strategies, bringing about an integration of solutions, and working out compromises on the basis of tentative progress. Lindeman concentrated on problem identification and decision making around solution overtures but did not continue into the phases of implementation and evaluation of outcomes.

Dunham (1958) later proposed a nine-step model that focuses on solving the problem through logical planning, with less attention to participant involvement. The stages include: recognition of a need or problem, analysis of the need or problem, fact-finding, planning, gaining official approval, action, recording and reporting, making adjustments, and evaluation.

Batten (1967), in his formulation, highlights interactional matters, particularly the stages through which group members typi-cally move, from passive residents to committed citizens aware of their situation. Batten proposed that, in order to go from one stage to the other, the worker must stimulate the process by raising the right questions. His list of stages follows with examples of the worker role in parentheses: (1) People are vaguely dissatisfied but passive (worker stimulates people to understand why they are dissatisfied); (2) People become aware of the need (worker encourages people to think about desirable changes); (3) People become aware of what type of change they are looking for (worker stimulates people to consider what actions they can themselves take to bring about the change); (4) People decide whether or not they want to act (worker aids people to examine optional means of getting organized); (5) People plan what to do and whether they are able to do it (worker helps them think of obstacles, crises, the need to shift direction, and so forth); and (6) There is an assessment of satisfaction with the results (worker encourages people to examine how far they have come and what else they want to accomplish).

Ross (1967) has formulated a set of practice areas providing an aggregate picture (analytical and interactional) of problem-solving activities, but not in sequential order. His six proposed areas, with some illustrative roles, include: system maintenance (organizing and organizational archive), planning (priority rating of community needs), facilitating relationships (mediation), mobilizing initiatives (fund raising), fostering innovation (leadership development), and interpretation and education (publications).

Henderson and Thomas (1980) more recently have taken the practitioner as the point of departure, examining the detailed steps required by the professional from beginning to end. The nine stages in this model are planning and negotiating entry into the community, getting to know the community, determining a general approach, making contacts and bringing people together, forming and building organizations, helping to clarify goals and priorities, keeping the organization going, dealing with friends and enemies, and separating and terminating.

Brager, Specht, and Torczyner (1987) offer a more general perspective. The worker's "first task in working with the community is to map out the intricate patterns of economic and social relationships by which the community carries out its purposes and functions." They suggest further that "organizers seek to work with and to change some of these patterns by developing an organization to promote effective relationships, maximize assets, generate power, and increase the emotional, social, and material resources of its members" (p. 51).

Locality development is not a linear, mechanical process that can be articulated in tightly compartmentalized stages; even experts do not agree upon specific stages. The processes described above do have similarities and reflect some key dimensions. A practitioner's day, nevertheless, may be composed of numerous meetings with people and activities that may seem on the surface irrelevant to the implementation of locality development.

Yet the activities serve to establish contacts, make both the worker and the cause visible, help set the agenda, and stir "the pot" in the community. Biddle and Biddle (1965, p. 224) observe that community developers have "a habit of being around and accessible in a community meeting place—a coffee shop, a bench under some trees in the market square or wherever people gather to gossip, to watch the passerby and enjoy their company, until such time as both curiosity and familiarity prompt the first exchange of greeting and inquiry." This illustrates that the role of a community developer is in many respects informal, complex, and emergent.

Problem solving in locality development is based on the logic of identifying and delineating the causes of the problem, making the problem visible and widely agreed upon, devising intervention, and implementing the planned intervention. In itself this is not at all unique, but it does contain special features. What is distinctive is the multiplicity of individuals and groups that are intimately and integrally brought into all aspects. Locally based groups are the core medium that locality development practitioners rely on to solve problems and foster community capacity.

INTERACTIONAL AND GROUP DEVELOPMENT ROLES

A key task of locality development practitioners is establishing self-sustaining representative organizations. Mondros and Wilson (1993) noted that "involving, engaging, and sustaining a large and strongly identified group of participants is important to achieving organizational goals" (pp. 69–70). Yet we know that 50 percent of voluntary neighborhood organizations may become inactive after their first year of existence (Prestby & Wandersman, 1985; Yates, 1973). Furthermore, many of the surviving organizations develop oligarchic structures that separate out active leaders, who by default become the experts, from the rest of the local citizens (Cnaan, 1991). Thus, maintenance of a genuine ongoing neighborhood organization represents a greater challenge in many ways than its formation.

Mondros and Wilson (1993) suggest that voluntary community organizations should be highly accessible. That is, they should encourage as many people as possible to join while losing as few as possible. These organizations make themselves accessible for new people, accept them willingly, avoid insider jargon, and hold open meetings at convenient locations and times. They accept members' suggestions and willingly discuss them, do not rely heavily on a small and traditional cadre of leaders, and maintain amicable and frequent contacts with many other organizations. Mondros and Wilson also discuss recruitment and engagement techniques such as focusing on those people who are likely to join with fellow residents, forming cogent messages that communicate, using multiple recruitment methods, providing orientation for new members, and facilitating easy access to committees.

Brager and Specht (1973) propose a model of community organization built on four stages of group development and two types of tasks—technical (or analytical) and interactional—to be carried out within each stage. The four stages include socialization of groups, primary group formation (developing affective relations), forming an organization, and mediating the relations between individuals and institutions. This model has the virtue of emphasizing more than one dimension at any stage. On the negative side, however, it seems to present all tasks as the purview of the practitioner, who then becomes more a leader than an enabler.

Cnaan and Adar (1987) have proposed a detailed model for fostering and nurturing what they define as instrumental groups. While group work is a key practice tool in social work, it is used in this context not to deal with members' psychological or adjustment problems, but as a means of purposively creating a unit of people willing to work collaboratively on solving tangible problems. The Cnaan and Adar model

is based on tasks to be carried out in order to enhance the likelihood that a group of people will function conjointly with effectiveness. The tasks and the emphasis placed on them varies, according to the life cycle (stage of development) of the group and its circumstances. Based on work with many practitioners, Cnaan and Adar note that groups do not necessarily progress linearly through stages but often regress to an earlier stage.

These authors use a five-stage process that may loop back: (1) preliminary development work; (2) creating the initial group; (3) establishing internal mechanisms and operative planning; (4) execution of the plan and goal attainment; and (5) summing-up and reevaluation. Within each of these five stages Cnaan and Adar have identified four specific interactional dimensions: (1) ideological–value dimension; (2) organizational–administrative dimension; (3) activity–professional dimension; and (4) interpersonal–social dimension. The model, then, entails a variety of activities that should be performed by group members and/or professionals to assure that the four interactional dimensions are covered in each of the five stages.

Kahn (1991) focuses on organizing techniques at the local level. He spells out a large number of scenarios for use in mobilizing groups of people: leadership, forming an organization, membership, constituencies, meetings, communication, and practical operation of the organization. Kahn's approach is a more comprehensive and updated version of an earlier work by Huenefeld (1970). In a similar vein, Rubin and Rubin (1992) have provided a rich account of how to run three types of meetings (the membership meeting, decision-making meeting, and training session), which are the backbone of locality development.

It is important that the process of bringing grassroots people together to form an organization takes profoundly into account the varied cultural patterns, values, and aims of local racial and ethnic groups. The poverty and discrimination experienced by minorities make them a prime constituency for efforts directed at improving their life circumstances, either by developing their own services or by applying pressure to external institutions for the transfer of resources. Indeed, Hutcheson and Dominguez (1986) found that in Atlanta 40 percent of the Latino population participated in an activity of a Latino voluntary association at least once in the past 12-month period.

In addition, as Kahn indicates (1991), there is a strong need to organize cross-racial and intercultural coalitions in order to create broad-based community instrumentalities. This requires particular alertness to group differences (for example, the disinclination of Korean communities to form formal representative organizations as compared to those put together along family lines or through churches).

There are some guides to this kind of culturally informed interactional process. Rivera and Erlich (1992) have compiled a volume of illustrative case studies of work with diverse populations, such as Native Americans, Chicanos, African-Americans, Puerto-Rican and Chinese Americans. This book enables the reader to look at cultural differences across a multiplicity of groups and situations. Burghardt's (1982) *The Other Side of Organizing* also examines cultural diversity and the relevance of culture in various community organizing roles. Several of the selections in the locality development and other sections of the book in hand also deal with the subject.

The formation and maintenance of community-based groups is a highly engaging and complex process, in which unexperienced practitioners can easily fail. The practitioner has to be able to attend to personal needs, interpersonal issues, educational factors, cultural variations, external pressures and so forth—without losing sight of the overall task goal and without taking control of the group away from the local leaders. Such a process requires patience, willingness to accept and work with others, sensitivity, and readiness to respond to the changing needs of the group, without becoming lost in the process. Not every person can do this work. In the next section we address the issue of who are employed as community developers and the settings in which they work.

EMPLOYMENT OF LOCALITY DEVELOPMENT PRACTITIONERS

Community developers can be employed by a variety of organizations, including local government, private social-welfare organizations, churches, and local initiative entities. We will describe these settings briefly.

In quite a few countries in the world, locality development is an official function of the local government, sometimes through programs and policies of the national government. In Hong Kong, India, Israel, Sweden, and the U.K., by law or through formal regulations, each local authority employs community developers and, in some cases, will even have a designated department for this purpose. Such workers and units are sometimes considered part of the social welfare department or alternatively as part of an adult education and/or recreation department. It is interesting to note that in some of these countries a key role of such practitioners is to form neighborhood-based representative organizations and citizen boards with a chief aim of enhancing democratic processes.

These workers may be assigned to planning tasks but rarely to social action. In Israel, when the community workers of the City of Jerusalem engaged in social action, they were moved from one department to another, sanctions were applied, and their activities were curtailed. Similarly in Great Britain. In Kuwait, where community organizers are also employed by local authorities, they are prohibited from engaging in either social action or group formation and are restricted to rather conventional roles. Locality development also takes place through several arms of the United Nations, including the World Health Organization, the World Bank, and others. In the United States, the Peace Corps, A.I.D. (Agency for International Development), and Agricultural Extension have conducted governmentally sponsored programs.

However, generally in the United States locality development has been carried out through private/voluntary sources. Historically, the settlement house movement involved itself in neighborhood work and social reform efforts needed to improve neighborhood conditions, symbolized by the endeavors of Jane Addams, Lillian Wald, and Robert Woods, among others. Religious organizations, such as the Friends Service Committee have sponsored programs in this country and overseas, providing a model for the establishment of the Peace Corps.

Churches and synagogues have taken an active role in locality development in a variety of ways. Saul Alinsky's well-known social action projects were financed by the Catholic Church through the Industrial Areas Foundation, but congregations have been much more involved in locality devel-

opment than in social action. Currently, in emerging ethnic neighborhoods containing new immigrants from Southeast Asia, Latin America, and the Caribbean, churches are often the first community institution to take steps to unite these people and work with them to obtain the resources needed to improve their life conditions.

In many communities, an umbrella organization of interfaith congregations is one of the key sources of employment of community developers in the United States. The Campaign for Human Development that operates under the United States Catholic Conference employs community developers in areas where local organizations ask for this assistance. These practitioners help form local citizens groups to promote social change and self-reliance and, after a few years, are assigned to a new location.

While social workers are familiar with the locality development area of practice and have been active in it, they are sometimes not aware of other auspices and patterns for the conduct of locality development. Union organizers use the skills of locality development in building solidarity within the organization, relating the membership to community institutions, and assisting them to address community problems that affect them. In rural development, people with agricultural and technological expertise are the leading professionals. In some instances individuals with business education are the main organizers, especially when economic development is the focus of change. Health educators engage citizens around wellness and disease-prevention concerns. Urban planners comprise another group of professionals often involved in community development, especially when the issues at hand involve housing, transportation, parks, or zoning.

Lay people who gain firsthand experience in organizing and are then solicited by local agencies to come on board as paraprofessionals make up another group of community developers. The paraprofessional designation refers to individuals with relevant life experience and skills, who lack formal training. In communities where the process of development extends over years, some residents acquire the capabilities necessary to do the work.

These individuals perform effectively in building a bridge between local citizens and agencies or authorities. Locality development provides a means for upward mobility for some. Local residents have been identified as an enormous source for spearheading locality development (Huenefeld, 1970). Kahn (1991) asserts that change is most frequently the result of local initiatives carried forward by residents, often out of frustration, who bring neighbors together to create organizations and seek change.

Chavis, Florin, and Felix (1993) have proposed ways of establishing entirely self-run local bodies through empowering activities instigated by an external support organization. These authors have developed what they call "enabling systems," that is, "a coordinated network of organizations that nurtures the creation and maintenance of a grassroots community development process through the provision of resources, incentives and education" (p. 48). These organizations enact the professional function of providing a foundation to spur local self-help activity. In this approach, instead of hiring individual community developers to enter the local community, a system of experts is brought in for a limited period to train and support self-sustaining grassroots leaders.

Chavis, Florin, and Felix describe a variety of enabling systems: some train potential leaders, others provide seed money for local grassroots activity, while still others provide data and information relevant to community needs. The authors also list various types of organizations that serve as enabling systems. For example, local chapters of the United Way of America provide training, prepackaged materials or tools for fundraising, community planning guides, conferences, and publications. The Citizens Committee for New York City annually supports 3,000 volunteer neighborhood organizations with small grants and printed materials. The federal government allocates 44 million dollars to the Community Partnership Demonstration Program to support programs in 150 communities, and the Henry Kaiser Family Foundation has launched community health promotion programs and a corresponding enabling system in seven southern states and the District of Columbia.

As financing for community development and other human services dwindles, professionals can anticipate that these enabling system activities will become more significant. For a foreseeable period of time, professionals may increasingly serve in supportive roles with indigenous leaders and staff, rather than as primary practitioners.

THE OUTLOOK FOR LOCALITY DEVELOPMENT

A few studies have been carried out to determine which models of community organization are typically applied by practitioners. In one of the first studies of its kind, Cnaan and Rothman (1986) found that Israeli community organizers, both in their perception and in actual activities, distinguish between locality development, social planning, and social action in their professional work. Furthermore, the authors discovered that locality development was both perceived as the most relevant model of community organization and the one most practiced. This study discovered that the gap between perceived importance of a practice mode and the one actually used in practice was the smallest for locality development. Thus, community organizers in Israel identified locality development as a distinct model, perceived it as most important, and practice it to a substantial extent.

In a more recent study that is ongoing, the Cnaan and Rothman results are being examined from a cross-cultural perspective. Using the same study instrument originally employed (a 30-item questionnaire), and also focus groups and in-depth interviews, Matts Mattsson in Sweden (1992), Carmen Diaz and Nilsa Burgos in Puerto Rico, Mohammed M. Eweiss in Egypt, Marta Jara-Jubilar in Chile, Rama Pandy in India and the United States, Masaaki Yoshihara in Japan, and Ram Cnaan in the United States have tentatively arrived at findings similar to the earlier study. Locality development, apparently, has a high degree of use by professionals on a cross-national basis.

As noted above, locality development is a means to energize people and to teach them through experiential means to act on their own behalf in order to improve their quality of life. There is, and likely always will be, a need to aid local citizens to find their collective voice and participate in decision making and policy making around matters that impact on their well-being. Unfortunately, these actions are often not self-generated, and professional intervention of a nonintrusive nature is required to motivate people and inculcate effective skills of self-help. The analogy of teaching the skills of fishing rather than providing a fish for one meal bears reiteration. It brings home the notion of fostering personal com-

petency in the same way that locality development conveys the notion of promoting community competency and social cohesion. In the face of potent contemporary trends engendering community disintegration, locality development stands as a countervailing community building force.

REFERENCES

Batten, T. R. *The Non-directive Approach in Group and Community Work.* Oxford, U.K.: Oxford University Press, 1967.

Biddle, W. W., and L. J. Biddle. *The Community Development Process: The Rediscovery of Local Initiatives.* New York: Holt, Rinehart, & Winston, 1965.

Biklen, D. P. *Community Organizing: Theory and Practice.* Englewood Cliffs, NJ: Prentice-Hall, 1983.

Bingham, R. D., and R. Mier. *Theories of Local Economic Development.* Thousand Oaks, CA: Sage, 1993.

Brager, G. A. "Advocacy and Political Behavior." *Social Work*, 13(2) (1968): 5–15.

Brager, G., and H. Specht. *Community Organizing.* New York: Columbia University Press, 1973.

Brager, G., H. Specht, and J. Torczyner. *Community Organizing*, 2nd ed. New York: Columbia University Press, 1987.

Bryant, R. "Conflict and Community Work: A Case Study." *Community Development Journal* 14(2) (1979): 1–7.

Burghardt, S. *The Other Side of Organizing.* Cambridge, MA: Schenkman, 1982.

Chavis, D. M., P. Florin, and M. R. J. Felix. "Nurturing Grassroots Initiatives for Community Development: The Role of Enabling Systems." In T. Mizrahi and J. Morrison, eds., *Community Organization and Social Administration: Advances, Trends, and Emerging Principles*, pp. 41–67. New York: Haworth, 1993.

Cnaan, R. A. "Neighborhood Representing Organizations: How Democratic Are They?" *Social Service Review* 65 (1991): 614–634.

Cnaan, R. A., and H. Adar. "An Integrative Model For Group Work in Community Organization Practice." *Social Work with Groups, 1987* 10(3) (1987): 5–24.

Cnaan, R. A., and J. Rothman. "Conceptualizing Community Intervention: An Empirical Test of 'Three Models' of Community Organization." *Administration in Social Work* 10(3) (1986): 41–55.

Coleman, J. S. *Community Conflict.* New York: Free Press, 1957.

Cox, F. M. "Communities: Alternative Conceptions of Community: Implications for Community Organization Practice." In F. M. Cox, J. L. Erlich, J. Rothman, and J. E. Tropman, eds., *Strategies of Community Organization: Macro Practice*, pp. 232–243. Itasca, IL: Peacock, 1987.

Dunham, A. *Community Welfare Organization: Principles and Practice.* New York: Crowell, 1958.

Dunham, A. "What Is the Job of the Community Organization Worker?" In E. B. Harper and A. Dunham, eds., *Community Organization in Action*, pp. 463–471. New York: Association Press, 1959.

Durkheim, E. *The Division of Labor in Modern Society*, G. Simpson, trans. New York: Free Press (original work published in 1893), 1933.

Epstein, I. "Professional Role Orientations and Conflict Strategies." *Social Work* 15(4) (1970): 87–92.

Friedmann, R. R., P. Florin, A. Wandersman, and R. Meier. "Local Action on Behalf of Local Collectives in the U.S. and Israel: How Different Are Leaders from Members in Voluntary Associations?" *Journal of Voluntary Action Research* 17(3&4) (1988): 36–54.

Garkovich, L. E. "Local Organizations and Leadership in Community Development." In J. A. Christenson and J. E. Robinson, eds., *Community Development in America*, pp. 196–218. Ames, IA: Iowa State University Press, 1989.

Goetz, E. G., and S. E. Clarke. *Comparative Urban Policies in a Global Era.* Thousand Oaks, CA: Sage, 1993.

Goulet, D. "Ethics in Development Theory and Practice." In D. S. Sanders and J. K. Matsuoka, eds., *Peace and Development.* Honolulu, HI: University of Hawaii School of Social Work, 1989.

Henderson, P., and D. N. Thomas. *Skills in Neighbourhood Work.* London: George Allen & Unwin, 1980.

Huenefeld, J. *The Community Activist's Handbook.* Boston: Beacon, 1970.

Hutcheson, J. D., and L. H. Dominguez. "Ethnic Self-help Organizations in Non-barrio Settings: Community Identity and Voluntary Action." *Journal of Voluntary Action Research* 15(4) (1986): 13–22.

Kahn, S. *Organizing: A Guide for Grassroots Leaders.* Silver Spring, MD: National Association of Social Workers, 1991.

Kettner, P. M., J. M. Daley, and A. W. Nichols. *Initiating Change in Organizations and Communities.* Monterey, CA: Brooks/Cole, 1985.

Khinduka, S. K. "Community Development: Potentials and Limitations." In F. M. Cox, J. L. Erlich, J. Rothman, and J. E. Tropman, eds., *Strategies of Community Organization: Macro Practice*, pp. 353–362. Itasca, IL: Peacock, 1987.

Lappin, B. "Community Development: Beginnings in Social Work Enabling." In S. H. Taylor and R. W. Roberts, eds., *Theory and Practice of Community Social Work*, pp. 59–93. New York: Columbia University Press, 1985.

Lindeman, E. C. *The Community: An Introduction to the Study of Community Leadership and Organization.* New York: Association Press, 1921.

Marris, P., and M. Rein. *Dilemmas of Social Reform*, 2nd ed. Chicago: Aldine-Atherton, 1973.

Mattsson, M. *Community Work in a Political Framework: An International Research Project.* A paper presented at Inter-University Consortium on International Social development, Washington, DC, July 1992.

Mier, R. *Social Justice and Local Development Theory.* Thousand Oaks, CA: Sage, 1993.

Mondros, J. B., and S. M. Wilson. "Building High Access Community Organizations: Structures as Strategy." In T. Mizrahi and J. Morrison, eds., *Community Organization and Social Administration: Advances, Trends, and Emerging Principles*, pp. 69–85. New York: Haworth, 1993.

Morris, D., and K. Hess. *Neighborhood Power: The New Localism.* Boston: Beacon Press, 1975.

Perlman, R., and A. Gurin. *Community Organization and Social Planning.* New York: John Wiley, 1972.

Pray, K. L. M. "When Is Community Organization Social Work Practice?" *Proceedings, National Conference of Social Work,*

1947. New York: Columbia University Press, 1948.

Prestby, J., and A. Wandersman. "An Empirical Exploration of a Framework of Organizational Viability: Maintaining Block Associations." *Journal of Applied Behavioral Science* 21 (1985): 287–305.

Rivera, F. G., and J. L. Erlich. *Community Organizing in a Diverse Society*. Boston: Allyn and Beacon, 1992.

Ross, M. G. *Community Organization; Theory, Principles and Practice*. New York: Harper & Row, 1967.

Rothman, J., and J. E. Tropman. "Models of Community Organization and Macro Practice Perspectives: Their Mixing and Phases." In F. M. Cox, J. L. Erlich, J. Rothman, and J. E. Tropman, eds. *Strategies of Community Organization: Macro Practice*, pp. 3–26. Itasca, IL: Peacock, 1987.

Rubin, H. J., and I. S. Rubin. *Community Organizing and Development*, 2nd ed. New York: MacMillan, (1992).

Sade, P. *A Man Is a Closed Room, His Heart Broken, and Dark Falls Outside* (Ish beheder sagor, libo shabor, ubahotz yoredet affela). Tel Aviv: Schocken, 1993.

Tonnies, F. *Community and Society (Gemeinschaft and Gesellschaft)*, C. E. Loomis, trans. East Lansing, MI: Michigan State University Press (original work published in 1912), 1957.

Warren, R. L. *The Community in America*, 3rd ed. Chicago: Rand McNally, 1978.

Yates, D. *Neighborhood Democracy*. Lexington, MA: D. C. Heath, 1973.

York, A. S. "Towards a Conceptual Model of Community Social Work." *British Journal of Social Work* 14 (1984): 241–255.

14.

Sylvia Martí-Costa and Irma Serrano-García

NEEDS ASSESSMENT AND COMMUNITY DEVELOPMENT: AN IDEOLOGICAL PERSPECTIVE

Community development is a process which, through consciousness-raising, promotes and utilizes human resources, leading to the empowerment of individuals and communities so that they can understand and solve their problems and create new circumstances for their livelihood. As part of this process, needs assessment may be utilized as a central method to facilitate the modification of social systems so they become more responsive to human needs.

At the individual level, community development promotes psychological growth and enhancement by channeling energies into self-help projects and through the genuine participation of individuals in those decisions that affect their lives. The basic assumption that underlies this reasoning is that most human beings can solve their problems when they obtain access to resources and create alternatives. The emphasis is on their strengths and their development (Rappaport, 1977).

Awareness of problems and of change possibilities is achieved by raising an individual's consciousness from its current or real level to its possible capacity. Real consciousness is defined as an individual or groups' understanding of reality at a given time. Possible consciousness is the maximum understanding that can be achieved by an individual or group according to its material circumstances at a given historical moment (Goldman, 1970).

Consciousness-raising includes critical judgment of situations, the search for underlying causes of problems and their consequences, and an active role in the transformation of society (Ander-Egg, 1980). It is an awareness of human dignity and is essential in the exploration of the relationship between the social order and human misery and in the discovery of the shortcomings inherent in our society (Freire, 1974). It facilitates individual and collective participation in building a new and less oppressive social order, thus affecting the general well-being of the population by enhancing the relationship between individuals and society. Needs assessment is valuable in the consciousness-raising process, because any social movement should start from and respond to the felt needs of the population, in other words, their real consciousness.

Community development can foster consciousness-raising through the involvement of individuals in change efforts. Community development activities need to be grounded in a specific political commitment that responds to the liberation of the powerless groups of society. This does not ignore the participation of the powerful in the maintenance or change of the present social order. It does, however, require a personal and professional commitment to the oppressed because of the mission of prevention—understanding and relieving human suffering.

Contrary to this view, many social scientists have fostered the value-free, apolitical, and ahistorical character of their disciplines throughout several decades (Moscovici, 1972; Weimer, 1979; Zuñiga, 1975). This position, which may be referred to as "the myth of neutrality," distorts the real value-laden and political nature of theory, methods, and practices and thus serves to alienate us from ourselves and others (Ander-Egg, 1973). It creates divisions and distrust within our ranks and resentment from those that participate as "subjects" or recipients of our work, feeling used, manipulated and misunderstood. Thus, it is necessary to examine this myth which has resulted in the social sciences serving the dominant groups of society.

The "myth of neutrality" has reasons for its existence. In some cases it has been sponsored by individuals who clearly believe in it, but in most cases, it has been accepted inadvertently by social scientists. One of the ways in which this occurs is by considering objectivity and neutrality as synonymous and inseparable concepts which are highly desirable in social scientific endeavors.

Those that hold that neutrality and objectivity must go together state that social scientists should not take political stances toward the object of their studies because this will hamper their research efforts (Myrdal, 1969). To them objectivity is defined as the capacity to study facts as they occur, without adhering to previously formed opinions and judgments and with the willingness to abandon positions that are proven false, inadequate, and unsatisfactory (Ander-Egg, 1977). Neutrality, its inseparable counterpart, is defined as a valueless stance before the objective reality (Martí, Note 1).

It is said that if researchers are not neutral, they cannot be objective (Martí, Note 1). This does not ring true as both concepts are different and clearly distinguishable, and while the pursuit of objectivity is desirable and necessary, the search for neutrality is not only impossible, but unwarranted. Objectivity is desirable because its definition implies the existence of defined values and positions which one is willing to change when an examination of reality requires it. Neutrality is impossible because every activity takes place in a particular political context.

If the political nature of the social sciences is recognized and accepted then an explicit definition of social scientists' values is necessary. It is our position that this value stance must be characterized by a commitment to the disadvantaged and powerless groups within a given society. This commitment is to the abandonment of a spectator role and the activation of a professional's mind and art to the service of a cause (Palau, Note 2). This cause should be the significant transformation of inequities in society which implies activism, risk, initiative, and a willingness to fight for clearly defined points of view.

To summarize, needs assessment is an integral part of community development, the process of consciousness-raising. It implies a political commitment which undermines the traditional view of a neutral science and a firm commitment to the exploited, underprivileged and powerless groups in society.

This paper will show that needs assessment is a political process that can be conceptualized as a tool for the organization, mobilization and consciousness-raising of groups and communities. This implies (1) that the diverse uses of needs assessment methods be placed on a continuum, ranging from the perpetuation of control and the maintenance of the social system to the achievement of radical social change; (2) an emphasis on multiple techniques of needs assessment that facilitate collective activities, leadership development, growth of organizational skills, and participation of community members in interventions within research (Irizarry & Serrano, 1979); and (3) the belief that it is necessary to examine ideologies and values

as they influence objectives, the selection of needs assessment techniques, intervention strategies, conceptual frameworks, and the utilization of obtained data.

NEEDS ASSESSMENT

Purpose

Needs assessment is part of a process used to plan social service programs (Pharis, 1976; Siegel, Attkisson, & Cohn, 1977). It is used to determine the problems and goals of the residents of a given community to assure that an intervention will respond to the needs of the population that is being sampled (Warheit, 1976).

The purposes that sustain the use of needs assessment methodology can be placed on a continuum (Table 14.1) according to their political roles. Towards the top of Table 14.1 are purposes that foster system maintenance and control; towards the bottom are ones that promote social change and consciousness-raising. Social system maintenance and control efforts include those activities which are carried out to maintain and/or strengthen the status quo. They also include first order change efforts which alter some of the ways in which the system functions but not the ideology on which it is based (Watzlawick, Weakland, & Fisch, 1974). Radical, or second order, social change efforts imply consciousness-raising and structural and functional alterations.

In consonance with these definitions, the very bottom of the continuum shows needs assessment as a mechanism used by community residents for participation and control in decision making. Needs assessment becomes a technique that facilitates second order social change.

The very top of the continuum lists purposes that foster system maintenance and control, including those that are used to obtain additional funding for already established community programs (Siegel et al., 1977) so as to guarantee their continuation. In the middle of the continuum, but still focusing on maintenance and control efforts, are included purposes such as (a) planning for decision making and program evaluation (Murell, 1976); (b) gaining additional input toward personnel recruitment; (c) describing, measuring and understanding different aspects of community life (Siegel et al., 1977); (d) determining discrepancies between residents' and professionals' points of view (Ronald, Titus, Strasser, & Vess, Note 3; and (e) obtaining knowledge about community resources so as to link these to agency services.

In analyzing this continuum it is important to notice that most needs assessment efforts are directed towards consumer satisfaction and agency survival. These are legitimate and necessary goals; however, if technique development is limited to these goals, it will be incomplete and unsatisfactory. Needs assessment methodology, if it is to respond to a commitment to the powerless and to the fostering of social change, must (a) emphasize techniques that, singly or in combination, facilitate grouping and mobilizing people; (b) foster collective activities; (c) facilitate leadership development; and (d) involve residents in the entire research process. These characteristics are essential so that the technique can facilitate consciousness-raising.

Categorization and Evaluation of Techniques

At present there is a great diversity of needs assessment techniques. In some instances it is suggested that different techniques be combined focusing on diverse kinds of

TABLE 14.1
Continuum of Needs Assessment Purposes

Political Role	Purpose
Control System Maintenance	Guarantee the economic survival of service programs
	Respond to interest group pressures
	Provide services required by communities
	Program evaluation
	Program planning
	Public policy decision making
Social Change	Measure, describe, and understand community life styles
	Assess community resources to lessen external dependency
	Return needs assessment data to facilitate residents' decision making
	Provide skill training, leadership, and organizational skills
	Facilitate collective activities and group mobilization
	Facilitate consciousness-raising

interventions (Aponte, 1976; Pharis, 1976; Siegel et al., 1977). Others suggest that only one technique be used with one line of intervention preferred (Clifford, Note 4; Evans, Note 5; Zautra, Note 6). In order to respond to the goals of organization, mobilization, and consciousness-raising in communities, the multiple technique approach is more desirable since a more precise view of reality is obtained. More data are gathered which will vary quantitatively and qualitatively, thus providing a thorough appraisal of community needs. Another reason for the combined use of techniques is that their limitations and deficiencies can be balanced. However, it is also important to study how each individual technique contributes to the goal of greater mobilization.

Needs assessment techniques can be grouped in three different categories defined by the contact they provide between the researcher and community residents. This contact is extremely important as it may be used to foster collectivization, mobilization, leadership development, and resident involvement (Ander-Egg, 1980; Sanguinetti, 1981), characteristics that are essential to a new focus on needs assessment goals.

No Contact with Participants. In this category, techniques permit no relationship between the intervener and the participants. These techniques are rates or percentages under treatment, social indicators, social area analysis and dynamic modeling (Kleemeir, Stephenson, & Isaacs, Note 7; Bell, 1976; Murell, 1976; Pharis, 1976). In general terms, these methods try to determine community needs by utilizing qualitative and quantitative data from several sources, such as demographic records and other social indicators. They are based on the assumption that community needs and problems that appear in official statistics are representative of community prob-

lems. The major limitation of the "non-contact with the participant" techniques lies in their absolute lack of direct mobilization potential. Since the residents are not involved in the needs assessment project—in fact, it can even happen without their knowledge—their involvement in social action efforts is not to be expected.

Contact with the Agency or Community. The "contact with the agency or community" category includes observation (Ander-Egg, 1978), service provider assessment (Kelly, Note 8), key informants (Pharis, 1976), behavioral census (Murell, 1976), surveys (Clifford, Note 4; O'Brien, Note 9), nominal groups (Delbecq, Van de Ven, & Gustoffsen, 1976), and community forums (Kleemeir et al., Note 7) among other techniques. The interaction that these techniques allow for takes place basically through three means: observations, interviews, and group meetings.

Observation facilitates interaction by the observer's mere presence in the setting. Interviewers interact individually and in groups with community residents, service providers, or other key informants to directly obtain data. This interaction takes place openly, as in community forums, or in a more controlled manner, as in nominal groups.

Key informants, nominal groups, community forums, and surveys respond to the goals of mobilization and consciousness-raising in the community. The first three techniques encourage community input by eliciting residents' discussions and introspections about the collective nature of their problems and needs. They serve to strengthen communication networks in the community and they facilitate the process of program planning. Survey techniques share some of these qualities if the survey is constructed, coordinated, and administered by community members. This process generates great involvement and knowledge and the ready acceptance of results by the rest of the community (Sanguinetti, 1981).

The nominal group technique has these, and other, advantages. Because of the structured nature of its process (Delbecq et al., 1976), it (1) maximizes the amount, diversity, and quality of the problems and alternatives proposed; (2) inhibits the control of the group by a few vocal persons (Siegel et al., 1977); (3) allows conflicting opinions to be tolerated; (4) fosters creativity; (5) facilitates attention to the contributions of marginal group members; and (6) emphasizes the role of needs assessment as the basis for program creation and planning. These four techniques have the highest mobilization potential.

Combined Techniques. This category includes convergent analysis (Bell, 1976), community impressions (Siegel et al., 1977), community meetings/surveys (Kleemeir et al., Note 7), and others. Convergent analysis techniques include techniques of service utilization, social indicators, and surveys. Each technique is used with a specific objective in mind and it is expected that, overall, the information offered by the techniques should give an estimate of those persons whose needs are not being satisfied.

Community impressions and community meetings/surveys have several common elements. The former include the techniques of key informants, data revision, and community forum. The latter includes the first two steps in addition to a survey, allowing the data to be validated and permitting additional verbal input from participants. Although all these techniques require a lot of energy and effort, they are the best alternative in the needs assessment process because they combine high mobilization potential with the more traditional criteria of representativeness, validity, and reliability.

Criteria to Judge the Adequacy of Techniques

Given the diversity of techniques, it is necessary to develop specific factors or criteria that should be considered in judging the adequacy of a technique. Some authors have examined this issue and have proposed criteria for the selection of techniques. These criteria include: the nature of the problem, the skills of both the researcher and the participants, available resources (League of California Cities, 1979), representativeness, the specificity required of the information (Murell, 1976), and the amount of political risk that the sponsoring group desires to tolerate (Aponte, 1976).

Although all these criteria are useful, additional criteria should be considered if the needs assessment effort is to contribute to community organization and mobilization. These criteria are presented in Table 14.2 and contrasted with more traditional views. The following dimensions are used as a guideline for this comparison: the goals, sources, content, and processes of the assessment.

A major distinction between the two sets of criteria is their goals. One set emphasizes prevention and promotion and the awareness of the collective nature of needs. The other works from a remedial perspective which focuses on the individual and on fostering dependency on external resources. The impact of these differences is most noticeable in the assessment process since a collective focus requires a collective intervention and an individual focus does not.

An evaluation of previously mentioned techniques according to the community organization and mobilization criteria appears in Table 14.3. As can be seen, key informants, surveys, nominal groups and community forums are the most adequate

TABLE 14.2
Suggested Criteria to Evaluate the Adequacy of Needs Assessment Techniques

Dimensions of Needs Assessment Process	Criteria	
	Criteria That Foster Mobilization	Traditional Criteria
Goals of Assessment	Prevention and promotion	Treatment
	Awareness of collective nature of needs	Individual focus
	Encourage collective action	Foster dependency on external resources
Source of Input	Community residents Marginal groups	Service providers Total population
Content of Assessment	All perceived needs Internal community resources	Assessment of needed services
Processes of Assessment	Facilitate community involvement and control of process	Assessment carried out by "experts"
	Facilitate face to face interaction between intervener researcher and participants	Lack of community participation Interaction highly controlled by scientific standards
	Data belong to participants	Data collection and future planning controlled by agencies
	Planning and collective action carried out by intervener-researcher and participants	

techniques. It is important to stress, however, that no single technique can be seen as valid for all times and circumstances; therefore, they should be tailored to the particular situation in which the needs assessment is conducted.

NEEDS ASSESSMENT AND COMMUNITY DEVELOPMENT

Irizarry and Serrano (1979) have developed a model, Intervention within Research, which integrates needs assessment into a community development approach. It uses needs assessment as its methodological foundation and the concept of problematization as its ideological guideline (Freire, 1974). Problematization, our translation for the term *problematización*, refers to the process whereby consciousness-raising takes place. If the latter is seen as the goal, then problematization involves the different strategies whereby it can be achieved.

The model conceptualizes the processes of intervention and research as simultaneous and interdependent. It also assumes that all phases of the model should be permeated

TABLE 14.3
Evaluation of Needs Assessment Techniques According to Their Potential for Mobilization
Organization and Consciousness-Raising

Criteria	Social Records	Computer Use	Observation	Social Indicators	Dynamic Modelling	Systems Model	Surveys	Key Informants	Forum	Nominal Group	Service Provider Assessments	Behavioral Census	Key Persons
Obtains information from community residents							X		X	X			X
Obtains information from marginal groups	X						X		X	X			X
Achieves change in services provided			X				X	X	X	X	X	X	X
Facilitates identifying a wide range of needs		X	X	X			X		X	X			
Facilitates development of internal resources								X	X	X		X	X
Control of information by residents			X	X			X	X	X	X		X	X
Oriented toward prevention			X						X	X			
Collective view of problems									X	X			
Commitment to residents' participation in general									X	X			
Commitment to residents' participation in research							X		X	X			
a. data collection							X		X	X			
b. instrument construction							X		X	X			X
c. data analysis							X		X	X			X
d. data returns									X	X			X
Fosters relationship between residents and intervener								X	X	X			X
a. more time together								X	X	X			X
b. dialogue								X	X	X			X
Facilitate collective activities									X	X			X
a. two or more persons									X	X			
b. two or more persons regarding common problems									X	X			
c. adding the discussion of possible solutions									X	X			
d. initiate collective action									X	X			

with explicit ideological inputs that lead to consciousness-raising.

The objectives suggested for this model include: (1) the creation of collective efforts to solve community problems as defined by community residents; (2) the achievement of individual and group participation in the analysis of social reality; (3) the creation of grass-roots organizations; and (4) the development of political skills among participants, resulting in their increased involvement in public affairs.

The model includes four phases. The first phase, familiarization with the community, includes a review of all written and statistical material regarding the community, and several visits to the same. This approach provides knowledge regarding the community's history, its structures, and the processes which facilitate the intervener's entry into the community. It should emphasize the early identification of key persons in the community through informal communication or through more structured means.

The second phase, which arises from a later revision of the original model (Martí, Note 1), is characterized by the creation of a core group that must be composed of both key community persons and interveners. This core group has planning, coordination, and evaluation responsibilities throughout the entire process of intervention within research.

The creation of this core group has positive psychological and operative repercussions. Since the group is formed with community people, a more effective dialogue can take place. It is also possible to increase their commitment and guarantee the group's continuance in this way. In addition, the key person can acquire skills through modeling or training that will be useful to future community work.

One of the most important tasks of this group is the direction and coordination of the needs assessment. This begins with the core group taking an active role in evaluating the relevance of the different needs assessment techniques to their particular community. The group's next step is the consideration of alternative actions to develop an effective propaganda campaign to inform residents of the needs assessment. In this effort it is essential to obtain the support of other organized groups in the community.

The core group should direct the needs assessment process per se as well as the process of returning the analyzed data to community residents. This can be done through letters, individual visits, group meetings, or community assemblies. The method used will be determined by the needs assessment technique previously used, by the number of participants it entailed, and by the number of human resources available. The data should be returned promptly and should be explained in simple terms.

The third phase, formation of task groups, includes group activities suggested by the needs assessment. In this phase, short- and long-term goals are defined and further action plans developed. To carry out these activities an organizational structure must be created. It is suggested that for this purpose a general community meeting should be held where task groups are formed around the needs assessment priorities. This general meeting should be planned and conducted by all participants with the support and guidance of the core group.

In addition to the task groups, workshops and other social, cultural, educational, and recreational activities must be fostered. Workshops should concentrate on the development of skills so as to help community groups deal effectively with outside forces that rally against their efforts. Some possible topics for the workshops are leadership, skills to deal with service agencies, interpersonal communication, propaganda, and organizational skills. Particular attention should be given to internal group processes so that the task groups' decision making will improve, their leadership struggles diminish, and their cohesiveness increase. We believe that this last characteristic is particularly important and that both the workshops and group tasks should emphasize cohesiveness.

The last phase in the model, involvement of new groups, is initiated after some of the short- and long-term goals of the task groups are achieved. This involves the development of new goals which should help in bringing together other community groups. The steps described should be repeated in a cyclical manner because needs change throughout the process and the community may develop other goals and interests.

CONCLUSION

This paper has presented an alternative ideological framework to evaluate and direct needs assessment efforts. It has also presented a model for its use for community development. Community residents can and should control intervention within research efforts that directly or indirectly involve them and scientists should facilitate this control. If some of these changes are incorporated into current needs assessment efforts, scientists will be more responsive to the people to whom their major efforts should be directed.

REFERENCE NOTES

1. Martí, S. *Hacia una identificación de necesidades en el sector femenino del Barrio Buen Consejo.* Unpublished M. A. thesis, University of Puerto Rico, 1980.

2. Palau, A. *La investigación con la técnica de observación: ¿Para quién y desde dónde?* Unpublished manuscript, 1977. (Available at Sociology Department, University of Puerto Rico, Rio Piedras, P.R.).

3. Ronald, L., Titus, W., Strasser, G., & Vess, J. *Views of Mental Health: A First Step in Needs Assessment.* Paper presented at the 87th Annual Convention of the American Psychological Association, New York City, 1979.

4. Clifford, D. L. *A Critical View of Needs Assessment in Community Mental Health Planning.* Paper presented at the Second National Conference on Needs Assessment in Health and Human Services, Louisville, Kentucky, 1978.

5. Evans, P. *A Model for Conducting Needs Assessment and a Report on National Ratios.* Paper presented at the 87th Annual Convention of the American Psychological Association, New York City, 1979.

6. Zautra, A. *Quality of Life Determinants: Some Guidelines for Measuring Com-munity Well-Being.* Paper presented at the Second National Conference on Needs Assessment in Health and Human Services, Louisville, Kentucky, March, 1978.

7. Kleemeir, C. P., Stephenson, D. P., & Isaacs, L. D. *Developing a Needs Assessment Approach for Community Consultation and Education.* Paper presented at the 87th Annual Convention of the American Psychological Association, New York City, 1979.

8. Kelly, M. *Halton Region Services for Children: A Needs Assessment.* Unpublished manuscript, 1978. (Avail-able at Faculty of Social Work, Wilfrid Laurier University, Waterloo, Ontario, Canada.)

9. O'Brien, D. *Merging the Technical and Community Catalytic Functions of Citizen Surveys: Toward a Theoretical Frame-work.* Paper presented at the Second National Conference on Needs Assess-ment in Health and Human Services, Louisville, Kentucky, 1978.

REFERENCES

Ander-Egg, E. *Hacia una metodología de la militancia y el compromiso.* Buenos Aires: Ecro, 1973.

Ander-Egg, E. *Diccionario del trabajo social.* Barcelona: Nova Terra, 1977.

Ander-Egg, E. *Introducción a las técnicas de investigación social*. Buenos Aires: Humanitas, 1978.

Ander-Egg, E. *Metodología del desarrollo de comunidad*. Madrid: UNIEUROP, 1980.

Aponte, S. F. "Implications for the Future of Needs Assessment." In R. A. Bell, M. Sundel, S. F. Aponte, & S. A. Murell (Eds.). *Needs Assessment in Health and Human Services*. Louisville: University of Louisville, 1976.

Bell, R. A. "The Use of a Convergent Assessment Model in the Determination of Health Status and Assessment of Need." In R. S. Bell, M. Sundel, J. F. Aponte, & S. A. Murell (Eds.). *Needs Assessment in Health and Human Services*. Louisville: University of Louisville, 1976.

Delbecq, A., Van de Ven, A., & Gustoffsen, D. *Group Techniques for Program Planning: A Guide to Nominal Group and Delphi Processes*. Glenview, Illinois: Scott, Foresman, & Company, 1976.

Freire, P. *Pedagogía del oprimido*. México: Siglo 21, 1974.

Goldman, L. Conciencia adecuada, conciencia posible y conciencia falsa. In L. Goldman (Ed.), *Marxismo y ciencias humanas*. Paris: Galiemard, 1970.

Irizarry, A., & Serrano-García, I. Intervención en la investigación: Su aplicación al Barrio Buen Consejo. *Boletín AVEPSO,* 1979, *2*, 6–21.

League of California Cities. "Social Needs Assessment: A Scientific or Political Process." In F. Cox, J. Erlich, J. Rothman, & J. Tropman (Eds.), *Strategies of Community Organization*. Itasca, Illinois: F. E. Peacock, 1979.

Moscovici, S. "Society and Theory in Social Psychology." In J. Israel & H. Tajifel (Eds.), *The Context of Social Psychology*. New York: Academic Press, 1972.

Murell, S. A. "Eight Process Steps for Converting Needs Assessment Data into Program Operations." In S. A. Bell, M. Sundel, J. Aponte, & S. Murell (Eds.), *Needs Assessment in Health and Human Services*. Louisville: University of Louisville, 1976.

Myrdal, G. *Objectivity in Social Research*. New York: Random House, 1969.

Pharis, D. B. "The Use of Needs Assessment Techniques in Mental Health Planning." *Community Mental Health Review,* 1976, *1*, 4–11.

Rappaport, J. *Community Psychology: Values, Research and Action*. New York: Holt, Rinehart, & Winston, 1977.

Sanguinetti, Y. La investigación participativa en los procesos de desarrollo de américa latina. *Revista de ALAPSO,* 1981, *1*, 221–238.

Siegel, L. M., Attkisson, C. C., & Cohn, I. H. "Mental Health Needs Assessment: Strategies and Techniques." In W. A. Hargreaves & C. C. Attkisson (Eds.), *Resource Materials for Community Mental Health Program Evaluation*. Rockville, Maryland: National Institute of Mental Health, 1977.

Warheit, George J. "The Use of Field Surveys to Estimate Health Needs in the General Population." In R. A. Bell, M. Sundel, J. Aponte, & S. A. Murell (Eds.), *Needs Assessment in Health and Human Services*. Louisville: University of Louisville, 1976.

Watzlawick, P., Weakland, J., & Fisch, R. *Change: Principles of Problem Formation and Problem Resolution*. New York: Norton, 1974.

Weimer, W. *Notes on the Methodology of Scientific Research*. New York: Wiley, 1979.

Zuñiga, R. "The Experimenting Society and Radical Social Reform." *American Psychologist,* 1975, *30*, 99–115.

15.

Mohan L. Kaul

SERVING OPPRESSED COMMUNITIES:
THE SELF-HELP APPROACH

INTRODUCTION

The East Akron Community House, a settlement house in Akron, Ohio, invited the author to "develop a program of community development with a view to achieve social justice and equal opportunity through democratic processes and nonviolent methods." This work began in early 1970 in an area that reflected years of general neglect, where residents complained about stray dogs, run-down dilapidated housing, scattered rubbish, congestion, abandoned cars, vacant houses, lack of open spaces, dark and dangerous streets, and a continuous smell of chemicals in the air. However, a closer look revealed that poverty, crime, powerlessness, and, above all, a sense of hopelessness were the deep-rooted problems. In spite of the seemingly insurmountable obstacles, area residents were surprisingly warm and friendly, demonstrated genuine pride in their homes, and unmistakenly indicated a readiness for change. These ingredients pointed to a situation where the existing dormant human resource could be motivated to engage in a self-help process with a definite outcome of a satisfying community life in the foreseeable future.

The author left the East Akron Community House after eight block clubs and a council of block club presidents were established and their membership was actively engaged in neighborhood improvement projects. Since then, the author's association with block clubs has included membership in one of them, periodical review of the process, occasional consultation, and attendance in selected neighborhood activities.

Akron, often referred to as the "Rubber Capital" of the world, is located in heavily industrialized northeastern Ohio. Its present population is 237,077,[1] a decline of 38,348 persons during the last 10 years, indicating the consequences of rubber and other related industry cutting back or moving out of Akron.

There are approximately 22,000 people in four neighborhoods of East Akron. One neighborhood of approximately 5,000 people is situated in the immediate vicinity of East Akron Community House (the only settlement house in the city of Akron). It is a predominantly black neighborhood where the block clubs are located, and it is referred to as East Akron Neighborhood in this paper.

The East Akron Neighborhood was 20 to 25 years old when East Akron Community House was established in 1915 to aid the assimilation and acculturation of European immigrants. Within one generation, they prospered and moved out of the neighborhood. The second group of people who came to live in this neighborhood were Appalachian whites. They followed

---

[1]"The Census: Town by Town," Akron Beacon *Journal*, September 6, 1981.

the earlier residents' example and left the neighborhood within the decade of 1940–1950. Black people are the third population group to find their first homes here[2]; many of them are longtime residents and would like to live in this neighborhood as long as they can.

East Akron Community House determined in 1969, "to muster the resources and skills needed to enable residents to influence and/or control decision making process and neighborhood serving institutions."[3] During the same time period, settlement houses around the country, in response to their constituencies' demands, were in the process of or were working toward neighborhood control. It was also during this time when maximum feasible participation concept propounded by the War on Poverty was being seriously debated and analyzed.[4]

COMMUNITY DEVELOPMENT

In East Akron Neighborhood, a program of community development was seen as a method of motivating people directly affected by neighborhood problems to organize and undertake well-planned action steps as a group, for dealing with such problems. Such a definition may seem to be somewhat narrow, but is realistic and manageable. The term "community" referred to, "an aggregate of families and individuals settled in a fairly compact and contiguous area, with significant elements of common life, as shown by manners, customs, traditions, and modes of speech." The word development implied the element of self-help and citizen participation in a decision-making process for the growth of community spirit and community activities. Citizen participation meant active involvement of individual residents in joint endeavors for better living conditions within the neighborhood.

Community development as a method of solving neighborhood problems is based on the assumption that social change can be brought about more effectively in geographical areas where people live, since the well-being of an individual is directly related to the place he (or she) calls home, the street he lives on, and the neighborhood where he raises his family. Geographic communities, comprised of populations with multiple needs, need assistance in recognizing their common needs, and organizing as a means to achieve common goals assumes pooling of resources, reinforcement of self-confidence, and development of a sense of power to deal effectively with neighborhood problems. Cooperation among residents is somewhat expected. However, cooperation is not seen as an ultimate good; individual efforts are still valid.[5]

ORGANIZING

The idea of neighborhood organizing was not new to the community, since attempts were made in the past by concerned residents to get together with their neighbors. Additionally, some service agencies in the

---

[2]Homer L. Pettengill, a long-time Executive Director of East Akron Community House, provided the information in 1970.

[3]Pettengill.

[4]There was a strong movement for local control of the settlement houses, nationally. EACH decision may have been influenced by that also. For comparative community case studies see Ralph M. Kramer, *Participation of the Poor* (Englewood Cliffs, NJ: Prentice-Hall, Inc., 1969).

[5]Murray G. Ross, *Community Organization* (New York: Harper & Row Publishers, 1967), 77.

area had taken steps to organize residents around specific issues. Such attempts had invariably been a passing phenomenon. The most recent attempt by the Community Action program of the War on Poverty had not materialized. During initial contacts, the resident position to the idea was favorable but had indicated some apprehensiveness about it.[6] Obviously, organizing was a feasible idea. But, maintenance of the groups organized was the challenge.

It was therefore assumed that organized groups are likely to keep up their initial momentum if the local leadership is developed to meet the challenge. In a general way, leaders who could work with people and stimulate them and could help the groups use all the abilities and experiences of its members were not known to the residents.[7] On the basis of a preliminary study it was found that there were not many who had such a specific minimum leadership experience. There were some with church-related experience, others had political experience at the precinct level, and quite a few had a life-long informal problem-solving experience. Their methods of helping included listening and referral. Apparently, there was a need for development of existing leaders.

Since residents were keen to meet with their neighbors on the block to share common concerns and to get to know each other, the strategy to organize, therefore, focused on initial socializing. It was assumed that, once the residents got together, appropriate leadership would develop if appropriate steps were taken. It was also understood that socializing as a means to achieve the goal of initial organizing could become an end in itself unless the organizer skillfully identified rallying points to develop ideological commitment to achieve social change.

Organizing focuses on the location of common problems and joint efforts aimed at their solution. Ecklein and Lauffer's view of organizing "as a means of achieving and guiding local control over problems that originate elsewhere in society"[8] appeared to be in tune with a genuine desire of the residents to exert some local control on those facets of community life that were historically directed from outside—such as education, employment opportunities, housing, social services, and political process of two major political parties. Neighborhood improvement, as an overall noncontroversial and worthwhile initial goal emerged as a top priority and block organization was accepted as a means to achieve it. The idea to hold meetings in a house on the block had a tremendous appeal and was perhaps in line with Kahn's thinking that "block organizing is a highly manageable technique usually an urban technique."[9] The term "block club" was readily agreed upon, as everybody seemed to be familiar with it. It was understood to mean a group of concerned residents who get together to improve their block by working together. In view of the limited resources and the experimental nature of the project, a 25-block area comprised of 4,000 to 5,000 people with census tract 5034 as its core area was determined as the program implementation area; it was chosen for its proximity to the Community House, resident's knowledge of the agency,

[6]This is primarily an impressionistic view gathered during initial contacts with local residents.

[7]Community Action Training, Inc., *So, You're on a Committee*, 1975, p. 20.

[8]Joan L. Ecklein, and Armaud A. Lauffer, *Community Organizers and Social Planners* (New York: John Wiley & Sons, 1972), 11.

[9]Si Kahn, *How People Get Power* (New York: McGraw-Hill, 1970), 36.

and readily available demographic information. Streets in the implementation area were designated as blocks on the basis of a face-to-face relationship and identification with the street as one's residence. To create a general sense of accomplishment in the neighborhood, a pilot block was selected. The resident concerns on this block appeared to be resolvable with minimum effort, and the residents were willing to make that effort. However, it was understood that residents would need assistance in: getting together, identifying common problems, building relationships, finding resources, and selecting action steps toward problem resolution. It was also assumed that pilot block accomplishments would generate a positive environment for organizing the neighborhood.

Community organizers have successfully used inclusion of formal leaders in developing community associations[10] since enhancement of social relationships is seen as bringing about greater capacity to deal with common problems. This approach was slightly modified to suit the East Akron Neighborhood. It was assumed that the realistic way to motivate the residents to come forward and participate in a neighborhood organization effort would be through identification of a contact person who may or may not be a formal leader. The contact persons were seen as concerned citizens who are willing to volunteer their time and effort to achieve changes on the block. Often, they are longtime residents and feel a sense of belongingness towards their neighborhood, they are well-known in the area, and they are generally trusted.

The organization was primarily to be neighborhood based and would not be equipped to use conflict and confrontation as deliberate strategies in its formative stage. In that sense the block clubs organization was to be different from five types of mass organizations; Alinsky-type programs (1959), the mass organization as part of civil rights movement (1963, 1968), the Mobilization for Youth (1964), the Community Action Program of War on Poverty (1965), and The Welfare Rights Movement (1966).[11] The Community organizer, "a qualified social work practitioner with specialized training in community organization,"[12] was to be a catalyst in the initial stages of organization.

Block Club-Council of Block Club Presidents, a two-level, input and feedback structure, was envisioned as the only grassroots organization accessible to the residents in order to voice their concerns, seek help and support, volunteer for services, and participate in a decision-making process to deal with those concerns. Block clubs would deal with block concerns and the Council of Block Club Presidents would have the responsibility to deal with the problems affecting the entire program implementation area. It was hypothesized that such a viable human resource structure would develop maturity, creativity, flexibility, and confidence as it began to undertake

---

[10]Murray G. Ross, op. cit., pp. 168–173.

[11]For details, the following references are suggested: Saul D. Alinsky, *Reveille for Radicals* (Chicago: University of Chicago Press, 1946).

Frances Piven, "Participation of Residents in Neighborhood Community Action Programs," *Social Work* (Jan 1966) 4, 74.

OEO, *Community Action Program Guide* (Washington, DC: Government Printing Office (Feb 1965), Vol. 1.

Richard A. Cloward, and Frances Piven, "Birth of a Movement: The War on Poverty," *The Nation* (May 8, 1967).

[12]Arthur Dunham, *The New Community Organization* (New York: Thomas Y. Crowell Company, 1970), 6.

problem-solving activities. Development of such a working structure became the primary objective of the community development effort, and any problem resolution was seen as a by-product during early stages.

The methodology to organize block clubs developed as a carefully implemented step-by-step process that included: an on-foot survey,[13] a working map, problem observation, informal meetings, house calls, establishing linkages, unit gatherings, finding and getting natural leaders interested,[14] resident involvement in the planning committees, and block formation meetings. The first eight block clubs were organized during 1970–71 and a Council of Block Club Presidents was formed. This concluded the first phase of organization; a neighborhood structure was in place and ready to work for neighborhood improvement. Its first major challenge came sooner than anticipated. The structure successfully mobilized human resources to close a notorious bar in the neighborhood in early 1972.[15] The presence of the bar had created danger to life and property for more than a decade. This single event strengthened and stabilized the block club-council leadership and created an overall environment of neighborhood power and self-confidence in the community. The organizing phase was completed in 1975 when 22 block clubs were organized. As the block clubs got

organized, the Council of Block Club Presidents was expanded accordingly to accommodate each new block club.

A summary of their accomplishments[16] is presented to illustrate the wide range of programs and activities of block clubs and the council. This is not a total list.

Recreation and Cultural

Over the years, the block clubs have developed meaningful, locally suited recreational and cultural programs that include an annual Labor Day parade and beauty pageant. A softball league, summer picnic, family night, and Christmas light decoration contest are some of the other regular features.

The sustained efforts of the block clubs have resulted in providing much-needed three parks for the neighborhood: Homestead mini park, Talbot-Whitney mini park, and Joy Park.

Health and Sanitation

Rodent population in the neighborhood is now under control. Trash barrels have been placed on vacant lots and rotten trees have been removed. Stray dogs are no longer a nuisance.

Political Action

A neighborhood elementary school was reopened after remaining closed for one year. Voter registration is a regular activity of the block clubs. Police community relations have improved. Abandoned cars have been removed. High gas billings are protested, and appropriately adjusted.

---

[13]The assumption is that events in the neighborhood can be better understood by walking as compared to riding in a car.

[14]Not necessarily a formal leader: a person who is respected by his or her neighbors and is more likely to be listened to.

[15]For a detailed discussion refer to Mohan L. Kaul, "Block Clubs and Social Action: A Case Study in Community Conflict," in *Journal of Sociology and Social Welfare* (March 1976) 4, 437–450.

---

[16]Information in this section is based on the data supplied by Grady Appleton, Director, Neighborhood Organization and Development, East Akron.

Candidates for political office seek block club leaders for support.

Neighborhood Beautification

Lawncare, flower gardens, street paving, sidewalk projects, proper maintenance of home lawns, clean-up and fix-up projects, and planting and trimming trees on devil strips are some of the ongoing activities for beautifying the neighborhood.

Safety

Missing traffic signs and additional street lighting have been secured. A neighborhood citizens alert program to deter house burglaries is in place. Block homes for school children during emergencies are available. Overweight trucks are no longer driving on residential streets.

Housing

The housing task force has secured homestead exemptions, grants, and loans. A number of vacant houses have been rehabilitated.

Miscellaneous

Other activities include a community-sponsored annual family Christmas dinner, telephone and personal contact with shut-ins, Kelly Avenue street extension project, food buckets for Christmas and Thanksgiving, assistance to disaster victims, raising money for children who need shoes, and much-needed help to senior citizens by filling forms, cutting grass, raking leaves, shovelling snow, and providing transportation.

Block Club-Neighborhood Council is primarily a self-help project and is very cost effective. East Akron Community House provides staff services for the Council of Block Club Presidents and assists block clubs as and when necessary. Local universities and colleges place their students for field work experience here and local newspapers have written about the project favorably. Other citizen groups in the city have made inquiries.

The community organization effort initiated in 1970 has stood the test of time during the last 13 years. It is alive and well and will achieve significant objectives in the near future. The success of this project is primarily due to the effective pattern that has developed over the years as a result of an on-the-job training provided by the Block Club-Council of Block Club Presidents structure.

CITIZEN PARTICIPATION AND LEADERSHIP DEVELOPMENT

Each block club has four officers: president, vice president, secretary and treasurer. Generally, at least one additional person gets involved with block club leadership. This person may not be interested in running for office or does not get elected for office. Taking into consideration the entire block clubs organization (20 active block clubs, and a Council of Block Club Presidents), more than 100 persons are involved in leadership roles on a day-to-day basis. Each block club President is also a member of the Council of Block Club Presidents and gets to be nominated to at least one of the eight standing committees of the council. The Block Club-Council of Block Club Presidents provides at least three levels of participation: very active participation for block club presidents; active participation for three officers and one member of each block club; and regular participation for the remaining membership of the clubs. During any one month, 200 to 250 residents of the neighborhood are involved in a decision-making process directly related to neighborhood programs, activities, and problem solving. On a short notice, a group of 100 persons can be mobilized to go to the city hall for a meeting.

Officer's training, orientation workshops, refresher courses, and overnight retreats for planning and policy formulation are regular features of the organization. This has enhanced the personal growth of a large number of residents in addition to the development of effective leadership for block clubs and the council.

To collect the significant data regarding the block club Leadership, a survey was undertaken in 1980 wherein 78 leaders participated. The sample included: 20 presidents; 11 vice presidents, 19 secretaries, 14 treasurers, and 14 regular members of 20 active block clubs serving a population of approximately 5000 people. It was found that 72% of the leaders had less than $10,000 income per year, only 50% had completed high school, 80% were not born in Ohio, 63% were 55 years and over, and 27% were male and 73% were female. The findings substantiate the assumption that local natural leadership can be effectively activated if it is provided an opportunity for true participation. A direct relationship to high education, high income, or younger age was not established.

CONCLUSIONS

The main assumption of the self-help approach—that people can be organized around common concerns in geographical areas where they live and an attainable problem-solving program can be identified, initiated, and accomplished on a self-help basis—is substantiated by the survey.

A second assumption that a vigorous neighborhood-based organization can be developed if the accomplished projects are truly community identified and community initiated is also well documented.

The first block clubs organized in the early seventies were seen as vehicles of change on a long-term basis rather than organizations built around specific issues. It was assumed that block clubs would become a part of the neighborhood life and that an effective leadership pattern would emerge. The survey indicates that, prior to the organization of block clubs, only a few individuals had some indirect leadership experience at the neighborhood level. However, church-related and political-party work were the two most common leadership experiences of the respondents. The block club activities and projects over the years, ranging from achieving a better garbage pick-up service and meaningful advocacy and appropriate political activism to reopening of a closed elementary school, seem to have accomplished the objective of providing a natural setting for training neighborhood leadership.

During initial contacts, residents had indicated their willingness to meet with other neighbors on the block to share common concerns and to get to know each other. It was feared that once the block residents got together, socializing as a means to achieve block organizing could become an end in itself unless other rallying points were skillfully identified to develop ideological commitment to achieve social change. The survey indicated that the local leadership was aware of this possibility, and maintained a well-planned balance between the residents' need to socialize and their commitment to achieve change.

The self-help approach is not intended to be applicable to all communities. It is not appropriate for those areas where the urban decay is apparently insurmountable. In essence, the self-help approach is a practical-realistic approach to serve only those oppressed geographical areas where (1) a community can be identified, (2) the residents indicate a genuine interest in community welfare, and (3) a majority of residents are willing to work with their neighbors for achieving a better community life for all. The self-help approach is also based on the premise that residents need assistance in getting organized and that social workers as catalysts can activate the dormant strength of selected communities by assisting the local natural leadership for initiating the organization process.

16.

Meredith Minkler

COMMUNITY ORGANIZING AMONG THE ELDERLY POOR IN SAN FRANCISCO'S TENDERLOIN DISTRICT

In inner-city single-room occupancy hotel (SRO) neighborhoods such as San Francisco's Tenderloin District, large numbers of low-income elders live on "the bottom rung on the housing ladder" (Ovrebo, Minkler, and Liljestrand 1991, 179). Often just a step removed from homelessness, many of these residents confront daily the interrelated problems of poor health, social isolation, and powerlessness as a result of poverty and social marginalization (Minkler in press).

Yet the elderly residents of the nation's impoverished and high-crime "Tenderloin districts" also possess many strengths and competencies. This chapter presents a case study of the Tenderloin Senior Organizing Project (TSOP) to demonstrate the role of community organizing as a vehicle for individual and community empowerment in a population previously labeled "unorganizable." After a brief description of the setting in which this project took place, the chapter examines TSOP's theoretical underpinnings and historical development. Particular attention is devoted to TSOP's evolution from a program that tried to "empower the elderly" to one in which elders and their neighbors could empower themselves. Project outcomes are des-cribed, as are a number of the problems and challenges faced in the course of TSOP's sixteen-year history.

Portions of this chapter are based on "Community Organizing among the Elderly Poor in the United States: A Case Study," *International Journal of Health Services* 22(2) (1992): 303–316. Copyright© 1992 by the Baywood Publishing Company, Inc., Amityville, N.Y. All rights reserved.

BACKGROUND

A culturally diverse "mixed-use" residential area, the forty-five-block area North of Market Street district, the Tenderloin, is home to large numbers of elders on small fixed incomes, younger people with physical and mental disabilities, immigrants, and homeless people. Three hundred times more densely populated than the city as a whole, this neighborhood for years has had the highest crime rate in San Francisco. The city's failure to enforce housing codes or building ordinances, the absence of any major grocery store chain, and the highest density of alcohol outlets in the city (North of Market Planning Coalition 1992) contribute to such prevalent problems as inadequate and unsafe housing, undernutrition, and alcoholism (Minkler in press).

Although the Tenderloin suffers from a plethora of unmet needs, it also has many strengths on which to build, including its multiculturalism. The Tenderloin has for years had its own multilanguage newspaper. Several large and widely respected churches, a comprehensive and progressive local health center, and an active neighborhood planning coalition and housing clinic were among the "building blocks" identified by early TSOP organizers as potential supporters, allies, and advocates in the effort to create an environment in which residents could become empowered.

The overall goal of TSOP was to facilitate such empowerment by assisting elderly residents and their neighbors as they worked to organize and improve their community. The project's objectives were to draw out the competence, self-confidence, and leadership skills of residents (Ferrante 1991) and to reduce social isolation by enhancing social support networks within Tenderloin SRO hotels and other low-income residences.

THEORETICAL BASE

Three major conceptual domains guided the project from its inception. The first, social support, is based on the large body of evidence demonstrating the critical role of social support and social interaction in influencing health status (Bloomberg, Meyers, and Braverman 1994; Cohen and Syme 1985; House, Landis, and Umberson 1988). Whether through "buffering stress" or contributing to an increased sense of "control over destiny" (Syme 1993), interventions that build supportive networks may be particularly important in neighborhoods like the Tenderloin, where social marginality and isolation are endemic.

A shortcoming of many social support theories lies in their tendency to focus on the individual and his or her supportive network as the sole unit of analysis. Empirical studies thus often overlook the more macrolevel changes that may take place as individuals and communities, empowered by increased social support, work collectively to attack those shared problems that have contributed to their oppression. In applying theories of social support to the Tenderloin, TSOP staff and volunteers attempted to look beyond individual-level outcomes of increased social support to focus as well on institutional- or community-level changes (Minkler 1992).

This perspective is in keeping with TSOPs second theoretical underpinning— the approach to empowerment theory elucidated by Brazilian educator Paulo Freire (1968, 1973) as "education for critical consciousness." Freire's educational methodology centers on a relationship of equality and mutual respect between group participants and "teacher-learners," with the latter using a process called problem-posing to ask questions that challenge members of the group to look for root causes and other consequences of the problem under discussion and eventually develop a plan of action. Although TSOP originally was conceived of, in part, as a "Freire project" through which student facilitators would attempt to use this educational approach in leading hotel-based support and discussion groups, the regular applications of this methodology proved difficult. Ongoing discussions of the root causes of problems, for example, often proved impractical when residents were motivated to organize quickly around problems demanding immediate action. Consequently, although Freire's education for critical conscious- ness continued to provide an important philosophical and ideological base for the project, the method per se was not employed in a regular and rigorous fashion (Minkler 1992).

Of greater day-to-day usefulness in TSOP's work has been a third, eclectic approach to community organization best typified by the philosophy and methods of the late Saul Alinsky (1969, 1972) and sup- plemented by the work of John McKnight (1987, 1993) and Michael Miller (1985, 1993). Alinsky viewed the low-income community as powerless and disfranchised in relation to the "haves" and to society as a whole. The goal of his approach was to facilitate a process whereby people coming together around a shared interest or concern could collectively identify a specific issue or target, garner resources, mobilize an action campaign, and through their collec- tive action help realign power within the community.

In recent years, TSOP has increasingly drawn on the work of several post-Alinsky theorists and organizers who go consider- ably farther than Alinsky did in identifying and stressing the strengths of the local community and in developing creative methods for capacity building. The emphasis of McKnight and his colleagues on helping communities identify their pre- existing resources or assets has been a central conceptual underpinning of the

TSOP approach. Similarly, TSOP has bor- rowed from community organizer and the- orist Michael Miller (1993) the notion that "action rooted in deeply held values is more likely to be sustained than that which relies solely on addressing a specific injus- tice." The relationship between commu- nity organizing and democratic citizenship is stressed by Miller, who argues that dis- cussions of values should form part of the community organizing process. Through such discussions, community members ideally begin to challenge such values as rugged individualism, consumerism, and a status system that exploits the poor and causes them to internalize their oppres- sion. By helping residents see their work in relation to deeper values and ideologies, TSOP attempted to apply Miller's approach and make it a fourth conceptual project base.

PROJECT ORIGINS AND EVOLUTION

Originally known as the Tenderloin Senior Outreach Project, TSOP was established in 1979 with the dual goals of (1) improving physical and mental health by reducing social isolation and providing relevant health education and (2) facilitating, through dialogue and participation, a process whereby residents would work together in identifying common problems and seeking solutions to those shared prob- lems and concerns (Wechsler and Minkler 1986). Specific methods included helping residents form discussion and support groups, and later tenants' associations and interhotel organizations and coalitions, that could serve as vehicles for increasing com- munity competence or problem-solving ability, and bringing about concrete changes (e.g., reductions in the neighbor- hood crime rate) that in turn could promote individual and community well-being (Minkler in press).

Architects of what was to become TSOP began by conducting a community assessment, which revealed that forty-three different "helping agencies" and organizations existed in this forty-five-block area. Of these, one in particular—St. Boniface Church—appeared universally respected by residents. Following Alinsky's (1972) admonition to organizers to establish their legitimacy by linking with a preexisting organization, the first project volunteers—students in a graduate community organizing class at the University of California at Berkeley—became St. Boniface volunteers and as such approached hotel managers about the possibility of serving refreshments in the hotel lobby one morning a week as a means of encouraging resident interaction. With the help of these inducements, an informal "coffee hour" and discussion group was formed in an initial hotel; the group met weekly and included a core of eight to twelve residents and two outside facilitators. As levels of trust and rapport increased, members began to share personal concerns around issues such as fear of crime, loneliness, rent increases, and their own sense of powerlessness.

Student facilitators used a combination of organizing and educational approaches to help foster group solidarity and, eventually, community organizing. A Freirian problem-posing process was used as appropriate, for example, to help residents engage in dialogue about shared problems and their causes and to generate potential action plans. Similarly, Alinsky's (1972) admonition to create dissatisfaction with the status quo, channel frustration into concrete action, and help people identify specific, winnable issues was among the community organizing precepts followed. Finally, drawing on social support theories

stressing the importance of social interaction opportunities per se, the student facilitators attempted to create a group atmosphere conductive to meeting the social, as well as the more political and task-oriented, concerns of group members.

As the first hotel discussion group became an established entity, more student volunteers were recruited, and seven additional groups were organized in other Tenderloin hotels. To provide coordination and continuity for the project, staff secured a small foundation grant to fund a part-time director, and TSOP became incorporated as a nonprofit organization with a twelve-member board of directors. In recognition of the importance of building on community assets, TSOP invited representatives of a popular neighborhood church, the powerful local planning coalition, and the neighborhood health clinic to join the board, along with community residents and allies from the business and professional communities.

Among the early issues identified and confronted by several of the hotel groups was the problem of undernutrition, particularly lack of access to fresh fruits and vegetables. After much discussion of alternative approaches, the residents of three hotels contracted with a local food advisory service and began operating their own hotel-based "minimarkets" one morning per week. In a fourth hotel, residents organized and ran a modest cooperative weekly breakfast program, thereby qualifying their hotel for participation in a food bank where large quantities of food could be purchased in bulk at reduced prices. Still other residents worked with TSOP staff to produce a "no-cook cookbook" of inexpensive and nutritious recipes. Later published by the San Francisco Department of Public Health, the cookbook was distributed free of charge to hundreds of residents of the Tenderloin, and more than one thousand copies were sold outside the community to generate additional money for the project. Early activities like these were important in making tangible changes (e.g., improved food access) but, more significantly, in contributing to resident feelings of control, competence, and collective ability to bring about change. Moreover, these early accomplishments gave residents the self-confidence needed to confront more difficult challenges in the future.

Although each hotel group developed and retained over time its own unique character, several common trends among the groups were evident. In all but one hotel group, for example, decreased reliance on outside facilitators was observed over time, with broader resident participation in discussion and decisionmaking. Greater concern for residents throughout one's hotel was increasingly witnessed among TSOP members and was particularly well demonstrated during stressful times, as when several hotels were temporarily evacuated in the aftermath of San Francisco's October 1989 earthquake.

Another trend observed in the groups, and one critical to TSOP's evolution, was the realization among residents of the need to look beyond hotel boundaries and work with residents of other hotels and community groups on shared problems. TSOP residents of several hotels thus identified crime and safely as their key area of concern and formed an interhotel coalition to begin work on this problem. The coalition in turn started the Safehouse Project, recruiting forty-eight neighborhood businesses and agencies to serve as places of refuge, demarcated by colorful posters, where residents could go for help in times of emergency. Coalition members also convinced the mayor to increase the number of police patrol officers in the neighborhood and, through this and other measures,

helped effect a dramatic reduction in crime, including an 18 percent reduction in the first twelve months after the coalition's inception ("Safehouses" 1982).

Two other outcomes of TSOP's organizing around the crime issue are worthy of note. First, having experienced success in increasing personal safety and well-being, the TSOP elderly began turning their attention to the safety needs of other vulnerable groups. Elderly TSOP members, for example, had their Safehouse materials translated into Cambodian and Vietnamese, and they arranged for articles about the project to appear in the Asian-language pages of the community newspaper. They were also able to recruit several Asian merchants in the neighborhood to open safehouses, bringing the total to more than one hundred at the height of this project.

Second, even though the Safehouse Project received considerable local and national publicity, several of the project's resident founders began to critically question the narrowness of the crime prevention approach they had developed. Their discussions of the root causes of the high crime rates in poverty neighborhoods and their involvement, albeit sporadically, in areas such as advocacy for the homeless, job training for the unemployed, and voter registration reflected increasing appreciation of the need for working toward broader social change. As E. Richard Brown (1991) notes in critically analyzing the TSOP experience: "Successful actions that resulted in desired changes in the health related environment may reduce the needs to which community members originally responded, but they may also increase community members' organizational skills, experience, leadership, and feelings of empowerment. They thus may encourage further action for more far reaching goals of social change."

INCREASING COMMUNITY COMPETENCE: PROGRESS AND PROBLEMS

TSOP's commitment to "starting where the people are" (Nyswander 1956) by helping residents organize around issues, such as crime and nutrition, that they themselves had identified was in keeping with the organization's commitment to empowerment. Yet even with resident-initiated goals and activities, there was often a danger of slipping into the inadvertent creation of dependency. By the mid-1980s, for example, the cooperative breakfast program and hotel-based minimarkets, as well as a health promotion resource center that TSOP residents planned and originally ran themselves, had begun to look more and more like direct service activities. Although residents remained interested in reaping the benefits of these programs, they lost interest in running them themselves, and project volunteers and staff were alternating their organizing roles with direct service-type functions.

TSOP staff discussed with residents the increasing tensions and contradictions between the organization's desired role in stimulating community organization and leadership development and its de facto service role. In the words of former project director Diana Miller: "We needed to clarify that what we do is build public power. [TSOP's role] was getting distorted because the organizers were spending a lot of time and energy on mutual aid programs" (Vanover 1991, 45).

After these discussions, and with the support of the board of directors, TSOP began gradually to terminate its direct service programs. The Health Promotion Resource Center, for example, was spun off to another community-based organization, while the minimarkets and cooperative breakfast program were gradually phased out. At the same time, and in a further effort to clarify the project's mission, TSOP formally changed the O in its name from Outreach to Organizing and adopted a new mission statement that stressed the organization's values and its commitments to drawing out and building on the skills of residents and creating community competence through organizing.

TSOP's new operational model, which remained in place until the project's closure in 1995, involved entering new hotels and residences only at the request of residents. Through personal conversations, the TSOP organizer clarified the organization's role as being not one of advocacy *on behalf of residents* but one of helping residents advocate *on their own behalf*. He or she would begin dialogues about some of the advantages organizing over help seeking and challenge residents to take the next step, speaking to a few of their neighbors and helping to form a small committee made up of individuals identified as potential leaders. Working with committee members on "thinking organizationally" (Miller 1993), or strategically and tactically the organizer would help residents form a tenants' association, which in turn would identify issues, assess resources, and mobilize to achieve collectively set goals (Ferrante 1991). A total of fourteen tenants' associations were established with the help of TSOP and achieved a number of impressive victories.

Critical to TSOP's goal of fostering community empowerment and problem-solving ability was its emphasis on leadership training. Through one-on-one and small-group activities, residents were helped to improve interpersonal skills, learn to facilitate meetings, and discover ways of working through (or against) bureaucracies to bring about change.

Early approaches to leadership training included a day-long leadership training conference attended by eighty residents and three "media workshops" in which TSOP members met with journalists and reporters, who helped them practice articulating their concerns to the press. Of greatest importance, however, was the ongoing nurturing of individual and small-group leadership, including the extensive use of role-plays prior to confrontations with landlords, meetings with city officials, and so on. Through these "trial runs," TSOP members could practice creating and responding to alternative hypothetical scenarios and could learn to function effectively as leadership teams. Such exercises, and the selection and preparation of back-up leaders on any given issue in the event that a designated leader was ill on the day of a planned action, were among the strategies that enabled TSOP to develop a strong leadership cadre from among its membership.

More advanced leadership training was undertaken during the later years of the project, with twenty TSOP members attending intensive national leadership training programs sponsored by the San Francisco-based Organize Training Center. Led by a prominent Alinsky-style organizer, the four-day training covered such topics as issue selection, values and critical reflection, and negotiation processes. Reporting back on the experience of one such training, one elderly participant said: "The workshop gave me an overall theoretical construct in which to place the things our tenants' association had learned from our TSOP organizer . . . so I could better grasp how one thing (such as values) ties into the next (such as action). I saw how our individual work can lead to building part of a community. Who would have thought an atheist in an apartment in a major city would be sharing concerns with a Lutheran pastor who

ministers to farmers in rural Nebraska?" (Miller 1993).

Although TSOP has been concerned with individual and community empowerment since its inception, the TSOP model's change over time reflected the organization's more sophisticated understanding of what empowerment entails and the preconditions necessary for its achievement. By helping residents create their own tenants' organizations and cross-group organizations rather than playing a direct role in their creation, and by offering resources (e.g., leadership training) as requested, the newer TSOP model was more effective in fostering true community organizing and empowerment.

TSOP continued to experience its share of problems, including residents tiring or "burning out" on some issues they had earlier decided to tackle, occasional power plays within groups, and leadership turnover as a consequence of illness, transiency, and other problems. Ethical issues also arose, as when the proposed closing down of the cooperative breakfast program was strongly opposed by one very elderly and disabled resident for whom the breakfast had become a high point of the week. As TSOP shifted to a "pure" community organizing project, it also discovered that its goals (e.g., community empowerment and leadership development) were less attractive to most traditional foundation and corporate sponsors than were such tangible "deliverables" as hotel-based minimarkets and health promotion resource centers. Moreover, even progressive foundations that understood and applauded TSOP's new directions tended to avoid refunding the same project, such that new sources of income continually had to be located. With an overworked board and no staff or volunteers specifically devoted to raising money, TSOP's two full-time organizers found themselves unable to respond to many requests to help organize in new buildings because they were too busy engaging in extensive fund-raising.

PROJECT ACCOMPLISHMENTS AND THE PROBLEM OF EVALUATION

As with many efforts aimed primarily at community organization and empowerment, separating TSOP's methods from the outcomes of those processes is difficult. Of at least equal difficulty, moreover, is determining project impacts on such health and social outcomes as malnutrition, depression, and social isolation in a neighborhood where concurrent adverse developments (e.g., cutbacks in supplemental security income [SSI] checks and escalating violence deriving, in part, from the drug epidemic) have often conspired to exacerbate these problems (Minkler in press). Finally, the strong objection of many residents to "being studied" led to a reluctance of project staff to engage in or allow formal evaluation efforts until very late in the organization's history. In spite of these limitations, however, a number of project outcomes can be examined.

TSOP's greatest achievement was its formation of eight hotel-based support groups and fourteen tenants' associations. The support groups met weekly over periods ranging from six months to, more typically, several years and averaged eight to twelve regular members. All but one of these groups moved from staff or student volunteer facilitation to resident facilitation or cofacilitation, and from discussion of issues to the taking of concrete actions to bring about change.

A number of tangible victories were achieved by these groups. Members of one support group organized a protest against a sudden (and illegal) 30 percent increase in rent, which as a consequence of resident organizing was reduced to 10 percent. In another hotel, residents demanded and got a change in the landlord's harsh eviction policy, and in a third they pressured successfully for architectural changes to make their shared bathrooms wheelchair accessible. Support group organizing also focused on accommodating the purely social or spiritual needs of residents and included the planning of elaborate holiday parties and memorial services for some group members who had passed away.

Finally, resident organizing sometimes led to cross-group activities (for example, with the formation of a Tenderloin chapter of the Nuclear Freeze and of the interhotel coalition Tenderloin Tenants for Safer Streets) and to increased involvement with and on behalf of younger groups. On a 1982 visit to TSOP, Gray Panthers' founder Maggie Kuhn called the project "the best example I've ever seen of the Gray Panthers' motto—'age and youth in action.'" She made this comment in reference to the fact that elderly TSOP support group members had increasingly broadened their focus to work with younger disabled people, persons who were homeless or unemployed, and advocates for children in this very heterogeneous neighborhood.

In several instances, TSOP support groups formed the basis of subsequent tenants' associations that were able to build upon the formers' effective leadership base and prior collective organizing efforts. The early victories of one such organization included getting a hated furniture rental policy abolished, substantial rent rebates, and pet deposits reduced from $300 to $100 (Goldotlas 1988).

Other tenants' associations were formed in buildings where no previous organizing had taken place. Victories achieved by the fourteen tenants' associations that TSOP helped to create included:

- Appealing to the Rent Board and winning $10,000 in compensation for a hotel elevator that had been out of service for five months
- Getting management to install in a hotel lobby a vending machine with low-cost, nutritious foods
- Successfully protesting a provision in a new lease agreement that would have limited residents' rights to freedom of speech and expression
- Winning improved pest control and upgrading of substandard plumbing and wiring
- Getting an agreement for lead-based paint removal
- Winning an out-of-court settlement against a prestigious local law school that owned four neighborhood buildings and had reneged on promised internal security
- Getting hot water turned on in a building that had gone without it for ten years (Ferrante 1991; Miller 1993; Minkler in press)

Like the earlier TSOP support groups, the tenants' associations went beyond their buildings' borders to work with other groups, organizations, and agencies on problems affecting the larger community. Through collaboration with several local businesses and the San Francisco Department of Public Health, for example, residents were able to secure the cleanup of a vacant lot that had become such a noxious and rat-infested dumping ground that its odors had prevented neighbors from opening their windows (Miller 1993). Similarly, tenants' association members successfully negotiated with the San Francisco Department of Parking and Traffic Safety for a senior crossing sign and an increase in

pedestrian crossing time after the death of a resident at a local intersection.

Unfortunately, measurement of actual changes in health and quality of life that may be attributed, at least in part, to TSOP organizing efforts is difficult. In a few instances, TSOP was able to collect "hard data" on project accomplishments. An evaluation of the minimarkets, for example, included twenty-four-hour diet recalls that demonstrated a significant increase in the consumption of fresh fruits and vegetables among participants (Wechlser and Minkler 1986). Similarly, the marked decline in the neighborhood crime rate during the first two years of TSOP organizing in this area was attributed by the chief of police in large part to tenant organizing and to the increased community solidarity that it inspired (Minkler in press).

Qualitative data, albeit often anecdotal, has suggested potential impacts on health and well-being. Many residents, for example, reported that, as a consequence of group participation through TSOP, they no longer felt depressed and lonely. A formerly depressed woman in her early sixties commented: "I can't tell you what a difference the group had made in my life. When I moved to the Tenderloin three years ago, my husband had just left me. All I kept thinking 'Who's going to want me now?' I think I would still be alone in my room if it weren't for [TSOP]" (Minkler in press).

Changes in health habits, including smoking cessation, decreased alcohol consumption, and improved adherence to medical regimens, were attributed by a number of residents to their involvement with TSOP. A mentally disabled resident who had frequently failed to take her prescribed medication reported that she had become religious about taking it now that she was heavily involved in several TSOP activities that relied upon her leadership skills. And a younger TSOP member remarked, "TSOP is the only group I belong to not because I'm poor or disabled or HIV positive but because of my strengths" (Minkler in press). Although such stories are difficult to translate into hard outcome data, they provide important anecdotal evidence of the effectiveness that TSOP groups and activities may have had in improving health and particularly in reducing depression among participants.

TSOP's focus on developing leaders and on increasing the problem-solving capacity of individuals and groups resulted in some important outcomes in terms of community empowerment. Several tenants' associations, for example, became recognized by management as the organized voice of building residents. In some of these residences, landlords now meet regularly with the associations to discuss the latter's concerns, whereas in other buildings tenants' associations have a regular hand in decisionmaking on any issues that might affect them (Miller 1993; Minkler in press).

Effective tenants' association outreach to and collaboration with other community groups, local businesses and agencies, and such government bodies as the Department of Public Health, the Department of Housing and Urban Development, and the Department of Public Safety were indicative, in part, of the former's growing sophistication in problemsolving. The formation of interhotel groups and coalitions such as Tenderloin Tenants for Safer Streets and the TSOP Leaders' Council suggests a growing identity with the community beyond one's individual building, and this, tool appears to have contributed to neighborhood empowerment. Joint mobilization to bring down the crime rate, arrange for vacant lot cleanup, and in other ways improve quality of life for members of the neighborhood are outcomes that may be illustrative of the increased problem-solving ability, on the community level, that TSOP helped to foster.

An extensive formal evaluation based on structured interviews with residents, unstructured interviews with key informants, and documents review was conducted during TSOP's final year of operation (Shaw 1995). The survey research component of the study compared 150 residents of TSOP-organized and nonorganized buildings. Significant differences between the two groups were found along fourteen dimensions, including social isolation, morale, feelings of safety, perceived ability to improve building living conditions, and overall quality of life. Unfortunately, however, the study failed to document statistically significant changes in health or sense of empowerment and also pointed to major organizational limitations, including lack of adequate strategic planning,

Although the evaluation produced important data on numerous aspects of TSOP's accomplishments and problems, the largely quantitative nature of the study may have limited its ability to capture some of the essence of the project. An alternative approach grounded in the philosophy and methods of empowerment evaluation might have overcome these difficulties. As Stephen Fawcett et al. (1996, 183) note, empowerment evaluation works toward the competing ends of "maximizing community control" and "understanding . . . the processes outcomes of a community initiative" or organizing effort. Empowerment evaluation ideally involves community members in all phases of the evaluation process and values qualitative, as well as quantitative, data so that the stories of community members and others become a critical part of the database. In both these respects, empowerment evaluation would, in retrospect, have been more in keeping with TSOP's philosophy and methods than was a more tradition survey research approach.

PROJECT CLOSURE AND REPLICATION EFFORTS

TSOP's closure after sixteen years came as a result of the increasing difficulty of raising the project's annual budget (approximately $100,000), most of it from private foundations. As suggested in the project evaluation, improved long-term strategic planning and earlier, more concerted efforts to develop a diversified funding base might have helped prevent the project's demise. At the same time, the general absence of government support for efforts such as TSOP and the increased competition among community groups for individual, foundation, and corporate dollars as a consequence of severe government cutbacks make the closure of projects like this one an all too frequent reality.

Several years prior to closure, however, and in response to growing numbers of requests for technical assistance from other community groups, TSOP developed a detailed project replication manual (Ferrante 1991). Outlining steps and barriers to starting and maintaining a grassroots organizing project, the guide includes discussions of such topics as the role of the organizer, choice of strategies and tactics, and the role of values in organizing, with case study examples and quotes from TSOP residents used to illustrate the points made. The manual was distributed upon request to organizers in the United States and Canada, and several replications have been attempted. A disabled veteran in New York City, for example, used the early TSOP model to help organize chronically schizo-phrenic veterans who had recently entered a residential treatment center (Pounder 1988). And in Vancouver, British Columbia, a government-funded project operates in nine SRO hotels and has achieved high credibility with the Ministry of Health (Jones and Sommers 1994). Replication efforts like these and the inclusion of the TSOP model in an innovative "health education models project" currently being developed by the Centers for Disease Control represent an important potential means of helping to ensure that the TSOP approach can continue to be refined and built upon in the years ahead.

CONCLUSION

The TSOP experience offers a number of lessons for those concerned with community organizing for health. Prominent among these are (1) the importance of community, rather than outside organizer, definition of need; (2) the need for a preliminary community assessment, as well as ongoing efforts to uncover and build upon community strengths; (3) the need to implement theories and methodologies flexibly, adapting them as necessary in order to ensure their greatest possible relevance in real-world contexts; (4) the importance of building in comprehensive, participatory, and empowering strategies for community organizing project evaluation; and (5) the need for attending early on to broad strategic planning, including the development of a diversified funding base (Minkler in press).

But as the TSOP experience also demonstrates, even the most committed community organizing effort will have limited success in improving health and quality of life in neighborhoods like the Tenderloin without a broad societal commitment to the reduction of social inequalities. A project like TSOP can make significant inroads in helping reduce feelings of social isolation and powerlessness endemic in low-income inner-city communities, especially as these feelings are often intimately tied to poor health. By helping to identify and nurture indigenous leaders, and by helping to build tenants' associations and other structures that can act as a unified voice for residents, TSOP was able to help the latter increase their power in fighting for and getting small but important changes in their health and living conditions. Furthermore, changes such as a drop (albeit temporarily) in the neighborhood crime rate, increased social support, and improvements in access to inexpensive, nutritious foods can have a direct bearing on malnutrition, depression, and other health and social problems prevalent in low-income communities (Minkler in press).

Yet conditions in the Tenderloin District, like those in many inner-city neighborhoods in the United States, have actually deteriorated over the last two decades as a result of broader economic and social conditions over which even the best-organized communities have little or no control. The economic problems of the early 1980s, combined with the politics of retrenchment that have continued to the present, have taken a particular toll on the poor. Severe cutbacks in SSI, subsidized housing, Medicaid, and a plethora of health and social service programs, combined with the growing epidemics of drugs, violence, and AIDS, wreak havoc on communities like the Tenderloin (Minkler in press).

Against this backdrop, the victories of organizations like TSOP take on added significance. Yet they also are dwarfed by the magnitude of the problems confronted, which can be adequately addressed only through a more fundamental societal-level commitment to reducing the social inequities

that lie at the base of such problems. When poverty remains perhaps the single greatest risk factor for disease and premature death, and when the links among poverty, alienation, and a plethora of health and social problems are documented in study after study (Adler et al. 1994; Haan, Kaplan, and Syme 1989), our failure to deal with these more fundamental problems becomes increasingly troubling. Projects like TSOP do not operate in a vacuum, and without a broader social commitment to reducing social inequalities, the problems plaguing inner-city communities like the Tenderloin will continue largely unabated into the twenty-first century (Minkler in press).

At the same time, however, and while health educators and other concerned professionals increase our commitment to working for broader social change at the societal level, we must not lose sight of the very real impacts a project like TSOP can have in the lives of both individuals and communities. In the words of one elderly TSOP leader who credited the project with keeping her from succumbing to severe clinical depression: "I thought when you're way down like this, way down below the poverty level, you're powerless. But I realized you can make the big shots stand up and listen. It was amazing to me to learn that if you work together you can do something" (Ferrante 1991, 8).

REFERENCES

Adler, N. E., T. Boyce, M. A. Chesney, S. Cohen, S. Folkman, R. L. Kahn, and S. L. Syme. 1994. Socioeconomic status and health: The challenge of the gradient. *American Psychologist* 49: 15–24.

Alinsky, S. D. 1969. *Reveille for radicals*. Chicago: University of Chicago Press.

_____. 1972. *Rules for radicals*. New York: Random House.

Bloomberg, L., J. Meyers, and M. T. Braverman. 1994. The importance of social interaction: A new perspective on social epidemiology, social risk factors, and health. *Health Education Quarterly* 21 (4): 447–463.

Brown, E. R. 1991. Community action for health promotion: A strategy to empower individuals and communities. *Journal of Health Services* 21 (3): 441–456.

Cohen, S., and S. L. Syme. 1985. *Social support and health.* New York: Academic Books.

Fawcett, S. B., A. Paine-Andrews, V. Francisco, J. Schultz et al. 1996. Empowering community health initiatives through evaluations. In *Empowerment evaluation: Knowledge and tools for self-assessment and accountability,* ed. D. Fetterman, S. Kaftarian, and A. Wandersman. Thousand Oaks, Calif.: Sage.

Ferrante. L. 1991. *The Tenderloin Senior Organizing Project's replication manual.* San Francisco: Tenderloin Senior Organizing Project.

Freire, P. 1968. *Pedagogy of the oppressed.* New York: Seabury Press.

_____. 1973. *Education for critical consciousness.* New York: Seabury Press.

Goldoflas, B. 1988. Organizing in a gray ghetto: The Tenderloin Senior Organizing Project. *Dollars and Sense* (January–February): 1–19.

Haan, M. N., G. A. Kaplan, and S. L. Syme. 1989. Socioeconomic position and health: Old observations and new thought. In *Pathways to health: The role of social factors,* ed. J. P. Bunker, D. S. Gromby, and B. H. Kehrer. Palo Alto: Stanford University Press.

House, J. S., K. R. Landis, and D. Umberson. 1988. Social relationships and health. *Science* 241: 540–545.

Jones, J., and J. Sommers. 1994. Grant proposal. Vancouver, Canada: Vancouver Second Mile High Society. Unpublished.

McKnight, J. 1987. Regenerating community. *Social Policy* (Winter): 54–58.

_____. 1993. Local social community development and economic development issues. Paper presented at the annual meeting of the American Public Health Association, San Francisco, California, October 27.

Miller, M. 1985. *Turning problems into actionable issues.* San Francisco: Organize Training Center.

_____. 1993. *The Tenderloin Senior Organizing Project.* Louisville, Ky.: Presbyterian Committee on the Self-Development of People.

Minkler, M. 1992. Community organizing among the elderly poor in the U.S.: A case study. *International Journal of Health Services* 22 (2): 303–316.

_____. In press. Empowerment of the elderly in San Francisco's Tenderloin District. In *Society and health: Case studies,* ed. B. Amick and R. Rudd. Cambridge, Mass.: Harvard University Press.

North of Market Planning Coalition. 1992. *Final report: Tenderloin 2000 survey and plan.* San Francisco: North of Market Planning Coalition.

Nyswander, D. 1956. Education for health: Some principles and their applications. *Health Education Monographs* 14: 65–70.

Ovrebo, B., M. Minkler, and P. Liljestrand. 1991. No room in the inn: The disappearance of SRO housing in the United States. *Journal of Housing for the Elderly* 8 (1): 77–92.

Pounder, R. F 1988. Social teaming for schizophrenic adults: The Lanchester model. Ph.d. diss. prospectus, Teachers College.

Safehouses now easing the fears of elderly residents. 1982. *Los Angeles Times,* November 21.

Shaw, F. 1995. Tenderloin Senior Organizing Project evaluation. 'Woodland, Calif: Wellness Foundation. Unpublished report.

Syme, S. L. 1993. Control of destiny: A key to good health. Paper presented at the fiftieth anniversary symposium Shaping the Future of Public Health: Perspectives from Berkeley, University of California School of Public Health, Berkeley, California, April 17.

Vanover, J. 1991. Some seniors in San Francisco: An interview with Diana Miller. *Organizing* (Spring-Summer): 44–47.

Wechsler, R., and M. Minkler. 1986. A community-oriented approach to health promotion: The Tenderloin Senior Outreach Program. In *Wellness and health promotion for the elderly,* ed. K. Dychtwald. Rockville, Md.: Aspen Systems.

17.

Jack Rothman and Mayer N. Zald

PLANNING AND POLICY PRACTICE

One characteristic of modern society is the systematic attempt to use tools of rational analysis to lay out pathways to achieving future-oriented goals. As organizations, both private and public, have become larger and developed professional staffs, and as the environments they deal with have become more complex, planning and policy decision-making have become full-blown enterprises. Corporations, governmental agencies, social welfare agencies, community federations, and others have resorted to planning activities to gather information and chart their future courses. Rational, future-oriented decision-making is a hallmark and indeed a widely accepted definition of social planning and policy making. We will use the term *planning* to encompass both concepts.

In this essay we will start by examining planning broadly as a function of the modern state. We will go on to look at particular characteristics of planning in the free-enterprise or capitalist society. We will then focus briefly but more specifically on historical forces that have given rise to planning in the field of social welfare in the United States. We will follow with applications to the field of human services.

THE SOCIETAL CONTEXT OF SOCIAL PLANNING

In this initial section we will nest planning and policy making in the social structure of society. Our questions are sociological and political rather than normative and metathe-oretical. When does planning work? Whose goals are served by planning? What are the social and institutional uses of planning? What are the social functions and dysfunctions of planning? Is planning activity in the community and welfare arena different in kind from planning in the economic sector? We do not intend to offer a sociological theory of planning but rather to identify some of the problematics of the planning function in society.

Planning and the State

As a general proposition, the growth of government and the state apparatus in modern times has been accompanied by an increase in planning activities (Shonfield 1965). Yet, modern societies have varied widely in their attitudes toward national planning. Socialist states have attempted comprehensive economic and social planning as techniques for realizing goals of economic growth and national development. These plans not only have established goals for specific industries, but have rationed the allocation of labor and capital. Moreover, these plans have included large social-welfare components such as plans for housing, education, and medical care.

Obviously, the adoption of national planning is related to the ideology of ruling elites and national social structure. Comprehensive five-year plans have been adopted in Communist and Socialist countries. The more fragmented or multilayered the political structure and the more the ruling elites are committed to capitalist laissez-faire ideology, the less likely they are to attempt to adopt national comprehensive planning. Capitalist states with strong central governments are more likely to adopt "indicative planning" where specific industries are singled out for aid and development. And legislation adopted in capitalist countries may plan and allocate resources for the implementation of specific social welfare objectives such as, for instance, the subsidy of thousands of low-income housing units, or plans to establish a nationwide system of community mental health centers.

What have been the results of comprehensive planning on the societal level? It is impossible to review the literature here.[1] But several general conclusions emerge. First, comprehensive planning coupled with a rationing system of resource allocation leads to systematic pathologies of production. The plans emphasize physical unit counts rather than quality criteria, and the production of inferior goods is pandemic. Moreover, there is a tendency to overemphasize the production of goods which meet raw quantity requirements at the expense of differentiated products not measured in the plan. Second, unless goals are constantly updated to record the increments in actual production, goals are rarely fulfilled. Third, comprehensive national plans have endemic problems of work incentives, labor, allocations and stockpiling raw materials to an excessive degree. . . .

Over all, the information shortcomings and incentive shortcomings of national planning have led to either planning as ritual or attempts to mix market pricing systems with indicative planning focusing upon a more limited set of objectives.

Yugoslavia was the prime example of this adaptive response. In spite of the vast increases in information processing capacity provided by modern computer technology and the planning theoretic devices provided by input-output analysis and other programming devices, long-range comprehensive planning eluded achievement. In capitalist societies it is not even attempted.

Social and Economic Planning in the United States

Although the notion of comprehensive societal planning has never been fully accepted in the United States, sectoral, policy-specific, and organizational planning is widely used. There are many examples: State prison systems develop planning models of needed facilities, taking into account projected prison populations, assumptions about crime rates, populations at risk, and sentencing policy. Forest products companies project wood-footage needs and plant seedlings now for harvesting in twenty years. Assuming market goals, large corporations project capital needs for five- and ten-year periods; moreover, large corporations have strategic planning staffs examining new product trends and attempting to project political and economic climates into the future. The Social Security Administration projects revenue needs, given demographic trends, eligibility rules, and benefit formulas. Local councils develop plans for hospital facilities. Universities attempt to develop models of projected enrollments and develop strategies for growth or retrenchment of faculty and facilities.

There is, of course, wide variability among organizations in the extent to which they engage in formal and explicit planning activities. Large organizations with larger professional and administra-

---

[1]For a summary of the problems of comprehensive planning in Socialist societies see Lindblom (1977).

tive components are more likely to engage in planning than smaller ones. Organizations that have longer time horizons in the procurement of resources, the development of products, or the demand for services are more likely to engage in planning than those with shorter time horizons. (It takes five to seven years to develop a new car model, while dress styles change yearly.)

Organizations with leaders trained in management-by-objectives techniques and other planning-oriented styles are more likely to engage in these techniques. And, finally, organizations that are required by external agencies to develop plans as part of their procurement or legitimation or the receipt of funds are more likely than others to engage in the production of planning documents. For instance, to receive federal grants for law enforcement activities or for community mental health centers, states and committees have had to develop planning bodies and plans for services.

Obviously, there is a difference between planning and implementing plans. What kinds of organizations are more likely to implement their plans? Implementation in its simplest form (that is, the translation of plan into action) depends upon the commitment of allocating authorities to the plan. One common problem in private organizations is that the planning group may not be integrally connected to the decision-making authorities. To the extent that planning officers are removed from central authorities, their plans may be pigeonholed. The same problem occurs to an even greater extent in public organizations. Public organizations are to a large extent dependent upon decision-making bodies (legislatures, elected executives) for the establishment of goals and the allocation of resources. These are in turn beholden to constituencies composed of diverse and often conflicting elements.

Since these external interests may have different priorities for the organization and competing demands for resource allocation, we suspect it is more likely that the planning documents of public organizations gather dust or are radically modified than are those of private organizations that engage in long-range planning. Ironically, these same private organizations often express disparagement of planning for public enterprises.

In both public and private organizations the inability to attract resources from outside and the decline of slack resources within organizations inhibit planning implementation. These issues particularly have plagued planning in social welfare. Moreover, as we have indicated, in both private and public organizations, planning is part of a social and political process. It serves ends and purposes apart from its formal or stated functions of gathering information and choosing pathways to goals. Rationalist schools of planning theory have not always been sufficiently sensitive to these realities.

Planning in Social Work and Social Welfare

At some minimal level, planning in social work and social welfare can be said to have occurred when a person or agency, motivated by concerns for clients or beneficiaries, anticipates future needs or programs rather than responding "spontaneously" to demands. Charity is transformed from a spontaneous response to a supplicant in need to a planned system when individuals or organizations anticipate philanthropic demand and set up rules and policies, services and organizations to respond to that anticipated need or demand. The Poor Law is thus an early instance of planning.

A caseworker can be said to engage in planning when he or she conceptualizes a goal of treatment or service delivery and anticipates or shapes alternative courses of treatment or service.

In the last century explicit planning emerged as agencies, both public and private, became aware that their ad hoc and uncoordinated efforts led to inadequate and inefficient provision of services. Sometimes clients would go to several agencies, requesting and receiving financial support from more than one source, without one agency knowing that another had helped. The community council case register movement (Social Service Exchange) began early in the century. Although these agencies may have been more effective at controlling multiple applicants (see Litwak and Hylton 1962) than they were for actually planning and implementing plans for whatever services were to be provided, the community chest and council movements represent an early attempt to assess community needs and to argue for rational decision making in projecting the development and location of community agencies. It is important to note that once a commitment to planning emerged, a methodology was required. The development of the community survey can be seen as an emergent methodology for community planning (Byington 1911; Colcord 1939; Warren 1955).

Another early attempt at planning is found in the efforts of welfare agencies to plan for emergency relief. Whenever a major cataclysm occurs there is large-scale and sudden disruption of the goods and services available to a population. In preplanning periods individual agencies respond in an ad hoc fashion to such needs. The emergence of agencies such as the Red Cross, the development of emergency planning committees, and the legislation of federal and state loan and service provisions are all attempts to plan in advance for unforeseen disasters, to forecast need, and to develop repertoires of response.

This perspective on social welfare planning is consistent with Lauffer's definition: "Social planning refers to the development, expansion and coordination of social services and social policies" (1981:583). Lauffer goes on to state that planning is a method of rational problem solving and that it is conducted at both the societal and the local level.

Both the community council movement and the development of emergency and disaster relief agencies are making plans for the delivery and coordination of service at the local community level. Large-scale planning has also been attempted for specific social welfare programs at the national level. The development of the Social Security system required a projection of the number and size of beneficiary claims and revenues from taxation. The planning system of Social Security has been buffeted by changes in mortality rates, changes in the economy, and political actions that have added claimants and enlarged benefit levels (Derthick 1979; Cates 1981).

Another national example of social welfare relevant planning can be seen in the development of the Comprehensive Community Mental Health Act of 1963. Here we see an effort to use federal incentives (the federal subsidization of local services) to encourage the planning and development of mental health services in a setting close to the patient's home, the provision of outpatient and preventive services, the setting up of provisions for noninstitutional alternatives, community consultation, and local boards.

The tasks of planning in these different cases vary substantially in the complexity of the planning activity: the number of components of the plan; the time horizon of the plan (short term to long term); the locus of the planning (private local agency to national government); and in the representation of interests (client, professional, political). They differ from planning in non–social-welfare arenas not in terms of the difficulty or ease of planning but in that the values to be served by planning are those of the liberal, caring society. It is these values of a humane industrialized society that link these planning efforts to the helping professions.

These humane impulses have led to other forms of organized response to need. Settlement houses, for example, strove to change conditions of life in the neighborhood through social reform or advocacy. They, together with YMCAs and other locally based organizations, also were concerned with citizen participation, public education, and personal development of participants. Planning theory reflects these various empirical crosscurrents of action and practice.

PLANNING THEORY

Planning theory emerged as a response to the need to engage in planning activity. It arose as an answer to questions about how one ought to conduct such activity. It has been a normative exercise. For example, writers have asked what is the best way to plan. What are the limits of different kinds of planning? What alternatives are there to the standard practices? As a normative exercise, scholars have examined planning activity in specific situations as a tool of rationality and choice. They have been concerned with its limits and blind spots. Less often, scholars have raised empirical and descriptive issues: Who plans, in what situations, with what results?

. . .

Rationalistic Decision-Making Theory

The modern era of planning theory was marked initially by a rationalistic model of decision making, crystallized in the writings of Herbert Simon (1957). Planning was viewed as a process whereby through use of proper rules of logic an optimal solution to a problem is determined. Persons are seen as utility-maximizing beings whose relations to others are defined in instrumental terms. Classic decision-making theory involves following a task-oriented set of basic steps, including ordinarily: (1) setting a goal; (2) identifying all the alternative means of attaining the goal; (3) evaluating means in order to arrive at the single best solution; and (4) implementing the decision. Hudson characterizes the approach as examining "problems from a systems viewpoint, using conceptual or mathematical models relating ends (objectives) to means (resources and constraints), with heavy reliance on numbers and quantitative analysis" (1979:389). This may entail use of forecasting and analysis techniques such as multiple regression analysis, Markov chains, econometric modeling, and Bayesian methods. In social work planning literature the work of Kahn (1969), in particular, has been identified with procedures of rational decision making.

Both in social work and in urban planning, the rationalistic approach has been associated with the idea of comprehensiveness. Comprehensive land use planning was the modus operandi in city planning for an extended period of time, and social work planning, according to Lane, was to entail "a progressively effective adjustment between social welfare resources and social welfare needs" (1959:65). Community chests and councils viewed their role to be that of fostering and steering comprehensive social welfare planning at the community level.

Despite, or perhaps because of, its elegance and simplicity, the rationalistic comprehensive concept has been subjected to criticism from various quarters. A variety of limitations has been attributed to the model, including limits to rational cognition, limits to analytic cogency, limits to environmental control, limits to professionalism, and limits of value dissonance.

Limits to rational cognition pertain to the amount of knowledge or information that may be gathered and digested in any decisional situation. In practical terms, far more information was required than could be acquired. The number of alternatives to be identified, documented, and weighted was legion. Technical difficulties in assembling data presented obstacles: the loss or transformation of data through aggregation or mathematical modeling; unavailability of organizational information; delays in data acquisition; faulty or falsified data; computer breakdowns, and so on. Limits to analytic cogency simply mean that what is logical may encounter fierce opposition by those who have not been consulted, or whose narrow "irrational" interests are threatened. Analytic purity is complicated by pluralism of values existing in most urban settings. Rationalism is most applicable when one can assume a unitary set of values (a general public interest), or at least a set of values that are not rancorously contentious. In other words, there are personal and organizational dynamics in formulating or implementing a decision that go beyond its intrinsic analytic features. This duality in planning has been recognized through conceptualizing "analytic" and "interactional" (Perlman and Gurin 1972) or "technical" and "sociopolitical" (Gilbert and Specht 1977) aspects of planning.

Limits to environmental control relate to the "turbulent" (Emery and Trist 1965), broader social context in which planners operate. The 1960s and 1970s were times of uncertain and shifting social, political, and economic currents, followed by an era showing signs of similar contextual instability. When the national or community political economy is unpredictable, the more narrow technical area of planning is subjected to unforeseen dislocations. "It is a feature of modern social dynamics that the future does not unroll incrementally but in a disjointed series of crises, breakthroughs and transformations" (Friedman and Hudson 1974:8). This has placed a high burden on the rationalist formulation.

Limits to professionalism suggest that while the planner does not have all the answers, some answers do lie uniquely with other sources. In particular, it is brought out, individuals affected by new services or facilities have a distinctive understanding of their needs and how to fulfill them. Thus families, neighborhood groups, and ethnic and racial communities are viewed as having important contributions to make to decisions concerning delivery of services. The concept of informal helping networks has come to the fore in this connection. Such networks have joined in constructive partnership with planners, both in decision making and in the actual delivery of services at the grass-roots level. The requirement for cost constraints is another factor which has curtailed professionalism and generated increased interest in the idea of self-help networks.

A final limitation deals with value dissonance. Rationalism has been criticized by many for projecting an image of the planner as technocrat. This image is of a policy scientist or systems analyst, surrounded by printouts, engaged in model-building, standing apart from community politics, and devoid of contact with ordinary citizens. The one "best" solution arrived at by the planner in isolation through technical gadgetry is seen as imposed on hapless populations without their input or consent. "Urban renewal as urban removal" conveys the sense of this view. This critique takes rationalism to task for its failure to incorporate an element of citizens' participation into its theoretical structure, which places it in dissonance with basic democratic values.

Rittel and Webber (1973) have pointed to a significant weakness in rationalistic theory. The theory assumes problems that are definable, discrete, and responsive to purposeful manipulation. In the current scene, however, these authors tell us, planning has been obliged to deal with "wicked" problems. These elude bounded definitions, have no clear end point, suggest innumerable potential solutions, are unique and incomparable in each instance, and are enmeshed with other problems of which they are symptoms. Rationalism requires somewhat benign, docile problems. Instead, society spews forth wicked and incorrigible ones. The theory was not up to coping with this discrepancy.

According to Galloway and Mahayni (1977), the evaluation of planning theory can best be understood through application of the work of Kuhn (1970) on the structure of scientific revolutions. A paradigm develops, is articulated, and wins general professional acceptance. Later anomalies appear and a crisis ensues. Alternative competing paradigms appear. In the view of Galloway and Mahayni, the dominant rationalist paradigm broke down in the turbulent 1960s and is being superseded by other approaches.

A useful way to obtain an overview of the main theoretical orientations to planning extant today is through a schema developed by Hudson (1979). Hudson sees rationalistic theory still retaining a foothold on professional thinking, but he suggests that four alternative theoretical positions

have also gained currency: incremental planning, transactive planning, advocacy planning and radical planning.[2]

Although planning theory has always acknowledged an implementation aspect or phase, most of the writings have concentrated on decision making. However, in recent years implementation has been given a prominent place as a defined area for theoretical explications (Pressman and Wildavsky 1973; Bardach 1977; Williams and Elmore 1976; Hargrove 1975; Smith 1973). It was as though the struggles and defeats of the Great Society programs, particularly the War on Poverty, brought home to planners and policy analysts the recognition that careful follow-through is essential for the success of the most clearly formulated plan.

Several variables have emerged in implementation studies which are associated with the attainment of planning goals. Conditions identified as facilitating implementation include such variables as commitment of top leaders, organizational capacity, the commitment of implementers, and interest-group support. Variables found to impede implementation include magnitude of change, number of actors involved, alternative preferences of actors, intrinsic complexity of the plan and its timing. Although the label "implementation"

---

[2]The Hudson schema has much similarity to the "Three Models" formulation of Rothman (1979). Transactional planning has features in common with Rothman's "locality development." Hudson breaks social planning into rationalistic (which he designates "synoptic") and incremental. He also subdivides social action, arriving at advocacy planning and radical planning. Both authors view the various approaches to planning not as competing and incompatible initiatives but as available planning strategies providing alternatives that may be used selectively in relation to given planning contexts and objectives. They both also discuss favorably the mixing of different traditions or models for particular planning purposes, taking into account the attributes of the different approaches which permit or impede combining among them.

may be different, the theoretical issues examined duplicate conceptual work in such theoretical schools as planned change, organizational development, diffusion of innovations, and political science studies of governmental bureaucracies and of interest groups. Nevertheless, the recent impetus by policy science groups may generate fresh ideas and promising reformulations of earlier efforts.

As a starting point in describing the previously mentioned emergent method for generating theory, we draw on Friedmann and Hudson's definition of planning "as an activity centrally concerned with *the linkage between knowledge and organized action*." (1974:22; emphasis in the original). In keeping with this view, one of the authors has developed a research utilization or social research and development methodology for systematically applying social science research in such a way as to construct social intervention strategies (Rothman 1974; 1980). The approach eschews a "grand theory" approach to planning but starts with more delimited planning issues or problems, such as establishing an innovative program in the community or bringing about a wider level of citizen participation in the planning process. The method proceeds through a series of steps: delineating knowledge areas that contain relevant data; determining appropriate descriptors and key words for retrieving data; evaluating, assembling, and synthesizing data; formulating generalizations concerning the phenomena under consideration; and converting descriptive propositions into prescriptive application guidelines. The methodology proceeds further into field testing and development work so that planning strategies are not only evaluated for workability but are also put into operation to facilitate practice implementation. The objective is to arrive

at middle-range theory which is both tested in the user environment and "packaged" for planning practitioners in user-ready form. Since the approach has been detailed elsewhere, it will not be discussed further here.

Social Planning Roles

Planning roles grow out of problems or needs in the society. But the planner does not necessarily define these. The planner is not an autonomous private practitioner, but one of a contemporary breed of professionals who is organizationally based and an employee of a bureaucratic structure. It is the governing bodies of such structures (boards of directors, commissions) that typically establish policy and set the agenda. However, this often takes place in collaboration with planners, who are in a strategic position (formally and informally) to influence decisions about organizational goals.

The character of the employers of planners has shifted over the years. In the early part of the century most of the employers were voluntary philanthropic agencies including community welfare councils, community chests, and specialized agencies in fields such as housing, child welfare, health, and the like. At the same time, settlement houses provided a base for neighborhood organizing and community development. With the advent of the New Deal in the 1930s, the federal government assumed a greater role in social planning. But throughout the 1930s, 1940s, and 1950s voluntary agencies were probably the major arena for planning jobs. This situation shifted drastically in the 1960s and 1970s. Government bodies at the federal, state, and local levels took on heavy responsibility for social programs and vastly overshadowed voluntary planning activity. The political outlook and social philosophy of the New Frontier and Great

Society Democratic administrations provided the impetus for this development.

The Reagan-Bush administrations checked this century-long trend. The expansion of federal activity in planning has been halted. Responsibility is being pushed back on voluntary agencies, private enterprise, and local and state levels of government. At this writing it is too early to predict what balance between governmental and voluntary planning efforts will be reached by the Clinton and subsequent presidencies. One can only note that this is an era in substantial flux.

As planners carry out their roles, a variety of skills is brought to bear. Arthur Dunham (1948) engaged in an early attempt to define this area. In his view, professionals need to exert "creative leadership" around specific tasks, and also facilitate group process in collaborative decision making. In other words, they should be able to expedite both task and process goals. For this reason, according to Dunham, they need, among other qualities, a sound knowledge of the social welfare field as well as interactional capabilities in dealing with people.

A roughly similar twofold schema was developed in a study by Rothman and Jones (1971). It is presented in slightly abridged form below.

Technical or task-oriented skills included the following:

A. Designing
    1. Fact-finding, needs assessment, and social-survey techniques
    2. Policy analysis
    3. Program development
B. Expediting
    4. Decision-making techniques
    5. Political liaison
    6. Legislative drafting and enactment
    7. Administrative procurement
C. Implementing
    8. Administrative role and function
    9. Fund raising and proposal writing
    10. Consultation
    11. Staff development and supervision
    12. Promotional, educational, and public relations techniques
    13. Evaluation

In the interactional domain the following skills areas were identified:

A. Managing Organizational Processes
    14. Initial organizing
    15. Participation
    16. Committee technology
    17. Leadership development and training
B. Exerting Influence
    18. Coalitions and their formation
    19. Bargaining
    20. Advocate role and conflict
    21. Broker role
    22. Identifying and influencing the power structure
C. Conducting Interpersonal Relations
    23. Interviewing
    24. Use of self
    25. Leading group discussion

These are presented as fairly generic skills which should be the equipment of any planner. However, not all planning agencies or situations call for using the full array. The type of agency, its mission, and the model of planning it follows all influence planner role performance. In larger agencies with abundant resources and a multiplicity of projects, staff may be able to specialize. In small agencies the jack-of-all-trades may be required. As new methods develop—nominal group process or computer-aided simulation modeling, for example—they are absorbed into the skill repertoire of planners.

Roles are related to emerging emphases in practice. . . . One of these is community-based services, an outgrowth of deinstitutionalization in fields such as mental health, mental retardation, and corrections. There are also increased activities in rural areas in connection with problems of ecology (water resources, topsoil erosion, and disposal of toxic wastes) and nuclear reactor construction. In addition, planning more and more reflects the interaction of local organizations involved in competition for grant funds.

To these may be added some fields of service that will gain greater attention in the period ahead. With an aging population, gerontology can be identified as a field requiring expanding planning. Health is another, in part in relationship to the aging phenomenon. Work-related services, including industrial social work, will likely expand as efforts to reindustrialize and enhance worker productivity are heightened. Refugee resettlement may also continue to rise in importance as an aspect of international political conflict and instability. Areas which will probably decline include mental health and child welfare. The state level will become a more significant arena for social planning as will the locality.

Skills receiving increased emphasis include needs assessment, proposal writing, computer technology, and research on laws and regulations. In addition, sophisticated use of media—videotapes, recordings, slides, and computer applications—for promotional and other purposes seems to be gaining in importance.

. . .

Social and Political Uses of Planning

Planning theory has largely been a goal-oriented exercise in which rationality is viewed as good and planning is advanced as a method or process in the service of rationality. Rational analysis is the medium for reaching desired future states.

Here we turn to uses of planning as an instrument of political and social control and as a ritual of justification. The emphasis is not upon planning as a rational device for the achieving of announced social ends, but as a device for maintaining power, for reaching consensus, and for justifying decisions that may be taken on other grounds.

Any social process can be used for purposes other than its manifest intent. Merton has referred to these as latent functions (1957). Three intrinsic features of planning activities lend themselves to use for other than their manifest purposes. Planning takes time, thus inhibiting current action. Planning requires explicit statement and ordering of objectives into priorities, thus it may become an instrument of conflict resolution and consensus formation. Planning leads to the generation of written documents. These documents may serve to legitimate actions of funders and review agencies, even if the written plans are not carried out.

Planning as Stalling. Any planning activity consumes time. Information must be gathered, alternatives scouted. When groups are pressing for action, yet authorities are unsure what alternative is reasonable (or whether any action ought to be undertaken), a proposal to study action alternatives and plan future steps may be adopted. The proposal to plan gives symbolic reassurance that the group's demands are being met, when in fact authorities are buying time. The results of the planning process may or may not lead to material change, but in the short run authorities buy political acquiescence (see p. 56).

Planning and Consensus Formation. When goals and priorities are clear, planning is transformed into a technical process—the efficient means to achieve ends. But where goals are not clear, where affected parties have different priorities and where authorities are loath to announce goals and priorities *ex cathedra*, the planning process may facilitate debate and the ordering of priorities. It encourages an orderly registering of preferences and a search for compromise solutions.

In a penetrating doctoral dissertation Kenneth McNeil (1973) has examined a number of local community committees and planning boards that operated between politicians, bureaucracies, and citizens in Nashville, Tennessee. These included the local zoning committee responsible for enforcing zoning restrictions, a committee to study the location and design of a new airport, the public health commission, and others. In all these areas there is room for different priorities. Bureaucrats, professionals, and citizens may value ends and means differently. The planning process, which includes the representation of different groups and a procedure for gathering evidence, holding hearings, allows a consensus to emerge. Not only may a compromise consensus emerge, but the process provides the legitimacy of due process. Losers may at least believe that they have had a chance to state their case. In this regard, planning activity takes on a quasi-judicial role in community change. Communication and consensus-building along these lines have been referred to as "process goals" in the social work planning literature (Rothman 1964).

We suspect that planning activities take on this quasi-judicial consensus formation function whenever strong competing interests confront a decision with long-range consequences and central authority is unwilling or unable to override one or another of the competing interests. The planning process in many confederated community organizations, such as local United Way agencies, resembles the quasi-judicial conflict resolution. Interestingly enough, capital allocation processes in some large corporations and in universities also resemble this process (Pondy 1964).

Documents and the Planning Process. Planning leads to written documents. These documents may be part of the ritual of allocation in grants economies. Kenneth Boulding has drawn our attention to the growth of the grants economy—governmental bodies, international agencies, and philanthropic foundations give grants to countries and organizations for delivery of services or the production of goods, even though the granting agency does not receive or use those goods or services (Boulding, Pfaff, and Pfaff 1973).

To receive the grant, the grantee may have to produce a plan. The plan becomes a justificatory document when the grantor must legitimate his allocation of funds. In the extreme case the grantor does not examine whether the plan is in fact implemented, whether the plan leads to any of the intended results, or whether the money is used for the original purposes. No penalty may be incurred for failure to carry out the plan. When plans are used for justification, without audit of expenditure or sanctions for failure, we can speak of planning documents as rhetorical instruments used as justificatory devices for the transfer of funds (Porter and Warner 1973; Wildavsky 1972).

There are other latent functions of planning activity. The planning process helps solidify networks of agencies and personnel who share information. In a sense, planning serves as a coordinating device, even if the formal plan is not adopted (process goals, again). Thus agencies may learn of each other's intentions and problems. Moreover, planning activity may institutionalize search and scanning activities in organizations, forcing review and reconsideration of established ways. Planning can legitimate a predetermined course of action, or justify moving ahead when there is no rational basis for a particular action path—the opposite of stalling (see Vinter and Tropman, 1970, for an analysis of the uses of community studies). At this point, however, we can only speculate on these by-products of planning, since systematic evaluations of empirical cases are few and far between.

Beyond that, it behooves planning specialists to observe latent functions of planning such as these with a clear eye, both to use them in a deliberative way in practice when considered appropriate, or to defend against them when they are applied to the detriment of one's clients or organization. These functions can be seen as planning tactics that can shape the course of intervention in the service of planning objectives.

In a socially and ecologically complex world, expert social planning and management by large, rationalistic bureaucracies with specialized professionals and technicians are essential elements of national survival. At the same time, the impulse of such bureaucracies, and their sponsoring governmental regimes, to become heavy-handed, arrogant, rigid, and self-serving is well known. The countervailing influence of local concerns and particular interests helps keep planning fluid and responsive to human requirements. Left alone entirely, however, the perpetual crush of pluralistic adversary pressures can lead to a neo-Darwinian nightmare of chaos and inequity. Both rationalistic-centralized and adversarial grass-roots modes of action have virtues and benefits. Their mix and interplay provide a healthy balance in the real world, at least until more ideal planning theories come into being to guide human affairs.

SUMMARY

It might be said that the state of the planning art is currently at a metatheoretical level. Much of the theory is highly abstract and anecdotal in character. There is an insufficiency of rigorous literature involving systematic evaluation. There is also lack of attention to mixed models of planning. Theorists generally pursue a single model while ignoring others. Accepting the validity of mixed models, one can examine planning issues with greater refinement. For example, it would be possible to identify certain problems or areas which should be subject to controlled central planning and others which ought to be left to the free play of the market. Similarly, organizations need a mixture of planning and mutual adjustment.

REFERENCES

Bardach, E. *The Implementation Game.* Cambridge, Mass.: M.I.T. Press, 1977.

Boulding, Kenneth, Martin Pfaff, and Anita Pfaff. *Transfers in an Urbanized Economy: Theories and Effects of the Grants Economy.* Belmont, Calif.: Wadsworth, 1973.

Brager, George A. and Harry Specht. *Community Organizing.* New York: Columbia University Press, 1973.

Branch, Melville. "Critical Unresolved Problems of Urban Planning Analysis." *Journal of the American Institute of Planners* (January 1978), 44(1):47–59.

Burchell, Robert and James Hughes. "Planning Theory in the 1980's—A Search for Future Directions." In Burchell and Sternlieb, eds., *Planning Theory in the 1980's,* 1979, pp. xvii–liii.

Burchell, Robert and George Sternlieb, eds. *Planning Theory in the 1980's.* New Brunswick, N.J.: The Center for Urban Policy Research, 1979.

Byington, Margaret F. *What Social Workers Should Know About Their Own Communities.* New York: Russell Sage Foundation, 1911.

Cates, Jerry. "Social Security: Organization and Policy." Ph.D. dissertation, University of Michigan, 1981.

Colcord, Joanna C. *Your Community: Its Provisions for Health, Education, Safety, and Welfare.* New York: Russell Sage Foundation, 1939.

Cox, Fred M., et al., eds. *Strategies of Community Organization*, 3d ed. Itasca, Ill.: Peacock, 1979.

Davidoff, Paul. "Advocacy and Pluralism in Planning." *Journal of the American Institute of Planners* (November 1965), 31(4):331–38.

Derthick, Martha. *Policy Making for Social Security.* Washington, D.C.: Brookings Institution, 1979.

Dunham, Arthur. *The Job of the Community Organization Worker.* New York: Association for the Study of Community Organization and Community Chests and Councils of America, 1948.

_____. *The New Community Organization.* New York: Crowell, 1970.

Emery, F. E. and E. L. Trist. "The Causal Texture of Organizations and Environments." *Human Relations* (February 1965), 18(1):31–32.

Etzioni, Amitai. *The Active Society: A Theory of Society and Political Processes.* New York: Free Press, 1968.

Friedmann, John. *Retracking America: A Theory of Transactive Planning.* New York: Anchor Press, Doubleday, 1973.

Friedmann, John and Barclay Hudson. "Knowledge and Action: A Guide to Planning Theory." *Journal of the American Institute of Planners* (January 1974), 40(1):2–16.

Galloway, Thomas D. and Riad G. Mahayni. "Planning Theory in Retrospect: The Process of Paradigm Change." *Journal of the American Institute of Planners* (January 1977), 43(1):62–71.

Gilbert, Neil and Harry Specht, eds. "Social Planning and Community Organization Approaches." In *Encyclopedia of Social Work*, pp. 1412–25, 17th ed. Washington, D.C.: NASW, 1977.

_____. *Handbook of the Social Services.* Englewood Cliffs, N.J.: Prentice-Hall, 1981.

Haggstrom, Warren. "Can the Poor Transform the World?" In Kramer and Specht, eds., *Readings in Community Organization Practice*, pp. 301–14. Englewood Cliffs, N.J.: Prentice-Hall, 1969.

Hargrove, Erwin C. *The Missing Link: The Study of the Implementation of Social Policy.* Washington, D.C.: Urban Institute, 1975.

Harper, Ernest B. and Arthur Dunham, eds. *Community Organization in Action: Basic Literature and Critical Comments.* New York: Association Press, 1959.

Hudson, Barclay. "Comparison of Current Planning Theories: Counterparts and Contradictions." *Journal of the American Institute of Planners* (October 1979), 45(4):387–98.

Kahn, Alfred J. *Theory and Practice of Social Planning.* New York: Russell Sage Foundation, 1969.

Kramer, Ralph M. and Harry Specht, eds. *Readings in Community Organization Practice.* Englewood Cliffs, N.J.: Prentice-Hall, 1969.

Kuhn, Thomas. *The Structure of Scientific Revolutions.* 2d ed. Chicago: University of Chicago Press, 1970.

Lane, Robert P. "The Nature and Characteristics of Community Organization—A Preliminary Inquiry." In Harper and Dunham, eds. *Community Organization in Action: Basic Literature and Critical Comments*, 1959, pp. 60–70.

Lauffer, Armand. "The Practice of Social Planning." In Gilbert and Specht, eds., *Handbook of the Social Services*, 1981, pp. 583–97.

Lauffer, Armand and Edward Newman, eds. "Community Organization for the 1980's." *Social Development Issues*, special issue of the journal (Summer and Fall 1981), (5): 2–3.

Lindblom, Charles. *The Intelligence of Democracy: Decision Making Through Mutual Adjustment.* New York: Free Press, 1965.

_____. *Politics and Markets: The World's Political-Economic Systems.* New York: Basic Books, 1977.

Litwak, Eugene and Lydia F. Hylton. "Inter-Organizational Analysis: A Hypothesis on Coordinating Agencies." *Administrative Science Quarterly*, 6(4) (1962):395–420.

McNeil, Kenneth Edward. "Citizens as Brokers: Cooptation in an Urban Setting." Ph.D. dissertation, Vanderbilt University, 1973.

March, James Q. and Herbert A. Simon. *Organizations*. New York: Wiley, 1959.

Merton, Robert K. "Manifest and Latent Functions." In Merton, *Social Theory and Social Structure*, pp. 19–84. Glencoe, Ill.: Free Press, 1957.

Morris, Robert and Robert Binstock. *Feasible Planning for Social Change*. New York: Columbia University Press, 1966.

Peattie, Lisa. "Reflections on Advocacy Planning." *Journal of the American Institute of Planners*. 34(2) (1968):80–87.

Perlman, Robert. "Social Planning and Community Organization." In *Encyclopedia of Social Work*, pp. 1404–12. 17th ed. Washington, D.C.: NASW, 1970.

Perlman, Robert and Arnold Gurin. *Community Organization and Social Planning*. New York: Wiley, 1972.

Pondy, Louis. "Budgeting and Inter-Group Conflict in Organizations." *Pittsburgh Business Review* (April 1964), 34(3):1–3.

Porter, David O. and David C. Warner. "How Effective Are Grantor Controls: The Case of Federal Aid to Education." In Boulding, Pfaff, and Pfaff, *Transfers in an Urbanized Economy*, 1973, pp. 276–302.

Pressman, J. and Aaron Wildavsky. *Implementation*. 2d ed. University of California Press, 1973.

Rittel, Horst and Melvin M. Webber. "Dilemmas in a General Theory of Planning." *Political Sciences* (June 1973), 4(2):155–69.

Ross, Murray. *Community Organization: Theory and Principles*. New York: Harper and Row, 1955.

Rothman, Jack. "An Analysis of Goals and Roles in Community Organization Practice." *Social Work* (April 1964), 9(2):24–31.

_____. *Planning and Organizing for Social Change: Action Principles from Social Science Research*. New York: Columbia University Press, 1974.

_____. "Three Models of Community Organization Practice, Their Mixing and Phasing." In Cox et al., eds., *Strategies of Community Organization*, 1979, pp. 25–45.

_____. *Social R & D: Research and Development in the Human Services*. Englewood Cliffs, N.J.: Prentice-Hall, 1980.

Rothman, Jack and Wyatt Jones. *A New Look at Field Instruction*. New York: Association Press in Cooperation with the Council on Social Work Education, 1971.

Shonfield, Andrew. *Modern Capitalism*. London: Oxford University Press, 1965.

Simon, Herbert A. *Administrative Behavior: A Study of Decision-Making Processes in Administrative Organization*. 2d ed. New York: Macmillan, 1957.

Smith, T. B. "The Policy Implementation Process." *Policy Science*. 4(4) (1973): 197–209.

Spiro, Shimon. "The Knowledge Base of Community Organization Practice." In Cox et al., eds., *Strategies of Community Organization*, 1979, pp. 79–84.

Vinter, Robert D. and John E. Tropman. "The Causes and Consequences of Community Studies." In Cox et al., eds., *Strategies of Community Organization*, pp. 315–23. 2d ed., 1970.

Warren, Roland L. *Studying Your Community*. New York: Russell Sage Foundation, 1955.

_____. "Application of Social Science Knowledge to the Community Organization Field." *Journal of Education for Social Work* (Spring 1967), 3(1):60–72.

Wildavsky, Aaron. "Why Planning Fails in Nepal." *Administrative Science Quarterly* (December 1972), 17(4):508–28.

Williams, W. and R. F. Elmore. *Social Program Implementation*. New York: Academic Press, 1976.

Wolf, Eric. "They Divide and Sub-Divide, and Call It Anthropology." *New York Times*, November 30, 1980.

18.

Charles E. Snare

WINDOWS OF OPPORTUNITY: WHEN AND HOW
CAN THE POLICY ANALYST INFLUENCE THE
POLICYMAKER DURING THE POLICY PROCESS

When is the policymaker likely to use a policy analyst's information as political information or as a means to influence constituents? When are decision-makers likely to change their agendas midstream? When are policymakers likely to seek information that confirms their views? When are decision-makers likely to change their views about an issue? When will persuasion be effective? When will manipulating the decision-making process be productive? What role should the policy analyst play in order to have the greatest impact? What part of the policy process is the most critical with regard to swaying the policymaker? In other words, when do the "windows of opportunity" occur for the policy analyst so that the analyst may have an impact on the policymaker and ultimately the policy process?

"When" and "what" depend on a number of factors. Three germane ingredients are the type of decision-maker, the stage of the policy process, and the role the policy analyst performs. By far the most neglected area in this equation has been the personality differences in policymakers. Webber (1987, p. 613) has indicated that earlier research has not considered the impact of policymakers' differing orientations on the use of policy information. Bozeman (1986, p. 527) said, "it is increasingly clear that policy analysis is not sufficiently attentive to the *psychology* of decision-making." Consequently, it is vital for the policy analyst to understand the decision-maker. Furthermore, and equally important, this awareness must be embedded in a comprehension of the interplay of the policymaker's personality, the policy process, and the role the analyst adopts. This is not to suggest other factors do not play a role; rather, these components are central features essential to discerning the windows of opportunity. Numerous factors can and do influence policy behavior of decision-makers. However, these inferences are channeled through the individual policymaker.

This article explores the windows of opportunity. In the first section, it examines the type of roles the policy analyst may play. The next section defines two types of decision-makers—the pragmatist and the crusader. A discussion of how the two types of policymakers perceive and comprehend the different stages in the policy process is addressed in the third section. The last section delineates the windows of opportunity for the policy analyst.

WHAT ROLES CAN THE POLICY ANALYST PERFORM?

Scholars have posited a variety of roles the policy analyst may embrace. Such roles have included Kingdon's (1984) policy entrepreneur, Meltsner's (1976) technician, Moore's (1983) framework of the advocate, technician, and policy broker, or Jenkins-

Smith's (1982) typology of the objective technician, issue advocate, and client's advocate. The latter two typologies are noteworthy because they enunciate the idea that there is more than one role the policy analyst can adopt. The ensuing discussion proposes a framework for understanding the various roles the policy analyst can perform. The roles, as shown in Table 18.1 are the policy expert, policy advocate and policy troubleshooter.

The policy expert role is one in which the analyst provides the policymaker with information and furnishes guidance. Such an expert may even generate options and outline the likely consequences and trade-offs of each option. The expert policy analyst wants to get down to the nitty-gritty of the problem. In other words, the expert tends to focus on the substance of the problem. Disagreement is highly valued and may be on means and ends. However, the policy expert is inclined to remain aloof from politics. Politics is someone else's business. The policy expert prefers an environment in which the policymaker is uncommitted and the problem is discernible. The more ambiguous and amorphous the problem, the more difficult it becomes to delineate the probable consequences of alternative courses of action as well as the potential trade-offs. The policy expert role can vary from encompassing a "technician," as Meltsner (1976) describes, to one of the "consulting critic" (Pal, 1985). The latter includes those who have been brought in to review the policy question undertaken by different policymakers. The technician, on the other hand, is not viewed in this light. Therefore, the technician, in one sense, is a minimalist position while the consulting critic is the maximalist position.

The policy advocate is a political actor with a goal or plan. Such an analyst seeks to map out and implement a strategy for gaining acceptance of his/her agenda. The advocate possesses an internal blueprint of how the world should be and seeks opportunities to shape policy in that direction. Thus, this type of policy analyst concentrates one's efforts on the ends not the means. Unlike the expert, the advocate has an intense desire to be an active participant in the political process. The advocate is task-oriented, thinking in terms of "let's do it." Gaining acceptance of one's policy choice includes mobilizing coalitions. Thus the advocate not only pushes his/her vision, but seeks to implement it. Information is tailored to fit one's position. The line between theory and ideology is blurred. The ideal environment consists of an uncommitted decision-maker or a like minded decision-maker. If the facts are not in one's favor, then a more ambiguous situation is preferred.

The policy troubleshooter, like the policy advocate, is an active player in the political process. However, the troubleshooter's goals are quite different. Instead of pushing a cause, the troubleshooter seeks to make the political process run smoothly for the decision-maker. Such an analyst focuses on the process aspects rather than the substance of problems. The troubleshooter sees oneself as an integral part of the decision-making group who is concerned with finding a reasonable compromise when intense conflict clouds an issue. This may entail providing psychological support and building consensus. For instance, Sorensen (1963, p. 61) refers to these advisors as individuals who see their role as one of a mediator and are pleased that they can ease policymakers' problems. Often the troubleshooter is a sounding board who helps evaluate the options. The ideal environment is a committed decision-maker or an uncommitted decision-maker who has finally chosen a direction. A second-best alternative that is implemented is better

TABLE 18.1
Roles of the Policy Analyst

	Expert	Advocate	Troubleshooter
Function	Provide information and guidance; generate options and consider consequences	Information and policy shaped by cause/ideology; implement now	Sounding board; evaluate rather than generate options; conciliator
View of self	Expert	Champion of a cause	Fixer
Disagreements	Highly valued	Only on means	Minimize conflict and disagreement
Program focus	Substance of problem	Substance of one's concern	Political process
Ideal environment	Uncommitted decision-maker with concrete problems	Uncommitted or like-minded decision-maker; unclear problem if facts not in one's favor	Committed decision-maker; a second-best alternative implemented is better than the best never implemented
Motto	"Let's get to the nitty gritty"	"Let's implement 'the' plan"	"Let's make the process run smoothly"

than the best alternative never implemented. The degree of ambiguity in the issue(s) of concern is irrelevant to this analyst. The policy troubleshooter is similar to Sabatier's (1987) policy broker. The relationship may develop into what Ripley (1985, pp. 208–217) calls a clinical relationship. It may also evolve more in the direction of a trusted "advisor" (see Goldhamer, 1978). In some ways, the troubleshooter may also act as the "client's advocate" in Jenkins-Smith's (1982) terms. However, the latter two may also be part of the policy advocate's role.

WHAT ARE THE PERSONALITY TYPES OF POLICYMAKERS?

Based on his extensive experimental research, Snyder (1987), a psychologist, has proposed that people tend to either possess a principled conception of themselves or a pragmatic conception of themselves (Snyder and Campbell, 1982). This distinction is equally important in how a person approaches situations. As Snyder (1987, p. 202) observes, the pragmatic individual often approaches a situation by asking, "Who does this situation want me to be and how can I be that person?" On the other hand, the principled person asks, "Who am I and how can I be me in this situation?" Similarly, Hermann (1984, 1989) and Stoessinger (1979) have observed two broad differences in political leaders. On one hand, some leaders are less sensitive to the context (i.e., a crusader in Stoessinger's terms), whereas others tend to be more sensitive to the context (i.e., a pragmatist in Stoessinger's terms). The growing consensus in the literature suggests that some people (such as Ronald Reagan, Newt Gingrich, Margaret Thatcher, Libya's

Muammar al Qadhafi, and the Ayatollah Mohammed Ali Khamanei of Iran) are guided by their traits, attitudes, schemas, and dispositions while others (such as George Bush, Bob Dole, and U.S. President Bill Clinton, Jordan's [late] King Hussein, and President Hashemi Rafsanjani of Iran) are more attuned to cues (Hermann, 1984, 1989; D'Amato, 1967; Ring and Wallston, 1968; Snyder, 1987; Stoessinger, 1979; Snare, 1992a).[1] Such a conceptualization to explicate personality differences of policymakers seems appropriate not only because of the experimental findings but also because researchers in different fields are drawing similar conclusions.[2]

Pragmatist: Pragmatists consider themselves as flexible and adaptive, and therefore becomes the facilitator or catalyst to make things work. Such decision-makers use external cues about the problem and/or what others think to form their views. Hence, it is important to know something about others' opinions (important constituents or power-holders) and incoming information since pragmatists look to the environment to guide their behavior. Additionally, if the pragmatist has a position on an issue, then contextual information is sought about timing and constituent opinion (Hermann and Preston, 1994).

In their relationships with others, pragmatists evaluate others in terms of their suitability for specific activities. Such decision-makers choose those who help them play the roles preferred at the time. Pragmatists have no problem having relationships with others based on what is appropriate for that situation. For instance, Hermann and Preston (1994) have noted that Bush organized his advising system differently depending on whether the situation was perceived as threatening or nonthreatening. However, Clinton's advisory style depended upon his degree of expertise in the area.

The pragmatist does not regard what one does and what one believes as necessarily equivalent (Snyder, 1987, p. 40). Beliefs and attitudes can vary from one context to the next and compromise is considered a positive attribute by such a policymaker. However, in politics this may not always be beneficial. For instance, Clinton was known as one who "can be rolled" (Drew, 1994). With Bush, the "read my lips, no new taxes" statement came back to haunt him in the election.

Crusader: The crusader regards what one does and what one believes as equivalent (Snyder, 1987, p. 40). The crusader's social world is constructed in a homogeneous manner so there is a propensity not to differentiate or segment the world (Snyder and Campbell, 1982, p. 199). Such a policymaker is a theory-driven, top-down information processor who is less willing to deal with discordant information.

In relationships with others, crusaders evaluate others on the basis of their similarity to themselves and the affection they inspire; in other words, a friend is someone who likes you and whom you like (Snyder, 1987). Ergo, crusaders tend to surround themselves with those of similar ideological bent and /or those who will help them implement their vision. Hermann and Preston (1994) also suggest that the advisory system built by the crusader tends to be fairly stable over topics, time, and situations.

WHAT IS THE ROLE OF THE POLICYMAKER'S PERSONALITY IN THE POLICY PROCESS?

It should be of no surprise that crusaders and pragmatists vary their interpretation, focus, and even their ultimate purpose of the policy process. That is, policymakers have different conceptualizations of the policy process. As

Greenstein (1994, p. 67) has recently pointed out in his historical reconstruction of an early 1961 Eisenhower–Kennedy meeting (along with some close associates of each), there was quite a diversity of perception with regard to that one specific episode.[3] The subsequent discussion elucidates how the crusader and the pragmatist structure the four policy stages—agenda-setting, formulation of alternatives, accomplishing tasks, and evaluation and decision about future policy.[4]

Agenda-setting: The agenda-setting stage is the process by which the policymaker decides what one is going to do (Kotter and Lawrence, 1974, p. 49). As shown in Table 18.2, crusaders create their agendas by "inside initiative."[5] Such policymakers believe they know what the agenda should be and are willing to risk rebuff. These principled persons go about "pulling" people along. Crusaders are advocates and entrepreneurs, a driving force behind ideas—their own ideas. For instance, Howard Baker, Reagan's Chief of Staff, disclosed that he soon learned some of Reagan's positions were simply not open for discussion (Heineman, Bluhm, Peterson, and Kearny, 1990, p. 61).

Pragmatists create their agendas by a "mobilization initiative." These decision-makers seek cues in the environment in order to establish their agendas.[6] Once pragmatists find an agenda, they prod people along. In other words, others define the agenda and pragmatists push the ball down the desired path. Pragmatists want to be catalysts that make the ball ultimately move. Without a definitive position, such decision-makers may be viewed as seldom taking a stand, as was the case with Carter (Bennis and Nanus, 1985, pp. 36–37).

Table 18.2 outlines two subdivisions of the agenda-setting stage—problem recognition and problem definition. Problem recognition refers to the process of fixing attention to one problem rather than another (Kingdon, 1984, p. 121). Although both the crusader and the pragmatist are likely to recognize disasters, crisis, or the like, the crusader often recognizes problems via internal cues (i.e., one's beliefs) whereas the pragmatist often recognizes problems via external cues or by monitoring what Kingdon (1984) calls the "political stream" (i.e., national mood, political forces, and public opinion).

During the phase of problem recognition, a comparison is made between how things ought to be and how things actually are (Billings, 1989). Billings asserts that research suggests if there is a discrepancy between them, then one must change either one's behavior or change how one views the problem. Since crusaders are unlikely to change their views if incongruity exists, this type of policymaker will be prone to view the situation or issue as a problem to be considered. On the other hand, pragmatists tend to focus on how things are. If there is a lack of consensus or if this type of decision-maker tends to be more information-focused rather than people-focused, then it may be regarded as an issue not to be dealt with. For instance, in 1991 and early 1992, George Bush contended there was no recession. The data led him to believe this was the case even though many voters did not have this perception.

The definition of the problem, the second subdivision under the agenda-setting stage, refers to how the problem is represented or described. As Caplan and Nelson (1973) have noted, problem definition exerts a major influence on problem solution. In one sense, one could assert it has a more lasting effect with regard to the crusader.[7]

For crusaders, the germane question is: Does the problem match one's view or schema? If it does, and there exists a discrepancy between what ought to be and

TABLE 18.2
Flow of Policy Stages and Types of Policymakers

	Stages	Crusader	Pragmatist
I.	Agenda-setting Problem recognition Definition of the problem	Inside initiative* Internal cues Self	Mobilization initiative* External cues Others
II.	Formulation of alternatives Information collection Decision	Focus on means Inductive analysis of means Substance-oriented	Focus on ends* Analyze problem to be solved Process-oriented
III.	Accomplishing the task	Seeks compliance*	Wants to know what's happening
IV.	Evaluation and decision about future policy Bias Purpose	Beliefs are supreme Are goals accomplished? Accountability and ability to proclaim success	Constituents and/or information are supreme Is everyone happy? Influence constituents; do goals need to be redefined?

*Denotes extreme focus by the policymaker.

what is, then the government must take action, which may entail eliminating present government action. Action must be taken because not only does a discrepancy exist, but a match between the problem and one's views also exists. This confluence of conditions results in the problem being defined in terms of his/her beliefs. The ramifications of such definition are far-reaching. At that point, crusaders know what their goals are, that the goals are hierarchical, the ends are known or seem to be known, and the goals and ends are legitimate. In other words, by simply defining the problem within their domain, crusaders draw upon their experiences and beliefs to instantaneously arrive at legitimate goals and ends. Defining the problem is almost equivalent to the solution. It is the beginning of the end of the policy process. What is left is finding the best means and implementation. If learning or change is to occur for crusaders, this is the critical stage.

On the other hand, for pragmatists, definition of the problem is the end of the beginning. Such policymakers define the problem via others. What ought to be is based on others' views and this may change. Pragmatists tend to be aware of shifting opinions and coalitions among those they are leading within their regime (Hermann, Hermann, and Hagan, 1987, p. 325). Consequently, the pragmatist has a propensity to be aware of two facets: the degree to which there is a fit between the facts and the views of others, and the degree to which there exists generally accepted definitions of the problem or generally accepted recognition that a problem exists (i.e. "we know there is a problem, we just do not know how to define it").[8] If either of these two conditions do not exist, pragmatists will wait until the appropriate time. A confounding aspect in all this depends also on whether other priorities exist (Billings, 1989). This may place this problem on hold or even remove it from being an issue. Pragmatists may place the issue on the back burner for the time being. Additionally, at this stage, they are very likely to keep the problem and potential goals vague in order to obtain a broad base of support. This would seem to be the case with Clinton on the budget issue in late 1995. From 1992 until the elections of 1994, Clinton defined the budget issue as one of reducing the debt, which he believed reflected the national (or his constituency's) definition of the problem. However, Gingrich defined the debt issue as one of balancing the budget which is reflective of his beliefs.

Formulation of alternatives: The second stage in the policy process, formulation of alternatives, involves two subordinate stages—collection of information and making a decision. Crusaders (having defined the problem, and understanding the causes, consequences and solutions) approach this stage as would a public executive who wants to know the best method or means to accomplish the task. These policymakers are seeking to find the optimum way of implementing their goals. Ergo, others they bring into the decision-making process will help them collect information and decide on the means. Crusaders are very open and flexible when it comes to deciding on what means are to be used, as was the case with Stockman regarding spending reduction (Smith, 1988). However, crusaders tend to ignore political considerations and questioning of ends. Accordingly, crusaders will crave ammunition to defend their views. For instance, Reagan went to other advisors when he did not secure the advice he wanted to hear, as was the case during the Iranian initiative. Weinberger and Shultz were not supportive, so Reagan relied on National Security advisors (Meltsner, 1990, p. 100). Moreover, even when the crusader discusses ends, it is more of a ruse to lead everyone to believe all sides were considered.

The pragmatist, who focuses on ends, is a voracious collector of information. At times, this may be deleterious in the sense that the pragmatist becomes consumed in collecting information, as was the case with Carter. Information may consist of either or both wanting to ascertain if there exists a broad base of support or support is likely to be forthcoming and information about the problem itself. In this information stage, one may be influenced into redefining the problem. Thus, the distinction between problem definition and information collection at times is murky and blurred.

At the decision stage, the decision-maker becomes process-oriented. Pragmatists seek legitimization so as not to be victims of political fallout. Much bargaining, negotiating, and compromising usually occurs since multiple and conflicting alternatives, even about ends, are likely to exist. Pragmatists tend to play one of two roles: broker or coalition builder. As brokers, they are establishing deals and building a power base. In the role of coalition-builders, they are attempting to push the preferences they have embraced and are seeking support. If compromise breaks down, no decision is likely. As the amount of disagreement increases, pragmatists will make the goals even more vague, try to please everyone, and/or recede from some of their initial positions. For example, Bill Clinton continued to water down his health care plan as support evaporated. The pragmatist has a tendency to get caught up in the process; rather than focus on what one is trying to accomplish.[9]

Accomplishing tasks: Implementation, the third stage of the policy process, refers to undertaking the task of one's agenda. Crusaders are likely to play authoritarian roles in the sense that they are "seeking compliance." Consequently, this stage is important, if not critical, to crusaders. Hence, they will either be very skillful at pushing, prodding, or running over others to carry out the plan, and/or they will surround themselves with staff that is skilled. Crusaders tend to ignore constraints on trying to make a program work (see Kotter and Lawrence, 1974, p. 234). They will work around constraints and not give in to rebuff. However, crusaders may redefine means. Gingrich, with regard to the debt issue, came to the conclusion that closing down the government was not a useful means to balancing the budget as it was beginning to redefine the problem in the public's mind.[10]

Pragmatists want to know what's happening. They want feedback on what resources were actually committed and whose interests were affected. How much resistance or what constraints exist? Does anyone care anymore? If few care or numerous constraints appear, the pragmatists will focus on other issues. However, if the issue is relevant to them or their constituents, then pragmatists will redefine the options or even the problem depending on their constituency.

Pragmatists are not above employing coercive tactics.[11] In situations of consensus (i.e., similar outlook on the problem and not an extreme degree of uncertainty), pragmatists will be confronted with clearcut goals and methods. In this case, coercive means may be acceptable or even expected, especially if the socio-political norms allow such behavior. For example, President Hafez al Assad's repressive measures in Syria, where all members have a stake in maintaining the regime, are expected and supported swiftly, at least by the power-holders, which in this case are Assad's constituents.

Evaluation and decision about future policy: Crusaders interpret this stage from the standpoint that their beliefs or causes are paramount. Crusaders are very susceptible to the confirmation bias in the sense that they seek to substantiate that their goals have been achieved and were successful. Thus, they want to know if the goals were accomplished and how much better the world is because of this. If the problem still exists, then it must be the *means* and the process reverts back to the formulation stage again. Crusaders will accept that a program did not accomplish its goal, but will not accept that their beliefs are inappropriate. Their beliefs are a nearly impenetrable foundation. It would take overwhelmingly clear-cut evidence to undermine them. Of course, from the nation's standpoint, if the crusaders' goals/beliefs do not coincide with those of society, accomplishment of the task is not a positive outcome.

Nevertheless, the purpose of the evaluation stage is twofold with respect to crusaders.[12] One purpose relates to accountability. The crusader desires to control the individuals or organizations who are responsible for the program implementation. For instance, Newt Gingrich in January 1996 punished those who did not vote to reopen the federal government by dropping them from a list of those to visit in the fund-raising tour. Second, the crusader will want ammunition with which to proclaim victory or success. The latter may include impact studies that focus on economic well-being and/or quality of life, in Ripley's (1985, p. 176) terminology. The bottom line is, the lives of society in general and individually are improved in some way.

On the other hand, pragmatists take a different slice when it comes to the evaluation stage. Their constituents and/or information are supreme. Thus, these policymakers are interested in finding out if everyone is happy. Are the power-holders and/or the public disgruntled? The purpose of this stage is also twofold in relation to the pragmatist. One purpose is to ascertain if the goals need to be redefined. This may be because new information is now available or one's constituents have changed their positions. On one hand, this can be very positive. In essence, this is what Pressman and Wildavsky (1984, pp. 255–256) call learning evaluation—striving to unearth faulty assumptions and policy designs. This may occur. However, the flip side can also eventuate. Pragmatists' external focus on others and information may lead to a different outcome. Instead of learning, they may find that by that their constituents are focusing on a new problem, which is considered more pressing. Consequently, the original problem falls by the wayside. Constituents must continue to press the original problem or at least consider it important, otherwise it may be forgotten. It is also possible for pragmatists to get bogged down in information, never quite obtaining enough information to move onward with regard to this problem.[13]

The second purpose of the evaluation stage may be to influence the external political environment. This is an effort to sway the responses of outsiders. Similar to the first purpose, attitudinal impact studies, as Ripley (1985) defines them, are considered important by pragmatists. Such evaluation studies may discern how policies and programs affect the attitudes of constituents or powerholders in the regime.[14] Pragmatists, unlike crusaders (who are more task-oriented), tend to view evaluation from an interpersonal standpoint.

WHERE ARE THE WINDOWS OF OPPORTUNITY AND TO WHAT DEGREE ARE THEY OPEN?

Initially, a policy analyst might prefer a wide-open window of opportunity—in other words, a policymaker who is willing to listen to anyone. However, as previously implied, this allows many actors to potentially have an impact. Thus, a wide-open door lets many into the ballpark, but few may get to play. Consequently, those windows that are open only ever so slightly may be the ones with huge payoffs.

The following discussion proposes a number of windows of opportunity that are available depending upon the type of policymaker and the role the policy analyst plays. The first part centers on general observations relevant to all policy analysts, while the second concentrates on observations for each of the three types of policy analysts.

General observations: There are two general revelations for the policy analyst are evident from this essay that are relevant to understanding the windows of opportunity: When does the crusader learn and when does the pragmatist learn? Does persuasion and manipulation work equally well for both types?

Learning and change occur in the crusader and the pragmatist in disparate ways and at different stages of the policy process. This has important ramifications for the policy analyst. It is at the agenda-setting stage where learning and change are likely to occur in crusaders. One open window occurs before crusaders define the problem. However, if they interpret the problem in an old classification scheme, then change will be very difficult. It would take overwhelming evidence for that to happen and this does not occur often in the policy arena. Change is likely to occur when the gap between image and information is sizable, unambiguous, memorable, and stable (Fiske and Taylor, 1984, p. 178). This would be exemplified by Reagan's change of policy toward Marcos as the public, Congress, and presidential advisors ultimately clashed with his view (see Jentleson, 1990).[15]

If the crusader has already defined the problem, two avenues may prove fruitful.

One avenue involves the creation of new categories. This increased differentiation would allow belief change along a new dimension while still allowing the crusader to continue to oppose the object/issue based on the old dimension (Schlegel and DiTecco, 1982, p. 46). In other words, "subtyping" occurs, as was the case with Reagan in regard to Gorbachev. Another avenue that can be pursued is forceful disagreement by a valued person, which may ultimately involve exiting or quitting. Snyder and DeBono (1985, p. 590) assert that a credible source may have an impact. However, this probably will only be effective if one has an extremely close relationship with the policymaker that has developed over years and/or if it is someone of equal or greater standing. This tactic can not be employed very often otherwise it will be ineffective. A valued subordinate, who has been loyal for a considerable period of time, may also have an impact. For instance, Jalloud, Qadhafi's No. 2 man, left Libya in protest of Qadhafi's aggressive foreign policies (see "Arabia," 1987, p. 23). Presumably, Qadhafi lured Jalloud back with the understanding that such activities would be lessened.

On the other hand, the evaluation stage is when learning and change seem to occur with pragmatists. It is at this stage that they *may* be inclined to learn about flawed designs and assumptions. As indicated earlier, this is not necessary but one of a few possible outcomes. It is imperative to keep the pragmatist focused. It is little wonder in the Clinton camp that there were placards declaring, "The economy, stupid." The policy analyst's major chore is to keep pragmatists from drifting off to some other issue because that other issue has now become important to their constituents. This is less likely to occur if the issue contains some personal relevance for the policymaker.

When the issue is of interest to the sensitive pragmatist policymaker, Hermann (1984) found a strong relationship between personality and behavior. Thus, it may be "ego involvement" (see Greenwald, 1980), a germane historical analogy, and/or sunk costs that may propel a leader to be more consistent. In the Gulf War, Bush had made up his mind to take certain action long before the formal decision was reached (Crabbe and Mulcahy, 1995, p. 254). The Munich analogy was the driving force behind his strong position and ultimate action.

This discussion implies that each type of policymaker learns only during one particular stage. While this is not the case, it is asserted that particular stages are where the most enduring learning and change tend to occur. However, a different kind of learning can occur for each type. For instance, crusaders may learn at the evaluation stage; however, the learning is limited to the means and not the ends. Crusaders may be willing to concur that the means were defective. As for pragmatists, learning may occur at agenda-setting and formulation of alternatives stages, during which they are open to new and creative ideas.[16] However, since the pragmatist may often be continually redefining the problem, the lasting impact may be negligible. Learning and change may be directly related to pragmatists' constituents' willingness to change and learn. Snyder (1987, p. 52) contends that pragmatists will exhibit such behavior if it is circumstantially appropriate, such as with social norms or values. If the policymaker believes or comes to believe that what one says needs to match one's behavior, then there is a greater tendency for this to occur. Clinton, for instance, has not folded with respect to Medicare and other entitlement issues during the budget debate with Congress in early 1996.

Another germane factor related to attitude-behavior consistency relates to the degree of ambiguity in the environment. If there exists a fairly unclouded, stable consensus on the part of the constituency on what to do, how to do it, or that something should be done, then expect pragmatists to pick up the ball and run with it. Embracing the general consensus, they will then attempt to have their behavior match. This would seem to be the case with Franklin Delano Roosevelt and many of his proposals during the depression (see McElvaine, 1984), in direct contrast to what he advocated during the 1920s.

A second observation important for all types of policy analysts relates to the type of influence tactics that are likely to be effective. Is persuasion or manipulation a more resourceful tactic? Manipulation tactics encompass framing the issue (Moaz, 1990). This may also include arranging meetings in which dissenters are not present. Persuasion tactics utilize others and/or information (i.e., data) to change preferences. In such cases, the use of others and/or information is a pivotal factor in showing the legitimacy of one's view.

Does the tactic matter? Absolutely. Persuasive tactics are more advantageous with the pragmatist while manipulative tactics prove more productive with the crusader. Framing the issue is the decisive component in how crusaders interpret the situation or issue. Crusaders seek to confirm existing beliefs or schema. Thus, the persuasion tactic in attempting to urge crusaders to change their views will be futile. For instance, David Stockman (1986), Office of Management and Budget director under Reagan, states that his persuasive tactics with Reagan on defense spending were fruitless. He recounts that Reagan and Weinberger shared a strong preference for increasing the defense budget where

Stockman was concerned with the national debt. Stockman was overconfident in numbers, believing the facts and figures would overwhelmingly demonstrate his position. In the end, Stockman lost out. His tactics were bound to be useless with Reagan, the crusader. For Stockman to even have a chance of influence, he should have attempted to frame the issue in a different way so as not to link it to defense spending.

It is the opposite with pragmatists, with whom persuasive tactics are more likely to be effective. For example, Garrison (1994) provides a detailed study of advisors' actions in U.S. President Jimmy Carter's administration during the discovery of the Soviet brigade in Cuba in the fall of 1979. She describes how Cyrus Vance and Zbigniew Brzezinski utilized various manipulative and persuasive tactics. The case study is interesting because it illustrates how important persuasive tactics can be.[17] Vance's employment of senior statesmen was especially valuable. Given that Carter is a pragmatist, the outcome is not surprising. While both Vance and Brzezinski tried to frame the issue in a different way, this manipulative tactic was fragile as the pragmatist tends to seek out some of the various ways the problem may be defined. At most, what may be important to the pragmatist is how the important constituents or power-holders frame the issue.

Observations about each type of policy analyst: This discussion can be examined on two levels. One can consider it from a descriptive standpoint or from a prescriptive view about the roles the policy analyst may perform. From a prescriptive standpoint, there has been a tendency by some to consider one role the best or most appropriate for the analyst to embrace. For instance, Jenkins-Smith (1982, p. 91) says that the most widely held and criticized style of analysis for the policy analyst is the objective technician. Recently, Lester (1993, p. 269) has asserted that, if policy analysts are to have significant impact on policy, then they must abandon the role of "neutral technician" and instead adopt the role of "issue advocate." Such a statement neglects the complicated relationship between the policy analyst, policymaker, and policy process, which has been described herein. There is no role for the policy analyst that fits all situations and types of policymakers. Furthermore, the role one plays provides a unique set of opportunities.

Policy expert: A policy analyst, especially one who is a "consulting critic," will prefer the pragmatist. Such a relationship between the critic and the pragmatist offers the opportunity to define the problem or possibly even ask if the right questions are being posed. Even the technician expert may have moments where such questions are considered as the line, which is sometimes blurred for pragmatists, between the agenda-setting and the formulation stages. Pragmatists value information that can help them to analyze the problem and/or build a coalition in the formulation stage. However, with pragmatists, the information provided may play second fiddle to what their constituents are seeking. In other words, policy experts often do not account for the political aspects.

During the implementation stage, pragmatists are concerned with "what's happening," according to Ripley (1985, p. 138). Such studies seek to extract a variety of factors that influence implementation. Pragmatists may call upon policy experts in the evaluation stage. As stated in the earlier discussion of pragmatists, they may be searching for ways to redefine goals. It is at these instances when policy analysts may engage pragmatists in learning and change. Of course, the earlier caveats apply. It is not necessarily the case that learning will result; rather, conditions are favorable for it to occur.

With crusaders, policy experts are unlikely to play a role in the agenda-setting stage. They will be called in after the problem is defined. Crusaders are not interested in delineating the trade-offs or explaining the consequences—they are interested in bolstering their views. For an example, Ripley (1985, p. 173) outlines Reagan policy on CETA. Ideology was superior to reports. For an expert to have an impact on the problem definition, access and proximity to the policymaker are essential. It may be, as Hedrick Smith (1988) illustrates with Stockman under Reagan, one is retained on the basis of the knowledge one possesses with respect to a specific and important issue.

Crusaders will also value the expert in analyzing the means during the formulation stage. Ironically, the door is wide open in this area and the expert may have an immense and lasting impact on the process. Furthermore, crusaders may treasure experts during the evaluation stage to ascertain accountability. Crusaders are interested in information focusing on compliance.

Policy advocate: Such analysts may play a significant role in the policy process if their beliefs coincide with those of the crusaders—an infrequent occurrence. In this case, the advocate and the crusader will define the problem in the same way. The advocate is useful for mobilizing others and building coalitions, as well as proclaiming success of the project in the evaluation stage of the process. This advocate may find a home in such an environment. However, such an analyst will not agree with the crusader on every issue. Consequently, at some point the advocate is faced with the question of exiting or choosing to be loyal. To some extent, it will depend upon the type of advocate one considers oneself. For instance, the minority influence literature says that if one is perceived as acting out of principle, being consistent, advocating a position at some personal cost, and exhibiting a sense of reasonableness, then one may have an impact (see Gaenslen, 1992, pp. 186–187). Added to this, another condition must be present with the crusader: The analyst must be loyal for one to have credibility (Calvert, 1985).

On the other hand, advocates with dissimilar beliefs are unlikely to be part of the policy process, since crusaders will not choose such individuals. If they were initially included in the process, these advocates would soon be frozen out (e.g., Thatcher's modus operandi).

Pragmatists pose a different challenge for advocates. Advocates may find themselves initially expending much of their energies during the agenda-setting phase—hoping to frame the issue their way, especially if the pragmatists are uncommitted. However, pragmatists will seek out different definitions and the competition will be fierce. Advocates' persuasive skills may be important if they are to have an influence (see earlier discussion about Carter). Advocates hope either for clear-cut information data that supports their case or for a problem that is ambiguous.

Advocates may not be part of the formulation and implementation stages, during which pragmatists may redefine the problem or compromise on both ends and means. Nonetheless, advocates may resurface again in the evaluation stage, when pragmatists are interested in influencing their constituents.

Troubleshooter: The troubleshooter has little interest in the agenda-setting stage of the policy process, and therefore will have no ideological conflict with the crusader. Concomitantly, crusaders are seeking those who will implement their vision and troubleshooters who can make the process run smoothly. However, the troubleshooters have two major stumbling blocks in dealing with crusaders. Crusaders are substance-oriented, while troubleshooters are process-oriented. Crusaders are inflexible when it comes to their cause; troubleshooters see the benefits in compromise and the desirability of a second- or third-best alternative being carried out rather than the best alternative never being implemented. Even with such differences, the crusader may offer the troubleshooter the opportunity to be part of the inner circle as long as loyalty is demonstrated. If this arises, crusaders tend to rely on the same group of individuals over a variety of situations. Thus, one becomes a valued player with respect to the process and an active, consistent participant.

Pragmatists offer troubleshooters the opportunity to build consensus and reach compromises among conflicting parties. The pragmatists' emphasis on process is in keeping with the desires of troubleshooters. While these aspects provide troubleshooters with a more challenging environment than that of crusaders, there are two major liabilities in working with pragmatists. At times, pragmatists will be perceived as gadflies, overly influenced by constituents or new information. More importantly, pragmatists have a tendency to change their advisors and analysts according to the appropriateness of the context. Thus, it may be much more difficult to be part of that inner circle or have any sense that one is a vital-part of the process spanning a number of issues. One's time with the pragmatist may be very limited, as was the case with David Gergen in the Clinton administration.

It is easy to see why the three types of analysts sometimes feel disillusioned, frustrated, or snubbed. Experts can easily become disillusioned with crusaders who have defined the problem in the wrong way or with pragmatists who apparently define the problem one way only to change their minds the next day. Advocates can easily become frustrated and will eventually have to make the choice of exiting or choosing to be loyal to the crusader; they will see such the pragmatist as being too wishy-washy and indecisive. Troubleshooters may feel neglected and excluded from the process (or its relevant parts), especially by the pragmatist who will call upon a variety of people at different stages of the process. It is possible for troubleshooters to find an ideal situation with crusaders if they are part of the inner circle; otherwise, they are used for implementation and forgotten until the next relevant issue.

With each of the policy analysts, there is one stage in the policy process that is secondary. With respect to the expert it is the implementation stage, while it is the formulation stage for the advocate. For the troubleshooter, the agenda-setting stage has secondary importance. Thus, each type expects to play a different role as well as perceives the various stages in a distinctive manner.[18]

CONCLUSION

Further research could delve into a number of areas. It would be useful to delineate subsets of the two types of policymakers (crusaders and pragmatists). This would be especially valuable for pragmatists, since there is a difference between those who focus on others as opposed to those who concentrate on the issue and/or information. A second study could include other facets not included in this study, such as the number of players involved, the importance of the stage in the policymaker's term (i.e., honeymoon period), and issues such as access, proximity, and Koenig's (1960) idea

of "favorite advisor." A third study might seek to determine if the policy analyst plays more than one role. Hess' (1976, p. 23) discussion would imply that this is rare. Another study could apply this model to a specific case.

I am not advocating that policy analysts tailor their research or behavior to always fit the policymaker. I am advocating understanding when the policy research and analysts are likely to have an impact. Then policy analysts can ask themselves if they want to (or should) influence a particular situation. This essay has attempted to shed light on the idea that the interaction between the policy analyst, policymaker, and policy process is quite complex. Until now, this area has been overlooked; however, it merits attention.

ACKNOWLEDGMENTS

I would like to thank Margaret Hermann, Randall Ripley, Marcia Whicker, and three anonymous reviewers for their useful comments, as well as Karen Andrews for her editorial feedback. Nevertheless, all errors rest with the author. An earlier version of this paper was presented at the 1994 annual meeting of the Southern Political Science Association in Atlanta, Georgia.

FOOTNOTES

1. Actually, there is probably a continuum with policymakers differing in their degree of being a pragmatist or crusader. See Hermann, Hermann, and Hagan (1987, pp. 335–336) for further discussion. Even though this paper posits a variety of typologies and attempts to arrange things neatly, reality is often unkind to typologies. Barber (1965, p. 261) refers to the temptation to fit all reality into one of the boxes as the "intellectual seduction of typologies." That is, the effort of this paper is not to deify typologies,

but to spur the analysis of the policy process and policymakers.

2. Hermann and Preston (1994, p. 85) call attention to a similar distinction in the group dynamic literature and organizational literature

3. The "crusader" and "pragmatist" labels have nothing to do with the content of one's beliefs; rather, they relate to how one interacts with the world (i.e., what is important and how information is stored, interpreted, and utilized). The crusader is a top-down information processor, whereas the pragmatist is a bottom-up processor. This has significant implications on the beliefs embraced, how others are viewed, and the policy process itself.

4. The four policy stages, or waves of activity, may occur in sequence or as successive iterations and reiterations.

5. The terms "inside initiative" and "mobilization initiative" are taken from Cobb, Ross, and Ross (1976, pp. 126–127) in their reference to models of agenda-building. This author has changed the usage of these terms to reflect the crusader and the pragmatist in the agenda-setting stage.

6. I am making a subtle distinction between attentiveness to information and responsiveness. The pragmatist monitors the environment fervently but this does not automatically equate with responsiveness.

7. Of course, the crusader and the pragmatist sometimes define the situation in the same way. For instance, the Japanese attack on Pearl Harbor sparked a national consensus to go to war. Pragmatists, following public as well as their constituent consensus, would follow along. War-minded crusaders may have been advocating this action for some time. Dissenting views might come from extremely peace-oriented crusaders, pragmatists with strong peace positions, or pragmatists whose base of support advocates peace.

8. It is important to recognize that pragmatists' understanding of the views of others is likely to come from policy analysts and/or advisors. Thus, at times, the pragmatists' embraced position may not reflect the constituency's position. For instance, Bill Clinton was surprised by inimical opposition from members of Congress and the public to his proposal to lift the ban on gays in the military. Clinton saw it as an issue of discrimination, whereas others saw it as an issue of morality or military readiness.

9. Since all policymakers delegate at times, once the problem is defined the decision-maker authorizes someone to act. With respect to crusaders, the delegate is likely to be someone who embraces their vision. Pragmatists will select someone who is "socially attractive" (Snyder, 1987), depending on what the pragmatists consider to be socially attractive. For President Bush this meant loyalty, while for John F. Kennedy or Bill Clinton it related to experts.

10. The willingness of a crusader to modify means relates to both circumstantial and personality factors. Some crusaders are more adept at monitoring the situation (high conceptual complexity). Qadhafi of Libya falls into this category (Snare, 1992b). Saddam Hussein's behavior, as is evident by his actions during the Gulf War, would suggest he is less so.

11. Hermann and Kegley (1995) have asserted the type of regime impacts such behavior.

12. The following discussion utilizes the insights of Pressman and Wildavsky (1984), Goldenberg (1983), and Ripley (1985, p. 176). These authors outline a variety of schemes with regard to the purposes of program evaluation, types of evaluations, and major types of impact of programs respectively. However, I have utilized their distinctions but have suggested that different types of decision-makers focus on different purposes, types of evaluation, and types of impact in the evaluation stage.

13. Pragmatists with a position will not likely be deterred, as was the case with President Kennedy after the Bay of Pigs fiasco. Kennedy just changed the means.

14. One could also speculate that decision-making process studies would also be considered useful by the pragmatist. See Ripley (1985) for an explanation of such impact studies.

15. Additionally, expertise plays a role in all this. Experts are less willing than novices to shift beliefs, schema, or attitudes as they have more invested (Fiske and Taylor, 1984, p. 174). This is why, as Larson (1994, p. 28) suggests, hard-liners in the State Department and National Security Council were less convinced than was Reagan by evidence the USSR had changed under Gorbachev.

16. "Snyder and De Bono's (1985, p. 596) research suggests personal or social attractiveness of a source may have an impact on the pragmatist's attitudes. Such sources may set the agenda, define the problem, and formulate the alternatives as was the case with the CIA in the Bay of Pigs fiasco.

17. "Garrison (1994) may not agree with my interpretation of her study.

18. "This paper also has implications for understanding the utilization of social science research by policymakers. Policy researchers have lamented because policymakers have made little use of policy research. Weiss (1990) relates the point that policy researchers have been repeatedly lectured to make themselves "user friendly" (i.e., research addresses the question, involve them in the research process, write short summaries, talk to them, and so forth) to decision-makers. This advice has failed. It is evident from this paper why such a strategy did not work. Others have recommended that the users must become better consumers of knowledge by being more open to research. (See Lester's 1993 discussion of this matter.) Again, this seems to overlook the critical components of what is actually happening in the process.

REFERENCES

Arabia. (1987, May). *The Islamic World Review*, p. 23.

Barber, J. (1965). *The lawmakers*. New Haven, CT: Yale University Press.

Bennis, W. and Nanus, B. (1985). *Leaders: The strategies for taking charge*. New York: Harper and Row.

Billings, R. S. (1989, November). Notes on a chapter for *The Factors Shaping the Decision to Change Course in Foreign Policy*. Paper presented at Mershon Center Conference, Columbus, OH.

Bozeman, B. (1986). The credibility of policy analysis: Between method and use. *Policy Studies Journal, 14*, 519–539.

Calvert, R. (1985). The value of biased information: A rational choice model of political advice. *Journal of Politics, 47*(2), 530–555.

Caplan, N. and Nelson, S. (1973). On being useful: The nature and consequences of psychological research on social problems. *American Psychologist, 28*, 199–211.

Cobb, R., Ross, J., and Ross, M. (1976). Agenda building as a comparative political process. *American Political Science Review, 70*, 126–138.

Crabbe, C. and Mulcahy, K. (1995). George Bush's management style and Operation Desert Storm. *Presidential Studies Quarterly, 25*(2), 251–265.

D'Amato, A. (1967). Psychological constructs in foreign policy behavior. *Journal of Conflict Resolution, 11*, 294–311.

Drew, E. (1994). *On the edge: The Clinton presidency*. New York: Simon and Schuster.

Fiske, S. T. and Taylor, S. (1984). *Social cognition*. Reading, MA: Addison-Wesley Publishing Company.

Gaenslen, F. (1992). Decision-making in groups. In E. Singer and V. Hudson (Eds.), *Political psychology and foreign policy* (pp. 219–245). Boulder, CO: Westview Press.

Garrison, J. A. (1994, September). *Disunity between all the president's men: Political games among presidential foreign policy advisers*. Paper presented at the meeting of the American Political Science Association, New York, NY.

Goldenberg, E. (1983). The three faces of evaluation. *Journal of Policy Analysis and Management, 2*(4), 515–525.

Goldhamer, H. (1978). *The adviser.* New York: Elsevier.

Greenstein, F. (1994). Taking account of individuals in international political psychology: Eisenhower, Kennedy, and Indochina. *Political Psychology, 15*(1), 61–74.

Greenwald, A. (1980). The totalitarian ego: Fabrication and revision of personal history. *American Psychologist, 35*(7), 603–618.

Heineman, R., Bluhm, T., Peterson, E., and Kearny, A. (1990). *The world of the policy analyst: Rationality, values and politics*. Chatham, NJ: Chatham House.

Hermann, M. G. (1984). A study of 53 heads of government. In D. Sylvan and S. Chan (Eds.), *Foreign policy decision-making* (pp. 53–80). New York: Harper and Row.

Hermann, M. G. (1989, May). *Leaders and foreign policy decision-making*. Paper presented at the Comparative Foreign Policy Workshop, University of Stockholm, Sweden.

Hermann, M., Hermann, C., and Hagan, J. (1987). How decision units shape foreign policy behavior. In C. Hermann, C. Kegley, and J. Rosenau (Eds.), *New directions in the study of foreign policy* (pp. 307–333). Boston, MA: Allen and Unwin.

Hermann, M. G. and Kegley, C. (1995). Rethinking democracy and international peace: Perspectives from political psychology. *International Studies Quarterly, 39*, 511–533.

Hermann, M. G. and Preston, T. (1994). Presidents, advisers, and foreign policy: The effect of leadership style on executive arrangements. *Political Psychology, 15*(1), 75–96.

Hess, S. (1976). *Organizing the presidency.* Washington, DC: The Brookings Institution.

Jenkins-Smith, H. C. (1982). Professional roles for policy analyst: A critical assessment. *Journal of Policy Analysis and Management, 2*(1), 88–100.

Jentleson, B. W. (1990). Discrepant responses to falling dictators: Presidential belief systems and the mediating effects of the senior advisory process. *Political Psychology, 11*(2), 353–384.

Jones, C. (1984). *An introduction to the study of public policy.* Monterey CA: Brooks/Cole.

Kingdon, J. (1984). *Agendas, alternatives, and public policies.* Boston, MA: Little, Brown, & Company.

Koenig, L. (1960). *The invisible presidency.* New York: Rinehart.

Kotter, J. and Lawrence, P. (1974). *Mayors in action.* New York: Wiley.

Larson, D. W. (1994). The role of belief systems and schemas in foreign policy decision-making. *Political Psychology, 15*(1), 17–33.

Lester, J. (1993). The utilization of policy analysis by state agency officials. *Knowledge, 14*(3), 267–290.

McElvaine, R. S. (1984). *The great depression.* New York: Times Books.

Meltsner, A. J. (1976). *Policy analyst in the bureaucracy.* Berkeley, CA: University of California Press.

Meltsner, A. J. (1990). *Rule for rulers.* Philadelphia, PA: Temple University Press.

Moaz, Z. (1990). Framing national interest: The manipulation of foreign policy decisions in group settings. *World Politics, 43,* 77–110.

Moore, M. H. (1983). Social science and policy analysis: Some fundamental differences. In D. Callahan and B. Jennings (Eds.), *Ethics, the social sciences and policy analysis* (pp. 271–291). New York: Plenum Press.

Pal, L. A. (1985). Consulting critics: A new role for academic policy analysts. *Policy Sciences, 18,* 357–369.

Pressman, J. and Wildavsky, A. (1984). *Implementation.* Berkeley, CA: University of California Press.

Ring, K. and Wallston, K. (1968). A test to measure performance styles in interpersonal relations. *Psychological Reports, 22,* 147–154.

Ripley, R. (1985). *Policy analysis in political science.* Chicago, IL: Nelson-Hall.

Schlegel, R. and DiTecco, D. (1982). Attitude structure and the attitude-behavior relation. In M. Zanna, E. Higgins, and C. Hermann (Eds.), *Consistency in social behavior: Volume 2. The Ontario symposium* (pp. 17–49). Hillsdale, NJ: Erlbaum.

Smith, H. (1988). *The power game: How Washington works.* New York: Random House.

Snare, C. (1992a). *Personality and political postures: The case of the clerical rulers of Iran.* Unpublished doctoral dissertation, The Ohio State University, Columbus, OH.

Snare, C. (1992b). Applying personality theory to foreign policy behavior: Evaluating three methods of assessment. In E. Singer and V. Hudson (Eds.), *Political psychology and foreign policy* (pp. 103–134). Boulder, CO: Westview Press.

Snyder, M. (1987). *Public appearances private realities: The psychology of self-monitoring.* New York: W. H. Freeman.

Snyder, M. and Campbell, B. (1982). Self-monitoring: The self in action. In J. Suls (Ed.), *Psychological perspectives on the self* (pp. 185–207). Hillsdale, NJ: Lawrence Erlbaum.

Snyder, M. and DeBono, K. (1985). Appeals to image and claims about quality: Understanding the psychology of advertising. *Journal of Personality and Social Psychology, 49*(3), 586–597.

Sorensen, T. (1963). *Decision-making in the White House.* New York: Columbia University Press.

Stockman, D. (1986). *The triumph of politics: Why the Reagan revolution failed.* New York: Harper and Row.

Stoessinger, J. (1979). *Crusaders and pragmatists: Movers of modern American foreign policy.* New York: W. W. Norton.

Webber, D. (1987). Legislator's use of policy information. *American Behavioral Scientist, 30,* 612–631.

Weiss, C. (1990). The uneasy partnership endures: Social science and the government. In S. Brooks and A. Gagnon (Eds.), *Social scientists, policy, and the state* (pp. 97–111). New York: Praeger.

Zanna, M. and Olson, J. (1982). Individual differences in attitude relations. In M. Zanna, E. Higgins, and C. Hermann (Eds.), *Consistency in social behavior: Volume 2. The Ontario symposium* (pp. 75–103). Hillsdale, NJ: Erlbaum.

19.

Wolfgang Bielefeld, Richard K. Scotch, and G. S. Thielemann

NATIONAL MANDATES AND LOCAL NONPROFITS: SHAPING A LOCAL DELIVERY SYSTEM OF HIV/AIDS SERVICES

The HIV epidemic of the 1980s and 1990s has been the singular American public health crisis of recent decades. Over a million people have been infected with the HIV virus, and tens of thousands of them have died (Rushing, 1995). The stigma associated with the disease has slowed and complicated response to the epidemic, leading to the development of many new institutions specifically created to fight the disease. In many communities, new systems of nonprofit organizations have sprung up to serve people affected by the disease. The growing HIV epidemic, the local political economy and culture, and federal resources and mandates combined to create a distinctive service system in less than a decade.

This case study of the evolution of an HIV/AIDS service delivery system in Dallas, Texas focuses on the organizational and institutional consequences of the federal Ryan White Comprehensive AIDS Resources Emergency Act of 1990, which provided millions of dollars to local nonprofit agencies along with specific mandates governing their expenditures. Personal interviews were conducted in 1994 with individuals who were involved with the HIV/AIDS service system since the mid-1980s, most of whom still work for local service agencies. Archived materials and newspaper articles concerning AIDS services in Dallas supplemented the interviews.

To examine the service delivery system in detail, a structured survey dealing with organizational and interorganizational characteristics was administered in 1994 and early 1995 to representatives of 34 of the 36 organizations identified as currently providing HIV/AIDS services in Dallas. Of the 34 responding agencies, 2 were Dallas County government health providers, 23 were nonprofit agencies, and 9 were for-profit firms. This reflects today's complex human service delivery systems, which often are comprised of a mix of public, nonprofit, and for-profit providers (Salamon, 1992, pp. 57–89). When we examined the nongovernment providers, we found that there were a number of statistically significant differences between the nonprofit and for-profit organizations. Nonprofit organizations had significantly larger budgets, used significantly more government and private funds, and generated significantly less funds from fees for services (an average of only 4 percent of their total income). All of the nonprofit groups surveyed received some public funds, with 17 of the 23 receiving more than 70 percent of their revenue from government sources.

The for-profit organizations were quite different from the nonprofits. In particular, they generated an average of 51 percent of their income from fees, and half of them received no revenue from government sources. These findings indicate that federal funding and federal mandates are more important to nonprofit organizations. This article focuses on how federal funding impacts nonprofit organizations, excluding for-profit firms from its analysis.

THE HIV EPIDEMIC, NONPROFIT ORGANIZATIONS, AND PUBLIC POLICY

Local systems of nonprofit organizations have become increasingly complex, with different types of agencies playing diverse roles influenced by varying inter-organizational relationships. Such complex systems rarely evolve on their own; they typically are the product of external forces.

The current service delivery system for persons living with AIDS is a striking example. The HIV epidemic is a recent and dramatic occurrence that has challenged and at times overwhelmed existing local health and human service systems. By 1990 in Dallas, there had been 2,366 HIV cases diagnosed, leading to 2,096 deaths (Dallas County Health Department, 1994).

In the first decade of the epidemic, rapid increases in the number of infected people strained the capacity of health and human service agencies. The severity, variability, and uncertainty of medical conditions related to HIV/AIDS have made treatments expensive. In addition, many individuals infected with HIV were caught in the gap between private and public health insurance, placing financial responsibility for their treatment on local public hospitals and public health authorities. The average cost of AIDS care in 1988 was estimated at $60,000 per patient (Hellinger, 1988). Those with AIDS needed multiple medications, emotional counseling to cope with the illness and society's response to it, and

financial support for basic needs such as food and rent. Medical and subsistence needs were often complemented by psychosocial supports such as "buddy" services, psychological counseling, and peer support groups.

The stigma of HIV—which has been associated with homosexuality, promiscuous sexual behavior, and intravenous drug use—makes it difficult to marshal resources for fighting the disease using traditional public health strategies. Of the cases diagnosed in the 1980s nationwide, more than 70 percent were linked to gay sex, and another 8 percent were traced to a combination of gay sex and intravenous drug use. In Dallas, these numbers were even higher: The county health department linked 83 percent of the diagnosed cases to gay sex and 11 percent to a combination of gay sex and intravenous drug use (Dallas County Health Department, 1994). Those with AIDS often faced discrimination where they worked, making it difficult for them to support themselves and maintain private health insurance even when they were still healthy enough to work. It is difficult to assess the extent homophobia influenced public health decisions in the 1980s, but most independent studies confirm that it had an important effect (Kayal, 1991; Panem, 1988; Perrow and Guillén, 1990; Rushing, 1995; Shilts, 1987).

New voluntary systems of human service providers were created in many cities to respond to the HIV epidemic and to complement strained pubic health agencies. Frequently, these emerging systems had roots in new or existing gay community organizations (Perrow and Guillén, 1990). However, the cost of medical care for AIDS patients administered through public hospitals and clinics remained with local governments. As the caseload continued to grow rapidly through the late 1980s and the epidemic spread into new socioeconomic groups, local expenditures climbed into the billions of dollars at a time when local tax bases were shrinking, limiting expansion of the public service system. Local officials were compelled to seek assistance from the federal government.

The need for external support was particularly acute in Dallas, where local government had long neglected all but the most basic public health services. Throughout the history of the epidemic, virtually no local tax dollars have been used for AIDS prevention or treatment. Despite the rising number of cases, critics charged in a lawsuit that the public hospital, Parkland Memorial, was slow to provide AIDS-specific services, and for many years provided AIDS patients extremely limited access to medical services (Dallas Gay Alliance et al. v. Dallas County Hospital District et al., 1989).

A watershed for the development of AIDS services in Dallas and the nation occurred in 1990 with the passage of the Ryan White Comprehensive AIDS Resources Emergency Act (Public Law 101-381), a federal response to the AIDS emergency facing public hospitals in many of the nation's largest cities.

The act's goal was to keep people living with AIDS out of hospitals by funding community-based health-related services such as home health and outpatient care, and subsidizing the cost of basic needs such as medicine, food, and housing. As a package, these services would constitute a comprehensive service continuum coordinated through a system of case management. In keeping with the times, the act maintained a high level of local discretion, with grant administration left to local officials. In the case of Dallas, the responsible local official was the county judge elected to chair the Dallas County Commissioners Court, the legislative body for Dallas County.

THE IMPACT IN DALLAS OF THE RYAN WHITE CARE ACT

The availability of substantial federal funds had several important effects on the service system in Dallas. First, HIV/AIDS services in Dallas increased rapidly. Between 1990 and 1994, the number of agencies providing federally funded AIDS services rose from 13 to 28. Funding through the Ryan White CARE Act added nearly $2 million to service providers' budgets in the program's first year, 1991–92. Federal funding increased to more than $7 million by 1994–95.

Table 19.1 shows the characteristics of the nonprofit HIV/AIDS service providers in Dallas in 1994. The table shows that providers average 20 years old and have provided HIV/AIDS services for about six years. While most of them (78 percent) provide other services, about 53 percent of their personnel effort was directed toward HIV/AIDS services. In addition, they received an average of $350,260 to provide these services, virtually all of which was spent during the same fiscal year. Finally, they employ an average of about nine full-time equivalent people in their HIV/AIDS services programs and use an average of about 22 full-time-equivalent volunteers.

New financial resources enabled existing agencies to provide more services, including those outside the health care core and social support services deemed less essential, more expensive, or having a less direct impact. Our organizational survey documents this expansion. During the interviews, respondents were handed a list of services and asked which of six health care services (e.g., primary health care, dental, hospice), four economic assistance services (e.g., emergency assistance, food, housing), and eleven social services (e.g., "buddy," day care, substance abuse) they provided.

TABLE 19.1
Characteristics of Dallas' Nonprofit HIV/AIDS Service Providers

Provider Characteristic	Mean	Standard Deviation	Range
Age of organization (in years)	19.7	24.8	1 – 89
Years providing HIV/AIDS services	5.7	3.7	1 – 12
Percentage of personnel effort to HIV/AIDS	52.9	40.2	1 – 100
HIV/AIDS income (in thousands of dollars)	350.3	493.7	6.8 – 2,058.3
HIV/AIDS expenditures (in thousands of dollars)	334.6	500.6	0 – 1,918.6
Employees (full-time equivalent)	9.3	9.0	1 – 30
Volunteers (full-time equivalent)	21.7	65.6	0 – 298

The data showed that 48 percent of the surveyed organizations provided health services, 56 percent provided economic assistance services, and 78 percent provided social services. In addition, the amount of an agency's income from government sources, virtually all of which is provided directly or indirectly by the federal government under the Ryan White CARE Act, was found to be significantly correlated to providing more economic assistance and social services ($r = .60$ and .64, respectively; $p < .01$). However, the amount of government income was not significantly related to the number of health services provided.

Not only was there a supply-side stimulus to providing services, but the demography of the epidemic in Dallas was changing in the early 1990s as well. While the vast majority of cases were still gay white men, new cases were appearing among African-Americans and Hispanics, and among women and children. A more diverse group of people living with AIDS demanded more culturally diverse service providers.

The combination of federal mandates and local politics increased diversity within the service system. Federal requirements

mandated that services be expanded to serve all population groups affected by the epidemic, and required that those groups be represented on the local councils that set priorities and allocated federal funds. Increased diversity in HIV services and program governance was also encouraged by the flow of federal dollars through the Dallas County Commissioners Court. County oversight resulted in providers extending their services into the minority neighborhoods of Dallas. An outspoken African-American member of the Dallas County Commissioners Court effectively raised the issue of the lack of funding for agencies based in the African-American and Hispanic communities in Dallas. The result was a significant increase in the proportion of Ryan White CARE Act funding allocated to newer minority agencies, and a mandate that existing AIDS agencies expand their involvement beyond the gay Anglo community.

Six of the nonprofit agencies surveyed for this study have predominantly minority leadership and primarily serve minority neighborhoods. These agencies are newer to the delivery system; on average, they have provided AIDS services only half as long as other agencies. Three were founded after the passage of the Ryan White CARE Act. Minority agencies are also smaller. Their average HIV/AIDS program income was $126,300, compared with $434,200 for other agencies. They also were far more dependent on government funding, which was responsible on average for 92 percent of their income, compared with 65 percent for income at those agencies not categorized as minority. Consequently, they received very few private donations and no self-generated income. They appear to fill specific niches in the service system and provide fewer overall services. They averaged 3.3 services per agency, compared with 5.1 services for other agencies. Perhaps reflecting the difficulty in obtaining the greater resources required for health care delivery, minority agencies are less likely to provide health care services. Only 33 percent of them reported providing health care services, compared with 53 percent of the other agencies.

Federal mandates affected long-term AIDS service providers as well. These providers added new sites and expanded outreach efforts in minority neighborhoods. Survey respondents reported the percentages of clients in five age categories, five income categories, and five racial/ethnic categories (white, African-American, Hispanic, Asian, and Native American). A Herfindahl index of concentration (Shughart, 1990, pp. 68–70) was calculated for each of these demographic dimensions, measuring the degree to which the clients of an organization were dispersed among the dimension's categories. Higher scores indicate less diverse clienteles. Government funding was significantly negatively correlated with concentration in the racial categories ($r = -.72, p < .01$), indicating that agencies receiving more government funds were more likely to have racially diverse clients. No similar relationship was found linking government income with the concentrations of clients by age or income.

During the early years of Ryan White CARE Act funding, tensions rose as new agencies competed for funding, and also from cultural clashes between gay-oriented organizations and more traditional and often culturally conservative minority service providers. By the final year of the five-year funding cycle, accommodations and working relationships appear to have been reached among representatives of the various affected populations.

Federal requirements and a conservative Dallas County government, which operated as a fiscal intermediary, led to the development of an extensive system of grant management and fiscal accountability, and a highly elaborate and formal system of fund allocation. Even though local funds were not involved (except those supporting the county hospital and public health department), the Dallas County Commissioners Court kept a close eye on how federal funds were expended.

Prior to the Ryan White CARE Act, nonprofit agencies providing services to people living with AIDS acted fairly autonomously, although many participated in a centralized case management system established in 1986. Public health agencies and voluntary groups centered in the gay community independently made decisions about the content and administration of AIDS services in Dallas. After its passage, The Ryan White CARE Act imposed new controls over local HIV/AIDS services, along with directives by the federal Health Resources and Services Administration (HRSA), and substantive and administrative requirements imposed by Dallas County officials.

Pursuant to the Ryan White CARE Act, the Dallas County Commissioners Court

TABLE 19.2
Average Importance of External Actors and Their Influence on Organizational Functioning

External actors	Importance[a]	Average Percentage of Organizations Reporting Actor Influence[b] on		
		Goals	Structure	Personnel
General public	6.1	21%	4%	9%
Community leaders	6.1	30	13	13
Local media	4.7	9	4	0
Private funders	4.4	17	9	13
Local politicians	3.4	9	0	0
Government funders	9.0	70	39	26
Gov. regulators	7.3	17	44	48
Legislature	4.9	4	0	0
Professionals	3.7	0	9	30
Clients	4.3	30	13	13

External actors	Techniques	Services	Clients	Evaluation
General public	9%	13%	17%	13%
Community leaders	9	17	9	17
Local media	4	0	0	9
Private funders	4	17	13	26
Local politicians	0	9	0	4
Government funders	39	70	52	57
Gov. regulators	61	30	22	35
Legislature	13	0	4	9
Professionals	35	9	4	4
Clients	9	30	9	26

[a]Organizations were asked to rank those actors which impacted their HIV/AIDS services in terms of their overall importance (1=most important). Rankings were recoded so that higher numbers represented more importance (10=most important).

[b]Organizations were asked if actors had any influence over the organizations HIV/AIDS program(s) in terms of: the goals of the program, how it was organized to accomplish the program, the types of personnel used to run the program, the techniques or procedures used to deliver services, the types of services provided, the types of people served, the evaluation of the impacts of the program on clients.

appointed a governing body for AIDS programs called the Health Services Planning Council (HSPC). The Health Services Planning Council reflected local traditions of centralized administration and avoidance of controversy through strong fiscal control and a rejection of outspoken political advocacy. While membership in the Dallas Health Services Planning Council included many key figures from the long-time service providers who had constituted the earlier, voluntary AIDS Coordinating Committee, an appointed leadership with strong ties to Dallas' conservative political establishment and the local Republican party often dominated its deliberations.

Attendance at monthly coordination meetings became mandatory for representatives of funded agencies; paperwork and cash flow reports were channeled into a centralized, formal, and apparently efficient system. Survey results suggest that agencies employed additional administrative staff in response to demands for accountability. The amount of income that HIV/AIDS service providers received from the government was significantly, positively correlated with the number of administrative personnel ($r = .80$, $p < .01$). Agencies with more government funds also reported more staff engaged in fund-raising, government relations, and grant writing activities, although only fund-raising showed a statistically significant relationship.

Survey respondents were also asked to rank 10 types of external actors (including such groups as the general public, community leaders, the media, politicians, funding sources, and clients) in terms of their "overall importance" to their agency, with higher numbers indicating increased importance. Respondents were then asked if any of these external actors had any influence over seven specific aspects of their organization, including their choice of goals, strategies, personnel, service delivery techniques, types of services, types of clients, and method of service evaluation. Table 19.2 shows the average overall importance given to the external actor's and the percentages reporting each actors specific organizational impacts. The table clearly shows how important the Ryan White CARE Act funding is to these organizations. Governmental funding entities were far and away the most important actors overall, and were most often cited as having an impact on four of the seven aspects of organizational functioning (choice of goals, types of services offered, types of clients served, and method of service evaluation). For the remaining three areas of organizational functioning (organizational structure, agency personnel, and service techniques), government regulators were cited most often as an external influence. Indeed, government regulators were perceived as the second most important external actor overall.

Finally, in implementing the Ryan White CARE Act, the federal Health Resources and Services Administration also emphasized the importance of a "continuum of care" for people living with AIDS that would keep them out of the hospital as long as possible. Establishing and maintaining such a continuum has been a major focus of the Dallas Health Services Planning Council, which promoted several mechanisms to encourage close coordination of services among providers, including participation in centralized case management, mandatory attendance at coordination meetings for both agency administrators and direct service staff, and solicitation of collaborative proposals.

The impact of these mandates is strongly reflected in our survey responses. Respondents were asked with which HIV/AIDS service providers they cooperated on a regular basis and which they considered to be direct competitors for clients or funding. The data showed that, overall, cooperation was far more common for agencies than competition, with the mean number of others cooperated with (15.4) far exceeding the mean number of competitors (5.0). We also found a significant positive correlation between agency income from government sources and cooperation with others ($r = .75$, $p < .01$). Moreover, personal observations indicate that cooperation positively influences local fund allocation decisions.

ORGANIZATIONAL IMPACT OF FEDERAL MANDATES

Agencies providing services for people living with AIDS provide a unique opportunity to study a service system that was created virtually *de novo* in a relatively short span of time. The number of agencies serving people living with AIDS and the types of services they provided increased markedly in Dallas as the result of federal funds. Several of the new agencies were centered in the county's minority communities, and providers as a group increased their work with people of color. Far greater fiscal and program accountability was imposed on nonprofit service providers by county officials. Providers within the HIV/AIDS service system also achieved a high level of cooperation among themselves in response to federal mandates.

These findings reflect the success of the Ryan White Comprehensive AIDS Res-ources Emergency Act in expanding services and incorporating service providers into a coordinated and accountable system serving the entire affected community. In the case of AIDS services in Dallas, government intervention not only increased available resources; it also achieved intended results in terms of structure and a more effective service delivery system. A working partnership between federal funding entities, local government administrators, and nonprofit service providers has been accomplished in a relatively short time. We believe that additional research on the relationship between local nonprofit organizations and government programs will help to further identify the elements that foster such success.

ACKNOWLEDGMENT

The research for this article was supported in part by a grant from the Aspen Institute's Nonprofit Sector Research Fund.

REFERENCES

Dallas County Health Department. (1994). *Acquired immunodeficiency syndrome (AIDS) surveillance report – 12/22/94*. Dallas, TX: Author.

Dallas Gay Alliance, Inc. et al. v. Dallas County Hospital District, d/b/a Parkland Memorial Hospital et al. CA 3-88-1394-H (N.D. Tex. 1989; plaintiffs' statement of specific "live" issues).

Hellinger, F. J. (1988). National forecasts of the medical care costs of AIDS: 1988–1992. *Inquiry, 25*, 469–484.

Kayal, P. M. (1991). Gay AIDS voluntarism as political activity. *Nonprofit and Voluntary Sector Quarterly, 20*, 289–312.

Panem, S. (1988). *The AIDS bureaucracy*. Cambridge, MA: Harvard University Press.

Perrow, C. and Guillén, M. F. (1990). *The AIDS disaster: The failure of organizations in New York and the nation*. New Haven, CT: Yale University Press.

Rushing, W. A. (1995). *The AIDS epidemic: Social dimensions of an infectious disease*. Boulder, CO: Westview.

Salamon, L. M. (1992). *America's nonprofit sector: A primer*. Washington, DC: The Foundation Center.

Shilts, R. (1987). *And the band played on*. New York: Penguin Books.

Shughart, W. E. (1990). *The organization of industry*. Homewood, IL: BPI/Irwin.

20.

Katherine L. Armstrong

LAUNCHING A FAMILY-CENTERED, NEIGHBORHOOD-BASED HUMAN SERVICES SYSTEM: LESSONS FROM WORKING THE HALLWAYS AND STREET CORNERS

THE PROCESS OF ORGANIZATIONAL AND COMMUNITY CHANGE

Contra Costa County began its long journey toward the development of neighborhood-based, family-centered services when its Board of Supervisors and the Youth Services Board (YSB), a policy making body made up of the Directors of Social Service, Probation, Health, Community Services, and the County Executive, Superintendent County of Schools, Juvenile Court Judge and children's advocates, made a commitment to translating the county's successful Inter-Agency Family Preservation Program into system-wide change. The county's access with Family Preservation taught a number of valuable lessons. Through an inter-agency commitment to families it had prevented out-of-home placements, reduced foster care costs, and helped improve the family life of participants. The county now had tangible evidence that concentrating on the entire family, engaging families as active partners, and assisting families within the context of the community resulted in better functioning families and cost savings. Just as significant as these improvements, the county had learned that Social Services, Health Services, Probation, and Community Services could work together successfully when presented with a common

goal, a unified structure for delivering services, and a mandated reporting of results.

Much of the success of this undertaking can be attributed to the fact that both the Board of Supervisors and the Youth Services Board were committed to creating a human services system that was community-based, family-centered, comprehensive, and involved inter-agency collaboration. All involved were committed to improving the well-being of the county's children and their families and preventing the costly family crises which now absorbed most of the county's resources and attention.

A consultant was hired for a three-year period to assist the YSB realize this goal of strengthening families. During the next three-and-a-half years the consultant:

- drafted the vision statement and strategic plan, obtained feedback, made necessary improvements, and communicated the vision to every significant group in the county;
- staffed and directed the work of the YSB and its newly created interagency managerial planning body, the Service Integration Management Team (SIMT), in carrying out the day-to-day work of designing and implementing community-based service integration;
- completed the analysis needed to select the key neighborhoods for development;

337

- engaged and motivated neighborhood residents, leaders, and community agencies in the two communities selected for piloting the new system of services;
- participated in extensive negotiations with unions, agency staff, and community-based organizations;
- helped develop the programmatic and physical infrastructure for relocating inter-agency, integrated services into the neighborhoods;
- consulted on the development of a proposal to become an AB-1741 service integration pilot county, the state's fast track for state waivers; and
- assisted with training and staff development issues.

Developing a Vision and Strategic Plan

The YSB faced the daunting challenge of determining how to decentralize county-wide services into a neighborhood-based service delivery system while confined within a rigid web of state and Federal regulations and categorical funding. In addition, YSB members were preoccupied with making severe budget cuts. In this environment, it was important to carve out a change process that allowed for risk-taking, and gave staff time to learn from mistakes, but also imposed as little disruption as possible on the entire human service system.

The first step was to create a unified vision, agree on a set of operating principles and draft a strategic plan. This process took a year and entailed intensive communication and collaboration with staff at many levels within each of the County Departments of Social Services, Health, Probation, Community Services, and the Juvenile Court, the schools, community groups, and children's advocates.

YSB members soon agreed that the development of neighborhood-based, family-centered, integrated services should be targeted to those communities with the highest number of residents living in poverty, and to neighborhoods in which there lived a significant number of clients known to three or more departments or receiving at least four different services. Members decided to pilot this new approach in the identified high risk neighborhoods that also had community leaders receptive and willing to form partnerships with the county.

The process for targeting communities included a data match of the client files from Social Services, Health Services and Probation. Through a geographical mapping of the data match findings, the YSB identified nine neighborhoods where service utilization was greatest, where there lived a large number of families using four or more services of the departments of Social Services (Child Welfare and Income Maintenance) Health, and Probation. High on the list of the nine eligible communities were the county's unincorporated areas of North Richmond and Bay Point/West Pittsburgh. The population characteristics of these unincorporated areas reflected many high risk factors (for example, 50% of residents have not graduated from high school, 34% are unemployed, a high number of children are in kinship foster care, the immunization rate is lower than average, and the infant mortality and morbidity rates are higher than average).

Fortuitously, at the same time the Board of Supervisors and the YSB were completing the strategic plan and finishing up the analysis of the county's service utilization, both North Richmond and Bay Point community members were beginning to organize. Leaders from these communities had recently approached the Board of Supervisors demanding changes in the way all services (including police, transportation, and employment) were delivered to their residents. This new pressure on the board to dramatically change the way services were provided to these two neighborhoods influenced the YSB to choose North Richmond and Bay Point for its first two pilot service integration centers.

Learning About the Neighborhoods and Engaging Residents

One of the key operating principles guiding the service integration effort was a commitment to design the neighborhood services system to meet the needs of families and residents. This required an extensive needs assessment of the communities and establishing new opportunities to hear from clients and residents about what they needed and wanted. The vehicle chosen for this endeavor was to join with the local schools to apply for a California State Department Healthy Start planning grant. The Healthy Start Program, begun in 1991, provides funding to schools with a large percentage of students living in poverty to work partnership with parents, county, city and community based organizations to improve the health and educational performance of their students. With funding obtained via Healthy Start, both North Richmond and Bay Point conducted focus groups, interviews, and town meetings, and completed a resource mapping of the available services, programs, and strengths in the community. The Healthy Start planning process brought many people to the table for the first time and started the dialogue among parents, community-based organizations, schools, and county services about community needs.

During the next year, as the Healthy Start planning effort was under way, North Richmond residents successfully advocated for the creation of a local governance structure, the Municipal Advisory Council

(MAC), that reported directly to the Board of Supervisors. Community leaders now had a means to advocate for more access to and accountability from the Board about how county services were delivered in their neighborhood. The North Richmond MAC developed its own strategic plan, incorporating the results from the Healthy Start needs assessment as well as findings from their systematic review of county-delivered services in the community. The North Richmond MAC leadership worked closely with the consultant and county staff guiding the process of county service integration for the North Richmond community. With support from the Zellerbach Family Fund, the MAC was able to fund their own priority projects and hire local people to deliver the programs. In the Bay Point community, a MAC had been authorized during the previous year and a MAC council member was involved with the Healthy Start needs assessment planning process and service integration planning and implementation.

YSB's motivation to improve local access to services and the new grassroots pressure placed on the Board of Supervisors created the needed tension and catalyst to spark dialogue ensured that the system changes were responsive to clients and families who lived in the neighborhoods. The consultant helped establish a mutually supportive and interactive process that allowed community building efforts to proceed independently, but in relationship to the extensive, internal department-level planning required before any services could actually move from central offices to the neighborhood or shift from categorical services to a family-centered and holistic approach.

Negotiating with Staff

Preparing staff for work in the new neighborhood-based, family-centered, service integration teams had two stages. The first stage involved staff selection and training, including:

- deciding what programs and staff, in what combinations, would be located in the neighborhoods;
- developing new job descriptions and determining how staff would be supervised and managed;
- drafting a training curriculum;
- gaining union support; and
- recruiting and selecting staff.

The second stage began immediately after all staff members had been selected, trained and located in the neighborhood centers. This stage required a reassessment and modification of everything that had been decided and begun during the first stage. A range of unanticipated conflicts emerged when staff were transferred from categorical programs, with no history of working together, into new teams responsible for serving the same clients and community.

Language was a huge problem. Workers used similar words, but the same word often had completely different meanings to the social worker, the eligibility worker, the public health nurse, the probation officer and the substance abuse counselor. It took some time together before the team members realized that they were all using different definitions, and even longer to develop common language and definitions of "family-centered, community-based, comprehensive, inter-agency case management," "community involvement," and "partnerships."

Personnel had difficulty respecting each other's work. Tension ran high between disciplines as they struggled with each other in forming a common approach to clients and their needs. Categorical rules and regulations continued to obstruct team relations and cause daily frustration. Departments found it challenging to cope with members of their own staff who were now functioning very differently from their mainstream workers. Turf issues among service providers remained at the heart of every discussion.

Contra Costa County staff struggled with the notion of self-managed teams because the traditional top-down supervision and control did not fit the demand for flexibility in a decentralized service system. However, the concept of a self-managed team was very troublesome for practically everyone—unions, managers, and staff—and continues to evolve as a new form of practice with more experience and training. The county engaged in extensive union negotiation for at least six months before the teams were recruited and selected, and union negotiations continue to be a key aspect of the implementation process. Union members participate in the SIMT and are among the staff operating in the two neighborhood centers. Five different unions were involved in negotiations about every operational issue and assignment of work tasks. Individual unions had concerns which dealt primarily with their own membership; thus, complying with one union's request sometimes placed management in conflict with another union. Management's responsibility was to help everyone reach some consensus before operations could proceed. Many of the initial discussions revolved around issues of safety, workload, and people working outside of existing job classifications. Together, labor and management worked through the design of the management information system, site selection and renovation, site configuration, job descriptions, confidentiality, training, staff development, and how the self-managed team concept would work.

The multitude of day-to-day frustrations quickly became serious obstacles to changing service delivery, raising many reasons to question the whole concept of neighborhood-based service integration. Commitment had to be constantly articulated and communicated by the Board of Supervisors, the YSB, and the County Administrator to all participants to keep everyone on track and moving through these difficulties. This was a top-down change process, but many at every level wanted the same changes. Throughout the entire process, participants continued to struggle with a simple fact: while most of us are in favor of making improvements, few like to make changes in their own world; almost all of us prefer that someone else do the changing.

Negotiating with the State

At the same time the SIMT was working through the operational issues, a study was completed which documented a list of state and federal waivers needed to blend categorical funding streams and redirect staff time from paperwork into prevention activities. This in-depth analysis of departmental operations documented how clients moved through the programs, from intake through exit, noting non-productive activities and requirements imposed on the departments. The county applied for and obtained AB-1741 status, which allowed five county pilots to receive waivers needed to support service integration.

Negotiating with Community Representatives

There were two key aspects to team members' work with communities. One involved establishing new kinds of relationships with the center's new clients, those who receive direct services from the team members. The other aspect required establishing a positive working relationship between the team and the community as a whole. This meant working with the MACs and with the Healthy Start Program as well as other community groups and representatives. This was a new experience for staff and involved considerable on the job teaming and experimentation.

Staff were able to establish new positive relationships with their clients more easily than developing a community-wide perspective necessary to build constructive neighborhood relationships. All client participation in the neighborhood centers was voluntary. Team members had to go door-to-door and persuade clients to transfer their cases from the central office to the neighborhood center. This dramatically changed the relationship between workers and clients and set the stage for the kind of individualized attention clients are now receiving. Because workers had to persuade their clients to join the center, staff members felt very responsible for adapting services to better meet client needs, and they assertively advocated with department management to change rigid policies and procedures that affect client services.

While the county engaged in restructuring, re-configuring and dealing with internal issues, the neighborhood representatives were becoming more organized and began advocating for specific service priorities: jobs, increased public safety, and increased after school recreation. There was ongoing tension between what the community viewed as its primary needs and what the county could actually provide under existing categorical funding until the waivers were approved.

The teams continue to learn how to work with neighborhood leadership. Turf struggles exist in the neighborhoods and it is not always clear who is speaking for whom.

It is not uncommon to find significant disagreements among neighborhood groups about what is best for the community. Staff have found that the best methods for adapting to community work involve patience, perseverance and relationship-building.

PRACTICE PRINCIPLES FOR MANAGING ORGANIZATIONAL AND COMMUNITY CHANGE

The management principles that impact leaders in the process of change center on four broad tasks—making a personal commitment, re-defining ourselves and our roles, planning for implementation, and moving from planning to action.

Making a Personal Commitment

Implementing a new vision of human services is time-consuming, tedious, and hard work, but not impossible. It requires a personal investment in converting the existing set of mandated department activities into a transforming vision. There usually is broad consensus about the merit of a family centered, neighborhood-based strategy. However, if one lacks passion and the necessary energy, it is impossible to move through the overwhelming inertia that exists in the public sector or to cope with the multiple roadblocks and barriers faced at every turn. Directors of Departments of Social Services interested in promoting family-centered, neighborhood human services should consider the following soul-searching questions:

- Does the vision of a family-centered, neighborhood human service system truly reflect our own vision of the ideal?
- Do we really believe that this vision, if implemented, will make the difference in the lives of our clients, workers and the community?
- Is this a good time to handle the increased responsibilities associated with the needed changes?
- Are we prepared to deal with the inertia, ingrained practices and the resistance we will uncover as we try to change ourselves and our department's practice?
- Are we willing to devote the necessary attention to managing change while handling the ongoing pressures imposed on us by the state or county?
- Are we willing to invest the effort to learn new habits and competencies related to:
  - re-engineering techniques and entrepreneurial approaches;
  - communications, public relations, public education;
  - organizational development processes;
  - motivating and engaging clients as partners;
  - identifying and working with strengths; supporting self sufficiency and responsibility;
  - worker self management/decentralized decision making and community governance?

Individuals usually come to the point of implementing a vision because they are "called" and are compelled to do whatever is required to make it happen. For example, one director became committed to such a vision after a soul searching and an "up close look" at the daily operation of his department. His beliefs about how staff and clients should be treated were so different from the way they were being treated that he had to change the department or give up his career.

Redefining Ourselves and Our Roles

A second major decision involves determining how we personally will participate in day-to-day change efforts and how involved we will be in overseeing the efforts required to transform our departments. For example, will we be out front, highly visible and attached to this effort? Or, will we delegate this responsibility to a high level person who can handle the day to day planning, communicating, and implementing and provide the support necessary for success?

Most directors of social service departments are so busy that they have few opportunities to observe how their departments are working, how workers' needs are changing, and how clients are treated. Most directors work under incredible pressures and spend much of their time on budgetary crises, smoothing relations with the Board of Supervisors, and coping with state and federal officials. Middle managers and their supervisors handle day-to-day operations. Even middle managers are not always clear about how their clients move from intake to termination and what services look like from the clients' perspectives.

It is essential that directors find ways to understand more fully how their organization functions, what must be changed, and how it would function if it were truly a client-centered, community-based, integrated system of support for families. This does not mean that the director needs to micro-manage the operation, but time must be spent on understanding what is going on before identifying strategic opportunities for improving service delivery. In Contra Costa County it made a big difference that two of the County Supervisors and the County Administrator were 100% invested in this endeavor and knew the details of what was going on.

Planning for Implementation

After struggling with the issues of assessing one's commitment and re-defining one's

role, one can turn to the hard work of planning and preparing for the implementation requirements. The actual work of implementing the vision is akin to flying a plane while making design improvements, knitting a sweater while wearing it, or renovating a house while living in it. In order to get started, Contra Costa County found it worked best to create a neighborhood-based system of service integration within and parallel to the existing county operations. In this way a "micro world" could be created for learning and testing how to do this work. This approach is less risky than throwing the entire department into upheaval; however, one must be comfortable with operating in two different and sometimes conflicting worlds at the same time. Also, one must be vigilant that this experiment is not just another project with no tie to real policy. Everything learned must be connected to improving services county-wide or else stakeholders will lose faith.

Staff must be found within the department that can work on two interdependent efforts—that of building a new infrastructure to support neighborhood services and that of community organizing and mobilizing. An individual who is very good at action planning and program and systems design, who knows the county services and how these fragmented services must be restructured, is not always the best person to work in a community involving community residents and clients in neighborhood improvement. But, the two efforts are mutually supportive and must operate with common agreement about priorities and expected results.

There are four sets of tasks that must be addressed in this planning stage. These include: (1) developing the programmatic frameworks and infrastructure for supporting community-based work; (2) determining how to obtain active community participation and partnership; (3) creating staff "buy-in" and ensuring staff success; and (4) building intra- and inter-organization collaboration. The elements of each are noted as follows:

Program Infrastructure

- Adopting prevention-oriented service models;
- Creating a unified, coherent management information system;
- Obtaining county, state and federal waivers;
- Building a management structure for operating decentralized teams;
- Developing community-focused budgets, which reflect blended funding sources.

Community Development

- "Unlearning" the past and building trust;
- Supporting the creation of neighborhood leadership;
- Clarifying community priorities;
- Creating a local governance structure;
- Bolstering self-help and mutual assistance;
- Employing neighborhood residents;
- Directing funds to community-identified priorities.

Staff Development

- Building trust and developing vision;
- Facilitating consensus on vision and values;
- Ensuring appropriate skills and competencies.

Collaboration

- Creating partnerships between county departments;
- Forging links with local businesses, funders, civic organizations and community-based organizations.

The successful accomplishment of these tasks requires certain organizational and leadership qualities. The organization must be a "learning organization" that uses data and information to correct operations. It must be organized to learn by doing, utilizing information from the management information system to improve day-to-day practice. In addition, the organization must replace protecting the department's image with a willingness to take risks and learn from mistakes, and it must ensure that everyone involved feels responsible for success and shares a comparable personal vision. Organizational leadership qualities that are required include "walking the talk," an ability to make and communicate decisions that are consistent with the vision. The leader must function as a cheerleader and rewarder, creating and providing incentives, as an educator, motivator, sales person and mobilizer. He or she must practice persistence, perseverance, and patience, be willing to "make it up as you go," and correct mistakes with little rancor. Most importantly, the leader must clearly and constantly communicate successes, lessons, and implications of changes as they occur.

Moving from Planning to Action

The action steps which must be undertaken to transform an existing system into a family-centered neighborhood human service system can be overwhelming. However, success can occur if all those involved work together with a well-organized action plan. Multiple activities and tasks can be carried out simultaneously and within common time frames if all agree on the operational plan for dividing up the tasks and responsibilities. For example, in Contra Costa County, the entire process from beginning to test-pilot stage took three-and-a-half years by taking small steps, one day at a time, which produced significant progress.

Figure 20.1 outlines elements of the four action areas that needed to come together to ensure project success. Each of these areas involved a number of specific action steps that kept the project moving forward to create an effective systems-level change. All were interactive and moved forward with overlapping time frames.

Establishing the vision involved educating and informing as well as listening and soliciting feedback at many levels within the County and the community. Participants needed to be allowed and assisted to articulate their reservations as well as their enthusiasm in order to develop and affirm their ongoing support. Developing the program infrastructure encompassed the "nuts and bolts" of program planning, while creating the community action plan and building the collaborative teams involved the promotion of strong and effective working relationships between individuals and organizations. The community action plan process required facilitating mutually-supportive working relationships between the neighborhood governance structure, schools, agencies and residents. The collaborative team building process focused on effective working relationships between neighborhood center staff and clients and community members. A final step involved the selection of a neutral party to evaluate the efforts and communicating with all parties to improve the quality of life in the neighborhood.

These steps are only highlights of a complex process of systems change. Much of the change process involves exploring uncharted territory. Once a vision is developed and key leaders adapt it as part of their own personal quest, the journey begins; however, it has no predictable end point. Much of the progress made and speed of the change process will depend upon the

process used to bring people together, the personalities of key individuals, success in focusing participants' energies on joint, positive action, and, of course, seizing unusual opportunities as they present themselves. If leaders have a great deal of energy, are passionate about this work, have good partners, and are patient and persistent, it can be done. Staff reported that working in the neighborhood Family Resource Center is the most difficult work they have ever done, but it is also the most meaningful. Over and over again staff report such comments as, "This is the first time in 16 years I actually enjoy coming to work everyday." Workers believe they are making a difference in the lives of their clients. Clients reported that they are shocked by the difference in the way they are treated. Many for the first time are served in a helpful, respectful manner.

THE CONSULTANT'S ROLE IN FACILITATING CHANGE

There are many different definitions of what a consultant is and what a consultant does. To some, a consultant is an expert who helps people clarify their intentions, helps design a process for achieving the organization's goals, and coaches everyone through an implementation process.

Each consultant also brings a value system and, in this case, a commitment to neighborhood-based, family-centered, interagency service integration. This involves promoting community participation in all aspects of neighborhood life and insuring that resources are distributed consistent with the needs and wants of the neighborhood.

The consultant's role changes over time in response to the presenting needs and requirements of the job. There were three phases of the work in Contra Costa County:

FIGURE 20.1
Project Action Steps

Establishing a Shared Vision and Agreeing on Desired Outcomes
• Obtain commitment from the Board of Supervisors, County Administrator, other department heads and school administrators;
• Educate management and staff about the strategic pian and common vision;
• Involve all relevant advisory boards, community coalitions, schools and community-based organizations;
• Assess the current operating processes for serving clients and identify elements that are inconsistent with a neighborhood-based, family-centered approach;
• Work with the state to eliminate regulations and finance systems that impede the new strategic direction.

Developing Program Infrastructure
• Select neighborhoods based upon defensible criteria;
• Assess needs and share information sharing about the new partnership;
• Develop a process for instituting local governance;
• Identify and recruit local leaders;
• Investigate funding streams;
• Develop management information systems, budgets, and management structures;
• Develop client consent and participation forms and procedures;
• Select staff;
• Begin joint training and staff development;
• Place the county service teams into the neighborhood.

Creating a Community Action Plan
• Facilitate the development of mutually-supportive working relationships between the neighborhood governance structure, schools, agencies, and residents;
• Monitor interactions to ensure movement toward a common set of program objectives and outcomes;
• Engage partners in developing the program infrastructure;
• Assist partners in developing a common community plan that specifies outcomes to be achieved, performance expectations, a monitoring process, and each partner's roles and responsibilities for achieving success.

Building Collaborative Teams
• Monitoring relationship building;
• Providing mediation and problem solving support "on-call";
• Resolving client-specific problems;
• Involving participants in training activities in the community;
• Promoting neighborhood opportunities to celebrate progress, life-cycle events, and holidays for children.

• The start up phase or the visioning process;
• The implementation planning and designing of a new system;
• Beginning operation of the pilot.

During the first phase, the consultant was responsible for drafting the vision, the set of operating principles and the strategic plan. The consultant was charged with gaining commitment and "buy in" from multiple agencies, levels in the organizations, communities, and decision makers. This was a full time job of motivating, communicating and listening to many different groups. During this stage, all of the disparate interests had to be brought into some form of agreement about the future. The consultant along with the YSB was identified with the effort, but it was the consultant's responsibility to keep everyone moving forward together.

Once the Board of Supervisors passed a Board Order in December 1992 mandating community-based, family-centered, inter-agency service integration teams to be located in the two neighborhoods of North Richmond and Bay Point, the Service Integration Management Team (SIMT) was created. As a result, the neighborhoods became associated with a larger group of concerned people, representing the departments and programs.

The consultant was the technical expert to the SIMT and helped guide the implementation planning process, structuring the work committees, overseeing the participation of all departments in making decisions, communicating with various county departments and coordinating with parallel projects related to neighborhood services. It was the consultant's responsibility to be well-informed about all of the possible methods for structuring service integration and to know and understand the "state of the art" information about the myriad of infrastructure issues that had to be dealt with (for example, financing, management information systems, self-managed teams, and evaluation) and tracked through written records of the plan, time lines, accomplishments and agreements. The consultant was a cheerleader that kept the process moving forward, serving as an activist in the community-building process and responsible for much of the day to day work of assisting the Healthy Start planning efforts, developing the North Richmond MAC, and creating communication channels between the community and the SIMT.

With the launch of the neighborhood family service centers, the County appointed a high level manager responsible for the operation and management of the neighborhood pilots. The consultant became more of an observer to the operation and shifted to a liaison role between the county and outside parties (foundations and state agency representatives), making the necessary connections to resources and expertise that could facilitate the full operation of the neighborhood centers. Specifically, the consultant conducted a technical review of all programs to determine which state and federal waivers were required to support service integration. This was done in collaboration with the County Administrator's analyst who was completing a full scale review of the existing financing mechanism and making recommendations for actions needed to maximize existing funding sources and waivers required to blend categorical funds to support the service integration efforts.

During all three steps the consultant was the person who reminded everyone about the shared vision, since everyone had many other priorities throughout the change process. The consultant maintained the county's memory on this entire enterprise and ensured communication links to the many different people who needed to be included.

The greatest challenge was coping with the slow pace of the change process. This was the consultant's only assignment, and she wanted everything to happen now. Her preferred pace was impossible for department management staff who had many competing demands on their time and energy. Allowing others a more relaxed pace, while maintaining the forward motion of the project was an ongoing balancing act.

In reviewing this experience, it seems that the consultant may have two major advantages over the appointment of an internal department manager when helping the county plan and implement neighborhood service integration. A consultant has the freedom and opportunity to speak his or her "own opinion about the truth of the circumstances" to upper management, the Board of Supervisors and the children's advocates without fear of reprisal. The consultant holds a neutral position with respect to any department or particular discipline; he/she is not required to promote the interest or defend the reputation of one department over another.

In a bureaucracy, middle managers, supervisors, and front line workers often find it difficult to say exactly what they think to upper management. Usually there are limited opportunities for their opinions to be heard and included in upper management discussions and when there is a chance to speak one's views, many worry about the repercussions of speaking up or being overly candid. Staff from different departments often reflect different organizational cultures and "ways of doing things." Even when they find it difficult to rationalize the decisions of their superiors, they are often expected or personally believe that they should present their department's "best possible face."

In contrast, the consultant's job is to present as truthfully as possible an impartial view of the circumstances and a thorough analysis of the options for action. At times, during this particular project, the consultant's opinions about what should be done in negotiations with the unions, departments and community were ignored. She walked a fine line between pushing a position that was vital to the success of the effort and accepting that others may actually better understand what is best for the program. She learned from her mistakes as to which decisions required more persuasion and which circumstances needed an accepting, open attitude. This is a luxury which a consultant can indulge more easily than a civil servant.

The consultant is often alone when presenting an unpopular view. When staff see that upper management's response to unpleasant facts is constructive, then agency staff become more actively involved by seeing how safe it is to advocate for change.

A second advantage of hiring a consultant is that the county can hire one person who has the skills and experience required to work with both public agencies and neighborhood advisory groups. While most departments have staff who could perform in either arena, they are more than likely functioning in job classifications and current assignments which make them invisible or inaccessible to upper management. Many eligibility workers are community leaders in their neighborhoods. Many front line supervisors have learned how to get different agencies to work together when serving the same client. However, it is uncommon for a public agency to search through the bureaucracy and find these people and reassign them to a team to work inside and outside the organization. Most social services departments do not function with the kind of flexibility needed to maximize the talents and abilities of employees, regardless of classification and formal education.

CONCLUSIONS

In Contra Costa County, the process of integrating services has caused some very dramatic changes in thinking and in practice. At the beginning of the change process, no one knew how it would end up or how it would look, and no one really knew exactly how to manage the process. The project was successful because participants learned to share a strong, sustained commitment to the vision of community-based, family-centered, inter-agency service integration over an extended period of time. This commitment led to shared planning, shared operations, and mutually supportive communication. Changing the system required the following critical elements:

- Commitment and leadership from the top levels of county government were needed to keep the process on track. Commitment and leadership from the community were necessary to keep the system changes responsive to the neighborhood's needs and to mobilize local participation and ownership.

- At least one person, in this case an outside consultant, was needed to keep an eye on the larger picture, bridge gaps and keep the dialogue open, thereby keeping everyone working together toward a shared goal.

- New ways of thinking about government, communities, workers, purposes, and service provision were needed, along with a thorough understanding of the technical information available on systems change and systems improvements.
- Participants in the process recognized the need to celebrate small changes as precursors to a larger change.

21.

Robert Fisher

SOCIAL ACTION COMMUNITY ORGANIZATION: PROLIFERATION, PERSISTENCE, ROOTS, AND PROSPECTS

Social action is a distinctive type of community organization practice (Burghardt, 1987). As articulated by Rothman (1968), in a seminal essay that provides the conceptual framework for this volume, it is different in a number of critical respects from other forms of community intervention, such as community locality development and community social planning. The "classic" social action effort is grassroots-based, conflict-oriented, with a focus on direct action, and geared to organizing the disadvantaged or aggrieved to take action on their own behalf. It has a long and important history, including, for example, such practitioners and efforts as Saul Alinsky and the numerous Industrial Areas Foundation projects associated with the "Alinsky method" since the late 1930s; Communist Party community organizing in the 1930s and 1940s; civil rights efforts in the 1950s and 1960s; the work of Cesar Chavez and the United Farm Workers; Community Action Programs and the confrontational organizing of SDS, SNCC, the Black Panthers, the Brown Berets, and La Raza Unida in the 1960s; and the wave of community-based social action since the 1970s organized around identity groups based on gender, sexual orientation, ethnicity, race, or neighborhood (Fisher, 1994; Fisher and Kling, 1993). Unlike community development and social planning efforts, social action focuses on power, pursues conflict strategies, and challenges the structures that oppress and disempower constituents. It is the type of community intervention that most lives up to the social justice and social change mission of social work, and yet, because of its oppositional politics, tends to be the least practiced within social work institutions and social service agencies.

Community-based social action, however, is not a static phenomenon. Social action is always changing in response to the conditions and opportunity structures in which it operates. In the 1980s, for example, one hallmark of community-based social action, as practiced by Alinsky groups and many others, was its withdrawal from a singular emphasis on conflict theory and confrontational politics. Involved in developing housing projects, organizing community development projects, and handling job training grants, these efforts, the heirs to classic social action community organization, now look more like a blending of social action with community development and social planning (Fisher, 1994).

This essay seeks to contribute to the expanding knowledge of community-based social action by making four essential points. First, because community-based

Parts of this essay appeared earlier in Robert Fisher, "Community Organizing Worldwide," in R. Fisher and J. Kling, eds., *Mobilizing the Community* (Newbury Park, CA: Sage, 1993).

social action is an evolving and ever-changing phenomenon, we must now view it beyond our national borders, as a global phenomenon. The community development literature has done this for more than a generation. Moreover, unlike in the past, when social action efforts were said to last no more than six years, current efforts persist much longer and often become important community institutions. Second, these social action community organizations share common characteristics, reflective of what some observers call the new social movements. Third, new social theory and histories of social action efforts have reconceptualized contemporary community-based social action as primarily a product of post-1945 social movement organizing. These movement roots help further distinguish community-based social action from other forms of community organization and help explain why Rothman's model of social action continues to have salience for the study of grassroots oppositional movement efforts. Fourth, like all eras, but perhaps even more so for the current one, our contemporary context poses both significant opportunities and immense barriers to effective community-based social action practice. It is these changing conditions and the responses of organizers and organizations to them that are significantly expanding and altering our knowledge and understanding of social action.

PROLIFERATION AND PERSISTENCE

Two things are certain about contemporary community-based social action organizing. It is both a widespread and a long-term phenomenon. Once thought of as confined to narrow geographic areas (like New York City or Chicago) or to a specific historical era (like the late 1960s and early 1970s),

proliferation and persistence, not provincialism and short-term existence, are the hallmarks of contemporary efforts. Without doubt, community-based social action has a long history in both social work practice and social work education (Burghardt, 1987; Fisher, 1994). Most social action, however, occurs outside of social work. That has always been the case. Since the 1960s, when the social work profession first began to take a very strong interest in social action approaches to community organization, grassroots organizing has become the dominant form of popular resistance and social change worldwide. Instead of not "enjoy[ing] the currency it once had," (Rothman with Tropman, 1987, p. 7) these efforts have proliferated widely outside the social work profession, and within as well as outside of the United States.

Jeff Drumtra (1991) provided sketches of citizen action in 38 countries. His research emphasized how recent political reform in 25 countries in Asia, Africa, and Latin America now allowed for wide voter participation in free elections with multiple candidates. Durning (1989, p. 5) goes further. In a comparable comparative study he argues that people are coming together "in villages, neighborhoods, and shantytowns around the world," in response to the forces which endanger their communities and planet. Paget (1990) estimates two million grassroots social action groups in the United States alone. Lowe (1986) sees a similar upsurge of activity in the United Kingdom. The same is true for most of Western Europe. Grassroots social action organizing and urban protest have been key elements of politics in the West since the late 1960s. But community-based social action is not limited to Western industrial states. What happened in the West is only part of a widespread escalation of urban resistance throughout the world. The picture shows "an expanding latticework covering the globe," Durning (1989, pp. 6–7) continues. "At the local level, particularly among the close to 4 billion humans in developing lands, it appears that the world's people are better organized in 1989 than they have been since European colonialism disrupted traditional societies centuries ago." Community organizing efforts, with hundreds of millions of members, have proliferated worldwide in the past 20 years, extending from nations in the West to those in the South, and, most recently, with extraordinary results, to those in the East (Frank and Fuentes, 1990, p. 163).

Similarly, the persistence of grassroots social action, as well as their proliferation, is another hallmark of our contemporary era. Many efforts have come and gone in the past decade. But the old rule of thumb that social action community organizing, like that pioneered by Saul Alinsky, lasts no more than six years, is no longer valid. ACORN celebrated its 20th anniversary in 1990, National People's Action (NPA) did so two years later, and COPS soon thereafter. Citizen Action, TMO in Houston, the New Jersey Tenants Union (NJTU), and many others recently passed the ten-year mark, with no signs of declining despite having to organize in very adverse conditions. Grassroots efforts tied to national issues, such as pro-choice, gay rights, and the environmental movement, not only persist but continue to grow.

THE NATURE OF CONTEMPORARY SOCIAL ACTION

But what is the nature of contemporary, community-based, social action organizing? Are these community-based social action efforts all of the same piece? Do prior models (Rothman, 1968; Fisher, 1994) capture the complexity of current efforts? If a global proliferation exists, what are the shared, essential characteristics of contemporary, community-based, social action organizing? Building on the insights from new social movement theory (Epstein, 1990; Melucci, 1989), contemporary social action organizing worldwide shares the following characteristics:

First, the efforts are community-based, that is organized around communities of interest or geography, not at the site of production (the factory) or against the principal owners of capital as was the case of most pre-1960s organizing (Offe, 1987).

Second, the organizations are transclass groupings of constituencies and cultural identities such as blacks, ethnics, women, gay men, neighborhood residents, students, ecologists, and peace activists. Labor becomes one, not *the*, constituency group. Class becomes part of, not *the*, identity (Brecher and Costello, 1990; Fisher, 1992).

Third, the ideological glue is a neopopulist vision of democracy. The groups reject authoritarianism: in the state, leadership, party, organization, and relationships (Amin, 1990). Their organizational form is most often sufficiently small, loose, and open to be able to "tap local knowledge and resources, to respond to problems rapidly and creatively, and to maintain the flexibility needed in changing circumstances" (Durning, 1989, pp. 6–7). Some see contemporary social action as "nonideological," because the organizations dismiss the old ideologies of capitalism, communism, and nationalism and because they tend to be without a clear critique of the dominant system. But others argue that ideological congruence is their essence. Their "neopopulist" principles and beliefs are what make them so important and filled with potential (Dalton and Kuechler, 1990; Offe, 1987;

Boyte and Riessman, 1986; Fisher and Kling, 1988; Boyte, Booth, and Max, 1986).

Fourth, struggle over culture and social identity play a greater role in these community-based efforts, especially when compared to the workplace-based organizing of the past, which focused more on economic and political issues. "After the great working class parties surrendered their remaining sense of radical political purpose with the onset of the cold war," Bronner (1990, p. 161) writes, "new social movements emerged to reformulate the spirit of resistance in broader cultural terms." Feminism. Black Power. Sexual identity. Ethnic nationalism. Victim's rights. Of course, culture and identity—grounded in historical experience, values, social networks, and collective solidarity—have always been central to citizen social action (Gutman, 1977). And, of course, identity and constituency efforts include economic and political issues. But as class becomes increasingly fragmented in the postindustrial city and as the locus of workplace organizing declines in significance, resistances that emerge increasingly do so at the community level around cultural issues and identity bases (Touraine, 1985; Fisher and Kling, 1991).

Fifth, strategies include elements of locality development self-help and empowerment. An aim is building community capacity, especially in an era hostile to social change efforts and unwilling to support them. Some of the more effective efforts go beyond community capacity building to target and make claims against the public sector. They see the future of community-based social action as interdependent with political and economic changes outside their communities. They understand that the state is the entity potentially most responsible and vulnerable to social action claims and constituencies

(Piven and Cloward, 1982; Fisher, 1992). But most contemporary community-based organizing seeks independence from the state rather than state power. As Midgley (1986, p. 4) points out, central to the rationale of community participation "is a reaction against the centralization, bureaucratization, rigidity, and remoteness of the state. The ideology of community participation is sustained by the belief that the power of the state has extended too far, diminishing the freedoms of ordinary people and their rights to control their own affairs." Community capacity building becomes a natural focus, reflecting anti-statist strategies and decentralization trends of the postindustrial political economy.[1]

---

[1] This argument of a common new social movement form plays out a bit differently in other parts of the world. One key difference is that the old social movements in the Third World (South) and Second World (East) were nationalistic and communistic, respectively, not social democratic as in the West (Wallerstein, 1990). Given their subordinate position in the world economy, the old social movements—in the South, for example—did not have the power to deliver material security or political liberty. They often became arms of Western imperial control. In response, community movements "mushroomed" all over the South. Like counterparts in the West, they are community-based, constituency or identity oriented, neopopulist in ideology, and focused on self-help strategies. But in the South, community movements put greater emphasis on material needs (Frank and Fuentes, 1990). Where old social movements achieved distributional victories only for a few, as in the southern hemisphere, or where such victories did not include significant minority segments, as in the United States, new social movements struggle to achieve a minimal standard of living and get basic services like housing and healthcare. Where material victories have been won, primarily among the more affluent in the United States and Western Europe, the social base tends to be the educated middle class (Merkl, 1987). But where basic material needs still remain to be won in the South and among the oppressed and disenfranchised in the West, new social movement forms include the poor and powerless and interweave struggle over postmaterial and material objectives.

HISTORICAL ANTECEDENTS: THE ROOTS OF IDEOLOGIES AND STRATEGIES

One of the key causes for this common form of social action organization is the common heritage of citizen resistance since the end of World War II. It is this common heritage that continues to structure and inform contemporary efforts. For our purposes I emphasize five major historical roots: the (1) community-based resistance of Saul Alinsky, (2) liberation struggles of people of color, (3) urban decentralization and citizen participation programs, (4) new left movement, and (5) new social movements. Of course, this is not to suggest that the heritage of community resistance does not include efforts prior to 1945 (Fisher, 1984; Fisher, 1992). Nor is it to suggest that all contemporary community mobilization efforts build on each of these antecedents or that these are the only sources. Admittedly, roots are more numerous and entangled than here suggested, but the following five are essential to contemporary community-based social action.

Of course, basic survival concerns are important even in those groups in the West professing to hold to "postmaterialist" values. Survival is tied to ridding the world of nuclear weapons, toxic wastes, domestic violence, or AIDS, all of which cut across class lines. Relatedly, the politics of identity, concern for personal and political freedom, and the desire to belong to a supportive and habitable community are of concern to new social movement efforts worldwide. Democratic self-help—community empowerment—is their essence. Predictably, new social movements develop easily among the affluent and around postmaterialist issues. But they succeed better as agents of transformative social change when they combine both distributional and postmaterialist objectives. The distributional demands ground identity in a class politics that understands, at least implicitly, the need in a postindustrial global economy to target the public sector and struggle for state power as well as develop democratic alternatives at the grassroots.

(1) Community-Based Resistance of Saul Alinsky

While the organizing projects of Saul Alinsky during his lifetime never amounted to much in terms of material victories and while his projects only took off when the southern civil rights movement shifted to northern cities in the 1960s, the community-based, constituency-oriented, urban populist, confrontational politics developed by Alinsky in the United States provides one of the earliest models of the community-based social action form (Fisher and Kling, 1988). Beginning just before World War II, Alinsky's work in Chicago built on the older, union-based models of social action, such as the Congress of Industrial Organizations and Communist Party United States of America (Horwitt, 1989; Fisher, 1984). From these it drew its labor organizing style, conflict strategies, direct-action politics, and idea of grounding organizing in the everyday lives and traditions of working people. But Alinsky's model added something new: a kind of labor organizing in the social factory (Boyte, 1981). The community organizer was the catalyst for change. The task was to build democratic, community-based organizations. The goal was to empower neighborhood residents by teaching them basic political and organizing skills and getting them or their representatives to the urban bargaining table (Fisher, 1994; Boyte, 1981). Both the site of production (supporting labor demands) and the public sector (making City Hall more accountable) served as primary targets of Alinsky organizing.

This was an insurgent consciousness of "urban populism," based in neighborhood "people's organizations," oriented to building community power, discovering indigenous leaders, providing training in democratic participation, and proving that ordinary people could challenge and beat City Hall (Boyte, 1986; Booth and Max, 1986; Swanstrom, 1985; Horwitt, 1989). At their weakest, Alinsky efforts sought to replace the political program and ideology of the old social action efforts with the skills of democratic grassroots participation, the abilities of professionally trained organizers, a faith in the democratic tendencies of working people to guide organizations toward progressive ends, and a reformist vision of grassroots pluralistic politics. At their best, however, Alinsky efforts continue to empower lower- and working-class, black and latino community residents and to demand expanded public sector accountability and public participation in an increasingly privatized political context (Fisher, 1994; Horwitt, 1989; Rogers, 1990; Delgado, 1986; Kahn, 1970). Alinsky may not be the "father of community organizing," but, especially in the United States, his work and the work of his successors has been seminal to social action community organizing (Boyte, 1981).

(2) Liberation Struggles of People of Color

Much more significant in terms of impact are the liberation struggles of people of color throughout the world since the 1950s. The civil rights movement in the United States and the national liberation struggles in the southern hemisphere served as important models for a community-based, ethnic/ nationalist politics oriented to self-determination and sharing the political liberties and material affluence of the societies that exploited people of color. As a model for grassroots direct action and insurgent consciousness, the southern civil rights movement spawned most of what was to follow in the United States and established important precedents for others throughout the world (Branch, 1988; Morris, 1984; Reagon, 1979). The liberation struggles in Africa, Asia, Latin America, and the Middle East, as well as specifically early efforts in Ghana, Vietnam, Iran, Guatemala, and Cuba, not only provided models for people worldwide, including activists in the civil rights movement in the United States, but symbolized the mobilization of a worldwide liberation struggle of people of color. The demand for national self-determination for all people (not just those of European descent), the opposition to policies of racism and imperialism, and the plea of the civil rights movement for "beloved community" helped pierce the consensus politics of the 1950s and early 1960s. More recent liberation struggles in Nicaragua, El Salvador, and South Africa, to name but a few, continued to challenge conservative, racist, and imperialist paradigms in the 1980s and 1990s.

The continuous liberation struggles of people of color emphasize three lessons critical to the insurgent consciousness of contemporary community activism. First, citizen insurgency is not a political aberration. It is a legitimate and important, informal part of the political process to which all those without access to power can turn. Second, if oppressed people—often illiterate, rural peasants with few resources—could mobilize, take risks, and make history, then people of other oppressed or threatened constituencies can, with sufficient organization and leadership, do the same. Third, strategy must include both community self-help and constituency empowerment, on the one hand, and the struggle for state power, or at least the targeting of the public sector as the site of grievances and as a potential source of support, on the other. This dual quality of building community capacity and targeting the state, though not always in equal balance and often in tension, as exemplified in struggles between the Southern Christian Leadership Conference (SCLC) and the Student Nonviolent Coordinating Com-mittee (SNCC), was as true for the civil rights movement in the United States as it was for the liberation struggles in the Third World (Carson, 1982).

(3) Urban Decentralization and Citizen Participation

The struggles of people in the southern hemisphere dramatized the exploitative nature of the imperial postwar political economy at the very moment in the 1960s that some progressive capitalists, political leaders, and planners in both the public and voluntary sectors found themselves unable to address mounting urban problems at home. From 1960 onward, as liberal leaders such as presidents Kennedy and Johnson in the United States advocated for modest social reforms and a more democratized public sector, pressure mounted for urban decentralization and citizen participation. The Community Action Program of the 1960s in the United States and the Urban Programme of the late 1960s in Britain were among the most noted of public projects seeking "maximum feasible participation" at the grassroots level. But such programs proliferated widely, making state-sponsored municipal decentralization and community participation an international phenomenon (Kjellberg, 1979; Blair, 1983; Midgley, 1986; Chekki, 1979).

Of course, such postwar programs differ dramatically from Alinsky and liberation movement efforts in their origins and problem analysis. They are initiated largely by reformers in the public and voluntary sectors—professionals such as urban planners and social workers, who either seek modest structural change or find themselves too constrained on the job to do much more in their agencies than deliver needed services at the grassroots level. As such, these initiatives represent a more institutionalized, more formalized wing of the community-based social action phenomenon. They tend, as well, to implement decentralized structure and democratic participation into public agencies without a sense for the contradictions inherent in doing so, but with a knowledge of the importance of linking the state and grassroots activism. The state becomes not the target of democratic insurgency but the employer and supporter of citizen initiatives (Merkl, 1985). At their worst, these measures defuse and coopt insurgency. At their best, contemporary organizing draws from this legacy a commitment to serving the people, to advocacy, and to citizen participation: (a) Deliver services at a grassroots level where people will have better access. (b) Include more people, even lay people, in the decision-making process at a more decentralized level. (c) Make sure they have real power to make decisions and control resources. (d) Struggle from within the state bureaucracies and agencies to achieve economic and participatory democracy for the greatest number of urban dwellers.

(4) The New Left Movement

Despite the efforts noted so far, urban problems and tensions continued to escalate in the 1960s. In response, direct action movements mounted, especially in the United States. Early SDS (Students for a Democratic Society) and SNCC (Student Nonviolent Coordinating Committee) community organizing projects focused on "participatory democracy" and "letting the people decide," seeking not only to pressure local and national policy but to create "prefigurative," that is, alternative, social groups (Breines,

1982; Evans, 1979). They also developed a critique of American policy abroad and the liberal consensus at home. They built a movement in opposition to the politics of both corporate capital and the old social movement. After 1965, organizing adopted more nationalist and Marxist perspectives; Black Power efforts, for example, were less concerned with participatory democracy and more interested in challenging imperialism abroad and at home, winning "community control," and building black identity (Jennings, 1990).

Such efforts in the United States were part of an insurgent trend in the West. Massive peace protests in the United Kingdom registered strong disapproval of Cold War policies, directly challenging social democratic regimes. These early efforts, among others, initiated a widespread "New Left" movement throughout the West, one which was soon to expand beyond university sites and student constituencies to develop, according to Ceccarelli (1982, p. 263), into "an unprecedented outburst of urban movements": Paris and West German cities in the Spring of 1968; Prague, Chicago, and Monterrey, Mexico, during that summer; in Italy the "Hot Autumn" of 1969 and the urban conflicts of the early 1970s; squatters in Portuguese cities after the April Revolution; and urban social movements in Madrid and other Spanish cities after Franco. All testify to a massive grassroots mobilization which developed rapidly, and perhaps even unprecedentedly, throughout Europe, the United States, and parts of the Third World (Ceccarelli, 1982; Teodori, 1969).

Concern for and experimentation with participatory democracy, nonhierarchical decision making, prefigurative cultural politics, linking the personal with the political, direct-action tactics, and constituency based organizing (students, the poor, etc.) characterized new left insurgent consciousness (Jacobs and Landau, 1966; Breines, 1982). Unlike the new social movement resistances to follow, the new left emphasized the formation of coalitions or political parties tied to national revolutionary/emancipatory struggles. There was a sense in the late 1960s, in cities as disparate as Paris, Berlin, Berkeley, and Monterrey, that "successful and autonomous urban movements are not a real alternative outside the context of a revolutionary national movement" (Walton, 1979, p. 12). The struggle over state power, over who should make public policy, fueled local organizing efforts. Grassroots efforts were for most activists a democratic means to larger objectives which transcended the local community. This strategy persists, in a more reformist form, in certain notable national efforts since then, such as the Green parties in Europe, the Workers Party in Brazil, and the Rainbow Coalition idea in the United States (Spretnak and Capra, 1985; Alvarez, 1993; Collins, 1986).

Community-based social action efforts which followed tended to borrow more heavily from the "newer" side of the New Left. These activists saw community organizing, alternative groupings, and grassroots efforts as at least the primary focus if not the sole end. They emphasized democratic organizational structure, the politics of identity and culture, existential values of personal freedom and authenticity, and the development of "free spaces" where people could learn the theory and practice of political insurgency while engaging in it. So did much of the New Left, but the other, more Marxist segments, closer in style and politics to the old labor-based social action, adhered strongly to older concerns with public policy and winning state power (Evans,

1979; Evans and Boyte, 1986; Carson, 1982).

(5) New Social Movements

Despite a marked backlash worldwide against the radical activism of the late 1960s, the 1970s and 1980s witnessed not the end of community-based activism but the proliferation of grassroots activism and insurgency into highly diversified, single-issue or identity-oriented, community-based efforts. These efforts, the subject of this essay, include women's shelters and feminist organizations, efforts in defense of the rights and the communities of oppressed people of color, struggles around housing, ecology, and peace issues, gay and lesbian rights and identity groups, and thousands of neighborhood and issue-based citizen initiatives, complete with organizer training centers. While these organizing efforts vary from one national and local context to another, they share a common form and movement heritage. Based in geographic communities or communities of interest, decentralized according to constituencies and identity groups, democratic in process and goals, and funded most often by voluntary sources, they serve as the archetype for contemporary social action.

The roots of their insurgent consciousness, while not always direct, can be found in the ideals discussed thus far: (1) that ordinary and previously oppressed people should have a voice and can make history, (2) that citizen and community participation, which gives "voice" to people previously silent in public discourse, is needed to improve decision making, address a wide range of problems, and democratize society, (3) that "by any means necessary" covers the gamut of strategies and tactics from revolutionary to interest-group politics, (4) that culture, whether found in a traditional ethnic neighborhood, battered women's shelter, counterculture collective, or gay men's organization, must be blended with the quest for "empowerment" into an identity- or a constituency-oriented politics, and (5) that "the personal is political," articulated first by radical feminists in the late 1960s, guides people to organize around aspects of daily life most central to them, while keeping in mind that struggles over personal issues and relationships—personal choice, autonomy, commitment, and fulfillment—are inextricably tied to collective ones of the constituency group and the larger society.

Most commentators tend to see the focus on democracy as the essence of new social-movement insurgent consciousness and the source of its potential. As Frank and Fuentes (1990, p. 142) put it, the new social movements "are the most important agents of social transformation in that their praxis promotes participatory democracy in civil society. Pitkin and Shumer (1982, p. 43) go further, declaring that "of all the dangerous thoughts and explosive ideas abroad in the world today, by far the most subversive is that of democracy. . . . [It] is the cutting edge of radical criticism, the best inspiration for change toward a more humane world, the revolutionary idea of our time." And these democratic projects have had profound impact: empowering participants, teaching democratic skills, transforming notions of political life, expanding political boundaries, returning politics to civic self-activity, strengthening a sense of public activism, raising new social and political issues, struggling against new forms of subordination and oppression, and even advancing agendas of the middle class to which formal, institutional politics remain closed (Roth, 1991; Slater, 1985).

But while the emphasis on democracy unites these efforts, it also helps detach them in the western industrialized nations from the material needs of the poor, and it contributes to their fragmentation into a plethora of diverse, decentralized community organizations. The pursuit of democracy, without sufficient concern for equality, has resulted in the failure of the new social movements to address the material needs of the most disadvantaged. Moreover, the new social movement origins in culturally oriented, identity-based efforts tend to fragment social change efforts in general (Fisher and Kling, 1993). For example, the diversity and flexibility that theorists of postmodernity attribute to contemporary society are nowhere more evident than in the variety of these new social movement efforts. A commitment to diversity embodies their emphasis on democratic politics. It encourages each constituency or identity group to name its own struggles, develop its own voice, and engage in its own empowerment. This may be the future of politics, a "postmodernization of public life," with its "proliferation of multiple publics [and] breaking down of rigid barriers between political and private life" (Kaufmann, 1990, p. 10). But the central challenges to these efforts require more immediate and realistic strategies. How do they encourage diversity *and* counteract fragmentation? How do they influence or get power at levels—the city, state, and nation—beyond their own limited universes *and* at the same time build community capacity? How do we organize grassroots social action efforts *and* at the same time build a larger social change movement or political party, the size of which can only accomplish the needed, large structural changes?

PRACTICE IMPLICATIONS

Without question, the fragmentation of contemporary social action weakens the possibility for coherently imagined challenges to current problems. To address this problem of contemporary organizing, the historical dialectic of domination and resistance must be understood and fashioned in terms of the *interplay* between class, community, and the search for new cultural orientations. In this regard Kling and I have offered elsewhere the following sets of strategies (Fisher and Kling, 1991).

First, mobilization in the fragmented metropolis demands that broad coalitions be sought between various constituency groups, and that community politics be more cohesively integrated with electoral activity. Single community-based efforts are not large enough to challenge the enormous power of corporate capital or centralized government. Because community problems almost always originate beyond local borders, the ability to effect change depends to a great extent upon coalition-building. The success of coalition-building, however, ultimately will be based upon whether specific ways can be found to break down the racial and cultural barriers that are so entrenched in the United States and growing again in Western Europe.

Pressure group politics, even through powerful coalitions, is not enough; movements must also struggle to win and hold power, not simply to influence it. The electoral arena must become a prime target for social movement mobilizing while, at some later point, political parties serve the critical role of formalizing and structuring relationships between loosely formed coalitions and constituency-based groups (Boyte et al., 1986; Delgado, 1986; Spretnak and Capra, 1985). We offer such advice knowing how coalition and electoral efforts draw already scarce resources away from the fundamental task of grassroots organizing. But the local and the global are equally necessary, and numerous models of such dually focused practice have emerged over time.

The experience of leading organizing efforts in the United States, such as IAF, ACORN and Citizen Action, and in Western Europe, such as the Green parties, illustrates how, while still focusing on the grassroots, they recognized the importance of coalition-building and electoral activity.

Second, as others argue (Evans et al., 1985) we need to bring the state back in, and use legislative policy to challenge the ideology of privatization and free enterprise that meets so well the needs of international capital. The state, of course, is not inherently an ally of low- and moderate-income people. But in the late 20th century, where private sector targets disappear in the electronic global economy, and where, in a new social movement context, the community replaces the workplace as the locus of organizing, a legitimized and expanded public sector becomes a critical ingredient for continued citizen action. Without it public life cannot even begin to be restored; without it grassroots mobilization devolves into self-help strategies which further fragmentation and perpetuate the use of private, voluntary solutions to massive, public problems (Fisher, 1993).

For example, take the worldwide push for privatization (Barnekov et al., 1989). By undermining government legitimacy and responsibility, it results not only in a declining public life and fewer public services, but also in loss of access to a potentially accountable and responsible public sector, *the* major victory of pre-1945 social movements and a crucial target of some of the earlier antecedents to current social action efforts (Fisher, 1988; Fisher, 1992; Piven and Cloward, 1982). Increasingly, in our current context, as the public sector declines as a source of grievances or solutions, citizen action is undercut. Contemporary resistance focuses its attention on community-based self-help and empowerment partly because the state—one of the primary arenas and targets for antecedents such as Alinsky, the civil rights movement, national liberation efforts, and the new left—has been delegitimized. But contemporary social action community organization requires a public-sector arena and target because, unlike union organizing, which had some power at the site of production, in our current era of high-velocity global capital and declining labor activism, where it is much more difficult for workers and citizens to affect the private sector, community-based social action efforts have the state as the entity most responsible and vulnerable to their constituencies (Fisher, 1992; Piven and Cloward, 1982).

Third, we must move to a more consciously ideological politics. We must seek new, centering narratives, or, at least, more common programs that can draw the decentered narratives of our time toward a focal point. New formations and groupings will make mobilization on local levels more potent, perhaps, but they will not resolve the fundamental divisions that plague the effort to challenge broad, culturally entrenched structures of domination, prejudice, and exploitation.

Organizers must continue to teach the techniques of organization—the knowledge of how to bring people together to identify common grievances; to get them to communicate with each other across differing and even conflicting agendas; to enable them to run effective meetings; and to empower them to recognize what sorts of strategies are most suitable for particular contexts, and identify those points in the political regime most vulnerable to the pressures of collective action. But among the organizer's most valuable skills remains the ability to challenge the accepted vision of things and to develop ideological congruence with other oppositional efforts. Good organizational leadership—and good community practice—lies with understanding what is involved in moving people beyond their received notions of how they are related to other cultural and identity-based groups. An authentic commitment to "human solidarity, mutual responsibility, and social justice" demands that people engage in a profound reexamination of the values on which their society and way of life are based. Such transformations of consciousness do not emerge without intervention and engagement.

An organizing ideology for our times needs to combine the new postmodern demands for autonomy and identity with older, modernist ones for social justice, production for human needs, rather than profit, and the spirit of connectedness and solidarity among people, rather than competition. Day-to-day organizing, if it is to move beyond fragmented values and cultures, still needs to be informed by this sort of centering, oppositional ideology. To continue to open activists and constituencies to broader conceptions of social action and social change remains the primary responsibility of the organizer in the 1990s.

REFERENCES

Alvarez, S. "Deepening Democracy: Social Movement Networks, Constitutional Reform, and Radical Urban Regimes in Contemporary Brazil," in Fisher and Kling, eds., *Mobilizing the Community*, op. cit., 1993.

Amin, So, et al., *Transforming the Revolution.* (New York: Monthly Review Press, 1990).

Barnekov, T., R. Boyle, and D. Rich. *Privatism and Urban Policy in Britain and the United States.* Oxford: Oxford University Press, 1989.

Blair, H. W. "Comparing Development Programs," In *Journal of Community Action I,* 1983.

Bonner, A. *Averting the Apocalypse: Social Movements in India Today.* Durham: Duke University Press, 1990.

Boyte, H. *The Backyard Revolution.* Philadelphia: Temple University Press, 1981.

Boyte, H., and F. Riessman. *The New Populism.* Philadelphia: Temple University Press, 1986.

Boyte, H., H. Booth, and S. Max. *Citizen Action and the New American Populism.* Philadelphia: Temple University Press, 1986.

Branch, T. *Parting the Waters: America in the King Years, 1954–1963.* New York: Simon and Schuster, 1988.

Brecher, J., and T. Costello. *Building Bridges: The Emerging Grassroots Coalition of Labor and Community.* New York: Monthly Review Press, 1990.

Breines, W. *Community and Organization in the New Left, 1962–1968: The Great Refusal.* New York: Praeger, 1982.

Bronner, S. E. *Socialism Unbound.* New York: Routledge, 1990.

Burghardt, S. "Community-based Social Action." In *Encyclopedia of Social Work,* 18th ed. New York: NASW, 1987.

Carson, C., Jr. *In Struggle: SNCC and the Black Awakening of the 1960s.* Cambridge: Harvard University Press, 1982.

Ceccarelli, P. "Politics, Parties, and Urban Movements: Western Europe." In N. Fainstein and S. Fainstein, eds., *Urban Policy Under Capitalism.* Beverly Hills: Sage, 1982.

Chekki, D. *Community Development: Theory and Method of Planned Change.* New Delhi: Vikas Publishing House, 1979.

Collins, S. *The Rainbow Challenge.* New York: Monthly Review Press, 1986.

Corbridge, S. "Third World Development." *Progress in Human Geography* 15 (1991): 311–321.

Dalton, R., and M. Kuechler, eds. *Challenging the Political Order: New Social and Political Movements in Western Democracies.* New York: Oxford University Press, 1990.

Delgado, G. *Organizing the Movement: The Roots and Growth of ACORN.* Philadelphia: Temple University Press, 1986.

Drumtra, J. "Power to the People," *World View.* (Winter 1991–92) 4: 8–13.

Durning, A. B. "Action at the Grassroots: Fighting Poverty and Environmental Decline." *Worldwatch Paper* 88. (January 1989): 1–70.

Epstein, B. "Rethinking Social Movement Theory." *Socialist Review* 90. (January–March, 1990).

Evans, P., et al., eds. *Bringing the State Back In.* New York: Cambridge University Press, 1985.

Evans, S. *Personal Politics: The Roots of Women's Liberation in the Civil Rights Movements and the New Left.* New York: Vintage Books, 1979.

Evans, S., and H. Boyte. *Free Spaces: The Sources of Democratic Change in America.* New York: Harper and Row, 1986.

Fisher, R. "Where Seldom Is Heard a Discouraging Word: The Political Economy of Houston, Texas." *Amerika-studien* 33 (Winter, 1988): 73–91.

Fisher, R. "Organizing in the Modern Metropolis." *Journal of Urban History* 18 (1992): 222–237.

Fisher, R. "Grassroots Organizing Worldwide." In Robert Fisher and Joseph Kling, eds. *Mobilizing the Community: Local Politics in a Global Era.* Newbury Park, CA: Sage, 1993.

Fisher, R. *Let the People Decide: Neighborhood Organizing in America,* rev. ed. Boston: Twayne, 1994.

Fisher, R., and J. Kling. "Leading the People: Two Approaches to the Role of Ideology in Community Organizing." *Radical America* 21 (1) (1988): 31–46.

Fisher, R., and J. Kling. "Popular Mobilization in the 1990s: Prospects for the New Social Movements." *New Politics* 3 (1991): 71–84.

Fisher, R., and J. Kling, eds. *Mobilizing the Community: Local Politics in a Global Era.* Newbury Park, CA: Sage, 1993.

Flacks, D. "The Revolution of Citizenship." *Social Policy* 21 (1990): 37–50.

Frank, A. G., and M. Fuentes. "Civil Democracy: Social Movements in Recent World History." In Amin et al., eds., *Transforming the Revolution: Social Movements and the World-System.* New York: Monthly Review Press, 1990.

Gottdiener, M. *The Decline of Urban Politics.* Newbury Park, CA: Sage, 1987.

Gutman, H. G. *Work, Culture, and Society in Industrializing America.* New York: Vintage, 1977.

Horwitt, S. *Let Them Call Me Rebel: Saul Alinsky, His Life and Legacy.* New York: Alfred Knopf, 1989.

Jacobs, P., and S. Landau. *The New Radicals: A Report with Documents.* New York: Vintage Books, 1966.

Jennings, J. "The Politics of Black Empowerment in Urban America: Reflections on Race, Class, and Community." In Kling and Posner, op. cit., 1990.

Kahn, S. *How People Get Power: Organizing Oppressed Communities for Action.* New York: McGraw-Hill, 1970.

Katznelson, I. *City Trenches: Urban Politics and the Patterning of Class in the United States.* Chicago: University of Chicago Press, 1981.

Kaufmann, L. A. "Democracy in a Postmodern World." In *Social Policy.* (Fall 1990): 6–11.

Kjellberg, F. "A Comparative View of Municipal Decentralization: Neighborhood Democracy in Oslo and Bologna." In Sharpe, op. cit., 1979.

Kling, J., and P. Posner, eds. *The Dilemmas of Activism: Class, Community, and the Politics of Local Mobilization.* Philadelphia: Temple University Press, 1990.

Laclau, E., and C. Mouffe. *Hegemony and Socialist Strategy: Towards a Radical Democratic Politics.* London: Verso, 1985.

Lehmann, D. *Democracy and Development in Latin America: Economics, Politics, and Religion in the Postwar Period.* Cambridge: Polity Press, 1990.

Lipsitz, G. *A Life in the Struggle: Ivory Perry and the Culture of Opposition.* Philadelphia: Temple University Press, 1988.

Logan, J., and T. Swanstrom, eds. *Beyond the City Limits.* Philadelphia: Temple University Press, 1990.

Lowe, S. *Urban Social Movements: The City After Castells.* London: Macmillan, 1986.

Mansbridge, J. *Beyond Adversary Democracy.* New York: Basic Books, 1980.

Merkl, P. *New Local Centers in Centralized States.* Berkeley: University Press of America, 1985.

Merkl, P. "How New the Brave New World: New Social Movements in West Germany," *German Studies Review* X. (February 1987): 125–47.

Melucci, A. *Nomads of the Present: Social Movements and Individual Needs in Contemporary Society.* Philadelphia: Temple University Press, 1989.

Midgley, J. *Community Participation, Social Development, and the State.* London: Methuen, 1986.

Molotch, H. "Urban Deals in Comparative Perspective." In Logan and Swanstrom, op. cit., 1990.

Morris, A. *The Origins of the Civil Rights Movement: Black Communities Organizing for Change.* New York: Free Press, 1984.

Offe, C. "Challenging the Boundaries of Institutional Politics: Social Movements Since the 1960s." In C. Maier, ed. *Changing Boundaries of the Political: Essays on the Evolving Balance Between the State and Society, Public and Private in Europe.* Cambridge: Cambridge University Press, 1987.

Paget, K. "Citizen Organizing: Many Movements, No Majority." *American Prospect.* (Summer 1990).

Piven, F., and R. Cloward. *The New Class War: Reagan's Attack on the Welfare State and Its Consequences.* New York: Pantheon, 1982.

Pitkin, H., and S. Shumer. "On Participation." *Democracy* 2. (Fall 1982): 43–54.

Reagon, B. "The Borning Struggle: The Civil Rights Movement." In Dick Cutler, ed. *They Should Have Served That Cup of Coffee.* Boston: South End Press, 1979.

Rogers, M. B. *Cold Anger: A Story of Faith and Power Politics.* Denton, TX: University of North Texas Press, 1990.

Roth, R. "Local Green Politics in West German Cities." In *International Journal of Urban and Regional Research* 15 (1991): 75–89.

Rothman, J. "Three Models of Community Organization Practice." From *National Conference on Social Welfare, Social Work Practice 1968.* New York: Columbia University Press, 1968.

Rothman, J., with J. Tropman "Models of Community Organization and Macro Practice Perspectives: Their Mixing and Phasing." In F. Cox et al., *Strategies of Community Organization,* 4th ed. Itasca, IL: F. E. Peacock Publishers, 1987.

Rude, G. *Ideology and Popular Protest.* New York: Pantheon, 1980.

Sharpe, L. "Decentralist Trends in Western Democracies: A First Appraisal." In L. J. Sharpe, ed., *Decentralist Trends in Western Democracies.* London: Sage Publications, 1979.

Slater, D., ed. *Social Movements and the State in Latin America.* Holland: Foris Publications, 1985.

Spretnak, C., and F. Capra. *Green Politics.* London: Grafton, 1985.

Swanstrom, T. *The Crisis of Growth Politics: Cleveland, Kucinich, and the Challenge of Urban Populism.* Philadelphia: Temple University Press, 1985.

Teodori, M. *The New Left: A Documentary History.* New York: Bobbs-Merrill, 1969.

Touraine, A. "An Introduction to the Study of Social Movements." *Social Research* 52. (Winter 1985): 749–787.

Wallerstein, I. "Antisystemic Movements: History and Dilemmas." In S. Amin et al., op. cit, 1990.

Walton, J. "Urban Political Movements and Revolutionary Change in the Third World." *Urban Affairs Quarterly* 15 (September 1979): 3–22.

22.

Warren C. Haggstrom

THE TACTICS OF ORGANIZATION BUILDING

The organizer lives in a world in which everything is called into question, subject to change, where half-perceived and complex structures constantly dissolve and reform before him. a world of possibility in which he [or she] takes a hand to reshape the future. . . .

The organizer cannot afford to believe that he knows his world well because he is engaged in a course of action under barely tractable, constantly changing, and mostly invisible circumstances which contrast sharply with the neat flatland of the sociological theorist.

To build organization in low-income areas is something like playing a long game of blindfold chess in which no player is sure of the rules. The chess pieces move by themselves; skillful players help get this movement channeled into planned patterns, strategies, and tactics. There are standard beginning lines (e.g., house meetings vs. dramatic large public meetings) and some established principles of play ("rub raw the sores of discontent," "the social situation sets the limits for moves"), but much depends on attention to detail, immense energy, and individual brilliance in capitalizing on whatever happens. Finally, these chess pieces can throw an ineffective player right out of the game.

It follows that the question, "How does one build an organization of the poor?"

cannot be answered in the same way as the question, "How does one build a house?" or "How does one build a great football team?" One can only relate a history of past organizations of the poor, a description of those currently functioning, and principles to which some able organizers more or less adhere. The following remarks are directed to the [last-named] task.

THE STARTING POINT

The physical structure and location of a low-income area carry collectively held meanings to the people of the area, meanings which affect the relevance of the physical context to their lives. For example, a hospital may carry the meaning of being a slaughterhouse or of a place in which patients are "treated like dirt." A row of slum houses may mean at once inferiority and deprivation and reassuring familiarity to slum dwellers. Of seven unmarried mothers living in public housing, six may be respectable women and the seventh a scandal—all in accordance with criteria which are not known outside the neighborhood in question. . . .

The social situation in low-income areas, consisting of such collectively held sets of meanings, can vary tremendously around any physical situation. It is a key responsibility of the organizer to come to know the social situation and, further, he must consider as well his own meaning as a stranger in the neighborhood. He starts work where he and the people of the neigh-

---

Although masculine pronouns are used in this selection, in all cases "he" should be understood to imply "he or she." *Ed.*

borhood are in a social situation which slowly becomes intelligible to him. If people want their windows fixed and the welfare check increased, the organizer helps them to begin to act on these problems even though he may privately believe they would be better off working to open up additional jobs. He is limited by the fact that people consciously and unconsciously misrepresent where they are, and, sometimes, they do not understand how to be relevant to the organizer since he has not clearly defined himself and his purpose in the neighborhood. One can come closest to starting where the people are when one begins in an atmosphere of mutual trust which develops when the organizer places himself clearly on the side of the people with whom he is working and states as plainly as possible his purpose in the neighborhood, but does not presume to define for them their problems or the solutions to their problems.

The people, with the help of the organizer, start to work on problems. Very shortly, their action is contested and the problems are transformed into issues with established institutions opposing the action of people in low-income areas. For example, when a number of people in one city began to seek additional money for school supplies for their children, the Commissioner of Welfare at first acceded to the request. When the number of people making such a request becomes large enough, the commissioner began to deny many of the new requests. At that point, the requests became demands and the resulting struggle drew an increasing number of people into sustained activity of value in building organization. Through a process of struggle around issues perceived in the neighborhood as central the organization develops power which can be used to resolve problems of many varieties.

When an organizer helps people to begin to act on central problems, that is, to make their own decisions about resolving their own problems and to begin to implement those decisions, by that very fact the organizer deliberately creates conflict since the problems of low-income areas cannot be resolved without negative consequences for the self-perceived self-interest and traditional ways of thinking and acting of various advantaged minorities. Until the problems are resolved, so long as the organizer maintains neighborhood action he will by that fact maintain conflict, and requires no artificial strategies leading to artificial confrontations.

THE WAY TO BEGIN

People are usually immersed in private lives centered about work and home. The organizer pulls and jolts them into the public arena.

In the beginning, the organizer is simply another stranger trying to convince people to do something. The organizer is like a salesperson—and is met by the evasive tactics which people use to ward them off. A salesman has only to persuade people to one act, to make one purchase. An organizer has the more complicated job of pulling people into new lives, into long-extended alternative lines of action. . . .

Because people do not yet know him, the organizer has to be credible, creating a convincing picture of what might be, relying on the emotional contagion produced by fire and enthusiasm as well as on the factual account that he gives. Since all this should be appropriate to the people with whom he is talking, he modifies his presentation at first as he talks with different persons and groups until working out an approach which is most effective for him (although not necessarily for other organizers) in the neighborhood in which he is working (although not necessarily in the other neighborhoods).

The organizer starts by persuading people to come to a meeting or begin action. He listens, describing the meeting or action as it is relevant to the situation of those with whom he is talking. He appeals to self-interest, builds anger, works along friendship and relationship networks and other formal and informal social structures. He recruits members without appearing too eager to recruit members; they must see themselves as acting on their own initiative. When people have decided to attend a meeting, join a delegation, etc., then an organizer does his best to make certain that their intention is carried out. People may be reminded again and again of the event, some are provided with transportation, etc.

Once at a meeting an organizer concentrates on moving those attending into decision and action through whatever formal structure may exist. He may make certain that decisions are made to do something concrete about sore points of acute concern: the speeding car that killed Bobby Smith, the lack of police protection for Mrs. Jackson, the slum landlord who runs down the neighborhood, etc. He may ask action-oriented questions, or he may suggest alternatives by describing what other organizations have done in similar situations or on similar problems.

From the point of view of the organizer, the sole point of meetings is to prepare for action just as the sole point of organization is to provide a structure through which action takes place. Thus, he or she helps to clarify alternatives around concrete and immediate courses of action, makes certain that whatever process results in decisions is both legitimate (in accordance with the rules) and efficient (a course of action is

undertaken which is likely to attain the objective intended or otherwise to build the effectiveness of the organization).

At first, people defend themselves against accurately seeing their position in the community and against admitting their discontent to themselves and others. An early objective of action is to provide people with experiences which destroy these defenses. A second early objective is to provide people with experience in responsible planning in defining social paths along which they can make actual gains. . . .

The legitimation for action is provided in meetings, but specific action events may develop from the general responsibility of a committee or other group of work in some area, and not directly from meetings. . . .

For example, in one city, people representing a small neighborhood, with the help of the organizers of a large organization, went to a district sanitation inspector to appeal for better street cleaning. During the course of the discussion the supervisor mentioned that there was no point in putting additional equipment into such neighborhoods since the residents didn't care whether their streets were clean or dirty. When the story of this insult was widely reported (the organizer helping the report along), a large number of people wanted to do something to change street-cleaning practices which they had never before clearly understood to be deliberately discriminatory. They planned a series of actions, including sweeping their own streets while newspaper reporters recorded the event, had the implied backing of the large organization, and several times carried the debris to the homes or businesses of politicians who were responsible. They picketed the district sanitation office and protested at the central sanitation office of the city. Since the city had received national beautification awards and the mayor wanted to maintain its reputation and since the various politicians involved feared that their reelection would eventually be jeopardized, the embarrassment was enough to end the discrimination. . . .

During the course of the several actions, people for the first time saw their relationship to one city service with stark clarity; this alone drove them to action. The insights provided through the experience of people in action are the fuel for a dramatic and broadening rhythm of action. The landlord who denies that blacks are good tenants; the school principal who "confesses" that neighborhood parents do not want their children to get an education—both can become focal points around which a good organizer builds action. As groups of people become drawn into a series of actions, each group working on its own problems but in relation to a common organization, there develops a body of accurate knowledge, enhanced levels of skill, and a larger number of active persons. Together, these enhance to the greatest extent possible the opportunity for each member to resolve his problems through the organizational structure.

ORGANIZER RESPONSIBILITY

An enabler is relatively passive, accepting the prevailing views, and helping people with their problems as defined by current neighborhood perspectives. An organizer is sensitive to current neighborhood perspectives, but may disagree aggressively with people while he remains clearly on their side.

For example, it is common in low-income areas for people to scapegoat their neighbors: "they don't care," "they run down the neighborhood," "people around here will only complain, they never do any-

thing," etc. In this fashion, people repeat the outside stereotypes of low-income areas and develop a rationale for not themselves venturing into organizational efforts. An organizer who agrees with the condemnation not only undercuts neighborhood confidence in the possibility of organizing, but also finds himself rejected as possibly concealing a negative opinion of *everyone* in the neighborhood. Or, the members of an organization may decide on an action that is certain to fail, or which is clearly in violation of the constitution of the organization, or clearly leads to violence, to a collapse of democratic process, etc.

In all these cases, an organizer may find it necessary to disagree aggressively with the members, not to convince people of his own point of view on issues, but rather to make it possible to organize, to build effective organization. The people provide the content of action. The organizer has the responsibility to create and maintain the effective democratic structure of action, that is, a structure through which each neighborhood person has as nearly as possible an equal opportunity effectively to secure self-realization. The organizer, thus, must sometimes assert vigorous, aggressive leadership, even though he is not a member of the organization, and although such leadership should never include projecting his own substantive orientations upon the neighborhood.

On the other hand, the organizer should always refrain from leadership or participation when his intervention is not clearly necessary. For example, when a delegation visits a city official, the preparation ahead of time may not have been enough and the meeting may threaten to dissolve into confusion. An organizer has the responsibility to intervene forcefully to ensure that an effective case is presented. Such intervention should occur rarely, and the organizer should refuse to participate above that minimal level even when urged to do so. To the extent that an organizer has to intervene, to that extent the members will not see the victories as *their* victories, will not maximally acquire knowledge and skills themselves, and will not develop effective organization.

Thus, the role of the organizer is extremely complex. He or she must stand by the side of the people and see the world from their perspective. But he must also be able to go outside that perspective to analyze and decide accurately what he should do in order to build organization. He should never be a member of the organization and should place the organization in the hands of the membership, but he also should know when and how to intervene to protect the essential characteristics which he is responsible for ensuring in the organization. He must be a passive enabler and an aggressive leader at the time when each is required of him, must use his own judgment to determine when he should do either, and therefore must not *need* to play either role.

In his role of energetic intervener, an organizer does not actually place himself in opposition to the neighborhoods. Instead, he allies himself with the long-term objective self-interest of the people in building organization through which they can act effectively, and he seeks to break up collective distortions and orientations which make impossible the creation of such an organizational structure. With this one exception the organizer stays as close as possible to present neighborhood points of view. By this strategy he makes certain that it will be very difficult for enemies of the organization to isolate him from the neighborhood by attacking him as an outsider, as being on someone else's side, etc. Further, the gradual identification of neighborhood

persons with their organization makes it increasingly likely that through, rather than outside of, the organization, they will seek solutions to problems which for the first time become perceived as problems rather than as conditions of existence.

For example, where there is no organization, children playing on busy streets may be injured or killed without any response in the neighborhood. People assume that nothing can be done except, maybe, to watch the children more closely. "Life is like that." The presence of an organization provides a new remedy: "We can get a traffic light." Thus, getting a traffic light becomes a problem which, in the resulting struggle with the relevant city department, is itself transformed into an issue.

The organizer, therefore, not only creates issues and conflict; prior to that he or she creates problems where none were perceived before by creating opportunities where none had been before.

Inexperienced organizers typically fail to understand the necessary self-discipline, the requirement to act (or not) always to build organization and never through needs of the organizer which are irrelevant to or destructive of the building of organization. An organizer who is committed to racial integration cannot organize for racial integration in a community in which people oppose or are indifferent to this stance. . . . An organizer who admires a certain neighborhood leader cannot remain passive while that leader transforms the organization into his own political organization or social club. . . .

The people in a low-income neighborhood may decide not to adopt the kind of organizational structure recommended by an organizer. What then? Should the organizer try to manipulate or coerce the people into accepting what he recommends?

An organizer does not seek to impose himself on a neighborhood; instead he offers his services on the clearly stated basis that he will help build organization with certain characteristics, with the clear understanding that the organizer has responsibility to ensure that the organization meets certain criteria and that the organization belongs and will belong to the members. At first, the members do not yet understand the requirements of organization very clearly; they must be helped to clarity as rapidly as possible and should be made aware that at any time they can discharge the organizer. In short, the organizer must have a legitimated and mutually agreed upon relationship with the organization, a relationship which the organization can cancel whenever it may wish. When the organization achieves permanent status, it may be wise to outline in a written agreement the rights and responsibilities of the organizer and of the organization with respect to each other. . . .

THE STRUCTURE OF SOCIAL ACTION

Any structure through which the poor act on the sources of their problems will be under attack from local governmental and other established institutions. The attack may not be direct; it may consist of subtle attempts to talk organization members out of their concerns, to divert attention to other questions, to ridicule the organization in informal discussions, etc. Attacks by established institutions on an organization of the poor tend to be indirect as much as possible, while it is to the advantage of an organization of the poor to bring these subtle, half-concealed attacks into the arena of open confrontation.

An open attack on the organizational effort in low-income areas usually sharpens the issues and can be used to quicken the pace of organization. Established institutions, realizing this, may choose to attack the sponsors of organization (whoever pays the salary of and supervises organizers) rather than the organizational effort itself. . . .

The sponsor of organization may have any of a wide variety of structures providing only that it is able to refrain from emasculating the work. However, there are fewer alternatives for the structure of the organization being built. It may be a direct membership neighborhood council or an organization of previously existing organizations. In any case, the point is to build a clearly defined structure through which people in low-income areas can act. Thus, although the organization of the poor may carry on social activities, provide services to members, and constitute a forum for militant rhetoric, the basic orientation has always to be the expression of power through the greatest possible number of members acting together to resolve the central problems of their lives.

For people to be able to act through a structure, it must be democratic. Any large number of people can act together democratically in complex activities only when the rules for their participation are clearly stated and equally applied to all members. Complex activities also require specialization of roles (e.g., the spokesperson, the chairperson, the secretary, the committee member, etc.) and a clear definition of the relationships among the roles. Thus, rules must be explicit and generally accepted in accordance with which members of the organization have a formally equal opportunity to participate in decisions and occupy various positions. The organizer is responsible to ensure that such a structure is developed and that formal equality is reflected as far as possible in actual practice. Since many low-income people are learning for the first time to maintain organizational roles, these structural requirements must be communicated and legitimated more vividly than would be necessary with memberships with more organizational experience.

It is common for an inexperienced organizer to attempt to develop movement through the natural relationships among people rather than to create an explicit structured set of interpersonal relationships and decision processes. The movement which results from the former course either is temporary and effective only in carrying out simple activities, or it becomes complex but the instrument of one person rather than of the widest possible portion of the general membership. In either case, the resulting organization is a relatively ineffective structure, relatively unavailable for collective action by the poor. . . .

One way to create [an effective] structure is to hold a series of preliminary unstructured small or large meetings with people in the neighborhoods in which organization is being developed (after organizers have been invited in by neighborhood persons and institutions). In those preliminary meetings issues can be clarified, leadership can become visible in the neighborhood, and a general interpretation can be made by the organizer of the nature of such a proposed organization. Then, an initial general meeting can decide whether to organize, can elect temporary officers, and provide preliminary committees (to develop a constitution, begin action, etc.). A permanent structure (officers, committees, constitution, by-laws, etc.) can be adopted at a later meeting. After such a beginning, there is a legitimated democratic process for replacing persons in various positions, a process which makes it less easy for the organization to become the captive of a single leader, and less likely that the organization will dissolve, turn into a social club, or meet others of the usual disastrous fates of democratic organizations.

THE SOCIAL SITUATIONAL CONTOURS OF CONFLICT

. . . The meaning of a move in a conflict depends on the nature of the move, its context, and may also vary to different audiences. For example, depending upon the context, when a Commissioner of Public Welfare increases clothing allotments this may be understood by everyone as an act of generosity or, alternatively, of weakness. Or, it may be perceived as an act of generosity to members of the welfare establishment *and* as an act of weakness to members of the organization demanding the increase. Further, the divergence of interpretations of the same public act in a conflict situation tends to make the reactions of each side incomprehensible to the other. When the organization renews its pressure, persons in the welfare establishment may believe that the organized welfare clients are simple-minded puppets of organizer manipulation and agitation, and also amoral and naturally parasitic. The organized welfare clients, on the other hand, may believe that the commissioner is trying to deprive them of their rightful allotments, that this is why he is not giving straight answers to their questions.

In a conflict situation the objective consequences of an act by one side or by another, or the intentions behind the act, may be almost irrelevant. The act is one point around which conflict swirls, and a common interpretation may eventually be made as both sides, usually first really brought together by the conflict, begin to know one another better. . . .

SOCIAL ACTION AS MORALITY DRAMA

The organizer conducts the conflict which draws to itself the fascinated attention of a large portion of the entire community. The public conflict creates an audience and actors who play to the audience. The actors invent their own lives in a performance not to be repeated. The organizer ensures that the play is seen as a struggle between the forces of good and the forces of evil (although there will be no consensus concerning which side is which). Through helping keep the initiative with the organization of the poor, through breaking up existing perspectives by unforeseeable improvisations, through drawing the powerful into a conflict in the spotlight of public attention, the organizer enables that organization to begin to control the opponents, thus creating the first interdependency for previously dependent people. From that point, the organizer works with a process which includes the opponents; no longer does he work *only* with the organization of the poor. He conducts the play in which one group of actors (the organization of the poor) creates and controls the conflict, and in which the other mainly responds and attempts to avoid the conflict. The actors write their own lines, but the organizer helps them to improve the performance. There is rehearsal prior to a public event (role-playing) and an analysis afterward. As the play continues, the skills of the poor begin clearly to rival, and then to outstrip, those of the opposition. The public conflict then communicates the ability of the poor to the community which had previously depreciated that ability. . . .

Besides achieving a diminution in dependency and a lesson in equality, the organizer has the task of institutionalizing the new relationships so that, as the audience departs, the poor find themselves with a stable level of power, greater than before, and incorporated into the new community status quo.

The institutionalization of a new social position for the poor is possible because, although the conflict may subside, and the audience may leave, the ability of the organization to create the conflict and draw the audience has been established. Thus, the actions of the poor now acquire a new meaning. . . .

SYMBOLIC CONCESSIONS

When the organization becomes powerful enough, it will force concessions from opponents. The mayor will appoint a Human Rights Commission, the urban renewal agency will agree to more citizen involvement in relocation of people from the demolition area, the state legislature will pass a resolution setting forth state policy on housing code enforcement, the public education system will announce classes for adult poor, trade unions will state that they no longer exclude anyone from apprenticeship programs on racial grounds, public welfare publicly decides no longer to support slum landlords by paying rent for welfare recipients in slum housing, the police chief assures the organization that there is now a new complaint process to which he pays personal attention, etc.

All these are promissory notes, issued under pressure. It is a responsibility of the organizer to make certain that they are converted into the legal tender of actual changes in practice which benefit the people in low-income areas, that they are not merely used as symbolic substitutes for the actual resolution of problems. When the leaders of an organization of the poor are appointed to this community and that board, the result is usually that they become part of the opponent apparatus by which the lives of the poor are controlled. Until enough experience develops in the organization it is often possible for opponents to take the edge off campaigns against them by making agreements which they intend never to keep. Especially in the early stages of organization, the organizer helps keep attention focused, not on promises and agreements announced with however much fanfare, but on whatever actually occurs in the lives of people in the low-income areas as a consequence of such announcements. When an opponent has agreed to a concession, a new line of action must usually soon be directed to force the opponent to carry out the agreement. Only after a period of time does it become clear to everyone concerned that agreements must be kept or painful sanctions will be imposed by the organization. The organizer repeatedly calls the attention of members, often by Socratic questioning, to what is actually happening within the low-income area, and brings out discrepancies between opponent promises and performances. The organizer agitates; the organization acts; a reluctant opposition is coerced into honesty.

KNOWING OPPOSITION TACTICS

Persons in positions of power have long experience in frustrating opposition to them. An organization of the poor gradually develops equivalent or even superior expertise through its own experience. The organizer helps members, and especially leaders, to think through the strategies and tactics of opponents.

He must, for example, understand the usual initial "cooling out" approach in which someone with a friendly and disarming manner attempts to persuade the neigh-

borhood to accept something other than what is being demanded. He must know that opponents may replace an old and hated injustice with a new injustice about which anger has not yet been developed, as happened, for example, when alienation in public housing was substituted for exploitation by private slum landlords. He must be alert to the use of rules and regulations to confuse critics. For example, when a delegation went to talk with a welfare commissioner, the members were told that their demands could not be met because everything in welfare is done according to the rules—federal rules, state rules, county rules—and pointed to a huge manual to support his statement. If they had not been prepared, the members would not have been able to describe numerous instances in which public welfare workers used wide discretion in interpreting and applying the rules.

The organizer must know the divide-and-conquer techniques, as, for example, when concessions are offered to leaders or to some portion of an organization in order to create illegitimate advantages and unfair disadvantages within the organization.

Opponents typically portray the organization to the rest of the affluent community as threatening some revered symbol: the nation, the American way of life, law and order, and the appeal for unity against subversion, for harmony rather than disruption, etc. They taunt the people for needing organizers, offer concessions provided the organizers are discarded, praise the people while attacking the organizers as outsiders trying to tell the people what to do. The organizer helps the people to understand the nature of the attack and to turn it back on the attackers in various ways. For example, the organization may publicize the extent to which the opponents violate other symbols: the right to equal opportunity, the value of self-help, the defense of mother and children. . . .

The current action requires development of moves against the vulnerable points of opponents. The organizer jogs members into thinking through what the opponent needs that the organization can provide, interrupt, or otherwise affect. Does a public agency fear public scrutiny? An organization of the poor can draw public attention to it. Does a member of the city council need a thousand additional votes? An organization of the poor can affect many more than that number. Does a department store need a positive image? A margin of profit? A mass organization may be able to affect the one by bringing employment discrimination into the open; the other by a combination of picket lines and boycotts. Does a social agency need to pretend that it is meeting needs? A people's organization can demonstrate unmet needs by helping ten times as many people with legitimate need to apply for help as the agency has openings. Does a school claim that the parents of the neighborhood are not interested in education? The parents can seek public funds to sponsor their own school, picket and boycott the existing school, make it clear that their interest in education is as intense as their opposition to the existing school. Do a variety of people and organizations want to avoid the fray, to stay neutral? The organization can focus public attention on their neutrality, force them to examine the issues, force them to take sides. Since most people with detailed understanding of the issues will agree with the orientation of a mass organization of low-income people, or at least do not want the opposition of such an organization, forcing neutrals to take sides will result in increasing support for it in the affluent community.

Since low-income people lack resources, it is useful to get opponents to work for the organization. If persons in authority are drawn into attack on the low-income people or on the symbols dear to them, the attack itself will build organization more quickly than any number of organizers could do by themselves.

An organization has often to map possible lines of action by opponents in order to make it easiest for them to meet organizational demands. It is not enough only to attack the destruction by urban renewal of low-income neighborhoods; the organization may have to secure competent technical counsel to prepare alternative feasible plans for neighborhood rebuilding, plans which will not violate the professional standards of city planners while having the advantage of support by the people of the neighborhood . . . .

All the moves mentioned above have been tried and found useful in one or another context. No one can say whether they would be useful again in other contexts. One could also consider modifications. Could clients or tenants engage in collective bargaining in order to work out new contractual agreements with a public welfare agency or a public housing authority? Could a low-income area organize to spend the bulk of its entire income in accordance with organizational decisions? What would happen if the poor used cameras and tape recorders to create a record of their treatment compared with that given affluent persons in shops, public offices, banks? Can low-income areas organize a "hiring hall" for jobs of all kinds, the analogue of industrial unionism on a community basis? . . .

THE KNOWLEDGE BASE OF ACTION

In a conflict situation, the organization does what is unexpected, dividing and confusing opponents, keeping them off balance. It seeks out and tackles points of weakness: the fact that bureaucratic organizations depend on clients or customers or constituents, provisions and communication, all of which may be affected at unpredictable times in unpredictable ways; the fact that powerful persons usually need to be jolted before they even begin to take seriously the lives of low-income people; the fact that people and organizations operating on routines cannot tolerate disruption. . . .

The knowledge base of social action must constantly be reformed; the organizer senses changes needed, inspires daily examinations and theoretical reanalyses of the event process. A series of demonstrations which had been projected for weeks may be abandoned without notice; an enemy of years' standing may become a friend; the major issue of one day may have been entirely replaced by another the next day; a drive to force landlords to repair housing may be replaced by a plan for public housing operated by the tenants. Academic observers may be surprised at the apparent lack of a predictable, consistent set of alliances, tactics, orientations, by the organization. However, the organization learns to follow the single principle of building power in the low-income area; it would be disastrous to that ambition if the organization were to become predictable to academic observers. . . .

CAMPAIGNS

The organization grows through actions and activities. Either is carried on by a series of campaigns of strictly limited duration. The actions may include a month of daily picket lines around city hall to protest police brutality, or a two-month period of voter registration and voter education ending in a massive directed vote, or a six-hour sit-in at a public official's office, or a two-hour play-in by children at city hall. The activities may consist of a two-day fund-raising barbecue, a week-long fundraising carnival, a two-week chest X-ray campaign, a monthly tour of scenic places for elderly persons in the neighborhood, an annual one-day fashion show. Actions are directed toward securing change in the relationship of the low-income area to the affluent community; activities contribute only indirectly to this outcome: directly they occur within established inside-outside relationships. However, in either case, a large number of people will only become involved for what is known in advance to be a limited period of time after which there will be a time of relative quiescence. It is a responsibility of the organizer to make certain that a series of campaigns is developed, involving the problems and issues and interests and skills of the widest possible number of persons in the area being organized. And, since the organization exists primarily for action, the organizer should ensure that campaign *activities* do not come to occupy the major attention of the membership.

Through such a series of campaigns, the number of persons identified with the organization continues to increase. Provided there is maintained an action emphasis, the pressure on the opponents of the organization will continue to mount. . . .

SERVICES

To some extent, outposts of the affluent community in areas of poverty (welfare, medical care, public housing, private business) are not likely to be responsive enough to organizational demands to supply adequate services sensitively tailored to the self-perceived needs of low-income people.

To that extent, the organization can itself sponsor temporary services which will eventually disappear when the area being helped is no longer one of poverty. From the point of view of the affluent community it is prudent to spend a given sum of money (a) more efficiently than it is now spent, and (b) without being open to blame for the inadequacies and inequities involved in the extention of services to a dependent and hostile population. It will therefore become attractive for the affluent community to finance services which will be operated under the direction of organizations of the poor. The organizer will need to acquire some understanding of the pitfalls and advantages of this eventual outcome, and help the organization to secure needed services in such a way that the organization is strengthened and retains its action orientation and in a way that avoids the stigma which attaches to many service programs operated by low-income people. . . .

The organizer should not get so involved in the tough daily struggle of creating organization that he loses sight of the minimum long-range outcomes which will validate the amount of effort by the organization.

WHAT WILL NOT WORK

. . . First, there is no easy or quick way to build powerful organizations in low-income areas. Power only comes to an organization after a large number of people have acquired the skill to work efficiently through the organizational structure. It takes several years to meet these conditions. Building mass demonstrations in a short-lived movement or campaign may leave a residue of change, but they do not provide a structure through which power is exercised. Or, one can pull together existing organizations and groups into an organiza-

tion of organizations in a convention with mass attendance, but the people who attend such a convention are not yet organized. All that has happened is that groups which previously met separately now meet once together and maintain some subsequent communication. The long, hard work of building a single powerful organization will require additional years. It is important in organizational work that some power be exercised very nearly at the beginning, but the early exercise of power does not mean that a structure has yet been created through which the exercise of power is effective and routine.

Second, an organizer can "look good quick" by organizing at once a mass action effort. However, if he or she does not also concentrate on creation of a structure and decision process through which people themselves can act effectively, his flash flood of action will soon disappear or leave behind an organization run by one person or a clique, not a structure through which the neighborhood can act.

Third, an organizer may have made a brilliant analysis of the need for a revolutionary social transformation, or have a beautiful vision of participatory democracy. But, if he or she projects these perspectives of his upon a low-income population with immediate and concrete problems, even if he also pays attention to these latter problems, he will find that his organization will be small, weak, sectarian, and easily isolated. An organizer must always be directly relevant to present neighborhood perspectives.

Fourth, it is sometimes argued that the appropriate structure for organizational work is that of the storefront church or some other type of organization [of] which low-income people are already members. This argument takes the culture of the poor into account, but not the fact that storefront churches and other organizations in low-income areas do not *do* much, do not perform complex tasks. In addition to the requirement of conforming to neighborhood traditions there is the other requirement of creating a structure adequate to carry on action and activities and operate services simultaneously and efficiently on a wide variety of problems and issues. Over any length of time this requires a division of labor, specialization, differentiated explicit role structures. Primitive structures do primitive tasks.

Fifth, existing social welfare institutions usually cannot sponsor organizational work in low-income areas because they cannot tolerate the conflict, because they define the problems of low-income people from outside rather than working with the definitions of low-income people, because they start from a position above the poor and reach down rather than starting with a working respect for low-income people.

Sixth, an organizer cannot follow a political organizational model since such models are developed solely to deliver votes and since they deliver votes by the politician doing things for people rather than by people doing things for themselves. A neighborhood acts through a political organization only in a very limited way. . . .

AWARENESS OF CHANGE

. . . In social action, the power of the poor shifts imperceptibly through their efforts. The public welfare worker is a little more alert to guard their rights, the politician a little more concerned about their opinion, the police officer less inclined to acts of brutality or corruption in the low-income neighborhood and a little more inclined to protect the rights of the people. The neighborhood continues to see the public welfare worker, the politician, the police officer, on

the basis of years of experience. It is one task of the organizer to arouse the people from their bad dream which includes an underlying fear of their own weakness and inferiority, to point out and describe the changes which are taking place even outside the areas of concrete actions by the neighborhood organization. It is a task of the organizer to go beyond the creation of an account of neighborhood action to helping the people in the organization create an alternative and more accurate view of their world and of their position in it. The assumption that blacks and women are excluded from an apprenticeship training program may be generally believed, no longer true, and an important belief for the behavior of young blacks and women. The assumption that the barriers to professional education are fixed and unchangeable may be important and no longer accurate. The organizer points out changes [and] possibilities and helps an appreciation of them to become incorporated in the everyday thinking of most people in the areas of poverty in which he is working.

THE NEW TRADITION

An organizer helps an alternative account of the world to develop in the organization. An organizer may relate the story in detail again and again of how this leader stood right up to the commissioner and told the truth, or how that demonstration led to an increase in police protection or how the voting power of the organization has the council passing ordinances which they never considered before. The action of neighborhood people becomes fixed in a positive account which creates a clear context whereby people can gain self-esteem through action, whether or not individual employment or other opportunities are open to them. . . . A positive collective identity becomes rooted in the past, and no longer subject to the vicissitudes of an uncertain world. This identity is publicly known throughout the neighborhood; it can be revived at any time as it bolsters self-esteem in contemporary actors.

An organizer who recounted traditions would normally be merely a neighborhood bore. But when the account is credible and about what neighborhood people have accomplished in combat on crucial issues against great odds, the account is often quickly grasped and long relished.

Thus, an organizer not only learns to listen carefully when talking with people, but also learns to provide through his words a concrete, vivid, compelling, and credible picture of the situation, a picture that is intended to upset the existing definition, force people to take sides about a proposed course of action, and outline such a course with clarity. This concrete, vivid, compelling and credible picture is often essential for getting movement under way, even though it stereotypes a wide variety of people and events under single labels and thus distorts reality through oversimplification and selection. People learn first to think about action while making only the major distinctions. Later, and through their own experience, people make the exceptions and fill in the details . . . .

The fact that an organizer creates an oversimplified sketch of action space should not be taken to mean that the people of low-income areas think in simple terms. Rather, just as the first knowledge of university students about a new area is stereotypic, for the same reason people who begin collective action must begin on the basis of the major relevant ideas and would be immobilized by a complete and detailed account which would not be easily incorporated in action.

THE LOCUS OF RESPONSIBILITY

The success of action can be undermined in two major ways: (1) it does not attain its objectives and, (2) it attains its objectives, but someone other than members of the organization is seen as responsible for the result. If the enemy is perceived in the neighborhood as having simply decided to give the people what they want, the action may be seen as ending well, but it is a failure as social action. It only becomes a social action success when the outcome is understood in the low-income area to be a direct consequence of organizational activity. Similarly, if the intended outcome is perceived in the low-income area as directly due to the intervention of the organizer, it is a social action failure. The organizer must ensure that the responsibility for securing an intended outcome is always placed squarely on the organization membership. Thus, the organizer typically ensures that meetings are well attended, that the necessary work gets done, that the organization holds such an initiative that an action favorable to the organization by an opponent is perceived as stemming from this initiative. But, the organizer accomplishes these ends as unobtrusively as possible in view of the fact that he may sometimes need conspicuously to intervene and that he must maintain a relationship of candor and responsibility with the people he helps. He interprets his role: "It is your organization, you will call the shots, do the work (and it's hard work)!" . . . Constant attention to placing responsibility with the people of low-income areas not only ensures that action has the most positive outcome for the skills and self-concept of the people involved, but also more people are more likely to become and remain active in an organization structured to increase their self-responsibility.

DEVELOPING THE PERSPECTIVES
OF THE PEOPLE

People begin to act for themselves rather than have someone act for them. This requires that people also learn to think for themselves and not merely rely on the organizer's thinking. As much as possible, the organizer helps develop from the action itself a tradition of success; he or she does not only create the tradition and tell it to the people. . . .

Instead of outlining action possibilities for organization members, the organizer will often ask questions which help people to think through action alternatives for themselves and strategies of action by their opponents. Insofar as efficiency is not too greatly reduced, responsibility for thought as well as for action is placed in the neighborhood, not merely with leaders or with organizers.

For example, suppose that an organization is trying to stop the illegal distribution of narcotics by licensed pharmacists in its neighborhood. After learning that state officials will do nothing, the members begin to think of securing legislative remedy. The organizer could simply explain the difficulty of getting legislation, especially in the face of well-financed opposition. But this approach would leave him more vulnerable to the constant attack by opponents: "The idea behind your organization is a fine thing. But aren't you people grown up yet? Do you need an organizer to do your thinking for you?" It would also mean that members may agree, but would not act with much conviction on the basis of ideas that were not their own. An alternative is preferable. The organizer may ask a series of questions about exactly how the organization can use its energy most effectively. Can you put much pressure on the legislature at this stage? Are there any other ways to act? What about direct pressure on drug-

gists in the neighborhood? What has the best chance to succeed? The organization may in any case seek legislation, but the decision will be made after a realistic examination of alternatives and will clearly be that of the organization itself.

A more complex problem arises when the organizer must respond to attempts (very common in organizational work) to isolate him from the members. For example, suppose that opponents of the organization spread the word that, although the organization itself is basically a good idea, it is hurt by the presence of an organizer who is a "Communist." The line of questioning by the organizer must help the members to an accurate appraisal of the attack: that the allegation is false and that it is an attempt to weaken the organization. . . .

It is not easy to help people to think for themselves in areas outside their usual experience. The organizer can only do it well through self-discipline and great respect for the people (to prevent manipulation in . . . the direction of organizer biases) and through having become perceived in the neighborhood as responsible and trustworthy. People are often afraid to act, uncertain about whom they can depend on, ignorant of the extent to which they are vulnerable to one or another disastrous outcome. The organizer must be the kind of person who can be counted on. He helps them undertake actions on the basis of assumptions which, through their own experience, people discover to have been valid. Even when it would be easier to agitate people by building up unfounded fears, the organizer maintains a relationship of honesty with neighborhood people, helping them to see accurately the possible disasters as well as limitations in the successes before them. Any other approach would lead to initially dazzling demonstrations or other actions followed by a decline in the organization as its members lost confidence in the organizer. For example, suppose people in one area are considering a rent strike to force landlords to fix up slum dwellings. The rent strike would get started very quickly if the organizer stressed only the facts that attorneys will represent the tenants, that money is available for legal expenses, that rent strikes do not appear to be illegal, etc., but did not mention the fact that tenants could probably be evicted after thirty days for nonpayment of rent. After the first few evictions, the reputation of the organizer and of the organization would have been destroyed beyond recovery. Over time, a self-confident critical elaboration of an adequate neighborhood perspective stems from the experience of having acted on a reasonable appraisal of alternatives and possibilities with the help of an organizer who is responsible and honest.

TRANSFORMATION OF RELATIONSHIPS

The relationships in a low-income area are primarily: (a) friendship, familial, or neighbor relationships, all object relationships with persons within the area, and (b) ecological dependency relationships with persons and institutions outside. In the beginning, to some extent people simply shift their dependency from other persons and institutions to organizers. On first appearance, an organizer is interpreted within the context of usual ways of relating. He or she is an outsider on whom people depend for the provision of skills and resources. The organizer is also like a friend. Therefore, at first, he is likely to be loved, at the same time hated, deferred to, and depended on. One task of the organizer is to transform this personal relationship (in which people find it difficult to accept a substitute for him) into a role relationship in a structure with which people identify. He is successful (a) to the extent that members value him as a resource, but in relationships of interdependence in which members make the important decisions and do much of the work; and (b) to the extent to which members want an organizer without needing a specific organizer, and (c) [to the extent to which members] value him for his contribution to the organization rather than for the broad range of his unique personality characteristics. In other words, the relationship of an organizer to the organization becomes gradually depersonalized and egalitarian from a beginning point of personalization and dependency. . . .

SUCCESS

Success occurs when the people in low-income areas can, through organization, solve a wide variety of central problems which they could not solve before, when through organization they can become effective acting persons rather than passive objects of action. Many people are swept into action, not by direct active membership in the organization, but through identification with an acting neighborhood-based mass organization. That organizer has succeeded who has ensured the creation of such a structure which expands the area of freedom for persons in the action area. . . .

As an organization accomplishes a number of things over a period of time, an organizer has to work actively against its decline into a bureaucratic skeleton going through routine motions while major collective problems remain unresolved. Because of the tendency of organizations to fossilize, organizers will very likely be needed to maintain an action emphasis for as long as one can plan ahead. . . .

23.

George Brager

AGENCY UNDER ATTACK: THE RISKS, DEMANDS, AND REWARDS OF COMMUNITY ACTIVISM

In the early 1950s, the initial years of my work life, community organization referred largely to the coordination and collaboration of social agencies and/or to a cooperative planning process conducted by professionals with an educated, largely middle-class citizenry. The participation of low-income service users in influencing institutional decision making, was at best a peripheral element in the field, and although "grassroots" organizing took place in the country, it was not by and large considered a part of social work. It was not until the concept of citizen participation emerged as a major idea—a prized value and the great nuisance of the social legislation of the 1960s—that organizing low-income consumers of services found currency as a mode of practice in schools of social work. A significant contributor to this development was Mobilization for Youth (MFY), an agency on the Lower East Side of New York City.

This paper focuses on one aspect of the Mobilization for Youth experience: a virulent attack on the agency by New York City officials and the right-wing press. MFY's social change-oriented community program was the primary target of the onslaught, and the experience illustrates some of the risks, demands, and perhaps the rewards of community activism.

Mobilization for Youth was designed to demonstrate ways of helping residents of an inner-city slum to deal with problems caused by living under the corrosive conditions of poverty, deprivation, and discrimination. Initially planned as an attempt to combat delinquency through interventions involving an entire community, it became the model for the War on Poverty. It is not hyperbole to assert that the Economic Opportunity Act of 1964 and the many programs that sprang up to implement it stemmed in considerable measure from the MFY experience. In *Maximum Feasible Misunderstanding*, a book by Daniel Patrick Moynihan that is hardly laudatory about community action programs in general or Mobilization for Youth in particular, he writes:

The first OEO Community Action Guide . . . clearly shows the influence of MFY. Preschool education (such as Head Start), legal aid for the poor (not just to defend them, but to serve them as plaintiffs), a theory of community organization, an emphasis on research and evaluation, and most especially the insistence on the involvement of the poor, all these were the legacy of Mobilization for Youth.[1]

Mobilization's program was based on opportunity theory, as developed by Richard Cloward and Lloyd Ohlin. To reduce delinquency, it was held, it is necessary to expand objective opportunities available to impoverished youth; thus youth employment and education became major components of the program. It was also necessary, in this schema, to attack factors that prevent youth from taking advantage of whatever opportunities do exist; a network of specialized services to individuals, group members, and their families was therefore included as well.

But Mobilization's mandate was to develop programs that represented innovation in content, method, structure, or auspices. It does not require theoretical sophistication to hold that poor youngsters need jobs, that their education should be better, or that individuals in trouble require help in order to maximize their life changes. Nor does espousal of these notions guarantee programmatic innovation. A primary source of MFY's innovation stemmed from the rather simple idea that if services were to be organized meaningfully, social class variables had to be taken into account in program planning. An understanding in class terms of reciprocal relationship between the "defects" of the clients and those of the institutions with which they interact suggests specific targets for intervention.

The engagement of the low-income community was featured in most MFY's activities, but in none was it more emphasized than in its community organizing program. According to Mobilization philosophy, poverty was viewed as the problem, and power, in the hands of those suffering the consequences of poverty, was necessary for its solution. Power, in the sense of the ability to affect one's life chances, can be provided to an individual through a network of services. It is also possible to try to vest power in a group, the group with the most at stake. With power, citizens can press for additional or improved services, express and demand redress of grievances from public and private institutions, develop leadership skills, and offer their youth some optimistic evidence of what the future might hold. A challenging social action program was viewed as the vehicle by which this might be accomplished.

The social action program was a lightning rod that drew controversy to the agency. Slightly more than two years after operations had gotten underway, on Sunday, August 16, 1964, blazoned in bold capital letters on the front page of the New York *Daily News*, then a right-wing tabloid, were the headlines: "YOUTH AGENCY EYED FOR REDS: City Cuts Off Project's Funds." Two days later, in similarly, dramatic style, front-page headlines read: "CITY TO PROBE YOUTH AGENCY: Mayor Reveals Curb on Cash," and the next day again, "LIST 45 LEFTIES IN YOUTH GROUP." Thus began an intense attack on the agency that continued unrelentingly for the next five months. Featured on the front pages of New York's seven dailies, some of which were friendly and some stridently negative, the organization was ultimately transformed.

In the maelstrom of August 1964 to January 1965, as a codirector of the agency, I was absorbed—immersed—all day, every day, whether at work or at home, in the events of the crisis. I spent every weekend during the five-month period recording the week's events In a diary. Yet, in the 32 years since then, I could not bring myself to read what I had written. Jack Rothman's invitation to contribute to [*Reflecting on Community Organization*] finally provided me with sufficient incentive to revisit the event.

The planets must have been in proper alignment during MFY's development; stated differently and without the astrological metaphor, the formation of the agency was made possible by a favorable confluence of political circumstances. Led by Henry Street Settlement, the social agencies of the Lower East Side of New York City had come together in 1958 out of their concern about gangs that roamed the neighborhood. They proposed to develop a community-wide program that would saturate the neighborhood with services, and thus draw funds for their ongoing programs in a time of fiscal strain. "The problem is not so much how to do it," one of the early documents read, "since the methods are known; the problem is to find sufficient means to meet the whole problem."

The proposal was submitted by the settlement group to the National Institute of Mental Health (NIMH), which suggested it be withdrawn and resubmitted as a request for funds for a planning period. Influenced by the Ford Foundation's Grey Areas community development initiative, NIMH was receptive to a community-oriented approach to reducing delinquency and interested in the possible use of the Lower East Side as a laboratory to test new perspectives. In granting funds for a two-year planning period to begin in June 1960, NIMH posed a number of stipulations. The program had to be innovative, include a significant research and evaluation component, and have a university affiliation. This is the basis for the inclusion of the Columbia University School of Social Work in the group. NIMH also required that the group had to demonstrate community "readiness" by establishing a broad collaborative structure to receive funds—thereby providing the incentive to create a new agency.

A significant element in MFY's development was the creation of the President's Committee on Juvenile Delinquency (PCJD). The Kennedy administration owed its narrow victory in 1960 to the heavy vote in key cities and particularly to the black vote in these cities. Kennedy had to find a way to reward that support without antagonizing other important constituencies.[2] Directly providing funds for community programs to largely Democratic-controlled cities while bypassing largely Republican statehouses was eminently attractive in that regard, and Mobilization was on the scene with a community approach to delinquency, a politically benign and compelling issue. PCJD headed by Robert Kennedy, then the attorney general (and the president's brother), included the secretaries of Health, Education, and Welfare and the Department of Labor, and wielded immense influence in Washington. Its executive director was David Hackett, a close school friend of Robert Kennedy. Lloyd Ohlin, an MFY planner and Columbia professor, was recruited as PCJD's program director, clearly the result of the administration's interest in promoting urban programs like Mobilization for Youth. The President's Committee became MFY's patron, running interference for the program in obtaining sanction and funds from federal departments and the New York City government.

In June 1962, President Kennedy announced at a press conference on the White House lawn that the United States and New York City would support MFY's community demonstration to prevent juvenile delinquency. The agency had been required to include others beyond the original group on its board, and now as reconstituted, the board was composed of roughly one-third of the original social agency members, with the other two-thirds divided between Columbia University and New York City representatives. It was to become painfully clear during the upcoming attack on the agency that, as is typical of coordinating groups, the primary loyalty of MFY board members was to their home organizations.

Winslow Carlton, a patrician philanthropist and former chair of the board of Henry Street Settlement, headed the 60-member group, and a tripartite administrative structure was adopted with three coequal directors, one primarily responsible for administration (Jim McCarthy), one for research (Richard Cloward), and one for program (myself). Approximately 14 other executives headed discrete program areas and were supervised by a deputy program director and myself. Since MFY's directors had primary access to the agency's financial resources through their relationship with its funding sources (NIMH, the Ford Foundation, the President's Committee, and City officials), their influence on agency operations was considerable.

Larger social forces also contributed to shaping Mobilization's actions and reaction before, during, and after the attack on the agency. The early sixties were a time of ferment and change; idealism was stirred and hopes burgeoned that something might be done about poverty in America. Few Americans were untouched in some way by the great social upheavals of the period—the marches and demonstrations launched by the civil rights movement, and the disruption associated with the student revolt and the protests against the war in Vietnam. During the sixties, the pursuit of social change occurred with great immediacy and militancy, and Mobilization inevitably reflected this societal coloration.

On a purely personal note, those were heady days. Mistakenly or not, social workers felt certain that the ways to improve social conditions were known. To be so close to the country's seat of power at Mobilization enhanced for us the meaning and value of our professional contribution. The exhilarating feeling that stemmed from the fact that what we did as social workers could make a significant difference was something I had not felt before, nor have I felt it since.

Although community organizing accounted for only 7 to 10 percent of Mobilization's expenditures, it provided the content for most of the controversy. The project's encouragement of community participation in the 1963 March on Washington generated anonymous complaints to the FBI. Its support of a group of Puerto Rican mothers who questioned a school's program contributed to the antagonism of the educational bureaucracy, and culminated in a public outcry against MFY by the district's principals. Landlords complained to local political leaders about MFY's activities regarding housing violations. Some local political leaders themselves looked askance at attempts to activate the minority community and complained about Mobilization's reformist coloration. Perhaps most antagonistic of all were the police, from whom the *Daily News* derived most of its raw "data" on "subversives" at MFY. Agency lawyers had been aggressively representing neighborhood youth at the station house, and worse still, MFY joined in a public campaign to create a Police Civilian Review Board, an anathema to the police in those days.

Although these activities may be seen as the genesis of the crisis, as important perhaps was the advent of federal funds to combat poverty. Antipoverty money put MFY in the position of competing with the City for federal resources. For example, the U.S. Department of Labor awarded significant money to Mobilization's youth employment program while it gave short shrift to the City's similar but less professional effort. In addition, a tense internal power struggle over "ownership" of the City's antipoverty efforts took place between the city administrator, to whom MFY was accountable, and the City Council president. The victor was the City Council president who became the City's new Poverty Czar. MFY no longer had a friend in City Hall, and its close association with the city administrator did little to endear it with this now newly powerful official.

It is true, nonetheless, that MFY's activities were perceived as threatening to City Hall and provided sufficient cause for it to go on the offensive. As stated by one high-level City official, "You can't treat the mayor like this; you can't kick him in the ass; after all, he's paying for it." The fact, too, that the attack came during the Johnson–Goldwater presidential campaign provided the political incentive for Republicans to join the agency's other adversaries.

Once an attack takes place, real or imagined grievances can be expected to fan the flames of the conflagration. For example, we had been unwilling to entrust the local neighborhood council of social agencies with implementing the MFY proposal to organize the low-income residents of the Lower East Side, and the council's executives became an active source of false and damaging rumors. Further, MFY had subcontracted about one million dollars to the original social agency group to provide social services, a larger sum than was contained in their original wish list. The lure of the contracts "bought the agencies off," as the planners intended, but an undercurrent of dissatisfaction persisted. Not only had their expectations risen but other programs such as youth employment and education had been accorded greater prominence than their own. As a consequence, although the agency directors were generally supportive, some of them were considerably less so than would otherwise have been the case.

In retrospect, it may be argued that MFY's social action program was overextended. However, there would have been legitimate dilemmas had we wanted to rein it in. (Though, admittedly, reining it in was not on our agenda.) One concern was the need to be seen as standing with the community, to maintain the agency's credibility with its constituency of the poor during those times of minority and civil rights activism. Further, community groups organized by MFY were a source of pressure on the agency to "do the right thing." Our initial contract had provided that community groups would be free to make their own decisions without endangering Mobilization's support as long as they did not break the law. It might, of course, have been possible to persuade participants that an action could seriously compromise the agency and to ask them to desist on that ground. But, then, what is the cost of emphasizing risks to the agency when community action itself entails risks to its low-income participants?

Community agitation brought the issue of subversion in its wake, and early rumblings about the radicalism of some staff began to surface. The red scare spearheaded by Senator Joseph McCarthy had swept the country a decade or so earlier, when legitimate criticism of social injustice was defined by many as serving the ulterior motive of promoting Soviet interests. Thus, a man of Martin Luther King Jr.'s stature was perceived by FBI director J. Edgar Hoover as sufficiently suspect to warrant investigation. While there were, of course, people who joined the Communist movement, their numbers were slim, and the party itself was marginal. Yet, the reputations of members, ex-members, and nonmembers had been ruined and their careers destroyed. These were unsettling times, and those who believed that people should be judged by their behavior rather than their beliefs fought a rear-guard action. By 1954, however, Senator McCarthy had been discredited, and by 1962 the fervor had abated.

One might accuse Mobilization's leadership of political naivete for ignoring the early warnings about "subversives" on staff. But the accusation is easier to make in retrospect, in light of the outcome, than it was at the time. Or perhaps it was hubris on our part, though in view of our civil liberties ideology, we could not have done otherwise. Indeed we would ourselves have been roundly attacked by important constituencies, including most liberal groups, if we had been publicly perceived as employing a political means test as grounds for hiring or firing. Further, Hackett, the executive director of the President's Committee, had on his own sought the advice of an FBI specialist who indicated that, given the size and scope of the Mobilization program, the evidence in the FBI files was not damaging or of concern. As we analyzed the issue, it did not seem in the interest of any of our major partners to publicly criticize the agency. The City was the only MFY sponsor that we considered to be potentially negative, but it did not seem possible to us that the administration of liberal New York City could gain any benefit from a major replay of a McCarthyite red scare. (The analysis was essentially correct, for the attackers lost a great deal more than they gained as a result of their actions. What the analysis failed to take into account, however, was that behavior may be impelled by impaired judgment and irrationality as well as by self-interest.)

The virulence of the attack shocked all of us. We were accused of printing incendiary leaflets, "fomenting" rent strikes, and encouraging "racial disorders" (the time was one month following riots in Harlem). The story also asserted that "official investigators have found that groups of well-indoctrinated youngsters from the Lower East Side had journeyed up to Harlem to . . . indoctrinate youngsters of their own age." According to the *News*, "one high law enforcement official" confirmed the paper's findings, and concluded that this is a "classic example of a takeover procedure by the Communist movement."

We hurriedly called a press conference that Sunday and issued a release denying the accusations. As was true then and later, reporters were a source of rumors, information and opinion. According to a *New York Times* writer, the only truly damaging aspect of the story was a Paul Screvane quotation that gave official sanction to the charges. Screvane was the City Council president, a Democrat, and associate of the Mayor, who had been appointed to head the recently created Anti-Poverty Operations Board. The *News* reported Screvane as saying that "We have heard of the employment of people of this type, and this is why we have been investigating. I would have to consider very carefully the continuance of this kind of program if it is infiltrated with people of leftist leanings." Privately, Screvane denied approximately two-thirds of the quotation to Carlton, which was only Screvane's first falsehood to MFY among many made during the course of the conflict. (One observation culled from reviewing the crisis diary is the discomforting frequency with which people who were engaged in the conflict were fast and loose with the truth, even to nonadversaries and friends. Worse still was the political advantage they gained from their dissembling.)

If the planets (or political circumstances) were well aligned for MFY in its formation, the alignment during the conflict was reversed. The agency's sources of political support had sharply diminished by August 1964. President Kennedy had been assassinated, and Bobby, the agency's godfather, was preparing to leave the Department of justice to run for the Senate from New York. With the move, Bobby's leverage vanished; he was now the seeker of City support rather than a sought-after Washington power broker. Hackett was leaving, too, and would single-mindedly pursue Bobby's altered political interest, which now conflicted with the agency's. Circumstances couldn't be worse in the City, either. As noted earlier, the acrimonious power struggle within the City had resulted in the loss to the City Administrator's office of the oversight function for poverty and human resources development, leading to the resignation of the official from that office who monitored the MFY program and was its strong advocate. Even the long-time liaison persons to MFY from both the Ford Foundation and NIMH were no longer on the scene. Politically speaking then, it might be said that MFY was being held together by Scotch tape. The timing for a challenge to the agency's legitimacy was perfect.

Initial reaction to the civil liberties issue was to stand firm. The project directors indicated at an emergency staff meeting on August 17 that they would continue to resist political means testing, as they had in the past. And at the board meeting that afternoon, Carlton surprised and pleased us when he, too, affirmed that the agency's criteria remained performance on the job. Unfortunately, his position was to erode the very next day.

On August 18, Carlton assured Senator Javits, a moderate Republican, that Mobilization would fire any current Communist it discovered on its staff. An old political warrior, Javits felt strongly that it would be damaging for MFY to countenance Communists in its ranks, but he also advised caution to avoid being accused of witchhunting. He suggested that the board acquire a panel of experts who had successfully fought subversives in the past as a cover to legitimate its actions. The political lesson was standard fare: How things were perceived was more important than the actual facts.

The three project directors met with David Hackett from midnight to 2:30 A.M.

on August 18 to appeal for a statement from the attorney general. An FBI name check had indicated that there were three lower-level staff who were currently members of extreme leftist groups and about 33 other who had once been members but appeared to be no longer. Among them was the agency's deputy director and my longtime friend, who had joined the Communist party in college. Hackett made, made again, and then further remade the point that if we did not fire the three MFY staff members who were identified by the FBI as current Communists, we were "dead." Further, the niceties of fairness or due process had to be overridden since the three had to be out of the agency by 8:00 P.M. the next day. Kennedy could not defend us by saying that there were only a few Communists on staff, and if he interceded, he risked being "sandbagged" by enemies in the Justice Department once he left to run for the Senate.

Subsequently, Hackett leaned heavily on Carlton, who agreed to firing the three following an immediate appearance without a lawyer at a board committee hearing. This precipitated a series of internal arguments, negotiations, caucuses, and renegotiations during which a position was forged, "cleared" with Washington, and accepted by the board. Mobilization would not maintain current Communists on its payroll; full and complete hearings would be held; past political association would not constitute grounds for dismissal; and a "noted counsel" would be hired by the board with Department of Justice approval to look into the charges leveled against the agency.

I recorded this retreat in my diary as follows: "Cloward seemed almost stunned through all of this, and talking to him, I almost broke down. We were both racked by the moral dilemma. On the one hand, there was the violation of principle and the injustice to the three staff members. On the other, we were convinced that without this agreement the project was doomed. Further, if we made a public fight without Washington's support, the virulence of the conflict could lead to tarnishing the names of numbers of staff."

The risk of hiring a special counsel was clear to all of us. Carlton had agreed to give the Department of Justice prior approval, raising the question of who exactly was the counsel's employer, whether he would be accountable to MFY or to the Department of Justice. A number of safeguards were put forward and adopted by the board. He was, for example, to be responsible to the board alone and would transmit reports only to it. As it turned out, the safeguards were later ignored.

A number of highly respected lawyers declined the position before Carlton found and hired Philip Haberman. We learned with dismay that Haberman had been the associate counsel of the Rapp-Coudert Committee, a forerunner in legislative Red hunting. But, said Carlton, he had a "liberal" civil liberties position. In fact, it became apparent over time that Haberman saw himself as saving MFY but that there was a wide chasm in his and our thinking about how to accomplish that end. He was highly protective of MFY's leadership (particularly Carlton), and hoped to find a few subversives to root out—to demonstrate that his investigation was not a whitewash and that the subversive infiltration had not constituted a "takeover." In a statement Haberman prepared to announce his appointment, he wrote "The leadership of MFY is beyond suspicion, but like many other service organizations, it may have been secretly invaded by Communists and subversives. Such people may always be expected to exploit their positions by promoting civil disorder and anti-social objectives."

Carlton, who was with Haberman and Hackett in Washington, adamantly refused Jim McCarthy's appeal to revise the statement before it was released. "He's wild," said McCarthy. Since Hackett was more likely than Carlton to respond to pressure, I decided to phone him. I argued that the release would further panic the staff. Hackett listened and, I suspected, put Carlton on the extension to hear my argument. He suggested I call Carlton in five minutes; when I did, Carlton was still unwilling to reconsider the release but no longer threatened to fire anyone who refused to issue it. He did, however, put Haberman on the phone, and the latter agreed to delete the offending sentences. Not that it mattered: The *Times* article on Haberman's early background included some quotations from years before that were even more alarming.

At his first meeting with the board, Haberman tried to soften the impression of him conveyed in the *Times* article. While partially successful, he said enough to cause uneasiness. Most disquieting was Haberman's response to one board member's proposal that the group adopt guidelines to reassure staff and others that a rule of law would be followed. Haberman protested vehemently to a simple unequivocal statement that past membership was irrelevant to Mobilization employment, insisting that it could also constitute evidence of current activity. When a civil libertarian lawyer on the board agreed that Haberman was correct, an attempt was made to redraft the proposal. It was abandoned because an equivocal statement appeared more threatening than no statement at all.

Haberman's argument and Carlton's, too, implied that past membership could be a significant criterion in the case of higher-level staff. In the first days of the conflict, it was understood that it would take a face-saver for Screvane to achieve a settlement, and there was speculation about what his "price" might be. Hearing Haberman and Carlton, it was a fair presumption that one of 20 top executives might be tagged as the "patsy." I felt an all-consuming gloom, even terror: Not only might the agency be destroyed but the reputation of people about whom I cared a great deal as well.

Haberman's investigation was only one of the probes to which MFY was subjected. The City Department of Investigation entered the fray early, but privately warned that it would not conclude its work until after the Johnson–Goldwater election in November. The City subpoenaed staff and commandeered agency personnel files, raising internal questions and disagreements about how to protect staff from the political juggernaut. Since MFY was formally "cooperating" with the City's investigation, staff was instructed to answer questions regarding their activities at MFY; political affiliations were out of bounds, however. Some of us were critically concerned about maintaining staff anonymity, and had for a time some partial success at preventing unfair exposure. John Marchi, a Republican State Senate committee chairperson, launched still another inquiry, and on October 6, Congressman Adam Clayton Powell, a Democrat and chair of the House Committee on Education and Labor, requested a resume of all personnel, the names of those who had recommended them, and their salaries. This, we were assured, was a probe tactically meant to ward off or counteract unfriendly investigators. In mid-October Haberman called a meeting of all of the investigating parties in order to coordinate their efforts. The gathering can best be described as a circus, with the parties scrapping among themselves over who was entitled to which set of papers.

An organization facing a major conflict with elements in its environment will often generate internal conflict as well. This point runs counter to logic and crisis theory; one would expect people who face a common threat to pull together. But solidarity does not occur so neatly in complex organizations in crisis. The different perspectives, stakes, and values of the organization's participants have great force when issues have major significance for them. The very intensity of the external challenge—the life and death nature of the struggle—is likely to further aggravate potential internal disagreement and erode trust. Such was certainly the case at MFY, most particularly between the board president and special counsel on the one hand and the agency's codirectors and other executives on the other. The tensions mentioned earlier continued throughout the period.

By mid-September Jim McCarthy had resigned as administrative director, ostensibly for health reasons. McCarthy had been a loose administrator and over the years had made enemies of numbers of City officials. His decision to leave, however, was impelled by personal issues. Soon after McCarthy's departure, the School of Social Work quietly decided that Cloward would eventually be withdrawn as a project director in order to direct the research program independently of MFY. On two different occasions during the period, I composed letters of resignation in the fantasy that my protest would cause some retreat by the City or prevent the implementation of one or another of Carlton or Haberman's positions. The letters may have been cathartic, but they were never submitted. With additional experience, I decided that it would be more effective to refuse to implement policies that violated strongly held values of mine and take the risk of being fired. Thus, when the City investigation began to question staff about their politics and did little to protect their anonymity, I sent a memo to staff with copies to Carlton and the City, indicating that I would no longer direct them to attend the City's interviews. Although Carlton must certainly have viewed my act as insubordinate, he never raised the issue.

There was no shortage of contentious issues. The agency's unwillingness to counterattack was one source of friction. Early in the crisis there was consensus that MFY had to act cautiously in relation to the City since the project would eventually require City support. With time, however, and Screvane's clear and continued enmity, a counterview developed that "cooperation" had failed, and that aggressive resistance or an attempt to inflict political pain was worth trying. Worse, Mobilization was cooperative even when political exigencies did not require it to be. The State did not provide either funds or sanction, and when the Marchi committee launched its investigation, the City Department of Investigation privately but strongly advised that we challenge the legitimacy of its jurisdiction. Carlton's philosophy was to win through wooing, however, and he opted for cooperation.

MFY lobbied influentials, made appeals to elite community associations and social service groups, held rallies, and undertook campaigns such as a petition drive. Some community groups conducted protest activities as well, though this caused mixed feelings on the part of the agency's directors, who were afraid that MFY would be accused of "using" clients (and public funds) to advance agency interests. In all, MFY's defense floundered. It was unduly reactive, responding primarily to the challenge of others, and at no point did it develop a coherent or overarching strategy.

Another major source of contention was Carlton's intention to subcontract the community organization program to another agency, and separate the entire organizing staff from MFY. (The subcontractor could then decide who among the group it wished to hire.) Stiff resistance by the executive staff and others and the obviousness of the ploy resulted in the plan's ultimate demise.

Internal conflict increased with the surfacing of a discussion paper on housing prepared by one of the community organizers for program planning purposes by an agency committee. The paper had come into the hands of the director of the local council of social agencies, and he covertly circulated it locally and in Washington. In enumerating housing problems on the Lower East Side, the paper suggested that the court system was "real estate controlled and a tool of landlords." It proposed a program that concentrated on "direct action, including rent strikes, local political contacts, mass delegations to courts and City agencies, etc.," as well as other ideas and language that were inherently innocent but were volatile in the paranoid climate of the MFY crisis.

Haberman called me to schedule an appointment, but would not tell me what the subject of our meeting was to be. Hardly reassuring was his reason for secrecy: "I don't want you to have time to prepare your defenses," he said. I had forgotten about the existence of the housing paper, but he saw it as a prima facie case of Marxist theory. He paled when I told him that other executives and I had participated in the housing meeting. It would, of course, need to be thoroughly investigated "to stem the damage." (His report ultimately charged us with poor judgment rather than subversive intent.)

The expertise of those who were considered competent to evaluate Mobilization's community program was another issue that festered throughout the crisis. We held that a lawyer was an inappropriate arbiter of the program, and that professionals had the right to be judged by their peers. Eventually, this view prevailed, and a blue ribbon panel of social workers and social scientists was organized to evaluate MFY's community initiative.

Tensions culminated in an executive staff revolt and a highly charged board meeting on October 28. Two days prior to the meeting, a memo from Mobilization's administrative and executive staff was circulated appealing to the board "to reassert its moral and legal responsibility to prevent the devitalization of MFY." The statement listed instances in which the board was ignored or by-passed by Carlton or Haberman. For example, although the board had authorized a special panel to review the community program, "before the panel had held its first meeting, Carlton had advanced plans to contract the entire operation to organizations outside the Lower East Side." Cited, too, was the violation of the board's agreement with the special counsel that his reports would be confidential, to be released only by the board. The statement also decried the fact that, soon after the *News* attack, the board had said it would seek the assistance of politically knowledgeable persons and public relations experts, but had not done so. "Our response to charges, in every instance, has instead been to lend credence to them by promising to investigate."

Some board members from Columbia and the local agencies caucused to review how they might support the executive staff appeal. It is not hyperbole to suggest that MFY was in fact in receivership, at least informally. Carlton and Haberman ignored board directives and made major decisions concerning the various investigations and MFY's dealing with the City, following

clearance with Washington and in response to its "advice." The executive staff was, of course, less interested in board hegemony than in protecting MFY's program and personnel, but the issues of board primacy and program integrity were interrelated.

The board caucus was also convinced of the need to assert its policy role and made common cause with the executive staff. It planned to introduce a motion reaffirming the initial charge to the special counsel that he would report solely and confidentially to the board. The motion was to be introduced by one of the local board members during the discussion of the issues raised by the executive staff. The motion also included the proviso that actions in relation to program and executive and board structure must follow established procedures and be subject to board approval prior to discussion with outside persons.

At the board meeting itself it was clear that our adversaries had also organized. Six or seven of the City board members appeared although no City member had attended since the *News's* salvo of August 16. Carlton outmaneuvered us as well. The board would meet first in executive session, he declared, to discuss whether it would agree to entertain the staff document. Haberman and I would make a statement if we wished, but we were to leave the meeting until a decision was reached on recognizing the staff paper. Haberman and Carlton both threatened to resign if the board entertained the paper. In the knowledge that there was a motion to be made later, I said that entertaining the statement was less important than dealing with the issues it raised. It was agreed that they could be discussed subsequently.

Unfortunately, the motion was never offered. An executive committee meeting of the board had been held prior to the full meeting, at which Haberman had apologized for releasing an interim report to Washington and at which he had accepted his accountability to the board. The designated presenter thought, therefore, that the motion was no longer necessary, ignoring the other prescriptions it contained. Although 10 to 12 others had attended caucuses, none tried to fill in the breach and offer the motion themselves.

The staff "mutiny" (as Carlton characterized it) was poorly conceived. The conflict should have been spearheaded by board members rather than staff. Further, circulating the document in advance allowed the opposition to mobilize its forces. Nevertheless, the collapse of the board/staff position need not have occurred. I suspect that the motion was not introduced because the members were at that point emotionally spent by the intensity of the conflict over the staff paper. There is probably a limited amount of energy that members without a critical stake in an issue can be expected to expend. In addition, many board members were high-level administrators of organizations that depended on good relations with the City, and they would be cautious about antagonizing it.

The School of Social Work is a case in point. Leadership of the Columbia board contingent rested with the School's associate dean. The associate dean (who was to become a welfare commissioner in a subsequent City administration) expressed principled support for Mobilization's programs and the defense of civil liberties throughout the crisis. Curiously, however, the support rarely translated into action. Proposals for School intervention were met by such comments as "they wouldn't help; they'd only make things worse." Thus did his gloom cast a pall over suggestions for School action. Essentially, his stance provided a prescription for passivity from a moral high ground with no imputation of self-interest. The situation changed following a rally organized by New York's schools of social work at which Columbia was roundly criticized for its notable silence throughout the entire Mobilization attack. The next morning, an emergency meeting of faculty was held to propose that the School speak out in support of Mobilization; otherwise it would be viewed with disappointment by its students and social work constituency. For the first time in three months of the crisis, the associate dean revealed his concern that the School "ran the risk of losing a number of projects sponsored in conjunction with the City."

Although the failure of the October 28 meeting resulted in my feeling a deeply personal sense of loss, a more objective evaluation suggests that the meeting was a standoff. Subsequently, Carlton and Haberman behaved less cavalierly and consulted more frequently than heretofore. A dynamic of the internal discord was that neither side wanted to push the other over the edge; whenever it came close to that, accommodations were sought.

Mobilization's fortunes began to shift in its favor following the national election. Screvane's interim report on November 10 was dismissed even by the Republican press. The *Herald Tribune*, which had supported Goldwater, called it "a report that indicts by implying more than it proves." (A few years later, Screvane ran for mayor. I note with what I hope is pardonable satisfaction that he was vigorously condemned by liberal Reform Democratic clubs in the city for his stance on MFY, and he lost the race.)

Most significant in the changing climate was the November 17 site committee report of the President's Committee. Its panel was headed by Leonard Cottrell, the highly respected director of the Russell Sage

Foundation, and consisted of a settlement house director, an educator, a criminologist, two foundation officials, and an attorney. In addition to recommending continued funding of MFY by all of its sponsors, its support of Mobilization's organizing effort was unequivocal. "Of all the projects supported by the President's Committee," it said, "MFY has been outstanding in its efforts to involve local residents in actions to improve their social conditions."

Because of Mobilization's good publicity, Haberman's report was anticlimactic. The report was moderate and supportive, although he told me privately that there was more to the housing business than he had been able to ferret out. He appeared eager to return to his law practice, and was, in part, disconsolate about the agency's current good fortunes, since it damaged his self-conception as the hero who would save MFY.

On the basis of the President's Committee's endorsement, it now seemed possible for me to leave MFY without an imputation of guilt. I had decided to do so for personal reasons. The City's endorsement was not yet assured, but a procedure for clearing names with the City's personnel department appeared to be the minimum requirement it would exact. (HARYOU-ACT, a fraternal community action program in Harlem, had agreed to a City name check and was fingerprinting its staff.) Implementing a political means test was not only distasteful to me but might be professionally damaging as well. I was convinced, too, that the vibrancy, idealism, energy, and innovation of Mobilization—its sense of mission— could not survive the battering we had taken. Fortuitously, I was offered a high-level job in the Department of Labor and accepted it. Federal employment had the considerable advantage of demonstrating that I was not "subversive," and certainly

not someone skillful enough to forge a coalition of Stalinists, Maoists, Trotskyites, and Castroites, per the whispered accusation of the executive director of the local council of agencies.

On January 15, with the release of Screvane's final report, the crisis may be said to have concluded. The City had retreated from almost all of its accusations, including the misappropriation of funds, a charge that was added during the course of the conflict.[3] No clean bill of health, however, could mitigate the consequences of the bruising experience.

MFY, as do all embattled organizations, sought to maintain stability in a hostile environment through increasing formalization, emphasizing means over ends, the instrumental over the substantive. Rules and procedures served to increase predictability, enhance the control of lower-level staff, and provide a defensive posture in the face of criticism. One example of post-crisis control was the newly "efficient" payroll procedures, causing one executive to state in a memo that the indigenous nonprofessionals employed by the agency were barely able to "stand the blows of the accounting department." One afternoon he found one such staff member "crying in the middle of the street, and another so angry as to be in a state of near-paranoia."

Personnel and training had been combined functions at MFY, led by a social worker. Subsequently, the functions were separated, and a new personnel director was hired. He was an administrator with prior experience in the City Personnel Department whose job application promised that he could help the agency avoid hiring subversive staff.

Staff turnover was considerable. In the eight months prior to the attack, 9 percent of the staff departed; in the eight months following its inception, turnover had grown to almost 25 percent. Particularly hard hit was the community organizing and group services program. Here, there were 16 resignations, and only seven persons hired to replace them. (In a letter to the Ford Foundation, Carlton indicated that by holding unfilled positions vacant, the agency could meet expenses incurred by special studies of personnel and fiscal operations.)

A serendipitous outcome of the Mobilization experience was the pathway into academia that the agency provided. After a six-month stint at the Department of Labor, I was sufficiently "rehabilitated" to gain a position teaching community organization at Columbia. (However painful the MFY experience was, it resulted in enormous learning for me, particularly with regard to the inseparability of policy and politics, as well as the dynamics of organizational stasis and change.) Other staff who gravitated to universities were: Charles Grosser, Harry Specht, Frances Piven, Robert Pruger, Sherman Barr, Gertrude Goldberg, Marilyn Bibb, Pat Purcell, and Phil Kramer. (One might presume they needed the rest!)

Although the organization was severely damaged, its ideas gained increased legitimacy, probably as a result of the program's added visibility, the widespread support it was able to garner, and the commitment of adherents around the country. Nationally, Mobilization may be said to have provided the impetus for lawyers to serve welfare clients and other impoverished citizens, to aid the poor as plaintiffs as well as defendants, and to challenge social policies and laws that were detrimental to low-income people. Mobilization's impact on professional thinking in social work has also been considerable. Among its achievements were (1) initiating the idea of employing local low-income workers in community programs, (2) advancing the concept of the

social worker as an advocate of the poor, (3) recognizing the need of the poor for legal assistance in their relationship to agencies administering benefits, (4) reintroducing the notion of subsidized work training for youth, and (5) a dual programmatic focus on both structural change and individual adaptation.

If Mobilization demonstrated that poor people can be organized to deal with the social problems that afflict them, it may also have demonstrated that it can be done only at the cost of seriously risking damage to the parent organization. Indeed, the attack on MFY was subsequently echoed nationally by numbers of community action programs that also came under the gun. In effect, of course, funders call the tune, and while some organizations can develop their own leverage or even insulate themselves from sponsor direction, there are limits to their ability to respond to the requirements for social change in impoverished communities. A political balancing act is necessary to avoid arousing sponsor intercession while remaining true to the needs of the low-income constituency.

The ability of social work agencies to pursue social change on behalf of and with disadvantaged citizens depends on the political climate of the times: how aroused its citizens are and how much political clout they have. Social idealism may burgeon in one period, die in the next, flower again, and subside once more. What grassroots community organizers in social work must strive to do, then, is to push the parameters of the possible and take advantage of opportunities that the times permit.

ENDNOTES

1. Daniel P. Moynihan, Maximum Feasible Misunderstanding (New York: Free Press, 1969), p. 123.

2. Frances Fox Piven, "Federal Interventions in the Cities," in *Handbook on the Studies of Social Problems*, ed. E. E. Smuggle (New York: Rand McNally, 1969).

3. Joseph H. Helfgot, *Professional Reforming: Mobilization for Youth and the Failure of Social Science* (Lexington, MA: D. C. Heath & Co., 1981), pp. 94–95.

BIBLIOGRAPHY

Brager, George, and Harry Specht. 1973. *Community Organizing*. 1st ed. New York: Columbia University Press.

A Proposal for the Prevention and Control of Delinquency by Expanding Opportunities, A Demonstration Project Conceived and Developed by Mobilization for Youth, Submitted to the National Institute of Mental Health for a grant, December 9, 1961.

Grosser, Charles F. 1973. *New Directions in Community Organization: From Enabling to Advocacy*. New York: Praeger.

Pearl, Arthur, and Frank Reisman. 1965. *New Careers for the Poor*. New York: Free Press.

Zimbalist, Sidney E. 1970. "Mobilization for Youth: Search for a New Social Work." *Social Work* 15, no. 1 (January):123.

24.

Steven Soifer

MOBILE HOME PARK LOT "RENT CONTROL": A SUCCESSFUL RURAL LEGISLATIVE CAMPAIGN

In a companion article (Soifer, 1998), I presented a rural tenant organizing model that drew upon a modified version of the community organizing model used by the Association of Community Organizations for Reform Now (ACORN). The article discussed the application of this model to organizing tenants in Vermont. The result was the formation of a statewide tenants association called Tenants United For Fairness-Vermont (TUFF). TUFF has grown into an organization comprised of 23 tenant associations with 750 members from low-income public housing projects and mobile home parks.

This article describes a successful rural legislative campaign conducted by TUFF that achieved lot rent stabilization in mobile home parks across Vermont. This article uses three different community organizing typologies (Delgado, 1994; Mondros and Wilson, 1994; Rothman, 1995) to analyze the campaign, and highlights differences between rural and urban legislative initiatives. In addition to organizing local tenant associations, another method of promoting tenants' rights is to implement statewide policy changes that affect renters. TUFF's lobbying efforts have been very effective in bringing about legislative change for Vermont renters. With other groups, TUFF helped pass legislation during the 1994 and 1995 Vermont legislative sessions that implemented a statewide mobile home lot rent increase appeals process and extends the protection of the state's landlord-tenant law to mobile home park residents.

Five years before TUFF's existence, Vermont mobile home park residents had tried to pass rent control legislation to regulate escalating lot rents in the state. From 1988 to 1994, average lot rents had increased 58 percent, or twice as much as the Consumer Price Index during the same period of time (Pfeiffer, 1995). Prior to TUFF's involvement, there had been no success on this issue; the proposed legislation never even got out of its assigned legislative committee.

At TUFF's very first meeting, the mobile home park resident representatives raised their concern about the lot rent issue. While TUFF's organizer had some reservations about the issue (whether it was winnable, whether such a "radical" measure could pass the Vermont legislature, and what such a loss could do to a new organization [Bobo, Kendall, and Max; 1991]), skyrocketing lot rents was clearly an issue of deep concern to the state's mobile home park residents.

At subsequent TUFF Board meetings, leaders planned their legislative priorities for the 1994 session. For mobile home park resident representatives at these meetings, rent control was the key issue. Other TUFF board members from low-income housing projects had their own concern—winning legislation that would force state landlords to pay their tenants interest on their security deposits. In true coalitional style, TUFF decided to push both these issues during the legislative session, hoping to win at least one of them. From the organizer's perspective, the easiest legislation to win seemed to be the interest on security deposits.

At this point in its development, TUFF received the first of many grants. This allowed the group to hire a part-time lobbyist (a former TUFF VISTA volunteer) to work on these two bills. Reflective of Mondros and Wilson's (1994) framework,

the organization was adopting both a grassroots organizing and a lobbying model—or an "insider-outsider" strategy for securing passage of the two bills.

Another mobile home park residents' organization in the state—the Vermont Mobile Home Owners Association (VMHOA)—was already planning to reintroduce a rent control bill during the 1994 legislative session. Once the TUFF Board decided to make this issue one of its top priorities, Tuff's lobbyist immediately began to talk with VMHOA representatives and other key people about amending the proposed legislation and to reframe the issue as rent stabilization.

TUFF's lobbyist was successful in this endeavor. When the legislation was introduced, it became known as H. 572—The Mobile Home Lot Rent Stabilization Bill. Moreover, a Republican state representative was the key sponsor—further increasing the chances of becoming legislation. The modified bill would permit mobile home park owners to make small lot rent hikes regularly. Increases above the Consumer Price Index (CPI) would be allowed if the owner could provide a cost basis for it. However, if the lot rent increase was above the CPI, the landlord had to give 60-days' notice to residents and the state. The state then had ten days to approve it. If the state denied the increase, a state commission would hear the case and make a final decision within 60 days. TUFF's other bill—the interest on security deposits or H. 771—would require the state's landlords to return tenants' security deposits with interest. TUFF estimated that landlords statewide received a windfall of about $1 million by not giving tenants interest on the deposits.

The 1994 legislative session was politically divided and potentially divisive; the state's governor was a moderate Democrat, the Lieutenant Governor was a moderate Republican, the state senate was Republican controlled, and the state house of representatives was controlled by the Democrats.

TUFF decided to kick off its legislative campaign with a newspaper story. A friendly reporter was fed an exclusive that received front page coverage in the Sunday state capitol's newspaper (Dillon, 1994). Then, the following Monday—Valentine's Day— about 20 TUFF members tied a bedsheet-sized valentine for legislators, "Have a heart—Vote Yes on H. 572 and H. 771," to the pillars across the front entrance to the statehouse. Being a slow news day (Vermont's legislature doesn't meet on Mondays), TUFF got excellent press coverage on the television stations, radio, in the state's newspapers courtesy of the Associated Press, and in the state section of *USA Today* (Associated Press, 1994a; Associated Press, 1994b; Associated Press; 1994c; Associated Press, 1994d; Across the USA, 1994).

The speaker of the house sympathized with the plight of mobile home park residents, so he agreed to place the rent stabilization bill (and the interest on security deposit bill) in a sympathetic committee—the House General and Military Affairs Committee. However, as the committee deliberated on the legislation, it became clear that except for the chair and a few representatives, the committee was only lukewarm to pro-tenant legislative initiatives. Moreover, there was heavy opposition forming from the pro-landlord groups, especially from Apartment Owners Inc. (AOI).

There were a umber of committee hearings on TUFF's bills during February and March. At these meetings, TUFF brought in expert witnesses and had 10–15 tenants present continuously (which was enough to fill the hearing room). As the deadline approach for bills to be reported out of

committee, it looked like there might not be a vote on either piece of legislation. After intense lobbying of the committee chair, TUFF was able to convince him to hold a vote on the interest on security deposits bill. Though a close vote, TUFF lost, and H. 771 died in committee.

After this loss, TUFF's lobbyist convinced the committee chair to hold a public hearing on H. 572. Although the hearing was held during the day on very short notice, TUFF and its ally VMHOA were able to turn out over 100 people, an excellent showing in a state the size of Vermont. Though TUFF got little press coverage, a movement was born at this point, and those in the statehouse knew it. Thus, Mondros and Wilson's (1994) mobilizing model of organizing becomes relevant to the analysis.

Before pushing for a vote on the rent stabilization bill, TUFF discovered that one of the primary reasons the bill might not get out of committee was because the governor didn't support rent control. He had promised AOI that he would not back this idea. Armed with this new information, TUFF decided to try to meet with the Governor about the issue. When his scheduling secretary said he was too busy to meet with the group, the organization decided to surprise the Governor with an unannounced visit. Since one of TUFF's Board members had access to the Governor's schedule, the group knew where he was every day.

TUFF picked a time the Governor would be in his office, brought along 25 members and a friendly reporter, and simply showed up at his office. When one of TUFF's leaders told the Governor's secretary that the group wanted to meet with him, the secretary told him the Governor had a very busy day and couldn't meet with the group. At that point, the leader, prepared for this response, informed the secretary that that was fine, and that the group would just show up at the Governor's press conference that afternoon (which TUFF knew about ahead of time) and ask him about H. 572 after he announce the appointment of a new cabinet member. Nervously, the Governor's secretary asked TUFF members to wait as she went to talk with him. Ten minutes later, TUFF had a meeting with him!

The ten-minute meeting with the Governor was extraordinary and very empowering for the mobile home park residents. Initially, the Governor refused to support what he called rent control. As park residents explained the bill to him, and someone asked if he could support a "temporary moratorium on rent increases," his eyes lit up and he said yes, much to the amazement of those present (Pfeiffer, 1994a, p. 9). Whether or not the final outcome was influenced by the reporter's presence is unclear; it certainly didn't hurt.

By the end of the week, the Governor's commissioner for housing and community affairs, who was asked by the Governor to come up with some new language, presented a slightly modified bill before the House General and Military Affairs committee. That same week, it was reported out of committee on a favorable 7–2 vote, and TUFF had won its first battle! (See Pfeiffer, 1994b.)

The Administration's proposal set a 5 percent limit on lot rent increases for one year, thus instituting a moratorium. Larger rent increases would be permitted if mobile home park owners could show significant capital improvements to the park. Furthermore, the state's Department of Housing and Community Affairs would require mobile home park owners to report to the state their data on the history and current status of mobile home lot rents throughout Vermont (Vermont Press Bureau, 1994).

TUFF was confident the compromise legislation would pass the Democratically controlled House. In addition to the inside work being done by the organization's lobbyist to line up votes, TUFF members began to show up regularly at the statehouse. When the vote took place, about 30 TUFF members were present, occupying most of the back row benches in the House chamber. All 150 representatives were aware that their constituents were there, and a few House members even introduced their constituents from the floor! The vote was almost unanimously in favor of the bill (Associated Press, 1994c), with only a few, very conservative Republicans voting against it. TUFF members were really beginning to feel empowered in the legislature, and legislators were beginning to feel their presence.

TUFF's biggest battle, however, loomed ahead. The bill now went to the Republican-controlled Senate. One news reporter, favorably impressed by the organization's efforts thus far, wondered aloud how TUFF could possibly expect to win the issue in the Senate. Another news reporter, also duly impressed with TUFF's efforts to date, wrote a story for the local Sunday paper, in which he stated: "Whether they're packing a public hearing, hounding reporters for a story or making an unannounced visit to the governor's office, the tenants this year have been a textbook example of citizens' influencing their citizen legislature." Furthermore, he wrote, "lawmakers and lobbyists agree that the tenants themselves have done the most to push the issue." Even the landlords' lobbyist, in the same story, observed about TUFF's work: "It's a magnificently organized effort" (Pfeiffer, 1994c, p. 1C).

TUFF's strategy in the Senate was twofold. First, the organization's lobbyist talked with each of the 30 senators to ascertain their positions on the issue. Also, he frequently talked with the Republican lieutenant governor, who as majority leader, would cast the deciding ballot if there was a tie vote. At one point, he set up a cordial meeting between the lieutenant governor and about a dozen mobile home park residents, in which she promised to think hard about whether or not she could support the bill. Convincing her that the bill was temporary rent stabilization and not rent control was helpful. Eventually, she told TUFF's lobbyist that she was supportive of the bill, a key victory for the organization that would make a difference later.

Second, TUFF's grassroots mobilizing effort was also paying off. The Senate General Affairs Committee, which was assigned the bill, was evenly split between Democrats and Republicans, but chaired by a Democrat who supported the bill. She agreed to schedule a public hearing on the bill. Said the local newspaper: "In another display of force, tenants, some of whom are organized in a group called TUFF (Tenants United For Fairness), crowded into the well of the house for a public hearing" (Pfeiffer, 1994c, p. 1C). There were over 150 people present at the hearing.

As the Senate committee deliberated on the bill, TUFF consistently turned out 10–15 members to hearings, occupying all available chairs. On the day of the Senate committee vote, though, the ranking Republican on the committee pulled a slick parliamentary maneuver, forced a tie vote, and therefore killed the bill. All seemed lost.

After the committee meeting ended, the Democratic chair pulled TUFF's lobbyist aside, and explained to him that there was still one chance to save the bill. If TUFF's lobbyist could get a Democratic senator to sponsor H. 572 as an amendment to yet another piece of legislation related to mobile home parks that was being voted on in the Senate the following day, it might be

possible to salvage it. TUFF's lobbyist briefed the organization's members still at the statehouse, and proceeded to find a friendly Democratic senator willing to help out. During a late night strategizing session, a plan was worked out. This was done in relative secrecy so that the Republicans and the landlords' lobbyist would not find out what TUFF was planning to do the next day and thus try to organize against the effort.

The following day, after a night of phone calls, about 40 TUFF members and allies arrived early at the statehouse. This group occupied all the chairs and benches in the Senate chambers, including the second floor balcony, effectively surrounding the senators. When the Senate Journal came out that morning, the Republicans knew what was up. Shortly after the morning session began, the Republican senator who had killed the bill in committee the previous evening called for a recess in order to rally his colleagues to kill the amendment. Again, things looked difficult for TUFF's effort.

However, a TUFF ally pointed out to those present that party caucuses were open meetings, and therefore TUFF members and its allies could join the Republican caucus! So, 40 mobile home park residents, with the media in tow, followed the Republicans into the lieutenant governor's office, eavesdropping in on one conversation after another. Finally, the lieutenant governor, clearly exasperated with the situation and annoyed at her Republican colleague for calling the party caucus, told him the caucus was over and it was time to return to the Senate floor. Upon returning, the Senate approved TUFF's amendment by a 19–9 vote, and the whole mobile home park legislative package passed favorably 27–1 (Associated Press, 1994f; Pfeiffer, 1994d). TUFF was victorious! As the newspaper reported it, "Mobile home owners outmaneuvered a Senate committee Thursday and won the right to appeal large rent increases. 'There's joy in Mudville today,' exulted Bev Ball of Montpelier, one of about 40 mobile home owners who crowded into the Senate chamber to hear the debate." Said Ball of the Republican senator who killed the bill in committee, he "kicked our buns yesterday, but I'll tell you we boxed his ears today" (Lewis, 1994, 1B). The Associated Press wire service story stated that "the effort by residents, coordinated by the advocacy group Tenants United for Fairness, was unusual at the Statehouse" (Associated Press, 1994g, p. 3). The lobbyist for the landlord's group AOI, who showed up after the vote occurred and didn't even know about the amendment, was flabbergasted. He was also fired from his job. The governor eventually signed the legislation into law.

The final legislation, which had been amended a few times, allowed 30 percent of mobile home park residents to petition the state's Housing and Community Affairs Department to appeal rent increases of 10 percent or more if lot rents were less than $170, or 5 percent or more if rents were greater than $170 per month (Lewis, 1994).

Since H. 572 was only a one-year moratorium, TUFF had to tackle the issue again in the 1995 Vermont legislative session. Already having exercised its political muscle and proven its strategic prowess, the 1995 effort was a lot easier. Once again, the bill sailed through the Democratic House (Pfeiffer, 1995). In the Republican Senate, there was significant opposition, and in light of the uncertain outcome, mobile home park owners and TUFF agreed to a compromise bill, H. 371, which the Senate passed. Essentially, this legislation set up a mediation process between landlords and tenants if lot rent increases exceed 10 percent (for lot rents at or less than Vermont's median lot rent market price) or 5 percent (for lot rents at or greater than Vermont's median lot rent market price). If the parties cannot agree, then mobile home park residents can file for relief in court from the excessive rent increase (Vermont Legislature, H. 371). It's too soon to tell whether this process will actually work.

DISCUSSION

The formation of TUFF and its successful legislative campaign is an example of successful, rurally based community practice. Through a mixture of good grassroots organizing, hard work and research on several key issues, and some plain luck, TUFF and its members achieved a significant legislative victory. The passage of the lot rent stabilization bill was an important boost to solidifying the organization and an empowering experience for all involved.

There are several organizing typologies and legislative principles which are helpful in contextualizing TUFF's organizational work in general and its legislative campaign in particular.

Delgado (1994) discusses three basic community organizing frameworks used in the United States: direct membership, coalitions, and institutionally based. The effort in Vermont most closely parallels the direct membership approach, perhaps best exemplified nationally by ACORN. Features of this approach include working with low- to moderate-income people to form small, grassroots direct action organizations of the local, regional, and state levels to engage in multi-issue campaigns. Leadership for the organization comes from within locally organized groups, and the organizer works with these leaders to formulate issues and devise and implement strategies and tactics.

TUFF initially used a modified version of the ACORN organizing model. The ACORN model falls nicely within Rothman's classic model typology (locality development, social planning, and social action, which helps conceptualize the Vermont organizing effort [see Article 1]. The social action model involves the following characteristics: a disempowered population engaged in a power struggle with the "enemy" over limited resources that often plays itself out dramatically in the political arena. The organizer is on the side of the oppressed group, acting as a catalyst to unify the targeted population to confront its oppressors, with the goal of creating social change.

Mondros and Wilson's (1994) practice method framework helps to further delineate the Vermont social action organizing effort. The authors posit three practice methods, grassroots, lobbying, and mobilizing, which are analyzed along 15 different dimensions (p. 240).

The grassroots model has a local focus, works with a low- to moderate-income constituency, tries to create an alternative power base, is easily accessed, attempts to empower people and alter the balance of power in the community, targets the power elite, counts on people rather than money, and engages in conflict strategies (Mondros and Wilson, 1994).

The lobbying model has a different focus. It concentrates on the state or national level, has a middle class constituency, operates from a pluralistic perspective, doesn't have easy access, attempts to bring about incremental change, targets legislators, seeks to educate the public, and counts on more collaborative and persuasive strategies (Mondros and Wilson, 1994).

Finally, the mobilizing model is a fluid one. It can work on the local, state, or national levels; its constituency varies; it focuses on mass education; access can be easy or difficult; it plays on the theme of social justice; it targets organizations or institutions; activists fuel the effort; and disruptive tactics are its main strategic focus (Mondros and Wilson, 1994).

Certainly, the Vermont example drew from each of these methods, phasing them in and out as necessary to win its campaign.

Beginning with the grassroots organizing framework, TUFF engaged in local organizing efforts with low- to moderate-income people to create formal organizations which could challenge powerholders through strategies to win victories for members. Staff played an important role, conceptualizing and strategizing with members on various issues. Later on, as the organization developed into a statewide network, it naturally began to incorporate elements of Mondros and Wilson's (1994) lobbying framework. The organization hired a lobbyist, put together expert testimony on several bills, and worked for incremental change through the political process in hopes of persuading legislators to support their efforts. Finally, as the organizing efforts around lot rent stabilization blossomed, TUFF's campaign transformed itself into a statewide movement, fitting well the Mondros and Wilson (1994) mobilizing framework. Mass education was used to mobilize a highly interested constituency to work for social justice. On very short notice, it was possible to involve hundreds of people in the lot rent stabilization campaign, and even have them engage in some disruptive tactics to achieve their goals.

Not all community organizing efforts fit the Mondros and Wilson (1994) frameworks so well. In fact, most probably adhere to one framework consistently. The most important observation from this case study is that the effective employment of more than one of these frameworks (and ideally all three) allows community organizing efforts to shift the balance of power between the haves and the have nots, with important benefits to oppressed populations.

Perhaps rural community organizing efforts lend themselves easily to mixing and phasing Mondros and Wilson's (1994) three frameworks, in part due to a scarcity of resources. That is, given how small the organization's budget was and how few staff resources there were, it was necessary to improvise along the way in terms of strategies, tactics, and methods. TUFF's organizational flexibility and its ability to adapt to new situations allowed it to seize certain opportunities and convert them into small "wins" along the way to its major goal—lot rent stabilization.

Much of TUFF's success can be attributed to the effective use of basic lobbying or legislative advocacy principles. Haynes and Mickelson (1997) discuss various policy advocacy models that have proved useful in understanding how social workers can effect change in the political realm. Dear and Patti (1982) and Richan (1996) have written about lobbying techniques and laid out numerous practice principles for social workers to follow. While it is beyond the scope of this paper to discuss these principles in detail, they will be briefly highlighted below in the context of TUFF's campaign.

According to Richan (1996), agenda setting is a key step. TUFF was clear about what it wanted and what constituted real change in lot rent control, and knew what and when it was willing to compromise.

Interestingly, TUFF followed the majority of Dear and Patti's (1982) seven basic principles to the letter. The organization's bill was introduced before the session began, pushed for open committee hearings in both the House and Senate, got the Governor's support, had important biparti-

san support (in particular, the Lieutenant Governor) and used parliamentary procedure well (in particular the amendment process) to get what it wanted. Several other of their principles, such as convincing influential legislators to support the bill and majority party sponsorship of it, were not possible in this case, given the nature of the bill and the legislative make-up. However, in the House, TUFF did have a Republican sponsor the bill, and the House leader (a Democrat) was supportive of it.

For several reasons, rural grassroots legislative campaigns may be easier to run and win than urban ones. A well-organized effort can have a greater impact because it takes fewer letters, calls, visits, demonstrations and/or actions to have am impact. Furthermore, rural state legislatures are generally part-time legislatures and tend to have fewer professional or career legislators. Part-time legislators don't have aides, and consequently they are less insulated, more accessible, and more open to the influence of their constituents. While travelling distances, especially in large rural states, could be a problem, given Vermont's small size and because most of the active campaign participants lived within a 25-mile radius of the state capital, this was not an issue for TUFF.

What were the key ingredients to TUFF's legislative success? First, there is no substitute for solid grassroots organizing. Second, it is essential to fight for issues that move people emotionally from the grassroots up and stir their dreams. Third, good organizers and well-developed grassroots leadership are crucial. Finally, organizational flexibility, seizing the momentum built, knowing how and when to compromise, and pushing toward the final victory are all necessary, too.

Solid community organizing efforts, whether urban or rurally based, empower disadvantaged communities to bring about important changes, both on micro and macro levels. When effective, empowered groups can wield significant power and effect important policy changes at local, state, and even federal levels.

CONCLUSION: IMPLICATIONS FOR SOCIAL WORK PRACTICE

Several implications for social work education can be drawn from the example above. First, it is important to share case examples from rural practice to balance the predominant classroom use of urban community organizing case examples.

Second, flexibility in the use of community organizing models, strategies and tactics is important. A community practitioner must be well versed in the various methodologies and models of community practice, being able to integrate, synthesize, and shift between them as necessary. In today's economic and political climate, rigid adherence to one particular methodology or paradigm could lead to the quick demise of any organizing effort.

Third, knowing policy advocacy practice models and knowing and practicing lobbying skills are extremely useful. Too often, social workers are hampered by not wanting to "get their hands dirty" in the political process. Yet, to bring about real change for our constituents, political campaigns such as the one described in this paper are often the sine qua non of real improvements in people's lives.

Finally, the empowerment process and perspective is vividly illustrated in this case example, and should always be kept in mind in social work practice and teaching. Through TUFF, low and moderate income renters, whether in low-income housing projects or mobile home parks, really began

to take charge of their own lives and get actively involved as citizens in the political process. By building an effective statewide renters' organization, TUFF was able to wield significant influence and power and actually shift the power relations between renters and landlords in the state of Vermont. Whether this power shift lasts remains to be seen.

REFERENCES

Across the USA: News from every state. (1994, February 15). An organization of mobile home tenants is seeking a law. *USA Today*, p. 10A.

Associated Press. (1994a, February 15). Affairs of the heart. *Valley News*, p. A3.

Associated Press. (1994b, February 15). Tenants lobby for house bills. *The Times Argus*, p. 10.

Associated Press. (1994c, February 15). Vermont tenant groups organize to seek limits on rent increases. *Battleboro Reformer*, p. 2.

Associated Press. (1994d, February 18). Activists push for protection for tenants in Vt. *The Burlington Free Press*, p. 2B.

Associated Press. (1994e, March 17). Mobile home residents "pleased." *The Burlington Free Press*, p. 3B.

Associated Press. (1994f, April 22). Mobile home bill passes. *Bennington Banner*, p. 5.

Associated Press. (1994g, April 22). Mobile homeowners watch as Senate backs bill regulating park evictions. *St. Albans (Vt.) Messenger*, p. 3.

Bobo, K., Kendall, J., & Max, S. (1991). *Organizing for social change: A manual for activists in the 1990s.* Arlington: Seven Locks Press.

Dear, R. B. & Patti, R. J. (1982). Legislative advocacy: seven effective tactics. In M. Mahaffey & J. W. Hanks (Eds). *Practical politics: Social work and political responsibility.* Silver Spring, MD: NASW.

Delgado, G. (1994). Beyond the politics of place: New directions in community organizing in the 1990s. Oakland: Applied Research Center.

Dillon, J. (1994, February 13). Mobile home tenants push for rent control. *The Sunday Rutland Herald* and the *Sunday Times Argus*. p. 1A.

Haynes, K. S. & Mickelson, J. S. (1997). *Affecting change: Social workers in the political arena* (3rd edition). New York: Longman.

Lewis, M. (1994, April 22). Senate empowers trailer park tenants. *The Burlington Free Press*, p. 1B.

Mondros, J. B. & Wilson, S. M. (1994). *Organizing for power and empowerment.* New York: Columbia University Press.

Pfeiffer, B. (1994a, March 4). Mobile home park tenants win support for rent legislation. *The Times Argus*, p. 9.

Pfeiffer, B. (1994b, March 5). Tenant request gets some action. *Rutland Daily Herald*, p. 9.

Pfeiffer, B. (1994c, April 17). Mobile home tenants take lawmaking into own hands. *The Sunday Rutland Herald* and the *Sunday Times Argus*, p. 1C.

Pfeiffer, B. (1994d, April 22). Mobile home park fee bill wins senate passage. *The Times Argus*, p. 11.

Pfeiffer, B. (1995, March 29). Mobile home rent review bill moving through house. *The Times Argus*, p. 4.

Richan, W. C. (1996). *Lobbying for social change* (2nd edition). New York: The Haworth Press, Inc.

Soifer, S. (1998). A Rural Tenant Organizing Model: The Case of TUFF-Vermont. *The Journal of Community Practice*, 5(3), 1–14.

Vermont Press Bureau. (1994, March 5). Bill capping rent increases goes to house. *The Times Argus*, p. 1.

PART THREE
ADMINISTRATION AND MANAGEMENT

Introduction

THE PLACE OF ADMINISTRATION

The administration perspective recognizes that community intervention, as well as the other methods of social work, is practiced overwhelmingly within organizations (Lauffer, 1984; Vinter and Kish, 1984). The functioning of those organizations is a necessary, but not sufficient, condition to effective and efficient intervention by the community practitioner. Administration has, after some uncertainty, come to be recognized as a basic method of social work practice in and of itself (Weinbach, 1998). The journal, *Administration in Social Work*, publishes a range of relevant articles in this area. Often, community practitioners and administrators are one and the same person, and it is the role, not the person, that shifts. Increasingly, schools of social work offer specialties in administration, and some schools of social work are developing joint ventures with schools of business for these purposes. In addition, some schools of management, such as Yale and UCLA, have trained for the "nonprofit" sector, which includes the gamut of human service agencies.

Organizational structures comprise the *vehicles* through which services and programs are mounted and implemented. The organization provides resources, legitimation, personnel, knowhow, "goodwill," and other instrumentalities through which action is articulated.

Organizations are often the *targets* of professional activity, as well. Frequently the practitioner's goal is the modification of policies or practice of some external organization or institution in the community. Service agencies seek clients and information from other organizations and make reciprocal referrals. Planning agencies coordinate programs among agencies. Locality development agencies bring community agencies into deliberative processes with citizens' groups in order to assess community needs and collaborate in developing ameliorative actions. Social action organizations often pressure organizational entities to drop certain policies and programs that are viewed as detrimental, or to adopt new ones.

Organizations also serve in many instances as the *context* within which practice takes place. An existing pattern of cooperation and communication among organizations may lead a change organization into one mode of action (working on an equal level with all organizations); a climate of distrust and conflict will suggest a different *modus operandi* (working with different factions). Likewise, if agencies generally exhibit high levels of professionalism or have an ample resource base, the form of action by a change agency will be different than when agencies have a low level of expertise or are poor in resources available for programmatic purposes.

If organization is the framework within which action takes place, administration is the practice of running, developing and changing organizations. Administration is the means through which organizations are shaped and directed to pursue particular goals and carry out particular strategies and programs. While administration is viewed as a delineated method of practice, it also cuts across all other methods of practice. Administration provides a basis for steering the work of direct-service organizations. It does the same for all three modes of community intervention, whether social planning and policy, locality development, or social action. Tasks from the rendering of clinical aid to individual clients through to the design of legislation policy at the federal level are typically articulated through organizational processes having a significant administrative component.

Particular elements of administration can be singled out to identify facets of the practice. Parsons (1960) has identified these, respectively, as institutional, managerial, and technical levels of administrative function. First of all, there is the institutional level, the matter of choosing the goals that an organization should pursue and determining the strategies and programs that are consistent with attaining those goals. This requires the ability to assess community needs, design programs, maintain community relationships, and facilitate consensus among organizational constituencies. Next, there is the managerial level, involving the execution of broad strategies in an effective way. The tasks of implementation require the ability to mobilize people, information, and resources so as to make an impact on the needs or problems being addressed. Finally, there are the technical tasks of delivering programs and structuring organizational operations. These tasks focus on the mechanics of delivering services to clients and ensuring that there are enough supplies to run the agency, getting the right staff people to the right place at the right time, acquiring and keeping in good condition the equipment and facilities necessary for program implementation, and so forth.

ADMINISTRATION AND COMMUNITY INTERVENTION

Having described the administrative function, it would be useful to examine it cross-sectionally, employing some of the practice variables that were used to analyze different modes of community intervention. We will do this type of analysis suggestively, selecting out a few practice variables to illustrate the utility of the approach.

Looking first at ***characteristic change tactics and techniques***, in *community intervention* different modes lean in the direction of either consensus or conflict. Locality development relies heavily on the former, and social action on the latter. *Administrative practice* often involves the use of formal authority as a mode of influence, and generally favors stability, goodwill, economy, and efficiency of operation. However, this is a preferred rather than an "ordained" tactic.

Examining ***practitioner roles*** provides interesting insights. *Community intervention practitioners* function in the role of enabler, fact-gatherer, and activist, depending on the given model of action. *Administrative practitioners* tend to rely on their position as an authority figure in a core role, such as executive, associate executive manager, or supervisor.

The ***medium of change*** shows variations in emphasis. Grassroots *community practitioners* work with many types of groups—block clubs, associations of all kinds, committees and task forces, and the like. Planners also deal with data and formal organizations. For *administrative practitioners* the key medium is the human service agency itself. Changes in structures and programs within the agency are the media through which change typically occurs.

In each perspective there is a somewhat different orientation toward the ***power structure***. *Community practitioners* have variable relationships to the power structure, from employees and allies to militant adversaries, depending on the strategic approach. From an *administrative practice* point of view, the chief executive often *is* the power structure as the implementor of programs and services and a key authority figure. It is interesting that sometimes practitioners who become administrators find themselves the targets of the very techniques they had used against their predecessors.

The conception of the ***beneficiary role*** varies within each perspective. In *community practice*, beneficiary roles are varied, from active to passive, depending on the approach employed. *Administrative practitioners*, particularly in service-providing agencies, tend to view beneficiaries in the same way as planners, that is, as consumers of the agency's product. In this sense, consumer/clients are subordinate participants in the organizational system. In administration, then, often the beneficiary role is passive, entailing recipient forms of participation. The consumer may be active in seeking and reacting to services, but is typically not active in determining the form and availability of services. Progressive agencies vary in this by encouraging the latter form of participation.

Beyond these basic comments about administrative practice, there are four other matters that merit discussion here. These will be treated sequentially and include administrative strategies in changing times, interpersonal factors in administration, organizational culture, and program development.

CHANGING TIMES AND EMERGING ADMINISTRATIVE STRATEGIES

Everyone agrees that we are living in changing and stressful times. On the political level, acrimony and bitterness prevail, and electoral outcomes shift from favoring one party to favoring another, and back again. Economic currents are producing unprecedented trends, with global developments adding a new, powerful, and unpredictable force. The human services field is under pressure and moving in novel directions, There is less funding available generally for programs; governmental responsibility for citizen well-being is being curtailed in deference to privatization and public/private partnerships of various kinds; and there is a great deal of competition among community organizations for resources. A free-enterprise environment with market-oriented values has made an entry into the human services, replacing traditional professional norms of empathy and cooperation.

In this atmosphere, according to Menefee, agencies need to bring a different kind of administrative thinking into play. Effectiveness is associated with being able to survive by functioning strategically in the current context. Strategic administration, in the author's view, means being adroit rather than humanistic, and includes components of planning, managing, and leading.

Strategic planning takes cognizance of the information age that is upon us. It makes use of information networks to assay what is happening in the external environment of the agency. This involves a surveillance process, using good communication to gather information and appraise it thoughtfully to advance the goals of the agency. Internal operations require accurate data as well. Such data assist in redesigning programs, reducing unnecessary costs, joining in collaborative programs with other organizations, and demonstrating successful outcomes.

Managing strategically, in Menefee's view, focuses on matters of efficiency and financial solvency. This involves greater accountability through monitoring and evaluating performance across the board. To accomplish high-level goals necessitates recruiting staff to attain the highest level of professionalism. It also entails establishing self-managing teams of staff, and productively engaging the board of directors as a resource.

Finally, leading strategically calls for the administrator to make appropriate linkages with the community in order to gain support and garner resources from the public. In a complex and often opaque environment, the organization needs to acquire a reasonable degree of visibility. The administrator also has to be astute in determining when it is beneficial to form alliances with community groups, when to go it alone, and when to compete.

INTERPERSONAL FACTORS IN ADMINISTRATION

The analysis by Menefee emphasizes the task or mission dimension of administration, with a focus on material outcomes. This emphasis on efficiency is not universally accepted (Kanigel, 1997). And there is an interpersonal or socioemotional administrative dimension that he leaves in the background, but which is brought out in the next article by Gabel, also in the context of the changing environment of the human services field. Gabel addresses leadership characteristics that are needed in relating to the managed care dynamic in the mental and physical health fields.

Many administrators, Gabel states, are personally opposed to or ambivalent regarding the tightening up of services that is a feature of contemporary human service developments. A commitment to quality of services, we know, is the overriding concern of many professionals (Moore and Kelly, 1996). The executive who is successful in pushing a managed care program forward may be perceived as "selling out," but to diminish the viability of organization by bucking the trend may lead to demoralization among staff. The administrator in such circumstances has to engage in introspection in order to resolve internal conflicts and arrive at a self-supportable position.

Having achieved such clarification, the administrator also needs to help staff work through concerns about programmatic change. This may involve initiating group discussions about values, new skills that are required, sources of support for making the transition, and the meaning of success or failure. The professional role involves both adapting to new policies and working to oppose or modify them. Staff members need to clarify for themselves whether to accept changes in the operations of human service organizations, fight these changes, or move over into other more compatible arenas of service. These personal and human factors are part of the administrative mix.

ORGANIZATIONAL CULTURE

The culture of the organization provides the social climate in which the executive and the staff operate in carrying out their functions, and it also presents a target for administrative change. It is sometimes necessary to adjust or revamp the climate in order to construct a better atmosphere in which to implement the mission of the agency.

There are many definitions of and approaches to organizational culture. One of the most helpful for community practitioners is developed by Robert Quinn (1989) in his book, *Beyond Rational Management*. Not only is the conceptualization helpful, but Quinn provides materials that allow practitioners to assess their own orientation and that of their agency (available in an easy-to-administer booklet called the PRISM SET). Although we do not reproduce Quinn's writings here, they merit a brief summary.

Quinn identifies two key dimensions—flexibility versus control, and internal versus external focus. These can be organized into four organizational culture types—the clan culture, the hierarchy culture, the market culture, and the adhocracy. The accompanying model illustrates his thinking.

FLEXIBILITY

Clan	**Adhocracy**
Internal Focus	External Focus
Hierarchy	**Market**

CONTROL

The clan style is one that emphasizes membership and connection, but can create an "us" versus "them" mentality. The hierarchy is one that emphasizes rules and procedures, and provides regularity, but can lead to what Quinn calls "trivial rigor" (what Robert Merton has termed the "means ritualism" of the "bureaucratic personality").

The market style emphasizes accomplishment and results, but may also have an excessive focus on short-term results and lack human compassion. And, finally, the adhocracy is a style that emphasizes ideas and creativity, but may result in much chaos.

There are a few key points to stress here. First, organizations, and persons, have dominant "styles." Some aspects of style are positive, but, as just suggested, "too much" of any style can turn a strength into a weakness. Thus, some attention to all styles is needed for an organization to be successful. If a specific administrator does not have all of them, and it is likely that she or he will not, then the administrative team will be especially valuable in providing scope. It is vitally important for administrators to be aware of culture, and to be sure that a balance of cultural components is maintained. Social work agencies tend to fall into the clan and hierarchy cultures, and thus need to take special care to draw upon market (results-oriented) and adhocratic (idea-based) cultural styles.

An interesting case study that deals with organizational culture is presented in the article by Roche. She describes a crisis in a battered women's service agency brought on by a staff revolt. The staff objected to a change away from feminist norms and toward a more traditional modus operandi, involving a shift from communalism to individualism, from politics to service, and from shared power to a hierarchical chain of command. There was dissatisfaction with the increasing bureaucratization and depoliticization of the organization that was in response to pressures from conservative quarters to emphasize resource maintenance issues. The staff wanted the organization to reflect a commitment to feminist politics (Naples, 1998).

The staff pushed for a feminist-based organizational climate valuing strength in diversity, respecting reflection and analysis as a component of action rather than as a diversion, and normalizing struggle as a component of organizational work. In the Quinn formulation, it appears that adhocracy and clan factors were being advanced over hierarchy and market factors.

PROGRAM DEVELOPMENT

Program development is an important aspect of administrative practice within agencies and has a good deal of overlap with the social planning aspects of community intervention. Program development provides a means for systematically designing and structuring organizational interventions to meet the needs of clients. As with problem solving more generally, as discussed in Part One, it starts with assessment of need, specifies objectives, lays out the mechanisms of implementation, and provides for monitoring and evaluation.

A comprehensive approach to program development is presented in the selection by Hasenfeld. He treats the various aspects of problem solving identified above, but in addition focuses on some aspects that are somewhat unique to administrative program planning. For example, specifying the program technology for aiding the elderly may involve choosing between a meals-on-wheels approach, cooperative cooking arrangements, or a hot-lunch program at neighborhood schools. Assuming that the meals-on-wheels concept is selected on the basis of valid criteria (its known success elsewhere, available resources, client receptivity), the necessary tasks of implementation need to be identified. This may mean organizing volunteers with cars, arranging weekly visits by a nutritionist, preparing the meals in the kitchen offered by a neighborhood church, and the like.

To implement the program the personnel factor must be addressed: Appropriate staff must be recruited and trained. For example, it might be necessary to hire a nutritionist to guide or oversee meal preparation in the programs that were suggested above. Next comes the question of developing an appropriate delivery structure. Activities that occur simultaneously or in close proximity might well be grouped together. Those that have different time and space requirements ordinarily should be grouped separately. Routine and nonroutine tasks need to be treated differentially.

There are also certain program-development activities that have an external focus and are similar to those conducted in social planning. Hasenfeld includes among these mobilizing support for the service, acquiring financial resources, and developing interagency relationships.

Clearly, people holding an administrative position can perform community intervention functions in the course of their work. There exists the possibility of role differentiation within the position. As an example, an administrator might decide that the best way to enhance service to clients in a clinically oriented program is to bring them together to see if they wish to form an action group to lobby for legislation geared to improving their situation. This community intervention piece of work could produce material benefits (funds to allow more frequent contact with counselors) as well as psychological benefits (greater feelings of mastery resulting from these empowerment actions). The relationship between administration and community intervention is varied and complex, but can be carried out in a way that is mutually reinforcing and cumulative in impact.

—Jack Rothman
John E. Tropman

REFERENCES

Hasenfeld, Yeheskel. *Human Service Organizations.* Englewood Cliffs, NJ: Prentice-Hall, 1983.

Kanigel, Robert. *The One Best Way: Frederick Winslow Taylor and the Enigma of Efficiency.* New York: Viking, 1997.

Lauffer, Armand. *Strategies of Marketing.* New York: Basic Books, 1984.

Moore, S. T., and M. J. Kelly. "Quality Now: Moving Human Services Organizations Toward a Consumer Orientation to Service Quality." *Social Work 41*(1) 1996: 33–41.

Naples, Nancy A., ed. *Community Activism and Feminist Politics: Organizing Across Race, Class and Gender.* New York: Routledge, 1998.

Parsons, Talcott. *Sources and Process in Modern Societies.* New York: Free Press, 1960.

Quinn, Robert. *Beyond Rational Management.* San Francisco: Jossey-Bass, 1989.

Vinter, Robert D., and Rhea Kish. *Budgeting for Non-Profit Organizations.* New York: Free Press, 1984.

Weinbach, Robert W. *The Social Worker as a Manager: A Guide to Success*, 3rd ed. Boston: Allyn and Bacon, 1998.

25.

David Menefee

STRATEGIC ADMINISTRATION OF NONPROFIT HUMAN SERVICE ORGANIZATIONS: A MODEL FOR EXECUTIVE SUCCESS IN TURBULENT TIMES

What trends and forces will impact the non-profit human services industry in the near future? How will these trends affect non-profit human service organizations (NPHSO)? How can agency directors position their organizations to succeed in this future? Such questions weigh heavily on the minds of many NPHSO directors, and rightfully so. Their administrative responsibilities are: (1) to identify emerging trends and anticipate their impact, (2) to create vision and purpose, and (3) to introduce and sustain innovation (Menefee & Thompson, 1994). To fulfill these responsibilities, agency directors must think and act strategically (Bryson, 1988). How does one think and act strategically, given the unparalleled changes occurring in society today? This study describes the visions and actions of twenty-one executive directors of NPHSOs who are responding effectively to the onslaught of opportunities and threats in their agency's environment.

Managing the relationship between the agency and its environment is essential for survival (Schmid, 1992). The importance of a leader's ability to think and act strategically relates positively to the amount of uncertainty and turbulence in the agency's environment (Bryson, 1988). It is critical that NPHSO directors understand what it means to think and act strategically. These skills will mean the difference between agency growth, maintenance, or decline. It is also essential that students of social work administration acquire the ability to think and act strategically when they assume leadership positions in human service organizations. These abilities will influence not only their career success but that of their agency as well.

LITERATURE REVIEW

Administration is strategic when it concerns itself with the welfare of the organization vis-à-vis its environment (Hasenfeld, 1992). Administrators think and act strategically when they accurately assess and plan for the future. They think and act strategically when they manage the agency's internal conditions, structures, or processes so that the agency is more responsive to the needs of its clients. Administrators think and act strategically when they actively influence their environment in ways that promote the agency's welfare. Strategic administration, therefore, requires that executive directors plan, manage, and lead strategically.

Strategic Planning

The strategic planning process enables top management and the board of directors to make fundamental policy decisions and develop strategies for implementing those decisions (Bryson, 1988). Assessing the environment, analyzing stakeholder expectations, identifying strategic issues and goals, and formulating a vision and mission are four essential steps in this process.

An ability to read the environment (Morgan, 1988) is an increasingly important competency for executives and board members (Kluger & Baker, 1994). They should be able to assess accurately the social, political, economic, and technological trends so that they can identify the opportunities and threats these trends represent to the organization. Reading the environment also requires evaluating internal organizational arrangements. Executives should be aware of and manage the strengths and weaknesses of the agency to maximize opportunities and minimize threats. They accomplish this by strategically altering the processes, structures, and conditions within the agency.

Examining the needs and expectations of primary stakeholders is critical. They reveal the agency's formal and informal mandates (Bryson, 1988). These mandates may occur at a variety of levels depending on the size, scope, and purpose of the agency. Executive directors should consider these needs and expectations in strategic planning. Otherwise, stakeholders may question the legitimacy of the agency when important needs and expectations go unsatisfied (Hasenfeld, 1983).

Strategic planning also requires that the executive director and board identify and prioritize the fundamental policy issues facing the organization and develop long-term goals to address those issues (Bryson, 1988). Fundamental policy issues are those that if not addressed will result in severe negative consequences or loss of important opportunities for the agency. Agency management then identifies strategic goals and measurable performance standards that describe what the agency must do to address its fundamental policy issues.

The director and board must also define and communicate the agency's vision and mission (Bennis, 1989). The mission is the business of the agency, the client needs it serves, and the variety of technologies it uses to meet those needs (Goodstein, Pfeiffer, & Nolan, 1985). The process of formulating the mission should systematically involve all levels within the agency (Peters & Waterman, 1981). This approach tends to maximize stakeholder ownership, an essential condition for agency success. The vision is a description of what the agency will become over time (usually 3 to 5 years) as a result of achieving its strategic goals. The vision evolves from the products generated out of the strategic planning process. It is a realistic picture of the agency's preferred future.

Strategic Management

Strategic management is the process of transforming strategic goals into action (Higgins & Vinczc, 1983; Hatten & Hatten, 1987; Hax & Majluf, 1984). It begins with developing annual business plans throughout the agency. Using a participative process, directors develop specific objectives, program steps, performance standards, schedules, and budgets. Staff identify needed financial, material, and human resources. Strategic management also superimposes accountability criteria on program and service activity and generates outcome measures for evaluating agency and unit performance (Elkin & Molitor, 1984).

A primary vehicle for strategic management is the self-directed work team (Orsburn, Moran, Musselwhite, & Zenger, 1990). These teams form around the delivery of specific services to "customers" and do not necessarily conform to the formal organizational structure. The director delegates the responsibility and authority for monitoring and managing the internal operations of the agency to these work teams (Schmid, 1992). Each team develops a mission statement, defines stakeholder expectations, identifies key results areas, develops indicators and measures of performance, sets challenging but realistic goals, and develops data collection methods for obtaining feedback on performance. They meet on a regular basis to identify, analyze, and solve problems related to work processes, administrative policies, and/or interpersonal problems. With the executive director's approval, teams implement changes that improve their performance. In this way, they contribute to the organization's mission while giving the executive director the freedom to focus on the relationship between the external environment and the agency.

Strategic Leadership

Schmid (1992) tells us that under conditions of rapid change, leaders must be more active in managing the external environment while delegating the responsibility and authority for managing daily operations to others within the organization. Executive directors are highly active in building and using support networks that will provide fiscal, legislative, and community support for their agencies. They cultivate and nurture long-term relationships with potential funding sources, legislative committees, complementary service agencies, referral sources, and private for-profit organizations. They submerge themselves in highly political arenas to gain support and exercise influence over impending decisions that affect their agency. Executive directors work with various groups to advocate for clients, changes in policy, or specific legislation. They work collaboratively with other agencies in the development of new programs or services; they build service linkages between service providers; and, they develop formal partnerships or contract with other agencies to provide services. Clearly, the executive director performs these duties as a leader, constantly thinking and acting to position the agency to achieve its strategic goals. Strategic leadership, then, is the application of processes and technologies required to influence positively the exchange relationships between the agency and its environment, so as to maintain the domain of the agency.

Strategic planning, management, and leadership are three major dimensions of the executive director's role. With this model in mind, it would be beneficial to learn how effective executive directors envision the future, anticipate its impact on their agency, and respond strategically.

METHOD

Procedure

This study took place in Baltimore, Maryland from August to October 1994, just before the last national congressional elections. Researchers collected data during twenty-one, one hour face-to-face interviews of 50lc3 NPHSO executive directors. The sample was purposely selected based upon three criteria. First, executive directors had to be nominated as among the most successful in the City by at least three representatives from a nominating panel of sixteen professionals selected from local foundation directors, University of Maryland School of Social Work faculty, Maryland Association of Nonprofit Organizations, and other agency executive directors. Second, executive directors must have established durable cash flow streams as evidenced by substantial increases in total annual support and revenues from first year of tenure until end of fiscal year 1994. Third, executive directors must have been employed by their agencies for at least five consecutive years between 1982 and 1994. Application of the first criterion yielded twenty-nine potential subjects. Application of the second and third criteria together with subject refusals due to time constraints reduced the total sample size to twenty-one. To qualify as a participant, each of the twenty-one executive directors must have met all three of the above criteria.

Four weeks before data collection, subjects received a letter requesting their participation in the study. The letter described the study's purpose, time commitment, and procedures for maintaining confidentiality. To obtain consent, researchers made a follow-up phone call to each director approximately two weeks before data collection. Demographic data on the agency and the director were collected during a pre-interview survey.

One hour face-to-face interviews occurred at their place of work. Interviews began with introductions and a review of the study's purpose. Next, the interviewer defined driving forces as "trends we presently perceive that we believe will have an important impact on our future." Finally, each subject was asked the three open-ended questions introduced earlier in this study. Responses were audiotaped and transcribed to a word processor.

Financial data on total annual support and revenue were obtained from records held by the Maryland State Archives and the Office of the Secretary of State. Nearly all of the data were extracted from independent auditor reports submitted by certified public accounting firms. Where these reports were not available, the data were obtained from Internal Revenue Service Form 990s.

Subjects and Settings

The majority of subjects were Caucasian (18) females (11) who graduated with a Master's degree (in Social Work, Community Psychology, French Literature, Business Management, Education, or Nursing) approximately seventeen years ago. Two subjects arc African-American and one is Hispanic. Subjects averaged approximately fourteen years of management experience and nine years of job tenure between 1982 and end of fiscal year 1994. Annual salaries ranged from forty to more than eighty thousand dollars. Over the course of their tenure, subjects increased their agency's total annual support and revenues by an average of 507%, representing an average dollar increase of $3,107,248 (range = $288,393 to $15,718,668). The median increase was 270% or $1,539,509.

Agency median age is nineteen years and eighty-seven percent have undergone major changes in strategy and/or structure since their inception. The median number of salaried employees is thirty-five. The median number of separate operating locations for each agency is four. The average number of different job titles within each agency is twenty and the average number of sub-units is five. Agencies employ an average of six professions within their workforce. Typically, there are two supervisory levels between front line workers and the executive director, and the average number of employees reporting directly to the executive director is six. Thirteen percent provide some form of social control; fifty-two percent provide social care or maintenance; sixty-five percent provide socialization or prevention; thirty percent provide rehabilitation; and seventy-eight percent are involved in advocacy and social change (percentages are not cumulative since an agency can function in one or more of the above areas). Agencies provide a variety of services, including: housing for the homeless, adolescent development, volunteer services, family support services, hunger prevention, health care, disabilities, prevention of spouse abuse, child care, delinquency prevention, child advocacy, shelter, and remedial education.

Data Analysis

The data analysis simulated the assembly of a large complex jigsaw puzzle. Researchers grouped related statements to form dominant views followed by the integration of dominant views to form the entire picture. The following process was used to analyze the data.

Interviews produced seventy-four single-spaced pages of narrative. In five separate reviews, researchers extracted responses from the text and organized them into a conceptual framework. An intentional outcome of the reviews was data reduction and synthesis without altering the essence of the statements made by directors. This process yielded thirty-six single-spaced pages of statements organized by question.

Researchers used a traditional model (political, economic, social, and technological trends) to classify statements associated with the first question. Statements that were political in nature went under political trends; those that referred to technology went under technological trends, etc. In the rare instance where a particular statement fit into more than one trend, researchers copied and placed it appropriately. Statements within each trend were organized according to similarity of content. Dominant views emerged out of this process.

Dominant views consisted of groups of related statements under each trend type. For example, under political trends, dominant views were governmental retrenchment, increased accountability, and heightened reg-

ulatory pressures. The dominant view of "governmental retrenchment" consisted of a group of statements that reflected similar concerns about the withdrawal of government support for social services (i.e., "government cutting services," "government downsizing and re-engineering," "government cutting programs and combining funding," "potential for business replacing government as a major player," "government's decreasing role in service delivery," etc.).

While dominant views were evident in the text, individual statements comprising these views were not exact duplicates of one another. Instead, they represented different variations on the same theme. Although there were dissenting statements that did not fully conform to dominant views, these were very few and are not presented here. (The purpose of the study is not to contrast and explain differing views but to compose a common view of one possible future.) The researchers used the same analytical procedures to organize and present the data related to questions two and three.

The findings are actual statements or paraphrases of actual statements. Where paraphrasing was necessary, care was taken to use the exact content and phraseology of original statements by extracting them from the text and integrating them to form the actual paraphrase. Since not all related statements in a paraphrase fit together perfectly, the author took editorial license to modify the wording or structure of the statement while preserving its meaning so that the paraphrase would make sense to the reader. The findings are as follows.

TRENDS

Economic

The global economy will remain relatively stable or improve only slightly. The local

NPHSO will compete for funding in a global market and the competition will be more fierce than ever. Their ability to compete globally for limited resources will be a decisive factor in their survival. The global economy will also offer opportunities to the NPHSO that is able to compete for and capitalize on new business ventures in other parts of the world.

The U.S. economy will stagnate or slightly deteriorate over the next ten years. Our nation will continue to deplete its "reasonable wage" job base while multinational corporations export work to other parts of the world. The nation's middle-class will experience substantial job loss through private for-profit sector layoffs, reorganizations, and downsizing, and the public and nonprofit sectors will follow close behind. There will be some job growth in the service sector where low paying jobs will force more and more people into the ranks of the working poor. The net effect of this will be increased un- and under-employment. To maintain their standard of living, people will either work more hours or acquire second or even third jobs as the cost of living rises and wages stagnate. Social class differences will become more pronounced. Growing numbers of poor, a rapidly shrinking middle-class, and only slight growth of the upper-class will result in a restructuring of our society. The gap between the rich and poor will widen as the wealthy dissociate themselves from the troubles of the swollen underclass. The demand for social services will increase dramatically, but resources for such services will decline.

The funding pie is shrinking and it is being cut up into smaller and smaller pieces. There will be less money available to the nonprofit sector from all traditional funding sources, and what is available will be harder to obtain. Federal and state funds will be eliminated or severely reduced in the near future. Private foundations, currently overwhelmed by requests from nonprofits, will be "tapped out as well." Private for-profit corporations, also inundated by requests, will continue or slightly reduce current funding levels. Individual contributions will be less accessible because donors are becoming more selective in what they are willing to support.

Alternative funding strategies are emerging. NPHSOs may increase their fee for service rates or barter in-kind contributions. They may contract with government agencies to provide services or create private for-profit subsidiaries. They may joint-venture with other agencies providing complementary services. Fees for services will never be a major source of funds because many clients cannot afford it. In-kind contributions, although of great value, will not supplant the loss of government or foundation funds.

There is a short-term trend toward privatization. A force boding well for nonprofits is that government on the state and city level seems not to be able to expand greatly and will be looking more to contract out services. This trend will sustain itself while government funds last. However, as these funds become less accessible, nonprofits will rely increasingly on other revenue generating strategies that mirror those of the private for-profit sector. In the long run, "Privatization will become a dinosaur."

Political

It will become increasingly difficult to predict how politics will affect the nonprofit sector. One thing seems certain: there is a trend toward reduced liberalism in the country. The roles of government, private enterprise, and foundations in shaping the nonprofit industry will change dramatically.

The role of government will change from provider to overseer. The trend toward government divestiture of social services will continue. The government will be streamlined, funding of programs will be combined, and programs will be cut. At the same time, the government will demand better services from nonprofits. Federal oversight and regulation will increase. The level and depth of government scrutiny will influence how the nonprofit does business, affecting the mission, structure, financial, technological, and managerial aspects of organization. Governmental standards imposed upon nonprofits will likely have a negative impact by regulating services, overhead, and hindering mission. The increased regulation will lead to the demise of many nonprofits. In addition, governmental emphasis on accountability will increase. Nonprofit organizations will account for their services in a much more comprehensive way than ever before. They will have to justify the use of public funds, demonstrate the outcomes associated with their services, and provide evidence of efficiency in their daily operations. The process of reporting will become more sophisticated and comprehensive. Reporting will be ongoing and detailed, requiring performance measurements that focus on contractual outcomes. The emphasis on reporting will be on demonstrating that the agency has made a difference in the welfare of the clients they serve.

A new spirit of cooperation between the private for-profit and voluntary sectors will emerge. Nonprofits will work more closely with corporations to provide services aimed at mending social problems. However, competition between the nonprofit and for-profit sectors will exist where it becomes profitable for corporations to enter traditional nonprofit market niches. Nonprofit organizations will also find opportunities in providing services to employees of large national and multinational corporations. A growing awareness of the importance of the community as a resource will also change the relationship between the for-profit and nonprofit sectors. Out of self-interest, the charitable priorities of corporations will shift to resolving social problems in their immediate communities.

NPHSOs will be more likely to conform to the expectations of foundations. Foundations will take a leadership role in helping solve social problems by investing only in programs that work. They will demand more accountability from nonprofits regarding the use of resources and the quality of service outcomes. Through outcome funding, they will exercise greater influence over the planning, organizing, leading, directing and controlling functions within private nonprofit organizations. This influence will ultimately position private foundations to have greater impact on resolving social problems. The posture of private individual donors will mirror those of the foundations.

Social

The complexity, intensity, and intractability of social problems will continue to increase with a corresponding increase in the tolerance and acceptance of these problems as a normal part of our society. These conditions will set the stage for a growing level of anxiety and fear among the public regarding the potential direct impact these problems might have on individual safety and security. Increasing apprehension among the public will lead to a surge of quick-fix solutions aimed at solving social problems at the least possible cost. Initially there will be a tremendous shift away from prevention toward crisis intervention. When it becomes evident that social problems are not amenable to quick-fix, compartmentalized solutions, the pendulum will swing back toward preventive, comprehensive, systems approaches that will increasingly enlist the efforts of local communities including those directly affected by the problem. There will be more people involving themselves in solving social problems; more people assuming leadership roles in human services; and, a greater sense of community responsibility for social problems. Minority communities will increasingly take responsibility and action for addressing their own local problems, while working to change those problems that impact their communities at higher levels of government. Eventually, a community partnership model will emerge to fill the void created by federal and state divestiture of social services. This model will emphasize the collaborative work of many diverse groups located in and around a community as a mechanism for effectively addressing social problems within the community.

A variety of social problems will plague our society and these problems will continue to proliferate. This will result in a growing concern for cities and their ability to sustain themselves in the future. Urban flight, spurred on by those things that make people afraid to live in cities, will continue to drain the resources these communities need to survive. Poverty, crime, drug abuse, hunger, racial tension, teenage pregnancy, family dissolution, inadequate parenting, illiteracy, unemployment, school dropout rates, inadequate educational programs, and the like, will increase dramatically in the future. The demographics of the client population will also change. Due to the shrinking middle-class and growth of the underclass, the number of clients needing

services will increase disproportionately to the number of people in the population. The poor will become more multicultural, composed mostly of African, Hispanic, and Asian-Americans. In addition, there will be an increase in the numbers of elderly using social services.

Technological

Technology will have a profound affect on the nonprofit sector. Together with the growing emphasis on accountability, increased scrutiny and measurable results, computer technology will change the way nonprofit organizations do business. It is likely that agencies will communicate through local, metropolitan, or regional area networks so that data concerning agency services is immediately accessible to members of the network. In addition, electronic networks will likely improve the quality and effectiveness of services because they enhance case management activities by improving access to information and referral sources.

Service agencies will not be the only organizations connected to the network. A host of funders will link to networks, keeping track of strategic, operational, performance, and funding information that encourages service integration and collaboration among agencies at the lowest possible costs with the highest possible quality.

The transition from a system that primarily sanctioned services based on moral certitude to one that demands accountability based on measurable outcomes will be difficult for the nonprofit sector since they are comparatively far behind the private sector in both their computer and performance measurement technologies. In spite of this technological lag, the pressure from funding sources for NPHSOs to produce evidence of efficiency, effectiveness, and financial viability increases daily. Agencies that succeed will be those that expeditiously can overcome the gap between technological naiveté and performance measurement and reporting. Reporting will be on a continuous basis, generated from detailed technical data repositories that are part of a database management system. Clinical and administrative data aggregated across the organization will provide performance information to funders. Agencies and funding sources will collaborate in defining performance measures and setting outcome goals. Agencies will have to achieve outcome goals as a precondition for future funding.

The trend toward increased accountability, the infusion of technology, and the emergence of nonprofit networking will eventually force an overall improvement in the effectiveness and efficiency of service delivery within the industry. A reduction in the size of the industry will follow; those organizations that are most effective and efficient will succeed; redundant and less effective services will not survive. These conditions will result in a dramatically reduced number of nonprofit organizations and a smaller workforce.

Management and direct service technologies will improve as a result of the emphasis on efficiency, effectiveness, and service quality. Real change is expected in the status of the client and in the prevalence and magnitude of social problems. Eliminated will be agencies that cannot achieve the goal of ameliorating the social problems they address. A higher level of professionalism is expected of direct service providers as well as managers. Funding resources are going to expect more quality, improved performance, and better management, and they are going to require the agency to demonstrate these

outcomes. Emphasis will be on reducing redundancy of services, achieving cost efficiency, improving productivity, and achieving economics of scale in daily operations.

IMPACT ON THE NONPROFIT SECTOR

Over the next decade, these economic, political, social, and technological forces will have a profound impact on the size, structure, and function of the nonprofit human service industry. Initially, the number of nonprofit organizations will proliferate at approximately the same rate they are today; but when funding sources and levels begin to diminish, the industry will shrink as many nonprofits go out of business for lack of support. Eventually the decrease in sheer numbers of nonprofits (perhaps by one-third of the current volume) will lead to a reduction in the supply of services when the demand is greatest.

The downsizing of the nonprofit industry will not be a quiet one. As resources become even more difficult to obtain, the present collaborative model of service delivery encouraged by funding sources will dissolve into fierce competition. Agencies will compete with one another for all kinds of resources. In the wake of the competition, there will occur mergers, acquisitions, buyouts, and hostile takeovers among nonprofit organizations which form partnerships, associations, consolidations and the like, causing a general downsizing across the industry. Eventually, large conglomerate social services organizations will dominate the nonprofit sector landscape. Out of the inherent weakness in this system, there will emerge a community-based model that mimics that of settlement houses and charity organizations. In this form, the major function of the industry will shift away from crisis intervention to prevention.

STRATEGIES FOR SUCCESS

Plan Strategically

Executive directors will have to stay constantly aware of what is going on in the immediate and general environment. They will need to assess frequently the social, political, economic, and technological forces that are likely to have an impact on their agency. The executive director will have to build and maintain formal communication networks that produce reliable, valid, and timely information. These networks will provide detailed information regarding multiple stakeholder perceptions, expectations, and actions that may have positive or negative effects on the agency. Intimate knowledge of stakeholder posture toward agency direction, operations, and performance will be essential to survival.

Executive directors will have to look more closely at the internal operations of their agencies, scrutinizing them for strengths and weaknesses, capitalizing on the strengths, and working to remedy the weaknesses. All internal operations should be reviewed with an eye toward increasing efficiencies and effectiveness. This information is necessary to assess the agency's capacity to function under changing environmental conditions and to make decisions about what within the agency must change to improve performance under those conditions. Such information, in sufficient detail, will continuously inform the executive director about the internal status of the agency. This again will require formal management information systems that provide continuous performance feedback on all units within the agency. In the future, information on agency performance will flow

freely and continuously and be aggregated at multiple levels to inform its intended recipient of the need for improvement.

Agencies should revisit their mission or purpose on a regular basis and make changes where desirable. Remaining true to the mission is critical. Agencies should only involve themselves in services that are consistent with the mission and resist temptations to enter incompatible or irrelevant business for the sake of obtaining funds. Agency directors should develop new, innovative, and economically feasible programs to address old social problems. Service diversification is viewed as a strategy to meet client needs as well as to generate additional revenue.

Executive directors must also find creative ways of managing existing programs and services through such strategies as redesign, downsizing, continuous quality improvement, program mergers with other agencies, collaboration, joint venturing, and reduction in administrative overhead. Programs and services should be based on clear and concrete plans that include specific objectives, performance standards, outcome measures, program steps, schedules, and budgets. It will be critical that agency directors demonstrate measurable outcomes on a program by program basis as well as for the agency as a whole. Program and service plans must, therefore, incorporate measurable performance indicators and goals for each outcome that reflect real changes in the status of the client or in the prevalence of the social problems they address.

Nonprofits will have to manage their finances more effectively. Proper financial planning, budgeting, accounting, and reporting will provide funders with information for assessing the return on their investment. Finally, effective financial management will provide the executive director with the tools necessary for strategic decision making related to program and service operations. Again, the executive director will have to develop and maintain a formal information system to provide the level of detailed reporting on performance required by many external stakeholders.

Manage Strategically

"Manage the agency like a business" with an emphasis on efficiency, effectiveness, and financial solvency. To ensure maximum efficiency, agencies will have to re-engineer their structures and processes, eliminating unnecessary layers of management, reorganizing to achieve economies of scale, and removing redundant procedures that do not add value to the bottom line. Executive directors will achieve these efficiencies by systematically applying such management technologies as business process analysis, continuous quality improvement, and performance control techniques within the framework of inclusive, team-based administration. To promote service effectiveness, the executive director will have to engage direct service providers, clinical supervisors, and middle-managers in the process of monitoring the effects of the agency's service technologies on client outcomes, service quality, and client satisfaction. Tools such as single system research designs, cause-effect analysis, service cycle audits, and other total quality management techniques will aid in collecting and analyzing data specific to the impact agency services have on client progress.

The need for increased accountability will force agencies to develop formal systems for monitoring performance on an ongoing basis. These systems will employ measurable performance indicators to inform management and funding sources of the extent to which an agency has achieved predetermined outcomes as contracted in the program planning and budgeting phase of the management control cycle. Of course, the agency's capacity to comply with these demands will greatly depend upon its ability to develop and automate its information system. Executive directors in the future will have to invest in information technology to position the agency to provide an adequate level and degree of accountability, financial solvency, effectiveness, and efficiency.

Managing strategically will require that the executive director model and promote the highest level of professionalism within the agency. He or she will need a wide range of management competencies and skills. Self-awareness and insight into the effects of the self on others will be essential. A healthy appreciation of the effects of one's ego-involvement in problem solving and decision making on others will be important. A strong sense of commitment to and belief in the particular mission or purpose of the agency, and the ability to inspire that commitment in others, will be critical. The executive director must be able to make actionable, through the joint efforts of others, the mission and vision of the organization. Executive directors will have to develop an "entrepreneurial culture" that supports risk taking, open communication, creativity, initiative, commitment, autonomy, responsibility, and self management. The style of management must demonstrate a healthy respect for the participation of individuals and groups in the agency's decision making processes, especially when those decisions are likely to impact them directly. An emphasis on problem solving rather than blaming should prevail as a means for continuously improving the way the agency performs its work. At the same time, the executive director must be able to help others deal with ambiguity, uncertainty, and paradox within the organization and its environment.

Executive directors must be able to manage personnel effectively. They must find ways of educating the public, especially funding sources, of the importance of providing adequate compensation to employees. They must create a diversified and effective workforce, by hiring good staff, investing in their development, and empowering them to perform as well as their abilities will allow. Staff should train in such areas as client relations, problem solving, decision making, total quality management, and multiculturalism. They should train in effective time management, coping with stress, and adapting to change.

Throughout the organization, self-managing work teams should be identifying, analyzing, and solving problems related to internal structures, processes, and conditions of the agency. These teams would be responsible for monitoring and managing the performance of the organization while freeing the executive director to concentrate on issues external to the agency. Teams in each responsibility center would set their performance goals, establish performance indicators, develop data collection strategies, collect and analyze data relevant to their service, solve problems of deficiencies in goal achievement, and implement changes in various aspects of daily operations.

Managing strategically will also require the executive director to use effectively the board of directors for fundraising, promoting agency image, influencing legislative representatives, and protecting the agency against threats in the environment. Executive directors must pick their board members carefully, develop their strengths, keep them informed, and manage them effectively.

Lead Strategically

One of the major responsibilities of the executive director is to preserve the legitimacy of the agency's services. There are a variety of mechanisms to accomplish this. They include marketing, fundraising, public relations, advocacy, boundary spanning, interagency collaboration, networking and relationship-building, and politicking.

Executive directors will have to engage actively in marketing their agencies by selling their issue to the public, constantly keeping them aware of the importance of the social problems the agency is working to ameliorate. To generate support, the executive director must identify and develop relationships with individuals who are sympathetic to the agency's cause. These relationships will develop through actively courting and educating funding prospects over an extended time, keeping them informed of agency activities and purpose, inviting them to special events, involving them with various board members, and perhaps inviting them to join the board. In this manner, the agency builds an extensive base of volunteers and individual donors to ensure an infrastructure of support in the future. Several approaches to increasing financial support are particularly salient for the future: unrestricted grassroots fundraising, investing in a fund developer, avoiding over-dependence on a few funding sources, forming a for-profit subsidiary, pooling resources with other agencies, and reducing dependence on federal and state grants.

Diversifying revenue sources is a universally accepted approach to preserving the financial base of the agency in the future. Reliance on a single source of funding is very risky; the executive director must find new ways of generating revenue by staying aware of potential sources of funding, keeping an eye on the appropriate mix of funding, anticipating where the funds will come from in the future, considering non-traditional ways of generating revenue, and developing multiple revenue generating strategies and niches in the community. In addition, to be successful, executive directors must develop their competencies and skills in the nonprofit fundraising arena.

Strategic leadership means staying visible. Staying visible ensures that the agency's programs and services are viable in the community. Staying visible demonstrates the agency's commitment to a partnership with the community to improve social conditions. Staying visible attracts clients and potential funders. How do executive directors stay visible? They will have to be active, locally and nationally; they must speak out, advocate for the interests of their clients, and be activists for legislative change. Executive directors must create a strong lobbying system that involves staff from the agency as well as community residents, clients, board members, individual donors, and members of the power elite. This lobbying system should counteract misinformed public opinion and ill-advised legislative decisions. To develop and mobilize an effective lobbying system, executive directors will have to know their constituencies intimately and be able to organize them on very short notice. They will have to expand their networks to include other human service agencies and other organizations, public and private. Executives will have to be proactive in initiating and developing coalitions with individuals, groups, and organizations outside their agency, so that they can expand their

network of influence and support. They will have to be politically astute and visible in the policy making, policy influencing arena on a local and national level. They need to become familiar with politicians, their views and plans, and what they are willing and not willing to support. They must also educate these politicians regarding the specific benefits of social service programs so that they can make more informed legislative decisions. To garner and maintain political support for their purpose, agencies must have developed a strong group of constituencies in the community.

Strategic leadership means collaborating and competing strategically. Agencies must let go of turf issues and examine how they can collectively meet the needs of the populations they serve while remaining true to their missions. They must look for opportunities for collective ownership and explore the possibilities of partnerships, mergers, and acquisitions with other nonprofit entities. Executive directors will have to consider ways of collaborating with the for-profit sector and government agencies in the delivery of services. They must form alliances with other organizations to maximize cost efficiency and fiscal strength. Conversely, nonprofits must remain wary of ill intentioned competitors who masquerade as collaborators. They must prepare to compete fiercely for limited resources when collaboration is not a requirement or option. They must position themselves to compete for clients and for jurisdiction where appropriate. Study participants suggest, in this era of limited resources, that executive directors entertain positioning their agencies to be the "mergor rather than the mergee." Executives must know when to collaborate and when to compete, and the ability to engage in either will be a decisive factor in future success as the industry begins to downsize.

Finally, as the society moves into an era where litigation seems to be the first response to dispute resolution, agency directors must pay more attention to issues of risk, exposure, and liability.

CONCLUSION

This exposé is a wake-up call for agency directors. Expect diminishing financial resources, gradual divestiture of government responsibility, increasing accountability and regulation, deteriorating social infrastructure, and advancing information technology to transform the way you do business. Do not anticipate long-term financial support from corporate, foundation, or governmental sources. Witness the federal and/or state governments foster short-term codependency with nonprofits by privatizing services as a means of shifting responsibility for social welfare from the public to the private sectors. Watch the nonprofit industry grow initially in size and influence from the influx of these government funds, but be aware that privatization is a double-edged sword also demanding increased accountability. Know that, in the long run, government funds will diminish beyond their capacity to support the nonprofit industry while oversight, regulation, reporting requirements, and taxation increase the burden on your financial base. Be prepared to invest in costly but essential information systems to demonstrate to the federal and state governments, private foundations, and corporations that your agency is accountable for predetermined outcomes. Realize that your agency will become increasingly dependent upon and controlled by these funding sources to satisfy the public's need to know how money

is being used and with what effects. Also be aware that an increase in the complexity, intensity, and intractability of social problems will place greater resource and service demands on the agency while resource and service supply declines.

As the capacity of your agency to provide effective services becomes overburdened by increasing service demands, diminishing resources, and overregulation, do not feel alone. Other nonprofits will deal with similar threats to their existence. Perhaps one-third of them will go out of business under these conditions, but not until fierce competition drives them out or absorbs them in mergers, acquisitions, buyouts, or hostile takeovers. The survivors will truly be a new breed of nonprofit administrators, and they will share, in common, the ability to think and act strategically.

REFERENCES

Bennis, W. (1989). *Why leaders can't lead*. San Francisco, CA: Jossey-Bass Publishers.
Bryson, J. M. (1988). *Strategic planning for public and nonprofit organizations*. San Francisco: Jossey-Bass Publishers.
Elkin, R., & Molitor, M. (1984). *Management indicators in nonprofit organizations: Guidelines to selection and implementation*. Baltimore, MD: Peat Marwick and Associates.
Goodstein, L. D., Pfeiffer, J. W., & Nolan, T. M. (1985). Applied strategic planning: A new model for organizational growth and vitality. *The 1985 Annual: Developing Human Resources*, 275–290.
Hasenfeld, Y. (1983). *Human service organizations*. Englewood Cliffs, NJ: Prentice-Hall, Inc.
Hatten, K. J., & Hatten, M. L. (1987). *Strategic management: Analysis and action*. Englewood Cliffs, NJ: Prentice-Hall, Inc.
Hax, A. C., & Majluf, N. S. (1984). *Strategic management: An integrative perspective*. Englewood Cliffs, NJ: Prentice-Hall, Inc.

Higgins, J. M., & Vincze, J. W. (1986). *Strategic management and organizational policy.* Chicago: The Dryden Press.

Kluger, M. P., & Baker, W. A. (1994). *Innovative leadership in the nonprofit organization.* Washington, DC: Child Welfare League of America, Inc.

Menefee, D. T., & Thompson, J. J. (1994). Identifying and comparing competencies for social work management: A practice driven approach. *Administration in Social Work, 18*(3), 1–25.

Morgan, G. (I 988). *Riding the waves of change.* San Francisco, CA: Jossey-Bass Publishers.

Orsburn, J. D., Moran, L., Musselwhite, E., & Zenger, J. H. (1990). *Self-directed work teams: The new American challenge.* Homewood, IL: Business One Irwin.

Peters, T. J., & Waterman, R. H. (1982). *In search of excellence: Lessons from America's best-run companies.* New York: Warner Books.

Schmid, H. (1992). Executive leadership in human service organizations. In Y. Hasenfeld (Ed.), *Human services as complex organizations.* Newbury Park, CA: Sage Publications, Inc.

26.

Stewart Gabel

LEADERSHIP IN THE MANAGED CARE ERA: CHALLENGES, CONFLICT, AMBIVALENCE

Traditionally, a major route to leadership in mental health organizations or departments has been through recognition for and expectation of further achievements in clinical, research, or educational areas (Barton & Barton, 1983). The psychiatrist administrator has sometimes been noted more for clinical expertise and humanistic values than for administrative experience or management values (Levinson & Klerman, 1967). Relationships between psychiatric leaders and supervisees often have been collegial rather than executive or authority based (Marcos & Silver, 1988; Silver, Akerson, & Marcos, 1990). A shared vision and common clinical, research, or educational goals have been important pillars for successful leaders and organizations. The leadership function in mental health organizations has been changing, at least to a degree, for quite some time, however (Astrachan, 1980; Conway, 1982; Feldman, 1981). In a managed care environment especially, the leadership role calls for administrative and executive experience, recognition and support for financial imperatives, and management based on productivity standards.

What types of leaders are best suited to lead organizations through transition periods generally (Adamson, 1989; Bennis, 1989; Greenblatt, 1983; Hersey & Blanchard, 1969; Kaplan, 1983), and especially through the enormous changes required in what has been called the managed care era? What types of leaders will succeed or will fail to achieve various and inevitably modified organizational goals that are a necessary part of the managed care framework in which all mental health organizations now find themselves?

Numerous authors have written about what constitutes effective leadership and what personality characteristics (Kernberg, 1978, 1979; Zaleznik, 1977) or qualities are important for the effective leader (Cozza & Hales, 1992; Rachlin & Keill, 1992). Still, the question of what makes one individual effective as a leader compared to other non-effective leaders, remains elusive (Bennis & Nanus, 1985).

Bennis and Nanus (1985) argue that leaders are people who commit themselves to a particular enterprise, are resilient in the face of conflict, are able to be transformed by the conflicts they face, and are able to sustain a vision for their enterprise or organization. Effective leadership, transformative leadership, is able to

"shape and elevate the motives and goals of followers." "Transformative leadership . . . reflects the community of interests of both leaders and followers . . . . It is collective, there is a symbiotic relationship between leaders and followers, and what makes it collective is the subtle interplay between the followers' needs and wants and the leader's capacity to understand one way or another, those collective aspirations." (page 217)

Bass (1990) also speaks of an international aspect to leadership: "Leadership is an interaction between two or more members of a group that often involves a structuring or restructuring of the situation and the perceptions and expectations of the members . . . Leadership occurs when one group member modifies the motivation or competencies of others in the group" (pp. 19–20). Importantly, as Bass notes, this definition of leadership is sufficiently broad that leadership to some degree may be exhibited by numerous members of the group.

Burns (1978) emphasizes that "leaders address themselves to followers' wants, needs and other motivations, as well as to their own, and thus they serve as an *independent force in changing the makeup of the followers' motive base through gratifying*

their motives." (p. 20, italics in original). Leadership *"is exercised when persons with certain motives and purposes mobilize, in competition or conflict with others . . . resources so as to arouse, engage and satisfy the motives of followers"* (p. 18, italics in original).

Talbott (1987) argues that vision may be the most important component of leadership. The ability to inspire others to share in the leader's vision and to become involved in decisions and policymaking also is important. Risk taking, aggressively seizing opportunities, nurturing members and maintaining a task orientation are all involved in leadership. Effective leaders accurately perceive the reality of their organizations and the place of their organization in larger contexts; they are active, energetic, oriented towards action, eager to set and achieve goals, able to set priorities and to serve as an example for others.

Menninger (1992) emphasizes the importance of the leader being able to provide clear direction, resolve conflicts, and clarify goals. Shore (1993) argues that managed care is the most potent influence on mental health administration at present. He raises questions, however, of whether mental health clinicians, whose customary activities require enough "passivity" to pay attention to the needs of their patients, are suited to taking charge of complicated systems of care.

Implicit or explicit in all of these views of effective leadership is the need for the leader to develop a clear vision about his/her organization's future, to be clear about the organization's goals and values and to communicate this vision and these goals and values to non-leader members of the organization. The leader's task is to motivate, involve, and rouse other members of the organization toward new goals and priorities in the face of conflict, doubt or adversity. The task certainly will be easier if the leader is able to define a clear vision for the future and if influential non-leader organizational members also are clear about the future for the organization. Major problems arise, however, along with a strong likelihood of failure, when leaders do not have a personally satisfying vision of the future or when they themselves have ambivalence or conflict on a personal level that results in an incapacity to formulate a vision for the future or to lead others towards it.

The managed care era has come upon mental health with great force and rapidity. There are many threats to customary practices and assumptions inherent in its approaches. Many mental health leaders, while recognizing the need for cost containment and greater availability of mental health services to previously underserved members of the population, are openly hostile to, or at best strongly ambivalent about, the tenets and practices of managed care (Goldstein & Kalman, 1997). These conflicts occur at a time when mental health organizations are most in need of effective leadership of the type described. This paper explores the issues and impact, personal and organizational, of leadership conflict during a period of great organizational change, stressing the importance of the leader's relationships with non-leaders during this time of transition. It concludes with recommendations to enhance leadership efficacy during periods of transition and uncertainty.

The framework of the paper involves an exploration of the issue of success and failure of mental health leadership from the perspective of the individual leader's own reactions and attitudes as he or she participates in current revolutionary health care changes. There are several major tenets through which the paper evolves. The first is the concept of conflict. It is hypothesized that many leaders (and other mental health practitioners) are severely conflicted about the nature and value of required changes within a managed care framework. The degree of conflict experienced and the individual's responses in the face of this conflict help determine an individual leader's success or failure as he or she attempts to facilitate and maintain survival or growth in a particular organization. A second tenet of this paper is that most organizations, like most individuals, struggle to survive as identifiable and distinct entities, and that an important measure of a leader's success is the leader's ability to ensure the organization's survival in some form in the face of external threats. A third tenet is that the concepts of "success" and "failure" are elusive, and often reside in the eye of the beholder. This paper considers success or failure largely from the perspective of whether the leader is able to facilitate an organization's or a program's change, adjustment and survival in a new era without addressing the question of whether "survival" of that particular organization is desirable or not.

It also should be emphasized that the paper takes no position on the advisability or inadvisability of the managed care framework itself, but rather discusses the implications of conflict in leaders on individual organizations as mental health delivery systems undergo revolutionary changes. From an organizational perspective, conflict in the leader results in less likelihood of the organization's making changes in approach that would enhance its survival which, as noted, is an assumed organizational goal.

A fourth tenet of the paper considers, along with Bass (1990), that leadership is potentially multilayered, with leaders at varying levels in the organization having the ability to facilitate or retard organizational change depending on their own motivation, conflict, vision and the like. The strengths or weaknesses of an organization's leadership may therefore be exerted on several hierarchical levels.

In order to facilitate the discussion of the points noted above, a series of hypothetical "cases" will be presented as illustrations of "success" or "failure" of leaders in mental health organizations or programs. These "cases" are not real situations, but were developed by the author for the purpose of illustration.

ILLUSTRATIONS

Case 1

A well thought of private psychiatric hospital in a large city abruptly closed. Staff and patients received 6 weeks notice of the impending closure. The board of directors had voted to close the hospital after 2 straight years of large financial losses and no change in sight.

At a press conference, the CEO was clearly depressed. She talked about unscrupulous competition and the inability to compete when financial incentives, rather than the finest in mental health care, was the goal. She felt badly for the staff who were laid off and for the patients.

The medical director was angry and resentful. He was appalled by the poor quality of care practiced under managed care, the competition for mental health care dollars, and the society's acquiescence in providing so little mental health treatment, when clearly so much was needed. One week hospitalizations were an insult when the average patient needed to be hospitalized for at least 2–3 months to begin to achieve some understanding of his or her illness.

Postscript: The CEO was unemployed for 3 months. Ultimately, she left the area,

moved to another state, and found another job in health care administration. The medical director went into full time private practice. Already in his late fifties, he planned to retire in the next few years, earlier than he had previously anticipated.

Case 2

A large general community hospital that supported two psychiatry residents' stipends under an agreement with the medical center in that city saw its revenues from an adolescent psychiatry unit drop. Occupancy had fallen from 75% a few years previously to 50% currently. In response, the hospital administration hired a highly respected child and adolescent psychiatrist from the community with a large private practice who had been active in her professional society to become medical director of the unit. The hospital's CEO hoped to capitalize on the child psychiatrist's professional and community contacts to increase inpatient referrals.

The new medical director was not able to lure referrals away from other hospitals, however. She felt uncomfortable negotiating "deals" and uncomfortable with marketing the hospital's services. The child psychiatrist felt that she should not have to "sell" herself or the hospital. The latter should have a marketing or development office.

The psychiatry unit's occupancy continued to fall, and soon reached 40%, at which point it was closed. There were numerous staff layoffs, although some staff were re-hired for a new residential treatment program that was developed. One training position was eliminated. The residential program that ensued had a much lower staff to patient ratio than the hospital unit had had, and therefore seemed to have a better chance to survive financially. Its director was an administratively oriented social worker. The psychiatrist continued as a medical consultant 10 hours per week.

ORGANIZATIONAL FAILURE: THE REACTIONS OF LEADERS

Mental health professionals are confronted frequently in clinical settings with individuals whose mental health has deteriorated because of work place failure and job loss. These difficulties increase significantly during times of employment change, such as occurs during recessions or corporate downsizing. The reactions of leaders of mental health organizations that have been unsuccessful in surviving in a desired mode or in making organizational changes would be expected to be similar, although the author knows of no specific data available in this area.

The illustrations noted above are intended to highlight possible reactions of leaders, which appear likely to include depression, anger and feelings of confusion and injustice. Individuals would be expected to be resentful, to blame others, such as society or managed care, to feel devalued, misunderstood and blamed or made into the "fall guy." Hopelessness, demoralization, feeling used and compromised are also reactions that leaders may have when their organizations have not succeeded because of an inability to make changes necessary for successful functioning in a managed care environment. Some of these reactions are summarized in Table 26.1.

A good deal of the evaluation of these situations of individual (and organizational) failure unfortunately often comes to the question of blame or fault. Higher level executive or management leaders, includ-

TABLE 26.1
Reactions of Leaders Whose Organizations Have Failed

Case Illustration 1	Case Illustration 2
• Depressed	• Angry
• Angry	• Compromised
• Resentful	• Used
• Blaming of society, of managed care	• Blamed

Other Reactions of Leaders
• Devalued
• Misunderstood
• Demoralized
• Helpless to effect change
• Hopeless
• The "fall guy," unsupported

TABLE 26.2
What Happened? Whose "Fault" Was It?
Clash of Perceptions and Values

Traditional Professional Values	Market Oriented Professional Values
• Excellence of clinical care paramount	• Efficiency, cost containment crucial
• Provider autonomy in decision making essential	• Services must be compensated
• Availability of psychiatric care for all who need it	• Services without definite beneficial outcome are not endorsed
• Availability of psychiatric care for all who want it	• The least costly professional services or settings are preferred
• High quality training programs that are eagerly sought and that increase the number of psychiatrists in the field	• Education should not be subsidized by the private sector
• Research programs that increase understanding, and produce new knowledge	• Research should not be subsidized by the private sector

ing those in mental health organizations, are heavily identified with their roles. Failure in the eyes of those judging them may become a very troubling personal concern with which the individual must deal. The questions of "What happened?", "Whose fault was it?" must be addressed certainly. The following perspective offers a response to the question of blame and fault that rests less on an individual's inadequacies as a leader in a usual sense, however, and more on the individual's inability or unwillingness to address conflicts in that individual (or in the organization) between traditional mental health care values and more market influenced personal values.

LEADERSHIP FAILURE: UNRESOLVED CONFLICTS INVOLVING PERCEPTIONS AND VALUES

Traditional professional values may be in conflict with market oriented values, although in reality both systems have parts of the other, and the question is one of emphasis or balance. Table 26.2 indicates several potential areas of conflict between traditional and market oriented value systems. It can be seen that traditional approaches at least overtly give precedence to the professional's notion of excellent clinical care, the value of research, and the value of education in psychiatric and mental health programs. Organizations and delivery systems that function in a managed care environment are likely to stress more the importance of financial accountability, efficiency, "consumer satisfaction," clearly demonstrated outcomes and the importance of market forces. Psychiatrists and administrators whose values are strongly traditional in nature will feel conflict in accepting and then in leading others in adapting to a new system of care that challenges their assumptions. Leaders who are in mid or later stages of their careers would be expected to have increased conflict in comparison to those earlier in their careers, given their longer exposure to traditional values. Some leaders who are unsuccessful in maintaining the survival of their organizations or programs may be too conflicted about the need to introduce market oriented values into their organization's overall value system to be effective.

The unsuccessful leader may be less skilled and inexperienced in areas that have assumed major importance in the managed care era. Administrative, management, budgetary and personnel issues are very heavily emphasized in a more market focused health delivery system. A lack of skill or experience in these areas will contribute to the potential failure of the leader and of his or her organization.

Case 3: Reactions of the "Successful" Leader

A middle-aged psychiatrist had been in private practice. He had always been interested in the business and corporate aspects of health care, and in the potential for developing large systems of care. When the opportunity arose, he applied for a position as regional medical director of a national managed care organization that was coming to his area. A few years later, he and another entrepreneurial psychiatrist decided to start their own managed behavioral health care organization, which soon became successful. The psychiatrist's income rose dramatically. He found it exciting to create new systems of care that he felt were cost efficient and well managed. He felt that the care provided under his (and others') direction was good; that much of "unmanaged" care had little demonstrable benefit, and that managing resources was essential and ultimately to the patient's benefit. He, himself, continued to see patients, but on a very much more restricted, part-time basis.

The above case illustrates an extreme example of an individual who took full advantage of the managed care revolution to create his own managed care company. Many individuals, lining within the restrictions of one social or organizational system, recognize its limitations, and then, if the chance arises, reach for opportunity in another system. The type of leader in the above illustration, or the numerous other leaders who less dramatically reorient themselves and their organizations to satisfy the needs of a managed care approach may also feel conflict along the lines noted above. They, too, may rue the loss of freedom for individual clinicians, the lack of autonomy, the need to provide care with the recognition that ill-trained or inexperienced reviewers may undermine the practitioner's efforts. Yet, these more successful individuals also have come to accept the need to work within a new system. If they are leaders of organizations, they will likely convey this feeling to other members of their programs and this will aid the organization's survival.

A re-oriented organization may carry with it burdens of its losses and its institutional memory of what has been given up, but if it is successful, it also will be more secure and perhaps revitalized. Since most organizations, programs, and agencies are at increased risk of failure in the managed care era, leaders who have had major roles in successfully re-orienting their programs may have various personal reactions; they may feel fulfilled, accomplished, more powerful, and gratified. Such leaders very likely have learned new skills, administrative and financial. They have shown the ability to survive in a competitive environment and may feel renewed creativity and vision as part of the restructuring effort. Conflict may be (or may have been) present for the leader who has been successful in reorienting his or her organization, but it is likely to be less than for the leader whose organization or program has not survived.

Success Despite Conflict: Is It Success?

The above illustration of a psychiatrist who developed his own managed care organization with little or no conflict about the loss of traditional values describes only a very small number of individuals. Another scenario, probably more common, is that of the mental health leader who, in order to continue to provide care to patents, to safeguard his or her own position, the organization's survival, or the positions of staff, energetically endeavors to reorganize and restructure the mental health program so that it can function successfully in a managed care mode. This will mean great effort, major shifts in approach for the leader and for the staff and quite possibly downsizing the organization, which will mean staff reductions. If these types of efforts were made, and if they were successful, earlier illustrations above (1 and 2) might have had more favorable outcomes. How might these now "successful" leaders feel? Clinical care would be markedly different in nature (and often less comprehensive), education and training at the institution would likely be struggling and perhaps diminished (e.g., fewer residency or internship positions offered or taken), and the existence of research threatened (Campbell, Weissman, & Blumenthal, 1997; Moy, Mazzarchi, Levin, & Blake, 1997). Threats to training and to research suggest that there will be fewer professionals in the future to perpetuate the field and that new ideas and creativity will be diminished.

Unlike the leader in case 3 who has little or no conflict in developing a managed care model, leaders who are "successful" out of necessity rather than out of enthusiasm for the new model may feel demoralized and "unsuccessful" as trustees of a personally valued system of care. These leaders may feel that they have "sold out" their ideals, and may be angered or frustrated by those in their organization who benefit from job retention but who nonetheless project their own anger at managed care onto leader who seemingly has given up his or her (or their) values (Table 26.3). Despite success, conflict about the value of that success ensues.

LEADERS AND STAFF, SUPERVISOR AND SUPERVISEE: RELATIONSHIPS IN TRANSITION

Leaders stand in a dynamic relationship with organizational staff whom they supervise. As noted earlier, the leadership/staff relationship can be conceptualized in part as one in which both sides rely on the abilities and common organizational values of the other. Leaders of health and mental health care organizations cannot succeed if the staff of those organizations are inadequate, unskilled, or inexperienced and the reverse also is true. Organizations in the midst of radical transformation have mem-

TABLE 26.3
Success Despite Conflict: Is It Success?

Possible leader reactions:

• Demoralization

• Disrespect by others for lack of emphasis on previously shared clinical, educational or research goals

• Compromised, having "sold out," and given up on values, ideals

• Anger, mistrust of those supervised who cling to "untenable" models of care or clinical paradigms (while benefiting by maintaining their jobs when the program survives)

bers who are at different stages in their transition to a new model of care (Gabel & Oster, in press). Given the likelihood of shifting expectations between the leader and the organization's professional and non-professional staff during times of radical change, there is an increased possibility of conflict as clashes between the traditional and market driven value systems noted above are played out between individuals or groups.

Leaders in organizations that have or have not succeeded in organizational transformation will likely be affected by professional and non-professional staff members' reactions and attitudes toward them and their efforts. These attitudes in time may affect the leader's own morale and his or her ability to function effectively.

The Leader Who Has or Has Not Succeeded: Staff Reactions

Organizational failure results in many reactions that are directed toward the leader, including anger and bitterness about job loss (even by those staff members who had resisted organizational change). It also creates feelings of being unprotected and abandoned by the leader who, correctly or not, often is thought of as having arranged for a soft cushion on which to land for himself or herself regardless of the outcome for others in the organization. Numerous other reactions on the part of staff may also result as the organization appears to be failing. Sometimes these reactions are surprising, considering that many face job loss and employment uncertainty. Some individuals, for example, may feel vindicated, even though their own future is clouded professionally. They may argue that, with an uncompromising stance, the values of the field are retained and "unethical" or "partial" care will not be provided. Various types of reactions are noted in Table 26.4. The range of these reactions suggests the potential for considerable conflict within and among staff members themselves and/or between staff and the leader.

The leader who has succeeded in re-orienting his or her organization or agency also elicits various reactions from staff members. These include gratitude for jobs saved, admiration for skills related to the development of new programs and for the institution of new approaches necessary in the current era of mental health care delivery. In

TABLE 26.4
Considering the Leader Who Has Not Succeeded

Possible reactions/attitudes:

• Abandoned, unprotected

• Angry, bitter

• Rejected

BUT ALSO

• Sympathy, pity

• Grateful (values were retained although jobs were lost)

• Vindicated ("We knew he/she couldn't do it. This new model will never work") this case also, however, the situation is not straightforward, but rather ripe for conflict within and between staff or between staff and the leader. Reactions of staff members toward successful leaders of their organizations may include feelings of abandonment and anger because of the leader's perceived failure to uphold the organization's and the field's values as well as empathy since the leader and staff are now both perceived to have suffered similar losses. Both are still employed although both are fallen and demoralized (a condition that if true and if prolonged does not auger well for the organization). Reactions of these types are summarized in Table 26.5.

ORGANIZATIONAL LEADERSHIP: NEW RELATIONSHIPS IN A PERIOD OF INSTABILITY AND CHANGE

The foregoing parts of this paper have presented various perspectives on the reactions, fortunes and values of the leader in an organization confronting radical change. The reactions of leaders, themselves, as well as reactions of staff members to leaders, have been emphasized. This section offers guidelines for leaders as they pursue often unwanted organizational changes that affect themselves, their staff and the relationships within an organization.

During times of stability and shared value systems, relationships of leaders of an organization and staff members within the organization are expected to be relatively well established and to have at least moderately clear and known expectations on both sides. The previous sections of this paper emphasize the potential instability that is to be expected in relationships between leaders and staff as organizations attempt to shift at least partly from a more traditional value system in mental health to one heavily influenced by managed care and market forces.

This period of organizational (and personal) uncertainty calls for the development of an approach to aid the organization's adaptation to a new model of care. It calls for clarity on the part of the leader about the process of loss and mourning expected for the leader himself or herself and for the staff

TABLE 26.5
Considering the Leader Who Has Succeeded

Possible staff reactions/attitudes:

• Respect, admiration

• Appreciation, supported

• Gratitude

BUT ALSO

• Abandoned

• Angry, bitter

• Rejected (personal value system given up.
  The leader, as role model, has "sold out")

• Empathetic (similar losses)

as certain established practices are modified, relinquished, and grieved. It also calls for clarity on the part of the leader about the need to look toward the future and the development of new skills and approaches if the organization is to be successful. Flexibility is important. The issues of ongoing evaluations of work performance, adherence to established goals, criteria for success and for failure of the organization, and for the leader and other staff members must be addressed. Since the system of care and the expectations of the organization must change as new approaches are adapted, the leader is likely to be confronted and challenged more strongly by organizational members who are at different stages in accepting the need for, or the possibility of, a new model of care (Gabel & Oster, in press). At times such as these, a new balance or clarification of roles between leaders and staff members must be established to promote both change and security within the organization.

The first step in this process is for the leader to personally confront, understand, react to, and resolve (at least to a large degree) the internal conflicts noted earlier in this paper. The leader must address the meaning of his or her own losses as one model of care emphasizing what has been called traditional values gives way, at least partly, to a new, more competitive and market influenced, model of care. It is important to realize that while there are unique aspects to the current period of change, there have been other major shifts in mental health care delivery previously, such as when the community mental health movement challenged a more institutional approach. The leader must confront the meaning of success and of failure for himself or herself, and for the organization, as a managed care approach now is instituted. The leader must be prepared to accept the accolades and the criticism of staff members during this period of transition, change, and uncertainty.

This initial step in organizational change involves a leader who is able to move forward because his/her own conflicts have been resolved to a manageable degree. Getting to this point requires personal effort and introspection on the part of the leader, and may also require external facilitation through peers in the field or through professional consultation.

Once the organization's leadership is more firmly committed to whatever changes are considered necessary to adapt to a managed care framework (a process that also may benefit from external consultation (Gabel & Oster, in press)), it is important for leaders and staff to redefine and clarify their mutual roles and expectations (Table 26.6).

Table 26.6 provides guidelines for areas to be discussed with staff by the leader in various forums, staff meetings, groups, and the like. These discussions sometimes benefit from external facilitation. The approach advocated emphasizes the need for open dis-cussion between leaders and staff members at various levels, straightforward statements about differences between the traditional professional value system and a more market driven or business oriented value system, the degree of loss involved in changes in bal-ance between value systems, clarity about what values are essential to maintain pride and satisfaction in one's professional work and what values or practices can be modified or given up as practice patterns change. These discussions should include possible benefits of new approaches (along with the losses), impediments (walls) to personal change at all levels (leadership, staff, organization), and specific, concrete steps to address, overcome, or work around the walls or difficulties at all levels. These meetings and discussions

TABLE 26.6
Developing a New Balance in the Relationship of Leaders and Staff Members

Openly discuss (perhaps with a facilitator):

• Traditional professional values

• Current market driven/business oriented values

• Shifting roles/expectations of leader and of staff

• Issues of loss, mourning

• Negotiable/non negotiable values and activities (e.g. patient care)

• Issues of gain with a new system (personal, patients, society)

• What is needed to change (new skills, attitudes, activities)

• Impediments to change (personal, organizational)

• New skill levels needed (e.g. for leader, managerial, budgetary skills; for staff, how to do short term treatment). Consider consultation for both leaders and staff in the development of new skills.

• Approaches to leadership and decision making (a.g. authoritarian, consensual)

• Areas of help, support, leader and staff need from one another

• Issues of ongoing evaluation and responsibility; performance and feedback assessment

• Issues of shared success, shared failure; meaning of success and failure to each

with staff should emphasize clarity about organizational structure, decision making and responsibility. Clarity is also important with regard to performance evaluations, feedback, and individual and programmatic responsibilities, as noted earlier. Consequences and expectations for success and failure should be discussed in an open, supportive, and clear manner. It is important to provide support through difficult changes and major losses, to emphasize continually core professional, patient centered values, but also to require concrete task related changes in decided upon approaches.

SUMMARY

This paper describes various reactions and attitudes that leaders and non-leaders in mental health organizations may have as they confront organizational change in the managed care era. Conflict in the leader himself or herself about changes in organizational or treatment approaches is a major factor limiting necessary or adaptive organizational change. A description of possible leader and staff reactions to perceived success or failure has attempted to clarify ambivalent reactions on the part of the leader and the staff. A model for leader initiated organizational change that emphasizes the need for leaders to have addressed their own conflicts about the institution of new approaches is advocated. Open, supportive dialogue and clear decision making and outcome expectations on the part of the leader towards the staff also have been emphasized as aids in clarifying and strengthening the relationship between leaders and staff during a time of transition to a new model of care.

REFERENCES

Adamson, F. B. (1989). Cultivating a charismatic quality leader. *Quality Progress, 22,* 56–57.

Astrachan, B. M. (1980). Regulation, adaptation, and leadership in psychiatric facilities. *Hospital and Community Psychiatry, 31,* 169–174.

Barton, W. E., & Barton, G. M. (1983). The psychiatrist-administrator. In J. A. Talbott, S. R. Kaplan (Eds.), *Psychiatric administration: A comprehensive text for the clinician-executive* (pp. 179–185). New York, NY: Grune and Stratton.

Bass, B. M. (1990). *Bass and Stogdill's handbook of leadership: Theory, research and managerial applications* (3rd ed.). New York, NY: The Free Press.

Bennis, W. (1989). Why leaders can't lead. *Training and Development Journal, 43,* 35–39.

Bennis, W., & Nanus, B. (1985). *Leader: The strategies for taking charge.* New York, NY: Harper and Row.

Burns, J. M. (1978). *Leadership.* New York, NY: Harper and Row.

Campbell, E. G., Weissman, J. S., & Blumenthal, D. (1997). Relationship between market competition and activities and attitudes of medical school faculty. *Journal of the American Medical Association, 278,* 222–226.

Conway, A. (1982). Psychiatric management: Change in the 1980s. *Hospital & Community Psychiatry, 33,* 310–311.

Cozza, S. J., & Hales, R. E. (1992). Leadership. In J. A. Talbott, R. E. Hales, S. L. Keill (Eds.), *Textbook of administrative psychiatry* (pp. 31–58). Washington, DC: American Psychiatric Press.

Feldman, S. (1981). Leadership in mental health: Changing the guard for the 1980s. *American Journal of Psychiatry, 138,* 1147–1153.

Gabel, S., & Oster, G. D. (in press). Mental health providers confronting organizational change: Process, problems and strategies. *Psychiatry, Interpersonal and Biological Process.*

Goldstein, M. A., & Kalman, T. P. (1997). Satisfaction among private practice psychiatrists: Impact of managed care. *Syllabus and Proceedings Summary of the Annual Meeting American Psychiatric Association.*

Greenblatt, M. (1983). The unique contributions of psychiatrists to leadership roles. *Hospital & Community Psychiatry, 34,* 260–262.

Hersey, P., & Blanchard, K. H. (1969). Life cycle theory of leadership. *Training and Development Journal, 23,* 26–34.

Kaplan, S. R. (1983). Phases of development in psychiatric organizations. In J. A. Talbott, & S. R. Kaplan (Eds.), *Psychiatric administration: A comprehensive text for the clinician-executive* (pp. 167–175). New York ,NY: Grune and Sratton.

Kernberg, O. F. (1978). Leadership and organizational functioning: Organizational regression. *International Journal of Group Psychotherapy 28,* 3–25.

Kernberg, O. F. (1979). Regression in organizational leadership. *Psychiatry, 42,* 24–39.

Lee, C. (1989). Can leadership be taught? *Training, 26,* 19–26.

Levinson D. J., Klerman G. L. (1967). The clinician-executive. Some problematic issues for the psychiatrist in mental health organizations. *Psychiatry 30,* 3–15.

Marcos, L. R., & Silver M. A. (1988), Psychiatrist-executive management styles: Nature or nurture? *American Journal of Psychiatry, 145,* 103–106.

Moy, E., Mazzarchi, A. J., Levin, R. J., Blake, D. A., & Griner, P. F. (1997). Relationship between National Institutes of Health research awards to U.S. medical schools and managed care market penetration. *Journal of the American Medical Association, 278,* 217–221.

Rachlin, S., & Keill, S. L. (1992). Administration in psychiatry. In R. E. Hales, S. C. Yudofsky, & J. A. Talbott (Eds.), *The American Psychiatric Press textbook of psychiatry* (2nd ed.) (pp. 1445–1461). Washington, DC: American Psychiatric Press.

Shore, M. F. (1993). Thoughts on twenty years of mental health administration. *Administration and Policy in Mental Health, 21,* 117–121.

Silver, M. A., Akerson, D. M., & Marcos, L. R. (1990). Preferred management styles among psychiatrist-administrators. *Hospital & Community Psychiatry, 41,* 321–323.

Talbott, J. A. (1987). Management, administration, leadership. What's in a name? *Psychiatric Quarterly, 58,* 229–242.

Zaleznik, A. (1977). Managers and leaders: Are they different? *Harvard Business Review, 55,* 67–68.

27.

Susan E. Roche

WALKING THE LINE BETWEEN CAPACITY
AND CONSTRAINT: FEMINIST SOCIAL WORK
IN A CONSERVATIVE ERA

Feminist social work is about the liberation, inclusion, and empowerment of women and other groups who have been marginalized, exploited, oppressed, and abused (Bricker-Jenkins & Hooyman, 1986; Davis, 1994; Van den Bergh & Cooper, 1986). It is rooted in the experiences and analyses of women as a diverse population and is expressed through the practice of women social workers as well as male allies. Because feminist social work fundamentally and explicitly combines political and personal dimensions of practice, it not only attracts deeply committed proponents but intense opposition.

Among the sources of oppositional structures which feminist social workers must negotiate is a highly organized neoconservative movement against feminism and against the welfare state which permeates the federal and many state and local governments (Davis, 1991; Ferree & Hess, 1994; Hyde, 1995; Marshall, 1995; Whittier, 1995). They must also cope with the related pressures on human service agencies to psychologize their approaches to social problems and to label clients' situations with mental disorder diagnostic categories for funding purposes.

Under these conditions social workers are hard pressed to preserve their transformative feminist agendas. They often find scant support from colleagues or employers for methods aimed at creating a more socially and economically just society in which all people are actively valued. Rather than assessments and interventions aimed at transforming inequitable, inadequate, and abusive social relations into more inclusive and sustaining conditions, many human services are funded to "treat" individual "dysfunction." As my own experience attests, even community-based organizations (e.g., youth work agencies and parent-child centers) originally founded as alternatives to unresponsive, punitive bureaucratic agencies have retrenched their progressive practices in order to secure and maintain funding. How then as feminists and as social workers, can we walk the line between the capacity of our thinking and action[1] and the contradictory constraints of our political era?

I have found one source of answers regarding how social workers can maintain and apply feminist thinking and action in our work in my experience working with organizations within the battered women's movement. Many of these organizations carry out feminist practice traditions. Furthermore, they have amassed a base of experience and strategies for preserving these traditions and for dealing with opposition to them. Their survival is particularly susceptible to the vagaries of funders and local and state politics because their resource needs are dense, their budgets and staffs relatively small, and their ties to political elites often weak. Operating a shelter requires intensive capital investment for maintaining a secure residential facility, staffing, and other resources necessary to assist women in virtually starting over in their lives. Laws, enforcement protections, zoning and other regulatory permits, fiscal and in-kind contributions, and additional community supports on which most shelters depend render them vulnerable to the idiosyncratic reactions of their surrounding communities.

This vulnerability of battered women's shelters mirrors the resource uncertainties of many human service organizations, especially those whose ideologies and practices contradict the status quo. Thus, shelters for women who have been abused are particularly valuable institutions to examine when considering how to maintain feminist practice.

One of the strategies which members of movements have often used to maintain their morale in difficult times is passing on stories of struggle, perseverance, and success. Such stories provide hope and inspiration with which to sustain progressive commitments and creative resilience. The remainder of this article considers one such "critical incident" story of a battered women's shelter in New England with which I am familiar.

A CASE IN POINT

This is a story of the internal struggle and change process of a battered womens' organization regarding its feminist identity and practice dilemmas in light of concerns about its resource maintenance and organizational survival. It is a fairly common story in the United States (Roche, 1991). What is somewhat unique is that it is also the narrative of a group of women who ultimately elected not to yield their feminist organizational practice traditions despite

the increasing conservative constraints on them. Analytically, this case study documents events of one organization in a particular location and a specific era and considers their implications for maintaining feminist social work more generally. I hope that the thinking it generates will contribute to the development of practice conceptions which can be applied to resist the magnetic pull to give up on feminist social work agendas.

Conditions

Following a year of internal struggle, the executive director and several board members of this New England-based battered women's organization resigned. Despite, or maybe because of the relative stability that the organization had achieved since its founding, the process leading up to the resignations was by all accounts, emotionally charged, unpleasant, and demoralizing. Even so, the remaining staff and board members were dedicated to staying with the organization and utilizing a feminist approach to maintaining the organization and its activities.

At the time of the resignations, the organization's activities included a hotline, shelter, support groups, and individual advocacy for abused women. The organization also provided services for their children, community and professional education, a violence prevention project for teens, and a pre-employment project for single mothers. It conducted social policy advocacy locally and at the state level, and was a founding member of the community domestic violence task force and the community intervention program for men who abuse their female partners. Over its 14 year life span, the organization had evolved from a radical feminist collective to a United Way member agency with a board of directors, executive director, shelter, hot-line, advocacy, children's services and special projects coordinators, and 75 active volunteers.

I had served in a variety of volunteer and ad hoc paid capacities in the organization for seven years prior to the events of this story. As a volunteer, I had provided crisis and groupwork training for other volunteers, facilitated a support group for women residing in the shelter and the community, served on the board of directors' executive committee, personnel committee, served on multiple hiring committees, and provided supervision to an interim agency coordinator. During the first five years of my volunteer work with the organization, I was employed as the director of a community-based youth and family agency and later, as an independent social worker on a contract basis. At the end of those five years, I left my community to attend a doctoral program in a school of social work in another state.

In the year before I began my doctoral education, I was contracted by the shelter organization to develop and coordinate a pre-employment project for single parents and displaced homemakers, and the summer before I left, as the interim coordinator of children's services. A year later, I was employed for a summer as the interim coordinator of shelter services. Because of the flexibility of my summer schedule as a doctoral student I was able to cover the vacancies in the latter positions until they could be filled more permanently. As part of my responsibilities in each, I served on their permanent coordinator hiring committees. At the end of that second summer I returned to my doctoral program and was there during the nine months that the organization dealt with the most emotionally charged aspects of its internal struggle.

During these years, the executive director of the organization was an M.S.W. level social worker with many years of professional practice experience in other types of settings prior to her work for the shelter. She introduced the provision of family casework services to the women and children residing in the shelter and provided clinical supervision to the white, mostly bachelor's level educated paid staff. In the process, she applied a more psychological orientation to violence against women than had previously been used at the shelter.

One of the primary reasons that the director had been hired was to increase the organization's fiscal stability. Largely due to her management and public relations efforts, the organization had become more fiscally secure and was in the midst of a capital campaign. She had also developed a board of directors whose membership was more connected to the business community than had previously been the case. Actively working with the executive director, this board was key to the development of the broadly-based budget, business-like fiscal orientation and accounting procedures, and capacity to renovate and furnish the newly acquired building in which the shelter was housed. However, the changes that came with this increased professionalization and fiscal stability had paradoxical effects; they strengthened the organization's survival and acceptance in the social service and business communities and its income, while weakening its feminist movement approach and alienating many paid and volunteer staff members.

At the peak of the executive director's successes, some personnel who had long-term commitments to feminist organizing began speaking out against the organizational changes taking place (e.g., professionalization and bureaucratization). They pressured the director and the board to rescind some of them. This led to what amounted to a rebellion by most of the staff against formalization, centralization, and depoliticization. Those who most vocally pressed for change spoke against the incongruence which they perceived between the official feminist mission statement, principles of unity, and history, and the more traditional social service agency structure and processes. They pressed for a more inclusive, less formal professional organizational approach with a more democratic-collectivist structure and process and a more political orientation to the daily work with women and the public. They also reacted against the alienation felt by personnel who did not reflect the middle class, professional image which was being projected on behalf of publicly legitimizing the organization (e.g., at large scale fund raising events). Those staff and board members who defended these changes did so primarily on the basis that they contributed to the maintenance of organizational funding and the nonprofit status of the organization.

Months of tense meetings (sometimes public and sometimes closed) among various staff and board members ensued prior to the resignation of the director and some board members. The struggle polarized members in a conflict over the competing claims of grassroots movement feminism and professional bureaucratic administration. By all accounts, it was a hurtful, frustrating period. Even so, the women who first spoke out against the reduction of feminist practice, the women who resigned, the women who remained, and I all played key roles in the reconstruction process.

Those who first spoke out were willing to risk possible hostility, rejection, even firing. They were also tenacious, keeping the issues on the organizational agenda for over a year. Among the women who resigned, were some who had been instrumental in gaining credibility and increased security for the organization in the face of conserv-

ative external pressures. Their decisions to resign, though painfully made, were critical in opening the way for changes which built on the relative security that they had contributed to the organization. Although the intensity of the conflict ended with their resignations, the months of struggle and the inability to resolve it more harmoniously left emotional weariness and wariness in their wake. Among the women who stayed, were board members who believed in professional consultation, so much so that one of them offered personal funds to pay me to assist the organization through its transition. These women also gave the organization time to heal reflectively and regroup by suspending the personnel replacement process for two months. All of the women who stayed made the critical decision to participate fully in the assessment and planning process and to abide by its outcomes. These choices required their investment of hours of effort within and above their regular work schedules.

Actions

In order to reduce the residual tension and stabilize the organization, the remaining board members formed an ad hoc planning committee of volunteers and employees. A member of the planning committee called me and asked if I would work with the organization for two months as a consultant. By that time, I was developing my proposal for my dissertation research (a national study of battered women's shelters), studying global feminism, and consulting with battered women's organizations in the state where I was in school. All of these experiences contributed to my thinking about how to be of assistance to the shelter organization.

Our letter of agreement stated that I would develop proposals for the organization's staffing pattern, the children's services, the organizational structure, salaries, and the direction of the organization, particularly as a feminist organization. I was to develop these in conjunction with the board, staff, program volunteers, and consumers. Everyone agreed that the services to women and children were to be maintained during this period of "self-examination" and reorganization. I agreed to attend personnel committee, planning committee, and staff meetings periodically, and that additionally, I would attend other related organizational meetings on an ad hoc basis, as indicated.

Assessment Phase. I began a four-week assessment phase by studying all of the board and staff meeting minutes for the preceding twelve months. I also carefully reviewed a written summary of an organizational evaluation recently conducted by a board member and the written, open-ended comments by the staff solicited by the personnel committee. The recommendations of this summary indicated that the staff should be more involved in organizational planning and decision making, the organizational structure should be clearer with less of a hierarchy, and fiscal matters should be shared by all.

Following this, I sought additional input through interviews with and written comments from members of the organization (staff, board, and service users). These I requested from those who either did not participate in the first survey, or who had more to add. I also interviewed women outside the organization. These women included founders of the organization, former personnel, and former service users. I took part in meetings as a participant observer and participated in less formal discussions, which were a natural outgrowth of working on site. I noted differences and

similarities in interpretation and discrepancies in information, and I explored these during subsequent meetings and informal discussions.

In addition to these localized methods, I asked the National Coalition Against Domestic Violence (NCADV) to identify shelters around the country that were operating as collectives. Only four such shelters were identified. I interviewed one representative from each of three of these organizations by phone about how their shelters were structured and operated and how they dealt with the focus issues identified by the planning committee of the New England shelter.

The assessment process revealed four broadly distinctive perspectives among the members of the organization. These perspectives conveyed differences in how members perceived the issues of contention, their relative significance, and the best ways to address them. For theoretical purposes only, members who shared similar perspectives can be categorized into four groups as follows: (1) "radical/cultural feminists" whose thinking appeared most influenced by grassroots and lesbian feminism beyond the shelter; (2) "liberal feminists" who appeared most influenced by their professions; (3) "postmodern feminists" who appeared most influenced by their lesbian vantage points and by a combination of feminist scholarship and professional orientations; and (4) "nonsexist," service-minded members who appeared most influenced by a "liberal-humanitarian service" orientation (Figure 27.1). (For expanded definitions or uses, see Cummerton, 1986; Eisenstein, 1984; Kramarae & Treichler, 1992; Sands & Nuccio, 1995; and Weil, 1986.)

These groups also represented different viewpoints about the best place to draw the line between some of the most obvious

FIGURE 27.1
Continua of Contested Organizational Practice Perspectives

Communalism–	–	–	–Individualism
"Radical/ Cultural Feminists"	"Postmodern Feminists"	"Liberal Feminists"	"Non-sexist" Members
Politics–	–	–	–Service
"Radical/ Cultural Feminists"	"Postmodern Feminists"	"Liberal Feminists"	"Non-sexist" Members
Shared Power–	–	–	–Hierarchal Power
"Radical/ Cultural Feminists"	"Postmodern Feminists"	"Liberal Feminists"	"Non-sexist" Members

themes that emerged as points of struggle: communalism and individualism, politics and service, and shared and hierarchical power arrangements. Each pair of themes can be viewed as two ends of a continuum.

Radical/cultural feminists gave more emphasis in the discussions to the themes on the left end of each continuum. Postmodern feminists' emphases ranged along the middle between the constructs. The liberal feminist and the non-sexist members emphasized the ideas on the right end of the continua. Thus, the radical/cultural feminists advocated changing to a more democratic-collectivist organizational system (Rothschild & Whitt, 1986) as essential to the shelter's vision for social change. The liberal feminists advocated maintaining the formal structure and professional agency practices as essential to the shelter's non-profit status and funding. The postmodern feminists were less attached to a categorical organizational form than to a planning process to accommodate the differences among members and the political exigencies of the work; they advocated a process of dialogue and conflict resolution whereby a new organi-

zational form might be generated. The non-sexist members were nonplussed by the issues and the dissension over them and simply wanted to "help" individual battered women.

As strong feelings arose during assessment discussions, I listened and responded to them as pertinent information about the experience of the group. Taylor (1995) refers to such feelings as the "emotional subtext" and argues the importance of this subtext to the understanding of feminist organizations. Among the feelings were fear of rejection by each other and by funders and human service providers, confusion and frustration about how the group had arrived at its current position, guilt about the treatment of those who had resigned, and hope that the situation could improve.

Probably because the postmodern feminist group was most involved in leading the assessment and planning phases, our diversity and process emphases also predominated. For example, one of the last assessment methods I used was asking all members for their written input regarding what would characterize the shelter as a feminist organization. In this way, I could give everyone's values, hopes, and concerns equal consideration in summary form before moving into the planning phase. I shared the responses to this request so that everyone could be informed of the commonalities (of which there were many) and differences (of which there were not as many) they embodied. Significantly, reflecting on these responses produced a shared belief among the members that the direction of the organization should be toward its feminist heritage rather than away from it.

Planning Phase. By the "end" of the assessment phase, the original goals (i.e., to reduce tension, stabilize the organization, and maintain or improve the work with battered women) had been expanded to include reasserting the transformative feminist mission of the organization in all aspects of the shelter's practices, as well as maintaining its fiscal survival. These priorities illustrate the symbolic reorganization which was a dimension of the "organizational self-reflection" in which the members were engaged. The expanded list of priorities, by now shared by most of the members, guided the four-week planning process and the final proposal which resulted from it.

In part, the planning phase was also interventive in that during it, the common ground among the members was strengthened and the tension about differences was reduced. At this time, I intentionally placed less emphasis on each individual's interpretations and more on the meaning these events held for the group as a whole and on the organizational context. For example, I facilitated planning-related discussions regarding how to reorganize in light of historic, ideological, economic, and community contexts influencing the experience of

the organization, rather than its members' personalities. Similarly, I referred to discussions of the outcomes preferred by the four different groups of members described above as examples of manageable differences to be expected and to be accommodated by our planning process. I also emphasized developing a tolerance for uncertainty regarding the preferred structure and processes that would be proposed by the end of this phase in order to support the members to participate in a truly creative thinking process. On several occasions, I asked the members to join me in imagining their "new organization" emerging from the rich variety of their different standpoints.

As this phase progressed, the emotional climate of the discussions was changing and the group appeared to be growing more cohesive. Typical emotions that were strongly expressed during the planning discussions included anger at the encroachment by cultural and institutional forces on the autonomy to be self-determining as individual women and as an organization, pride in the collective commitments to maintaining a feminist agenda, caring about each other, and optimism about the future of the organization.

I also used several conceptual methods to facilitate this process. First, I referred to the issues of contention as "tactical differences," rather than as differences of purpose. I used two related methods to anchor this notion of differences: (a) amplifying and linking the shared feminist commitments to social change (i.e., ending violence against women) and to personal support (i.e., providing refuge and access to other social and material resources to individual abused women and their dependents); and (b) referring to the organization's long-standing "principles of unity." (At an earlier point in the organization's development, these principles had been articulated in three paragraphs explicitly referring to the shelter as a feminist organization.) The principles of unity summarized the organization's commitments, beliefs, and stances regarding the following subjects: violence against women and children, women's rights, the relationship between violence in the family and violence and discrimination in society, the organization's empowerment function, and the ways that men can support the organization's work.

Second, I frequently referred to analysis and action as inseparable and obtained agreement that analysis would be given more time as a mode of action than the group had typically devoted to it in the midst of daily demands. Thus, we were able to critically analyze the local sources of possible objections to feminist organizational practice (e.g., social service funders and larger, traditional social service agencies) and derive strategies from these analyses. We also explored comparisons between past organizational experiences with public and private funders, the media and other external influencers, and the experiences of individual battered women with informal and formal sources of support and struggle, and the women's coping, resistance and survival strategies (Kelly, 1988). This analytic process produced new approaches and criteria for making decisions regarding desirable organizational actions to take in specific situations with funders. I encouraged the group to consider how to apply the same creativity used by or on behalf of individual battered women in meeting the organization's survival needs. Applying this principle, the staff adopted the strategy of transforming funders' potential objections to non-traditional organizational approaches into interest in them. This thinking led to the formulation of strategic

rationale for feminist structure and processes that could be articulated to "outsiders" as means-ends congruence.

Third, I employed the architectural design principle of "form follows function" as a guide for creating a redevelopment proposal (the form), which was rooted in the mission statement and principles of unity (the organizational function). In drafting the proposal for organizational change, I formulated and evaluated every provision of the proposal according to its congruence with these two documents. The feminist philosophy of the shelter, which preceded and inspired the current members, was clearly articulated in both documents that referred to the organization as a resource operated by and for women and as an alternative to abusive structures.

The third conceptual device segued spontaneously for me one day at a staff meeting into a fourth, the notion of "standing the hierarchy on its side." In listening to a discussion in which hierarchy and collective were used as opposites, someone commented that she found herself agreeing with the arguments for both. When I asked them "why *not* both?" we recognized that the organizational maintenance responsibilities that are hierarchically assigned in traditional social service agencies (e.g., planning, budgeting, decision-making, administering, and evaluating) could continue to be carried out through a non-hierarchical arrangement. By the same token, the creativity and inclusiveness of feminist organizational ideals could be purposefully structured. In this way, the "best" features of both models could be combined.

Finally, to normalize the differences among and reduce the polarization between members beyond the reorganization process, I selected the concept of "coalition" as an operating metaphor for the organization. I used this metaphor as an explanatory label for the proposed structure and process as well as a practice guide for the challenges of organizational life that would continue. In using this term, I pointed out that the organization was and would continue to be comprised of women who shared a commitment to a common mission and had an array of different methodological leanings and experiences. This catalyzed a group discussion of the way that social class, education, personal experiences with abuse, and affiliations with other social structures shape these leanings, and of the richness and inherent challenges of such differences.

As a strategic structural concept, coalition appeared to enable the individual members to be open about their differences with less fear of hostile criticism than when the assessment phase began. It provided all four groups an accessible, shared language with which to participate in discussions about the new patterns that the organization might enact. To assist them with their continued development of this orientation, we all identified practice theory regarding coalition building that would provide the group a source of supportive thinking for the future (e.g., Bunch, 1987; Pheterson, 1990; Reagon, 1983).

Decision Phase. The proposal that I presented by the end of the planning phase comprised a series of recommended changes and implementation narratives that I hoped reflected the plurality of women, issues, and suggestions I heard throughout its development. I entitled each section of the proposal with a phrase from the mission statement, in keeping with the assertion I made in the introduction to the proposal that "this is the starting and ending point through which all that we do should circle." The sections included: I. Introduction, II. A Feminist Organization,

III. Ending Violence Against Women, IV. Supporting Women as Mothers and Individuals (Staffing Patterns), V. Supporting Women as Mothers and Individuals (Children's Services), VI. Differences and Discrimination (Organizational Structure: Communi-cation flow), VII. An Organization which Empowers (Organizational Structure: Functions), and IX. An Organization which Empowers (Organizational Structure: Acc-ountability).

In the proposal, I recommended a much flatter organizational structure than that which had evolved prior to the assessment phase. Concurring, the board of directors voted itself and the traditional hierarchical administrative structure out of existence and formed a more inclusive, less hierarchical organizational structure. The structure as described in the written proposal, made provisions for the decision making, accountability, communication flows, and organization's future that administrative functions typically accommodate.

The new policy body of the organization became known as "the steering committee" and was comprised of paid and volunteer staff members, former service users, and policy volunteers. The former executive director position was split into two administrative coordinating positions, one for fiscal matters and one for other organizational support functions (e.g., volunteer training, community education, and those I had been performing temporarily). Both of these staff positions were designated as standing members of the steering committee. The supervision structure was reorganized into several peer groups, eventually called "pods."

All paid staff members (including the two organizational-level coordinators) were appropriated the same amount of decisional authority and paid at the same starting rate, regardless of position or educational degree, as a means of expressing equal valuation of their roles and responsibilities. Future hiring decisions were to be made on the basis of related experience, ability to do the job, and willingness and ability to work in the new structure, rather than level of education. A consensus approach to decision making in staff and steering committee meetings was adopted and the members of both received training in this approach and in related conflict resolution methods. Organizational accountability and follow-through were conceived as responsibilities shared by all paid staff members with specific responsibilities for the aspects of the daily work in which they were most involved. The financial and organizational support coordinators were delegated the facilitation, scheduling, and document preparation responsibilities for a designated annual program planning and budgeting process.

Future Development. The issue of the membership role of women service users was identified as requiring further development. There was no question that former service users were welcome in any personnel capacity that they were capable of filling. The troubling questions had to do with women in crisis. The issues of concern involved the ethics and practicalities of on one hand, asking women in crisis to assume caretaker responsibilities for the organization, or for other women or their children, and on the other hand, condescendingly defining for women the limitations of their capacity to be of assistance. Underlying these questions was the uncomfortable theme of who the organizational feminist thinking and action actually empowered, personnel *and* service users or personnel *not* service users (Davis & Srinivasan, 1991). Not reaching consensus on an organizational position regarding this issue

of difference among women was the most acute limitation of the plan that was adopted.

Epilogue

Only one staff person and one volunteer who participated in the reorganization remain in the organization today. Nevertheless, with some revision, most of the provisions of the organizational change continue.

The structure and process adopted by the shelter in the case example remain (with the exception that as a result of a budgetary decision, the organizational support coordinator position no longer exists), and is once again up for review and possible reconstruction. Currently, the coordinators in the organization (e.g., hotline, shelter, children's services, court advocacy, community services, development, financial, membership services, administrative) incorporate the functions originally delegated to the organizational support coordinator into the rest of their responsibilities. Contrary to the original concerns, the organization has retained its non-profit status and the support of its funders. As hoped, the staff's articulation of the structure as integral to the mission of the organization increased the interest of community representatives of the major ongoing funder whose support has continued to this day.

Professionalization of the organization is no longer emphasized over valuing experience, consciousness, and native ability. Even though three members of the staff do have graduate degrees in social work (from a program that stresses social justice, human rights, and the work they do), personnel are not hired on the basis of their formal education. Rather, personnel are recruited and hired for their feminist philosophy, respect for all women who are abused and their children, ability to work within a non-hierarchically structured organization, and representation of the diversity of women the shelter serves.

An increased emphasis on diversity can be found in the revised mission statement. Policies and their implementation now more explicitly prioritize promoting social and cultural diversity and combating racism and other forms of oppression than when the reorganization proposal was adopted. According to one coordinator, the issue of service users' active participation as members of the organization continues to lack satisfying resolution despite these recent policy changes.

At this time, the organization is once again seeking a consultant who will assist in reviewing its current operating processes in terms of its effects on staff and consumers. Whereas originally, feminist practice was the issue of contention, today the concerns are about staff burn-out and turnover and how these in turn, affect the individual women and children who are served.

DISCUSSION AND RECOMMENDATIONS

I have shared drafts of this article with some current members of the organization in the case example in order to keep my interpretations closely aligned with their realities. In the light of our discussions, a number of points are significant to note regarding factors that contributed to the reassertion and continuation of the organization's feminism: the critical decisions of key people, their renegotiation of shared meaning, and their organization's historic developmental experiences and community resource contexts. The implications of their organization's past suggests principles that

should be applied to its own and others' current and future approaches to change in order to maintain their feminist commitments while also resolving the need for change. These principles include: normalizing struggle and change, keeping purpose central, finding strength in diversity, caring for our organizations, developing analysis as action, and sustaining these principles.

Normalizing Struggle and Change

Feminist social workers should normalize the existence of struggle and change as part of organizational life. Regardless of the type of organization feminist social workers are employed by, working in all types of agencies involves multiple professional, organizational, and ethical challenges as a matter of course. Moreover, as the most recent developments at the organization in the case example suggest, even the most systematically planned organizational change in response to the challenges is not permanent. This recognition should be incorporated into planned change efforts as well as into the general orientation toward welcome and unwelcome changes that are unplanned.

Specific challenges exist for feminist social workers in women-centered organizations such as battered women's shelters, and in agencies that are not women-centered. The constancy of struggling with personnel in other institutions (e.g., courts, social welfare departments, emergency rooms, and mental health centers) to gain their responsiveness to women whose lives are at risk can be demoralizing. Likewise, the lack of funding for, and the public policies against, sociopolitical action that is imperative on multiple levels can lead organizations and individual social workers away from their feminist missions and practices. When these situations have a politicizing effect on them (as they often do), tension is produced by the difficulties of maintaining both social action and individual support functions under working conditions characterized by long hours, relatively low salaries, and inadequate, uncertain human and fiscal resources. (This is part of what currently exhausts the members of the New England organization.) Understanding these challenges and the multiple changes that accompany organizational responses to them is part of the long-term work of feminism. Developing practice wisdom from our experiences with them is a requisite aspect of developing feminist resilience.

Keeping Purpose Central

Feminist social workers should remind themselves regularly of their purposes and the stakes involved in working toward their fulfillment as a means of keeping them central to their efforts. The purposes (i.e., mission and philosophy) can serve as focalizers in making difficult decisions, in preventing the severity of the internal struggle experienced by the New England organization, and in contributing standards for evaluating our efforts and holding ourselves and others accountable.

Regularly reminding ourselves of what is at stake in maintaining feminist practice involves remembering why this practice matters and why it is not universally valued. It refocuses us on the lives of socially marginalized women and children who are at multiple risk, and on the vision of the changes we are committed to on behalf of all marginalized and oppressed people. For the women in the case example and the women reading about them, it represented a call to carry forward what had been passed on to them by those who came before. It also represented the loss of their

place in the movement against violence against women should they not carry forth the feminist vision through their work in the organization.

Finding Strength in Diversity

If we are to maintain our feminist purposes, we must be skilled at activating our differences as our strength. Most fundamental are the many social status differences (e.g., race, social class, ethnicity, and sexual identity) among feminist social workers and between social workers and those we serve. Multiplying these differences are those having to do with personality, ideology, organizational setting, and personal experience with the difficulties that bring women into formal contact with social workers.

The case example illustrates what can happen when we move from a stance of difference as a basis of animosity and fear to difference as a basis of creative tension and multi-dimensional thinking. This is possible when difference is assumed, welcomed as normative, and bridged by our recognition of shared purpose. It also requires ongoing development regarding recognizing and struggling compassionately and effectively with one's own and others' internalized oppression and domination (Pheterson, 1990) to strengthen feminist consciousness and skill in transforming difference from a barrier into a genuine strength.

Caring for Our Organizations

Feminist social workers should ensure that some of us do for our organizations what our organizations are intended to do for our constituents. One of the best ways of caring for our constituents is caring equally for our organizations, because our organizations have the potential to reduce isolation and alienation and increase reconciliation and belonging. Thus, it is a feminist responsibility to build responsive organizational infrastructures that simultaneously support women and other marginalized and oppressed groups, feminist practitioners, *and* organizational survival.

In order to preserve sanctuaries for feminist thinking and action, individual social workers must commit themselves to organizational stewardship as rigorously as they commit themselves to direct practice. To carry out this commitment, we must be as knowledgeable about organizations and communities as we are about individuals, families and small groups. We must also adopt "both/and" practice orientations which do not separate these focuses of practice into "either-or" categories of specialization. When we do not adopt such orientations toward our organizational membership-as-leadership, we risk displacing our feminist mission and practices with the utilitarian, rational-technocratic premises, methods, and outcome measures of traditional organizational management theory and many funding institutions.

Developing Analysis as Action

Feminist social workers should understand and employ purposefully the principle of praxis, that our "activity consists of action and reflection" (Freire, 1970, p. 119). Our "activity is theory and practice; it is reflection and action" (p. 119). Meaningful action congruently combines the liberatory politics, equality of participation, and communal ownership of feminism with the professional ethics, ecosystemic knowledge, and reflective skill of social work. Developing our analysis as action can deepen our discussions about how to respond to the challenges to our feminist

mission and practices and expand the range of options to which we have access. It also can serve to offset the initial impatience toward the analytical aspects of strategizing that I have often observed in working with feminist organizations and teaching about social work practice.

To illustrate, at first, members of the organization in the case example often stated or implied that they do not have time in their daily work to analyze its historic and sociostructural influences. By our last meeting together this had changed noticeably as we evaluated the unanticipated impact of our work together. One member pointed out that she believed the new organizational structures and processes were responsive to their everyday realities because they had all invested in thinking about the broad contextual issues in addition to their more immediate concrete concerns. Many other members agreed with her. As this wrap-up discussion continued, recognition was also conveyed that analysis and action are inseparable when we center our efforts on our overarching feminist purposes. Someone else noted that it really is necessary to think about the broad influences (e.g., culture, economics, politics, and historical timing) on the issues with which they struggle if they are to maintain their feminist orientation as an organization. This led to the agreement that time should be built into staff and steering committee meeting agendas on at least a quarterly basis for broadly analytical discussions about the work in order to augment what was termed the "more practical" business.

Sustaining These Principles

Feminist social workers should also create and cultivate ongoing supports for sustaining the principles contained in these recommendations. This requires making temporal, emotional, informational, and tangible resources and opportunities accessible to ourselves within our own organizations and throughout our feminist networks.

The case example illustrates some very specific forms of resources and opportunities for sustaining the principles that I have recommended above. These include the following: organizational principles of unity; organizational mission statement; careful handling of critical incidents; feminist organizational consultation and development; new staff orientation about the organization's feminist history, philosophy, and processes; periodic staff training in feminist decision making, accountability, leadership, and conflict resolution practices; dedication of precious meeting time to thinking analytically together in order to maintain feminist mission, analyses and practices; and commitment of willingness, time, and active involvement. These and other resources and opportunities should not be allowed to fall by the wayside as luxuries that can be set aside until a less busy or stressful time; they should be given the same priority as the work with clients and the work to maintain the budget and legitimacy of the organization. This is why the designation of someone(s) within our organizations to coordinate and facilitate actions geared toward contributing to organizational resilience is so important. Employing the notion of standing the hierarchy on its side, this individual(s) does not have to hold hierarchically-structured power and authority in order to be able to carry out these activities as primary responsibilities.

IN CLOSING

In considering the lessons of the case example, the vitality of feminist social work practice appears to be a matter of the will, creativity and shared meaning among people, of timing, and of the characteristics of multiple communities (i.e., feminist movement, human service system, and funding). The particular impact of these factors as they are still being played out in the New England shelter demonstrates that although feminist social work would seem to have more and less conducive geographical homes, contextual factors are not deterministic. With thought and effort, they can be differentially negotiated and synergistically recombined as long as the feminist purposes are kept central.

It is critical that feminist social workers sustain their will to walk the line for women's safety, freedom, and full participation. If they do not, it is unlikely that anyone else will risk their credibility to do so, especially at a time when it is not the popular choice to make. There are no simple maps to follow in walking this line. The key to the survival and resilience of feminist social work in a conservative era lies in individual practitioners supporting each other to integrate and exercise creatively their feminist and professional social work strengths. Collectively, it lies in giving equal value and attention to the survival of the organization *and* its feminism, fostering genuine consensus about how to do this on a day-to-day basis, and generating new organizational modes of transforming the obstacles into opportunities and resources.

NOTE

1. As used here, feminist thinking and action refers to the analyses and activities that are directed at changing attitudes, policies, and practices which maintain and justify male domination and subordinate and abuse women. Feminist social work practice, therefore, is understood as the analyses and activities of social workers that foster such personal and social change.

REFERENCES

Bricker-Jenkins, M., & Hooyman, N. R. (Eds.). (1986). *Not for women only: Social work practice for a feminist future*. Silver Spring, MD: National Association of Social Workers.

Bunch, C. (1987). Making common cause: Diversity and coalitions. In C. Bunch, *Passionate politics: Feminist theory in action* (pp. 149–157). New York: St. Martin's Press.

Cummerton, J. M. (1986). A feminist perspective on research: What does it help us see? In N. Van Den Bergh, & L. B. Cooper (Eds.), *Feminist visions for social work* (pp. 187–210). Silver Spring, MD: National Association of Social Workers.

Davis, F. (1991). *Moving the Mountain: The women's movement in America since 1960*. New York: Simon & Schuster.

Davis, L. V (Ed.). (1994). *Building on women's strengths: A social work agenda for the twenty-first century*. Binghamton, NY: The Haworth Press, Inc.

Eisenstein, Z. R. (1984). *Feminism and sexual equality: Crisis in liberal America*. New York: Monthly Review Press.

Ferree, M. M., & Hess, B. B. (1994). *Controversy & coalition: The new feminist movement across three decades of change* (rev. ed). New York: Twayne Publishers.

Freire, P. (1970). *Pedagogy of the oppressed*. New York: Continuum.

Hyde, C. (1995). Feminist social movement organizations survive the New Right. In M. M. Ferree, & P. Y. Martin (Eds.), *Feminist organizations: Harvest of the new women's movement* (pp. 306–322). Philadelphia: Temple University Press.

Kelly, L. (1988). *Surviving sexual violence*. Minneapolis: University of Minnesota Press.

Kramarae, C., & Treichler, P. A. (1992). *A feminist dictionary*. London, ENG: Pandora Press.

Marshall, S. (1995). Confrontation and co-optation in antifeminist organizations. In M. M. Ferree, & P. Y. Martin (Eds.), *Feminist organizations: Harvest of the new women's movement* (pp. 323–338). Philadelphia: Temple University Press.

Pheterson, G. (1990). Alliances between women: Overcoming internalized oppression and internalized domination. In L. Albrecht, & R. M. Brewer (Eds.)., *Bridges of power: Women's multicultural alliances* (pp. 34–48). Philadelphia: New Society Publishers.

Reagon, B. J. (1983). Coalition politics: Turning the century. In B. Smith (Ed.), *Home girls: A black feminist anthology*. New York: Kitchen Table Press.

Roche, S. E. (1991). Social change and direct service: Striking the balance in battered women's shelters across the U.S. Unpublished doctoral dissertation. Rutgers University, New Brunswick, NJ.

Rothschild, J., & Whitt, J. A. (1986). *The cooperative workplace: Potentials and dilemmas of organizational democracy and participation*. Cambridge: Cambridge University Press.

Sands, R. G., & Nuccio, K. (1995). Postmodern feminist theory and social work. *Social Work, 37*, 489–494.

Smircich, L. (1983). Studying organizations as cultures. In G. Morgan (Ed.), *Beyond method: Strategies for social research* (pp. 160–171). Beverly Hills, CA: Sage Publications.

Srinivasan, M., & Davis, L. V. (1991). A shelter: An organization like any other? *Affilia: Journal of women in social work, 6*, 38 57.

Van Den Bergh, N., &, Cooper, L. (Eds.). (1986). *Feminist visions for social work*. Silver Spring MD: National Association of Social Workers.

Weil, M. (1986). Women, community and organizing. In N. Van Den Bergh, & L. B. Cooper (Eds.), *Feminist visions for social work* (pp. 187–110). Silver Spring, MD: National Association of Social Workers.

Whittier, N. (1995). *Feminist generations: The persistence of the radical women's movement*. Philadelphia: Temple University Press.

28.

Yeheskel Hasenfeld

PROGRAM DEVELOPMENT

INTRODUCTION

Program development and implementation is a common and crucial task of community intervention practitioners, yet it has not received adequate attention in practice theory. There seems to be an implicit assumption that, once the community practitioner has successfully mobilized action groups or planning task forces to grapple with important community issues, the function is essentially completed. Yet, the most critical element in any community organization activity is the emergence of some idea and design for a *program*, be it a direct service delivery, a training program, a coordination council, a fund-raising program, or the like.

The implementation of such a program, which in almost all instances requires the development of some organizational framework, is in the last analysis the true test of successful community organization, since the program provides in very concrete terms the outputs or services desired and needed by the community. Thus, the overall thesis of this paper is that the community intervention practitioner has the dual role of action mobilizer and planner, and of organizer and program implementer. In this paper, then, I discuss some of the major tasks and skills that the practitioner needs to know and fulfill in order to successfully implement a community-generated program. The term planner-organizer is used to designate the complexity of such a role.

Most frequently, the planner-organizer is asked to develop a program for direct-service delivery. Social action groups often develop service programs in order to serve people ignored by existing services, or as a means of gaining community support, or as a device to stimulate existing service providers to change their own programs. Examples include unions instituting information and referral services and recreation programs for retired workers, and the Black Panthers setting up a breakfast meal service and elementary school education program for neighborhood children. Thus, the discussion that follows will focus on program development for direct services. Nevertheless, the tasks and skills involved are clearly applicable to other types of programs.

Development of a new program is by no means an easy undertaking. It often requires a prolonged process of negotiation and planning. Launching a new service inevitably results in some disruption of the delicate balance that exists among various service providers. Some agency representatives may feel they were excluded from participation. Others may see the new program as a challenge to their own domain. While the planner-organizer may find it necessary to disagree with certain groups who oppose the program, he or she must have enough support and sufficient resources to withstand countervailing pressures.

Every new program requires resources — in particular, money and manpower. Without a fair chance of obtaining these, no effort to develop a new program is likely to succeed. The key to the success of a new venture could be the extent to which the planner-organizer is in a position to control at least some of the funds allocable to the relevant social service programs. Yet money without capable or trainable assistance is of little avail. And without facilities, legitimacy, or some other needed resource, both money and assistance may be expended without benefit to consumers. The planner-organizer must be willing to invest a significant proportion of time to mobilize needed resources and to influence this allocation.

THE SYSTEMS PERSPECTIVE

In considering the establishment of a new program or agency, the planner-organizer may find a "systems" perspective to be particularly useful. Each agency can be viewed as an open "system," composed of a set of interrelated units designed to achieve a common objective or complex of objectives. The activities of these units are aimed at (1) recruiting such *inputs* into the agency as money and credit, manpower, and clients; (2) transforming these inputs into actual services such as medical care, counseling, or community planning; (3) producing *output* in such forms as improved social services coordination, reduction in the incidence of need for protective services, etc.[1]

Service and Maintenance Functions

A second assumption underlying the systems perspective is that the activities of the agency staff are guided by two basic motivations. The first can be termed the goal-seeking motive leading to "service" objectives and the second the self-maintenance motive leading to "survival" objectives. The first motive informs those staff activities designed to achieve the *output* goals of the agency. The self-maintenance motive informs those efforts by staff to maintain the agency through enhancing its access to resources, expanding its services, building a positive climate of public support, etc. Clearly, no agency can achieve its service objectives without consideration of its maintenance needs or survival objectives. Yet if the agency invests all its energies in self-maintenance it will be accused of not accomplishing, indeed of subverting, its service objectives.[2] Both sets of activities are often in tension, causing intraorganizational competition for scarce resources. Improper allocation of these resources reduces the effectiveness of any service provider.

The interplay between the goalseeking or service function of an agency and its survival needs or maintenance function can be observed in its internal structure. From a systems perspective, five subsystems within an organization are identifiable, each fulfilling an important function without which the agency is likely to experience strain and possible disintegration. Each subsystem is characterized by the function it fulfills in the agency and by a common motivation of those participating in it. The subsystems may be characterized as: (1) the technical, (2) the environmental support, (3) the institutional, (4) the intelligence, and (5) the managerial subsystems.[3]

---

[1]See for example, D. Katz and R. Kahn, *The Social Psychology of Organizations* (New York: Wiley, 1966); F. Baker, ed., *Organizational Systems* (Homewood, IL: Richard D. Irwin, 1973).

[2]R. A. Scott, "The Factory as a Social Service Organization," *Social Problems* 15 (Fall, 1967): 160–75.

[3]D. Katz and R. Kahn, op. cit., Chapter 4.

Subsystems and Their Functions

1. The function of the *technical subsystem* is to provide a service. In a social service agency, it is generally designed to improve or maintain the well-being of a client or client population. The primary motivation of the agency staff providing these services is to achieve proficiency in these assigned tasks. The range of tasks they perform may include assessment of the client's needs; evaluation of the client's resources; counseling or treatment; and referrals to other service providers. The manner in which these tasks are performed is called the agency's service technology.

2. The *environmental support subsystem's* function is to manage or recruit those resources from the environment necessary to the performance of the tasks of the technical subsystems. At least five categories of resources must be brought into the agency: (1) money and credit to cover the costs involved in providing the services and performing other functions; (2) personnel such as administrators, social workers, counselors, clerical staff, and other support staff; (3) clients whose needs or interests can be served by the agency; (4) knowledge and expertise necessary for the successful implementation of the services; and (5) complementary services of other agencies necessary to ensure that the agency's services are effective.

Procurement and management of these resources requires a variety of transactions or exchanges with those external units in the environment (other systems) that control these resources. This requires that certain agency employees perform what systems theorists call "boundary roles": roles that are necessary to develop and facilitate transactions between the organization and its environment. Boundary relationships are generally managed by agency staff with special responsibility for these tasks. For example, when budget staff negotiates with state and national officials for the allocation of fiscal resources, it manages boundary relationships leading to input of fiscal resources. When personnel workers interview or recruit potential staff, intake workers screen potential clients, and various staff members develop relations with other social service agencies, each also performs a boundary role or assumes a boundary function. In most smaller agencies, many of these boundary relationships are likely to be fulfilled by the same person or persons. These activities enable the agency to achieve some mastery over its environment, leading to procurement of needed resources with some degree of certainty or stability.[4]

3. Staff performing *institutional subsystem* functions seeks to obtain social support and legitimation for the agency from the environment. Without such support, the agency cannot hope to obtain the resources necessary for other functions. Sometimes, legitimation is in the form of a legal mandate, such as the Housing Act, Medicare, the Social Security Act, or other legislation.

Without understanding the importance of these legislative acts, one should not ignore the importance of obtaining social support in the very community in which the program operates. This includes support from potential clients, various civic organizations, governmental agencies, and other social service agencies. Staff activities involve the development of ties with key community influentials, contribution of resources to important community functions, public exposition of the agency's services, etc. Such activities are oriented

---

[4]H. Aldrich, "Organizational Boundaries and Interorganizational Conflict," *Human Relations* 24 (1971): 279–293.

toward "institutionalizing" the agency in the community, assuring it will be perceived as integral and indispensable to the community's interests.[5]

4. The ability of the agency to develop effective linkages with its external environment as well as an effective service delivery system is dependent on the operation of the agency's *intelligence and feedback mechanisms*. The functions of the intelligence subsystem are: (1) to gather and interpret vital information about the conditions of the target population for which the service is developed and about other potential client populations, about new service opportunities, about the needs and attributes of the clients served, etc.; and (2) to provide feedback to the staff of the agency on the outcomes of their efforts. This may include information about the results of client referrals to various services, evaluation of staff activities in the counseling and treatment of clients, or assessment of the "progress" being made by those clients.

Intelligence activities can help the agency to reduce uncertainty about its efforts and can be used to plan on a more rational basis. Without adequate intelligence, any agency is in danger of finding itself off target or out of the mainstream of client needs.

5. Activities of the *managerial subsystem* cut across all the other subsystems in the agency. Management is in charge of making the key decisions regarding what services get delivered, by whom, and how; relations with the environment; and the use of intelligence. The major tasks of management are: (1) to coordinate the activities of the various subsystems in the agency; (2) to resolve conflicts between the various hier-

archical levels, and to elicit the compliance of staff to its work requirements; and (3) to effect coordination between the external demands on the agency and its own resources and needs. Management acts to achieve control and stability within the agency and to mediate and achieve a compromise between the various needs and demands of the subsystems of which it is composed.

From this rather brief overview, it should be apparent that each subsystem is dependent on inputs from the others in order to fulfill its function. The quality of the performance of each subsystem profoundly affects the quality of work done in other parts of the agency. A change in one subsystem is likely to affect the performance of the others. For example, increased intelligence activities may result in increased capacity to enlist new services for the target population, which in turn influences the ability of those performing the service technology of the agency to help those clients.

Starting a New Service or Program

An understanding of these systemic functions is necessary in any effort to establish a new service or program or to modify and expand an existing one. In choosing whether to work through an existing agency or to establish a new agency, the planner-organizer must consider the costs and advantages of building from what already exists as against building something entirely new.

Developing a new agency to serve certain needs has the clear advantage of freeing the planner from the constraints of existing arrangements. These may include competing objectives of ongoing community agencies as well as tradition, and the

[5]C. Perrow, *Organizational Analysis* (Belmont, CA: Wadsworth, 1970): 92–132.

custom of following established procedures. Overcoming such obstacles is by no
means easy. Consider, for example, the difficulties that might be anticipated in
attempting to shift the program focus of a
medical clinic serving primarily young
mothers and their children, to a medical
checkup program for the aging, or of
getting a citywide planning agency to
develop neighborhood planning "outposts."

Adding a new program to an existing
agency may result in serious coordination
problems between functional units, may
lead to conflict with other agency activities,
and may ultimately lead to its "benign
neglect."

On the other hand, establishing a new
agency is often costlier than expanding the
services of an existing organization. An
established agency is often well recognized
and supported in the community. Its staff
has the training and experience to run the
agency and knows how to handle all its
administrative details. Moreover, the
agency may have all the basic equipment
necessary for the new service or program.
New agencies often flounder because of the
lack of experience and expertise.

PROCEDURES IN ORGANIZING
A NEW SERVICE OR PROGRAM

Identifying the Need for Service

No new agency or program should be initiated unless it is propelled by the existence
of a concrete and viable need. Self-evident
as this may seem, attempts are too often
made to develop new services without a
clear definition and articulation of the
needs to be met. Lack of clarity and specificity of needs is likely to result in two
undesirable consequences. First, it makes it
far more difficult to mobilize community

support for the new program. Second, the
actual design of the program may be hap-
hazard, ad hoc, often leading to ineffectiveness and inefficiency. A cardinal principle
in program design is that the greater the
clarity of the program's objectives, the better its chances for success.

Identifying unmet needs in the community is a complex task that necessitates several steps. The concept of "need" itself
often defies adequate definition. What is
perceived as a need by one group may not
be so considered by another. Nevertheless,
there are a number of ways in which planners can get a quick orientation to needs.
The following are illustrative strategies:

1. Planners might start by examining
available statistical reports such as census
data, local Social Security office data,
county government surveys, health surveys. While information on the number of
potential clients in a given area, their distribution in various neighborhoods, their level
of income, housing patterns, health conditions and the like might not indicate what
they "need," such information is often suggestive.

2. The planner-organizer might then
take a second step: identifying the various
agencies in the area that serve the community. This involves finding out whom these
agencies serve and what types of services
they offer. Statistical reports issued by relevant agencies, the local welfare council and
the public social service agencies may be of
particular importance. Some communities
may have developed information systems
for a network of agencies that could provide invaluable data to the planner-
organizer.[6]

---

[6]See for example, CHILDATA. Council for
Community Services in Metropolitan Chicago.

3. A third step is to explore with the staff of the agencies that are current or potential providers of services to the target population the concerns and problems it has identified regarding gaps or inequities in services.

4. Very early in the process, planners should meet with community groups to discuss their wants, preferences, and interests.

5. A more systematic data-gathering procedure might be developed through a "needs survey" of the neighborhoods in which potential clients are most likely to reside. The facilities of a college or university or a local mental health center, as well as civic groups and volunteers, can be mobilized to conduct the survey. Questions should be designed to elicit information about the problems and unmet needs of those interviewed. A social-indicators–type survey is one of the most useful of the new devices to get at such information.[7]

An important concomitant of the planner's information-gathering activities is his or her effort to increase the community's awareness of the needs of the target population. Involvement of community leaders and representatives of agencies in determination of these needs sensitizes them to existing problems and lays the groundwork for mobilizing them into action. Awareness on the part of key groups and agencies in the community is often fundamental to the initiation of new programs.

Mobilizing Support for the Service

It is extremely difficult to develop a new program without the existence and active support of a group in the community that is highly committed to its development. The planner-organizer must often initiate and organize such an action group. The action group then gathers resources and influence, actively representing the new program's objectives, and fights for its support in the community. In short, it assumes an advocate function. Sometimes this group will be the planner's advisory council. At other times it will be a specially organized task force on transportation or protective services or some other need. Again, it may be a purely ad hoc coalition of interested parties.

What persons should the planner-organizer mobilize into such a group? Perhaps more than anything else, participants should share a keen interest in and concern for the welfare of the target population. To be truly responsive, it must include representatives of the clients themselves. Potential for influence is another criterion for inclusion. The greater the individual prestige of the members, the greater their potential for collective influence. Influential members may include representatives of civic organizations, financial institutions, church organizations, and the like.

The higher the level of understanding about the problems of the target population among members of this group and the greater their expertise in the delivery of services to them, the more realistic will be the group's efforts and the greater the credibility of its suggestions to the community. Planners often enlist members of professional associations, physicians, social workers, etc., to assure this expertise. Having representatives of community agencies in the group increases the chances that their support for a new program will be forthcoming.

The function of such a group might be: to formulate the overall objectives of the new program; to identify the target popula-

[7]D. Fruin, "Analysis of Need," in M. J. Brown, ed., *Social Issues and the Social Services* (London: Charles Knight, 1974): 27–56.

tion to be served; to identify sources of financial support for the new program; to present the program objectives to important institutions in the community (such as city council, county government, mental health board, United Fund); or all of these.

This group might also examine in detail the information and ideas developed by the planner-organizer. Although the group itself need not develop a detailed plan for action, consensus regarding the type of program to be developed is helpful. Sometimes, of course, consensus is difficult to reach. Participants must be aware that differences in opinion or in conclusion are possible, and that these experiences can be healthy. An action group should provide the arena where ideas can be exchanged, proposals explored, and creative thinking encouraged. Ultimately, the group should formulate a basic plan for a new program by identifying and agreeing upon its major objectives and the population it should serve.

It is from this action group that a body in charge of defining or reviewing the policies for the new program may ultimately be drawn. This may be formalized as a board of directors, as an advisory council, or as an internal task force within an existing agency. The importance of an action group of this kind cannot be overemphasized. In the founding stages of the new program, the planner-organizer will need to rely heavily on its support, energy, and creativity, and most importantly, on its ability to mobilize necessary resources for the program.[8] The existence of an advocate group is no less crucial when the planner decides to launch the program within an existing agency, than when an entirely new structure is to be developed.

[8]M. Zald, "The Power and Function of Boards of Directors: A Theoretical Synthesis," *American Journal of Sociology* 75 (July 1969): 97–111.

Assigning Responsibilities to a Board or Advisory Council

When the interest group has developed an adequate level of cohesion and formulated a basic statement regarding the mandate of the new program, it may be reconstituted as a formal board or council. It might then be given any of the following charges:

1. Development of a specific plan for the implementation of the new program
2. Responsibility for obtaining the basic resources to get the program started
3. Authority to hire or approve the director of the new program
4. Accountability for the activities of the program director and the disbursement of fiscal resources

The board or council must be helped to develop some internal division of labor to ensure that the necessary tasks will be fulfilled. This may involve designating members as president or chairman, secretary, treasurer, program planning subcommittee and the like. In addition, clear procedures for decision making must be formulated. These steps are of particular importance since the board's decisions are bound to have critical impact on the character and direction of the program.

Defining the Mission of the New Agency or Program

Establishment of a new program requires a carefully planned blueprint that specifies both mission and operational objectives. It requires a thoughtful assessment of the feasibility of achieving each objective and identification of the essential means for implementing it. Identified needs coupled with available resources and means must be translated into a series of program objectives aimed at meeting these needs.

The planner-organizer plays a crucial role at this stage. Possessing critical information regarding needs, as well as knowledge about potential resources, he or she must help the board, advisory council, or task force to reach consensus on what the organization's mission will be.

This mission is defined in terms of needs to be met, populations to be served, and services to be given. This mission, however, must be translated into operational terms. This requires first of all, *specification of the needs to be addressed.* These *needs are prioritized* (step no. 1), and *objectives specified* (step no. 2). It is not necessary that the most crucial need be acted on first. Sometimes what is most easily accomplished takes precedence on the planner's timetable. But the ultimate mission must always be kept in mind.

Specifying the Objectives

Specifying the objectives of the program is a process of moving from the general to the specific through careful assessment of alternatives. Assume, for example, that there is a consensus to focus on the needs and problems of aged persons living alone. In the process of identifying the needs of such a population there arises a growing awareness that they are most likely to experience problems in personal management. Such consensus does not lead directly to programs or services. Are these problems expressed in poor household management, in inadequate diet, in poor personal care, in social isolation? Which of these problems are of the greatest urgency? If agreement on the urgency of these problems can be reached, they may be ordered on a chart. In Figure 28.1, four specific problems are identified and ordered in terms of importance.

The next task (step no. 3) is to *specify* the "target" population to determine more exactly what older persons are to be helped by the new or expanded services. A similar process is followed to identify those who manifest the problems most acutely. These may be found in a minority population with low income, residing in a specific neighborhood. Agreements must be reached concerning this target population, as its characteristics will determine the feasibility of various alternatives for responding to the needs.

FIGURE 28.1

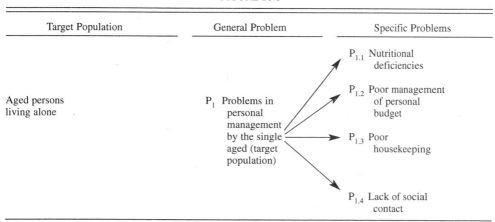

Target Population	General Problem	Specific Problems
Aged persons living alone	P₁ Problems in personal management by the single aged (target population)	P₁.₁ Nutritional deficiencies P₁.₂ Poor management of personal budget P₁.₃ Poor housekeeping P₁.₄ Lack of social contact

FIGURE 28.2

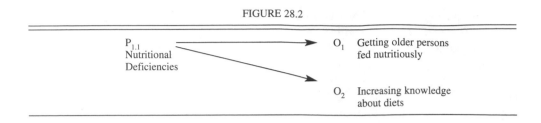

The choice of the target population should also reflect contingencies regarding the attainment of needed resources. Grants may be earmarked for certain categories of older persons. Certain agencies may be able to provide certain services only to older persons living in their geographical jurisdiction. Also, if it will take two years and $200,000 to develop a service for persons living in neighborhood X, while a similar level of service to persons in neighborhood Y is possible for far less and in only nine months, the choice of initial target population may be clear.

Next comes *exploring alternative program approaches* to dealing with specific problems of the target population (step no. 4). For example, in addressing the problem of nutritional deficiencies the objective may be to provide meals to a given population. Alternatively, the service might be an educational one, in which older persons are taught about proper diet (see Figure 28.2).

Similarly, in response to financial management problems, program objectives may include helping older persons to use their financial resources more efficiently, increasing access and use of banking services, and the like (see Figure 28.3).

Through this process a list of potential agency or program objectives can be developed.

Doing a Feasibility Study

After an inventory of alternative objectives has been formulated, a feasibility study of each (step no. 5) is necessary.

Some of the criteria to be used are as follows:

1. What would be the fiscal cost?
2. What would be the manpower requirements?
3. What facilities and equipment would be needed?
4. How receptive to the objective could the community be expected to be?
5. What would be the anticipated support of the objective by other community agencies?

FIGURE 28.3

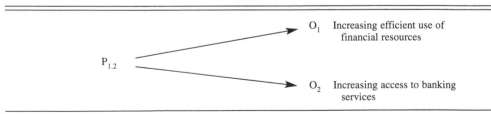

With such information on each objective, the planning task force must now shift its focus to the other side of the coin, namely *assessing the potential money and credit* the new program could hope to obtain (step no. 6). Some of the elements in such considerations are:

1. The availability of federal and/or state grants
2. Potential contributions by local government
3. Donations and contributions by local private organizations such as United Fund
4. In-kind contributions by social service agencies and social clubs
5. Availability of volunteers to offset or reduce staffing costs

In considering various sources of support, it is often necessary that the new program be affiliated with, or an integral component of, an existing agency. The auspice-giving or sponsoring agency may be able to allocate a certain portion of its budget for the new program, cut the administrative or overhead costs, or provide the organizational auspices required as qualification for grants.

Following the feasibility study, the board, council, or task force must then, on the basis of all the information on options and constraints, determine which services the new program will provide. This process culminates in a comprehensive policy statement specifying the consented objectives of the new program, the rationale for their adoption, the kinds of services to be provided, the clients to be served, and the individuals and groups who have assumed responsibility for the program and will be accountable for it to the public. Such a statement may serve as a charter, which may be required if the program is to become incorporated. In any event, it is a claim for domain and a statement of intent.

Obtaining Seed Money for Start-Up

Some planner-organizers assume that no project should commence unless all the resources needed to ensure its success are secured. This view fails to recognize that the most effective way to obtain needed resources may be to start the project and count on its visibility, demonstrated utility, and receptivity by clients to attract new resources. A program once started often generates its own momentum, attracting supporters unknown prior to the project's initiation and quickly developing spokesmen for itself in the community. This, of course, is not always the case. Many programs have foundered on inadequate funding, regardless of the need for the services. Every beginning necessitates some risk taking. The constraint of inadequate financial resources is a limiting factor, but it need not be an inhibiting one.

Nevertheless, basic "seed" or "start-up" money is often necessary. The planner-organizer, with a knowledge of federal and state funds and grants, and through contacts with local agencies, plays a crucial role in locating and obtaining funds. Together with the sponsoring agency or members of the board, task force, or advisory council, the planner-organizer may initiate or provide technical assistance toward: (1) the submission of grant proposals to federal or state governmental agencies or to private foundations; (2) fund-raising campaigns with the help of local civic associations, fraternal clubs, or churches; (3) solicitation of donations from industrial and commercial organizations; (4) competition for local or revenue-sharing funds; (5) presentations before the United Fund; (6) development of contracts with established community agencies, such as a community mental health board, for the provision of funds for the new program; (7) locating in-kind resources (such as facilities and equipment) through enlistment of the aid of social clubs and the news media; (8) mobilizing volunteers to provide the initial manpower needed to start the program.

The initial resources gathered for the new program must be allocated for two basic purposes: to set up the actual service or program, and to promote the program in the community, attracting additional resources. Often, because of inadequate financing, there is a tendency to ignore the second purpose. Yet if those resources are not allocated to promotion, the program may quickly reach a dead end. While it may be difficult to divert limited dollars from needed services, failure to do so may be shortsighted, ignoring the fact that organizations must survive to be successful. Promotion requires more than money, however. It usually requires the assignment of staff to carry it out.

Specifying the Program Technology

The program objectives formulated in the new program's policy statement do not necessarily define the means to achieve them. The "set of means" by which the objectives are to be accomplished is called the *program technology* of the organization.

As the technology becomes articulated, it provides a series of guidelines for the type of staff and skills needed and the daily tasks to be performed in serving clients.[9]

The components of a program technology can be derived from the program objectives discussed earlier. In the previous example, the problem of nutritional deficiencies led to identification of two objectives—getting older persons fed nutritiously, and increasing their knowledge about diets. In attempting to implement the first of these objectives, the planner-organizer should explore every possible type of service that relates to providing adequate meals for the aging. Schematically, the process can be presented as shown in Figure 28.4.

Thus S_1 may be a meals-on-wheels service, S_2 may represent a cooperative cooking program for small groups of older persons in a given neighborhood, and S_3 might be a hot lunch program at the neighborhood schools. The choice of the specific service may be based on such criteria as: (1) known success of similar programs elsewhere, (2) availability of expertise to implement it, (3) availability of other necessary resources, (4) receptivity by the aged to be served.

---

[9]On the concept of human service technology see Y. Hasenfeld and R. English, eds., *Human Service Organizations* (Ann Arbor: University of Michigan Press, 1974): 12–14.

FIGURE 28.4

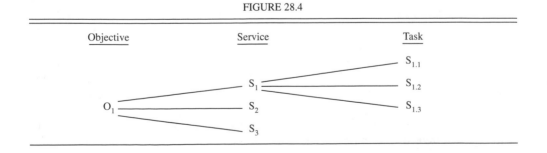

Objective	Service	Task
O_1	S_1	$S_{1.1}$
	S_2	$S_{1.2}$
	S_3	$S_{1.3}$

Assuming that the meals-on-wheels program has been adopted, the next series of specifications identifies the major tasks required to provide the service. For example, $S_{1.1}$ stands for organizing volunteers with cars; $S_{1.2}$, preparation of weekly visits by a nutritionist; $S_{1.3}$, preparing the meals at the kitchen of the local church, etc.

In short, this process provides a blueprint of all major tasks necessary to make the program operative.

Implementing the Program Technology

Once the choice of technology is made and its components identified, the new program can proceed to obtain the needed personnel. The program technology itself can be used to provide guidelines for the type of personnel required, and to specify the skills required of staff. It can, in fact, be used as the basis for writing job descriptions— although these should not be overly prescriptive or rigid.

Any program, in its initial phase, will require a great deal of flexibility from its staff. Staff may be called upon to switch roles and assume various tasks as the need arises, even though tasks calling for particular skills must be performed by qualified personnel.

The success of the meals-on-wheels program, for example, may hinge on the skills of a nutritionist needed to plan well-balanced meals. A program in which volunteers cook and deliver meals may only seem to be successful but in fact be missing the objective of getting older people fed nutritiously.

Once personnel are hired they must be given the responsibility to perform those tasks for which they are qualified. A nutritionist, for example, may not be the right person to supervise or organize drivers for the "wheels" part of the meals program.

There is often a tendency to assume that a higher level of credentials implies proficiencies in many areas. Yet a nutritionist with an academic degree may know little about counseling or working with volunteers. Often a volunteer is much better qualified.

Developing an Appropriate Delivery Structure

Division of labor, then, is all-important. Effective division of labor requires three critical organizational decisions: Who does what? In what order must various tasks be performed? Who is accountable for what is done? The first decision requires identification of the tasks to be performed and the persons to perform them. The second decision is related to sequence and coordination. Some tasks must be performed before others can be begun. Those that are performed sequentially may be separated among several work units. Other tasks must be performed together and belong to the same work unit.

In every organization there are certain sets of activities for which a supervisory person may be held accountable. The following principles may prove useful in guiding the development of an appropriate set of structural relationships.[10]

1. Those activities which need to be done simultaneously or in close proximity to each other are generally best grouped together. In the example given, the menu planning and the cooking activities should be in the hands of certain staff, while the handling of the delivery of the meals can be in the hands of another group. A set of

---

[10]P. R. Lawrence and J. W. Lorsch, *Organizations and Environment* (Cambridge, MA: Harvard University Press, 1967).

activities which must be closely coordinated should be conducted or supervised by a single unit supervisor.

2. Activities that have different time and space schedules and contingencies should generally be grouped separately. For example, the meals-on-wheels program should be separated from a group counseling program.

3. Tasks which can be performed through explicit routines should be separated from tasks that are nonroutine. For example, determination of membership, registration, and fee assessment are routine tasks. They should not be performed by those who provide consultation to community groups, a highly nonroutine activity.

4. Activities which require different ways of relating to the clients should be separated. For example, recreational activities for older people should not ordinarily be provided by the staff who give intensive individual counseling. While the same staff could conceivably do both, there ought to be a clear distinction between their two functions.

5. Staff should not be subjected to multiple supervision if at all possible. If it is necessary for more than one supervisor to relate to a particular staff person because of multiple roles that staff person performs, clear distinction must be made regarding the areas of jurisdiction of each supervisor.

The period of initial implementation of program technology is a period of trial and error. It requires a great deal of flexibility and no little tolerance for failure and for ambiguity. Open-mindedness and willingness to explore alternative routes are essential ingredients. During the early stages of program development, lines of communication with staff and clients must be kept as open as possible. Feedback is essential if the program is to adjust to unexpected exigencies. Staff who work directly with the community can provide invaluable information on the operationalization of the technology and its problems, its failures, and its successes.

It is probably desirable to have a "dry run" of the technology to test its organization and to acquaint the staff with its roles and duties. This can be accomplished through simulation techniques prior to putting the program into the field. Another approach is to select clients who are willing to volunteer for the service, even though the "bugs" in it may not have been fully shaken out.

Developing Inter-Agency Relationships

Concurrent with development of the technology of an agency or program is the development of a "support structure." This structure refers to the organization's patterned relationships to those elements in its environment that provide it with the resources necessary to attain its service and maintenance objectives. These elements include:

1. Clients or *consumers* of its service
2. Fiscal, manpower, technical, and other *resources* essential to the goal-oriented performance
3. *Complementary or supportive services* without which an agency's services would be unattainable, inadequate, or ineffective
4. Support or recognition from regulatory and auspice-providing bodies which give the program its *authority or mandate*

Managing the flow of these elements to and from the program requires establishment of a variety of exchange relationships with other organizations in the environment. This environment is described as an agency's "task environment." It is composed of all those groups and organizations whose actions directly affect the agency's goal attainment. Exchange activities leading to receiving elements from the task environment may take the form of: (1) competition, (2) contractual agreements, (3) cooptation, or (4) coalition formation.[11]

Agencies and programs are frequently in *competition* with each other for needed resources. One agency may compete with another for a federal grant by offering to serve more clients per dollar; it may compete to obtain better-trained staff by offering better benefits.

Human services agencies often make *contractual arrangements*, in which one organization agrees to do something for another (often in return for something). Without such arrangements, many services would be poorly performed or left undone. Examples abound. Agencies may exchange staff with complementary competencies on a temporary basis. One agency may do the mailing and publicity for another. A community group may contract with the Welfare Council to assess the service needs of a particular neighborhood. A county department of social services may purchase services from other agencies for its clients, including recreation, mental health, or protective services it does not have the staff to provide directly.

A new program or agency may also attempt to *coopt* key persons from other agencies whose services it seeks. Cooptation is accomplished through involving others in the design of a service or delivery of a ser-

vice program. Cooptation strategies are employed when involvement and its rewards are likely to give those who might otherwise oppose a program a greater appreciation for why it is needed and what it is intended to accomplish. Their involvement may not only nullify potential opposition, but may actually increase support.

When agencies pool their resources in a joint venture, they form a coalition. Coalitions differ from contracts in that the latter require explicit agreements about what one party will do for the other. Coalitions, on the other hand, are binding only insofar as working together leads to some mutual goal attainment.

It is not essential for parties in an exchange relationship to benefit equally from the exchange, or to have fully complementary goals. It is only necessary that each part perceive the relationship as being of some benefit to itself.

The choice of each of these strategies depends on numerous conditions, particularly those pertaining to the perceived status and desirability of the new program in the community. The more secure and the greater the importance attached to the agency's services, for example, the more likely it is to employ competitive and contractual strategies.

Enlisting Needed Elements from the Environment

In the discussion that follows, attention will be given to how agencies recruit resources or manage the flow of needed elements from the environment itself.

Clients. Clients can be recruited through referrals by other agencies informed about the new program. Clients may also be informed of a service through the news media. To reach some isolated clients, it is

[11]K. Benson, "The Interorganizational Network as a Political Economy," *Administrative Science Quarterly* 20 (June 1975): 229–46.

often necessary to launch a door-to-door campaign using volunteers.

Inadequate interpretation of an agency's services or intake policy may result in inappropriate referrals. An agency that turns away many ineligible clients causes a serious and unnecessary hardship to those clients and to its staff as well. It does harm to its own image, often damaging its relationships to other agencies. Thus it is critical for the new program to disseminate accurate and specific information about eligibility, both to the public and to other social agencies. Changes in eligibility criteria should be promptly communicated to all referral sources.

Permanent Sources of Funding. Often a new program must expend some of its initial and temporary resources on activities aimed at securing additional, more permanent sources of funding. Examples of such activities include: (1) entering into negotiations with the United Fund or United Way; (2) preparing grant applications to federal and state governmental agencies; (3) organizing a group of community influentials willing to sponsor an annual fund drive; (4) negotiating with local governmental bodies such as community mental health boards or county commissioners to incorporate the program under its sponsorship.

These and other activities require that certain staff members spend considerable time and energy meeting with potential funding sources, exchanging ideas, and presenting the agency's case.

It is often desirable to designate a specific staff position for such activities and hire a person with considerable experience in mobilization of resources.

Knowledge and Expertise. No new program can function without adequate access to at least the minimal amount of necessary knowledge and expertise. In the long run, the success of an agency may hinge on the quality of services it offers, and that quality may be in direct proportion to the knowledge and expertise of its staff. Inadequate and erroneous information could be disastrous.

The planner-organizer can mobilize expertise through: (1) enlisting the services of experts in the field from nearby institutes and universities; (2) consulting with and visiting programs of similar nature in other communities; (3) arranging information exchanges between the staff of the new agency and that of an established one in another area; (4) exploring the available literature on the problems or needs the program attempts to deal with; (5) obtaining consultation and relevant publications from appropriate state and federal agencies; (6) arranging for training and continuing education seminars.

Complementary Services. The effectiveness of any program is dependent in no small measure on the availability of complementary services for its clients. It is not enough to give one's own service well. No matter how highly specialized a service, the organization providing that service must still assume some responsibility for the general welfare of its clients. It cannot shy away from its obligation to make sure that clients receive other needed services.

This is particularly true when the effectiveness of the very services provided by the agency is dependent on the complementary services of other agencies. For example, if an agency develops a child-care program, it cannot in good conscience ignore the health needs of the children, and it may contract for periodic medical examinations with the local "well baby" clinic. A nutrition program for the aged might not be

successful unless it also enlisted cooperation from the outreach staff of the Information and Referral Service, the Visiting
Nurses Association, or the Mental Health
Crisis Center.

A new program must identify the crucial
services it will need to enlist from other
agencies and programs in order to meet its
own objectives. It is within the planner-
organizer's responsibility to see to it that
such services are or will be made available.
Without them, the new program may fail.

These complementary services can be
arranged through several means: (1) actual
purchase of such services from another
agency; (2) contract of exchange of services between the two agencies; (3) a unilateral decision by the other agency to
provide the needed services as a gesture of
goodwill; (4) a coalition of several agencies
with different services all committed to
serve the same clients.

Monitoring and Evaluation. Every program is subject to the monitoring and
evaluation of some overseeing agencies.
These may be state licensing organizations,
other governmental units, local administrative boards, professional associations,
citizens' groups, or other interested parties.
Often these regulatory agencies exert
considerable influence. They may impose
very specific requirements for the agency to
meet.

A state agency, for example, may annually audit the financial transactions of the
program, or it may check the extent to
which the facilities conform to state regulations. A professional organization may be
responsible for accreditation without which
outside grants cannot be received.

The planner-organizer must see to it that
the program has developed the appropriate
mechanisms by which it can meet the
requirements of these regulatory agencies.

This is not a mere bureaucratic formality.
Accrediting bodies and standard-setting
organizations are often the key sources of
legitimation and support of a new program.
For example, an agency approved for
internship of urban planners will gain considerable prestige and recognition in the
professional community and could, therefore, attract good staff. Similarly, an agency
that receives a favorable evaluation by a
state agency is more likely to obtain future
state grants.

Maintaining appropriate relations with
the various agencies and organizations
necessitates the establishment of "boundary
roles" for program staff. Persons in these
roles develop and maintain linkages
between the new program and relevant
organizations in its environment.[12] A staff
person may be designated as the liaison
with the state social service agency, county
government, local hospital, etc. The duties
of boundary personnel include: (1) establishment of the necessary relations with
outside groups and organizations; (2) resolution of whatever difficulties may arise in
the course of a relationship; (3) obtaining
relevant up-to-date information about the
activities of the partner to the relationship;
(4) establishment of contacts with key staff
in that organization or group who may be
favorable toward the agency; (5) alerting
the agency to new developments that may
alter the relations between the two.

The ability of an agency to seize on new
opportunities in the environment, to adapt
to new changes, and to be prepared for new
constraints depends on the effective job
performed by the occupants of these boundary roles. They serve as the ears and eyes of

---

[12]H. Aldrich and D. Herker, "Boundary Spanning
Roles and Organization Structure," mimeographed
paper (Ithaca, NY: Cornell University, 1974).

the agency, without which its ability to adapt, grow, and develop would be seriously hampered.

Legitimation and Social Support.   Underlying all the inter-agency relations described above is a pervasive need of the program to obtain legitimation and social support. The success of the program in achieving viability is dependent on its ability to become a recognized "institution" in the community. Once the program is perceived by key elements in the community as desirable, indispensable, and an important contributor to the general welfare of the community, it has been "legitimated." Legitimacy implies that the community is willing to accept it as a viable and necessary component of the service structure.[13]

Support and legitimacy do not come easily; neither are they cheap. Concerted efforts to achieve them must be made by program staff. Support generally requires at the very least a satisfied community group or gratified clients. This is the core of an agency's constituent base. This constituency should also include other social service agencies that benefit in some direct way from the services offered by the new program. The constituent base should also include community influentials and professionals who are committed to the well-being of the target population.

Other mechanisms to promote support for the program include: lectures and presentations by staff to various community groups; establishment of an influential board of directors; public visits to the agency's facilities; reports by the news media of the activities of the agency; etc.

But necessary as these are, none is sufficient without solid constituent support.

Getting Staff to Perform Adequately

Persons choose to work in organizations and agencies for a variety of reasons. They often join an agency staff with personal expectations and aspirations. The agency, on the other hand, expects them to perform in accordance with its needs, demands, and schedules. There may be many points of incongruity between personal aspirations of staff and organizational expectations. The larger the discrepancies, the greater the strains and the less likelihood that staff will perform adequately.[14]

Planner-organizers can help a new program determine adequate criteria for staff selection and realistic expectations for performance. Individuals who become employees of an agency make a contractual agreement whereby they accept the role requirements assigned to them in exchange for the various inducements provided by the agency (salary, work satisfactions, good working conditions).

A great deal of misunderstanding can be avoided if the agency specifies its requirements at the point of recruitment. Clearly written requirements can guide the agency to hire staff who have the needed skills, aptitudes, and attributes. Recruitment, however, is only a limited mechanism to ensure that staff will perform adequately. Socialization is a critical organizational process through which staff internalizes agency norms and values and learns specific role obligations. Two important socialization mechanisms are training and staff development.

---

[13]P. Selznick, *Leadership in Administration* (New York: Harper, 1957).

[14]L. W. Porter, E. E. Lawler, and J. R. Hackman, *Behavior in Organizations* (New York: McGraw-Hill, 1975).

In the final analysis, however, effective and efficient role performance by staff is predicated on the design of a work unit that is congruent with the tasks it has to perform.[15] Tasks can be categorized by two major variables: (1) *Task difficulty*, which refers to the degree of complexity, amount of knowledge needed, and reliance on nonroutine decision making. For example, determination of service eligibility may be a very simple task based on few explicit decision rules, while planning community services necessitates consideration of many factors, reliance on extensive knowledge, and complex decision making. (2) *Task variability*, which refers to the degree of uniformity and predictability of the work to be done. For example, preparation of monthly statistical reports is a relatively uniform and predictable task, while developing ties with various agencies calls for a variety of procedures.

Tasks which are low in complexity and variability call for a work unit structure which is essentially bureaucratic in the classical sense of the word. Tasks which are high in complexity and variability necessitate a work unit structure which is "human relational." In a bureacratic structure line staff has very limited discretion; there is a clear hierarchy of authority; and coordination of staff is based on an extensive set of rules and operating procedures. In a human relation structure, the discretion of line staff is high; relations with supervisory staff are collegial; and coordination is based on feedback from the other staff.

When the task has both complex and noncomplex components or variable and nonvariable elements which cannot be separated, a "mixed" structure will be most appropriate.[16] Based on the nature of the "mix" such a structure may provide line staff with high discretion in some specific areas and none in others. For example, the task of intake may be of such type. Workers may have high discretion in defining the problem of the client, but none concerning determination of fees, scheduling, and the like.

It can be readily shown that each structure is most efficient if appropriately matched with the characteristics of the tasks to be performed. This is so because the work unit structure is designed to elicit the behavioral and role prescriptions that each task requires.

When conflict arises between two units or among several staff members because of overlapping jurisdictions, lack of coordination, or lack of mutual understanding, an ad hoc task force to deal with the conflict may prove helpful. In a multi-service center, for example, a conflict could arise between the outreach staff and the counseling staff. The former may feel that they do not get any help in scheduling appointments and in coping with problems they encounter in the field. The counseling staff, on the other hand, may feel that it is asked to do the work of the outreach staff and that the outreach staff fails to understand what the counselors are trying to accomplish. To resolve the conflict, an ad hoc task force might be established with representatives of both parties to arrive at an acceptable solution, or an integrator position might be created.

The integrator role requires that a third party become the mediator between parties in the dispute. The integrator is generally a person with adequate knowledge of the activities of the units of persons he or she attempts to

---

[15]C. Perrow, op. cit., Chapter 3.

[16]Eugene Litwak, "Models of Organization Which Permit Conflict," *American Journal of Sociology* 67 (Sept. 1961), pp. 177–84.

bring together, and may be in an authority position in relation to both. In the example above, the integrator might be a person who has expertise in both outreach and counseling, so that his directive to both units will be respected. His function is to identify areas where coordination needs to be established and procedures that can be developed to minimize conflict. He also serves as a mediator, interpreting to each unit the issues and problems the other unit needs to solve.[17]

A further word: Conflict is not necessarily dysfunctional to an organization. To the contrary. It can help to effectively identify operational problems, philosophical differences, or staff deficiencies. Properly managed, conflict situations assure a changing and responsive pattern of agency operations. Conflict is often a symptom of healthy adaptation to changing needs and expectations.

Developing an Intelligence and Feedback System

There is a strong correlation between the extent to which an organization can adapt to changes in its environment and the effectiveness of its "intelligence" system. An effective system enables the organization to evaluate its own activities in relation to changes and developments in its environment. Without such a system, the organization may find that its services and modes of operation are rapidly becoming obsolete. An effective and efficient intelligence system can provide the program with the new information and knowledge required to adjust to changes from both within and without.

In general, an intelligence system fulfills three interrelated functions: monitoring the external task environment of the agency,

internal auditing of staff and client activities, and evaluation of the agency's outputs.

The *monitoring of the agency's external environment* is intended to alert the agency to important changes and developments in the various units upon which it is dependent. These include federal and state programs, the programs of local social service agencies, new legislation, etc. Monitoring activities can also be directed at identifying new developments in service techniques. Finally, external monitoring is required to inform the agency of changes in the character of the population it seeks to serve.

The main purpose of *internal auditing* is to inform the agency of the activities of the staff vis-à-vis the clients. Information generated by internal auditing enables staff to assess the progress of the clients and to determine future courses of action, and enables the agency management to evaluate the operation of the service technology. Without such evaluation, the agency has no way of determining whether it is achieving its service goals at some reasonable level.

Evaluation of agency *outputs* occurs after clients have been served by the agency. The emphasis is on what happened to clients and how many were served.

Fulfillment of each of these intelligence functions requires several steps: (1) collection of the necessary data; (2) analysis of those data so that they are useful and used; (3) transmission of relevant information to appropriate decision makers; and (4) interpretation of the information in order to generate additional knowledge. Since the final step of the intelligence process is the generation of knowledge, malfunction in any of the previous steps is likely to adversely affect the capability of the intelligence system to develop that knowledge.

Effective external monitoring systems are dependent on the performance of boundary personnel who maintain close ties

---

[17]P. R. Lawrence and J. W. Lorsch, op. cit., Chapter 9.

with external units and who actively scan the environment for new resources. Staff members assuming boundary roles may develop specialized working relations with a given set of organizations. The contact person gathers essential information about the availability of given resources and the conditions of their use, and transmits this information to staff members who can use it. This is a necessary function if the agency is to remain up-to-date on changes and developments in its environment.

Personnel who perform boundary roles must develop expert knowledge about the characteristics of the resources in their areas of specialization. They must also be able to develop cooperative and informative relationships with the major suppliers of these resources, and must develop analytic skills necessary to assess and evaluate developments and changes in the nature of the environment. Perhaps most important, they must acquire effective and efficient communication channels to decision makers within their own organization.

Internal auditing enables staff to carry out its activities on an informed and rational basis. Internal auditing is directed at (1) the case or client level, and (2) the operational or departmental level. The function of internal auditing at the case or client level is to provide staff with all the necessary information for decision making at every juncture of the client's career in the agency.

This often requires the use of a client "case record." Each client served by the agency should have a record which includes basic information about him, his own perception of his needs, and the service objectives for him. Actions taken by staff and periodic evaluations of the client's performance in the agency should be systematically recorded and the impact of those services noted. A client record could

be organized around topics such as background information, health status, income, housing, nutrition needs, and interpersonal problems. Each action or referral should be recorded in the appropriate topic section.

A scheme must also be developed for the uniform classification and codification of the information items to be used; and procedures for information gathering, update, and retrieval must be planned. This process requires that the basic information the agency plans to collect and use be classified and coded in a system of categories that are explicitly defined, unambiguous, and uniformly applied throughout the entire agency. This process can be used to enable staff to develop an orderly and rational sequence of services aimed at assisting the client to achieve his service goals. It can also be used to monitor the actions taken and to signal staff when new or different decisions need to be made.

Auditing procedures at the "operations" level attempt to answer basic managerial questions about the modes of operation of the agency or units thereof. These could include the analysis of all activities done for clients suffering from visual handicaps; the success of various treatment technologies; analysis of the type of referrals used by the agency; or the responses of staff to clients who drop out. The findings of such auditing enable the agency to evaluate its operating procedures and make necessary adjustments or changes.

Findings may specify such information as (1) the type of clients arriving at the agency, the range of problems they present, and the services they request; (2) assessment of the services given to different cohorts of clients, the consequences of those services, or whether adequate follow-up is done by staff; (3) the performance of various staff regarding size of case load; average number of contacts with clients; (4) type of resources or intervention techniques used.

Perhaps the most important function of an intelligence system is to enable the agency to evaluate its service outcomes. In the final analysis, an agency can justify its existence only if it can show competence in attaining its service objectives. To do so, it must develop reliable procedures to evaluate the use of its services. The problems involved in attempts to measure are extremely complex. They stem from the fact that there is no consensus regarding a norm of "success," nor are there valid and reliable methods to measure success.

There is, however, some risk of developing inappropriate *output measures*. This can be observed when the number of clients seen by staff becomes the measure of success. When this criterion is adopted by staff, it may gear its efforts to obtaining a high ratio of clients per worker while reducing the amount of time spent with each. There is also a tendency of organizations to adopt "symbolic" criteria when faced with the difficulties of developing substantive criteria. Symbolic criteria are testimonies by staff or clients, display of the "successful" client, self-evaluation, and other approaches that may be highly misleading and in fact could cover up serious failures by the organization.

Any evaluation of an agency may be painful in that it is likely to expose serious gaps between expectations and accomplishments. Such an exposure may undermine the legitimacy of the agency. Yet an agency cannot improve its services if it lacks adequate outcome measures or fears the consquences of such measures. In the long run, lack of adequate outcome measures may lead toward the deterioration of the organization.

An agency's service goals are often multidimensional, with various subgoals and tasks. The design of valid and reliable outcome measures requires recognition of this fact. In general, outcome measures should relate to the goals of each subsystem in the agency. Outcome measures differentiate between the initial state of the client at the point of entry and the terminal state of that client at point of exit from the agency.

In a complex service program, the new client goes through a series of assessments, which are often updated and corrected with the collection of additional information. These assessments may cover a range of attributes and problems, such as personal care, motivation to participate, health status, financial problems, etc. These include the gamut of areas in which the agency activity plans to intervene in order to improve the status of the client. At point of exit, these same attributes are reassessed and the amount of progress shown by the client through actual performance or his own evaluation is recorded. Because an agency may have succeeded more in some areas than in others, one measure cannot summarize the range of activities undertaken by the agency, nor can it reflect the complexity of attributes and problems presented by the client.

Multiple measures are necessary. Each of these should include concrete and precise descriptions of client attributes and behaviors. These measures must become an integral part of the service technology itself. They may serve as assessment devices for the client's progress in every stage of his association with the agency. In fact, they should logically follow the activities that have been specified in the service technology. They should be embedded in the daily work of the staff and not external measures imposed on the agency without direct reference to what it actually does. Needless to say, such measures must be constantly reexamined, updated and refined.[18]

Successful use of measures for service outcome necessitates a comprehensive and effective *follow-up* system. Without one, the information necessary for evaluation could not be obtained. The basic function of follow-up is to gather the necessary information regarding the consequences for the client of services given. It is the basic mechanism by which the agency can find out what has happened to its clients. Unfortunately, few service agencies have established such sophisticated measures. In a number of cases, in fact, output measures of the type described could be overly costly in relation to the sophistication of the services provided.

CONCLUDING NOTE

The process of establishing a new program is highly complex and requires considerations of many inter- and intra-organizational factors. It is not surprising, therefore, to find that while community workers and action groups may conceive of imaginative and innovative service programs, their ability and success in implementing them are at best modest. As was shown in the above discussion, each step in the process of implementation requires a particular set of skills, expertise, and resources. Inability to enlist them at crucial points in the program development may lead to failure or to detrimental consequences in the ability of the program to fulfill its objectives.

Thus, the systems approach used here alerts the planner-organizer to the intricate interrelations among the various building blocks of the program. It identifies the points at which the establishment of certain subsystems must assume priority over other organizing activities. Nevertheless, it should not be concluded that the model presented here is deterministic, in that each of the steps identified must be so followed. It should not be assumed a priori that an organization is a tightly coupled system in which each component must be closely articulated with all others. There is evidence to suggest that many programs may function quite adequately even if some components or subsystems are not fully developed or are not closely inter-linked. The systems approach advocated here enables the planner-organizer to assess at each point in the program development process the need for the establishment of certain organizational components. For example, the planner-organizer may find that a feasibility study is unnecessary since resources have already been earmarked for certain types of programs, or that whatever service technology will be developed, support of key groups in the environment is assured.

Moreover, it has been stressed throughout that agency or program development involves a great deal of trial and error in the face of many unknown parameters. The approach developed here merely attempts to identify the critical parameters the planner-organizer must consider and thus reduce some of the risks that are inherent in any program implementation.

---

[18]C. Weiss, *Evaluation Research* (Englewood Cliffs, NJ: Prentice-Hall, 1972).

APPENDIX
INTERNET RESOURCES—NONPROFIT

MACRO SITES—CAREER ORIENTED

http://www.nonprofitcareer.com/	Nonprofit Career Network
http://www.execsearches.com/exec/	Headhunter for nonprofit, public sector, and socially conscious organizations
http://www.philanthropy.com/jobs.dir/jobsmain.htm	The Chronicle of Philanthropy—Job openings

NATIONAL ASSOCIATIONS AND BOARDS

http://www.naco.org/	National Association of Counties
http://www.asaenet.org/main/	American Society for Association Executives
http://www.ncna.org/	The National Council of Nonprofit Associations
http://www.ncppp.org/	The National Council for Public-Private Partnerships
http://www.ncnb.org/main.htm	National Center for Nonprofit Boards

NONPROFIT RESOURCES—META SITES

http://www.nonprofits.org/	Internet Nonprofit Center
http://www.granted.org/	Community Resource Institute
http://comnet.org/index.html	Michigan Comnet
http://www.nonline.com/	Nonline Nonprofit Network
http://www.clark.net/pub/pwalker/ General_Nonprofit_Resources/	Nonprofit Resources Catalogue

STATE AND FEDERAL GOVERNMENT—NONPROFIT LINKS

http://www.nonprofit.gov/	Nonprofit gateway to federal government information and services
http://www.sbaonline.sba.gov/nonprofit/	Small Business Administration's nonprofit site
http://www.irs.gov/bus_info/eo/eo-types.html	IRS: Types of tax-exempt organizations
http://www.irs.gov/bus_info/eo/eo-tkit.html	IRS: Tax-exempt organizations tax kit

NONPROFIT MANAGEMENT

http://www.nptimes.com/	Nonprofit Times—The leading business publication for nonprofit management
http://www.pfdf.org/	The Peter F. Drucker Foundation for Nonprofit Management

NONPROFITS AND TECHNOLOGY

http://conference.pj.org/	Philanthropy News Network: Nonprofits and technology conferences
http://www.wecaretoo.coM	WeCareToo: Offers free website service and site management to nonprofits
http://www.icomm.ca/	An Internet service provider helping nonprofit organizations
http://ombwatch.org/npt/	Nonprofits' policy and technology project— U.S. Office of Management and Budget

NONPROFIT FOUNDATIONS AND THINK TANKS

http://fdncenter.org/	The Foundation Center
http://www.indepsec.org/	Independent sector
http://www.nira.go.jp/ice/tt-info/nwdtt99/index.html	A World Directory of Think Tanks (circa: 1999)

SOCIAL WORK LINKS

http://www.abecsw.org/	American Board of Examiners in Clinical Social Work
http://www.socialworkonline.com/resource.htm	Internet Resources for Social Workers—Meta site
http://www.naswdc.org/	National Association of Social Workers
http://www.cswf.org/	Clinical Social Work Federation

Name Index

Subject Index

Health and Human Services, Department of, 94
Helping relationship, 212–213
Henry Street Settlement, 381
Heterogeneity, of population, 121–124
HEW (Department of Health, Education and Welfare), 93, 94
HIV/AIDS services, delivery system for, 329–336
Housing, self-help approach and, 283
Housing and Urban Development (HUD), 97
Housing and Urban Development Act (1968), 6
Human ecology theory, 119–124
  application of, 120
  population size and, 120
Human service organization, nonprofit, 414–428

Ideological politics, 58
Ideology
  1865–1914, 68–69
  1915 to 1929, 78–79
  1929–1954, 87–88
  1955–1968, 92–93
  1969 and after, 95–96
Immigrant Protective League, 73
Immigration, 66
Immigration Act (1924), 78
Implementation, 16–17
  decisions, 55
Incentive-based approach, 19
Indian Reorganization Act (1934), 86
Indians. *See* Native Americans
Individualization, 103–104
Individual (micro) practice, 21–22
Industrial Areas Foundation (IAF), 33, 360
Industrialization, 66
Influence, interpersonal interaction, organized pressure, and, 17–21
Informal groups, 124–125
Information, globalization and, 113
Information society, 94–95
Institute for Democratic Socialism, 50
Institutional subsystem, 458
Institutions, privatization of, 108–112
Integrated practice, 200–207
Integrating Social Welfare Policy and Social Work Practice (McInnis-Dittrich), 24
Integration
  into community, 119
  residential, 129–130
Intelligence and feedback mechanisms, 459, 474–477
Internal auditing, 474
International affairs, 1929–1954, 85
International Ladies' Garment Workers' Union, 76
International organizations, privatization and, 109
Interorganizational relationships, 12
Interpersonal factors, in administration, 410–412
Interpersonal influence, 4, 17–21
Intervention. *See* Community intervention
Intervention within Research model, 273–276

Japanese-Americans, 75, 78, 89, 91
  World War II and, 87
Japanese Association for Issei, 75
Job Corps, 92
Journal of Progressive Human Services, 34
Justice Department, 86
Justice-oriented practice, social justice and, 222
"Just" therapy, social justice and, 224

Knights of Labor, 75
Knowledge, for service or program support, 470
Koerner commission, 51
Korean War, 88

Labeling perspective, 201
Labor, Chicano, 83
Labor union movement, 59
La Raza Unida, 33, 58, 350
Leadership. *See also* Small groups
  in mental health organizations, 428–439
  organizational failure and, 432–433
  relationships among staff members and, 435–437
  relationships in period of instability and change, 437–439
  strategic, 416, 425–427
  unresolved conflicts involving perceptions and values, 433–435
Leadership development, self-help approach and, 283–284
Leadership roles, in groups, 13
League of United Latin American Citizens, 83, 88
League of Women Voters, 55, 58, 83
Legislation, institutional subsystems and, 458–459
Legislative campaign, for TUFF, 394–402
Liberalism, 70
Line workers, role definitions of, 140–141
Linkages, for intervention modes, 243
Locality development, 29–31, 59, 155, 245–246, 304n
  beneficiaries, 42, 43
  boundary definition, 40
  change strategy and, 38
  collaborative tactics, 256–258
  community interests, 41
  conceptualizing, 253–255
  dilemmas in, 53, 54
  employment of practitioners, 262–264
  empowerment, 43
  future of community and, 251–253
  goals, 36
  intellectual roots for, 30
  interactional and group development roles, 260–262
  and orientation toward power structures, 40
  outlook for, 264–265
  practitioner roles and medium of exchange, 39
  problem conditions, 37
  problem-solving roles in, 258–260
  resident initiatives, 256–258
  theoretical grounding for, 255–256
Lonely Crowd, The (Riesman), 103
Louisville Convention of Colored Men, 74